Record OF THE CENTURY

Philomena Doogan

HarperCollins*Publishers*

In association with

HarperCollins Publishers, Westerhill Rd, Bishopbriggs, Glasgow G64 2QT

First published 1999

© HarperCollins, 1999 (text)
© The Scottish Daily Record & Sunday Mail Ltd, 1999 (images)

ISBN 0 00 472350 3

Reprint 10 9 8 7 6 5 4 3 2 1 0

All rights reserved. No part of this publication may be reproduced, stored in a retrieval system or transmitted, in any form or by any means, electronic, mechanical, photocopying, recording, or otherwise, without the prior permission of the publisher.

This book is sold subject to the condition that it shall not, by way of trade or otherwise, be lent, re-sold, hired out or otherwise circulated without the publisher's prior consent in any form of binding or cover other than that in which it is published and without a similar condition including this condition being imposed on the subsequent publisher.

Visit the book lover's website at

www.**fire**and**water**.co

Printed in Scotland by Edinburgh Press, Edinburgh

Introduction

Where else would Scots look for a record of the turbulent twentieth century than in the pages of their truly national newspapers, the *Daily Record* and *Sunday Mail*? Day in and day out, from the dawn of the century through to the new millennium, we have recorded the triumphs, tragedies and trivialities of Scotland's century. In the last 100 years, we have seen the human race at its very finest and its very worst. The Scottish people have suffered, survived and thrived – and we have reported every momentous event, every disaster, every celebration. Catching the moment in words and pictures is a hectic and hasty business, just as living it has been. Only when we reach the end-of-an-era vantage point and look back do we realise we have been writing and capturing the images of our history.

A nation's newspapers are actually a never-completed portrait of a people. So what do 100 years of *Daily Record* and *Sunday Mail* front pages tell you about the Scots? First, that we are most assertively and proudly what we think we are and that is a race to be reckoned with. One thing remains constant on every page – the Scottish character. Scots have had to be hard, because only a durable folk could have come through so much. We have shared so much with fellow-citizens of the United Kingdom, especially in the two world wars, yet our sense of special identity has never been in doubt. Tragedies have struck us as a community and drawn us even closer. Many created an anger that led to social crusades and political movements. The chronicle of the century starts with bubonic plague in the teeming tenements of Glasgow, moves on through decades of pit disasters, rail crashes, crowd calamities at football matches and the night in 1988 when, in a combination of the freakish and the unthinkable, death fell out of the sky onto the town of Lockerbie. Two tragedies stand out because they robbed us of our most precious possession, our children. Both the 1930 Paisley cinema horror when 69 children died, and the 1996 slaughter of the innocents at Dunblane Primary School stunned Scotland and shocked the world. Our papers were always on the scene, always reported the facts with professionalism and humanity – and went on to campaign for the changes that might prevent more horrors.

To reach so many people in such a tightly-knit society takes a special binding relationship between newspapers and their readers. The *Daily Record* and *Sunday Mail* have forged that bond and kept that mutual loyalty fresh over the years. They have shared the Scottish people's politics and aspirations – often, it seemed, before the people knew what they were thinking themselves … In 1932, when the then Scottish Secretary suggested "a Scottish Parliament within the British Union", the *Record*'s response was "Bravo!" During the years of misrule and strife, when Scots tholed a government they did not vote for and the dismantling of their industrial heritage, the *Record* and *Mail* were the voice of never-say-die opposition. And, if the Government had heeded the *Record* readers' referendum on self-government, we would have had our Scottish Parliament almost a quarter of a century before the dream finally came true!

The *Daily Record* was five years old when the century began. Our early-century front pages were not as they appear here; they were traditional broadsheet, without the breezy banner headlines of today's tabloids. From the very beginning, the papers were at the cutting-edge of newspaper production: the first daily newspaper to colour-print at speed, the world's first colour picture of a news event at the Abdication, the largest newspaper plant of its kind in the world at Anderston Quay, the first national daily to be put together with the help of computers, and still leading with the new plant at Cardonald and the move onto the Internet. Throughout, it has been technology at the service of news, but news presented in a specially Scottish and vibrant way. When the founders of the papers set out their aims 105 years ago, they declared: "Ours will be the task not to furnish a mere dull chronicle of events from day to day but to give a picture, vivid, accurate, and varied, of the web of human life as it is. Not the dregs, but the foaming, sparkling liquor itself will the readers be asked to drink". This book is our distillation of 100 years of Scottish life. Drink deep and hearty!

Tom Brown
The Scottish Daily Record
September 1999

Acknowledgments

My thanks go to everyone at the picture library of the *Scottish Daily Record* who helped me in researching and scanning the pictures for this book. I would also like to thank Sandra Guy and Helen Dow who helped me research through the old bound volumes of the newspaper, page by page and to Brian Glancey, Alistair Fyfe, James Leo and Jack McSharry for their invaluable input to the book.

Special thanks go to John Gordon who had the task of scanning and re-touching the front pages and other images and to Paul O'Donnell and Euan Cameron for their help with the images during the production of the book.

Finally, a particular mention must be made of the help and continuous guidance I received throughout from Colin MacMillan and Patricia Baird.

Philomena Doogan
Glasgow
September 1999

How To Stop Strikes. See Page 4.

The Daily Record.

PART XIV. OF "With the Flag to Pretoria" NOW ON SALE.

LARGEST SALE OF ANY MORNING OR EVENING NEWSPAPER IN SCOTLAND.

No. MDXIX—SIX EDITIONS. GLASGOW, MONDAY, SEPTEMBER 3, 1900. PRICE ONE HALFPENNY.

THE PLAGUE OUTBREAK.

NO NEW CASES REPORTED YESTERDAY.

93 PATIENTS NOW UNDER OBSERVATION.

STRANGE DEATHS ON SOUTH-SIDE.

The official bulletin issued at the Glasgow Sanitary Chambers in Montrose Street yesterday showed that there were, at midnight on Saturday, eleven cases of bubonic plague in Belvidere Hospital, one case under suspicion, and ninety-three contacts under observation. On making inquiry at the Chambers at a late hour last night it was learned that there were no fresh cases to report. It will thus be seen from the figures of yesterday that no additional cases of plague have come under the notice of the sanitary authorities since Friday, when it was officially reported that there were eleven in the hospital. The number of persons isolated, however, shows an increase of ten since midnight on Friday. The ninety-three persons under observation are about equally divided between the North Montrose Street reception house and the Weaver Street reception house, and so far as can be ascertained none of them have, up till the present, shown any decided symptoms of the disease.

Precautionary Measures.

The medical authorities of the city are meanwhile adopting the most stringent measures to combat the trouble, and are hopeful of successfully accomplishing their purpose, especially if their efforts are supplemented by the exercise on the part of the populace of every precaution as to cleanliness, etc.

In Rose Street and Thistle Street, in which thoroughfares the disease was first detected, the closes, stairs and back-courts leading to tenements where cases, or suspected cases, were discovered, are being thoroughly white-washed, and, in addition, the houses are being disinfected, the ashpits emptied and cleaned, and every particle of dirt likely to harbour disease removed from the buildings.

Dr. Chalmers, Medical Officer of Health, accompanied by Councillor Battersby, one of the members of the Health Committee, and a sanitary officer, visited the building at 57 Thistle Street yesterday between one and two o'clock. They made a careful examination of the houses, many of which are still occupied, and so far as could be learned they were in every way satisfied with what was being done to cope with the plague. While the investigation was being conducted a large crowd of men, women and children principally of the poorer classes, gathered in front of the entry, and from the manner in which they laughed and chatted to each other, it was evident that they did not fully appreciate the serious nature of the situation.

Dr. J. B. Russell, late medical officer of health for Glasgow, and now Medical Member of the Scottish Local Government Board, visited Glasgow on Saturday to make further enquiries with regard to the outbreak. Dr. Cantlie, of London, has also arrived in the city to make investigations on behalf of the British Medical Association.

The anti-plague serum which was ordered from the Pasteur Institute in Paris has now been received by the authorities, and the work of inoculation was started on Saturday forenoon.

A Strange Story.

At the Southern Police Office on Saturday evening Detective Kilgour reported the peculiar death of Mary Gardner (20), in her mother's house at 248 Mathieson Street, S.S., between the 27th and 30th ult.

From inquiries it seems that deceased has not been seen outside since last Monday, when she stated to some of the neighbours that her mother was ill. She, however, made no complaint regarding her own condition. On Saturday afternoon Mr. Somerville, factor of the property, called with the object of seeing Mrs. Gardner on business, but on approach-

DESTROYING THE LINE.

BRIDGES BLOWN UP BY THE BOERS.

GRAND WORK BY THE HIGHLAND BRIGADE.

The guerilla tactics of the Boers are being prosecuted with vigour. The Delagoa Railway, the control of which has been assumed by the British Military Authorities, has been destroyed at two points by the blowing up of bridges.

Otherwise the news from the seat of war this morning is unimportant. Lord Roberts reports further upon French's occupation of Barberton and also upon the brilliant operations of the Highland Brigade under General MacDonald.

President Kruger is still at Lorenzo Marques. It is stated that a Dutch warship will bring him to Europe. Mr. Reitz, the late Transvaal State Secretary, is also coming to Europe, and he will afterwards go to America.

FRENCH'S CAPTIVES.

BOER OFFICIALS TAKEN AT BARBERTON.

BRITISH OFFICERS RELEASED.

The following despatch from Lord Roberts was issued from the War Office yesterday:—

"Machadodorp, Sept. 15, 7.40 p.m.

"French reports all quiet at Barberton. Among his prisoners are the Landrost of the place and Commandant Vanderpost, late Chairman of the Free State Raad. General Schoemak was found in jail at Barberton. He fought against us at Colesberg, surrendered to General French when we occupied Pretoria, and was tried by court-martial and imprisoned by the Boers for treason, his crime being that he refused to break his parole.

"The following are the names of the officers released at Barberton on September 13:—

"LINCOLN REGIMENT—Colonel Roberts, Lieut. Lyall.

"IMPERIAL YEOMANRY—Colonel Spragge, Col. Holland, Lieutenant Ruttledge, Lieutenant Mitchell, Lieutenant Dupre, Lieutenant Woodnouse.

"LORD STRATHCONA'S CORPS—Cap. Howard, Intelligence Department; Mr. Goodson, New Zealand Mounted Rifles; Captain Bourne, Lieutenant Cameron.

"12th LANCERS—Captain Egerton Green.

"HIGHLAND LIGHT INFANTRY—Lieutenant Murray.

"IMPERIAL YEOMANRY—Capt. Rokeby, Capt. Robinson, Lieutenant Lane, Lieutenant Wright.

"BETHUNE'S MOUNTED INFANTRY—Captain Cathell

"BRABANT'S HORSE—Lieutenant Butler.

"BORDER MOUNTED RIFLES—Major Saugmeisters.

"EASTERN PROVINCE HORSE—Lieutenant Bertram."

PAGET AT HEBRON.

Lord Roberts reports that General Paget arrived at Hebron, north-west of Pretoria, on the 14th. He had driven off a party of Boers during his march from Pienaars River Station and had taken 10 prisoners and 1000 head of cattle.

HIGHLANDERS IN ACTION.

MACDONALD HEADS OFF A PARTY OF RAILWAY WRECKERS.

PURSUIT ACROSS THE VET.

WORK OF LOVAT'S SCOUTS BEYOND ALL PRAISE.

Koomati Poort yesterday previous to its abandonment on the approach of the British.

[REUTER'S TELEGRAM.]

Lorenzo Marques, September 17.

The Boers have destroyed Crocodile Poort Bridge and burned 300 railway trucks.

BOTHA SURRENDERED?

BOERS REPORTED TO BE RETIRING TO ZOUTPANSBERG.

[From our own Correspondent.]

Lorenzo Marques, Sept. 17.

Fugitive Boers state that Botha has actually surrendered, but of this there is no confirmation.

Kaap Muider Bridge has also been blown up, and the line blocked at Crocodile Poort by immense boulders of rock.

Dynamite mines have been laid in readiness to blow up Komati Poort bridge.

The Boers are falling back on the Zoutpansberg by the way of Selanti, from which district they will probably slink home. Those remaining at Komati Poort are mostly mercenaries, and they practically represent the belligerent element of the Boer army.

They have no homes in the country, and little to stake except the spurious promises held out to them at the commencement of hostilities.

ANXIOUS TO SEE THE END.

[REUTER'S TELEGRAM.]

Lorenzo Marques, September 17.

British troops are daily expected at Koomati Poort

Small parties of Boers who are continually arriving here say any further struggle is hopeless They are anxious to see war finished.

The Portuguese Railway officials decline to accept goods for conveyance beyond the frontier.

KRUGER & CO.

A VILLA FOR THE EX-PRESIDENT AT MESSINA.

[From our own Correspondent.]

Pretoria, September 17.

Mr. Kruger is reported to have taken a villa at Messina, Italy.

Mr. Reitz is going to Paris and thence to the United States, where he will probably stop.

The proclamation issued by Lord Roberts is having a salutary effect. It is very difficult, however, to reach the guerilla forces with it.

Part of the Rustenburg commando surrendered their arms yesterday.

The railway wreckers have desisted from their particular form of outrage which shows that this method of warfare is considered hopeless.

[REUTER'S TELEGRAM.]

Paris, Sept. 17.

A Brussels correspondent states that the Transvaal Consul at Naples is making arrangements for the reception of Mr. Kruger, and that the ex-President will be the bearer of the peace proposals for which he will ask European support.

DUTCH WARSHIP FOR KRUGER'S JOURNEY.

[From our own Correspondent.]

Amsterdam, Sept. 17.

It has now been arranged that the Netherlands warship Gelderland, now in Aden waters, shall bring Kruger to Flushing.

DUKE OF THE ABRUZZI.

HIS HIGHNESS TO LECTURE IN LONDON.

[From our own Correspondent.]

Rome, September 17.

Prince Louis, Duke of the Abruzzi, received to-day a visit at the Royal Palace at Naples from Admiral Fisher, the Commander of the Mediterranean Squadron, who congratulated him in the name of Queen Victoria on the splendid success of his expedition.

The Royal Geographical Society of London has invited the Duke to deliver a lecture on the scientific results of his expedition. The invitation has been accepted, and the Duke will go to London.

ORPHAN HOMES OF SCOTLAND.

OPENING OF ANOTHER CONSUMPTIVE HOSPITAL.

The biennial public thanksgiving service in connection with the Orphan Homes of Scotland and Consumption Sanatoria, at Bridge of Weir, held yesterday, was attended by a large concourse of people from all parts of Scotland. The occasion was also taken advantage of to celebrate the opening of the second sanatorium for consumptives, and the dedication of upwards of £40,000 worth of new property in connection with the Homes.

The proceedings opened with a prayer meeting in the Church Hall, conducted by Mr. Quarrier. Thereafter the 1300 children resident at the Homes formed in processional order, and marched across the field which separates the Orphanage

FROM THE SANATORIA.

At noon Sir Thomas Glen Coats, Bart., accompanied by Sir Robert Pullar, Perth; Lord Provost Hunter, Bailie Doig, and Chief Constable Dewar of Dundee; ex-Preceptor Dickson, Glasgow; Drs. M'Donald (Calcutta) and Ebenezer Duncan, Mr. R. A. Bryden, architect; Mr. and Mrs. Quarrier and others, ascended the improvised platform erected in front of the new sanatorium. Prayer and praise having been conducted, Sir Thomas Glen Coats declared the building open, and paid a high tribute to the administrative qualities shown by Mr. Quarrier and the resource he had dsplayed in grappling with the dread disease, consumption. With the opening of the new premises it was thought possible to deal with 240 persons each year, giving each an average of three months' residence; but when Mr. Quarrier's contemplated scheme of having six hospitals—three for men and three for women—was completed, it would be possible to deal with some 750 cases. In conclusion, Sir Thomas pointed out that they

OWED THE PRESENT HOSPITALS

to people in the East, and remarked that there was a large field to draw upon in the West.

Dr. Duncan, a member of the Advisory Board, spoke of the results of the two years' experience with the first hospital, and mentioned that 20 per cent. of the cases had been entirely cured and rather more than 40 per cent. cured sufficiently to pursue their daily duties. He would like to see Corporations and Parochial authorities following the example of similar bodies in England in supporting such institutions.

Mr. Bryden, the architect, presented a gold key to Mrs. Quarrier, with which she opened the door of the new hospital. The building, which is named "The Door of Hope," and is gifted by Mr. J. Carnegie, of Lochearnhead, was then opened for public inspection. It is beautifully situated on rising ground facing the south. The Gothic scheme of the Homes has been adhered to, and the architect has produced a very beautiful structure of red stone. It has been provided with an additional wing, in which the kitchen and dining rooms are situated, for the use of the patients of both hospitals.

BY THIS ARRANGEMENT

a large amount of space will be saved.

From one till two o'clock the chimes of the church played sacred and national tunes, and the sailor boys went through sail drill and showed the manner of saving life from a stranded wreck.

The dedication service, held in the church shortly after two o'clock, was presided over by Lord Provost Chisholm, Glasgow. Prayer having been offered by Dr. Ross Taylor and Dr. Wells, the Chairman delivered an interesting address. The whole work of the Homes was, he said, based on Christian love and simple faith. With a love and forbearance absolutely unprovokable, Mr. Quarrier had gone on in the steps of the Master, and had rescued thousands of poor children whose surroundings were dragging them down to criminality. The Second City had done much towards filling the Homes, and it would be well if wealthy merchants gave practical remembrance to that fact.

Lord Provost Hunter, Dundee, commended the work of the Homes, after which Mr. Quarrier expressed his indebtedness at the large and representative gathering present and his pleasure at the interest shown in the work. He directed the attention of his hearers to the cruelty of the County Council of Renfrew and the Parish Council of Kilmalcolm in rating the Homes and giving no corresponding advantages. (Shame.)

Other gentlemen also spoke.

CITY IN PANIC OVER THE PLAGUE

FEARS that an outbreak of the plague could sweep Glasgow sent the city into turmoil and medical authorities moved fast to try to calm public fears.

An official bulletin issued at the Glasgow Sanitary Chambers in Montrose Street on September 2 showed that there were 11 cases of bubonic plague in Belvidere Hospital, one suspected case and 93 contacts under observation.

Stringent measures were adopted by the authorities.

In Rose Street and Thistle Street, where the disease was first reported, closes and stairs and back courts leading to tenements where cases or suspected cases had been discovered, were whitewashed. In addition,

the houses were disinfected, ashpits emptied and cleaned, and as far as possible, all traces of dirt likely to harbour the disease removed.

The *Daily News* – which later evolved into the *Daily Record* – stated:

"For those who feel any alarm at the news of the plague in Glasgow, there will be timely comfort in the publication of Mr Baldwin Lathman's valuable paper on the climatic conditions necessary for the propagation and spread of plague.

"The disease, we are assured by Mr Latham, can make no headway where the conditions for its development and conveyance are absent.

"And we do not gather that they are present in England or Scotland. The cases

are sporadic, and the condition in this country is not favourable to an epidemic.

"Bombay and Poona have suffered terribly from the plague. But in Bombay such diseases are traceable to the blocking of the natural drainage outlets from the city, and the consequent stagnation in the movement of underground water.

"In Poona, Mr Latham found a revolting state of things and horrible stagnation of the subsoil. It was apparent that the ground was impregnated with filth of man and beast."

The newspaper concluded by pointing out that there were no such conditions in Glasgow or in any part of the United Kingdom which could enable the disease to take hold.

COMINGS...

Alistair Sim
Actor

GOINGS...

The Marquis of Queensbury
Creator of Boxing Rules

THE GREATEST OF ALL TONICS.

PHOSFERINE

THE ROYAL TONIC AND DIGESTIVE.

MR. LEWIS EXPRESSES HIS HEARTY THANKS FOR THE MARVELLOUS BENEFIT HE HAS DERIVED FROM PHOSFERINE. HE WAS A GREAT SUFFERER FROM INTENSE WEAKNESS AND NERVOUS PROSTRATION, RESULTING FROM INDIGESTION AND DYSENTERY.

AFTER UNAVAILING MEDICAL ADVICE, ON THE RECOMMENDATION OF A FRIEND, HE TRIED PHOSFERINE, AND, THANKS TO ITS AID, IS NOW QUITE WELL.

ROYAL COMMANDS.

Phosferine enjoys the distinguished honour of having received commands from
MEMBERS OF THE BRITISH ROYAL FAMILY.

QUARRIER HOMES PRAISED

The work of William Quarrier's orphan homes and consumption sanatoriums was praised at a public thanksgiving service in Bridge of Weir in September, attended by dignitaries from all over Scotland. Mr Quarrier was commended for his Christian efforts in rescuing thousands of destitute and homeless children from the slums of Scotland's cities, as was the success of his consumption hospitals where it was stated up to 40% of cases were cured.

HIGHLANDERS IN ACTION AGAINST THE BOERS

The Highland Brigade reported another successful action against Boer guerrillas in southern Africa in September. The commandos had been attempting to disable the Delagoa railway by destroying bridges over the Vet river near Brandfort. Under the vigorous leadership of 'Fighting Mac' MacDonald, the Brigade engaged the enemy near to Tafel Top and put them to flight, taking a number of prisoners and capturing a large quantity of weapons and other supplies, without loss to themselves.

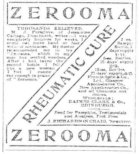

ZEROOMA

RHEUMATIC CURE

ZEROOMA

Grace before Meat_

YORKSHIRE RELISH

with it!

THE MOST DELICIOUS SAUCE IN THE WORLD.

WHAT IT COST

POUND OF BUTTER	1s
POUND OF BACON	9d
PINT OF BEER	2d
CIGARETTES	3d (10 Black Cat)
WOMEN'S SHOES	4s 6d
MEN'S SUIT	6s 11d
TON OF COAL	10s 9d
POSTAGE	1d
CAR	Ford Model T £175

THIS SPORTING LIFE

FOOTBALL	RUGBY UNION	GOLF	HORSE RACING	SHINTY
Scottish Champions Rangers	*Scotland vs England* Scotland 0–0 England at Inverleith	*British Open Winner* J.H. Taylor at St Andrews (309)	*Scottish Grand National Winner* Dorothy Vane at Bogside	*Camanachd Cup Winners* Kingussie at Perth
Scottish Cup Winners Celtic				

City Edition

THE KING: EDWARD VII. PAGE 4.

The Daily Record.

LAUREATE'S TRIBUTE. PAGE 4.

LARGEST SALE OF ANY MORNING OR EVENING NEWSPAPER IN SCOTLAND.

No. MDCXLII—SIX EDITIONS. GLASGOW, THURSDAY, JANUARY 24, 1901 PRICE ONE HALFPENNY.

SCOTLAND CONDOLES.

REPRESENTATIVE MEN BEWAIL THE NATION'S LOSS.

EULOGIES AND ELEGIES.

Public expression was yesterday given to the country's sense of the loss sustained by the death of Queen Victoria, at meetings of many of the Town Councils and other bodies throughout Scotland. The Corporations of Edinburgh and Glasgow, however, have deferred their meetings for this purpose till to-day. Telegrams of condolence have been general. Further official manifestations of the national mourning fall to be noted in the artillery salutes from Edinburgh Castle and the guardships, in the tolling of bells in many a town and hamlet, in the flags drooping at half-mast over public buildings. Correspondents everywhere note the depth and sincerity of private grief. Arrangements are generally contemplated for local funeral services on the day of the Queen's obsequies. Details are published of the ceremonial of the proclamation of the King in Edinburgh to-morrow.

EDINBURGH.

PUBLIC BODIES' EXPRESSION OF SYMPATHY.

In the fullest meaning of the expression Edinburgh was in mourning yesterday. From the flagstaffs on the Castle, the City Chambers, Piershill Barracks, public buildings and offices and business premises, flags were flying at half-mast. Signs of sorrow were everywhere observable. Many of the shop fronts in Princes Street were draped in black and the many evidences of regret at the death of her Majesty were common to all classes of the community. Business for the day was practically suspended, and all functions of a public character have been either abandoned or indefinitely postponed. The theatres and other places of amusement did not open in the evening. A special meeting of the Corporation of Edinburgh will be held to-day, at which a resolution of regret at the death of the Queen and sympathy with the members of the Royal family will be adopted. During yesterday the Royal, the Judges', the Professorial, and the Corporation pews in St. Giles Cathedral were draped in black. Minute guns were fired from the Castle during the afternoon. There were eighty-one discharges—one gun for every year of her Majesty's life. The first shot was fired at 3.30.

SCOTTISH LIBERAL ASSOCIATION.

The annual meeting of the Scottish Liberal Association next Tuesday, at which Sir Henry Campbell-Bannerman was to have spoken, has been abandoned; as has also the dinner of the Scottish Reform Club, at which Sir Henry was to have been the guest of the evening.

The following telegram has been sent to the Secretary of State for Scotland by Sir Thomas Gibson Carmichael on behalf of the Scottish Liberal Association:—

"The Executive of the Scottish Liberal Association express their deep regret at the death of her Majesty Queen Victoria, and their respectful sympathy with the members of the Royal Family. May I ask you the favour of forwarding this message."

THE LIBERAL CLUB.

A meeting of the members of the Scottish Liberal Club was held in the reading rooms yesterday afternoon to pass a resolution of condolence with the King and Royal Family. Mr. Lang Todd, the chairman, presided over a large attendance of members.

In submitting the resolution the Chairman remarked that the first sensation which filled their hearts was not that of the mere sorrow which one felt when one of the great ones of the earth passed away, but was a feeling more akin to that of personal loss which they felt when one who was near and dear to them had been removed by the hand of death. They would ever have before them the many and great blessings which had been showered upon the land during the long reign of her Majesty, many of which were due in no small measure to her wisdom as a ruler, and to her high virtues as a woman. Her kindly and loving sympathy with her people in all their trials and fortunes had especially endeared her to all her subjects.

The address of sympathy was read to the meeting upstanding. It was in the following terms:—

"To the King's Most Excellent Majesty,—Most gracious Sovereign, we, your Majesty's most dutiful and loyal subjects, humbly ap-

MERCHANT COMPANY'S CONDOLENCE.

The following address has been sent to Lord Balfour of Burleigh by the Merchant Company of Edinburgh:—

"On behalf of the Company of Merchants of the City of Edinburgh, I respectfully tender through your Lordship an expression of heartfelt grief at the death of our revered and beloved Sovereign, and of profound sympathy with his Majesty and the other members of the Royal Family in their bereavement.—Robert Weir, Master, The Merchants' Hall, Edinburgh."

THE UNIVERSITY.

The following telegram was despatched yesterday:—"His Royal Highness the Prince of Wales,—The University of Edinburgh submit to your Royal Highness and the Royal Family their deepest sympathy in the loss which has overwhelmed them and the Empire at large, in the death of her who for more than three score years has ruled with a beneficent majesty unequalled in ages past. (Signed) W. Muir, Principal and Vice-Chancellor."

EDUCATIONAL INSTITUTIONS.

The classes at the University did not assemble. The Edinburgh Board Schools were closed, as also those of the Merchant Company and Heriot Trust; the New Veterinary College, the Heriot-Watt College, and Royal (Dick) Veterinary College.

THE STOCK EXCHANGE.

The members of the Stock Exchange met during the morning, and the chairman, Mr. L. Brown Douglas, expressed the prevailing sorrow when he said that they had often drunk the health of her Majesty and joined together in singing "God Save our gracious Queen," but neither the health nor the hymn would ever be the same to them again.

The Committee agreed to suspend business, and accordingly the Stock Exchange was closed.

POLICE COURTS, ETC.

At the Burgh Police Court Bailie Telfer referred in sympathetic terms to the lamented death of the Queen, and the Court thereafter adjourned until noon.

The Sheriff, Small Debt, Appeal, and Bankruptcy Courts were also adjourned.

In the City Police Court yesterday Sheriff Orphoot, who presided, said:—The death of the Queen, who had so entirely won the affection, admiration, and respect of her people, is an event so impressive and so sad that I felt disposed, as a mark of respect to her memory, to suspend for to-day the sitting of this Court; but the effect of so doing would be to prolong the detention of the persons in custody and under charge, and that might inflict upon some of those persons a certain amount of hardship. We may be well assured that the Queen would not desire that any respect for her memory, or mourning for her loss, should take that shape. On the contrary, I think we shall best follow the lofty example which she set by doing the work which lies before us to be done; so while we feel that a great blank has been created in the national life, and while we feel the profoundest respect for the memory of the Queen, I propose to proceed with the business of the Court.

"THREE LESSONS."

At the usual daily service in St. Giles Cathedral yesterday afternoon the Rev. Dr. Cameron Lees said he was sure that all would join in wishing for our King a long, prosperous, and peaceful reign. Their minds were at present, however, fully occupied with the present, and the past was full of remembrances of her whom God had taken away from them. The sorrows of that day taught them three lessons, the universality of death, the supreme importance of character, and the great and far-reaching powers of a Christian life

conies in front of the building. In the early hours of the morning a meeting of the Municipal Buildings Committee was hastily convened by Councillor Shearer, and the character of the mourning decided upon. Two festoons of black were run along the outside balconies from George Street to Cochrane Street, the Council Chamber was heavily draped, as was the front of the gallery of the Banqueting Hall, and all the blinds were drawn. The work was most expeditiously performed by Messrs. Wylie & Lochhead, under the supervision of Mr. William Macleod, the keeper of the Chambers. Numerous other public buildings have been or will be treated in the same manner, including all the City Churches, Kelvinside Parish Church, St. Matthew's United Free, Battlefield United Free, Elgin Place Congregational, Pollokshields United Free, Crosshill United Free, Western Club, Clyde Trust Buildings, Stock Exchange, Conservative Club, Junior Conservative Club, and the New Club. In addition a number of commercial firms, including "The Daily Record," draped the windows of their offices; the shopkeepers who are privileged to display the Royal Arms on their premises swathed them in black, and many others, not so highly favoured, followed this example by substituting black for lighter coloured goods in their windows, and giving other evidences of the public sorrow. The principal hotels gave similar expression to the general feeling, the Royal Hotel in George Square following closely the scheme of the City Chambers, with the addition of black draperies round the principal entrance. Black ties and gloves were very generally worn by gentlemen, and many ladies attired themselves in their darkest garb. Indeed there was an unprecedented run on blacks all day, and orders poured in on the wholesale houses from all parts of the country. Of course, the demand was anticipated to some extent, but many of the largest houses declared that they would probably be unable to supply the trade in a day or two.

The classes at the University did not meet, several schools were closed, and at the training colleges the classes were dismissed. In the evening all the places of entertainments with only one or two exceptions were closed.

At the harbour the vessels of all nationalities hoisted flags at half-mast, and one rather touching incident was witnessed. On the arrival of the Italian vessel, Silvia, laden with grain, from Bona, Algeria, at the dock in the morning, one of the deputy harbourmasters went aboard, informed the master of the death of the Queen, and asked him to hoist his flag half-mast. On hearing the news the captain fell on his knees on the deck, clasped his hands, and offered prayer.

THE CITY'S CONDOLENCE.

Lord Provost Chisholm was at the City Chambers at an early hour, and despatched a telegram of condolence to the King by his former title Prince of Wales, it being understood that the kingly title should not be given until his Royal Highness had been proclaimed. The telegram was as follows:—

"To his Royal Highness the Prince of Wales, Marlborough House, London.

"With every section of her Majesty's devoted people, the citizens of Glasgow mourn the loss of their revered Sovereign. For upwards of sixty-three years her beneficent and loving sympathy have given her an unexampled place in the national history, in the lives of her subjects of every class, and in the admiration, not only of all English-speaking races, but of the whole civilised world. The citizens of Glasgow offer their humble and fervent sympathy with the Princess of Wales and all the other members of the Royal Family.

"The Lord Provost of Glasgow."

In reply to an inquiry by a "Daily Record" representative, Lord Provost Chisholm said he intended to call a meeting of the Magistrates of the city at the earliest opportunity and consult with them as to calling a special meeting of the Corporation, either to-day or Friday, at which the sorrow of the entire body of the citizens might be officially and adequately expressed and an address of condolence voted.

Later in the forenoon the Magistrates were summoned to meet at half-past eleven to-day to make the necessary arrangements for the meeting of the Corporation, and in the afternoon Sir James Marwick, the Town Clerk, issued a black-bordered circular calling the members together at noon "for the purpose of voting an address of condolence with H.R.H. the Prince of Wales and the other members of the Royal Family on the death of her Majesty the Queen."

MAGISTERIAL TRIBUTES.

It was arranged by the Magistrates and Judges on duty at the City Police Courts in the morning that prisoners charged with minor offences should be dismissed, and that those charged with serious crimes should be remanded till to-day. In announcing this decision when the Courts met the Magistrates made reference to the nation's loss.

At the Central, Bailie J. C. Robertson said they met under the shadow of a great national loss. The fears of the past few days had been

SMALLPOX IN GLASGOW.

WARNINGS AND PROMPT ACTION BY THE CORPORATION.

At the meeting of Glasgow Corporation yesterday—Lord Provost Chisholm presiding—Mr. Dick, convener of the Health Committee, alluded to the report by the Medical Officer of Health as to the prevalence of smallpox in the city. He was sorry to say that during the last seven days there had been 146 cases discovered. The Medical Officer of Health was very anxious indeed that people should understand the great desirability for revaccination, especially those in the better circumstances of life. They would see that the committee requested the Corporation to ask the Parks Committee to grant the use of Tollcross House as a Reception House. The committee had gone over the length and breadth of the city and could not get another place, and they therefore threw themselves on the tender mercies of the Corporation.

Bailie Steele seconded.

Mr. George Mitchell moved a direct negative, and pointed out that the necessary barricade would cost £500. He thought another plan might be tried which had been suggested, that there should be supervision of people in their own houses. Plans for the extension of the Weaver Street House had been shunted. If Tollcross were used they might as well shut Tollcross Park.

Mr. Roderick Scott seconded, and pointed out that a committee had been considering how to provide reception houses for nine years. That committee should be disbanded and another appointed, for within six hours he would get all the houses that were required, if he got the order.

Mr. Shaw Maxwell protested against the proposal, and suggested that

THE WEST-END MEMBERS

would object to such a house being put in Kelvingrove Park, just as the East End members did regarding Tollcross House.

Bailie King asked the Corporation to recognise the exigencies of the case, and pointed out that the fittings and equipment of the House made it suitable for the purpose. They must remember that there was an infectious diseases hospital in Ruchill Park.

Mr. Battersby—You opposed that. (Laughter.)

Bailie King—I opposed it before I had any experience in the matter, and having had experience we find people do not care one button. It has never detracted from the use of the park one iota.

Mr. Bilsland regretted that circumstances had arisen to dictate the request for the use of Tollcross House, but he recognised that they were face to face with an emergency, and he would not be responsible for refusing to afford the accommodation needed. But he did ask that the Committee should give a pledge that every possible endeavour should be made to get a permanent place on a more suitable site. He feared that if the request were readily granted the Committee would not feel the necessity to bestir themselves to provide a remedy.

Mr. P. G. Stewart suggested that the Art Galleries in Sauchiehall Street, which would soon be vacated, should be utilised.

The Lord Provost said the question before the Corporation was as to what should be done to preserve the health of the city, not as to the dilitoriness of the Committee in providing a suitable reception house elsewhere. There was no need to take an alarmist view of the fact that smallpox prevailed in the East-End. Efforts had been made to meet the difficulty which that entailed by finding a house elsewhere, and therefore he saw no other course before the Corporation than that they should, with regret, ask the Parks Committee for

THE USE OF TOLLCROSS HOUSE.

He could understand there being something stronger than regret on the part of the East-End representatives, but they must consider what was best to be done at that crisis.

Mr. Battersby traced the difficulty to the Committee's failure to provide a reception-house.

A discussion ensued, in which most of the East-End members took strong exception to the proposal; but Mr. Hugh Alexander appealed to them to withdraw opposition now that they had entered their protest.

Dr. Carswell desired that the crisis should be faced. He characterised the opposition as dictated by flippancy. He did not wish to be

NATION MOURNS QUEEN VICTORIA

SCOTLAND officially mourned the death of Queen Victoria at the meetings of many town councils and other bodies around the country.

In the country as a whole, there was a general sense of loss and there many public and private expressions of sadness and regret at the passing of the long-reigning monarch.

At Edinburgh Castle, Glasgow City Chambers and other public buildings and offices, flags were flown at half mast.

The people mourned too and shop fronts in towns and cities throughout the country were draped in black and numerous telegrams of condolence were sent from throughout the United Kingdom.

A special meeting of the Privy Council was held on January 23 which was attended by the new king, who took the customary oath.

He then intimated that, in deference to the wishes of his late mother, he had taken the title of Edward VII. The public proclamation of this was made the following day.

A special Army Order was issued announcing that the King had commanded officers to wear mourning ensignia on their uniforms for the duration of the official mourning period which was to run from January 23 to March 5.

The body of the Queen lay in state at St Paul's Cathedral before her coffin was taken to Windsor for burial.

The death of Queen Victoria was regarded by historians as also the end of an era. She had been on the throne since 1837 and was sovreign of such a massive empire that it was said that the sun never set on it. Her reign had also witnessed momentous changes in British society and huge upheavals in world politics.

THE EXHIBITION.

AUSPICIOUS OPENING BY ROYALTY.

IMPOSING PROCESSION IN THE CITY.

AT KELVINGROVE.

A MEMORABLE INAUGURAL GATHERING.

NEARLY 100,000 PERSONS IN THE GROUNDS.

CIVIC HONOURS.

DUCHESS OF FIFE CREATED A BURGESS.

OGDEN'S

"GUINEA GOLD"

CIGARETTES

ARE ALWAYS TO THE FRONT. BECAUSE THEY ARE THE BEST VALUE ON THE MARKET AT THE PRESENT DAY.

INTERNATIONAL EXHIBITION OPENS

The Glasgow International Exhibition was opened by Princess Louise, the Duchess of Fife. The 73-acre site in Kelvingrove Park featured a staggering array of exhibits from around the world in every field from heavy machinery to sweets and from international pavilions to local artists. An undeclared war waged between the older gas and the new electricity industries which meant that their respective sections blazed with light every night as each tried to out-do the other.

COMINGS...

Lewis Grassic Gibbon
Writer

DR WILLIAMS' PINK PILLS FOR PALE PEOPLE
Registered.

Dr. Williams' Pink Pills for Pale People

CURE
ANÆMIA, INDIGESTION, PALPITATION, CONSUMPTION, RHEUMATISM, ST. VITUS' DANCE, SCIATICA, NEURALGIA, PARALYSIS, ECZEMA, RICKETS, LADIES' AILMENTS, &c., &c.

Worthless substitutes are numerous, being intentionally made up to deceive unwary people. Look for the full name on the wrapper and

are sold only in a pink paper wrapper, surrounding a wooden tube, bearing the full name (seven words) printed in red.

Price 2s. 9d. per box, or 13s. 9d. for six boxes.

Mind you ask for Dr. Williams'

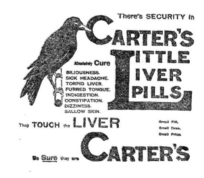

There's SECURITY in

CARTER'S LITTLE LIVER PILLS

Absolutely Cure
BILIOUSNESS.
SICK HEADACHE.
TORPID LIVER.
FURRED TONGUE.
INDIGESTION.
CONSTIPATION.
DIZZINESS.
SALLOW SKIN.

They TOUCH the LIVER

Small Pill.
Small Dose.
Small Price.

Be Sure they are CARTER'S

SMALLPOX IN GLASGOW

An outbreak of smallpox was reported in Glasgow in January. In the space of a week, more than 146 cases were discovered, many in the east end of the city. The Health Committee of the Corporation feared that if steps were not taken to contain it, it would spread rapidly, with an estimated 40 to 50 new cases daily. Vaccination was recommended, particularly for those living in the city's lodging houses and prisons. It was also suggested that Tollcross House be set aside as an emergency measure to receive the infected although the cost of doing so and the need to close Tollcross Park as a result led to opposition to this move. Other possible sites in Kelvingrove Park and in the former Art Galleries in Sauchiehall St were rejected.

THIS SPORTING LIFE

FOOTBALL	RUGBY UNION	GOLF	HORSE RACING	SHINTY
Scottish Champions Rangers	Scotland vs England England 3–18 Scotland at Blackheath	British Open Winner James Braid at Muirfield (309)	Scottish Grand National Winner Big Busbie at Bogside	Camanachd Cup Winners Ballachulish at Inverness
Scottish Cup Winners Hearts				

The Daily Record & Mail.

LARGER SALE THAN ANY OTHER MORNING OR EVENING NEWSPAPER IN SCOTLAND.

ESTABLISHED 1847.—No. 17,213. GLASGOW, MONDAY, APRIL 7, 1902 ONE HALFPENNY.

APPALLING CATASTROPHE.

COLLAPSE OF TERRACING AT INTERNATIONAL FOOTBALL MATCH.

EIGHTEEN MEN KILLED.

OVER 250 SPECTATORS INJURED.

HARROWING SCENES.

PROMPT AND ENERGETIC WORK OF RESCUE.

What was expected to have been one of the greatest football matches ever witnessed between the chosen representatives of England and Scotland became in the sequel the most memorable in the annals of the game—memorable unhappily not because of the play, but for an appalling calamity which occurred a few minutes after the kick-off.

The match was being played on Saturday on the Rangers' ground at Ibrox Park, in the outskirts of Govan, about two and a half miles from the centre of Glasgow. A portion of the high terracing at the west-end of the arena gave way, with the result that several hundred people were precipated to the ground beneath, from a height of about 40 feet. Over 270 in all received injuries necessitating their being medically attended to in the infirmaries or elsewhere: three were dead or practically on the point of death when lifted; and since then 15 others have succumbed to their injuries, making a death-roll up till last midnight of 18.

It is believed that never before in Scotland was a multitude of such dimensions as that which assembled at Ibrox Park crammed into a space so circumscribed. Conflicting estimates of the number of spectators were given, but the figure is believed to be about 70,000. It was quite apparent long before three o'clock that the terracing all round the track, no less than grand stands, was too crowded to admit of any more being safely accommodated.

The Fatal Swaying.

Still, newcomers pressed in by every avenue, and the spectacle soon became something more than impressive—it grew alarming. Especially was this the case when one turned one's eyes in the direction of the terracing at the west-end of the track. At every point and continuously round the enclosure there appeared a seething mass of humanity, so closely packed together that from the opposite side of the pitch the faces gave a prevailing flesh tone to the serried ranks, which banked up the east end and sides to the height of some fifty terraces and the west end to over a hundred terraces.

No one could fail to guess that very serious danger to the progress of the match, if not to life and limb, lay in that fearful crush at the west end. It is said that the lofty terracing there was divided into sections by crush rails made of cast iron, but if that were so—and there is no reason to doubt the statement—these railings, erected to prevent swaying on the part of the multitude, were smashed by the enormous pressure by telephone and telegraph to convey the injured to the infirmaries or to their homes. When the supply of stretchers gave out ingenuity found means of making rough and ready substitutes. Lieut. M'Fadzean, of the Govan police, procured a lot of timber from the engineer of the new railway now in course of construction near the Park and improvised stretchers.

The Melancholy Procession.

For the ensuing two hours there was a touching procession of the wounded from the field to the infirmaries. It struck the crowds of pedestrians encountered on the way with feelings of the deepest compassion and awe. A gentleman who witnessed the procession going to the Western Infirmary describes the scene as one never to be forgotten by those who looked on—the vehicles passing by filled with the injured, who bore evidences of the medical assistance they had received on the ground in the shape of bandaged heads and limbs. The procession crossed the river by way of the Govan horse-ferry. A crowd numbering several thousands gathered at the corner of Govan Road and Water Row, which leads to the ferry, but excellent order was maintained by the police. The other vehicular traffic willingly stood by and allowed the ambulances to pass without interruption. All along the route from the ferry up to the gate of the Western Infirmary great numbers of people awaited the passing of the mournful line of vehicles, and many anxious ones looked into the vans fearing to see there some of their relatives.

As at Govan, there was a staff of policemen at Partick Cross and at points along the route keeping the way clear. The car and other traffic was stopped in order to let the ambulances reach the infirmary as speedily as possible. The vans and cabs and so on entered the infirmary grounds by the western gate at Byars Road, and, having been relieved of the injured, they passed out by the southern gate, got on to the Dumbarton Road, and so returned by the ferry for more victims.

Meanwhile the football match was going on, and there is a very good reason why the committees of the respective Associations decided that it should be played. It may seem incredible, but the fact is undeniable that thousands and thousands of spectators were absolutely ignorant of the grave nature of the accident, and would have created a dangerous riot if the match had been put off.

The attention of the people was at first diverted by rather serious consequences which followed the crash in the west terracing. Those in the near vicinity of the part which fell crushed in their terror upon those in front, and that with such compelling force that they almost did to death the people at the bottom fencing. Youths and men who fainted in the terrible struggle were lifted over the heads of the crowd and handed over the fence by the dozen. Others had the breath almost crushed out of them at the fence and were in evident jeopardy of their lives.

KING EDWARD VII.

THE MONARCH'S CROWNING TO-DAY.

THE ABBEY CEREMONY.

ORDER OF THE HISTORIC SOLEMNITY.

WORLD-WIDE REJOICING.

The Monarch of the United Kingdom and Ireland and of the British dominions beyond the seas, Defender of the Faith, and Emperor of India, will be crowned in Westminster Abbey at five minutes past twelve to-day.

Simultaneously with the great event in London the whole of the British Empire beyond the seas and many foreign countries friendly to Great Britain are participating in the general celebration.

From the Antipodes comes news of universal rejoicing; the Cape Colony, Natal, the Orange River Colony, and the Transvaal are holding high holiday; in Gibraltar and at the outlying bulwarks of the Empire there are processions, illuminations, and the like.

In foreign towns, such as Bruges, Dusseldorf, Berlin, Copenhagen, The Hague, and Budapest there will be services at the churches, English or otherwise, and individual festivities suitable to the locality.

At the British Embassies and Consulates throughout the world there will be receptions, and no corner of the Empire will be without its contribution to the general pæan of congratulations.

On inquiry last night it was ascertained that the King, who had had an exceptionally busy day at Buckingham Palace, had suffered no undue fatigue as the result of his labours, and that the Crowning ceremony to-day was looked forward to without the slightest misgiving.

His Majesty was engaged with various affairs of State, including the matter of Ministerial changes. He gave separate receptions to the Emperor Menelik's envoy and the Prime Minister of Uganda, and held an important investiture of the insignia of various honours conferred in celebration of the Coronation.

The order of the processions from Buckingham Palace and York House to the Abbey today was issued last night by the Court newsman. The alterations from the original programme, as published in our columns some time ago, are only trifling. All the processions start half an hour earlier than was arranged for June 26th. Owing to the smaller number of foreign Princes there is one carriage the less, and Lord Kitchener has a place in the King's procession, riding with Admiral Seymour and General Gasalee immediately in front of the headquarters staff.

THE CROWNING.

FEATURES OF THE CEREMONIAL IN THE ABBEY.

From seven o'clock for two and a half hours those who are to witness the Coronation without joining in the great procession will take their places in the Abbey.

They will be seated on three sides of the theatre, which is at the crossing of transept and nave. North and south of it are places for Peers and Peeresses, and behind these, raised tiers for members of the House of Commons. Guests of the King and Queen will be accommodated in large Royal boxes on either hand of the area which is between the theatre and the high altar, and Peers of the blood Royal in chairs set in front of their fellows.

In that portion of the nave which is behind the nave altar screen, and thus in view of the theatre, there will be Cabinet Ministers, Colonial Premiers, foreign representa-

SCOTLAND'S REJOICING.

HOW THE GLAD TIDINGS WERE WELCOMED.

JOY BELLS RINGING.

A GENERAL FEELING OF THANKFULNESS.

Scotland yesterday gave free rein to her feelings of jubilation at the conclusion of peace. In the cities and large burghs to which the momentous news was telegraphed on Sunday evening, some of the effervescence had already found means of outlet by the ringing of bells, the partial illumination of public buildings, and mutual congratulations between individuals, but in many towns and villages it was only on the arrival of the morning newspapers that the information became public property.

In these cases, however, the delay but added to the general joy of the morning, and reports from our provincial correspondents show that not since the relief of Kimberley, Ladysmith, and Mafeking, and the occupation of Pretoria, has public feeling been roused to such a pitch of excitement. Lavish were the decorations, vociferous were the crowds, and brilliant were last evening's illuminations in all centres of population.

Glasgow always comes to the front on occasions of national rejoicing, and she did so yesterday. Although discounted, to some extent, by confident anticipation and published on Sunday evening to thousands of the citizens by the "Daily Record and Mail" through the instrumentality of the city churches, the news was the only topic of conversation all day, and the prevailing feelings were those of deep thankfulness that the country had at last seen the end of a terrible war, pride for the heroism of the troops which brought Britain the victory, and admiration for a brave and tenacious foe. The city from north to south, from east to west, was early decked with flags, the streets were crowded all day with sightseers and demonstrators, becoming in the evening, and especially in the centre of the city, more congested than they have been seen for many months, work in the large factories and yards was almost entirely suspended—in short, the day was regarded more or less as a general holiday. At three o'clock a special meeting of the Corporation was held, at which a telegram of congratulation was despatched to the King, and a brief thanksgiving service followed in the Banqueting Hall of the City Chambers.

CIVIC JOY.

GLASGOW'S LOYAL MESSAGE TO THE KING.

There was a large attendance of members at the hurriedly-summoned special meeting of the Corporation at three o'clock. Lord Provost Chisholm presided and wore his robes of office, as did also the Magistrates.

The Lord Provost said he was sure he could reckon on the cordial approval of all his colleagues, as well as of the citizens of Glasgow as a whole, when he said that he had thought it his duty to summon a special meeting of the Town Council in order that they, the representatives of the city, might give utterance to those feelings, deep and strong, which that day animated and swayed every heart amongst them. (Hear, hear.) It was not the tumultuous excitement of victory which filled them, and it was by no means the shout of triumph they were disposed to give.

I am sure (continued his Lordship) I speak for all when I say that the feelings that are deepest in our hearts at this moment are feelings of fervent gratitude to God Almighty, in whose hands are the hearts of all men, that the way of peace has at last been found

1902

18 KILLED IN BIG MATCH TRAGEDY

DISASTER struck the Scotland-England football match in April. A few minutes after the kick-off. at Ibrox Stadium, a section of the terracing gave way and three people were killed, with 15 later dying from injuries. More than 250 fans at the Glasgow ground were also hurt.

A major factor in the tragedy was the size of the crowd crammed into a limited space. The number of spectators at the ground, the home of Glasgow Rangers, was believed to have reached about 70,000.

They had turned out to see what was expected to be one of the great football matches but instead witnessed one of the major catastrophes in the history of Scottish and British football.

It was apparent long before the kick-off that the terracing was too crowded to admit any more people safely but fans continued to pour into the ground. The crowd on the terracings heaved and swelled like an ocean of bodies even before the game kicked off.

Shortly after the match began, a corner kick was awarded by the referee. It led to a surge among the thousands of fans packed onto the terracing behind the north-west end of the ground.

Spectators leaned forward to see the kick being taken and with a sickening crash, a huge part of the terracing at the highest point gave way and the people standing on it crashed down.

The gap left on the terracing was some 70 feet deep and 11 feet wide and the spectators who had been standing in this section were left lying mangled, bruised and bleeding in the wreckage.

Most of those who died suffered head or internal injuries as they crashed on to twisted wood and steel trestles and beams but other victims were suffocated by other people falling on them.

Rescue work started immediately, and police and ambulance reinforcements arrived to give assistance.

CORONATION JUBILATION

Cities and towns across Scotland joined in the celebrations as King Edward VII was crowned at Westminster in August. In Glasgow, as elsewhere, the drab buildings were transformed by flags, bunting and flowers. From early morning, people poured out onto the streets in the city centre and the revelry continued until the early hours. Three specially-illuminated trams celebrating the new king toured the city and brought streets to a standstill wherever they passed.

COMINGS...

Eric Liddell
Athlete

Fyfe Robertson
Broadcaster & Journalist

GOINGS...

William McGonagall
The World's Worst Poet

Drunkards Easily Cured

Miss Edith Williams, Wants Every Lady Reader of this Paper to Know How She Saved Her Father.

A new discovery, odorless and tasteless, which any lady can give in tea, coffee or food. It does its work so silently and surely that while the devoted wife, sister or daughter looks on, the drunkard is reclaimed even against his will and without his knowledge or co-operation. Send name and address to Dr. J.W. Haines, 2397 Glenn Bldg Cincinnati, O., U.S.A., and he will mail enough of the remedy free to show how it is used in tea, coffee or food. Nothing could be more dramatic or devoted than the manner in which Miss Edith Williams, Box 33, Waynesville, Ohio, U.S.A., cured her drunken father after years of misery.

MISS EDITH WILLIAMS.

wretchedness and almost unbearable suffering.

"Yes," she said, "our friends think it a miracle I cured him without his knowledge or consent by using a remedy secretly in his coffee and food. I hadn't seen him sober for half a day before in over fourteen years. But the very day he got the first dose of it he came home sober and said, 'Edith I don't know what has come over me but I hate the sight and smell of liquor and am going to stop drinking forever.'"

Golden Specific is sold by Lynch & Co., Ltd., General Agents, 192 Aldersgate St., London, E. C., and all respectable chemists. Free trial packages are sent from Cincinnati only.

Blood Poison Cured Free.

The Remedy is Sent Absolutely Free to Every Man or Woman Sending Name and Address.

BOER WAR FINALLY OVER

In June, news of the Boer surrender was relayed back to Britain and in Scotland, whose regiments had played such a prominent role in the South African war, there were widespread celebrations across the country as almost three years of conflict came to an end. In every city and large burgh, church bells were rung, flags and decorations raised, and buildings illuminated. Work in factories and yards was suspended as people spilled out onto the streets to celebrate. An unofficial general holiday was declared.

The war had begun badly for the Crown forces with a string of defeats and the loss of some 11,000 men, mostly through disease. However, under Lord Kitchener, the British progressively gained the upper hand over a difficult enemy who chose guerrilla tactics over set-piece battles.

THIS SPORTING LIFE

FOOTBALL	RUGBY UNION	GOLF	HORSE RACING	SHINTY
Scottish Champions Rangers	*Scotland vs England* Scotland 3–6 England at Inverleith	*British Open Winner* Sandy Herd at Hoylake, England (307)	*Scottish Grand National Winner* Canter Home at Bogside	*Camanachd Cup Winners* Kingussie at Inverness
Scottish Cup Winners Hibernian				

City Edition

The Daily Record & Mail.

LARGER SALE THAN ANY OTHER MORNING OR EVENING NEWSPAPER IN SCOTLAND.

ESTABLISHED 1847.—No. 17,473 GLASGOW, TUESDAY, FEBRUARY 10, 1903 ONE HALFPENNY.

DISASTROUS FLOODS IN SCOTLAND.

CLYDE BANKS BURST AT MANY POINTS.

UNPRECEDENTED SCENES.

RUTHERGLEN WORKS WATER LOGGED.

RESCUE OF EMPLOYEES.

THRILLING NARRATIVES OF SUFFERERS.

ENORMOUS DAMAGE.

Not within living memory has Scotland experienced such a continuous and disastrous storm of rain as that which subsided yesterday, leaving devastation in its wake on every hand. Not a single district throughout the length and breadth of the land escaped the phenomenal visitation, and the reports from our correspondents, both far and near, tell the same story of overflowing rivers, tiny streamlets swollen into great rushing torrents, acres and acres of land submerged, houses and workshops flooded, bridges swept away, railways inundated, and damage in many other ways.

Happily the loss of life attendant on the storm has been but very slight in comparison with what might have been expected under such dangerous and suddenly-created conditions, but farmers and others in the country districts have suffered severely from the loss of cattle swept away by the floods.

In no district has such havoc been wrought as in Glasgow and the West of Scotland. The Clyde on the south-side of the City burst its banks at four points; the Kelvin was in heavy spate and overflowed at the lower points, flooding wide expanses of the neighbouring lands; the Cart, too, swollen beyond all previous records, poured its waters over the banks.

The points at which the Clyde burst its banks in the Rutherglen district are indicated on the plan reproduced on this page. The first break occurred at the spot marked A, the second at B, the third at C and the fourth at D.

It is impossible to estimate the extent of the damage occasioned by the inundations, but it will reach an enormous figure, and, as will be seen from our reports, large numbers of workpeople have been temporarily thrown out of employment.

THE CLYDE BURSTS.

THOUSANDS OF ACRES COMPLETELY SUBMERGED.

Not for several generations has such a disastrous inundation been witnessed as that which occurred early yesterday morning on the level haughs between the river Clyde and the burgh of Rutherglen. Indeed, to find an approach to it, one must go back to March, 1832, while the flood which most approximates it in recent years occurred in March, 1885.

Yesterday thousands of acres of land were submerged to an average depth of ten feet—2½ feet more than 17 years ago and 3½ higher than in 1832. But the latest flood far surpasses in the damage caused either of these earlier occurrences. Seventy years ago the Clyde was a pellucid stream, with no huge factories on its banks. To-day it bears navies on its broad bosom, and the reaches above Glasgow furnish sites for some of the largest industrial concerns in the West of Scotland. About a dozen of these have been most seriously affected, and, though it is impossible to estimate, even roughly, the loss which has been caused, it must amount to many thousands.

The Third Burst.

When the third burst occurred at Farme Colliery the water dashed roaring over the adjacent ground in a solid wave several feet in height, and in an incredibly brief space of time had occasioned dreadful destruction. The Scotia Works of the Rivet, Bolt and Nut Company were inundated half way up the wall; then the Clydebank Finishing Works, belonging to Messrs. Andrew Robertson & Sons, Limited, were submerged, and the water flowed over Cambuslang Road, in the dip between Dalmarnock Bridge and Farme Loan Road, rising in the hollow to the top of the gas lamps and converting the roadway into a waterway fully ten feet deep.

The tube works of Messrs. Stewarts & Lloyds, Limited were next attacked, and the flood pursued its irresistible way into the similar works belonging to Messrs. Eadie & Son, to the extensive rope works of Messrs. John Todd & Son, Mr. Thomas M'Ghie's Scottish Plaster Works in Farme Road, and the steel rope works of Messrs. Allan Wylie & Co., until it was stayed by the railway embankment.

Fortunately for the workers the gravity of the situation had been fully appreciated for some time and all reached places of safety without sustaining injury. Some men, however, employed in the galvanising department in Messrs. Stewarts & Lloyd's establishment had rather narrow escapes. Operations were proceeding as usual and the galvanising tanks were full of molten spelter at a very high temperature. When the alarm was given the men had just time to leave the department before the water poured in and came in contact with the spelter.

The enormous quantity of steam thereby liberated caused an explosion which lifted the roof off and scattered portions of the walls of the shed, which measured about 100 feet long by 50 feet broad. The foundry also suffered severely. One of the foremen had to swim through the flood and in doing so swallowed so much of the filthy liquid that he had to receive medical attention, and an old man was dragged out of the water by three of his comrades who joined hands.

The Fourth.

While these scenes were being enacted the fourth and last burst occurred, about eight o'clock, at a point in the river bank near Clyde Bank Finishing Works, within a short distance of Dalmarnock Bridge. This break allowed a vast quantity of water, which had hitherto been dammed back, to escape into the bed of the river, and with the turn of the tide about noon the flood began to subside gradually.

On Dalmarnock Bridge, however, the water was still very deep, and a foolhardy attempt to cross, made by a man, a boy and two horses and lorries, was only prevented from having a fatal termination by the prompt action of some policemen and civilians. Although warned not to make the attempt, the man persisted, and when about half-way across the bridge the horses and lorries became completely submerged. The driver, seeing his peril at last, waved his cap for assistance, and two boats, manned by members of the police force and some civilians, went to the rescue. With some difficulty the man and boy were taken on board, and after the horses had been unharnessed, which was not accomplished without considerable danger, they reached safety at the end of the bridge. The vehicles perforce had to be abandoned.

Naturally the greatest alarm prevailed in Rutherglen and neighbourhood when reports of the disaster began to spread. The wildest rumours were afloat as to supposed loss of life, especially when the danger arising from the explosion in the works of Messrs. Stewarts & Lloyd's was added to that of the great inundation. The belief was entertained till well on in the forenoon that loss of life must have been inevitable, but this was dissipated when it was found that the workmen and women in all the different establishments had been rescued.

It is indeed a fortunate and remarkable circumstance that ruin so extensive and sudden should be created without expense of human life.

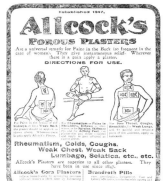

Established 1847.

Allcock's

POROUS PLASTERS

Are a universal remedy for Pains in the Back (so frequent in the case of women). They give instantaneous relief. Wherever there is a pain apply a plaster.

DIRECTIONS FOR USE.

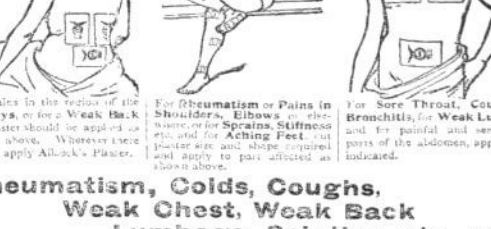

For Pains in the region of the Kidneys, or for a Weak Back the plaster should be applied as shown above. Wherever there is pain apply Allcock's Plaster.

For Rheumatism or Pains in Shoulders, Elbows or elsewhere, or for Sprains, Stiffness etc. and for Aching Feet, cut plaster size and shape required and apply to part affected as shown above.

For Sore Throat, Coughs, Bronchitis, for Weak Lungs, and for painful and sensitive parts of the abdomen, apply as indicated.

Rheumatism, Colds, Coughs, Weak Chest, Weak Back Lumbago, Sciatica, etc., etc.

Allcock's Plasters are superior to all other plasters. They have been in use since 1847.

Allcock's Corn Plasters relieve immediately by preventing pressure and cure within a short time by extracting the corn.

Brandreth Pills cure constipation, indigestion, liver and kidney affections, headaches with nausea and depressed temper caused by bilious sufferings.

KING AND QUEEN IN SCOTLAND.

MAGNIFICENT RECEPTION OF THEIR MAJESTIES IN EDINBURGH.

TRIUMPHAL PROGRESS TO DALKEITH.

MEMORABLE SCENES IN THE STREETS OF THE CAPITAL.

The reception accorded to the King and Queen on their arrival in Edinburgh yesterday evening, the formal introduction to the people of Scotland after their Majesties' ascension of the Throne, was in every respect worthy of the great occasion and in thorough accord with the traditional loyalty of the old metropolis of Scotland.

Never in the history of the city has a Royal visit been looked forward to with a keener sense of expectancy, and never has there been such a lavish display of the outward and visible tokens of appreciative welcome. Naturally beautiful by reason of her incomparable situation, the city has undergone a transformation which adds to the charm of the natural conditions, and which evinces in a degree which is unmistakeable the fervour and the loyalty of the citizens towards their illustrious guests.

From Holyrood Palace to Liberton; from the North Bridge to the Colinton Mains Hospital the city is ablaze with colour. In yesterday's gorgeous sunshine, even although the entire scheme of decoration had not been carried out, it was possible to obtain an idea of the whole effect which was alike pleasing to the eye, and a magnificent triumph to all concerned in the carrying out of the elaborate details.

The Waverley Station was beautified in a highly striking manner, while at Dalkeith the townsfolk had neither spared pains nor expense to show how pleased they are to assure the King and Queen of a genuine welcome. Edinburgh and Dalkeith yesterday evening had only a brief foretaste of what was to come to-day and to-morrow. It was sufficient to indicate that their Majesties were prepared to fulfil the high obligations in a spirit unstinted and ungrudging.

The route from the Waverley Station to Dalkeith was lined with crowds of interested spectators, who testified by the cordiality of their reception that what was really the homecoming of the King and Queen to Scotland afforded them unmeasured gratification. Their Majesties appeared deeply gratified by the welcome, which was of a character unprecedented in the recent visits of Royalty to the city.

A huge bonfire on Arthur's Seat carried the tidings of the arrival of the King and Queen throughout the vast stretch of country. The burning mass of combustibles made a magnificent sight, and was a fitting termination to a sincere and thorough regal welcome.

SCENE AT THE WAVERLEY STATION.

On arrival at the Waverley Station, Edinburgh, at 6.20, the King and Queen were greeted with every demonstration of loyalty and affection. Every preparation had been made for their proper reception, and the whole arrangements passed off without a hitch.

For about a couple of hours before the arrival of the Royal train the station entrances and exits were closed and only those having business were allowed entrance.

A highly decorative scheme of embellishment was carried out by the North British Railway Company, and the station was as unlike its normal appearance as it was possible to imagine. The decorative plan embraced a continuous line from the east end of the arrival platform to the station entrances. From the iron girders of the roof there was quite a bewildering display of flags, and prominent were the Union Jack and the ancient flag of Scotland—the lion rampant on the yellow ground. The supporting pillars of the roof were treated with a beautifully conceived design of flowering plants and shrubs. Evergreens were entwined round the pillars, and the plants were displayed in a highly effective manner.

As the place where the Royal saloon was to draw up the floral effect was beautified by a display of imposing magnificence. The pillars of the roof were hidden by large palms which, in the garish sunshine, had a fine cooling effect, and a number of flowering plants added a touch of colour which was most attractive. The suburban bridge was decorated with shields and flags, and the station exit had pendant baskets of Pampas grass, with evergreens.

Punctually in accordance with the police and military arrangements the station approaches were taken in hand, and for some time there was great bustle and animation in the allocation of the forces who were to line the routes and who were to act as guards of honour. The police arrangements were carried out under the personal supervision of Chief Constable Ross, and his force totalled some 970 men, including 400 from Glasgow. The police supervision extended from the Waverley Station to Cameron Bridge. The number of military details utilised apart from the guards of honour was 3420, and the whole line of route to Cameron Bridge was manned. The units were for the most part composed of Bluejackets, Royal Marines, Cameron Highlanders, Gordon Highlanders, Argyll and Sutherland Highlanders, Royal Artillery, and details from the first regimental district, and were in charge of Colonel Broadwood.

Blood Poison Cured Free.

The Remedy is Sent Absolutely Free to Every Man or Woman Sending Name and Address.

The Illustrations Above Plainly Show What this Grand Discovery Will Do.

BIG GREENOCK FIRE.

DISTILLERY AND OTHER BUILDINGS GUTTED.

STREAMS OF FLAME.

FOUR PERSONS KILLED: SEVERAL INJURED.

Greenock was last night the scene of a fire calamity such as has seldom if ever been paralleled in the history of the town. The damage is estimated to approach £100,000, and there has been the loss of at least four lives and serious injury to several other persons.

There were really two fires, the one being the direct outcome of the other. The first occurred in the stores of the Ardgowan Distillery Company situated at the head of Baker Street, and it was the blazing liquid which flowed from this building along the sewers that led to the second, and, so far as the effects on human life are concerned, the more serious disaster.

The outbreak was observed shortly after six o'clock originating in the upper flat of a seven-storey building in which, it is stated, there were about 15,000 casks, each containing fifty gallons of whisky. Within a very few minutes of the alarm being raised the flames burst through the roof. To the looker-on it seemed as if all the spirits on the top flat had caught fire. The flames mounted fifty or sixty feet above the highest point of the buildings, and at the same time the spirits from bursting casks ran down the walls and carried the fire to other parts of the building.

The fire brigade, under Superintendent Taylor, and assisted by about 500 bluejackets and marines from the Benbow, poured tons of water on the burning building, but they were quite unable to stay the progress of the fire.

Blazing like a hundred furnaces one floor was attacked after another until nothing remained but the walls of the greater portion of the building, and even the flames from the burning barrels and spirits still curled high above what had been the roof.

Less than three hours after the commencement of the fire the gables of the western section of the store began to collapse, the fall of each mass of stonework being succeeded by great bursts of fire that threatened destruction to adjacent buildings. The brigade and the bluejackets concentrated their efforts on the saving of the adjoining buildings, but despite all they could do some of the smaller erections were involved.

THE SECOND OUTBREAK.

At ten o'clock when it appeared as if the full strength of the brigade was necessary a great blaze burst out in the east end of the town near the Victoria Harbour, and a contingent was hurriedly sent off to cope with it. This later outbreak occurred in Springkell Street, and was a result of the fire at the distillery. The whisky from the distillery had, it seems, found its way into a sewer which crosses Springkell Street, and having caught fire it caused a serious explosion under the flour mill of Messrs. Muir & Son.

The gable came down and some half-dozen persons were caught and partly buried among the debris. Help was promptly rendered, but unhappily it was found that two, both boys of about fifteen, had been killed. Six persons at least received serious injuries and were conveyed to a police box to await the arrival of ambulance vans, and were afterwards taken to the infirmary.

It was stated that there were others under the debris, but it was impossible while the fire was in progress to institute a search. Several persons were reported to be missing and the gravest anxiety prevailed as to their fate.

The mill was speedily gutted, and the houses adjoining were in such peril that the unfortunate inmates had to rush for their lives.

Although not a densely populated neighbourhood the district contains many houses tenanted by working people, and great alarm naturally existed among hundreds of families. Myriads of sparks rose from the burning property, and falling thick on the adjacent roofs threatened to carry the conflagration to property in Rue End Street.

While the main detachment of the brigade directed their energies to the principal building sections poured water on the buildings which seemed likely at any moment to break out into a blaze, and there were several small outbreaks.

About midnight the outbreak at Springkell Street had been got pretty well under, but in this neighbourhood there remained a danger of fresh outbreaks, as the blazing whisky from the distillery continued to flow down the cut

RAINSTORMS WREAK HAVOC

SCOTS experienced their worst rainstorms in living memory with the ferocious downpour that struck the country suddenly on February 9.

It was a disaster for the nation although fortunately, the loss of lives due to the storms was very low in comparison with what might have been expected in such treacherous conditions.

Not a single district escaped the ravages on the phenomenal storms. Reports from every area told of overflowing rivers, and streams swollen into rushing torrents.

Farmers and others in country districts suffered severely. There was a huge loss of livestock that were swept away by the floods while thousands of acres of farming land were under water. In towns and villages across the country, houses and workshops were badly flooded.

Transport was also seriously affected Railway lines were hit badly by the delguge while bridges were swept away.

As a result, the flooding also affected large numbers of workers who were temporarily unable to get to or start work, in some cases forcing their employers to lay them off under their businesses could recover.

The havoc was worse in Glasgow and west central Scotland. On the south side of Glasgow, the River Clyde burst its banks at four points and the Kelvin was in heavy spate, overflowing at its lower points to flood wide expanses of adjoining land. The River Cart was also swollen beyond all previous records.

It was impossible to estimate accurately the bill to repair the damage caused by the storms but it was reckoned to have reached an enormous figure.

EDINBURGH WELCOMES THE NEW KING

In May, Edinburgh had its first opportunity to see the new king and queen as Edward VII and his consort, Queen Alexandra, arrived at Waverley Station. As with previous royal visits, the people of Edinburgh turned out in large numbers to cheer and no expense was spared in decorating both the train station and the route which the king's carriage would take to Dalkeith where the royal party was staying as guests of the Duke of Buccleuch. As the king and queen left Waverley, a huge bonfire was lit on the slopes of Arthur's Seat to announce the arrival of Scotland's newest monarch.

Why people drink OXO

OXO makes energy quickly. It digests and becomes a living force in the blood in a shorter time than any other food. OXO gives the system rapid and continuous nourishment—the nourishment of prime lean beef. When there is no time for a full meal, OXO will put real cash-earning energy into a lagging brain, or tired limbs, in such a business-like way that you reap the full benefit long before other foods could be half digested.

OXO IS LIEBIG COMPANY'S FLUID BEEF.

OXO

COMINGS...

Alec Douglas-Home
Conservative Statesman

GOINGS...

William Quarrier
Social Reformer

EIFFEL TOWER

You can neither make or buy a drink so healthful, so thirst quenching, so convenient, and so inexpensive.

LEMONADE

2 GALLONS FOR 4½

EIFFEL TOWER BUN FLOUR 1º⁰

DOUBLE BLAZE STRIKES GREENOCK

Greenock was the scene of a major blaze in June which destroyed part of the Ardgowan whisky bond. The seven-storey building contained around 15,000 casks of whisky when it caught fire and within minutes of the alarm being raised, flames were rising some 50 feet above the building. Despite the local fire brigade's efforts, the fire spread to neighbouring structures which began to collapse with the intensity of the flames. Whisky from the bond also found its way into a sewer and caught fire. This stream of blazing spirit caused a huge explosion and a second conflagration that gutted a nearby flour mill and for several hours, the entire neighbourhood was in danger as the blazing whisky continued to flow into the sewer.

THIS SPORTING LIFE

FOOTBALL	RUGBY UNION	GOLF	HORSE RACING	SHINTY
Scottish Champions Hibernian	*Scotland vs England* Scotland 10 –6 England at Richmond	*British Open Winner* Harry Vardon at Prestwick (300)	*Scottish Grand National Winner* Chit Chat at Bogside	*Camanachd Cup Winners* Kingussie at Perth/Inverness
Scottish Cup Winners Rangers				

City Edition

INFORMATIVE HANDBOOK ABOUT CANADA. Threepence; Post Free, 4d. DAILY RECORD AND MAIL, GLASGOW.

Daily Record & Mail.

LARGER SALE THAN ANY OTHER MORNING OR EVENING NEWSPAPER IN SCOTLAND.

IF YOU WANT YOUR COAST HOUSE LET ADVERTISE AT ONCE IN Daily Record & Mail

ESTABLISHED 1847.—No. 17,882 GLASGOW, THURSDAY, MAY 26, 1904 ONE HALFPENNY.

QUACK DENTISTS.

SCOPE OF THEIR OPERATIONS IN GLASGOW.

SCHEME OF SUPPRESSION.

Few callings have in recent years attracted so many recruits to their ranks as that of the dental surgeon. All over Scotland the growth of the profession has been quite remarkable. Unfortunately, however, there is now associated with it a very large number of bogus members.

This fact is, perhaps, more apparent in Glasgow than anywhere else. According to a leading dental surgeon there are at present at least a hundred "quack" dentists in practice in the city. So numerous, indeed, have they become that the qualified dentists have been compelled to take action in the shape of forming a defence union. Articles of Association have been drawn up, and it is expected that in the course of a few days the new union will be duly registered.

Conversing with a "Daily Record and Mail" representative yesterday, one of the pioneers of this protective movement went the length of saying that quackery was so rampant in dental surgery as to almost bring it to the level of a farce.

"Many citizens, not to speak of visitors to the city, are unable to distinguish between the qualified dentist and the unqualified quack, the result being that in many cases the latter is doing a more lucrative trade than the former.

"We thought," he continued, "that the law might intervene, but the authorities have declined to make a single prosecution, although all the facts concerning the bogus dentist have been placed in their hands.

"The unqualified dentists take care not to infringe the Dental Act by styling themselves 'Surgeon-Dentist' or 'Dental-Surgeon, or dishonestly using the letters 'L.D.S,' but they contravene the Act by putting after their names on the outside of their premises such words as 'Dental Consulting Room.'"

Strange as it may seem very few Jews or foreigners are among the quack practitioners in Glasgow, almost all of them being Scotchmen who have for years followed some other occupations. Former butchers, coal-hawkers, clerks, shopmen and representatives of other walks of life have now extensive dental businesses with no other qualification than the efficiency which daily practice has given them.

The fees charged by the unqualified dentist vary in proportion to the financial position of the client. One man may get a tooth pulled for a shilling while another may be asked to pay half-a-guinea, and sets of teeth are supplied on equally elastic terms.

As a rule the quack dentist employs young men who have served part of an apprenticeship with qualified dental-surgeons, and these, it is asserted, do not scruple when extracting teeth to administer gas or chloroform. Should a patient succumb while in the hands of a qualified dentist, or receive serious injury, the latter may be held responsible by law, but in the case of an unqualified practitioner no responsibility can be fixed according to the law.

The name of the new union, it may be added, is "The Registered Dentists' Defence Union of Scotland, Limited," and one of its objects is the suppression and prosecution of unauthorised practitioners.

van Houten's Cocoa
BEST & GOES FARTHEST.

RUNAWAY DISASTER.

BOY KILLED AND SIX PERSONS INJURED.

HORSE IN A CROWD.

The fancy dress cycle parade which took place in Govan on Saturday afternoon, on behalf of the local Gladstone Memorial Fund, was marred to a great extent by a serious disaster, which, occurring at the corner of Ure Street and Crossloan Road, resulted in the death of a four-year-old boy and the more or less serious injury of six other persons.

The procession, which was formed on Govandale Park, proceeded to Linthouse by Govan Road, and was returning by Langlands Road and Crossloan Road to Ibrox Park, where sports were to be held.

Shortly after four o'clock the procession passed along Crossloan Road, where a large crowd of people had assembled, among whom a number of the members of the clubs were walking and collecting money in boxes.

Immediately the parade had passed the corner of Ure Street, one of the collectors is stated to have rattled the box he was carrying, causing a horse attached to a lorry of vegetables (which was standing a few yards down Ure Street) to take fright. The lorryman at the time was engaged carrying vegetables into the shop and was standing at the rear of the vehicle, while the boy who was on the lorry was handing the vegetables to the man.

The horse at once bolted across the street, and on to the pavement at the corner. So little warning did the spectators get of the approaching danger that they had practically no time to get to a place of safety before the frightened horse was upon them. The animal dashed through the crowd and into Crossloan Road, knocking down seven or eight persons, several of whom were run over by the lorry.

The driver of the lorry, John Lundie (35), who resides in Steven Parade, Glasgow, did everything in his power to bring the horse to a standstill. The animal, however, continued its wild career along Crossloan Road, knocking down a lamppost and smashing about 15 feet of an iron railing in front of a tenement. It was only stopped when it ran against the wall of the building.

With so many women and children on the street at the time, there was naturally a great amount of excitement in the neighbourhood. The majority of those injured were carried into the surgery of Dr. Forbes Brown for treatment.

It was seen after examination that a little fellow named John Henderson (4½), who had a lacerated wound on the ear and was badly hurt about the head and body, was the most seriously injured. He was removed to the Western Infirmary in the ambulance wagon, where he succumbed to his injuries early yesterday morning. The boy was the son of an electrician residing at 21 Ure Street. The others were taken to their respective homes. Their names are:—

May Cameron (4) and James Cameron (6), sister and brother. The former had two ribs on the left side broken and severe bruises about the head, body and legs, and the latter slight bruises about the head.

Hannah Allan (7), daughter of a widow staying at 45 White Street; left thigh fractured.

Robert Hodgson (38), riveter, residing at 30 Shaw Street; injuries to back.

Elizabeth Gordon or Hodgson (39), residing at 30 Shaw Street; bruises on right ankle and left leg.

Barbara Hodgson (7), daughter of Robert Hodgson; bruises on right arm.

If you use OXO, you can get a handsome enlargement of your own or your child's photo free for six worth of OXO coupons.
OXO
OXO, 4, Lloyd's Avenue, London, E.C.

RAIN, SLEET AND SNOW.

SEVERE STORM THROUGHOUT SCOTLAND.

DAMAGE BY FLOODING.

The first really severe weather of the year was experienced throughout Scotland yesterday. Storms raged in most parts of the country, and at certain points along the East Coast the sea was very rough.

In the forenoon, when the wind and hailstorm was at its worst, a serious accident occurred at the works of Messrs. Malcolm, Ogilvie & Co., jute manufacturers, Dundee. The gable of the old factory, after the recent fire, was left standing, and being caught by the storm was levelled, the masonry crashing through the engine-room, and smashing the steam pipe caused a loud explosion. Seven or eight men standing by were felled, and the steam pouring out in great volume they were severely scalded and otherwise injured.

The injured were removed to the infirmary, where, after treatment, they were all, with a single exception, able to return home. The names of the injured are:—

GEORGE MALCOLM, Manufacturer—Cuts on hands.
J. G. LESLIE, manager—Cuts on hands and arms.
JOHN CHRISTIE (63), engineman—Scalds on face and arms and hands.
JOHN DOTT, beamer—Cuts on head and face.
ALEX. LEWTHWAITE, beamer—Cuts on head and face.
JOHN BIRNIE, boiler coverer—Cuts on hands and face and scalds.
JAMES COWIE, boiler coverer—Cuts on head and face and scalds.

In Edinburgh and district the weather was very stormy. Rain and sleet fell incessantly all day, accompanied by a high wind, the streets being practically deserted. Showers of snow fell in the afternoon, and Arthur's Seat, the Braids, the Blackford Hill, and the Pentlands are covered with snow.

TRAWLERS RUN FOR SHELTER.

In Aberdeen yesterday the weather was of the most violent character, while on the north-east coast generally it was very severe. Many of the trawlers arriving at the Aberdeen fish market reported having encountered very boisterous weather and heavy seas during the past week, and a large number had to put into Lerwick, Kirkwall, and other places for shelter.

In Market Street a young lady was blown off her feet, and as a result sustained bruises.

The scene at the harbour entrance was picturesque and terrifying, and the oldest of the pilots stated that not for 60 or 70 years had the water been so high.

At Arbroath yesterday the waves broke over the protection wall in dense masses, flooding the roadway below. The steamer Mergauser, which was stranded off the harbour lately, and is submerged, was rocked about in a violent manner, but she did not remove from her sandy bed. In the streets chimney cans were blown down.

A terrific wind storm prevailed in North Perthshire and the Central Highlands, accompanied by heavy showers of sleet and snow. The higher Grampians were wreathed in white.

Snow continued to fall heavily in East Lothian yesterday and the ground was last night covered to a depth of over five inches. On the Lammermoor Hills there were nearly two feet of snow. The railway between East Linton and Drem was gradually being covered with the rush of water from the high lying lands. Traffic was proceeding with great caution.

The first snowstorm of the season was experienced in Lanarkshire yesterday, and proved exceptionally severe. In the afternoon there was a depth of from six to eight inches of snow on the higher ground. In the evening rain came on, and the roadways were in a bad state.

To assure yourself the pleasantest of Christmas times and to add to the brightness and cheerfulness of your home, secure a

PIANOLA.

Not a tiresome and soulless mechanism, but an instrument that seems almost part of yourself, an artistic medium between you and the music you produce, and, therefore, a Pianola.

Should your inclination not run to a new METROSTYLE PIANOLA, you can buy a Pianola that has been used. Even second-hand PIANOLAS are superior to all other piano-players. They are the instruments that have secured for the Pianola its reputation, and that Paderewski, De Pachmann, Rosenthal, De Reszke, &c., have endorsed.

If you are interested in the piano-player idea, visit us. We carry a complete line of instruments at all prices, and guarantee them the best that can be had at the money.

Write for Catalogue "C."

J. MARR WOOD & CO., LIMITED,
42 BUCHANAN STREET,
GLASGOW.

PIPING HOT BOVRIL
Try it with a dash of cold milk.

WRECKED DISTILLERY.

OFFICIAL INSPECTION OF THE BUILDING.

NUMBER OF VICTIMS INCREASED.

Large crowds flocked to the scene of the Glasgow distillery disaster yesterday. They found, however, that Muirhead Street was closed against all traffic, and workmen were busy making the building safe for the inspection on behalf of the Dean of Guild. After that the proprietors expect to be able to estimate the damage.

One noticeable feature yesterday was the appearance of draff which had been showered out by the force of the outflow to a height of ten feet on the wall of the opposite side of the street. During the night the streets were cleared of the escaped draff by the Cleansing Department, and the shopkeepers

1904

ATTACK ON THE QUACK DENTISTS

FEW callings in the early part of the century attracted so many recruits to their ranks as that of the dental surgeon.

All over Scotland the growth of the profession had been quite remarkable. Unfortunately, however, a large number of bogus dentists had also begun associated with it.

This fact was more apparent in Glasgow than anywhere else. According to a leading dental surgeon, there were at least 100 "quack" dentists in practice in May 1904.

So numerous had the bogus dentists become that the qualified ones were forced to act and formed a defence union.

Articles of Association were drawn up, and it was expected that in the course of a few days the new union would be registered.

One representative, a pioneer of the proactive movement, went so far as to say that "quackery was so rampant in dental surgery that it almost brought the profession to the level of a farce."

Many people in the city were unable to distinguish between the qualified dentists and the unqualified quack with the result that in many cases, the latter was doing a more lucrative trade than the former.

The unqualified dentist was generally careful not to infringe the Dental Act by calling themselves "Surgeon Dentists" or "Dental Surgeons" or dishonestly using the letters "LDS".

However, they did contravene the Act by putting descriptions such as "Dental Consulting Room" after their names on the outside of their premises

Almost all of the quack dentists were Scotsmen who had been employed in other professions such as butchery, coal-hawking, and clerking.

The quack dentist often employed young men who had served part of an apprenticeship with dental surgeons, and did not hesitate to administer gas or chloroform when extracting teeth.

Should a patient receive serious injury while in the hands of a qualified dentist, the practicioner could be held responsible in law.

But in the case of an unqualified dentist, the law was powerless to act in such cases.

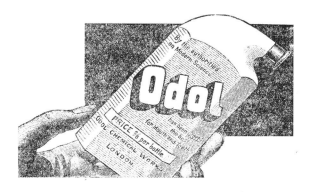

GLASGOW'S DEADLY ATMOSPHERE

The extent of the air pollution affecting Glasgow was revealed in February. Eight stations had been established around the city to measure soot deposits in the atmosphere and their results caused great concern. The gauge in Alexandra Park recorded the highest levels of pollution while that in Queen's Park registered the least. It was revealed that a staggering average of 64 tons of soot and other substances was dumped on the city from the atmosphere every day, chiefly as a result of industrial and domestic coal-burning. These deposits were seriously affecting both the fabric of Glasgow and the health of its inhabitants, with over 15,000 known cases of consumption in the city.

DRINKING CLUBS SQUASHED

Time was called in January on the nation's notorious drinking clubs, widely regarded as a major source of drunkenness, licentious behaviour and general disorder. The new Licensing Act for Scotland required all such drinking clubs to be registered with the local authorities and imposed stringent operating conditions. The success of the law in stamping out "these pernicious institutions" was remarkable in that few of their owners even bothered to apply for registration and simply closed. Of the clubs who did apply, most were respectable sporting, social or political clubs.

A BURNING ISSUE

The Scottish Burial Reform and Cremation Society reduced the cost of a cremation to £6 6s in an effort to improve business. Burial was still the preferred choice of most people and only 137 cremations had taken place in the 12 years that the Society's Maryhill crematorium had been operating. The Society claimed that even when cremation was specified in wills, there was often a delay in the formal reading of these by which time the deceased had already been buried.

COMINGS...

Jennie Lee
Labour Politician

THIS SPORTING LIFE

FOOTBALL	**RUGBY UNION**	**GOLF**	**HORSE RACING**	**SHINTY**
Scottish Champions Third Lanark	*Scotland vs England* Scotland 6–3 England at Inverleith	*British Open Winner* Jack White at Sandwich, England (296)	*Scottish Grand National Winner* Innismacsaint at Bogside	*Camanachd Cup Winners* Kyles Athletic at Kingussie
Scottish Cup Winners Celtic				

Ex-Convicts
AND
The Police.
See This Week's
Scottish Weekly Record

Daily Record & Mail.

LARGER SALE THAN ANY OTHER MORNING OR EVENING NEWSPAPER IN SCOTLAND.

"The HOLY LAND:"
LIFE IN A
GLASGOW SLUM.
See This Week's
Scottish Weekly Record

ESTABLISHED 1847.—No. 18,081 GLASGOW, FRIDAY, JANUARY 13, 1905 ONE HALFPENNY

APPALLING CATASTROPHE IN GLASGOW.

MODEL LODGING-HOUSE IN FLAMES.

TERRIBLE DEATH ROLL.

39 MEN SUFFOCATED.

GHASTLY SCENES AT THE MORTUARY.

IDENTIFICATION OF BODIES.

HEROISM ON THE ROOF.

HOMELESS MEN LODGED IN THE POORHOUSE

THRILLING NARRATIVES.

The most appalling fire disaster that has occurred in Scotland within living memory sent a thrill of horror through vast numbers of people in Glasgow yesterday who became aware of the facts.

In the early morning, just before six o'clock, while the thick fog that made outdoor enjoyment impossible on Saturday evening still rested like a pall on the sleeping city, thirty-nine men lost their lives by either suffocation or literal roasting, while twenty-four others received injuries which led to their immediate admission to the Royal Infirmary.

No more shocking calamity is conceivable than that of over 350 of the submerged classes occupying cubicles in a model lodging-house face to face with death in its most dreadful form. That was the experience at Councillor William Nicol's huge caravanserie at the corner of Watson Street and Græme Street, close to Glasgow Cross and High Street, at the hour indicated.

By a melancholy coincidence it was in Watson Street also that the Star Theatre panic took place.

Every cubicle in the place had its occupant. There had been the usual Saturday night scenes. Money was not so plentiful among applicants for admission as it sometimes it; there were a number of quarrelsome fellows and not a few had primed themselves with bottles containing spirituous drink. However the establishment was closed, and patrons and officials went off to bed in fairly good time.

Quietude reigned. Outside the police on the beat saw nothing throughout the night to tell of an approaching catastrophe without parallel in our city annals.

Suddenly on the cold, raw, foggy air of the morning rang out the terrible word "Fire!" Someone had seen a little glimmer of flame quivering through the gloom up near the roof of the lodging-house.

The alarm was responded to with all possible haste by the police at the Central Office and the Chief Fire Brigade, both, fortunately, within a few minutes' call.

But it was soon apparent that, while the property would be saved, there could be no hope for those who slept on the top flat. These, indeed, were cut off at once by volumes of smoke which rolled from one corner of the burning building and enveloped them before many of them, as judged by the positions in which their bodies were found, could have had time to move or make any attempt at escape.

The damage to the premises was largely confined to this corner, and is estimated at only £500. But when a search was instituted in the debris no less than thirty-nine bodies were removed and taken without delay to the they remain, as suffering from dislocations and shock.

How the fire originated is, for the present at any rate, a mystery. It is supposed that one of the men now dead who was under the influence of drink had risen to light his pipe and tossed a lighted match carelessly away, igniting the varnished wood separating his cubicle from that of another lodger.

It is also suggested that a lighted candle may have been in use, as it is not an unknown element in model lodging-house life for lodgers to break the regulations that forbid naked lights to be used.

To-day the catastrophe will be reported to the Procurator-Fiscal, and it is expected that an inquiry will be ordered, as in the cases of the Ibrox disaster three and a half years ago and other great calamities in this neighbourhood.

Meantime, the Police Mortuary is besieged by women in tears seeking to identify the bodies of friends or relatives. Already over twenty of the bodies have been identified. A pathetic feature is that many of the women who have gone through the process of identification were lodged in the Women's Shelter in the Calton district on Saturday night, and were distressed beyond measure on hearing of the fate that had befallen husband, father, or brother as the case might be.

A LIGHTED CANDLE.

VISIT TO THE SCENE OF THE AWFUL DISASTER.

A representative of the "Daily Record and Mail" called at the Watson Street Home yesterday, and was afforded every facility of questioning the staff on the disaster.

It appears that between midnight and one in the morning the warder on duty made his final inspection of the building and found all quiet, save only on the floor in which the fire occurred, where a man had lighted a candle. He reprimanded the man and the candle was put out. Rising at 5.30 a.m. he was going upstairs when he met a crowd of excited men shouting that fire had broken out. The fumes of smoke were rolling down from the upper storeys.

Instantly the iron gate was opened and the men allowed to make their escape into the open.

On the cause of the conflagration opinion was unanimous. The lot of men on Saturday night were particularly drunken; indeed, two men admitted to Barnhill afterwards confessed they had no idea when and how they had got to bed the previous evening. It is no uncommon occurrence to find a pillow badly burned, and it is thought that a man waking in the small hours, felt for his pipe, lighted it, and, after a few draws, fell asleep.

The partitions between the beds are of light, dry wood, and the fire once catching hold would fly from one to the other till the whole ward was in flames.

But, without doubt, it was insisted there would have been a far smaller death-roll had the men been sober. At ten, and even as late as midday men descended from the second floor, newly wakened and anxious to know what the stir was about.

The home was well filled on Saturday night: the first floor had 81 occupants, the second 120, while on the third, where the fire broke out, there were 106, and on the fourth 61—a total of 368.

On the first floor one of the warders sleeps, but in the others the men are left to themselves for the night, save when the midnight inspection is made.

FIREMASTER'S STORY.

A world of tragedy underlies the cold, bare, matter-of-fact statement which comprises the Fire Brigade's official record of the disaster.

In order to facilitate the work of the Press representatives, Captain Paterson makes up an account of all the fires to which the Brigade is called. An old book, which has done duty for many years, was filled up by the entering in of the particulars of other four fires which occurred on Saturday night and Sunday morning, so that curiously enough the first entry in the new book was that pertaining to the Watson Street tragedy.

According to Captain Paterson's statement, the Brigade was called by the fire alarm in the Cleansing Department yard at Græme Street at ten minutes to six o'clock to a fire which had broken out in the Watson Street Home, No. 2, at 39 Watson Street, tenanted by Mr. William Nicol. The building is one of four storeys, with a basement and attics, and is used as a model lodging-house for males.

A dense fog enveloped the city like a mantle, and when the firemen got to the scene of operations they found the haze was partially lightened by the flames, which had obtained a firm hold on the upper floor, shooting out of the windows.

As the cubicles on the upper floor and the attic were fully occupied, Captain Paterson at once saw that there was great danger of considerable loss of life, and accordingly he directed the energies of his men mainly to the removal of the inmates.

They found that a work of much difficulty, as their movements were greatly hampered by the occupants of the various floors—a was rescued from his perilous position on the roof and brought in safety to the ground.

About 40 dead men were taken out of the building, while 24 were removed to the Royal Infirmary by the St. Andrew's Ambulance Association suffering from partial suffocation, shock and burns.

Most of the men, it is certain, met death in the passages by suffocation, for it was there that they were found lying in all sorts of attitudes by the firemen. One man was found lying on his side grasping in his right hand a half mutchkin bottle of whisky. It was decidedly an instance of the ruling passion being strong in death, and it was also a vivid commentary on the class of people who flock into lodging houses, for it has to be remembered that the man, when alarmed, must have started from his sleep, clutched at his bottle of whisky, even neglecting his clothes to do so, and then rushed into the passage, there to be overcome by the thick smoke.

About 200 of the occupants, half mad wtih terror and blue with cold, were marched up to the police office in Albion Street, and taken care of there.

Police Casualty Surgeons Lothian, Fletcher, Chalmers and Green were early on the scene of the calamity, and superintended the dressing and removal of the injured. Valuable assistance, says Captain Paterson, was also rendered the brigade by the police in the rescue work and the removal of the bodies.

During the forenoon Lord Provost Bilsland and Councillor Cleland, the convener of the Watching and Lighting Committee, visited the scene of the fire. They also visited the Royal Infirmary and talked with the victims lying there.

NAMES OF THE DEAD.

The following is a list of those who had been identified up to midnight:—

James CASEY, newsvendor.
Manus BROADLEY (60), slater.
Robert EASTON (44), cattleman.
James MITCHELL (38), irondresser.
Alexander M'DERMID (39), labourer.
Patrick M'CABE (42), labourer.
James CAIRNS (52), cutler.
William ARNEIL (38), brass refiner.
Andrew RANKIN (36), engineer.
John CURRAN (48), baker.
Daniel EADIE (40), labourer.
James M'GARTHLAND (54), labourer.
James MITCHELL (36), irondresser.
James COLLINS (44), cabinetmaker.
Patrick CALLAGHAN, hawker.
—— BURNS (25), labourer.
Simon DOCHERTY, labourer.
John MORTON (46), bootcloser.
John BARRETT (40), labourer.
Patrick M'CUE (60), labourer.
John DACK, labourer.
Henry MITCHELL (19), carter.
James BROWN (28), labourer.

The man identified as Burns has also been claimed by a woman as her son John Callaghan.

LIST OF THE INJURED.

The following is a list of the injured lying in the Royal Infirmary:—

John GILLOGAN (50), labourer, shock.
John GIBSON (35), labourer, burnt on head, back, and right arm.
Hugh RICE (30), carter, burnt on arms and back, and suffering from shock.
Thomas SINCLAIR (60), hawker, burnt on back, arm, and right hand, and suffering from shock.
Hugh M'QUIN (32), labourer, cut fingers and foot, and suffering from shock.
James RAFFERTY (25), labourer, burnt on arms, back, and groin, and suffering from shock.
John HARKER (50), storeman, superficial burn on shoulder.
James M'INERNEY (61), french-polisher, burnt on back and hand, and injury to foot.
James CATTENACH (38), iron-turner, shock.
John WILSON (23), labourer, burnt on back, forearm, and hand, and suffering from shock.
John FARMER (49), shoemaker, shock.
Thomas BRADY (48), labourer, shock.
James JOHNSTONE (56), labourer, burnt on scalp, neck, face, and hands, and suffering from shock.
Owen FOLEY (48), labourer, shock.
James ALLEN (60), hawker, shock.
James COLLINS (70), cabinetmaker, shock.
Hugh CAVANAGH (53), shoemaker, shock.
Hugh O'DONNELL (37), tool-maker, burnt on hands, neck, scalp, and suffering from shock.
Patrick PRIOR (37), labourer, shock.
Robert HENDERSON (48), boilermaker, burnt on back and arm.
John DONALD (46), newsvendor, shock.
David HANNA (46), labourer, shock.
Charles M'DONALD (49), steelworker, burnt on arms, back, and scalp; dislocation of shoulder, and suffering from shock.
Robert WHITE (50), labourer, shock.

AT THE MORTUARY.

HEARTRENDING SCENES DURING THE IDENTIFICATION.

Bad news, says the old proverb, travels quickly, and how quickly it does travel was illustrated yesterday morning. A crowd at the entrance to the Police Chambers in Albion Street began to gather almost as soon as the victims were taken through the doors, and befofe long the usually quiet Sunday thoroughfare was a seething mass of people. Continuous queues, regulated by a number of police, streamed into the police office, up the narrow stone stair, and so into that quiet little room where thirty-nine persons lay in the awesome stillness of death.

Towards noon the crowd was so great and was so eager to gain admittance that other doors were rushed. Order was, however, quickly restored, and during the remainder of the day the large number of people who visited the mortuary were quiet and seemly in their behaviour.

The mortuary is situated on the second floor. Utterly destitute of furniture was the death chamber. The dead lay in rows, a narrow passage only being left—so narrow, indeed, that the visitor as he walked along brushed with his right foot the feet of one row while with his left foot he touched the heads of another.

Very still and stiff and quiet they lay in the robes provided by the police. From their passive faces no hint of suffering could be gleaned. Smoke-begrimed the faces were, and they were also for the most part faces of

POLICE DISCIPLINE.

AMAZING CHARGES AGAINST CITY CONSTABLES.

Serious reflections on certain members of the Glasgow Police Force were contained in questions put by Mr. Gibson at yesterday's meeting of the Corporation.

In the first place, he asked what reasons the Magistrates' Committee could give to the Council for deciding to compensate an East-End citizen for an assault committed upon him by a police officer who had since decamped, and denying compensation to an equally assaulted and robbed citizen who requested compensation last September.

"That is a question arising out of the Magistrates' minutes," the Lord Provost pointed out, "and you will have an opportunity of dealing with it when they come up."

Mr. Gibson, at a later stage directed attention to a paragraph in the Magistrates' Committee's minutes relating to an alleged unprovoked assault committed on George M'Cutcheon, 2 Cathkin Place, Shettleston, on the morning of Sunday, the 11th September last, by ex-Constable Maloney, then of the Eastern Division of Police. In consequence of the assault, M'Cutcheon sustained a loss of wages to the extent of £2 18s and incurred an outlay for medical attendance and medicines amounting to £2 10s.

M'Cutcheon's agent, it was stated, contended that payment of these sums should be made to him by the Magistrates, who, having considered a report on the case by the Chief Constable, showing, inter alia, that the ex-constable had deserted the service, and that his whereabouts were unknown, and that he had been dismissed the force in absence on the 21st September, agreed to recommend that, without any admission of legal liability, but purely as an "ex gratia" payment, the sum of £5 8s be paid to M'Cutcheon.

With reference to this affair, Mr. Gibson alluded to a minute of the Magistrates, also dated September last year, reporting that the Magistrates had received a letter from a legal firm in Glasgow enclosing on behalf of Mr. Duncan Campbell, 13 Sword Street—a locality also in the Eastern Police Division—a statement by him containing charges of theft and assault by a policeman. In this case, Mr. Gibson explained, the policeman knocked Campbell down, took his watch, and brutally assaulted him. When the case was reported to the Sheriff the policeman was liberated on £5 bail, and took the opportunity of immediately leaving the country, as the constable in the M'Cutchton case had done.

Mr. Gibson expressed the hope that something drastic would be done by the Chief-Constable to restrict, if possible, this dangerous and pernicious principle of allowing policemen in such positions to get bail for a miserable sum and to leave the country and escape punishment. He was amazed to observe that the Magistrates had decided to repudiate liability in the Campbell case, while in the M'Cutcheon case they had paid a sum of £5 8s.

Bailie George Mitchell pointed out that the decision of the Magistrates to repudiate liability in the Campbell case had been homologated by the Corporation.

Probably the best method, Mr. Gibson replied, would be to allow the present minute to pass and let those concerned in the Campbell case take what action they thought fit.

Chief-Constable Stevenson said the question raised by Mr. Gibson would be brought before the Magistrates.

Other questions to which Mr. Gibson desired answers were:—

If the Chief Constable can give this Council any information regarding the charge duly lodged with him of a lieutenant in a district police station having assaulted a female prisoner aged 14 years?

Since the case was reported to the Chief Constable, is it the case that the officer in question has resigned, and has been favoured with a certificate of physical incapacity by Dr. Boyd?

Is there no form of protection provided for a girl of such tender years that would prevent the possibility of her being criminally assaulted in a police cell by a police officer?

Was the case referred to reported by the Chief Constable to the Magistrates, and if not, why not?

What was the nature of the report of the Chief Constable regarding the state of police discipline in the Eastern district?

Is it the case that the police in the Eastern district occupy a most unsatisfactory position by comparison with other districts, and, if so, who is responsible for this state of matters?

If steps are being taken to prevent the continuance of the existing practice in the East-End of police officers committing brutal and unprovoked assaults upon citizens, and of such officers being allowed to leave the country in order to escape a court of law?

The Lord Provost pointed out that it was necessary, according to the Standing Orders, that the Chief Constable should have been furnished with notice of these questions.

Mr. Gibson said he would be very pleased to give him notice if necessary.

GLASGOW STEAMER WRECKED.

NINE LIVES LOST.

GHASTLY SCENES ON THE ANTRIM COAST.

EIGHT BODIES FOUND.

[FROM OUR OWN CORRESPONDENT.]

Belfast, Monday.

Friday's disaster in Larne Lough, by which two Coastguardsmen, a Customs officer, and a Larne youth lost their lives, has been ollowed by a still more terrible calamity—the total loss some time during Sunday night or Monday morning of the steamship Peridot, belonging to Mr. William Robertson, of Gordon Street, Glasgow, and the entire crew of ten with one exception, on the beetling rocks at Skernaghan Point, midway between Portmuck on Island Magee headland and the entrance to Larne Lough.

The Peridot, which was an iron screw steamer of 241 tons register, built in 1890 by Fullerton & Co., of Paisley, was one of the fleet of 51 vessels belonging to the same owners, and known as the Gem Line. She traded generally between Glasgow and the smaller Ulster ports, and occasionally called at Belfast.

Commanded by Captain O'Kane, a native of Carnlough, the ill-fated steamer, it would seem, arrived on Saturday at Carnlough with coal for the local limeworks. By Sunday morning the cargo was discharged, and the crew were allowed to proceed on shore to visit their friends, while the vessel was brought up alongside the limestone pier to load lime and iron ore for the return voyage.

As the day wore on a south-westerly breeze gave place quite suddenly to half a gale with strong rain squalls from the south-west, and, towards the afternoon, with the storm increasing momentarily in violence, the sea was lashed to fury, and it was very soon apparent that the Peridot, night as she was, was in imminent danger of being either dashed against the pier or rocking violently in the heavy seas, dragging her anchors, and being driven to sea.

Captain O'Kane at once summoned his crew aboard and all responded but one man, who at the moment could not be found. No time was lost in weighing anchor, and the vessel was headed, so it was understood in Carnlough, for Belfast.

A TERRIBLE SCENE

Nothing further was heard of the vessel until the Portmuck coastguards on the look-out this (Monday) morning noticed evidence of a wreck some little distance away and put out in their boat to investigate.

On reaching the place where the wreckage had been observed a terrible scene met their gaze.

The stern of the vessel, on which was her name board and port of register, was found firmly fixed in the rocks, while the forward part had been completely carried away. Lying among the rocks were the bodies of eight men, all of whom have since been identified.

They presented a ghastly appearance, being terribly mutilated, especially about the face, and in three instances it was found that the men's necks had been broken, but whether this injury had been sustained at the moment of death or subsequently while being tossed to and fro among the jagged rocks is not at present known.

THE ILL-FATED CREW

The crew is as follows. With the exception of Ferguson, the engineer, a Glasgow man, whose body has not yet been found, they were all natives of Carnlough and Glenarm:

Captain O'Kane—Master.
Patrick Black—Mate.
Alex. Ferguson—Engineer.
James Stewart—Assistant Engineer.
James M'Kenty—Fireman.
John M'Mahon—Fireman.
John Darragh—Seaman.
R. M'Kellar—Seaman.
Alex. M'Neill—Seaman.

They were nearly all married men with families, and when the news reached Carnlough and Glenarm some touchingly pathetic scenes were witnessed, the grief and despair of the wives and families of the victims being

COUNCIL QUIZZED OVER POLICE

SERIOUS questions about certain members of the Glasgow Police Force were raised at a meeting of the Corporation.

The Magistrates' Committee were asked to explain to the council why they had decided to compensate an East End citizen for an alleged assault on him by a police officer while denying compensation to another citizen who had also requested compensation for an alleged assault and robbery.

Attention was drawn to an unprovoked assault made on Mr George McCutcheon by an ex-Constable Maloney, then of the Eastern Division of the Police.

Because of the attack, Mr McCutcheon lost wages of £2 18s and also had to pay £2.10s for medical bills. Mr McCutcheon's agent contended that payment of these sums should be made to him by the magistrates.

The accused ex-constable had left the service and his whereabouts were unknown according to evidence from the Chief Constable.

It was agreed to recommend that, without any admission of legal liability, the sum of £5.8s should be paid to Mr McCutcheon. The council's attention was then brought to a minute of the magistrates in which a Mr Duncan Campbell accused another police officer, also in the Eastern Police Division, of theft and assault. This policeman had allegedly knocked down Mr Campbell, took his watch, and brutally assaulted him. After the case was reported, the policeman was freed on £5 bail. He took the opportunity to leave the country immediately, as the constable in the McCutcheon case had done.

Councillors expressed the opinion that something drastic would have to be done by the Chief Constable to curb such excesses in his force. And they also called for action to restrict, if possible, the "dangerous and pernicious principle" of allowing policemen in such positions to get bail for a "miserable" sum and then to leave the country to escape punishment.

A SEASONABLE PRESENT
that will Delight Everyone.

SCOTTISH . . . .
WEEKLY RECORD
MICROSCOPE.

In order to advertise SCOTTISH WEEKLY RECORD the Editor is offering you this powerful and scientifically constructed

MICROSCOPE

FOR **5/6** POST FREE.

The Ordinary Price for this Beautiful Instrument is 10/6.

It has an enormous magnifying intensity, and is made in highly polished Brass Tubing, has a movable reflector on pivots, and powerful lever, achromatically arranged.

It is provided with covered glass slip, with insects ready mounted, also spare glass slips for mounting other objects, and a pair of brass forceps. All in a very handsomely polished box, specially fitted inside to take all parts.

Send P.O. for 5/6 to-day to—

SCOTTISH WEEKLY RECORD,
RENFIELD LANE, GLASGOW.

COMINGS...

Duncan Macrae
Actor

James Robertson Justice
Actor

GLASGOW STEAMER LOST

A steamer trading between Glasgow and the Ulster ports was lost with all hands in November. The *Peridot* perished in heavy seas off Portmuck as it headed for Belfast from Carnlough after discharging a cargo of coal. Ironically, it had left the small Ulster port as the storm rose in the hope of finding a safer anchorage at Belfast.

Nothing more was seen of the vessel until Portmuck coastguards investigated a wreck on rocks at Skernagham Point. There they found the remains of part of the ship wedged on the rocks together with the bodies of several of its crew members.

Lotus Winter Boots

Men's Reol No.
654

21/-

Smarter than boots made to measure and better

Bought by many men for special purposes such as shooting or golfing; but is more often chosen for general hard wear by men who neither shoot nor golf. Illustrated style booklet and the address of the local agent sent on request.

The Lotus Shoe Makers Ltd,
Stafford.

MODEL-LODGING HOUSE FIRE DISASTER

One of the worst fires of its time struck Glasgow in November. A model lodging house in Graeme Street was engulfed by flames in the early morning, killing 39 people and seriously injuring 24 others.

The building was full with almost 350 occupants when the alarm was raised. All the casualties had been sleeping on the top floor of the building, where the fire was believed to have started. Thick smoke quickly filled the upper levels of the building, making it difficult for firemen to reach the trapped men. Their job was also greatly hampered by the panic-stricken occupants who blocked the main staircase in their rush to escape. Although the fire was quickly extinguished, nothing could have been done to save the victims.

THIS SPORTING LIFE

FOOTBALL	RUGBY UNION	GOLF	HORSE RACING	SHINTY
Scottish Champions Celtic	*Scotland vs England* England 0–8 Scotland at Richmond	*British Open Winner* James Braid at St Andrews (318)	*Scottish Grand National Winner* *Theodocian* at Bogside	*Camanachd Cup Winners* Kyles Athletic at Inverness
Scottish Cup Winners Third Lanark				

History of the Old "Central:"
THE GREATREX CASE.
SEE THIS WEEK'S
Scottish Weekly Record

Daily Record & Mail.

LARGER SALE THAN ANY OTHER MORNING OR EVENING NEWSPAPER IN SCOTLAND.

Holiday Competition
FOR CASH PRIZES.
SEE THIS WEEK'S
Scottish Weekly Record

ESTABLISHED 1847.—No. 18,472.　　　　GLASGOW, FRIDAY, APRIL 13, 1906.　　　　ONE HALFPENNY.

THE TRUANT SCHOOL OF GLASGOW.

FRONT OF SCHOOL AT SHETTLESTON.

Wing contains dining-room on ground floor, sick ward and nurse's room above. Similar wing, of which a corner is shown, contains school-room with dormitory overhead. Intervening space—corridors, storerooms, &c.

HOW BOYS ARE SAVED FROM PRISON AND THE STREETS.

(By C. W. PATTISON.)

WHAT doleful party of young lads is this?

They are bound for the Truant School at Shettleston.

A—h!

Well, well, wicked as they must be thus to wring the heart of teacher and School Board officer, surely they do not deserve all they seem to expect. You will follow, and see what fate o'ertakes them.

Panting behind, you reach the fine red building amongst the trees just in time to see them disappear through a side door. Here you wait in horrid fear, listening for sounds of woe. You are somewhat reassured by a smiling gentleman, who comes on the scene and conducts you round to another door, whence they will issue by-and-by to a very large asphalted playground, round which the school is built.

At last—they come! They have not been massacred—only weighed and measured, stripped and bathed. But you hardly know them again, soap and hope have so changed their countenances, whilst their bodies are uniformly clad in suits of stout grey tweed and cosy red jerseys, their discarded garments reposing meanwhile in the fumigator. You learn that they will stay here to be disciplined for three months. You turn away with a sigh of relief, but a tear in your gentle eye.

The Reformation.

You do not forget, however, and in about three months' time you turn up again. You are conducted to the schoolroom. The boys politely rise to salute, whereat you modestly blush. Here, it seems, half the inmates are assembled, the remainder being employed in the workshops—about one hundred boys altogether. There are no truant girls—perish the thought!

They are separated at lessons into three divisions, according to attainments on arrival or progress since. The lowest are practically in the Infant Room, the highest in Standard IV. Most of them quickly make up for time lost. Poor children, neglected at home, often half starved, it is their parents who ought to be caged and tamed.

Getting very much interested, you go on to the shoemaker's department, where the youthful cobblers are learning to make and mend strong, neat shoes; and then to the next room, where embryo tailors are stitching the grey suits aforesaid or patching the garments which have passed thither from fumigator and washing machine.

Twelve o'clock, and the whole school troops to the playground, there to engage for an hour in drill and marching. They go through a series of free exercises, in which they learn to use their muscles and to breathe properly. Without aid either of music or the teacher's voice, they pass from one to another, this forming valuable training for their minds as well as for their bodies. You look around for your proteges, but they are mostly altered out of recognition for such a passing acquaintance. They have grown in height, in weight—some to the extent of one stone—and on chest girth, while their now rosy faces beam with interest.

Three out of every twelve, it is expected, will reappear at the school for a second term of four months, and one or two incorrigibles for even a third term of six months, by which time their years and educational attainments (!) will doubtless permit of their leaving school. Every Friday fortnight a fresh lot arrives.

The boys have been up since six o'clock, and have done an hour and a half's housework, including making of beds and scrubbing, before breakfast. This consists of "Scotia's halesome parritch," with which many are probably making their first acquaintance, and good sweet milk. Then they have worship or "devotions" under Protestant or Catholic masters. At nine lessons begin.

One o'clock, and they march to the dining-hall, each equipped with a sauce no French chef can supply. A shelved table is run in from the kitchen on rails, and a plain substantial meal is quickly served. The long narrow deal tables and benches of this hall render it capable of being used for occasions when the school assembles, and there is an organ on the platform at one end.

Dinner and play over, at two o'clock the boys who were in the schoolroom in the morning go to the workshops, and vice versa. You take the opportunity of seeing over the establishment and hearing the views of the enthusiasts who teach them. Punishments are by no means prohibited, but are used with the greatest discretion. Although everything is done to make them happy and comfortable, the boys are made to feel in moral disgrace should they appear at the school a second time. Then the loss of their liberty tells, for every minute of the day is ordered, and they are never allowed even at play to hang around slouching with hands in pockets.

Saturday Football.

On Saturdays the time-table is pretty much the same, but in the afternoon they may be allowed to play football, and some of the most trustworthy—the oldest inhabitants, so to speak—may be taken for a walk. On Sundays they go twice to church or chapel, read suitable books, and sing and learn hymns.

Boys assist everywhere throughout the day—in laundry, kitchen, and garden. In the manual instruction room they learn to make all sorts of useful articles in joinery work. In every department, of course, they are bound to display their special bent, and in the needle room, where they are mending their shirts and stockings, you notice one little fellow who, you feel sure, will give his mother points on the family mending when he gets home again. What a history they must have to tell that day, and what a new life must here open out to those intelligent boys!

Five o'clock, and you repair to the gymnasium to watch them getting out their animal spirits, jumping, leaping, swinging, and swimming.

The Nightly Bath.

Supper at six o'clock consists of tea, coffee, or cocoa alternately, with bread and syrup or good margarine. Worship follows; then more gymnastics or singing, games, and the nightly bath. In the lavatory each boy has a separate towel, to minimise risk of skin disease by contagion.

By nine o'clock they are in bed and the lights are down. Each airy dormitory, with white scrubbed floor, is overlooked by a window from a master's room. There is a sick ward near at hand.

As you go down the road you are musing how many may here be saved from prison and the streets; at all events, you cannot imagine any boy who has been in such a school for even three months ever taking to the future to hooliganism.

LOCOMOTIVE AS BIRD-CATCHER.

As the 4.20 a.m. train from Glasgow Central to Aberdeen was passing Alloa Junction the other morning, a bird in the act of flying across the track was intercepted by the locomotive, which at the time was travelling at a speed of fully 60 miles an hour.

The engine - driver observed the incident, and on drawing up at Stirling, the first stopping - place, some six miles further on, he found this magnificent specimen of the Barn Owl clinging to the hand-rail in front of the engine's smoke - box, but quite dead. Strange to say, not a single feather was ruffled. The victim has been stuffed, and is regarded by admiring local railwaymen as a unique "catch."

A STORY IN BRONZE.

THE WONDERFUL "GATES OF PARADISE," WHICH MAY BE STUDIED IN DETAIL BY VISITORS TO GLASGOW'S ART GALLERIES AT KELVINGROVE.

IN the great entrance hall of the Glasgow Art Galleries stands a replica of the most beautiful gates of bronze in the world—worthy, according to Michael Angelo, to be the gates of Paradise, and the original of which is to be found in the grand old city of Florence. Apart from its magnificence there is in connection with the portal one of those humanly interesting little stories which sometimes bring the past so vividly before us, and "make the whole world kin."

In the year 1406 the municipality of Florence announced their determination to have completed the gates of the Baptistery. For that purpose they summoned to a competition the artists of Italy, who were to send in as a specimen of skill some "story in bronze." The matter made a great noise, for was there not, besides the substantial commission, the prospect of almost certain fame!

Beginning of the Work.

Lorenzo Ghiberti, a lad of twenty, the pupil and stepson of one Bartoluccio, an art worker, had just then gone on a ramble through the land, to see what was to be seen that could aid him in his profession, casting here and there small figures in bronze, wax, and stucco. To him came in all haste a letter from Bartoluccio, who seems to have had great faith in Lorenzo's powers.

Here was an occasion, wrote the stepfather, to show his genius and raise the family fortunes. The lad set out at once for home. To his excited mind even our modern facilities for travel would have appeared slow. As it was, "it seemed to him a thousand years before he could reach Florence." There he immediately set to work, aided in his youthful fervour by the anxious and experienced Bartoluccio.

The day of judgment drew near. Councillors, burghers, painters, sculptors—art authorities of all kinds, in short—had an anxious time. Before their slowly-formed decision had been arrived at, however, Filippo Brunelleschi and his friend Donatello had made up their minds about the matter. Brunelleschi, the designer in after years of that wonderful cathedral dome, was one of the competitors, and only a little older than Ghiberti. He and young Donatello, who was yet to make a name in sculpture, wandered through the exhibition, comparing and criticising with bated breath.

The Work of Genius.

Well, Filippo's was better than that—and that—and that! Surely he must win! But here they paused before Ghiberti's group, and criticism died on their lips. They could look on no more, but, with a chill at their hearts, drew into a corner, where they acknowledged to each other, as artists, that it was the best, and ought to win.

It did win, and Lorenzo Ghiberti was chosen to do the Baptistery gates. They were the work of a lifetime, each taking twenty years to complete—forty years in all; Ghiberti, however, executing numerous other works during that period.

THINK IT OUT.

If we sit down at set of sun
And count the things that we have done,
And, counting, find
One self-denying act, one word
That eased the heart of him who heard,
That fell like sunshine where it went,
Then we may count the day well spent.

But if through all the livelong day
We've eased no heart by yea or nay;
If through it all
We've done no thing that we can trace
That brought the sunshine to a face,
No act, most small,
That helped some soul and nothing cost,
Then count that day as worse than lost.

The youth William Munro who heroically saved a fellow workman from death at the oil refining works of Messrs. Walls & Company, Lochburn Road, Maryhill, yesterday.

YORKSHIRE RELISH.
THE MOST DELICIOUS SAUCE IN THE WORLD.
Sole Proprietors—Goodall, Backhouse & Co., Leeds.

RAW ITCHING ECZEMA
Blotches on Hands, Ears, and Ankles For Three Years. Relief from First Day's Treatment and

van Houten's Cocoa
BEST & GOES FARTHEST.

1906

SCHOOL FOR THE CLASS DODGERS

THERE was no more "dogging" classes for the boys who were sent to the Truant School at Shettleston in Glasgow.

The children were divided into three groups for lessons on their arrival, according to their levels of literacy.

The lowest were in the Infant Room, the highest in Standard IV. Most of them, quickly made up for lost time. Poor children, neglected at home and often half-starved, also quickly regained their health.

It was expected that three out of every 12 would reappear at the school for a second term of four months.

And one or two "incorrigibles" would be back for a third term of six months, by which time their age and educational attainments would permit them to leave the school.

The boys rose at 6am to do an hour and a half of housework before breakfast. Lessons began at 9am.

Lunch was at 1pm and consisted of a plain but substantial meal. Playtime was next and at 2pm, the boys who had been in the schoolroom in the morning, went to the workshops and vice versa. The youngsters learned to make and mend shoes.

On Saturdays the timetable was much the same, but in the afternoon they were allowed to play football and some of the more trustworthy were taken for a walk. On Sundays they went to church or chapel, read and sang, and learned hymns.

Throughout the day, the boys were expected to assist in the running of the school: in the laundry, the kitchen and the garden. At 5pm, the boys were in the gymnasium for a range of physical pursuits that included basic gymnastics and swimming.

Supper was at 6pm and consisted of tea, coffee or cocoa, with bread and syrup or margarine. Then there were games and the nightly bath. By 9pm, they were in bed and it was "lights out".

Each dormitory was overlooked by a window from a master's room.

The authorities reckoned that many of the boys were saved from prison or the streets.

WRECKED DISTILLERY.

OFFICIAL INSPECTION OF THE BUILDING.

NUMBER OF VICTIMS INCREASED.

MAID'S
AFTERNOON DRESS
(AS SKETCH)
MADE FROM GOOD
WEARING BLACK SERGE.

Neatly Made   Lined Throughout

12/6
OR MADE TO MEASURE 2/- EXTRA

MOORE, TAGGART & Co.

DISTILLERY CHAOS

An extraordinary accident threw the densely populated neighbourhood of the Gorbals in Glasgow into chaos as three massive distillery vats burst without warning. Each vat at the Loch Katrine Distillery contained some 60,000 gallons of liquid used in the distilling process and each was housed on a separate floor of the distillery. The accident occurred when the supports for the vat on the top floor collapsed and caused it to crash down on the others on the floors beneath it. The liquid poured out into the narrow streets surrounding the distillery in a massive tidal wave which caused great damage to surrounding buildings and anyone caught in its path.

ROYAL YACHT COMES TO THE CLYDE

It was announced in July that the King's new racing yacht was to be built on the Clyde. The king was returning to the sport of his youth when, as Prince of Wales, he won many competitions at both home and abroad racing in the *Britannia*. The new yacht was to be called *Britannia II*. It was also hoped that the royal patronage of the Clyde would encourage other commissions at a time when the popularity of traditional yachting was under severe threat from motor cruising.

CANADA

The cry for unskilled Labour greater than ever. Splendid opportunities for healthy men and women, Britain's nearest and greatest colony.

160 Acres Free

Get your own Farm; quit paying Rent; Happy Homes; Healthy Bracing Climate; Under the old Flag; Cheap Fares; Comfortable and Speedy Travel.

Work is found

On Farms for experienced or inexperienced Men, for Domestic Servants, for Navvies, Carters and all willing workers.

For Maps, Pamphlets, full information and directions, apply— J. BRUCE WALKER, Assistant Superintendent Canadian Emigration, 11-12, Charing Cross, London, S.W., or to JOHN WEBSTER, 35-37, St. Enoch Square, Glasgow.

COMINGS...
Andrew Cruikshank
Actor
Jack House
Broadcaster & Journalist

THIS SPORTING LIFE

FOOTBALL	RUGBY UNION	GOLF	HORSE RACING	SHINTY
Scottish Champions	*Scotland vs England*	*British Open Winner*	*Scottish Grand National Winner*	*Camanachd Cup Winners*
Celtic	Scotland 3–9 England	James Braid	Creolin at Bogside	Kyles Athletic at
Scottish Cup Winners	at Inverleith	at Muirfield (300)		Inverness
Hearts				

CITY EDITION.

Daily Record & Mail.

LARGER SALE THAN ANY OTHER MORNING OR EVENING NEWSPAPER IN SCOTLAND.

ESTABLISHED 1847—No. 18,769 GLASGOW, TUESDAY, MARCH 26, 1907 ONE HALFPENNY.

CONSULT LIST OF
Coast-Country Houses
TO LET
IN
Daily Record & Mail.

SEE
INTERESTING NOTICE
ABOUT
Coast-Country Houses
On PAGE 3 TO-DAY.

FILTHY HABIT

THE SPITTING NUISANCE ON TRAMCARS.

A GLASGOW CRUSADE.

The special efforts that have been put forth of late for the suppression of the filthy habit of spitting on Glasgow tramcars do not appear to have resulted in any real reform. Journeys on different routes during Saturday and yesterday revealed a state of affairs that demands even more stringent measures than those already adopted.

It is remarkable that it is only within the last few weeks Glasgow authorities have been induced to follow the English cities in affixing metal plates to the electrical standards with the words in white on a blue ground—"Please do not spit on the footpath." A step in advance in general manners would fall to the credit of the city if the footpaths could be kept clear of this nuisance, and it is to be hoped there will soon be a sensible improvement in that regard; but it is impossible to inculcate good manners in the ordinary pedestrian in a crowded thoroughfare with business movement at full pressure, or it is at any rate less possible to do so than in the case of a tramcar where thirty or forty people are more or less comfortably seated, and where the conduct of a single individual may cause annoyance to his fellow-passengers.

In the tramcar it is within the scope of the passenger's jurisdiction—as it is within the right of the conductor—to resent filthy habits. The disgust that even "strong" smokers express for the usual expectorating hooligan leads to the belief that a little encouragement would result in the formation of an effective public opinion which would check this spitting evil once and for all.

The Tramway Department has, of course, posted fresh notices, quoting the bye-law and the penalty enforcable in the double-deckers—on the upper decks, to be correct, for, singularly enough, one hardly ever hears a complaint of spitting on the lower decks. But these notices are being ignored just as have been for years the notice "Spitting is Forbidden" on the box protecting the trolley swivel. Complaint is made that the new notices might be replaced by notices in larger lettering or printed in red ink, so as to emphasise the necessity of having the evil put a stop to.

CONDUCTORS SNUBBED.

The difficulty of having offenders rendered amenable is no light one. A conductor who was questioned on the subject said he could not be always on the upper deck, and when he was if he ventured to protest against an individual indulging in the spitting habit he often found the passengers as a body anxious to "side" with the individual, passing rude remarks about the official and his authority, and boorishly intimating that he ought to "mind his own business."

He might have right and legality with him, but it is easy to imagine that a conductor who meets with treatment of this kind from a number of passengers is chary about interference another time. A prosecution here and a prosecution there, with light fines, do not seem to matter to the great army of boys and men who pollute the upper decks, or, what is infinitely worse, squirt saliva on the hats and clothes of persons entering or leaving the cars or others who may cross a street just at the point where a car is passing. This latter phase of the nuisance is so atrocious an outrage against public decency that witnesses of its almost daily occurrence are amazed at the number of apparently well-to-do folks who so far forget themselves as to indulge in it.

"The only plan I can suggest," said the conductor indicated above, "is that the public should do their best to help us to put down spitting. We cannot do it without their assistance. We do our best, but our best is very little, and we cannot be expected to keep the cars clean and free from disease germs as long as people are at liberty to do just as they please. The people who don't smoke attribute the spitting to the smokers. Well, I can tell you this—I have seen many a non-smoker, or men who said they were non-smokers, and their conduct in spitting was just as bad as the worst smoker or chewer of tobacco that you could find."

"It would do no harm," observed a car

RAID ON THE COMMONS.

800 WOMEN BESIEGE THE GATES.

RIOTOUS SCENES.

UMBRELLA ATTACK ON THE POLICE.

SIXTY ARRESTS.

The campaign of the Suffragettes in pursuit of votes had an alarming development yesterday, when for several hours a determined attempt was made to carry by storm the Houses of Parliament.

It was only by the strenuous efforts of a large staff of policemen that the effort was not successful, as many as 800 women delivering the opening attack.

After the first raid had been broken up, the women reassembled in Caxton Hall, whence they originally set out, and gathering fresh courage made a second attempt to get within the walls of St. Stephen. They were not more successful than on the first occasion, and left many prisoners in the hands of the enemy.

Altogether 61 persons, including two men, were taken into custody and afterwards liberated on bail.

THE BATTLE.

It is exactly a year since the Women's Social and Political Union initiated their campaign and adopted militant tactics, and the anniversary was celebrated by a "national convention" which was held in Caxton Hall in the afternoon.

The speeches consisted of a series of threats, and the developments of the evening were foreshadowed by pointed allusions to the impending raid.

Miss Kenney declared that if the evening's proceedings did not result in the Government taking into consideration women's demands, she was prepared to lead 1000 cotton operatives from Lancashire to storm the House of Commons—girls and women who were prepared to throw themselves against all obstacles, and continue the struggle until they were face to face, on the floor of the House of Commons, with the Ministerial Bench.

These premonitions of the coming attack culminated in the passing of a resolution "That a deputation now proceed to the House of Commons to demand from the Premier suffrage for women."

The hall was crowded, a large proportion of the audience consisting of supporters of the cause from the provinces, many having come from the North of England.

The plan of campaign had been carefully organised. A score of the stalwarts, headed by the indomitable Mrs. Despard, led the van, and practically the whole of the meeting followed in procession by way of Victoria Street. The police had information of the raid, and a large force, some of them mounted, and many in plain clothes, were in readiness in the vicinity of the House.

As the procession came round the corner of St. Margaret's Church they were in time to witness the ejection of a party who had previously gained access to the Lobby.

The women had got half-way across the street when a police charge was made. Several mounted officers urged their steeds amongst the women, and immediately there followed a scene of wild confusion. Parties of twos and threes rushed off in different directions, their objective being the St. Stephen's entrance. The police likewise broke their cordon, bolting in pursuit.

Many of the women tried conclusions with the guards at the Palace Yard entrance. Their efforts to get through were defeated, and the large iron gates were closed. The women then became wildly excited, screaming and shouting. Baffled in their attempts to effect an entrance, they next directed their attention to the police, and over the whole area between the Abbey and the Houses of Parliament a series of struggles ensued. The women refused to leave the vicinity, and wholesale arrests followed.

Groups of twos and threes were led off to Cannon Row Police Station. Some went quietly; others offered the most vigorous resistance all the way.

It was at considerable danger that any lady ventured near the scene. Little discrimination being used by the police in dealing with the crowd. One or two of those arrested disclaimed all association with the Suffragettes.

One dignified lady wearing the insignia of the Suffragettes, a "Votes for Women" badge created great amusement by the methods she adopted to irritate the police. At the most leisurely of paces she began to walk alongside Palace Yard. A dozen officers followed her, and a crowd quickly collected.

At the same measured tread she traversed the whole length of the House, refusing to be hurried, and her ruse was successful in attracting more officers as the crowd continued to increase. This weakened the defence at the entrance, and a succession of women singly tried to gain admission, one or two of them getting within the police bar by driving up in cabs. Without exception they were unceremoniously forced from the pavement.

At 7.30 a Yorkshire section formed a sort of forlorn hope, but so close was the observation of the police that their design was surmised, and their attempt frustrated. Three of them were among the last to be arrested.

A SECOND ONSLAUGHT.

At a quarter-past nine a second attack was made on the House. A strong detachment approached bravely singing one of the party songs.

The police, however, expected them, and had made elaborate preparations for their reception. A body of 50 or 60 constables were waiting in ambuscade, and when a signal was given that the Suffragettes had arrived they emerged and formed up in front of the Palace Yard and across from the House to the Abbey. A strong mounted patrol came trotting up, and kept the crowd of Suffragettes and the curious public continuously moving.

Most of the ladies fled before the horses, but about half a dozen, more intrepid than the rest, persisted and gained for themselves the honour of arrest.

The attempt to reach the legislators within St. Stephen's was, however, renewed again and again, and right up to ten o'clock the Suffragettes were being apprehended and taken in batches to the police station.

A LIST THAT SPEAKS FOR ITSELF.

The "DAILY MAIL" series of Sixpenny Novels is unique in that it needs no long explanation or recommendation. The books speak for themselves, and a perusal of the list already issued and those forthcoming is quite sufficient guarantee of the excellence of the series, from which all inferior works are rigidly excluded.

THE ETERNAL CITY, By HALL CAINE.
THE WOMAN WITH THE FAN, By ROBERT HICHENS.
VIVIEN, By W. B. MAXWELL.
BETTY WESLEY, By "Q."
THE SHADOWY THIRD, By HORACE A. VACHELL.
TRISTRAM OF BLENT, By ANTHONY HOPE.
A NINE DAYS' WONDER, By B. M. CROKER.
TALLY HO! By HELEN MATHERS.
THE GATE OF THE DESERT, By JOHN OXENHAM.
SUSANNAH AND ONE OTHER, By E. MARIA ALBANESI.
THE REFUGEES, By A. CONAN DOYLE.
THE CONFLICT, By Miss BRADDON.
MY SWORD FOR LAFAYETTE, By MAX PEMBERTON.
BEHIND THE THRONE, By WILLIAM LE QUEUX.
THE STAR DREAMER, By AGNES and EGERTON CASTLE.
MIRANDA OF THE BALCONY, By A. E. W. MASON.
LETTERS FROM A SELF-MADE MERCHANT TO HIS SON, By G. H. LORIMER.

READY JULY 20th.
A GENTLEMAN OF FRANCE. STANLEY WEYMAN.
THE CALL OF THE BLOOD. ROBERT HICHENS.

READY SHORTLY.
THE HEART OF PRINCESS OSRA. ANTHONY HOPE. (Aug. 31)
THE PHILANDERERS. A. E. W. MASON. (Aug. 31)
UNDER THE RED ROBE. STANLEY WEYMAN.
THE GARDEN OF ALLAH. ROBERT HICHENS.
THE GUARDED FLAME. W. B. MAXWELL.
THE BATH COMEDY. AGNES and EGERTON CASTLE.
POISON ISLAND. A. T. QUILLER COUCH.
THE HEART'S HIGHWAY. MARY E. WILKINS.
PETER'S MOTHER. Mrs. HENRY DE LA PASTURE.
LITTLE NOVELS OF ITALY. MAURICE HEWLETT.

6d. net. Everywhere.

FATAL HEAT WAVE

DEATHS IN IRVINE MOOR CAMP

PEDESTRIANS PROSTRATED

Only a few days have passed since cold, raw, and depressing conditions prevailed, and now we are in the midst of heat of tropical intensity. The almost stifling glow of Sunday's atmosphere, intensified by a broiling sun after mid-day, was the first indication of the approach of the present heat wave. Up to that point Sunday was the hottest day of the year, but the greater warmth of Monday, when the maximum temperature was 74 degrees in the shade, set up a fresh record.

Still greater heat was experienced yesterday, for even by noonday, when the temperature is not at its height, the thermometer stood at 74.1, being one-tenth of a degree above Monday's maximum. The later readings, as given by Prof. Becker, of Glasgow Observatory, showed that the maximum temperature was 80.6 degrees in the shade, being the highest this season.

This is an exceptional temperature, and has only been exceeded on nineteen occasions during the last forty years. The barometer at first showed an inclination to fall, standing 30.42 at ten o'clock on Monday night, 30.41 at ten o'clock yesterday morning, and 30.39 at noon. It, however, gradually rose again, so that there is the prospect of a continuance of the heat.

The sudden prevalence of oppressive conditions has proved overpowering to many, and several cases of exhaustion were reported yesterday. Here and there through the city elderly men and women were to be seen seated in shaded areas, and in the streets it was no uncommon occurrence in the afternoon to see groups round some old lady or weakly person who had been temporarily prostrated.

There was a continuance of the warm weather in Edinburgh yesterday, and during the forenoon and afternoon the atmosphere was very oppressive.

CAMP VICTIMS.

In the camps the effects have been still more serious. At Irvine Moor two fatalities are reported, while several cases are in hospital.

The men who died are James Doyle and Robert Sproul, both privates in the Fourth Argyll and Sutherland Highlanders, belonging to Paisley. Doyle was unmarried, and Sproul was a widower. It appears they took part in the big sham fight yesterday, and returned to camp after marching nearly twenty miles.

Neither of the two men complained or fell out on the march, but before they had been dismissed they collapsed and were conveyed to hospital. Sproul died about six o'clock, and Doyle about nine, neither having regained consciousness. Death was due to heat apoplexy.

Several other cases, all belonging to the Militia, were reported to have been removed to hospital last night, and at the Highland Light Infantry Volunteer Brigade camp at Gailes three slight cases are being treated.

During the progress of a sham fight at Llangollen, where the Royal Worcestershire Militia are in camp, Private John Perry, of Castleford, Yorks, suddenly collapsed and died.

A death from heat apoplexy is reported from Lancaster, the victim being an ambulance brigade superintendent named Roocroft.

CITY'S SPITTING IMAGE REMAINS

THE special efforts that had been suggested for the stamping out of the "filthy habit" of spitting on Glasgow tramcars did not appear to have resulted in any real reform.

In March, these efforts began when Glasgow Corporation decided to follow the practice that was then common in many large English cities of fixing notices to street lamps requesting people not to spit on the pavements.

It was said that it would not only be a step forward in improving the general good manners of Glaswegians if they would take heed of the signs but that it would also help reduce the spread of infectious air-borne diseases. Yet at the same time, it was acknowledged that it was virtually impossible to enforce any such bye-law against spitting in the street.

On the trams, however, the situation was felt to be different and that it would be possible to enforce the ban because it was within the rights of the tram conductor to forbid spitting and to eject those guilty of it.

The general disgust expressed by most people with regard to spitting led to the belief that with civic encouragement, public opinion would check the spitting habit once and for all.

To this end, the Tramway Department posted fresh notices, quoting the bye-law and making clear the penalty enforceable, namely, a fine.

The signs were displayed on every corporation tram, and particularly on the upper decks of double-deck vehicles. Significantly, there were hardly ever any complaints of people spitting on the lower decks.

PATRIOTIC GATHERING

The annual gathering of the Scottish Patriotic Association took place at the Wallace Monument in Robroyston near Kirkintilloch. A large crowd of some 500 people gathered in the fields near the monument and sang patriotic songs to the accompaniment of a brass band.

In his address, the chairman of the SPA, George Eyre Todd, told the assembled mass that they met "not for their own vainglory but to serve Scotland in the present by recalling the heroic deeds of her past sons". He also made an impassioned plea for the deeds of Wallace, Bruce, Knox and other Scottish heroes to be systematically taught in every Scottish school.

MERIT
is and has always been the foundation of popularity.

Here is the HUB OF MANY MERITS, so called because it embodies in one shell a high gear for the level—a low gear for the hill—a free wheel on both gears—and a brake of absolute efficiency.

It was the first hub to demonstrate the practicability of such a combination, and to-day retains a unique position in this respect.

EVERY CYCLIST
meets difficulties on both sides the hill—it will help you to overcome them all—dispel the toil of the laborious climb, and at the same time the dangers of the down hill spin.

If you would enhance your cycling pleasure you should write at once for descriptive booklet—study it—and then specify the

EADIE TWO-SPEED COASTER
in your new machine, or have it built into your old one.   Address   Dept.G.G.
EADIE MFG. CO., LTD., REDDITCH.

COMINGS...

Lex Maclean
Comedian

Basil Spence
Architect

GOINGS...

Lord Kelvin
Scientist & Inventor

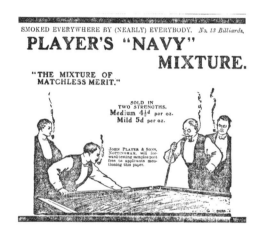

SMOKED EVERYWHERE BY (NEARLY) EVERYBODY.   No. 13 Billiards.

PLAYER'S "NAVY" MIXTURE.

"THE MIXTURE OF MATCHLESS MERIT."

SOLD IN TWO STRENGTHS.
Medium 4½d per oz.
Mild 5d per oz.

JOHN PLAYER & SONS, NOTTINGHAM, will forward testing samples post free to applicants mentioning this paper.

KILWINNING ANTI-POPERY TRIAL

There were riotous scenes in Kilwinning in Ayrshire in August following the trial of anti-Popery preacher, James MacDonald. Mr MacDonald had been charged with the use of abusive language with intent to cause a breach of the peace following his open-air preaching in the town earlier in the month.

At the trial several witnesses for the prosecution declared that MacDonald had insulted the Pope, abused their religion and repeatedly suggested that all female Catholics – particularly in Kilwinning – led immoral lives. For the defence, witnesses denied any that inflammatory language had been used.

In the end, MacDonald was found guilty and fined 40s but on leaving the court, a huge crowd had assembled and cheered and shouted when the preacher appeared. They rushed forward to shake his hand and it was only with great difficulty that the police prevented MacDonald being borne away on the shoulders of the crowd.

THIS SPORTING LIFE

FOOTBALL	RUGBY UNION	GOLF	HORSE RACING	SHINTY
Scottish Champions Celtic	*Scotland vs England* England 3–8 Scotland at Blackheath	*British Open Winner* Arnold Massey At Hoylake, England (312)	*Scottish Grand National Winner* Barney III at Bogside	*Camanachd Cup Winners* Newtonmore at Kingussie
Scottish Cup Winners Celtic				

RACY ARTICLES
FROM THE
Leading Football Players
APPEAR IN THE
Scottish Weekly Record.

Daily Record & Mail.

LARGER SALE THAN ANY OTHER MORNING OR EVENING NEWSPAPER IN SCOTLAND.

ESTAB. 1847—No. 19,249 GLASGOW, TUESDAY, OCTOBER 6, 1908 ONE HALFPENNY.

HOLIDAY CRUISES.
BOOKLETS and FULL PARTICULARS on APPLICATION.
UNION TRANSIT CO.,
381 ARGYLE STREET, GLASGOW.

LINERS COLLIDE IN THE FOG.

GLASGOW VESSEL SUNK.

THREE OFFICERS LOST.

FIREMEN ACCUSED OF UNGALLANTRY.

Information of a shipping disaster near the Tuskar Rock, off the coast of Wexford, was received in Liverpool last night, when Messrs. Elders & Fyffes' 3838 ton steamer Matina arrived with the crew and passengers of the City liner City of Dundee, a steamer of 3427 tons, and the property of G. Smith & Sons, Glasgow.

The latter left Liverpool at four o'clock on Saturday afternoon bound for Alexandria, and at twenty minutes past seven on Sunday morning she was struck amidships by the Matina, and sank in eight minutes.

The captain, second officer, and quartermaster of the City of Dundee were drowned, but the rest of the crew, 36 in number, were safely got on board the Matina along with the 13 passengers—seven ladies, five gentlemen, and a little child.

The scenes which followed the collision were on the whole in keeping with the highest traditions of British seamanship, and it was undoubtedly due to the heroism and presence of mind of the deceased captain, supplemented by the coolness of his crew and the admirable self-restraint of the passengers, that the loss of life under the circumstances proved comparatively small.

Captain Belton set his men a splendid example. Realising at a glance that his vessel was doomed, he immediately gave the order that first attention must be given to the ladies.

Upon seeing the hopeless condition of the City of Dundee, the Matina stood by and lowered two boats. At this moment several of the firemen of the City of Dundee pushed aside the passengers, and endeavoured to secure their own safety.

On the instructions of Captain Belton, the sailors forced them back, and the process of rescuing the more helpless began. Eight of the ladies had been taken on board the Matina, when one lady, having been separated from her baby, was no sooner on the Matina than she began to shriek for it.

The captain himself fetched the missing child, which was thrown safely into the arms of a man on the Matina. The City of Dundee then began to show a dangerous list, the lifeboats in their davits hanging over the Matina. Into these the passengers and crew clambered, and were thence transferred to the deck of the Matina.

Captain Belton was struck a heavy blow by a floating small boat and sank.

Scarcely had the last person left the City of Dundee when her boilers exploded, and she disappeared.

The passengers included Mr. and Mrs. Kent, a newly-married couple, who lost two hundred wedding presents. Twenty-nine foxhounds for Prince Kamil Pasha were all drowned.

The rescued crew and passengers presented a pitiable sight on landing at Liverpool. Few of them were fully clothed. Some of the crew had not had time to don more than their nether garments, while several of the lady passengers were clad only in their night-dresses. They were immediately taken to a clothing establishment to replenish their lost wardrobes.

KING'S TOUR IN THE HIGHLANDS.

THROUGH CULLODEN FIELD.

RELICS OF PRINCE CHARLIE.

The King had a long motor tour yesterday through some of the most historic parts of the Highlands of Scotland.

His Majesty left Tulchan Lodge shortly after noon on a visit to the famed Cawdor Castle, where Shakespeare has it that the "air nimbly and sweet recommends itself unto our gentle senses." It was hardly so yesterday when the King paid his first visit to the ancient castle.

The forenoon was dull and threatening rain, but when his Majesty was timed to arrive the mists which overhung the Cawdor Hills lifted and the sun shone out brilliantly. During his Majesty's stay of two hours ideal weather prevailed.

The route by which his Majesty motored was by Nairn and Grantown Road. It was intended to go by Clunas, but, being unable to ford Meikleburn, Nairnshire, which is at present in spate, the King and party had to return to Grantown Road and go by way of Foynesfield. This caused a delay of about 25 minutes.

At Cawdor Castle the King was received by Earl Cawdor and the Hon. Elidor Campbell, who were introduced by the King to his party. Accompanying the King in the Royal car were Sir Arthur Davidson, Lady Crewe and Mrs. Sassoon. In the second car were Lady Sarah Wilson, Lady Ilchester and the Hon. Mrs. George Keppell.

The house party at Cawdor Castle were the Earl and Countess Cawdor, Lady Welby, Lady Hatherton, Lady Edith Campbell and the Hon. Elidor Campbell. After luncheon the party visited the beautiful gardens and grounds of the Castle, which are one of the sights of Nairnshire. The visit being a private one, few people witnessed the King's arrival, but on his departure about four o'clock a large number of people had assembled near to the entrance gate, whose salutation the King graciously acknowledged.

RETURN JOURNEY.

Earl Cawdor accompanied his Majesty part of his return journey to Tulchan, which was by the way of Moy Hall, where his Majesty paid a visit to the Mackintosh of Mackintosh.

On the way to Moy the King passed through the battlefield of Culloden, which is divided by a public road. It was the first visit of a King to the historic spot since the fateful battle. King Edward made no stay. His Majesty could not fail to see the huge memorial cairn and the stones on the graves of the Highland clansmen that fell fighting for Prince Charlie.

At Moy Hall the King made a short stay, and had the opportunity of viewing the priceless Jacobite relics which find a resting place in the Castle.

In these he was greatly interested. They include Prince Charlie's cap and walking-stick and the bed in which the Prince slept before the battle. Another relic which interested his Majesty was the old anvil of the famous blacksmith of Moy, who with five men put Lord Loudon's army to flight, and saved the Prince from capture at Moy Hall.

The journey back to Tulchan was accomplished without incident.

A right Royal welcome is to be given to his Majesty when he visits Blairgowrie on his way from Balmoral to Dunblane. In an interview which the members of the Town Council had with Lord Dunedin, the latter stated that the King was averse to flags being hung across thoroughfares, but was pleased to see decorations along the sides of the streets. His Lordship also stated that he had advised the King

CLYDE BOAT DISASTER.

LUGSAIL CAPSIZED OFF GOUROCK.

THREE LIVES LOST.

OTHER DISTRESSING ACCIDENTS.

The capsizing of a lugsail boat on the Firth of Clyde yesterday was the cause of the loss of three lives, and boating accidents in other parts of the country were responsible for other deaths.

Gourock, the popular yachting centre, was the scene of the most serious of the mishaps. Shortly after ten o'clock a party of four men left Cardwell Bay in a 16-feet centre-board lugsail boat—the Uno—intending to cross the firth to Strone Point, four or five miles away.

It was a blustering morning with a strong wind from the west, and the water was pretty rough. When the little craft, with full canvas out, was about in mid-stream a sudden squall caught her and overturned her.

Three of the occupants were thrown into the sea, but the fourth appeared to have got entangled in the gear of the boat and was taken under water. Two of the others also sank.

A PERILOUS PLIGHT.

A curious feature of the accident was that the boat though below the water did not sink to the bottom, and two or three feet of the mast remained above the surface. To this the only survivor, Mr. James Mitchell Pattison, clung until help arrived, and he was rescued in a very exhausted condition.

The disaster had been witnessed from the shore and from some of the steam yachts anchored in the bay, and a crew of four men from one of the latter, the Petronella, immediately put off to the doomed men, boats also going from the shore. On reaching the Uno the yacht's boat took Pattison from his perilous position and with all haste got him ashore, where he was attended by Dr. Leitch, and was soon little the worse for his terrible experience.

For some time the other boats cruised about in the hope of picking up the other men, but the search was futile. The Petronella's boat then returned to mid-stream, where the mast of the ill-fated craft was still bobbing up and down.

THE VICTIMS.

Taking it in tow, the Uno was, with much difficulty, brought ashore at the Coastguard station at Gourock. Here, in the well of the boat, was found the dead body of Thomas Wood Morris, and it was removed to the police mortuary to await identification. It was also seen that the Uno's sheets were fast, showing that the squall had taken the party, all of whom were experts in handling a boat, by surprise. Later the boat was taken round to Cardwell Bay.

Mr. M'Leod, boat-hirer, and his two sons and others were among those who promptly went to the rescue immediately after the accident, and Mr. John Adams, boat-builder, of Cardwell Bay, went out in his motor launch and assisted in the trawling operations which were carried on throughout the afternoon and early evening. Neither of the two bodies, however, was recovered.

Needless to say the accident caused a painful sensation in the town, in which one, at all events, of the victims was well known. The men who lost their lives are:—

James M'MILLAN (56), Osborne House, Gourock. He was a foreman at the Gourock Laundry, and

SAILOR'S GRAPHIC STORY.

A graphic description of the disaster was given by one of the crew.

"I was on duty below at the time the Matina ran into us," he said. "The last vessel we had made was the Lusitania, which passed us about eleven o'clock on Saturday night. There was a thick fog all through the night, and it still enveloped us when we were nearing the Tuskar Light.

"Suddenly a large steamer loomed up through the mist, and, without the slightest warning, her bow crashed into us between No. 1 and No. 2 holds. The impact was such that two of the crew and one of the lady passengers were thrown into the water. Ropes were promptly thrown, and we managed to get them safely on board.

"The crew and the passengers had at the first concussion hurried on deck. The vessel which struck us, and which we afterwards found to be the Matina, inward bound, came alongside again, and the majority of us scrambled on board her.

"The officers of the City of Dundee at once took steps to ensure the safety of the passengers. By means of the Matina's lifeboat they were all transferred from the sinking ship.

"Just as the City of Dundee was sinking we saw the captain clinging to one of the ropes. Apparently through the swaying of the vessel as she went down he must have received a vital injury, for he threw up his arms, and, calling out "Good-bye," disappeared from view.

"How the second officer and the quartermaster lost their lives I cannot say, but evidently they must have been struck by some portion of the sinking ship."

Mr. Alexander Alderson, a director of Messrs. Allen, Alderson & Co., Alexandria, one of the passengers, said:—"I had with me my wife, her sister, my baby girl, aged two years and eleven months, and her nurse. At six o'clock on Sunday morning I heard the fogborn sounding vigorously. About seven o'clock I heard the toot of another horn close by us, and before I realised what it meant there was a fearful crash.

"I ran up on deck. The bow of the Matina seemed to have crunched right through us. The impact was so great that two portable engines weighing about six or seven tons snapped their chains and toppled into the hole made by the Matina.

"My first thought when I found that our vessel was on the point of sinking was for those under my charge. The ladies were safely transferred by the lifeboat to the Matina, but there was a difficulty about my little girl.

"I wrapped her in a blanket, and one of the sailors of the City of Dundee undertook to throw the precious human bundle on to the decks of the Matina. He measured the distance, and then was afraid to risk the throw.

"Captain Belton thereupon took the swathed child from his sailor's arms, and with a catch in his voice he remarked: 'I will try it.' A long swing backward, and the little one in its flannel casement went hurling through the air, to my intense relief landing safely in the arms of one of the crew of the Matina.

"I cannot testify too highly to the conduct of the officers and crew of the City of Dundee, and the act of the Captain in seeing everyone off his ship before abandoning the vessel to go to his own grave, as it proved, was one of noble self-sacrifice."

The City of Dundee was built by Workman, Clark & Co., of Belfast, and was sailing on charter from Messrs. Smith & Sons with the Ellerman-Papayanni Line. Her commander, Captain J. T. Belton, belonged to Hull, and was one of the founders of the Hull City Football Club, in which up to the time he sailed he was a prominent figure.

The name of the second officer was Lehan, of London, and of the quartermaster Burke, of Liverpool.

The Matina, which was laden with fruit from the West Indies, was damaged about the bows.

49 SAVED AFTER LINERS COLLIDE

THIRTY SIX of the crew of the Scots liner *City of Dundee* and 13 of her passengers were landed safely at Liverpool – by the ship that sank her in a collision in the fog.

Elders & Fyffes' 3838-ton steamer *Matina* arrived with the survivors of the sunken 3427-ton vessel that had been owned by G Smith & Sons, of Glasgow.

The *City of Dundee* left Liverpool on Saturday, October 3, and at 7.29am the next day, she was hit amidships by the *Matina* in fog near the Tuskar Rock, off the coast of Wexford in Ireland.

The Scottish liner sank in eight minutes and her captain, second officer and quartermaster were all drowned.

The rest of the crew and the passengers were taken aboard the *Matina* and brought to Liverpool.

During the collision, seeing the hopeless condition of the damaged liner, the *Matina* stood by and lowered two lifeboats.

Captain Belton, of the *City of Dundee*, gave the order that first priority must be given to the women aboard on board the stricken ship.

But on watching the lifeboats being lowered, several men pushed aside the female passengers and tried to make sure of their own safety. However, on the instructions of the captain, seamen forced them back.

As the *City of Dundee* began to list dangerously, passengers and crew clambered into the lifeboats hanging from the *Matina* and were then pulled to the deck.

Tragically, however, Captain Belton was hit by a floating boat and disappeared beneath the waves.

The people rescued from the *City of Dundee* had a narrow escape for only moments after the last of them were aboard the rescuing ship, the damaged liner's boilers exploded and she quickly sank.

CARNEGIE AWARDS FOR SCOTS UNIS

In April, the Carnegie Trust, set up to administer the vast sums bequeathed by the US steel magnate Andrew Carnegie for charitable purposes, awarded Scottish universities and colleges £194,000, to be distributed over 5 years. Edinburgh University topped the award league, receiving £52,500, followed by Glasgow University with £50,000, St Andrews £47,500 and Aberdeen University £40,400. The remainder of the award was distributed amongst technical, agricultural and medical colleges across the country. Later in the year, it was revealed that Lord Kelvin had left £5000 to Glasgow University in his will. The pioneering physicist had taught at the university for much of his career.

COMINGS...
John Wheatley
Judge

EDINBURGH LICENCES

Licensing courts met all over Scotland in April and the results of their deliberations were two-fold, namely the reduction in the total number of licences and the strict adherence to the 10 o'clock closing time. They even resisted attempts to extend the licensing hours to allow later opening in Edinburgh during the International Exhibition to be held in the capital over the summer. In terms of the number of licensed premises in Edinburgh, applications before the Court showed that there were 307 public houses, 394 licensed grocers and 23 hotels selling alcohol.

GOINGS...
Henry Campbell-Bannerman
Liberal Prime Minister

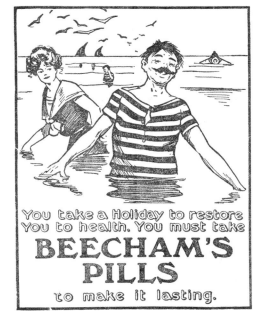

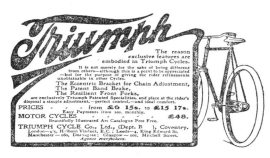

THIS SPORTING LIFE

FOOTBALL	RUGBY UNION	GOLF	HORSE RACING	SHINTY
Scottish Champions Celtic	*Scotland vs England* Scotland 16–10 England at Inverleith	*British Open Winner* James Braid at Prestwick (291)	*Scottish Grand National Winner* Atrato at Bogside	*Camanachd Cup Winners* Newtonmore at Inverness
Scottish Cup Winners Celtic				

CITY EDITION

Daily Record & Mail.

LARGER SALE THAN ANY OTHER MORNING OR EVENING NEWSPAPER IN SCOTLAND.

ESTAB. 1847—No. 19,448 GLASGOW, WEDNESDAY, MAY 26, 1909 ONE HALFPENNY.

DAILY RECORD & MAIL IS THE BEST AND CHEAPEST MEDIUM FOR LETTING COAST-COUNTRY HOUSES

HOME AND CONTINENTAL REMOVALS.
Our Complete Arrangements, coupled with Wide Experience, enable us to Conduct Removals in First-Class Style on Best Terms.
Give Us an Opportunity of Quoting.
UNION TRANSIT CO.
381 ARGYLE ST., GLASGOW.

OSCAR SLATER.

THE DEATH SENTENCE COMMUTED.

HOW HE RECEIVED THE NEWS.

ERRONEOUS RUMOUR EXPLAINED.

Yesterday we published a report that information had been received by us to the effect that the Secretary for Scotland had written to the authorities in Glasgow intimating that his Majesty saw no reason for interfering with the decision in the case of Oscar Slater, lying under sentence of death for the murder of Miss Marion Gilchrist in her house in West Princes Street, Glasgow, in December last.

The report proves to have been erroneous. In giving it we pointed out that we had been unable to obtain either confirmation or denial of the report, which we accordingly published for what it was worth, though in absolutely good faith.

The story we received was supported by every probability. Lord Guthrie, it may be recalled, in his summing up spoke in no qualified terms, and as his Lordship would be consulted upon any question of a reprieve, it seemed unlikely that the death sentence would be commuted. This, indeed, was the general opinion in official circles, and the decision of Lord Pentland has come as a complete surprise.

Yesterday afternoon, indeed, the City Magistrates met to complete the arrangements for the execution which it was fully believed would duly be carried out tomorrow morning.

Even the man appointed to carry out the execution had been ordered to Glasgow, and preparations were being completed at Duke Street Prison for the last dread act in the terrible drama.

At a late hour on Monday night we informed the Lord Provost of the information which had come into our possession. His Lordship informed us that he had not at that time received any intimation of the kind from the Scottish Office, but he added that the letter would probably be at the City Chambers the following morning.

At Duke Street Prison, also, nothing had been received at the time of our inquiry.

The fact that an official document had been received at the office of the Town Clerk, bearing on the envelope the words "On His Majesty's Service" and "Justiciary, Scotland," gave to our information a further balance of probability. This letter, as a matter of fact, was a reply from the Under-Secretary for Scotland to a letter from the Town Clerk's Department asking that, if possible, the reply of the Secretary for Scotland to the petition might be received by Monday. It was this, apparently, to which our informant alluded in saying that a letter had been sent to Glasgow, and, knowing the feeling in official quarters, he took it for granted that the letter was an expression of that feeling—and that a reprieve had been refused.

To say that the decision of Lord Pentland has occasioned surprise is but to very inadequately express the public view.

Until the definite reasons which have induced Lord Pentland to revoke the finding of the Court are known—if ever they are revealed—it is difficult to realise why Slater has been reprieved. Possibly the fact that the verdict of guilty was returned by only a majority of the jury may have weighed with him, but it is, after all, the law in Scotland in this connection that the majority rule. In England it is different, for there a man charged with murder must be unanimously condemned by the jury ere the death sentence is pronounced.

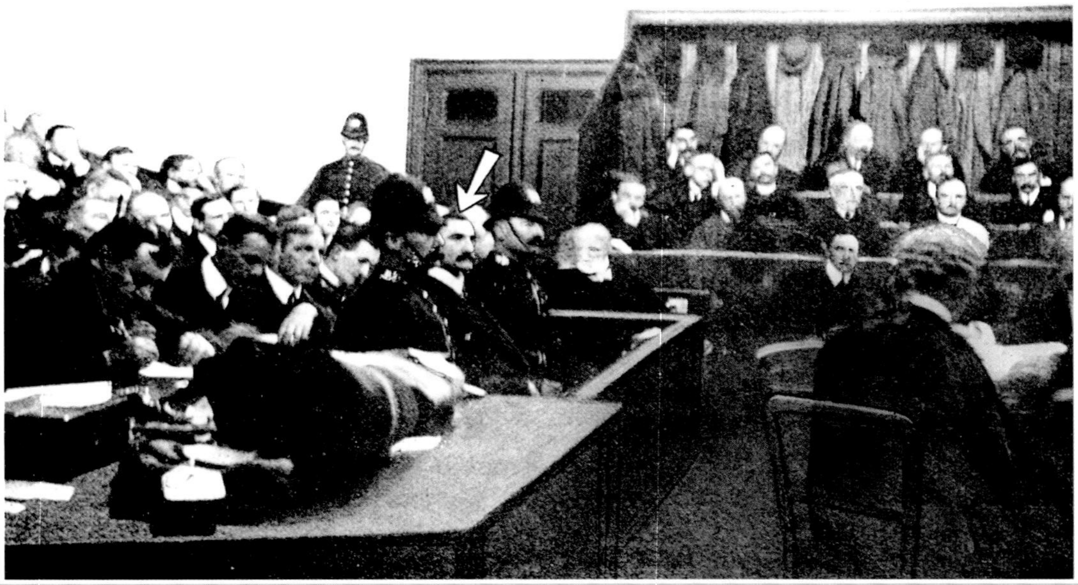

PENSION DAY.

NEW EPOCH IN BRITAIN'S SOCIAL PROGRESS.

HONOURING THE POOR FOLK'S CHEQUES.

TRAGEDY AND COMEDY OVER THE BORDER.

In after years January 1, 1909, will be one of the landmarks in the history of Britain's social progress, the day being set aside for distinction as the one on which the Old Age Pensions Act came into operation.

In England, Wales, and Ireland some 500,000 aged people had looked forward to yesterday as the day on which their coloured checks, ranging from 1s to 5s, would be honoured at the various Post Offices, while to-day has been as eagerly anticipated in Scotland, the public holiday preventing payment yesterday north of the Tweed.

The distribution was not without its humorous and pathetic aspects. In the former category comes a story from Braintree, where the town band paraded the town playing, "Hail, smiling Morn," and other jubilant tunes; while in the latter category must be placed an incident at Bishops Stortford, where an ex-Royal Artillery gunner, Ephraim Clary, who had been accepted for a 5s pension, died after he had signed his paper with a cross, and his widow was refused payment.

Two hundred pensioners, entertai[illegible] Newport, Mon., utilised the occasi[illegible] to send a message to the Prime Minister wishing him a happy New Year, and adding that it had begun well for them.

At Burton Latimer pensions were paid in crowns, which some of the recipients sold at enhanced values to souvenir hunters.

LIVELY CENTENARIAN.

An old lady at Oundle had to walk four miles, but exclaimed, "I don't mind; it's worth it." At Wood Green, London, the most venerable applicant was Mrs. Rebecca Clark, who is bordering on her 104th birthday. She disregarded the bad weather and, walking briskly to the nearest Post Office, smilingly cashed her cheque.

Generally speaking, so far as the Metropolis was concerned, there was not the early rush that had been anticipated. Some 41,000 claims had been made, of which number 32,488 had been duly investigated and recommended for pensions.

There was a steady stream of applicants at Bethnal Green, all bearing the marks of poverty and some of unmistakable destitution. All over, women greatly preponderated, seemingly outnumbering the male sex by ten to one.

The first recipients to put in an appearance at the Ludgate Circus Post Office were a venerable old couple, both of whom were nearly 80 years of age. Neatly dressed, the old people walked into the office arm-in-arm, and were courteously received by the clerks. "Here lass," said the old man as he handed over his two halfcrowns, "you be cashier. Put it in your purse."

One of the earliest claimants at Victoria Street was an old man of 75, who paced shiveringly outside the office at 7.30. The officials were considerably surprised at so early a visitor, but his book was quickly examined, the first cheque torn out, and the money handed over. He was only entitled to 2s, but all the seams and wrinkles in his worn face were brought prominently out by the beam of satisfaction which appeared when the florin was placed in his hand.

A Crimean veteran in his 77th year—George Hibbard—was the first applicant at High Road, Kilburn. He walked in on the stroke of ten wearing two Crimean medals, British and Turkish, and appeared to be pleased to know he was the first to put in an appearance. He received the two half-crowns smilingly from the young lady behind the counter.

One of the earliest of the Lewisham claimants was Wm. Constable, aged 79, who celebrated his golden wedding two years ago. The father of 24 children, he has lived in the locality all his life.

After 61 years at sea, and having been a captain in the merchant service, an old gentleman at a Catford office regretted that, at the age of 75, he should be compelled to avail himself of the kindness of the Government.

A pathetic incident at the Bethnal Green Office was the arrival of a tottering old couple, the man 85 and so infirm that he had to be assisted by his wife, a woman of 74. "This will be a great help to us. Bless the Lord for it," said the woman.

STATELY RECIPIENTS.

The few pensioners in the West End, chiefly old domestic servants and stablemen, drew their State New Year's gifts with true aristocratic disdain for haste in financial matters. No one so far forgot the stately tradition of the West End as to stand on the doorsteps of Post Offices in the fog. There was no democratic scramble at the counter of South Audley Street Post Office, and it was evident that the people living in the "gilded mansions" had thoughtlessly disqualified themselves for pensions by allowing their incomes to grow well over £30 per annum.

An octogenarian at Brentford after receiving his 5s wished the staff a happy New Year and invited the payer out to toast the occasion "round the corner." One pensioner in the Barnet district drove up in a cab. He lost a huge fortune in a forest fire. The most characteristic pensioner here was Captain Austin, an old Navy man who was present at the bombardment of Sebastopol.

Nearly 80 years of age, an old lady was waiting for the opening of the Sidcup Post Office. When she received the money tears ran down her cheeks as she thanked the clerk as though he were the donor of the pension.

The Mayor of Richmond treated all the old people in the borough who drew their pensions to a tea and entertainment. Carriages were sent for the infirm, and the proceedings ended with a cinematograph show.

In populous Irish centres such as Dubli[illegible] Belfast, and Limerick, the Post Offi[illegible] Officials were kept steadily busy

CAMP COFFEE
READY! AYE READY!
FISHING RODS AND TACKLE

IDEAL HOMES.

GREAT EXHIBITION OPENED.

BIG CROWD.

LORD INVERCLYDE AND HOUSING.

BRILLIANT SCENE.

Yesterday was indeed an epoch-making day in the history of Glasgow. The man in the street could not fail to realise that events unusual were happening. As the hands of city clocks turned towards "the wee short hour" a long procession of business men in morning coats bent their steps eastward to the City Hall in anticipation of the Roseberian oration on the Budget.

A little later there was a larger and more conspicuous stream of beautifully dressed ladies, accompanied in many instances by male escorts, flowing westwards for the opening of the great and unique Scottish Ideal Home Exhibition, promoted by the "Daily Record and Mail."

Within St. Andrew's Halls the finishing touches had been put upon the most magnificent home pageant ever presented to the Scottish public, and on every hand there was unstinted admiration for the wealth, artistic arrangement, and extent of the collection of all the harmonious units, which combine to realise an ideal home.

Viewed from the platform the scene in the Grand Hall is a happy blend of colour, beauty, and utility, the picturesque dresses of some of the lady attendants enhancing the picture. The platform itself is tastefully decorated with palms and plants with splendid specimens of photographic art, and the raised bandstand in the background.

But no one must run away with the false idea that when he has seen the exhibits in the Grand Hall, he has seen the Ideal Home Exhibition. There are no fewer than eight other large halls in addition to annexes, and these too are filled with strikingly suggestive stalls of fascinating features.

AEROPLANES AND TROPHIES.

For example, the unbounded popular enthusiasm created by the £1000 offer of a prize by the proprietor of the "Daily Record and Mail" for a non-stop flight in a heavier-than-air aeroplane between Glasgow and Edinburgh on a Scotch built machine has aroused the greatest interest in the clever invention and construction of the Mollinsburn blacksmith which was one of the first Scotch-built flying machines to accomplish actual flight.

It was found impossible to have this aeroplane placed in its original quarters at the Granville Street door, and it faces the visitor in the vestibule of the Berkeley Street entrance.

OPENING CEREMONY.

The opening ceremony took place in the Grand Hall at three o'clock. Sir Samuel Chisholm, Bart., LL.D., presided, and among those on the platform, besides Lord Inverclyde and the Hon. J. A. Burns, his son, were Treasurer Graham, Bailies Russell and Campbell; ex-Bailies W. F. Anderson, Burt, Martin, Willock, John Macfarlane, Nicol, and Morrin; Councillors Forsyth, Bostock, and M'Neil; Drs. Devon, Scott, and M'Lean; Messrs. Robert Blyth, Arthur Hart, W. F. Salmon, Daly, Ninian B. Stewart, David Fortune, Browning, Montgomerie, Dreghorn, Hewat, Stephen Henry, James Cunningham, C. H. Bowser, John Ingram, and others.

Telegraphic apologies were received from Mr. T. M'Kinnon Wood, M.P., Under-Secretary for Foreign Affairs; Mr. Alex. Findlay, M.P.; and Mr. A. Cameron Corbett, M.P., all of whom were detained in London on Parliamentary business.

The Chairman, in his introductory sentences, said he could not look around on the crowded benches and on the crowded area in front of him without making his first words those of congratulation to the promoters of that exhibition on the success which had attended their opening ceremony, nor could he look on those exhibits which were within reach of his eyes at the moment without congratulating those who had come on the fact that they had something worth coming to see.

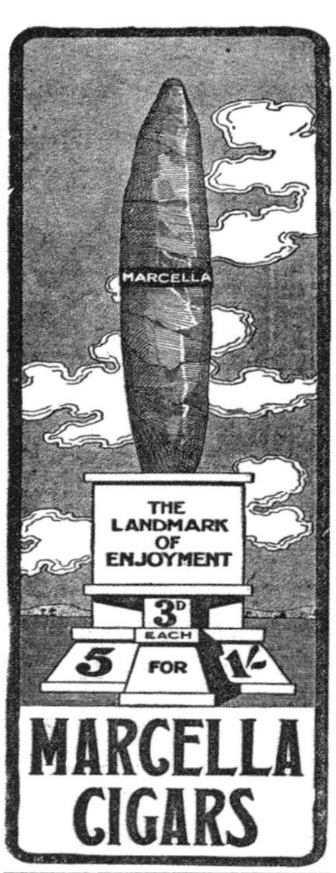
MARCELLA
THE LANDMARK OF ENJOYMENT
3D EACH
5 FOR 1/-
MARCELLA CIGARS

SLATER ESCAPES THE GALLOWS

OSCAR SLATER was sentenced to death by the High Court in Edinburgh on May 7 after a trial that had lasted four days.He had been accused of the murder, on December 21, the previous year, of Miss Marion Gilchrist, an old well-to-do lady who lived in a flat in West Princes Street, Glasgow.

When the judge, Lord Portland, asked for the verdict, the foreman of the jury replied: "Guilty, My Lord, by a majority."

The majority was nine to six and those six had found the murder charge not proven.

After the verdict, Glasgow city magistrates met on May 25 to complete the arrangements for the execution that was expected to be carried out two days later.

The man appointed to carry out the hanging had been summoned to Glasgow, and preparations were being completed at Duke Street Prison for the execution.

However, Slater received notice of a reprieve on the evening of May 25.

The *Daily Record* reported:

"Until the definite reasons which have induced Lord Portland to revoke the finding of the court are known, if ever they are revealed, it is difficult to realise why Slater has been reprieved.

Possibly the fact that the verdict of guilty was returned by only a small majority of the jury may have weighed with him, but it is. after all, the law in Scotland in this connection that the majority rule."

There was also the question of identification, which was considered the weakest part of the case for the prosecution.

And this was thought to have been the most likely point on which Lord Portland's decision rested.

Scots law at that time did not have any procedure for someone found guilty by the High Court to appeal against the verdict or sentence.

But after much public pressure over many years, the law was changed to allow such appeals.

And in 1928, Scotland was once more to hear of the case of Oscar Slater.

IDEAL HOMES EXHIBITION OPENS

The first Scottish Ideal Homes Exhibition was opened in September. Staged in the St Andrew's Halls, the Exhibition was a spectacular and colourful blend of the decorative, artistic, utilitarian and unusual. As well as everything to make the Edwardian home ideal, there were also less likely items, such as the first Scottish-built aircraft, designed by a Mollinsburn blacksmith to win the £1,000 prize for the first non-stop flight between Glasgow and Edinburgh.

On a crowded platform packed with civic dignitaries, the chairman of the Exhibition committee, Sir Samuel Chisholm, observed during his introductory speech that "there were few things more important than the making of a home attractive, bright and sweet, and if [people] could get their homes in that character universally, they would have gone a great way in the direction of solving many of the most important social problems."

AMERICAN ROLLER RINK WILL **OPEN TO-DAY.**

VICTORIA ROAD. S.S. GLASGOW.
CRAWFORD & WILKINS. - Managing Directors.
Under Same Management as London Olympia Skating Rink.

This Luxurious Roller Rendezvous for Society Skaters, where the Famous Winslow Skates, so essential for graceful gliding, are used exclusively, opens

TO-DAY
(SATURDAY), AT 10-30 A.M.

MILITARY BAND. PRIVATE GARAGE. AFTERNOON TEAS.
THREE SESSIONS DAILY. Books of Tickets at Reduced Rates.
MORNING—10.30–12.30. Admission Free. Skates, 1s.
AFTERNOON—2-5. Admission, Gentlemen, 6d. Ladies Free.
EVENING—7-10. Admission, 1s. Skates, 1s.
"If You would be Graceful, Learn to Skate."

COMINGS...

Nigel Tranter
Writer

Matt Busby
Football Manager

SCOTLAND'S FIRST OAPS

It was a particularly happy New Year for thousands of Scots who queued patiently outside post offices to receive their first old age pensions. The Invalid and Old Age Pensions Act came into force on January 1st but Scotland's first OAPs had to wait until the following day to collect their money because of the New Year public holiday. Single men and women over the age of 70 would receive a weekly pension of between 1 and 5 shillings, depending on their circumstances, while married couples received 7/6. Those eligible for a pension had had to register the previous September although the workshy, prisoners, paupers and the insane were all excluded.

THIS SPORTING LIFE

FOOTBALL	RUGBY UNION	GOLF	HORSE RACING	SHINTY
Scottish Champions Celtic	*Scotland vs England* England 8–18 Scotland at Richmond	*British Open Winner* J. H. Taylor at Deal, England (295)	*Scottish Grand National Winner* *Mount Prospect's Fortune* at Bogside	*Camanachd Cup Winners* Newtonmore at Glasgow
Scottish Cup Winners up withheld because of rioting fter two Celtic–Rangers draws				

PICTURES :: ARE :: A FEATURE :: OF :: TO-DAY'S ISSUE.

Daily Record & Mail.

THE ALL-SCOTLAND NEWSPAPER.

LARGER SALE THAN ANY OTHER MORNING OR EVENING JOURNAL IN THE COUNTRY.

ESTAB. 1847—No. 19,642 GLASGOW, FRIDAY, JANUARY 7, 1910 TEN PAGES; ONE HALFPENNY.

NO TIME TO LOSE - - - IF YOU WANT TO WIN THE SCOTTISH WEEKLY RECORD'S £100 PRIZE FOR BEST ELECTION FORECAST. SEND IN YOUR COUPON TO-DAY.

LAND REFORM IN HIGHLANDS.

MR. BALFOUR'S PROBLEMS.

SOLUTION WITH A "SAFEGUARD."

Mr. Balfour has addressed to Cameron of Lochiel, the Unionist candidate in Sutherland, a letter on land reform in the Highlands. The communication, which is dated from Prestonkirk, to "My Dear Lochiel," is in the following terms:

On the broad principles which should underlie land reform in the various parts of the United Kingdom I have already expressed myself on more than one occasion, and at a recent meeting in Edinburgh, which illness unfortunately prevented me attending, Sir Robert Finlay gave an admirable exposition of my general views. It may, however, be necessary, and it certainly is desirable, that I should add some thing with respect to the special problems which have to be faced in the Highlands and Islands.

I need not speak of amendments to the existing Crofter Acts, with regard to which I believe there is general agreement—such, for example, as the legalisation of sub-letting to tourists—but amendments of this character, though far from unimportant, do not touch the main difficulties by which we are confronted.

What are these difficulties? They arise in the main from three causes—

Overcrowding or congestion;
Want of employment; and
Excessive rates.

Congestion in the Highlands, as in Ireland, is, of course, a relative term. It does not mean that the proportion of population to acreage is large compared with what it is, or may be, in other districts, but that it is large compared with what an acre can produce in a region where neither soil nor climate are favourable to agriculture.

In places where congestion of this kind exists, and where there is land available for the extension of holdings, it is manifestly desirable that such extension should take place, provided that adequate steps are taken to prevent the enlarged crofts being again sub-divided, and thus, in the end, aggravating the very evils which we desire to remedy. I believe that in most cases there would be no difficulty in carrying out this reform by voluntary arrangement under the guidance of the Crofters Commission; but if such a difficulty unexpectedly arose there would be no objection to the compulsory acquisition of land, under proper safeguard, for the purpose of meeting what all must recognise as a great public need.

Employment, like agriculture, is in these regions necessarily limited by local conditions, and, so far as I am aware, there are, apart from farming, sport, and tourists, only two sources from which employment can be provided—fishing and afforestation. On fishing I needn't dwell. Much has been done in the past by Unionist Governments to improve the communication with the southern markets, and to provide local facilities for those engaged in the industry. If, as I suppose, more could be done in this direction it would be very desirable.

Afforestation stands in a somewhat different position. Public attention has only recently been directed to it, and, unfortunately, an excellent cause has been discredited by the wild advocacy of certain enthusiasts, and the extravagant hopes which that advocacy has occasionally raised. This is much to be regretted, since there seems great probability that in districts where soil, shelter, and means of transport are suitable planting might be made an economic success. Where this is the case afforestation would provide a demand for crofters' labour at the very time of year when there is little to be done upon their own holdings.

BURDEN OF RATES.

Of all the difficulties, however, which beset the land question in the Highlands one of the most pressing, and one of the most difficult, is that connected with rates. It is the burden of rates which, in addition to all its other evils, makes land purchase on the Irish system so hard of accomplishment, and compels us to supplement it by other and, in some respects, less satisfactory modes of tenure. Here again the Crofters Commission, or the Congested Districts Board, or perhaps a new body combining the functions of both, might, if possessed of increased resources, render invaluable aid. They could, by purchase or hiring, obtain control of land suitable for new holdings. These they might sell or, where sale was impracticable, lease in the manner which they thought most suitable to the conditions of the district. Congestion might thus be relieved without any extension of dual ownership.

THE CHARING CROSS BANK.

DEPOSITORS DISMAY.

SCOTTISH CLIENTS BADLY HIT.

"The affairs of the Charing Cross Bank are in the hands of the Official Receiver, Bankruptcy Court, London, to whom all applications must be made."

This brief, but pregnant, announcement was posted at the branches o the Charing Cross Bank in Scotland yesterday morning. It had already become known through the medium of the morning papers that the affairs of the bank had reached a crisis, and there was keen anxiety on the part of the depositors to know the worst. But there was nothing in the nature of a rush, for in no case were the premises of the bank opened.

There are sixteen branches in Scotland, these being situated in Glasgow, Govan, Partick, Edinburgh, Leith, Paisley, Greenock, Hamilton, Kilmarnock, Kirkcaldy, Perth, Dundee, Arbroath, Stirling, Inverness, and Aberdeen; and, though no definite information can be obtained, it is understood that the amount of deposits reaches a very large sum.

With its principal offices in London, and branches in the leading towns of England and Ireland, as well as those in Scotland, the bank, in its announcements, has claimed to have assets amounting to £1,607,949, against liabilities of £1,236,871 a surplus of £371,078. It claimed to be prepared to make loans of from £30 to £2000 on personal security, jewellery, stocks and shares, furniture, and the like, and it also conducted a brokerage business, buying and selling stocks and shares.

On deposits of £10 and upwards it allowed interest at the rate of 5 per cent. per annum, subject to three months' notice of withdrawal; 6 per cent. on deposits subject to six months' notice; and 7 per cent. on 12 months, with special terms for longer periods.

IN LONDON.

A notice, "The Bank has suspended payment. The affairs are in the hands of the Official Receiver, Carey Street," scribbled upon a sheet of typewritten paper met the many anxious depositors from all quarters, who, having read of the troubles of the Bank, hurried early yesterday morning to the head offices in Bedford Street, London, to make personal inquiry. Just before ten o'clock the first callers came, and gradually the gathering of waiting people grew bigger. At intervals the crowd outside numbered well over a hundred. Most the people were small tradesmen, business women, and mechanics. They came, read the notice, dashed behind the glass door, glanced at the front windows with blinds drawn, and then, after a short wait, moved away, usually bound for the Official Receiver's office.

Three policemen on duty by the bank were questioned by most of the arrivals." "Is there anyone inside now?" "Where is Carey Street?" "How much shall we get?" were the usual questions put, but the constables could only answer the second.

At the Official Receiver's office in Carey Street depositors in the bank were asked to give their names and addresses and the amounts of their deposits. One depositor, who made urgent inquiries, was told by an official in the office, "We are informed by the bank that there will be 20s in the pound."

Our London City Editor deals with the situation in his "Chat on 'Change" on page 2, and makes certain suggestions for the benefit of the depositors.

THE GLASGOW BRANCHES.

By ten o'clock yesterday morning, the hour at which the branch at 100 Sauchiehall Street, Glasgow, generally opens for business, a small knot of people was attracted by the typewritten announcement which was posted on one of the windows of the building. Similar notices were exhibited at the Govan and Partick branches; and here, also, numbers of people stopped to read the intimation, some lingering evidently in the hope of hearing the tale of some depositor, but the majority after satisfying their curiosity, passed on.

Practically the same thing repeated itself all day, and at no time was there any demonstration of public feeling in front of the branches. It was, of course, quite apparent that many depositors called to assure themselves that the business had actually suspended operations, and talking to one of them a "Daily Record and Mail" representative learned that he had deposited £15 some little time ago. "I thought it was safe," he added, "but I don't suppose I'll see a penny of it again."

Another depositor had what might be termed a mixed form of luck. There was already something to his account at the bank, and he arrived in Glasgow yesterday with a further deposit of £100, to find that, fortunately, he was too late. There was also the case of a Glasgow landlady, possibly not an individual case, whose savings (£100) were all invested in the bank. Her first intimation of the stoppage of payment was a copy of the "Daily Record and Mail" taken into the house by one of her lodgers, during the course of the forenoon.

A MANAGER'S STATEMENT.

Mr. J. B. [illegible], the manager of the Sauchiehall Street branch, was interviewed by the "Daily Record and Mail" yesterday afternoon. He was sorry that he could not supply even an approximate figure of the Glasgow deposits involved. "You can see my difficulty," he explained. "My connection with the Charing Cross Bank ceased last night, and I am now working on behalf of the official liquidator, so I cannot possibly give any information of that nature."

Another question brought out the statement that it was entirely a mistake to think that the bank's business in Glasgow was mainly connected with the industrial classes. "Of course," he said, "there are many cases in which the class you refer to will be involved, but we have done business with all classes of the community."

"Is the stoppage due to any lack of business at the Glasgow branches?"

DEATH OF THE KING.

PEACEFUL LAST MOMENTS.

PRINCE OF WALES' MESSAGE.

I AM DEEPLY GRIEVED TO INFORM YOU THAT MY BELOVED FATHER 'THE KING' PASSED AWAY PEACEFULLY AT A QUARTER TO TWELVE TONIGHT.—GEORGE.

This official announcement of King Edward's death was conveyed to the Lord Mayor of London in a telegram from the Prince of Wales.

The following was the official notification to the Home Secretary:—

6th May, 1910, 11.50 p.m.

His Majesty the King breathed his last at 11.45 p.m. in the presence of Her Majesty Queen Alexandra, the Prince and Princess of Wales, the Princess Royal and the Duke of Fife, Princess Victoria, and Princess Louise, Duchess of Argyll.

FRANCIS LAKING, M.D.
JAMES REID, M.D.
R. DOUGLAS POWELL, M.D.
J. BERTRAND DAWSON, M.D.

All the King's own children, it will be seen, were present at the bedside with the exception of the Queen of Norway. Queen Maud, on receiving a cablegram announcing the critical condition of her father, replied at once that she had left for London and would probably arrive on Sunday.

The physicians signing the bulletin were also in the death chamber.

The Queen an dthe other members of the family had been constantly going to and from the sick room, but for some considerable time before his death the King was not conscious of their presence. He was lying in a comotose state, from which he had a slight rally between nine and ten o'clock, after which, it is stated, though no official information on the point is available, that there was no return to consciousness.

The Archbishop of Canterbury also was present during his Majesty's last moments. The news of the death was promptly telegraphed to all members of the Royal Family not in attendance, Foreign Courts, and to the various Ministers of the Crown entitled to receive communications.

Shortly after midnight the various members of the Royal Family not resident in the Palace took their departure, and up to that time the public outside had no indication that the end hadcome.

It is expected that the news will be officially promulgated at St. Paul's Cathedral this morning.

THE END.

The Nation and the Empire, and indeed the whole English-speaking world, will learn with heartfelt sorrow of the death of the King in his 69th year.

His Majesty's end come with extreme suddenness, as it was only on Thursday that it was announced that the King was indisposed from a severe bronchial attack. Hopes entertained that his Majesty would recover were engendered by the bulletins issued during that evening, but when yesterday morning it was announced that the King's condition was critical the worst was anticipated.

During yesterday there was a continuous stream of callers at Buckingham Palace, servant that Lord Knollys had announced that no further bulletin would be issued until eleven o'clock this morning. The agitated servant, however, stated—"The King is dead."

"What time did it occur?" asked the Press representative.

"About 12.0," was the reply.

The crowd by this time were beginning to suspect something was the matter, and eager inquiries were made of various people who left the Palace.

At 12.42 an official notice was posted outside the Mansion House. It was very brief, as follows:—

11.45 p.m.

The King has just passed away.

This information had evidently come direct from the Palace.

It was received with due reverence. The company uncovered, and one of them remarking "God bless him," another adding: "His Majesty now knows the great secret."

OUTSIDE THE PALACE.

The news spread rapidly all over the West End of London, and, curiously enough, the large crowd which had gathered outside Buckingham Palace were unaware until nearly three-quarters of an hour later that King Edward was dead, no notice having been posted up outside. They waited in suspense, and no one suspected that his Majesty had passed away.

When the Prince and Princess of Wales left it was even thought that King Edward's condition had taken a turn for the better. The first intimation the crowd received was about twenty minutes to one, when a clergyman was seen approaching from one of the entrances to the Palace. The crowd immediately flocked around the gate. In a low voice, so low as to be only heard by those immediately near him, the clergyman announced that King Edward was dead. Hats were at once removed, and the crowd stood in reverend silence.

All the members of the Royal Family who were within reach were present at the King's bedside, and remained until the end. The news was at once conveyed to the Church of St. Mary Abbots in the Royal Borough of Kensington, where, by the special request of the Princess Mary of Battenberg, an intercessional service was being held. The service was closed with prayer.

For some time a crowd remained outside Buckingham Palace, but as the morning advanced it gradually melted away.

CONDOLENCES.

The Lord Mayor sent the following acknowledgment to the Prince of Wales:—

I tender to your Royal Highness an expression of most true sympathy and condolence from the citizens of London. May God in His loving mercy comfort you and the Princess. The prayers of the nation are with you, and they keenly share your sorrow.

The Lord Mayor also despatched the following message to Queen Alexandra:—

The City of London hears with profound emotion that God has called to Himself your august husband and our most gracious and beloved King, and desires to lay at your feet its loyal devotion and deep sympathy, praying that His loving hand may bless and comfort you and those that are so dear to you in this your hour of need and sorrow.

THE BULLETINS.

Two bulletins were issued yesterday, the first at eleven o'clock and the second at 6.30. The forenoon announcement was:—

11 a.m.

The King has passed a comparatively quiet night, but the symptoms have not improved and his Majesty's condition gives rise to grave anxiety.

6.30 p.m.

The King's symptoms have become worse during the day, and his Majesty's condition is now critical.

In each case the bulletin was signed by the five physicians in attendance on his Majesty:—

F. Laking, M.D., J. Reid, M.D., Douglas Powell, M.D., Bertrand Dawson, M.D., and St. Clair Thomson, M.D.

We were authoritatively informed at 10.30 that:—

There is no further change to record in his Majesty's condition, and no further bulletin or statement of any kind will be issued to-night for publication.

In response to his telegram of inquiry and sympathy, the Mayor of Windsor last night received the following significant message from Lord Knollys, the King's Private Secretary:—

Sincere thanks for telegram; deeply regret his Majesty's condition is most critical.

ANXIOUS PUBLIC.

SCENES AT THE ROYAL PALACE.

DAY OF WATCHING.

To the millions of the King's subjects the news of his Majesty's grave illness came as a great shock yesterday morning, and to-day the Empire will mourn his death. The following narrative of the progress of the monarch's illness, and the scenes outside Buckingham Palace and throughout the country were, of course, received before the notification of a fatal termination.

Two of his Majesty's physicians, Sir James Reid and Sir Francis Laking, as stated in yesterday's "Daily Record and Mail," remained all through the night within easy call of the King's apartment. A quiet night passing by the Royal patient had given the impression that he was making good progress, and to some early inquirers, notably Mrs. Asquith and Lord Rothschild, this news was given.

It is understood that the Queen and the members of the Royal Family generally all looked for a more favourable bulletin, and great therefore was the consternation caused when it was found that the first official report was distinctly unfavourable. Dr. Bertrand Dawson and Dr. St. Clair Thomson joined Sir F. Laking and Sir J. Reid at the Palace at about ten o'clock, and the fact that one of them is a well-known throat specialist did not tend to reassure the public as to the nature of the malady. At 10.10 Sir Douglas Powell joined the other four doctors. At 10.30 they had concluded their examination, consulted together, and issued the bulletin which said that his Majesty's condition gave rise to grave anxiety.

ANXIOUS WAIT.

The Prince of Wales was early at the Palace, and had anxiously awaited the professional pronouncement. The bulletin was shown to him immediately after it was drawn up, and greatly disappointed his hopes. It was not until very long after that copies of the notice were publicly displayed on the Palace railings, and the crowd which had assembled there were drawing the happiest conclusions from the circumstances that the guard-changing ceremony was going forward in the Fore Court as usual, and that the full band of the Irish Guards, posted quite close to the Royal residence, was playing a selection of lively airs. It was thought that the King was a great deal better, or this would not have been allowed.

When the notices were at length posted the people read the copies with the utmost gravity and concern.

Never since the King's memorable illness in the initial year of his reign had such a scene been witnessed at Buckingham Palace as was presented yesterday. From ten o'clock in the morning and throughout the day there was an almost constant stream of motor-cars and carriages bearing to the Royal residence people of note anxious to testify their sympathy and concern in the only practicable way by signing the Visitors' Book. For the first few hours the Royal servants and the police sought in vain to cope with the ever-increasing stream, and at length it was found absolutely necessary to open the Ambassadors' entrance in Buckingham Palace Road, and to provide additional visitors' books.

MANY CALLERS.

To give a list of the callers would be largely to reproduce the Court Guide, the Church, the Army, the Navy, and all classes of society being represented.

The Prince of Wales was for the whole morning at the Palace and, like the Queen and other members of the Royal family, saw his Majesty for a short time. On the occasion of the present illness, however, it was fully recognised by all concerned that it was desirable to give all possible quiet and repose, and his Majesty's Royal relatives did not attempt any prolonged stay in his room. Prince Christian walked to the Palace in the morning to make personal inquiries, and repeated the visit later in the day. Princess Christian called, and at luncheon time the Princess of Wales, the Princess Royal, and the Duke of Fife called, and remained. The fact that they and the Prince of Wales all joined the Queen and Princess Victoria at luncheon seemel to indicate some relaxation of the tension caused by the King's grave illness.

Shortly before 6.30 in the evening the bulletin stating that his Majesty's symptoms had become worse, and that his condition was critical, was issued at Buckingham Palace, and this caused general consternation. For some time previously the crowds in front of the Palace had been steadily increasing in the expectation of its issue. The Prince of Wales remained at the Palace, but the Princess had left some time before the bulletin was issued. The Princess was then seen to be weeping, having a handkerchief to her eyes. Prince Francis of Teck, Prince and Princess Christian, and the Princess Louise (Duchess of Argyll), also had taken their departure. Presumably these members of the Royal Family had been made acquainted with the unfavourable turn which his Majesty's illness had taken.

TOUGH TALKING ON HIGHLANDS

FORMER Conservative Prime Minister Mr Arthur Balfour spoke out in January on land reforms in the Highlands.

In a letter to the clan chief, Cameron of Lochiel, Mr Balfour said:

"I need not speak of amendments to the existing Crofter Acts, with regard to which I believe there is general agreement, such for example, as the legislation of sub-letting to tourists.

But amendments of this character, though far from unimportant, do not touch the main difficulties by which we are confronted.

These difficulties arise from the following causes:

Overcrowding or congestion; want of employment; excessive rates."

Congestion in the Highlands was worked out in terms of what an acre could produce in those areas where neither the soil nor the climate were favourable to agriculture.

In places where congestion existed, Mr Balfour recommended that where there is land available for the extension of holdings, this should take place, provided that adequate steps are taken to prevent the enlarged crofts being sub-divided again.

Also, in those districts where soil, shelter, and means of transport were suitable, tree planting might be made an economic success and unemployment reduced, he said. Afforestation would provide work for crofters' at a time of the agricultural year when there is little else to be done upon the holdings.

Of all the difficulties, however, which beset the land question of the Highlands, said Mr Balfour, one of the most pressing and difficult was that connected with rates.

He suggested that the Crofts Commission or the Congested Districts Board, or perhaps a new body combining the functions of both, could if they possessed an increase in resources render invaluable aid.

They could, by purchasing or hiring, obtain control of land suitable for new holdings. These they might sell or lease in the manner best suited to the district. Congestion might thus be relieved without any extension of dual ownership.

Reading the suspension notice at the Charing Cross Bank, Sauchiehall Street, Glasgow.

HARDSHIP CAUSED BY BANK COLLAPSE

In October, the Charing Cross Bank of London was placed in the hands of official receivers and in each of its 16 Scottish branches, notices of the suspension of business were posted. Because a large number of the bank's depositors north of the border were working class, a relief fund was set up, to be administered by the Royal Bank of Scotland. Advertisements were placed in the Scottish press inviting depositors deprived of funds by the bank's suspension to apply for interest-free loans from the fund. The large response highlighted the hardship that the bank closure had caused.

BOUND FOR THE NEW WORLD AND A NEW LIFE

In late March more than 3000 people left Glasgow bound for a new life in the USA and Canada – a record for a single day's departure. Vast crowds thronged Stobcross and Prince's Docks as the emigrants sought to board the *Pretorian*, the *Caledonian* and the *Cassandra*, the ships that would take them across the Atlantic. Amongst those leaving were a large number of well-dressed young women, most of whom were going to work as domestic servants. The quays were also filled with many mothers with young children going to join their husbands who had gone ahead to Canada and the Mid West in response to the various immigration societies' advertisements for Scots to populate and build the New World.

Liable to Winter Colds.

ANGIER'S EMULSION

Free Sample Coupon.

COMINGS...

Norman MacCaig
Poet

WHAT IT COST

POUND OF BUTTER
1s

POUND OF BACON
1s 1d

PINT OF BEER
2d

CIGARETTES
3d (10 Black Cat)

WOMEN'S SHOES
7s 11d

MEN'S SUIT
£2 15s

TON OF COAL
11s

POSTAGE
1d

CAR
Rover 2-seater £225

THIS SPORTING LIFE

FOOTBALL	RUGBY UNION	GOLF	HORSE RACING	SHINTY
Scottish Champions Celtic	*Scotland vs England* Scotland 5–14 England at Inverleith	*British Open Winner* James Braid at St Andrews (299)	*Scottish Grand National Winner* The Duffrey at Bogside	*Camanachd Cup Winners* Newtonmore at Kingussie
Scottish Cup Winners Dundee				

CITY EDITION.

THE CHEAPEST and QUICKEST WAY TO LET A COAST or COUNTRY HOUSE IS TO ADVERTISE IN THE DAILY RECORD AND MAIL.

Daily Record and Mail.

The All-Scotland Newspaper. Larger Sale than any other Morning or Evening Journal in the Country.

IN THE COUNTRY THE CHALLENGE OLD SCOTCH WHISKY HOLDS THE FIELD. ANDERSON & SHAW, LTD., GLASGOW.

ESTAB. 1847—NO. 20,060 GLASGOW, THURSDAY, MAY 11, 1911 ONE HALFPENNY.

THE SCOTTISH EXHIBITION.

INAUGURATION BY ROYALTY.

DUKE OF CONNAUGHT AND PATRIOTISM.

STRIKING TRIBUTES TO THE NATION.

RAINSTORM EFFECTS.

FIRST DAY'S VISITORS TOTAL 65,615.

Sunshine came late yesterday afternoon to redeem weather that proved lamentably inappropriate for such an august occasion as the opening by Royalty of an Exhibition whose essential mission is to bind Scotland more closely to the glories and victories of its past.

The beginnings of the outside ceremonies and processions, with the droop of sodden flag and the drip from flower-garland, had the suggestion of a gay parasol put up in rain. Naturally the streets had not the throb nor the volume of jubilant cheering that would, under brighter conditions, have been associated with the day, and on the 6¼ miles of route the people clustered for the most part in the porticos of shelter.

IN THE GRIP OF STORM.

In their closed carriage, the Duke and Duchess of Connaught must have sympathised with those who braved the batter of rain and the bluster of wind. The city which they saw was in the grip of storm, and the colours of beflagged buildings and cars were lost in the grey of a wet sou'-wester.

It was a big and crowded day, filled with manifestations of loyalty and ceremonials, including the presentation of the freedom of the city, a luncheon in the City Chambers, and the central function of opening "The Scottish Exhibition of National History, Industry and Art."

Fortunately all the white facades of the buildings of the Exhibition, so consistent in design, effective in architecture, and demonstrative of the magnificence and adaptability of the Baronial style, were gleaming in sunshine when it came to the visit by the Royal party of the principal features. So in spite of an unpropitious morning, the Exhibition was inaugurated in a brightness which, it is to be hoped, will endure throughout its run of months.

QUIET JUBILATION.

Glasgow was not absolutely en fete, as many firms did not join in the suggested lapse of business. Schools, however, were closed for the day, and the banks were only open an hour and a half in the morning. In the evening the grounds at Kelvingrove, radiant with illuminations and bustling with crowds, presented a picture that one can only wish perpetuated. The whole course of the ceremonies was unmarred by any serious accident.

Before leaving, his Royal Highness, speaking to Mr. Pettigrew, chairman of the Executive, expressed solicitude for the people who had stood the cold and rain for so long. He appreciated their loyalty very much. For himself personally during the whole of the tour through the grounds he had never felt any drawback from the weather.

EVENING CROWDS

Notwithstanding a recurrence of the rain enormous crowds visited the Exhibition in the evening, the numbers being calculated at 65,615. When lit up with electric light the buildings presented a spectacle of fascinating grandeur and beauty, while the effect on the waters of the Kelvin was entrancing. Continuous streams of visitors passed in and out of

THE PROCESSION.

ENTHUSIASTIC SCENES IN THE STREETS.

It was a quarter to twelve when the Royal procession, headed by Chief Constable Stevenson and Inspector Joseph Conway on horseback, left the station, followed by a number of mounted police. In the first seven carriages were the Corporation members, officials, and others who had been presented to their Royal Highnesses.

Staff Officers Major A. A. Wolfe Murray and Captain R. B. J. Crawfurd were seated in the eighth carriage; Miss M'Innes Shaw, Major the Hon. Leslie d'H. Hamilton, and Lord and Lady Pentland in the ninth; Mrs. M'Innes Shaw, Lieut.-General Sir Bruce Meade Hamilton, the Marquess and Marchioness of Tullibardine in the tenth; and Lord Hamilton, the Hon. Adele Emily Anna Hamilton, Major Malcolm Murray, and Miss Annie Evelyn Pelly in the eleventh carriage, which was followed by the Royal carriage with the Duke and Duchess of Connaught and Lord Provost M'Innes Shaw. Major-General Spens followed on horseback, and several mounted police brought up the rear.

ENTHUSIASTIC RECEPTION.

When the procession passed into Hope Street rain was falling heavily, and there was keen disappointment among the crowd when they saw that all the carriages were closed. A rousing cheer, however, was raised, which was taken up by the crowds which lined the route along Bothwell Street, St. Vincent Street, North Street, Kent Road, and Granville Street to the St. Andrew's Hall. Every point of vantage was occupied by cheering people, while from business premises and the windows of dwelling-houses men, women, and children waved flags and cheered lustily in demonstration of their loyalty.

Their Royal Highnesses seemed much gratified with their reception, and smiled and bowed their acknowledgments to the cheering crowds on each side of the closed carriage. A Guard of Honour, furnished by the 6th Highland Light Infantry, with band, under the command of Captain and Hon. Major W. M. Gale, was drawn up opposite the Granville Street entrance to the St. Andrew's Halls, and was inspected by the Duke of Connaught before he entered the hall.

Less than half-an-hour was spent in the St. Andrew's Halls, and the procession when re-formed proceeded to the Municipal Buildings by way of Granville Street, Sauchiehall Street, Buchanan Street, St. Vincent Place, and George Square. A Guard of Honour, furnished by the 5th Scottish Rifles, with band, and under the command of Captain and Hon. Major A. A. Kennedy, was drawn up at the City Chambers, facing the main entrance in George Square. It was also inspected by His Royal Highness.

The procession from the City Chambers to Kelvingrove was by way of George Square, George Street, High Street, Trongate, Argyle Street, and Kelvingrove Street. All along the route a large concourse of people were gathered, the weather conditions by this time having slightly improved, and cheer after cheer was raised as the Royal carriage passed. A Guard of Honour, with band, furnished by the 2nd Argyll and Sutherland Highlanders, under the command of Captain A. H. M'Lean, was drawn up in front of the concert hall and inspected by his Royal Highness.

THE RETURN.

Shortly after four o'clock the procession was again re-formed for the return journey to the Central Station, and was augmented by the Town Councillors.

In the first carriage were Councillors Bryce, M'Ewan, A. Maclure, and Carson; second, Councillors Sadler, Hutchison, Erskine, and Macnaughton; third, Councillors Muir, Nicol, Lyon, and Macdonald; fourth, Councillors M'Culloch, Kennedy, Drummond, and J. Stewart, of Townhead; fifth, Councillors Rosslyn Mitchell, Robert Mitchell, Hamilton Brown, and Hannay; sixth, Councillors M'Nell, Davidson, Whitson, and Cairns; seventh, Councillors W. C. Martin, Moir, Cosh, and Irwin; eighth, Councillors Forsyth, C. B. Young, Morton, and M'Connell; ninth, Councillors Hoey, Duncan Graham, William Maclure, and James Stewart, of Broomielaw; tenth, Councillors Nelson, Pratt, Gardiner, and Ure; eleventh, Councillors Barrie, Smith, Cohen, and Montgomery; twelfth, Councillors Dunlop, Hunter, Bruce Murray, and R. S. Brown; thirteenth, Councillors Watson, Willock, and D. M. Stevenson; fourteenth, Councillors Steele, Battersby, Robert Anderson, and Alexander.

These were followed by the Magistrates, Corporation officials, and others who formed the original procession.

By this time the sun had struggled through the clouds, and the carriages which formed the procession were thrown

THE THEATRE DISASTER.

DEATH ROLL TOTALS NINE.

LAFAYETTE AND SIX OF HIS COMPANY.

TWO SCENE SHIFTERS.

PROBABLE CAUSE OF THE FIRE.

THE KING'S SYMPATHY.

The fire disaster which overtook the Edinburgh Empire Palace on Tuesday night has proved to be a much more calamitous affair than was at first believed, and the terrible fate which has befallen Lafayette, the American entertainer who earned world-wide fame as the greatest living illusionist, together with six members of his company, has sent a thrill of horror throughout the country.

The Edinburgh Empire, thus fated to be the scene of the third and most disastrous theatre fire which has occurred in Scotland's capital during a period of half a century, was chosen as the house in which the "command" performance, by which the King had decided to honour the music-hall profession in his Coronation year, should take place.

Sir Edward Moss, the head of the combine which owns the hall, immediately the news became known to him, left London for Edinburgh to find on his arrival there that a telegram of regret and sympathy with the management, together with a request for full information regarding the occurrence, had been forwarded by his Majesty. The Royal message was as follows:—

"The King has learned from the newspapers with much concern of the calamitous fire which occurred at your theatre last night, resulting in the loss of life. His Majesty is anxious to have full particulars, and would be glad if the expression of his true sympathy, and that of the Queen, could be conveyed to the families of those who have lost their lives and to those who have been injured.—A. BIGGE."

Throughout the day a search was conducted amongst the debris and ruins of the stage in the hope that the announcement of the early morning of eight bodies having been recovered would not be added to. When work was suspended for the day about 7.30 the death roll stood at nine persons, and one man named S. Richards, a member of Lafayette's company, was still amissing.

LIST OF DEAD.

The following is the list of the victims:—

T. G. LAFAYETTE (38), residing at the Caledonian Hotel, Edinburgh, belonging to Los Angeles, California. Near his body was found a sword and shoe, both of which bore marks of fire.

Alice DALE (17), of New Inn, Hammond Street, Sheffield, who appeared in Lafayette's company as the "Teddy Bear."

Joseph COATS (14), also of Sheffield, who joined Lafayette's company a fortnight ago to appear as a midget.

John WHEELAN (40), of London, a trombone player in Lafayette's orchestra.

James BAINES (45), of Hackney, a 'cellist in Lafayette's orchestra.

Walter SCOTT, musician in Lafayette's orchestra.

Alexander JOSS (50), 357 High Street, Edinburgh, temporarily employed with Lafayette, married.

James WATT (63), 15 Arthur Street, scene-shifter.

A negro, six feet in height, believed to be Lafayette's drummer.

The Injured.

Charles MUNRO (24), Gifford Park, Edinburgh, who was removed to the Infirmary suffering from suffocation and shock.

Robert NELSON, 115 Buccleuch Street, Edinburgh, burns on face and legs and suffering from shock.

Thomas HAIG, Boroughloch Square, Edinburgh, suffocation and nervous prostration.

Henry MOORE, 43 Willowbrae Road, Edinburgh, shock (a member of Lafayette's company).

Fireman KENDALL, six stiches in one of his hands.

STORY OF THE HOLOCAUST.

PERFORMERS TRAPPED BEHIND IRON CURTAIN.

As fully reported in our later editions of yesterday, the fire at the Edinburgh Empire Palace Theatre was of a calamitous description so far as the loss of life was concerned.

Inquiries conducted yesterday amongst policemen, firemen, members of the audience, theatre employees, and members of the different companies appearing, all go to point to one end, and that is that the entire audience left the theatre in admirable order when once it was realised that a serious conflagration was raging, and that Lafayette, one of the best-known men in the variety profession, met his death gallantly endeavouring to save the lives of those who were dependent upon him.

Owing to the rapidity with which the flames spread, and the small space in which the outbreak was confined by the fire brigade, it was for a time impossible to get anything approaching accurate information as to the outbreak. There was a general consensus of opinion that the first sign of something being wrong was observed shortly after eleven o'clock on Tuesday evening, and until about three o'clock in the morning there were many contradictory rumours as to the nature, extent, and taken home, played the part of the "Teddy Bear." Joseph Coates (14), also found in a dressing-room suffocated, was waiting to go home. Most of the other remains were badly charred, and in some cases identification was established only with the utmost difficulty.

Throughout yesterday a staff of firemen were employed searching among the debris of the stage and its fittings, but the operations were hampered by the heavy iron fireproof curtain which had fallen on to the stage. It had prevented the flames from spreading from the stage to the auditorium, and after it had served its purpose it fell inward and covered the entire stage.

Until this curtain is removed it will be impossible to state definitely the number of the casualties. The entire stage of the theatre was burnt out and the roof was open to the sky. The roof of the auditorium was badly damaged, and the boxes and stalls were scorched by the heat.

When one takes into account the whole circumstances of the disaster, the marvel is that the death-roll is not greater. While the iron curtain was slowly descending a draught from the back of the stage drove the flames outwards across the stalls. It was the descent of the curtain which prevented the spread of the flames to the auditorium, and as it was owing to the draught forcing the cloth curtains outward the iron curtain did not fully descend by several feet.

MANAGER'S COOLNESS.

It was the coolness and promptitude of the manager in rushing to the front when he saw that something was amiss, and the prompt response of the band to his call for the National Anthem, when the whole audience rose and made for the doors, which were in the hands of capable attendants, and the whole audience, exceeding 3000 people, were able to leave the theatre without mishap beyond some slight crushing. There was no panic. Everything passed off in good order, and only the firemen, who by this time had arrived on the scene, the policemen inside the building, and the employees, knew of the fierce fight for life that was taking place behind the iron curtain.

The operations of the Fire Brigade were under the supervision of Firemaster Pordage, and the police were under the command of Chief-Constable Ross. Both discharged their onerous duties in a very acceptable manner, and but for their services, so promptly rendered, the casualties and the destruction of property might have been greater.

THE FIRST ALARM.

EXCITED NEIGHBOURS LEAVE THEIR HOMES.

One of those admitted to the Royal Infirmary suffering from shock was Charles Munro, who was standing on the stair leading to the gallery when the alarm was first raised.

About eleven o'clock dense volumes of smoke began to come through the door and windows and rolled into the pend at the side of the theatre. At that moment the gallery door opened, and some people came rushing out. The first was a young woman, who got the length of the small confectioner's shop near by when she fell to the street in a dead faint. She was carried into the shop, and there treated. Meanwhile the people came out of the theatre in a rapid but orderly manner. The houses of a row of tenement buildings which stood opposite the theatre were completely filled by smoke, and the inhabitants were in a state of great alarm, rushing down the stairs and into the street.

Munro, with several others, accordingly turned their attention to assisting the people from their houses, hurrying up the stairs, kicking at the different doors until the people came out. At one door they could get no response; so they had recourse to extreme measures, and burst it open. A woman, with a couple of children, were standing inside. The woman was hysterical, and the children were crying. The house was so full of smoke that they could hardly see their way about. The inmates, however, got safely out, and Munro again went back to the pend.

Here it was that he saw Lafayette. He was standing in the pend dressed just as he had been while on the stage. He appeared to be greatly perturbed, and when Munro came up to him he turned and said with some emotion, "I'll have to go in and get my horse." So far as is known these were his last words, for he at once went to a side door and disappeared amid the smoke that was coming from the burning theatre.

Seeing that nothing more was to be done in the pend, Munro turned once more to the tenements. It was then that he met with his accident. He had found his way to the top of a stair, kicking at the door as he went. When coming down again the smoke became so dense that he could not see where he was going. Thinking he was at the foot of the landing, he slipped his foot and fell down the stairs, hitting his head in his fall, and became unconscious. He knew nothing more until he found himself in the Infirmary being treated.

ORIGIN OF OUTBREAK.

STATEMENT BY SCENIC ARTIST.

Mr. C. B. Fountaine, the acting manager of the Empire Palace Theatre, in the course of an interview, referred to what he described just prior to the falling of the curtain of a little spurt of flame, which he knew had no part in the performance. This led Mr. Fountaine to remark that he believed the origin of the outbreak to be due to the fusing of a wire in some part of Lafayette's electrical fittings. Lafayette, he said, carried tons of scenery, and the staging was of an inflammable nature. The persons burned were engaged in some part of the flies. Some of the artistes seem to have left the stage and returned. Lafayette was one of these, and it is thought that he had gone back to try to save his horse and dog. The body found yesterday morning in the left-hand corner of the stage beside the charred remains of the horse, is supposed to be that of Lafayette. The remains of the lion lay on the other side of the stage. The boy and girl were waiting in the dressing rooms to go home with other members of the company and they were suffocated. The dressing-rooms remained intact.

Mr. Fountaine paid a fine tribute to the orderly manner in which the audience left the burning building. When he saw the little spurt of flame he ran to the front and shouted to the conductor "The King," and the orchestra struck up the National Anthem. The audience instinctively rose to its feet and turned towards the exits. The tremendous draught blew the draperies beneath the descending iron curtain, and prevented it quite reaching the floor. Through the few inches of space remaining,

APPALLING SCENES

"GOLDEN RAIN" OF DEATH.

RAGING FLAMES.

A gentleman who is well known in the city thus describes his experience:—

"The fire was the most appalling spectacle it has ever been my fate to witness. The fire started with a lamp suspended from the roof. I don't know what sort of a lamp it was, but all of a sudden what appeared like a shower of "golden rain" occurred, and the whole scenery burst into flames. The light curtain, which closes in from both sides, fell, and then one of the people on the stage—I think it was Lafayette—came forward and called out "Keep cool." The stalls were emptying in any case, it being the end of the performance, and there was no confusion. The fire was spurting out towards the stalls, but, although the flames were raging over their heads, the members of the orchestra struck up the National Anthem, and pluckily continued to play.

"The flames leaped towards those of us in the front seats, and the friend who was with me had his eyebrows and the side of his face scorched. The most wonderful thing, to my mind, about the whole occurrence, was the way the people behaved. There were shouts of "Women first," and, so far as the stalls were concerned at any rate, they were allowed to pass out. In fact, the women were assisted out. The men, following, left the theatre in a most orderly fashion. In a few minutes the stalls were empty, and as I looked across the pit the crowd was dispersing rapidly, but there was neither panic nor confusion."

A NOBLE SACRIFICE.

Interviews with those who were on and near the stage reveal the terrible nature of their ordeal, and also the unavailing gallantry of the artistes to save those in peril.

Lafayette's stage manager, who is the uncle of the little girl Alice Dale, said—"Our boys gave their lives for the audience. Had it not been for them scores of the audience would have been burned to death."

This gentleman himself did not leave the stage until he was satisfied that everyone was clear, and then he attempted to reach his niece's dressing-room, but he was driven back by flames.

Mr. Frank Benson, an artist appearing at the Empire, whose death had been reported, "thanked God he had escaped such an awful end." At the time of the outbreak, he said, he was in the wings. His attention was at first attracted by a shout of "fire" from a young woman on the stage. Looking round he noticed something burning dropping. Lafayette ordered the girl to stop calling out, and also ordered the fireproof curtain to be lowered.

By this time smoke had become so dense that Mr. Benson lost his bearings, and would have plunged into the flames had he not been stopped by a fireman. At that moment the body of the boy was found, and Mr. Benson assisted to remove it to a side room.

IN THE FLIES.

Mr. Arthur Jewitt, who figured in Lafayette's company as "The Rajah," said it was a most horrifying experience. In the piece the curtain falls immediately after the Rajah has been shot and whilst Lafayette drove the lion back to its den. Mr. Jewitt was waiting for Lafayette to take his "curtain" when he noticed that the artiste was missing. The cry of "Fire" was raised, and Mr. Jewitt rose to find that the whole place was ablaze, as he phrased it.

Proceeding to his dressing-room, situated in the flies, Mr. Jewitt there found Alice Dale, who cried, "Save me, Mr. Jewitt."

Mr. Jowitt replied "I will," but was forestalled by Baines, who snatched up the girl and made for a place of safety.

Both, however, perished in the flames.

Mr. Jewitt dashed down the stairs, and was driven back by the smoke to another dressing-room. He was on the point of being overcome when he heard a comrade shout, "This way, Mr. Jewitt," and, rushing headlong down two flights of stairs, he reached the open-air minus his helmet, but wearing his stage armour.

A BALL OF FIRE.

Mr. D. Mackenzie, one of the violinists in the theatre orchestra, said that whilst they were playing the finale of "The Lion's Bride" music he noticed sparks, and then a ball of fire. Someone told the conductor to strike up "The King."

"We saw the stage was on fire," added Mr. Mackenzie, "but we played the National Anthem to a finish. It was the longest 'King' ever played. Whilst we were playing the flames were licking towards us, and we should have been in imminent danger of death had we stayed another minute."

Descending to their rooms the members of the orchestra found the place filled with smoke, but they fought their way through it to the open air.

PUBLIC SYMPATHY.

Lord Provost W. S. Brown, Edinburgh, yesterday made public reference to the disaster, and on behalf of the citizens offered sympathy with the relatives of the victims. He also spoke of the lack of panic among the audience.

The Lord Provost received the following telegram from the Earl of Rosebery:—"I hope without intrusion that I may express my deep sorrow and sympathy on this terrible accident.—Rosebery."

A SPLENDID RECORD.

Sir Edward Moss, the chairman of the directors of Moss' Empires, the proprietors of the Empire Palace Theatre, yesterday evening granted an interview to the "Daily Record and Mail," in the course of which he expressed profound sorrow at the calamitous fire and its terrible results.

Sir Edward recalled that the present was the only time throughout his whole career that at one of his theatres lives had been lost.

At Cardiff a few years ago the theatre there was burned, but the Empire Palace made a first where there had been a fatality. He was sorry for the artistes, and his concern was to keep them in employment. To that end negotiations were proceeding for a continuance of the performances, and to-day he hoped to make a statement on the subject regarding the Empire Theatre.

NINE DIE AS BLAZE HITS THEATRE

NINE people were killed when a huge fire destroyed the Empire Palace Theatre in Edinburgh in May. Among the victims was the Great Lafayette, the American entertainer who earned world-wide fame as the greatest living illusionist. Six members of his company also died in the blaze.

Lafayette was a big favourite in Glasgow as well as Edinburgh where a popular feature of his shows was his spectacular colouring effects on the stage.

Lafayette, who was also dubbed "The Man of Mystery", was in the middle of his act when according to the evidence of some of those who were in the vicinity of the stage, something was seen falling from the roof, and immediately afterwards the whole of the stage was enveloped in flames.

The fire curtain was lowered, but owing to a draught forcing the other curtains to billow out underneath, it was unable to be dropped to its full extent.

The majority of the audience, after some struggling and amid a great deal of near-panic, managed to get out safely.

And, as far as the police were able to report, no serious injuries were sustained by any of the audience.

The flames spread rapidly in the theatre and in a comparatively short space of time, the whole of the Empire Palace was a raging furnace.

Despite all the resources at their command, the local firemen had great difficulty in confining the fire to the blazing ruins of the theatre.

KELVINGROVE EXHIBITION

Scotland and its history and culture was much more the focus of Glasgow's 1911 Exhibition than previous ones in 1901 and 1888. Exhibits on Scottish history included gems such as Bonnie Prince Charlie's baby rattle and Flora MacDonald's slippers. A mock Scots town – Auld Toon – was constructed in Kelvingrove Park from plaster, wood and canvas, looking so realistic that even moss was painted on the walls. Fittingly for an exhibition focussing on Scottish themes, the weather on the opening day was foul although for almost all of the rest of the 6-month event the sun blazed down. Almost 10 million visitors paid upwards of a shilling admission, leaving the organisers with a smallish profit of £20,000.

ROYAL COMMANDS.

Phosferine enjoys the distinguished honour of having received commands from MEMBERS OF THE BRITISH ROYAL FAMILY.

I. M. the Empress of Russia.	H.I.H. the Grand Duchess Olga of Russia.
H.M. the King of Greece.	H.R.H. the Crown Princess of Roumania
H.M. the Queen of Roumania.	H.I.H. the Grand Duchess Serge of Russia.
H.I.M. the Dowager Empress of Russia.	H.I.H. the Grand Duchess Xenia of Russia.

And the leading aristocracy and public generally throughout the universe

Cures Neuralgia, Sciatica, Lumbago, Gout, Rheumatism, Impaired Vitality, Debility, Brain Fag, Weakness, Nervous Exhaustion, Melancholia, Impaired Digestion, &c.

A Vitalising Tonic, imparting New Life and Energy to the Entire System.

Phosferine is the most powerful Nerve and Recuperative Tonic known. It removes Mental Depression, want of Tone and Nerve Power. It has remarkable Health-giving, Strength-giving, Energising, and Rejuvenating properties.

No other Medicine has received such absolute proof of its extraordinary properties in restoring Shattered Constitutions, and in giving back to the prematurely aged New Life and Energy.

Pale, weakly children and people suffering from broken-down health, brain-fag, nervous exhaustion, the weakening after-effects of severe illnesses, derive benefit from the first dose; it gives a new lease of life.

Proprietors: ASHTON & PARSONS, Ltd., 17 Farringdon Road, London, E.C. Bottles, 1s 1½d, 2s 9d, and 4s 6d. Post Free 1s 3d, 3s, and 4s 9d. Sold by all Chemists, Stores, etc.

The 2s 9d size contains nearly four times the 1s 1½d size.

CORONATION CELEBRATIONS

All across Scotland the celebrations of George V's coronation had been going on for almost a fortnight prior to the event. Public and private buildings were a riot of bunting, flags and streamers, and tramcars were ablaze with light-bulbs. In towns and cities, special dinners for pensioners and parties for children were a common feature of the celebrations. On Coronation Day itself, a public holiday was declared.

COMINGS...

Fitzroy Maclean
Diplomat & Soldier

Sorley Maclean
Gaelic Poet

THIS SPORTING LIFE

FOOTBALL	RUGBY UNION	GOLF	HORSE RACING	SHINTY
Scottish Champions Rangers	*Scotland vs England* England 13–8 Scotland at Twickenham	*British Open Winner* Harry Vardon at Sandwich, England (303)	*Scottish Grand National Winner* *Couvrefeu II* at Bogside	*Camanachd Cup Winners* Ballachulish at Lochaber
Scottish Cup Winners Celtic				

Public Opinion has Pronounced
FOUR CROWN WHISKY
Finest Whisky in the World.

CITY EDITION

Daily Record and Mail.

The All-Scotland Newspaper. Larger Sale than any other Morning or Evening Journal in the Country.

OWING TO THE ENORMOUS SUCCESS AND GREAT POPULARITY OF THE POLY.
RESTAURANT LOUIS XVI.
WE ARE ENABLED TO INCREASE THE VALUE OF THE ALREADY FAMOUS 3-COURSE
SHILLING LUNCH,
"MORE OF EVERYTHING,"
MAKING IT THE CHEAPEST AS WELL AS THE BEST IN THE CITY.

ESTAB. 1847—NO. 20,292 GLASGOW, SATURDAY, FEBRUARY 10, 1912 ONE HALFPENNY.

OUR NAVAL POLICY.

SUPREMACY TO BE MAINTAINED.

NO DANGER OF A RIVAL LEAD.

THE ADMIRALTY'S PLANS.

SPEECH BY MR. CHURCHILL IN GLASGOW.

Mr. Winston Churchill, First Lord of the Admiralty, spent a busy day in Glasgow yesterday. The right hon. gentleman, who arrived in the city from Belfast in the early hours of the morning, was entertained to luncheon at midday by the Clyde Navigation Trust, and he afterwards made a tour of inspection of one of the largest shipbuilding yards in the Clyde district.

Great public interest was displayed in Mr. Churchill's visit.

At the banquet the First Lord made an important speech on Naval policy, in the course of which he said:—

The Government is resolved to maintain the Naval supremacy which this country enjoys.

The Cabinet is firmly united on this point.

There is no chance whatever of our being overtaken in Naval strength unless we want to be.

There is no necessity for a Naval loan.

What is wanted is steady building and a regular plan; no sensational or violent departure from our existing methods is required or will be required.

We should be the first Power to welcome any retardation or slackening of Naval rivalry; we should meet any such slackening not by words but by deeds.

But if there is to be an increase—if there are to be increases upon the Continent of Europe—we shall have no difficulty in meeting them to the satisfaction of the country at large.

Mr. Churchill, who was accompanied by his wife, left Glasgow at 10.45 last night for London.

THE LUNCHEON.

Mr. Churchill was the guest of Sir Thomas Mason and the Trustees of the Clyde Navigation at luncheon in the offices of the Trust, Robertson Street. The company numbered about 100 gentlemen, including members of the Trust and many other representatives of the shipbuilding, shipping and commercial interests of the city.

Sir Thomas Mason, the chairman of the Trust, presided, and he was supported on his right by:—

Mr. Churchill, Miss Mason, the Marquis of Graham, Sir John Ure Primrose, Sir William Bilsland, Sir N. Dunlop, Sir Robert Balfour, Mr. William Beardmore, and Mr. Hugh Reid; and on his left by Mrs. Churchill, Lord Provost D. M. Stevenson, Sir Samuel Chisholm, Miss Stevenson, Principal Sir D. MacAlister, Sir A. M'Innes Shaw, the Hon. E. E. T. Fiennes, M.P. for Banbury; Sir Jas. Fleming, and Mr. Greenwood.

After the King's health had been duly pledged, Sir Thomas Mason rose to propose the toast of the health of their guest, and to ask them to accord a hearty welcome to the Right Hon. Mr Churchill upon his first visit to the Clyde as the First Lord of the Admiralty. (Applause.)

At the present moment, said Sir Thomas, and that for various reasons, we are deeply interested in the right hon. gentleman's visit. I would only refer to two of these—both of which are of great importance to this Trust, to our engineers, our shipbuilders, and the great army of workmen employed on the banks of the Clyde. You are all aware that the Clyde Navigation Trust have recently obtained Parliamentary powers to construct a large graving dock. Following precedent, we have thought it advisable to consult the Admiralty regarding the width of our new dock in order to meet, if we can at all possibly meet, their present and prospective requirements.

CHARACTERISTIC ZEAL.

The presence of the First Lord of the Admiralty here to-day is evidence of the deep interest of the Admiralty in our great undertaking, and affords another example of Mr. Churchill's earnest and characteristic energy in coming here to make himself intimate with the whole affair of the First Lord of the Admiralty, and that is a toast which is always well received, not because of the virtues of the individual who may occupy the post, but because of the great and noble Fleet over which, under the Crown, it is my duty to preside.

I can give you, he proceeded, a very good account of the British Navy. (Applause.) In ships it is possible to match every other Fleet in the world and show a clear superiority ship for ship. The numbers can be computed from the published returns. In guns I think there is no doubt that we possess in the latest 13.5 gun certainly the finest weapon that the British naval service has ever possessed, and probably, as far as we have any means of judging, far and away the finest gun in the world.

We believe that the Navy is not only at the present moment strong, but that it is in the highest state of preparation for any sudden call.

The rumours which have become part of the newspapers, during the last few months, that the Navy was during the last year unprepared are absolutely baseless (applause), and we hope that the creation of a naval War Staff will tend to render the propagation of these rumours absolutely impossible in the future. ("Hear, hear.")

WAR STAFF AN WORK.

The War Staff at the Admiralty is already at work; and the second part of that policy is now to be carried into effect, by which I mean the development of a class of officers, afloat and ashore, throughout the Naval service who will be consistently trained and accustomed over long periods of time, to interest themselves and educate their minds upon the highest problems of strategy and naval organisation. That, of course, is a much longer business than the creation of a more effective machinery at Whitehall, but it will be undertaken in the next few weeks, and there will be no delay in giving full effect to that part of the War Staff policy.

Well, now, gentlemen, let me say what after all you realise, but what it is still our duty to affirm, that the purposes of British Naval power are essentially defensive. ("Hear, hear," and applause.) We have no thought, and we have never had any thought, of aggression. We attribute no such thoughts to other great Powers. ("Hear, hear.")

There is, however, this difference between British Naval power, and the Naval power of the great and friendly Empire—and I trust it may long remain the great and friendly Empire—of Germany. The British Navy is to us a necessity, whereas the German Navy is to them more in the nature of a luxury. Naval power involves British existence. It is existence to us; it is expansion to them. We cannot menace the peace of a single Continental hamlet, nor do we wish to ("Hear, hear"), no matter how great and supreme our Navy may become, but, on the other hand, the whole fortunes of our race and Empire and all the treasure accumulated during so many centuries of sacrifice and achievement would perish and be swept utterly away if our Naval supremacy were to be endangered. (Applause.)

It is the British Navy which makes Britain a great Power. Germany was a great Power respected and honoured all over the world before she had a single ship. These facts ought clearly to be stated, because there is no doubt that there is a disposition in some quarters to suppose that Great Britain and Germany are on terms of equality so far as naval risks are concerned, but such a supposition is utterly untrue.

The Government is resolved to maintain the Naval supremacy which this country enjoys. (Applause.) The Prime Minister and his colleagues without exception are resolved to maintain it ("Hear, hear"), and they would, none of them tolerate my presence at the Admiralty for a single hour unless they were satisfied that all steps would be taken, and were being taken, to secure the safety of the Empire. In fact, I am not sure if I should tolerate it myself. (Laughter.)

INCREASED COST.

We now see, as far as the public prints inform us, that there are prospects of further Naval increases among the Powers of the European Continent; and that is a very serious matter, because not only are Navies increasing in size, but everything connected with Navies is increasing in cost. The ships are getting larger, longer, and—broader, Sir Thomas (Laughter and applause), all the appliances with which they are fitted are becoming every day more complicated and more expensive. The means of repairing these ships require every day more elaborate and more costly machinery. The accommodation for docking these vessels involves every year the provision of docks of a scale and dimension not hitherto foreseen.

The size of the guns increases, the size of the ammunition and the expense both of armament and ammunition, and the increase in horse-power of the new vessels now being added to the Fleets means a greater consumption of coal and oil, although there is no greater movement of the vessel. And there is no doubt whatever that the nations of Europe are at the present time pressing forward, and pressing each other forward, into an avenue of almost indefinite Naval expansion and expense. We may have our own opinion as to how far future generations will compliment the present age upon the Christianity, the wisdom, and the civilisation which have made this dreary, dangerous, and sterile competition so large a feature in our lives.

But there it is, and we shall have to meet it, and I am glad to tell you, Sir Thomas, to-day that there is no need whatever for alarm, there is no need for the arising of any excited panic, and there is no need for disparaging the resources of our country. (Applause.) We may face the situation with great composure, because it is just and true to say that at every point and in every detail we have it well in hand. We were never in a better position, and the country was never more united in its resolve to see the supremacy of the British Navy maintained. (Applause.)

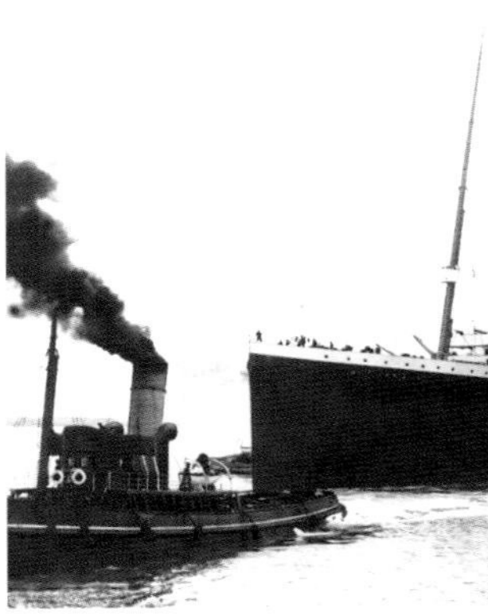

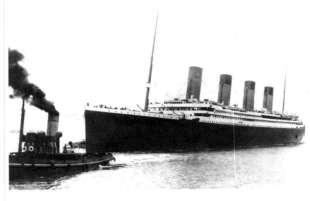

TITANIC SINKS AFTER COLLISION.

CRIPPLED BY ICEBERG IN MID-OCEAN.

MANY LIVES LOST.

LINERS DASH TO THE RESCUE.

EFFORTS TO SAVE THE PASSENGERS.

ANOTHER TRIUMPH OF WIRELESS.

TWO FATEFUL MESSAGES.

SINKING OF THE TITANIC WITH LOSS OF LIFE.

A NEW YORK MESSAGE TIMED 8.20 P.M. SAYS:

CAPTAIN HADDOCK, OF THE OLYMPIC, SENDS WIRELESS MESSAGE THAT TITANIC SANK AT 2.20 A.M., MONDAY, AFTER ALL PASSENGERS AND CREW HAD BEEN LOWERED INTO LIFEBOATS AND TRANSFERRED TO VIRGINIAN.

A FURTHER NEW YORK MESSAGE, TIME 8,40 P.M., SAYS THAT THE WHITE STAR LINE NOW ADMIT THAT MANY LIVES HAVE BEEN LOST.

Such is the fate which has befallen the world's largest vessel, which set forth on her maiden voyage from Southampton in the latter part of last week to the accompaniment of the hurrahs of the wondering throng on the quay and the farewells waved from those on board proud of the distinction of travelling by such a mighty vessel, and looking expectantly forward to a pleasant voyage.

And all went well until Sunday night. The vessel was making good progress, fully expecting to reach New York a day in advance of her scheduled time, when misfortune overtook her. She got into a field of ice, and in a dense fog which suddenly came upon her she collided with an iceberg, and was so badly damaged that she had to summon aid.

This is the season of the year at which

GREAT LOSS OF LIFE.

NEWS OF 675 SOULS ONLY SAFE.

LINERS SEARCHING SCENE OF DISASTER.

New York, Monday, 8.15 p.m.

The following despatch has been received here from Cape Race:—"Steamer Olympic reports steamer Carpathia reached the Titanic's position daybreak, but found boats and wreckage only.

"She reports Titanic foundered about 2.20 a.m. in latitude 41.16 longitude 50.14.

"All the Titanic's boats are accounted for. About 675 souls saved of the crew and passengers. The latter nearly all women and children.

"The Leyland liner California searching the vicinity of the disaster.

"Carpathia returning New York with the survivors."

8.40 p.m.

The White Star officials now admit that many lives have been lost.

8.20 p.m.

The following statement has been given out by the White Star officials:—

"Captain Haddock of the Olympic sends wireless message that the Titanic sank 2.20 a.m. Monday, after all the passengers and crew had been lowered into the lifeboats and transferred to the Virginian.

"The steamer Carpathia with several hundred passengers from the Titanic is now on her way to New York."—Reuter.

"HAVE STRUCK ICEBERG."

THE TITANIC'S STARTLING MESSAGE.

(From Our Own Correspondent.)

New York, Monday.

The Titanic, which sailed on her maiden voyage from Southampton on Wednesday, is to-day a wreck some 1200 miles east of New York and 300 miles south-east of Cape Race.

Her 2358 passengers and crew are being rapidly transferred to the liners Carpathia and Virginian, which were first of the many liners from whom assistance was demanded to reach the scene.

"Have struck iceberg. Am badly damaged. Rush assistance."

Such was the terrible message received at 10.35 p.m. last evening by the Marconi wireless station at Cape Race. Half an hour later came another message reporting that the Titanic was sinking by the head, and adding, "the women are being put in the lifeboats."

Already the Allan liner Virginian had been notified of the accident, and its captain informed his owners that he was proceeding at full speed to the assistance of the largest ship in the world. The weather was calm and the sea quiet. The position of the damaged vessel was given as 41deg. 46min. north latitude, 50deg. 14min. west longitude. At midnight the Virginian notified the shore station that she was 170 miles distant from the scene of the collision, and expected to reach the Titanic at ten o'clock this morning.

Twenty-seven minutes later the Virginian sent word that the signals from the Titanic were blurred and had ended abruptly.

Meanwhile the S.O.S. distress warnings had been sent to as many as 50 steamers, and soon the news reached New York that the Baltic, Olympic, and Carpathia were steaming to the aid of the Titanic.

CAPTAIN'S SILENCE.

Many hours of painful suspense followed. Urgent messages to Captain E. J. Smith of the Titanic, begging him to send particulars of the damage and condition of the passengers elicited no response. A wireless message sent by Mr. P. S. A. Franklin, vice-president of the White Star Line, inquired anxiously for information and full particulars of the probable disposition of the passengers, but remained unanswered.

THE SECOND CITY.

GLASGOW'S GREAT TRIUMPH.

BOUNDARIES BILL GOES THROUGH.

PREAMBLE PROVED.

Population Annexed - - -	256,249
Present Population - - -	784,496
	1,040,745

After hearing evidence and speeches for and against the Glasgow Boundaries Bill, in a protracted inquiry extending over several weeks, a Select Committee of the House of Commons has granted, not indeed the whole of the area claimed for annexation to the municipality, but more than sufficient to leave to Glasgow the proud pre-eminence of being "the second city of the Kingdom," and, if Calcutta's claims be admitted, "third" of the Empire.

A MILLION INHABITANTS.

That coveted honour was temporarily wrested from "the dark sea-born city" last year by Birmingham, when the Midland city swallowed up many populous places in its neighbourhood. By yesterday's decision, however, Glasgow will have, with the addition of Govan, Partick, Pollokshaws, and other areas in Lanarkshire, Renfrewshire, and Dumbartonshire a population of over 1,030,057, whilst Birmingham's population is put at 840,291. Govan, it may be interesting to note, is the fifth largest burgh in Scotland in respect of population.

The House of Commons Committee delivered its decision in the following terms:—

The Committee have found the preamble of the Bill proved with regard to Govan, Partick, Pollokshaws, and that portion of the County of Lanark west of Govan; also all portions of Lanark north of the Clyde, the County of Dumbarton, a portion of Renfrewshire north of the Clyde, and so much of the County of Renfrewshire south of the Clyde as lies within the southern section of the Glasgow main drainage area.

Put briefly, the decision of the Committee means that the following districts are in future to be included in the Glasgow area:—

GOVAN, PARTICK, POLLOKSHAWS, MERRYFLATS, SHIELDHALL, BRAEHEAD, SOUTH CALDERCUILT, BISHOPBRIGGS, ROBROYSTON, LAMBHILL, MILLERSTON, RUCHAZIE, SHETTLESTON, TOLLCROSS, BURNSIDE, WESTFIELD, TORYGLEN, MANSEWOOD, NEWLANDS, CATHCART, YOKER, SCOTSTOUNHILL, SCOTSTOUN, JORDANHILL, ANNIESLAND, KNIGHTSWOOD, TEMPLE, DAWSHOLM—Total population, 256,249.

The principal places excluded from the scheme by the Committee are Rutherglen, Thornliebank, Giffnock, Cardonald, Crookston, and Corkerhill.

The news of the decision of the Select Committee occasioned excitement in all circles. The non-appearance of Rutherglen among the districts amalgamated came as a surprise to many; otherwise the satisfaction seemed to be general, and the ambition of the Glaswegian for a city of a million inhabitants satisfied.

The population and valuation of the three most populous places which will be amalgamated with Glasgow are as follows:

	Population.		Valuation. £
Govan	90,700	....	441,991
Partick	68,100	....	408,601
Pollokshaws	12,930	....	51,629
	171,730	....	902,221

CITY'S PROGRESS.

Very steady has been the growth of the city of St. Mungo during the last century and a half. In 1740 the inhabitants numbered only 17,043, and in the following forty years, which embraced the period of thirty-six years during which the Tobacco Lords proudly walked the "plainstanes" in the Trongate, the total rose to 42,832. The tobacco trade was ruined by the American War, but other industries began to take root and develop, so that by the first year of the new century the city contained 77,385 souls.

Now there came the era of the steam engine and iron founding with such small beginnings as the plying of the Charlotte Dundas steamer on the Forth and Clyde Canal (1803), the introduction by Neilson of the hot-blast furnace (1828), and the opening of the Glasgow and Garnkirk Railway (1831). These among other agencies no doubt contributed to the increase of the population to 100,748 in the next decade to 1811, and to 202,426 in the decade to 1831. From this date the population advanced by leaps and bounds, reaching 359,696 in 1851, 477,732 in 1871 (including Govan, 19,200); 487,985 in 1881 (Govan, 49,426); and 658,198 in 1891 (including Govan, 63,625)

1912

CHURCHILL BOOST FOR CLYDESIDE

THE First Lord of the Admiralty, Mr Winston Churchill, spent a busy day in Glasgow in February Great public interest was displayed in Mr Churchill's visit.

His presence was seen as evidence of the deep interest of the Admiralty in Clydeside's commitment to ship-building. And it afforded an example of Mr Churchill's earnest and characteristic energy in coming to the city personally to acquaint himself with the whole affair, and to arrive at his own conclusions after investigation into the Clyde's set-up.

The First Lord's visit included an inspection of one of the largest ship-building yards on the Clyde.

Mr Churchill said he believed that the shipbuilding industry on the river was a question not only of local, but also national importance.

At a city banquet held later in the day Mr Churchill made an important speech on the nation's naval policy, set as it was against the backdrop of the growing political tension with Germany and the race to built greater numbers of bigger and better battleships:

"The Government is resolved to maintain the naval supremacy which this country enjoys.

"There is no chance whatever of our being overtaken in naval strength unless we want to be .

"What is wanted is steady building and a regular plan; no sensational or violent departure from our existing methods is required or will be required.

"But if there is to be an increase, if there are to be increases upon the continent of Europe, we shall have no difficulty in meeting them."

A LONG TAIL BUT A GOOD TALE

1909.

Showing the increase in deliveries of

MOLASSINE DOG FOODS.

The demand for August, 1910, being sixteen times greater than Jany., 1909.

1910.

There is a reason for this.

They are different from all others.

Other Foods feed Dogs only. Molassine Foods not only feed but keep dogs healthy, improve the coat, eradicate worms, and prevent unpleasant odours from the skin and excreta.

MANUFACTURED FROM THE PUREST INGREDIENTS ONLY AND FREE FROM ANY MEDICAMENT.

Call to-day at the nearest dealer's and buy some. Samples post free from

MOLASSINE
CO., LD.,
11 TUNNEL-AV., GREENWICH, S.E.

BURNS' HOWFF REPRIEVED

Fans of Robert Burns breathed a sigh of relief in November when the threatened dispersal of a number of important relics belonging to the Bard was averted. The crisis had arisen following decision of the current owners to put the Globe Tavern in Dumfries up for sale.

The Tavern, popularly known as "Burns' Howff" because of the frequency of the poet's visits to it, contained a number of items that belonged to Burns, including his favourite chair. The proprietors agreed to sell the pub to Dumfries Town Council and the local Burns Club for an undisclosed sum.

There had been a growing movement amongst the various Burns' Clubs at home and abroad to prevent the sale of the "Howff" to disinterested parties and this agitation was now to be channelled into a public appeal to fund the purchase.

THE SECOND CITY

After a protracted inquiry lasting several weeks, the Select Committee of the House of Commons examining the Glasgow Boundaries Bill backed the expansion of the city through the incorporation of a number of surrounding areas. These included Govan, Partick and Pollokshaws.

As a result, the city's population increased immediately by over 250,000, rising from 785,000 to over 1 million. Glasgow thus became "Second City of the Kingdom" and "Third City of the Empire" behind Calcutta.

COMINGS...

John Crofton
Pioneering TB Specialist

GRAND THEATRE.
NIGHTLY at 7.45.
THE GREAT THREE-PART PROGRAMME.
ALEX. KEITH AND CO. Present
"THE AGONY COLUMN."
THE WORLD'S LATEST AND BEST PHOTO.
PLAYS.
ILLUSTRATED SONGS.
PRICES—3d to 1s 6d. Book Seats at Muir Wood & Co.'s.

EMPIRE THEATRE.
6.45—TWICE NIGHTLY—9.
"THAT BAD LAD,"
GEORGE FORMBY,
In all his Latest Successes.
ELLA RETFORD,
The Charming Comedienne.
GLADYS BARNARD. BIOSCOPE.
HORACE WHEATLEY, the Irish Comedian.
LECARDO BROS., Acrobatic Eccentrics.
O. LEVATOR'S
WOLF HOUNDS,
An Extraordinary Exhibition of Canine Instinct.
CHARLIER,
The Continental Ventriloquist.
WILSON AND WARING
In a Refined Vaudeville Entertainment.
BOX OFFICE OPEN DAILY, 10.30 to 5.30.
'PHONES—Nat., 3731 Douglas; P.O., 2177 Douglas.

GOINGS...

Joseph Lister
Pioneer of Surgical Antisepsis

THIS SPORTING LIFE

FOOTBALL	RUGBY UNION	GOLF	HORSE RACING	SHINTY
Scottish Champions Rangers	*Scotland vs England* Scotland 8–3 England at Inverleith	*British Open Winner* Ted Ray at Muirfield (295)	*Scottish Grand National Winner* Couvrefeu II at Bogside	*Camanachd Cup Winners* Ballachulish at Perth
Scottish Cup Winners Celtic				

CITY EDITION.

Daily Record and Mail.

The All-Scotland Newspaper. Larger Sale than any other Morning or Evening Journal in the Country.

ESTAB. 1847—NO. 20,722   GLASGOW, FRIDAY, JUNE 27, 1913   TEN PAGES: ONE HALFPENNY.

GENTLEMEN,
BEFORE YOU TAKE YOUR HOLIDAY TRIP HAVE A LOOK IN AT THE "POLY."
OUT-FIT SALE.

THE BODY IN THE WOOD.
SPLENDID STORY OF DEREK CLYDE, and CHARLES PRIEST, Detective.   Prince of Scoundrels.
SEE THIS WEEK'S
Scottish Weekly Record
NOW ON SALE.

DUKE OF SUTHERLAND DEAD.

BREATHED HIS LAST THIS MORNING.

GREAT HIGHLAND LANDLORD.

RECORD OF USEFUL LIFE.

STORY OF LAST ILLNESS

(From Our Own Correspondent.)
Golspie, Friday.
The Duke of Sutherland passed peacefully away at 1 a.m,

We regret to announce the death of the Duke of Sutherland, who passed away early this morning at Dunrobin Castle, Golspie, to which he had journeyed a fortnight ago on the advice of London specialists.

While on a voyage to Ceylon, the Duke, who was in his sixty-third year, contracted pleurisy, which was followed by heart complications.

All hope was given up of his recovery yesterday, and, after slowly sinking during the day, he died after having been unconscious for several hours. In the last moments the Duke was being kept alive by the administration of oxygen.

Lord and Lady Castlereagh had, before the end, arrived at the Castle from Assynt.

The Duchess's private secretary has been despatched to meet Lord Alistair on his arrival from India. He is due back at the end of next week.

All the other members of the family are now at Dunrobin Castle.

The condition of the dying nobleman was indicated by the publication of the following bulletins yesterday:—

Golspie, Thursday Afternoon.

Now in grave condition. Going off in swoons of unconsciousness. End may be expected at any moment. Bulletins awaited with eagerness.

At a later hour last evening the following grave bulletin was published:—

Slowly sinking. Been unconscious for hours. End expected soon.

A GREAT LANDOWNER.

CAREER OF THE DUKE OF SUTHERLAND.

An outstanding figure in the modern history of the Scottish Highlands was the

It was with the coming of the first Duke of Sutherland that the north of Scotland really came into line with the southern counties, as at that period there was not such a thing in the north as a decently constructed road. He was the means of obtaining a grant from Parliament for the construction of roads and bridges, and the other holders of the titles have followed in his footsteps, with the result that roads and bridges are as they should be.

The fourth Duke, who has just departed this life, has excelled his ancestors in many ways. He has ever had the interests of his tenantry at heart, and was liberal in his dealings with them. His ear was ever open to the merest request, and received his personal attention. As a landlord, a more ideal one could not be found in Britain, and at the time of his succession to the title the crofters and cottars were not what could be called well off or prosperous.

He immediately set about to improve their position, and in the matter of rent gave liberal concessions all over—even going the length in the case of the very poor among his tenantry of striking off arrears and allowing them to start anew. The poorer class of the tenantry have never at any time during his tenure of the title been pressed for rent—in fact many cases could be instanced where he has allowed them to sit rent free for 20 years, on end.

For the prosperity and welfare of the crofters he has done more than any Act of Parliament has accomplished, or could accomplish in a decade or more. The people not only looked upon him as a landlord but as a friend whom they could approach at any time they found themselves in distress through adverse circumstances. In recent years he made large concessions in the shape of land to small farmers, crofters, and others in different parts of the county.

The Duke was born in 1851, and was therefore in his 63rd year. He succeeded his father in 1892, and was welcomed with open arms by the people, who long before his succession had learned to hold him in the highest respect, because of his disposition of kindness and large-heartedness. The people under his tenure of Dukeship have lived in peace and contentment.

The fisher population of the district have had a sincere and true friend in the Duke, and have benefited at his hands in many ways. Whenever a disaster took place, no uncommon occurrence in Sutherland, the Duke, along with the Duchess, were always the first to extend their sympathy in a practical way, and head the funds got up for the relief of the widows and orphans with a liberal donation.

If the fishermen were bereft of their boats through being broken up in the storm, to enable them to earn their livelihood and provide for those dependent on them, he would provide them with new boats. All in distress and trouble received help from the Duke, who seemed ever to anticipate their wants. There is a row of cottages in Golspie known as the Duchess' Cottages, where those who have no home find a roof to cover their heads.

At various times in the year tea, sugar, garments, sticks and coals were distributed to the deserving poor with a lavish hand, and many a blessing have the recipients called down on the Duke's head.

Both the crofters and fishermen have been specially catered for by the Duke. For the former a cattle show was inaugurated and handsome prizes offered for the best exhibits to encourage initiative in farming. This venture has been a great success, and the stock now put forward at these annual shows speaks volumes for the scheme.

The fishermen have had bestowed upon them reading and recreation rooms, where of a wintry evening they can pleasantly while away the time. The Duke was interested in all the good and charitable works in the county, and has done an immense amount of good to the people. Along with the Duchess, he was always on the outlook to improve the condition of the people, and even went the length of paying for the education of some of their sons and daughters. At present in various parts of

GREAT FIRE AT STEWARTON.

WOOLLEN MILLS IN RUINS.

DAMAGE £3000.

200 WORKPEOPLE OUT OF EMPLOYMENT.

The hosiery factory known as Robertland Mills, belonging to Messrs. Wm. Hannah & Sons, wool spinners, and situated at the river bank, Stewarton, was yesterday practically demolished by fire.

The outbreak occurred at the mid-day meal hour, and thanks to this circumstance no lives were endangered, as all the employees had left the building. Had the fire broken out a few minutes earlier, however, there would in all probability have been a loss of life among the workers.

The main building is one of three storeys, and the fire originated in the highest floor shortly after two o'clock.

The Stewarton Fire Brigade turned out, but the pressure of water could not reach the third floor. Kilmarnock Fire Brigade were then summoned by telephone, and Firemaster Campbell and his staff proceeded with the motor fire engine to the fire. The journey, a distance of fully five miles, was accomplished in the remarkably short period of nine minutes.

By this time the roof of the burning building had collapsed. The motor engine, however, proved of great assistance, and with three lines of hose, and strenuous efforts on the part of the firemen, an effective check was put upon the ravages of the flames, and they were prevented from spreading to the engine-house and stores. In other words, they were confined to the main building.

IN THE DANGER ZONE.

Another factory adjoining narrowly escaped destruction, as the flames were being blown in its direction by a strong wind.

For fully two hours the joint fire brigades struggled manfully with the raging tongues of flame, and had the satisfaction of ultimately gaining the mastery of the situation.

When at last the fire had weak and died, however, it was a sorry spectacle that was left, the building having been reduced to a gaunt mass of charred remains.

While the fire was at its height the spectacle was a brilliant one, and provided a great crowd of onlookers with an awe-inspiring sight.

Great sheets of flame leapt skywards to immense heights, and had the conflagration occurred at night it would have lit up the country for miles around. It was beyond doubt the greatest fire that has ever been witnessed in Stewarton.

A great amount of valuable machinery has been destroyed, besides large quantities of yarn and manufactured goods. It is impossible as yet to accurately estimate the damage, but the loss must be nearly £3000. The loss is covered by insurance. The factory is, of course, closed to-day and fully 200 employees are thrown idle.

SCOTTISH BOMB OUTRAGE.

DALKEITH PALACE DISCOVERY.

CHAPEL NEARLY BLOWN UP.

INFERNAL MACHINE IN HEATING ROOM.

A DEFECT SAVES THE BUILDING.

PAST WARNINGS.

The fears that were entertained some little time ago that Dalkeith Palace, the seat of the Duke of Buccleuch, would be made the object of a Suffragette attack have proved to have been only too well founded.

A bomb has been found in the chapel on the estate, which embraces the burial aisle of the Buccleuch family, and but for the timely discovery it is believed that the stately edifice would have been greatly damaged if not entirely wrecked.

When it first became known that the Suffragettes had marked out the historic house for their destructive work the Palace and estate were closely guarded, but if this supervision has been kept up the militant women have been able to evade the guards and almost complete their design.

As in England, in thus attempting to wreck such a building as the Duke of Buccleuch's Chapel, the Suffragettes have shown that in their zeal for votes no associations with the past are sacred.

Nothing could have so clearly demonstrated this as the placing of a bomb in St. Paul's Cathedral, which, perhaps excepting only Westminster Abbey, is regarded by all Englishmen as their most cherished historical pile.

If such attempts as the one made at Dalkeith are followed by the Suffragettes in Scotland with others the authorities may find that it will be necessary as it has been in England totally to exclude the public from what have been their favourite haunts for becoming acquainted with Britain of former days.

Since July last year, when a bomb was found in Mr. McKenna's room at the Home Office, there have been sixteen discoveries of supposed infernal machines.

Only two of the bombs are known to have exploded, but it is probable that some of the destructive fires have been started in this way.

DEATH OF THE BIG-HEARTED DUKE

THE 4th Duke of Sutherland passed away in June at Dunrobin Castle, Golspie. He was 63-years-old, and had contracted pleurisy, which was followed by heart complications.

The Duke was an outstanding figure in the history of the Scottish Highlands, with a varied and interesting.career.

The Duke was born in 1851 and succeeded his father in 1892, a move generally welcomed by the people on his estates since for long before his succession they had come to hold him in the highest respect, largely because of his disposition and his kindness towards them.

He devoted a good deal of time to politics and municipal work, while the Army and the Territorial force also had a share of his enthusiasm. Whatever cause he entered, he did so wholeheartedly.

It was the late Duke's ancestor, the 1st Duke, who began the movement to bring the infrastructure of the Highlands into line with the southern counties. At that time it was said that there was not such a thing in the north as a decently constructed road.

Through the efforts of the 1st Duke, a grant from Parliament was secured for the construction of roads and bridges. Subsequent holders of the title continued the process, with the result that roads and bridges increased in both quality and quantity.

The 4th Duke excelled his ancestors efforts in many ways. He always had the interests of his tenantry at heart and was liberal in his dealings with them. For the prosperity and welfare of the crofters, he did more than would have been possible through an Act of Parliament.

He was open to the smallest request for help and everyone received his personal attention.

His tenants looked upon him not simply as a landlord but as a friend whom they could approach at any time they found themselves in adverse circumstances.

COMINGS...

Jo Grimond
Liberal Party Leader

Record Bargains in ROYAL WORCESTER CORSETS.

TRERON et Cie.,
(SAUCHIEHALL STREET, GLASGOW.)
GREAT SUMMER SALE.

SUFFRAGETTE BOMB OUTRAGE

In May, the suffragette movement's bombing campaign spread north of the border when an explosive device was discovered in the chapel of Dalkeith Palace, the seat of the Duke of Buccleuch. The palace was the latest high-profile target in the increasingly violent "guerrilla" campaign being waged by suffragettes. In the past few months, 10 Downing Street, St Paul's Cathedral, Kew Gardens and Regent's Park – all in London – had all been attacked. Fortunately, the Dalkeith bomb was discovered and made safe before it could detonate.

GLASGOW CENTRE FOR ULSTER GUN RUNNERS

During the second half of the year it became increasingly obvious to the authorities that Glasgow had become the departure point for weapons being smuggled to Loyalists in the north of Ireland. The weapons – rifles, bayonets and ammunition – were originating not only in Glasgow itself but from other parts of the British mainland, such as Newcastle and London, and several consignments had been seized by detectives in Glasgow, Belfast and Londonderry.

This development came in the wake of a visit to Scotland and England by the Ulster Unionist leader, Sir Edward Carson. Sir Edward had established an Ulster Volunteer Force earlier this year and was calling for the arming of Protestants in order to oppose the parliamentary imposition of Home Rule for Ireland.

GOINGS...

James Howden
Marine Engineer

William Arrol
Bridge Engineer

VAUX'S STOUT
Sold in Large Bottles Everywhere.

Father says:
"A cup of 'Camp's' the finest thing on earth for putting life and go into one; and so delicious, so economical, so easy to prepare. he'd never be without it." Just you try it yourself.

CAMP COFFEE
Sold by all Grocers, everywhere.
R. Pa'erson & Sons, Ld., Glasgow.

THIS SPORTING LIFE

FOOTBALL	RUGBY UNION	GOLF	HORSE RACING	SHINTY
Scottish Champions Rangers	*Scotland vs England* England 3–0 Scotland at Twickenham	*British Open Winner* J. H. Taylor at Hoylake, England (304)	*Scottish Grand National Winner* *Couvrefeu II* at Bogside	*Camanachd Cup Winners* Beauly at Kingussie
Scottish Cup Winners Falkirk				

CITY EDITION.

£200 FOR PAPER HA'PENNIES. SEE GRAND NEW COMPETITION IN THIS WEEK'S SCOTTISH WEEKLY RECORD. OUT TO-MORROW.

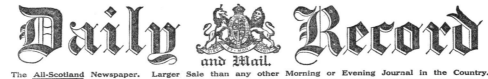

Daily Record and Mail

The All-Scotland Newspaper. Larger Sale than any other Morning or Evening Journal in the Country.

ADVERTISING REDUCES THE EXPENSE OF SELLING GOOD PRODUCTS, HENCE ADVERTISED GOODS ARE BEST VALUE.

ESTAB. 1847—NO. 21,062 | GLASGOW, WEDNESDAY, JULY 29, 1914 | TEN PAGES: ONE HALFPENNY.

AUSTRIAN DECLARATION OF WAR.

SERVIA'S FEVERISH PREPARATIONS FOR DEFENCE.

THE FIRST ACT OF HOSTILITY.

LOCALISING THE AREA OF CONFLICT.

GERMANY AND THE CONFERENCE PROPOSALS.

REPLY TO SIR EDWARD GREY.

The formal declaration of war was published at Vienna yesterday in a special edition of the Official Gazette. It is worded as follows:—

"The Royal Government of Servia not having given a satisfactory reply to the Note presented to it by the Austro-Hungarian Minister in Belgrade on July 23, 1914, the Imperial and Royal Government of Austria-Hungary finds it necessary itself to safeguard its rights and interests, and to have recourse for this purpose to force of arms.

"Austria-Hungary, therefore, considers itself from this moment in a state of war with Servia.

(Signed) "COUNT BERCHTOLD, Austro-Hungarian Minister for Foreign Affairs."

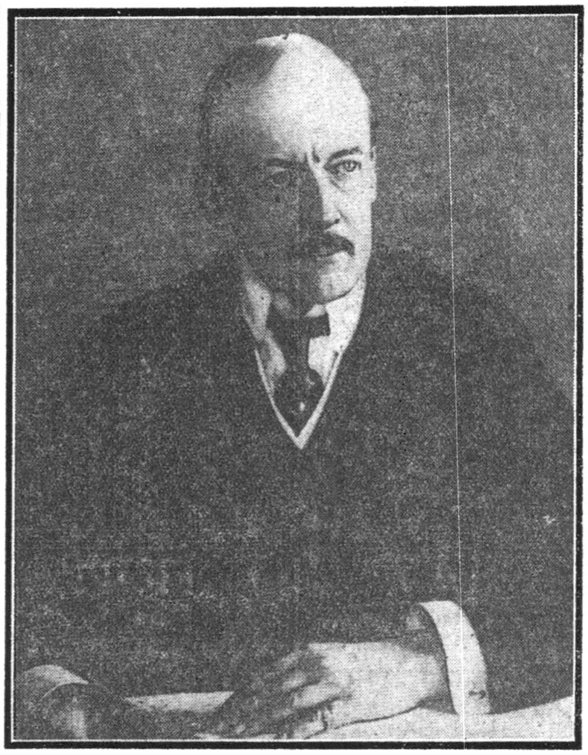

Count Berchtold, the Austro-Hungarian Foreign Minister, who signed the declaration of war.

FIGHTING BEGUN.

("Times" Telegram.)

Berlin, Tuesday.

The "Vossische Zeitung" reports from Vienna that fighting has begun on the Drina River between Bosnia and Servia. Servian Volunteers forced a passage, but lost many killed and wounded.

Further south, Servians are said to have pushed their pickets as far as Proboj in the Sandjak of Novi Bazar, where they are in contact with the Montenegrins.

The Drina is a tributary of the Save, and forms the boundary between Bosnia, which now belongs to Austria and Servia.—*(Per Press Association.)*

The Austro-Hungarian Government, as the telegram given above shows, has officially notified Servia of the declaration of war.

Almost simultaneously the Viennese newspapers made what is regarded as an inspired statement to the effect that Austria is in entire agreement with Sir E. Grey's desire to localise the conflict, but, as regards the suspension of military operations, things have gone much too far to allow anything to be done in that direction

The declaration of war has removed all ground for speculation on that head, but, while it destroys the hope which had been entertained that a conflict might be avoided, it does not, it will be seen, necessarily modify that of restriction of the area

The Austro-Hungarian Ambassador made a late call at the Foreign Office yesterday afternoon, and it is understood that his Excellency conveyed to the Department the grave news of Austria's decision. Subsequently Sir Edward Grey received from Servia confirmation of the news that war had been actually declared.

Mr. Asquith is a very infrequent visitor to Departments other than his own,

AUSTRIA.

SIR E. GREY'S SPEECH

INSPIRED STATEMENT BY NEWSPAPERS.

(Through Reuter's Agency.)

Vienna, Tuesday.

The evening newspapers publish the following evidently inspired statement:—

"In well-informed circles the view is held that, as far as the aim of Sir Edward Grey's proposals is to localise the conflict between Austria-Hungary and Servia, Austria-Hungary can declare herself in entire agreement with Sir Edward Grey's remarks; but as regards what he said as to the suspension of military operations, things have proceeded much too far to allow anything to be done in this direction."

A military censorship has been established at the central telegraph office.

In well-informed quarters Sir Edward Grey's speech is regarded as a good sign. It is remarked that it is natural and logical that an attempt to maintain peace should be made in this question, which affects the whole of Europe. The English proposal can, it is thought, only have the object of localising the dispute between Austria-Hungary and Servia.

It is also pointed out that, as a matter of fact, Sir Edward Grey has principally dealt with the differences with Russia, and that, in so far as the British proposal relates to the localisation of the dispute, people in Austria can be in agreement with it.

To-day's settlement on the Vienna Bourse passed off smoothly, and there were no failures.

There was a somewhat severe run yesterday and to-day on the First Austrian Savings Bank, the most important deposit institution in the Monarchy, a sum of £250,000 being paid out to 7000 depositors; but, on the other hand, over £83,000 were paid in by a thousand depositors.

The management state that, in contrast with their behaviour in the previous Balkan crisis, the public are keeping their heads and maintaining a very patriotic attitude. The bank, it is added, is prepared to pay a more confident feeling prevailed in the city yesterday, and, although both post and telegraph communication with Austria-Hungary is interrupted, and the only connection with Europe is the telegraph line from Belgrade to Kladovo and Bukharest, all sorts of reports alleged to be well founded and favourable to Servia spread everywhere. Confidence in this news increased by the fact that no hostilities occurred either on Sunday or to-day, and feeling is increasing that war may still be avoided.

Nevertheless military defence preparations are being carried on with feverish activity, and concentration of troops in different fortified positions is proceeding in complete order in spite of the short time at the authorities' disposal. The army headquarters will be established at Karsevac. General Pavlovics is acting temporarily as chief of the general staff.

Yesterday news of the arrest of General Putnik at Buda Pest became known through the newspapers. It was first received with incredulity, but when it was confirmed it aroused everywhere feelings of the deepest bitterness.

Perfect order prevails throughout Belgrade, and the police duties are being carried out by a volunteer corps of gendarmerie composed of students. According to the newspapers, 2000 volunteers had been enrolled at noon to-day. Red Cross flags are floating in various directions over the capital.

The German Minister, Baron von Grissinger, with other foreign representatives left for Nisch last Saturday.

King Peter arrived in the capital yesterday evening, and after a short stay returned to Riberska Banya, where he is undergoing the cure.

STEAMERS CAPTURED.

(Through Reuter's Agency.)

Nisch, Monday.

The Servian steamer Deligrad was taken possession of at Orchava by Austrians, and the passengers on board were detained.

The Austrians at once hauled down the Servian colours and replaced them with their own.

An Austrian tug, which had already the Servian steamer Morava, as well as several barges, took the Deligrad in tow.

exhorts its subjects to retain their reticence and tranquility, it rests confidently on the guardianship of the dignity and interests of Russia.

The "Petersburgski Kurier" learns from the Foreign Office that Great Britain's demarche was taken on her own initiative, and was not dictated by the Russian Government, which, for the time being, regards her diplomatic mission towards Austria-Hungary as accomplished.

The newspapers are unanimous in considering Servia's reply as adequate.

GERMANY.

CONFERENCE PROPOSAL.

UNFAVOURABLE OFFICIAL VIEW.

(Through Reuter's Agency.)

Berlin, Tuesday.

The following statement was made to Reuter's correspondent in an official quarter this morning:—

"Despite our sincere approval of Sir Edward Grey's object, and our sympathy with his efforts for the preservation of peace, we are unable to see that his idea of a Conference in London offers any prospect of finding a way out of the difficulty.

"Austria cannot consent to appear before a European tribunal like a Balkan State, and explain her actions, and allow her policy to be influenced by the decisions of such a Court.

"We are convinced that Russia, too, would not consent to such a course. As for Germany, she would be glad to join in any action which offered a prospect of success, but we cannot participate in an effort which offers none, and in our opinion an Ambassadorial Conference in London is calculated to increase rather than diminish the difficulties of the situation.

"The German Foreign Office is of opinion that conversations between the Powers will afford a better means to the desired end than the proposed Conference.

"It considers that, with the assurance that Austria intends not to annex any portion of Servian territory, and being well aware that Servia deserves chastisement, it should be content to stand aside until the Austrian military measures against Servia are completed, when opportunity might

WILD RIOT IN GLASGOW.

MRS. PANKHURST ARRESTED.

POLICE STORM THE PLATFORM.

WOMEN'S STUBBORN FIGHT.

REVOLVER SHOTS IN ST. ANDREW'S HALLS.

SEVERAL PERSONS INJURED.

Amid a scene of wild riot in St. Andrew's Hall, Glasgow, last night, Mrs. Pankhurst, the suffragette leader, was arrested. The meeting, which was held under the auspices of the W.S.P.U., had an audience of about 5000, the vast majority of whom were ladies.

Mrs. Pankhurst, despite the vigilance of the police, entered the hall by one of the main entrances wearing a large picture hat with a yellow feather and trimmings, and a thick black veil.

The Chairwoman, Lady Isabel Margesson, had scarcely taken her seat on the patform before Mrs. Pankhurst, who had come in by a side door, rose from her seat in the centre of a crowded platform, and, throwing off her hat and a dark cloak she wore, dramatically advanced to a place beside the president. But she appeared to be suffering from extreme nervousness.

Mrs. Pankhurst was greeted with a wild outburst of cheering.

The introductory remarks of Lady Isabel Margesson were very brief. She contented herself with merely introducing Mrs. Pankhurst.

Opening her address, Mrs. Pankhurst said, "I have kept my programme, and, in spite of His Majesty's Government, I am here to-night.

"Very few people in this audience, very few people in this country, know how much of the nation's money is being spent to silence women (Cries of "Shame"), but the wit and ingenuity of women has overcome the power of money and of the British Government."

TRIUMPH OF MILITANCY.

Continuing, Mrs. Pankhurst said it was well they should have that meeting that night, because in the House of Commons that day was being witnessed the triumph of militancy—men's militancy—and she hoped to make it clear to the people at that meeting that if there was any distinction to be drawn at all between the militancy in Ulster and the militancy of women, it was all to the advantage of the women. ("Hear, hear.")

She proposed that night to have a text. Texts were usually given from the pulpit. Her text was equal justice for men and women, equal political justice; equal legal justice; equal industrial justice, and equal social justice.

While Mrs. Pankhurst was speaking a lady steward hurriedly approached one of the platform party seated in the front row and excitedly whispered something to her. At the same moment there was a rush of half a dozen male stewards to the area door on the left of the platform.

The door was burst open to the accompaniment of a cheer from the corridor, and the forms of several stalwart detectives were seen backed by a mass of policemen in uniform.

STORY OF THE ARREST.

The platform was in uproar. The ladies in the two front rows scrambled to the edge of the platform, and half a dozen of them made a ring round Mrs. Pankhurst whose speech had come suddenly to a conclusion.

Before the leading officers could reach the platform an excited lady in a blue jacket flourished a diminutive iron hammer as if daring them to approach.

Several women who had been seated in the front row of the audience in the area rose up to bar the progress of the police, who were now streaming through the doorway. But the policemen, tolerating no obstruction, pushed the women back, upset the Press tables, which had been precipitately vacated, and drew up in a line with batons drawn across the hall.

A combined rush was made to scale the platform, but the excited occupants offered the resistance of violence. The weapons of defence were various, women suddenly crushed to the front wielding Indian clubs. Simultaneously the flower pots fringing the platform were thrown in the faces of the attackers.

Then a resourceful woman, observing that Inspector Walker had almost gained a foothold on the platform, picked up a chair and rammed one of the legs against his face. Fortunately it caught him on the forehead and not in the eye.

The operations of the women were diverted by bodies of policemen, who forced their way on to the platform by the two side entrances.

THE WORLD PLUNGES INTO WAR

EUROPE was a political tinderbox in 1914 and on July 28 came the spark that unleashed the horrors of the First World War.

A young Bosnian terrorist, Gavrilo Princip, assassinated the heir to the Hapsburg throne, Archduke Ferdinand of Austria-Hungary during a visit to Sarajevo in Serbia.

A formal declaration of war with Serbia was issued from Vienna and appeared in a special edition of the Official Gazette. It was worded as follows:

"The Royal Government of Serbia not having given a satisfactory reply to the note presented to it by the Austria-Hungarian Minister in Belgrade on July 23, 1914, the Imperial and Royal Government of Austria-Hungary finds it necessary itself to safeguard its rights and interests, and to have recourse for this purpose to force of arms.

"Austria-Hungary, therefore, considers, itself from this moment in a state of war with Serbia."

Because of the complicated and inter-related network of alliances between the various European states, this single declaration triggered a domino effect which by mid August embroiled all the Central European Powers in the War to End All Wars: on one side, Germany, Austria-Hungary, and their allies and on the other, the Triple Entente of Britain and the British Empire, France, Russia and their allies.

Initially, there was much enthusiasm for the war on all sides and thousands of men marched off to war in a patriotic haze.

The full horrors of modern warfare only became apparent once the senseless slaughter in the trenches had begun.

FAMOUS HAMPDEN VICTORY

While conflict loomed on the international stage, people's attentions at home were turned, perhaps albeit briefly, to a battle of another sort. At Hampden in April, Scotland met the Auld Enemy once again and on this occasion, proved too strong for them. The first half was an evenly fought affair with neither side able to break down the others defence. After the interval however, the Scots stepped up a gear and gradually took control of the game, so much so that the final score of 3-1 to the Scots flattered the visitors.

I SMILE all the WHILE I use GLOSSO because-

1. It saves time

YOU will get your polishing done quickly if you use GLOSSO. It gives a brilliant shine *in half the time*. You save time, too, because metals cleaned with GLOSSO *retain* their brilliant shine much longer. The Glosso shine lasts, so that you do not have to polish so often. Time is money—GLOSSO saves time.

GLOSSO
THE ONE-MINUTE METAL POLISH

A FREE SAMPLE will be sent on receipt of a POST CARD bearing your own *and your dealer's* name and address to Dept. G 27,

HARGREAVES BROS. & CO. LTD.
The 'Gipsy Black Lead' People,
HULL.

SUFFRAGETTE RIOT AS MRS PANKHURST ARRESTED

There were chaotic scenes at St Andrews Halls in Glasgow in March when police attempted to prevent Mrs Emmeline Pankhurst addressing a meeting of over 5000 suffragettes and their supporters. Mrs Pankhurst had evaded the police surrounding the hall by using a disguise and was greeted by wild cheering from the floor when she took the stage. She had barely begun her speech advocating political, social and employment equality when a band of stewards and police rushed the platform. In the chaos that followed, Mrs Pankhurst was arrested and taken away in a waiting police car.

COMINGS...

Tom Weir
Hillwalker & Broadcaster

GOINGS...

John Muir
Pioneering Environmentalist & Creator of the Yosemite National Park in the USA

WAVERLEY CIGARETTES
10 FOR 3d.
The manufacturers make them good.
Smokers make them popular.

THIS SPORTING LIFE

FOOTBALL	RUGBY UNION	GOLF	HORSE RACING	SHINTY
Scottish Champions Celtic	*Scotland vs England* Scotland 15–16 England at Inverleith	*British Open Winner* Harry Vardon at Prestwick (306)	*Scottish Grand National Winner* Scarabec at Bogside	*Camanachd Cup Winners* Kingussie at Glasgow
Scottish Cup Winners Celtic				

CITY EDITION.

Daily Record and Mail.

The All-Scotland Newspaper. Four Times the Sale of any other Morning Journal in the Country.

ESTAB. 1847—NO. 21,323　　　GLASGOW, MONDAY, MAY 24, 1915.　　　ONE HALFPENNY

Four Crown
Whisky Regd
The Sovereign Whisky of the Age.
ROBERT BROWN LIMITED, GLASGOW.

10,000
RECRUITS WANTED
AT ONCE
TO AUGMENT
GLASGOW'S
TERRITORIAL REGIMENTS.

LIKE NEUVE CHAPELLE.

TRAGIC HOME-COMING OF GLASGOW SOLDIER.

BLOOD-WELCOME TO SCOTTISH SOIL.

HELPING THE DOCTORS

If we ask ourselves why the disaster should so move and shock the nerves, even in days when the individual life is held more cheaply than ever before, the words of one of the soldier survivors, who told his story on reaching Glasgow on Saturday evening, will be sufficient answer.

Private G. Duncan Gordon, 2nd Gordons, who was janitor at Keppochill School before volunteering for service at the outbreak of war, had passed through Neuve Chapelle, not scatheless—he received a slight arm wound—but dry-eyed.

Tough and seasoned, with the memory of trench shambles and hospital sufferings, he nevertheless admitted a tear at Gretna Green.

Perhaps in that lies the painful contrast between slaughter on the field and death and holocaust through avoidable accident. Private Gordon felt this and expressed it in his own way.

But the effects of the disaster he must describe as "like nothing so much as a miniature Neuve Chapelle."

AFTER SEVEN MONTHS' FIGHTING.

He emphasised the tragedy of his home-coming, which other soldiers coming north have shared. After seven months absence, with the most critical fighting in it, he had been invalided home and had spent a few convalescent days at Margate. His furlough of seven days was to be spent at his Glasgow home, and he was just experiencing the Scots' jubilation at once again getting a glimpse of his native land when the London express in which he was travelling crashed into the debris of the first collision.

Habituated with the unexpected, he and his comrades, one of whom was a 6th Gordon, laughed, saying "we're damned near home, but we had better not crow till we're there." He left the train and ran

Lieut.-Colonel W. Carmichael Peebles, T.D., Commander of the 5th Royal Scots. (Collart.)

MEN OF GOVAN, CLYDEBANK, and PARKHEAD, DRINK

Tuborg
DANISH
LAGER BEER

It's refreshing, it's satisfying, and it's a drink, no matter whether you're hot or cold, you'll enjoy, but, what is more important, it won't impair your efficiency in the least.

BURNING MEN.

AGONIES WHICH COULD NOT BE ALLEVIATED.

SOLDIERS' PITEOUS PLEA.

DYING MEN IMPLORE RESCUERS TO SHOOT THEM.

EYE-WITNESS'S GRAPHIC STORY OF COLLISION.

A young farmer, who was probably the only eye-witness of the actual disaster, gave a vivid impression of what he had witnessed.

"My home is just over the way there," he said, pointing to a house a little beyond the field where the dead were lying, "and I was just finishing breakfast when I was startled by a terrific crash.

"I did not know what had caused it, but, surmising that something terrible had happened on the railway—for we are only too familiar with mishaps in this part of Dumfriesshire—I rushed from the house, and, looking towards the railway line, I was horrified to see the north-going Glasgow express dash into a mass of wreckage.

"I realised then what had been the cause of the crash which I had heard at breakfast. A collision had already taken place, and I had just been in time to witness the second.

"The scene at such comparatively close proximity was terrifying, and I had scarcely grasped the horror of it all when I was appalled to observe the whole mass of wreckage burst into flames.

"So far as I can recall, there was no smoke or fire until the second collision took place. A dreadful quietness seemed to hang over the place for a second or two, and then I saw figures running and crawling from the vicinity of the wreck.

"Without loss of time, I dashed across the intervening fields to render what assistance I could, but before I had reached the embankment the flames had got a good hold of the smashed carriages.

PARALYSED WITH HORROR

"An awesome scene presented itself as I approached. I saw a number of khaki-clad figures running distractedly about the wreckage, from which there came piercing screams and groans.

"At first the men seemed paralysed with horror, for they knew what I did not know at the moment of my arrival, that underneath the burning woodwork were hundreds of their companions.

"The men, however, speedily regained their nerve, and set about the work of rescue with promptitude. I immediately offered my services, and, although the work was heartbreaking, I did my best.

"The sights I witnessed will not be forgotten. One man was pinned beneath a huge mass of wreckage. The upper portion of his body seemed to have escaped injury, and he was quite conscious, but the frightful part of his predicament was that his legs seemed to me to be only charred stumps. He was removed after the greatest exertion on the part of the rescuers.

"Another man it was found impossible to remove from the debris until his hands were amputated.

"But the most terrible cases were those of men who had been scorched by the flames and were suffering agonies which we could not alleviate, for nobody could get near them, and, even if they could have done so, rescue would have been im-

WHAT CAUSED THE EXPLOSIONS?

NOT THE AMMUNITION WAGONS.

UNCOUPLED BY SOLDIERS' GALLANTRY.

(From Our Own Correspondent.)
Carlisle, Sunday.

At Carlisle Castle, the depot of the Border Regiment, our Carlisle representative this morning interviewed an officer and several men of the Royal Scots, from whom he obtained some new facts concerning the disaster. He also obtained the official return of the regiment as affected by the catastrophe.

It was thought on Saturday that only A and B Companies were affected, but C and D Companies have also suffered. This return is as follows:—

Killed, identified,	48
Killed, not identified,	114
Missing,	88
Injured,	154
Slightly injured,	66
Total,	470

Of the 66 men taken to Carlisle Castle 53 were only slightly injured, and were sent home on Saturday. The 13 remaining are all minor losses.

It is believed that B Company has been almost wiped out. Our representative interviewed this morning several men of the ammunition section. They stated that at the rear of the troop train were ammunition wagons; but the assumption that these wagons caused the violent explosions which followed the collision is incorrect. The explosions came from the gas tanks of the train immediately after the collision.

Such of the men of the ammunition section as were uninjured ran to the ammunition wagons, and, though in their stockinged feet and wearing nothing but their shirts and trousers—for they had been sleeping with most of their clothes off—they uncoupled the wagons, pushed them back, and then removed the ammunition to a position outside the danger zone.

COLONEL PEEBLES' HEROISM.

Private D. Rennie, one of these men, said—"There were about thirty men in our coach, and out of these four have been saved. I was sleeping when the collision occurred, but caught hold of the carriage rack and swung myself clear.

"The bravest men on the whole scene after the disaster," said Private Rennie, "were Colonel Peebles, our colonel, and a R.A.M.C. officer, whose name I do not know. Colonel Peebles threw off his coat and we among the flames with tools, breaking carriages and fighting to save the men."

Sergeant Robertson, explaining what happened in the collision, said in the first crash his coach toppled over to the left and the adjoining coach toppled over to the right. The latter was crashed into by the London express. Apparently all the men in it were killed, but the men in his coach escaped in rather a singular way. The coach toppled on to the trucks of a goods train stationed on the siding. Had the train not been there the coach would have

LIEUT.-COL. STANSFELD BADLY WOUNDED.

Official notifications have been received in Montrose of casualties sustained during last week-end, and these are heavy.

Lieut.-Colonel J. R. E. Stansfeld, D.S.O., nephew of Captain Stansfeld, of Dunnineld Castle, Montrose, who had already been twice wounded, has on this occasion met with injuries of a grave nature. He was Commanding Officer of the 2nd Battalion, Gordon Highlanders, and in leading his battalion on Saturday last he had both legs broken, his right limb having to be subsequently amputated.

Lieut.-Colonel Stansfeld got his D.S.O. in South Africa, where he acted as railway

MUSSELBURGH OFFICER

Sec.-Lieut. Ernest A. Meldrum (2/8th Gurkha Rifles), who has been killed in action.

staff officer. He took part in the relief of Ladysmith, and served elsewhere in Natal, the Transvaal and the Orange River Colony. He was captain and adjutant of the 2nd Gordon Highlanders when he went to the front, and has been several times mentioned in dispatches. His commission dates from October, 1899, and he was for a term adjutant of the 5th (Buchan and Formartine) Gordons.

Mr. A. Crowe, slater, 13 Christie's Lane, on Wednesday night received a field post-card stating that his third son, Sergeant Albert Crowe, had been killed in action. Sergeant Crowe, who had been attached to the 2nd Black Watch for the past six years, came from India with the Expeditionary Force and spent a short furlough in Montrose two months ago. He was quite a young man.

Sergeant James M'Innes, postman, who as a reservist became attached to the 3rd Gordons on the outbreak of war, and joined the 1st Battalion (to which he originally belonged) at the front ten months ago, lies in Eastbourne Red Cross Hospital with seven wounds. He was wounded on Saturday and has been operated upon, but has to undergo another operation. His wife resides in Bents Road.

INVERNESS MEN FALL.

LIEUT. URQUHART AMONG THE KILLED.

The Cameron Battalions in Flanders appear from unofficial reports already received to have had their full share in the

1915

226 DIE IN TROOP TRAIN CRASH

A MULTIPLE train crash on the Glasgow-London line in May claimed the lives of 226 people, including 214 Scottish soldiers.

The accident happened when a crowded troop train was one of five involved in a series of collisions at Quintinshill, near Gretna, 10 miles north of Carlisle.

Errors by signalmen were thought to have been responsible for what was the highest death toll in British railway history.

Shortly before 7am, the southbound troop train, heading from Larbert to Liverpool docks, crashed headlong into a Carlisle-Glasgow passenger train that was standing at Quintinshill. Its coaches were crushed, and as survivors struggled to escape, their train was then hit by an express travelling north.

Two other trains also waiting at Quintinshill also became entangled in the wreckage.

The trains then became engulfed in flames as the cylinders of the gas-lit troop train ignited. and in the course of a few minutes, half a battalion was wiped out.

Little more than 50 survivors answered the roll call after the disaster.

Ironically, many of the victims had survived the carnage of Flanders.

The whole neighbourhood was roused by the noise of the crashes and news of the tragedy was broadcast widely by telephone and telegram. This brought doctors and ambulance men, railwaymen and military officials together to form a massive rescue operation.

The magnitude of the disaster seemed too great to grasp and a more terrible scene was hard to imagine.

Morning mists had disappeared to show the beautiful valley in the bright morning sunshine.

And right in the middle of this beauty lay a tragic scene of horror.

SCOTS CASUALTIES BACK FROM THE FRONT

Over 100 casualties from the Highland regiments – primarily the Gordons and the Cameron Highlanders – returned from Flanders to Perth at the end of September for treatment at local hospitals, chiefly the Royal Infirmary and the local Red Cross hospital. The men had all received their wounds while taking part in a major British offensive to the north and east of Loos the previous week, where the fighting had been severe and the Germans had counter-attacked strongly.

KNITTED WOOL MOTOR WRAP

Suitable for either LADY OR GENTLEMAN.

In all Colours. Club Stripes &c. &c.

CASH ORDERS POST FREE

Write for ILLUST^D CATALOGUE

1/1½ BETTER QUALITIES 2/11½ & 3/11½

MOORE, TAGGART & C^O. CASH DRAPERS. CROSS · GLASGOW.

COMINGS...

David Stirling
Founder of the SAS

Ewan MacColl
Folk Singer

GOINGS...

James Thin
Bookseller

Mary Slessor
African Missionary

James Keir Hardie
Co-founder of the Labour Party

CRICKET. TENNIS. GOLF. CROQUET.

NEW SEASON'S DISPLAY.

LARGEST AND FINEST IN SCOTLAND.

Our Spacious Saloons are now fully equipped with Requisites for All Summer Games, and we cordially invite inspection. Our Large Output enables us to offer Goods at the Lowest Possible Prices.

CRICKET BATS—Our Stock this year is unique, comprising some of the Choicest Timber to be had. The Bats have been personally selected, and are wonderful value.

BALLS, STUMPS, BAGS, LEG-GUARDS, NETS, &c.

TENNIS. TENNIS.

Every care has been taken to secure the Finest Possible Selection of Racquets. Prices range from 6s 6d, and constitute the best value obtainable. Satisfaction is assured.

SLAZENGERS AND AYRES BALLS.

POSTS, NETS, MARKERS, BAGS, &c.

All Repairs Executed on the Premises by Practical Workmen.

70-Page ILLUSTRATED CATALOGUE POST FREE.

F. A. LUMLEY'S ATHLETIC STORES

80 and 82 SAUCHIEHALL STREET

(RENFIELD STREET CORNER),

GLASGOW.

THE BEST SCOTCH WHISKIES.

LANG'S LIQUEUR

AND

TAM O' SHANTER.

PROPRIETORS—

LANG BROS., LTD., GLASGOW.

WOMEN PULL THEIR WEIGHT

As more and more men enlisted, so the opportunities became available for women to break through the barriers of male-only industries. This was true, not only for war work like munitions, but in day-to-day jobs such as cab- and tram-driving. In Edinburgh in October, the latest addition to the ranks of working women included coal-carters.

THIS SPORTING LIFE

FOOTBALL	RUGBY UNION	GOLF	HORSE RACING	SHINTY
Scottish Champions Celtic	*Scotland vs England* No game played	*British Open Winner* No competition held	*Scottish Grand National Winner* Templedowney at Bogside	*Camanachd Cup Winners* No competition held
Scottish Cup Winners No competition held				

ALL THE LATEST WAR NEWS & PICTURES

APPEAR IN TO-MORROW'S

Weekly Mail and Record

THE BRIGHTEST AND BEST
SUNDAY PAPER PUBLISHED.

CITY EDITION

Daily and Mail. Record

The All-Scotland Newspaper. Four Times the Sale of any other Morning Journal in the Country.

ESTAB. 1847—NO. 21,592   GLASGOW, SATURDAY, APRIL 1, 1916   ONE HALFPENNY

A NATIONAL MINISTRY.

MR. LLOYD GEORGE ESSAYS ITS FORMATION.

MR. BONAR LAW TO CO-OPERATE.

DRAMATIC GATHERINGS AT THE KING'S PALACE.

Press Bureau, Wednesday, 10.10 p.m.

The Right Hon. David Lloyd George, M.P., had an audience with his Majesty the King this afternoon, and was requested by his Majesty to form a Government.

He has consented to undertake this task, with the co-operation of the Right Hon. A. Bonar Law, M.P.

KING'S ACTIVITIES.

ROUND TABLE CONFERENCE AT THE PALACE.

(From Our Own Correspondent.)

London, Wednesday Night.

There has been another dramatic development in the political situation this evening.

Mr. Lloyd George has been entrusted by the King with the formation of a National Ministry, which he will seek to constitute regardless of party differences.

In this supremely important task Mr. Bonar Law has agreed to co-operate with him.

This morning it was assumed that Mr. Bonar Law, who was summoned to an audience with the King at Buckingham Palace late last night, would undertake the formation of a new Ministry. The Unionist leader, however, after a fully occupied forenoon, went again to the Palace at one o'clock to-day and conveyed to the King the intimation that he was unable to comply with his Majesty's request.

Later in the day the King summoned Mr. Lloyd George to the Palace.

All the other Ministers were invited, and they began to arrive some time after Mr. Lloyd George had been closeted with his Majesty.

THE PALACE ASSEMBLY.

Among those who attended were Mr. Bonar Law, Mr. Balfour (who was out for the first time after his recent indisposition), Mr. Arthur Henderson, and Mr. Herbert Samuel.

Mr. Asquith, who motored from Downing Street, was the last to arrive.

The conference broke up shortly after 4.30.

Mr. Asquith was the first to drive away, and it was noticed that he appeared gravely concerned.

Mr. Lloyd George followed shortly afterwards.

Then came Mr. Henderson, Mr. Balfour, and Mr. Bonar Law, who were together, being the last to leave.

The King throughout the crisis has been unremitting in his efforts to bring about a solution, and his summoning of to-day's round table conference at the Palace has been the most significant incident of to-day's doings. The pur-

pledging the group to support any Government formed to carry out Mr. Lloyd George's policy.

PALACE AUDIENCES.

OFFICIAL ACCOUNT OF THE PROCEEDINGS.

The Court Circular of yesterday evening states:—

The King summoned the Right Hon. A. Bonar Law, M.P., to an audience last evening, and invited him to form an Administration.

The King held a conference this afternoon, at which the following were present:—

The Right Hon. A. J. Balfour, the Right Hon. H. H. Asquith, the Right Hon. D. Lloyd George, the Right Hon. A. Bonar Law, and the Right Hon. Arthur Henderson.

The King gave a further audience this evening to the Right Hon. A. Bonar Law, M.P., who intimated to his Majesty that he was unable to form an Administration.

The King summoned to an audience the Right Hon. D. Lloyd George, M.P., who undertook, at his Majesty's request, to endeavour to form an Administration.

TO-DAY'S PARLIAMENT.

Press Bureau, Wednesday, 7.50 p.m.

The House of Commons will meet to-day (Thursday) at 2.45 p.m.

In the exceptional circumstances no questions will be answered, and the proceedings will be formal.

The House will adjourn until Monday.

LONDON PRESS OPINION.

FAIRPLAY ASKED FOR THE NEW ADMINISTRATION.

The leading London newspapers have the following comment this morning:—

"Times"—

The "reconstruction crisis" ends in the only practical and straightforward way. The result, we are confident, will be hailed with the deepest satisfaction by the country and the Empire; by our Allies and our well-wishers; while it will chill the hearts of our enemies with a new conviction that we shall wage the war with redoubled vigour in the coming year.

The significance of a Government under the leadership of the Statesman who has been, throughout, the most vigorous and whole-hearted advocate of war to the uttermost cannot be missed. It is the best and most conclusive of answers to the "peace talk" which Germans and German emissaries are now strenuously seeking to revive, and which they will doubtless repeat more insistently now that Bukharest is in their hands.

ZEPPELIN RAID.

LONG LINE OF COAST VISITED.

9 KILLED: 29 INJURED.

Press Bureau, Wednesday, 8 p.m.

The following communique was issued by the Field-Marshal Commander-in-Chief, Home Forces, at 5.50 p.m. to-day:—

Zeppelin Raid.

The Zeppelin raid of last night covered a considerable extent of our eastern coasts. At least five or six airships actually crossed the shore, but reports received from reliable observers made at various times during the night at many points (some so far distant as Rattray Head in Scotland down to the north coast of Norfolk) would point to a possibility of a greater number of airships having been employed off our coasts.

The enemy, however, made only two attempts to penetrate inland.

About one hundred bombs were dropped, scattered over many localities. Their exact number is difficult to give, since a great number fell in uninhabited areas and some others into the sea.

Only in a single locality did the raiders cause any casualties or effect much damage. In this case the bombs which fell amounted to twelve explosive and four incendiary, with the result that eighteen houses were damaged.

6 men (including one soldier) and 3 women killed.

13 men (including 3 soldiers) and 8 women injured.

Total, 36 casualties.

The remaining 70 odd bombs occasioned only two casualties (1 soldier and 1 child slightly injured).

The damage affected one storehouse and a few cottages—mostly broken glass.

The raiders only twice came within the range of our anti-aircraft artillery, and on both occasions retreated out of range without delay.

17 BOMBS IN SCOTLAND.

Replying to Sir H. Daiziel, in the House of Commons yesterday, Mr. Tennant stated that a Zeppelin crossed the coast line on the east of Scotland on Tuesday night and dropped 17 bombs on agricultural land. The result in casualties and damage were nil.

GLASGOW CAR SMASH.

DRIVER SENT TO PRISON FOR ONE MONTH.

A sequel to the alarming tramcar accident which occurred in Bilsland Drive, Glasgow, on January 2, and which resulted in severe injuries to 62 passengers, was heard before Sheriff Thomson in Glasgow yesterday, when the motorman, George Logan, was brought up for trial.

The accused, who was represented by Mr. George Smith of the Town Clerk's office, pleaded not guilty to having driven the car culpably and recklessly. The car, it may be recalled, left the rails, overturned, and collided with a wall.

Evidence was led stating that immediately before the curve at which the accident occurred there was a notice posted by the Corporation warning drivers to proceed with caution.

Mr. David Brown, assistant engineer of rolling stock in the employment of the Corporation, said he examined the car after the accident and found the magnetic brakes working properly. The superstructure of the car was completely destroyed. He examined the rails, and found them in quite good order.

The speed of cars at this point was limited by the Board of Trade to eight miles an hour. That limit was well known to tramway employees. The weight of the car with the passengers on it would probably be fourteen tons.

Mr. John Boyce, an electrician, stated that he was in Bilsland Drive at the time the accident occurred. The car was travelling at an excessive speed. He thought it had not been stopped at the station in Shannon Street. He formed the impression that the car could not take the point whether or not the brakes were applied.

When the brakes were applied the car gave a jump and then ran off the rails. It bumped against the kerb and then fell against the wall. There was a good deal of screaming among the passengers. He assisted in extracting some of the passengers from the body of the car. Some seemed badly injured. About fifteen of them received first aid; others were conveyed to the infirmary.

THE RUNAWAY CAR.

Startling evidence was given by Mr. Malcolm M'Lean, another eye-witness. The car was going at an excessive speed. It did not stop at the station in Shannon Street. A young man ran past witness and told him to run as fast as he could after the car as something was likely to happen. Witness ran to see if he could be of any assistance, and he saw the car jump the rails and crash into the wall.

Margaret Fullerton, the conductor of the car, said accused told her he did not like the type of controller. She noticed accused on one occasion that day leave his controllers while the car was in motion and stand with his back against the door. He also applied the brakes suddenly.

The car did not stop at Shannon Street, and, going down the incline, it seemed to increase in speed. She would not say it was excessive speed, but it was not proper. Witness was injured in the accident about the head and hands, and was two weeks in the infirmary and five weeks off duty as a result of her injuries.

No witnesses appeared for the defence. The accused was found guilty. Mr. Smith asked for a pecuniary penalty, but this was objected to by Mr. J. D. Strathern, who prosecuted, on the ground of the extreme recklessness of Logan.

In this the Sheriff concurred. In the public interest, the very greatest care must be exercised by drivers, and such had been wholly absent in this case. He could not deal more leniently than in passing sentence of one month's imprisonment.

1916

SHERIFF JAILS TRAMCAR DRIVER

TRAMCAR driver George Logan went on trial at Glasgow Sheriff Court in April after an accident in which 62 passengers were badly hurt.

Mr Logan denied having driven the car recklessly but he was found guilty and sentenced to one month's imprisonment by Sheriff Thomson.

The accident took place on January 2 in Bisland Drive, Glasgow, when the tramcar left the rails, overturned and crashed into a wall. The superstructure of the car was destroyed.

An assistant engineer examined the car after the accident and found its magnetic brakes to be working properly.

The assistant engineer also examined the rails and found that they too were in working order.

The Board of Trade speed limit for tramcars at the spot where the accident took place was 8mph. A witness, Mr Boyce, said that he had been in Bisland Drive at the time of the accidentand had seen that that the car had been travelling at an excessive speed. He believed that it could not take the point, whether or not the brakes were applied.

When they were applied, the car gave a jump and ran off the rails. It bumped against the kerb and then fell against the wall. There was much screaming among the passengers, some of whom seemed badly injured. About 15 of them received

first aid at the scene, while others were conveyed to the infirmary.

Another witness also stated that the car had been going at an excessive speed and said that it had not stopped at the Shannon Street station. A young man ran past the witness and told him something was likely to happen. The witness ran to see if he could be of assistance and saw the car jump the rails and crash into the wall.

Sheriff Thomson told driver Logan: "In the public interest, the very greatest care must be exercised by drivers, and such has been wholly absent in this case."

He said he could not deal more leniently than by passing a sentence of one month's imprisonment.

STEAMERS

ALLAN ROYAL MAIL LINE.
GLASGOW to QUEBEC and MONTREAL.
Carthaginian ..Sat July .. i Pretorian ......Sat July 29
GLASGOW to BOSTON.
*Saxon Monarch .... Saturday, July 8
LIVERPOOL to QUEBEC and MONTREAL.
Scandinavian ..Fri. July 14 i Grampian..Fri. July 28
LONDON to QUEBEC and MONTREAL.
*Pomeranian..Wed. July 5 i Corinthian ... Wed. July 12
* Cargo on'y.
Apply to
ALLAN BROS. & CO., U.K., LTD., 25 Bothwell Street.

DONALDSON LINE.
GLASGOW to QUEBEC and MONTREAL.
Athenia ......Sat July 22 i Cassandra ....Sat. Aug. 5
Cabin Fare, £10 10s; 3rd Class, £6 15s. Accommodation unsurpassed. For Cheap Tickets to In'and Points in Canada apply to DONALDSON BROS., LTD., 56 Bothwell Street, Glasgow.

CUNARD LINE.
From LIVERPOOL to NEW YORK.
*Saxonia .....Sat. July 8 | *Carpathia ...Sat. July 15
* Cabin and Third Class Passengers only.
LIVERPOOL to NEW YORK and BOSTON.
Freight Service.
Valeria (New York) ....Sat. July 15
Pruth (Boston) ....Sat. July 22
LONDON to NEW YORK and CANADA.
*Ausonia ..Tues. July 11 | *Pannonia..Tues. July 18
* To Montreal—Cabin (£10) and Third Class (£6 10s)
Passengers.
† To New York—Cabin (£10) and Third Class (£6 15s)
Passengers.
BRISTOL to CANADA.
Folia (to Montreal)................Sat. July 8
From Avonmouth Dock.
Apply to LOCAL AGENTS or CUNARD LINE, 30
Jamaica Street, Glasgow, and Liverpool.

ELLERMAN'S "CITY" LINE.
Owing to the WAR the REGULAR SERVICE is SUSPENDED. The following Special Steamers have been arranged subject to Government requisition, and owing to limited space available and concession at Docks, no Cargo to be sent forward unless space previously booked.
CALCUTTA DIRECT.
Closing
Steamer. Glasgow. Liverpool.
CITY OF EDINBURGH ....July 8 July 17
BOMBAY and KARACHI.
CITY OF CAIRO ....July 27 July 29
Passages at Moderate Rates. Surgeon and Stewardess carried. Wireless Telegraphy.
For full particulars apply to
GEO. SMITH & SONS, 76 Bothwell Street, Glasgow.

ZEPPELIN RAIDS ON SCOTLAND

The war was brought to the home front in May when a huge Zeppelin raid was mounted against Britain's eastern coastline. The raid ranged widely from Rattray Head, north of Peterhead, all the way to Norfolk. At least half a dozen of the giant airships were actually sighted although reports of the bombing itself suggested that a greater number of Zeppelins were in fact involved.

It was estimated that about 100 bombs were dropped during the raids over many different locations and in total nine people were killed and over thirty injured.

COMINGS...

Jessie Kesson
Writer

Mary Stewart
Writer

WATERPROOF GARMENTS
FOR THE HOLIDAYS.
LATEST STYLES.
For LADIES and GENTLEMEN, MISSES and BOYS, In Cashmeres, Tweeds, Black Rubber Proof and Oilskins.

MOTOR CYCLING WATERPROOF
JACKETS & LEGGINGS A SPECIALITY.
CYCLING CAPES AND PONCHOS, from 4s 6d. Cycle Valve and Inflator Tubing, Patching Rubber, and Solution in Tubes and Boxes.
GOLF CLUB CARRIERS, from 4s. WITH HOOD, from 9s each.

CURRIE THOMSON & CO.
INDIA RUBBER AND WATERPROOF
MANUFACTURERS,
45 JAMAICA STREET
(Opposite ANN STREET), GLASGOW.

GOINGS...

James Connolly
Socialist & Irish Republican

THIS SPORTING LIFE

FOOTBALL	RUGBY UNION	GOLF	HORSE RACING	SHINTY
Scottish Champions Celtic	*Scotland vs England* No game played	*British Open Winner* No competition held	*Scottish Grand National Winner* No race ran	*Camanachd Cup Winners* No competition held
Scottish Cup Winners No competition held				

GRIM FIGHT FOR VILLAGE FORTRESS.
Read This Tale of Battle Amid Ruins.
Told in This Week's
WEEKLY MAIL AND RECORD.
NOW ON SALE EVERYWHERE.

CITY EDITION.

Daily Record

and Mail.

The All-Scotland Newspaper.   Circulation more than Double that of any other Morning Journal in Scotland

ESTAB. 1847—NO. 22,118   GLASGOW, THURSDAY, DECEMBER 6, 1917   ONE PENNY

GRAVE TRAM CAR ACCIDENT.

TWO MEN KILLED AND 40 INJURED.

GLASGOW DOUBLE-DECKER OVERTURNS.

Tramcar accidents, even of a serious nature involving the loss of life, are not unknown in Glasgow, despite the fact that the system is probably unexcelled anywhere. But until last night the record of the Department was unmarked by tragedy consequent upon the overturning of a car.

Two deaths have so far been reported, but the injuries received by others are so serious that they cannot yet be said to be out of danger; while the roll of those suffering from minor hurts is a lengthy one and contains upwards of 40 names.

The facts of the accident are easily told. It happened in Victoria Road, just immediately fronting the entrance to the Queen's Park, shortly after six o'clock, and to a car plying on the route between Netherlee and Kirklee.

The car carried at least its full complement, for the hour is one of the busiest in the day by reason that many workmen make their way home at that time from establishments such as that of Messrs. Weir, Cathcart.

Of those on board, witnesses declare, the great majority were men of the artisan type, and it was computed that only five or six women were in the car. Exactly what took place is the one point on which there exists any doubt.

Two explanations are, of course, possible. One is that the speed may have been excessive. There is a sharp curve at the point, and at the city end of the half-circle there is a stopping-place, where passengers may alight from or join cars. The other theory is that a defect may have developed in the brake, rendering it impossible for the driver to draw up in time to avert serious accident.

Which—if any—of these explanations is the correct one will be determined only by the inquiry, which will follow in due course.

FAILED AT THE CURVE.

The car seems to have left the rails when about half of the curve had been taken. Several who were in the smash assert that there was a sudden jolt, and then the car seemed to leap across the roadway, and impale itself on an iron railing which screens a bit of open ground fronting a row of large private residences.

In its progress the car smashed to pieces the coping stone and parts of the railing, and finally came to rest with a large part of the front portion of the vehicle lying over the basement of a dwelling.

The car was entirely wrecked. Glass panels were broken to smithereens and lay scattered in fragments all over the street. The roof, as indicating the violence of the force with which the car toppled over on its left side, parted company with the body, and rested like an open lid against the main structure.

Many thousands were attracted to the scene in the course of the evening, for news of the disaster spread quickly and far. A cordon of police kept the crowd in check, however, and they had to be content with a view of the wreckage from a respectable distance. All that met the eyes of those unprivileged to go closer was the under-body of the upturned vehicle.

For a brief period after the occurrence there was much excitement. People who occupy the houses adjoining heard the crash of the car as it dashed into the railing. Nervous women in a few instances concluded that bombs were being dropped, but a common impulse led most of them into the open, where they discovered the actual nature of the happening at their doors. No time was lost in summoning help. Police officers did all in their power to assist those imprisoned in the wreckage, and their efforts were ably supported by firemen who arrived with almost incredible speed from three different parts of the city.

WORK OF RESCUE

One of the first persons encountered by the rescuers was lying on the floor of the car. When a fireman essayed to help the man into a posture suitable for removal, he made the discovery that he was dead, and that the upper part of his head had been shockingly injured. It had been cut clean off in the smash, and a pool of blood lay at his feet.

Ambulance wagons arrived in a constant stream, and by this means those who appeared to be suffering from the more serious injuries were conveyed to the Victoria Infirmary.

No fewer than 41 persons were admitted to that institution in the course of the evening. Of these 21 were suffering from hurts which demanded their detention; the others, after receiving attention from the staff, were able to leave for their homes.

Much that is complimentary is said on behalf of the ladies and gentlemen resident in the vicinity, who threw open their doors, and did all in their power for the comfort of the injured. Medical men from several quarters were also assiduous in their efforts.

The second death took place at the Victoria Infirmary. In this instance also the victim was a man.

Callers from a wide area were arriving in little knots during the evening at the Queen's Park Police Station, many of them wet-eyed, to ascertain the fate of friends who were expected to be travelling home by a car about the time at which the accident took place but who had failed to put in an appearance.

A remarkable feature is that, although the hour was one at which the streets are thronged with pedestrians, nobody seemed to be in the way of the car when it leapt on to the footpath.

The driver of the car was James Gardner, 16 years of age, who resides at 157 Dumbarton Road, Partick. He has been taken into custody pending investigations.

THE KILLED AND INJURED.

The two men killed have not yet been identified; but the following is a list of the injured:—

INJURED.

Bessie Johnstone (17), machinist, 2 Shields Terrace, Kinning Park, head injuries.
Catherine Alexander, 201 Calder Street, head and face injuries.
Stafford Haynes (?), mechanic, 533 Victoria Road, fractured thigh.
William Small, c/o Murray, 129 Shields Road, bruises and back injuries.
William Welsh, mechanic, 18 Prince Edward Street, bruises and back injuries.
Alexander Wilson, mechanic, 99 Kelburn Street, Barrhead, shoulder and head injuries.
Matthew Chrystal, mechanic, 73 St. Andrew's Road, head injuries and shock.
William Reid, 7 Ardgowan Terrace, W., head injuries.
Alexander Fisken, 8 M'Kinlay Street, shoulder and hand injuries.
Isa Robertson, 26 Lilybank Road, shock and slight cuts.
Lily Young, 16 Bowman Street, cuts and head injuries.
Isa Clark, 8 Maxwell Road, shock.
Alfred Eadie, 100 Kelburn Street, Barrhead, general bruises and small cuts.
Thomas Christie, 67 Carlabar Road, Barrhead, general bruises and small cuts.
Harry M'Kenzie, 12 Kerr Street, Barrhead, general bruises and small cuts.
John Wilson, 1 Gladstone Avenue, Barrhead, general bruises and small cuts.
Moses Johnstone, 7 Paisley Road, Barrhead, general bruises and small cuts.
James M'Ewan, 168 Oxford Street, Glasgow, general bruises and small cuts.
Annie Chisholm, 23 Albert Road, Crosshill, severe head injuries.
Mrs. Aitken, 388 Victoria Road, shock.

BY-ELECTION AT DUNDEE.

TRIUMPHANT RETURN OF MR. CHURCHILL.

MAJORITY 5266.

In genial weather and bright sunshine polling took place in Dundee yesterday for the seat rendered vacant by the appointment of Mr. Churchill to the Ministry of Munitions. The register on which the voting took place was three years old. Owing to the war and the short time engaged in the campaign, it was impossible to compile an estimate of the number of electors. Thousands have gone to the war, many have removed from the city in the interval, while a number are still on holiday.

The three years old roll has 21,953 names, but taking all things into account,

Mr. Winston Churchill, M.P.

it was thought that not more than 11,000, or at the most 12,000, voters would be available.

At the close of the poll the boxes containing the papers were removed to the Sheriff Court-House and the votes counted. A huge crowd assembled in the Court-House Square to await the result, which was as follows:—

Churchill 7302
Scrymgeour 2036

Majority 5266

Mr. Churchill's poll at the three former contests he had in Dundee were 7079 in 1908, 10,747 in January, 1910, and 9240 in December, 1910.

Mr. Scrymgeour's poll on each of the above occasions was 655, 1512, and 1825.

EDUCATION REFORM IN SCOTLAND.

WHAT TO AIM AT.

REPORT BY NATIONAL COMMITTEE.

One of the lessons driven forcibly home by the war is that ample room exists for an improvement in our present system of education. In its various aspects this subject has for many months been engaging the attention of the Scottish Education Reform Committee, a body set up under the joint auspices of the Educational Institute of Scotland, the Secondary Education Association of Scotland, and the Scottish Class Teachers' Association.

The complete report of the Committee will be issued in the course of a few days. Meantime we are able to give that part of it which deals with moral education, a subject which, in the words of the report, " bristles with many difficult problems."

The Committee state that the political considerations which have determined the segregation, if not the exclusion, of religious instruction from the school time-table, have rendered the question of moral education one of distinct and special importance.

The greatest war in the world's history was neither more nor less than a war for the maintenance and establishment of international moral ideals. To save civilisation from the moral wreckage of this war, and to prevent similar wars, would be the great task of the moral education of the future. International solidarity through enlightened patriotism, religion and humanity, would be its aim, a task which would never be achieved until undertaken by the schools of all the civilised nations of the world. They should seek through the school to destroy false ideals of patriotism, convinced that no patriotism is real unless founded on principles consistent with those of humanity itself.

Again, the ideals of the good citizen of the future should be not material success, but happiness in work as the artist is happy, and happiness in service both for employer and employed; not competition but " mutual aid "; not self-interest but altruism; not quantity but quality; not getting but giving; not slacking but serving.

Implicitly and explicitly, teachers and managers of schools should condemn unsparingly the folly of mere money display and the parade of social standing.

There should be co-operation with the municipality, the Church, and the home in co-ordinating the culture of the school with the intellectual and recreative life of the community. Good music, art exhibitions, and a municipal theatre need not be confined to the larger cities or be beyond the reach of the smaller communities.

YORKSHIRE RELISH.

THE MOST DELICIOUS SAUCE IN THE WORLD.

Sole Proprietors—Goodall, Backhouse & Co., Leeds.

RAW ITCHING ECZEMA

Blotches on Hands, Ears, and Ankles For Three Years. Relief from First Day's Treatment and

SPEEDY CURE BY CUTICURA

1917

TWO DEAD AND 40 HURT IN CRASH

TWO men were killed outright and 40 other people were hurt in yet another tramcar accident in Glasgow.

Some of the casualties were so seriously injured that they were not expected to live.

The accident happened in Victoria Road, early in December.

The car was on the Netherlee and Kirklee route and was near to full with workmen making their way home. There were two explanations put forward for the main cause of the accident.

The first was that the speed may have been excessive – there was a sharp curve at the accident spot.

Another theory was that a defect may have developed which made it impossible for the driver to draw up in time to avert a serious accident.

The car left the rails about halfway round the curve.

Passengers reported that there had been a sudden jolt and then the car seemed to leap across the roadway and impale itself on an iron railing.

The car itself was wrecked in the accident. Glass panels were broken and lay scattered in fragments all over the street. The roof came off and lay resting beside the main structure.

Help was summoned and police officers did all in their power to assist those trapped. They were aided by firemen from three areas of the city.

GOINGS...

Elsie Maud Inglis
Surgeon & Reformer

MEN OF GOVAN,
CLYDEBANK, and
PARKHEAD,
DRINK

Tuborg

DANISH

LAGER BEER

It's refreshing, it's satisfying, and it's a drink, no matter whether you're hot or cold, you'll enjoy, but, what is more important, it won't impair your efficiency in the least.

From all Hotels and Bars.

Glasgow Agents—

Finlay M'Diarmid & Co., Ltd.,
Maryhill.

'Phone—Maryhill, 123.

MORAL INSTRUCTION ESSENTIAL IN SCHOOLS

After many months' deliberation, the Scottish Education Reform Committee published its findings on ways of improving the system of education north of the border. A key issue for the SERC, which had been set up under the joint auspices of the Educatonal Institute of Scotland, the Secondary Education Association of Scotland and the Scottish Class Teachers' Association, was the matter of moral instruction. This, according to the SERC, could only be done effectively if there was collaboration and agreement on the basic moral principles between all the agencies responsible for the child's moral welfare, namely the home, the school, and the church. It also recommended that moral instruction be made much more a part of the school timetable that it currently was.

CHURCHILL BY-ELECTION VICTORY

A by-election in July saw Winston Churchill returned as MP for Dundee. Following his resignation from the post of First Lord of the Admiralty because of the failure of the Dardanelles campaign in 1915, Mr Churchill had been commanding a battalion in France. He was recalled by the Prime Minister Lloyd George to be Minister for Munitions.

The war posed a problem for the electoral officers who, because of the number of men away on active service, found it impossible to compile an accurate electoral register. They were forced to use a register compiled in 1914.

Even with the greatly reduced turnout, Mr Churchill still managed to secure a majority of 5266.

THAT FINISHING TOUCH TO YOUR DRESSES WHICH MEANS SO MUCH

is added by wearing the correct Royal Worcester Kidfitting Corset.

It pays to buy a good corset. "The smarter the corset the smarter the dress." A poor corset will spoil the costliest gown, but a smart corset will make even the most inexpensive dress look becoming.

We carry a large stock of Royal Worcester Corsets—every type, every fitting, every price from 5/11 to 84/. We give expert service in fitting, and can promise you a Royal Worcester Corset that will fit you as perfectly as if it had been made expressly for you, but which has the infinite advantage of being an original design by the world's foremost corset artist—not a mere copy.

AT TRERON'S TO-DAY.

Monsieur Lacoute's Exclusive Designs.

Shapes Certified Correct.

Write for the new Illustrated Catalogue of Corsets—it will be sent you post free. We also pay carriage to every part of Great Britain and Ireland on all goods bought in Les Grands Magasins des Tuileries.

ROYAL WORCESTER
Kidfitting Corsets

LES GRANDS MAGASINS DES TUILERIES,
254-290 SAUCHIEHALL STREET, GLASGOW.

THIS SPORTING LIFE

FOOTBALL	RUGBY UNION	GOLF	HORSE RACING	SHINTY
Scottish Champions Celtic	*Scotland vs England* No game played	*British Open Winner* No competition held	*Scottish Grand National Winner* No race run	*Camanachd Cup Winners* No competition held
Scottish Cup Winners No competition held				

VACANT SITUATIONS
ADVERTISED IN THE
Record and Mail
ARE
QUICKLY FILLED.

Daily Record and Mail.
The All-Scotland Newspaper. Circulation More Than Double That of Any Other Morning Journal in Scotland.

SCOTS IN RAID VENDETTA.
Read This Thrilling War Story In This Week's
Weekly Mail & Record
On Sale Everywhere on Thursday.

ESTAB. 1847—NO. 22,410 [Registered at the G.P.O. as a Newspaper.] GLASGOW, TUESDAY, NOVEMBER 12, 1918 ONE PENNY

RE-ILLUMINATED GLASGOW.

AIRMEN FLASH ACROSS THE SKY LINE.

CEASELESS THRONGING OF THE PEOPLE.

What took place in Glasgow during the day will be found fully described in page 7, but the enthusiasm failed in those doings to expend itself.

Like a river in spate the tide of traffic flowed steadily citywards again in the evening. Pavements in the centre of the town rapidly became next to impassable. Inconveniences arising from the congestion were treated lightly, for the crowd, attired in Sunday best, and in happiest of holiday mood, saw everything through rose-coloured glasses.

Tired with their perambulating the sightseers naturally sought refreshment, and the waitresses in the numerous dining-rooms were unanimous in their verdict that never had they experienced such a time.

The tramway people were in similar plight. Drivers and conductors had their distinct, but very real, worries. The former found it a most anxious task to thread a way through the boisterous celebrants who overflowed from the plainstanes to the causeways, oblivious alike to warning bells and whistles. The latter endeavoured to keep within the restrictions anent overcrowding, and had a heart-breaking time of it with that section which always knows better than the responsible officials how things should be managed.

THRILLS FROM THE AIR.

The rejoicings in one particular assumed an unexpected form. Aeroplanes, a fighting weapon which has rendered such signal service during the war, appeared over the city, to the intense delight of the multitudes. Not content with a mere appearance, the flying men ... manipulated the machines gave an exhibition of their skill by carrying out a number of daring and thrilling evolutions.

As if in sympathy with the occasion, the sky was a lovely blue, and the aerial programme was thus seen under ideal conditions.

Augmenting the exhibition, a firework display was given by the airmen ere they ascended and vanished swiftly in the direction of their hangar.

Modifications have now, of course, been permitted in lighting. In the main these could not be put into effect last night, as the notice available was insufficient for many people. But there was an appreciable difference in the conditions of affairs at a number of points.

Shades, once orthodox and essential, had been removed, and obscuring, likewise necessary, had been scraped away. The brilliance, coming after so much that was subdued and dim, instinctively gave an added uplift to the spirit.

Not many in Glasgow kept the blinds raised after darkness fell and the gas had been lighted. Privacy was preferred to that form of rejoicing.

In the evening large sections of the promenaders visited the places of entertainment. Even standing room was impossible to find at most of these resorts half an hour before the curtain was drawn.

THE POPULAR CHORUS.

On till midnight processions continued to parade the streets. Each had its band—of a sort—at its head. To the quickstep the "musicians" played the demonstrators marched, rendering as they swung along a vocal accompaniment. Favourite tunes were essayed in large numbers. One of the happiest—and the people lining the kerb quickly apprehended its significance—was "I'll awa' hame to my mither, I will." It hinted of the return at an early date of the absent fighting men.

George Square remained to the close the great rallying place. In that vast meeting-ground the crowd was at its densest. Past it at some time or other of the day or evening all the processions paraded.

In the intervals between the excitement of following the progress of the numerous pipe, brass and assorted bands, the spectators amused themselves by throwing high into the air pink and coloured lights, and placing detonators beneath the wheels of the tramway cars.

Slowly the enthusiasm wore itself out, and by one o'clock the streets were again empty, save for the patrolling special, his blue-coated brother guardian and those whom necessity demanded should be abroad.

Arrangements are in progress for holding thanksgiving services in the churches.

IN THE WAVERLEY MARKET.

The jubilation in Edinburgh culminated in a great demonstration in the Waverley Market, Edinburgh, at night.

FAR FLUNG JOY.

TOWN AND COUNTRY CELEBRATE THE TIDINGS.

Many thousands of Clydebank people early decided to join in the celebrations in Glasgow, and the tramcar conductors had a worrying time in trying to keep their loads at the regulation number.

A procession was organised by the wounded soldiers at Dalzell House. Preceded by the Motherwell Boys' Brigade bugle band, the soldiers and nurses in motor cars made merry along the principal streets. The wounded soldiers carried an effigy of the Kaiser, which was afterwards burned.

In Hamilton, the regimental brass band and pipers of the Scottish Rifles paraded the streets playing patriotic airs.

Aeroplanes cruised over Musselburgh, and a light signal was dropped from one a few minutes after the good news arrived.

A mission band headed a procession of merry-making shipyard and munition workers at Renfrew.

Everybody in Kilsyth was more anxious than another to decorate the town. In a wonderful display of flags, bed coverings were even pressed into service.

Although Dunfermline has been a centre of the senior service during the war, the citizens received the good news philosophically. Sir William Robertson, the Lord-Lieutenant of Fife, was the first to receive the tidings.

Provost Lochhead and others addressed a meeting at Denny Cross, and a joint service was held in the Parish Church.

Joy bells were pealed all day in Dumfries, and the public were urged by the Provost and Town Council to leave their blinds undrawn to illuminate the town as much as possible.

As the home of the Gordon Highlanders, Aberdeen welcomed the news of victory with jubilation.

An effigy of the Kaiser was carried through the streets of Lennoxtown and afterwards kicked to pieces.

A Royal salute was fired by the Fleet at Cromarty.

A congregation of over 1300 assembled in Dunblane Cathedral at a united service which opened with the "Hallelujah Chorus," played on the grand organ.

Hamilton Town Council, at a special meeting, agreed to send telegrams of congratulation to the King, Prime Minister, President Wilson, Marshal Foch, Sir Douglas Haig, Sir Rosslyn Wemyss, Admiral Beatty, and General Pershing.

FESTIVE DUNDEE.

CHEERS AND MUSIC TO THE BOOM OF GUNS.

As early as 6 a.m. the news of the signing of the Armistice was known at Dundee, but it was not until the breakfast hour, 9 a.m., that the general public got to know. This came with the firing of guns, the buzzing of mill bummers, and the screech of fog horns from the boats lying in the river. By ten o'clock the whole city was seething with excitement.

Every mill, factory and workshop suspended work at breakfast time; and teeming thousands of workers made their way to the central thoroughfares of the city, singing lustily and cheering wildly. As if by a miracle, flags and bunting appeared from every window and shop, flagpoles flew the Union Jack, and by noon every public building was gaily bedecked.

Guns continued to boom, and star shells were sent up, while the excited crowds cheered themselves hoarse. Handshaking was indulged in at every turn; women were seen to weep and embrace each other; while stern men gripped hands, to the accompaniment of a glistening tear of joy. It was the day of all days in the old jute city, which had sent so many of its sons to compose the famous 51st Division.

As the afternoon wore on the streets became utterly impassable, owing to the multitude of processions. Rag-time bands that had done so much during the war to raise funds for benevolent purposes, now played to a different and happier tune. A military band turned out and paraded the streets, followed by a band of youthful pipers.

During the course of the day Lord Provost Sir James Don spoke from the front of the Town House to a vast concourse of people. He referred to the great event, and alluded to the noble part Dundonians had taken in the struggle.

ABERDEEN.

Aberdeen, the home of the Gordon Highlanders, rejoiced in a hearty and dignified fashion. Bunting was profuse on public and private buildings.

Enthusiasm reached a climax when a huge procession headed by Gordon Highlanders with bands playing and flags flying from their rifles marched through

VICTORY LOAN IN GREAT REQUEST.

STIRRING OPENING DAY AT EDINBURGH.

Following closely on the news that an Armistice had been signed, the opening ceremony of Edinburgh's "Feed the Guns" campaign was invested with special interest. It began and ended with a hearty rendering of the National Anthem, and was characterised throughout by a spirit of joyous, if restrained, enthusiasm.

Great cheering greeted the opening remark of the Lord Provost, Sir J. Lorne MacLeod, that the Armistice had been signed and the last shot fired. The "Feed the Guns" campaign they were inaugurating now became a Peace Loan

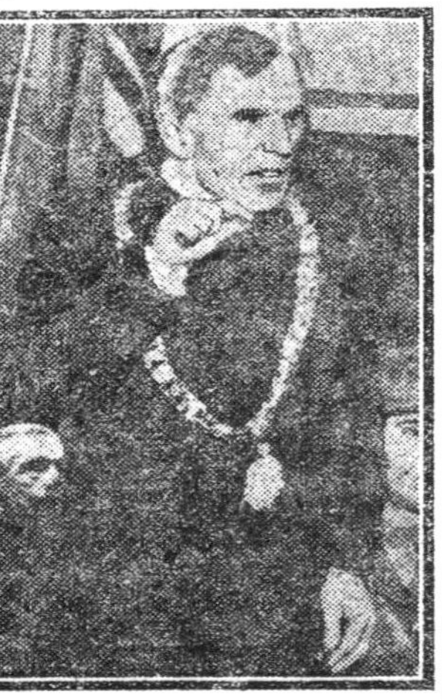

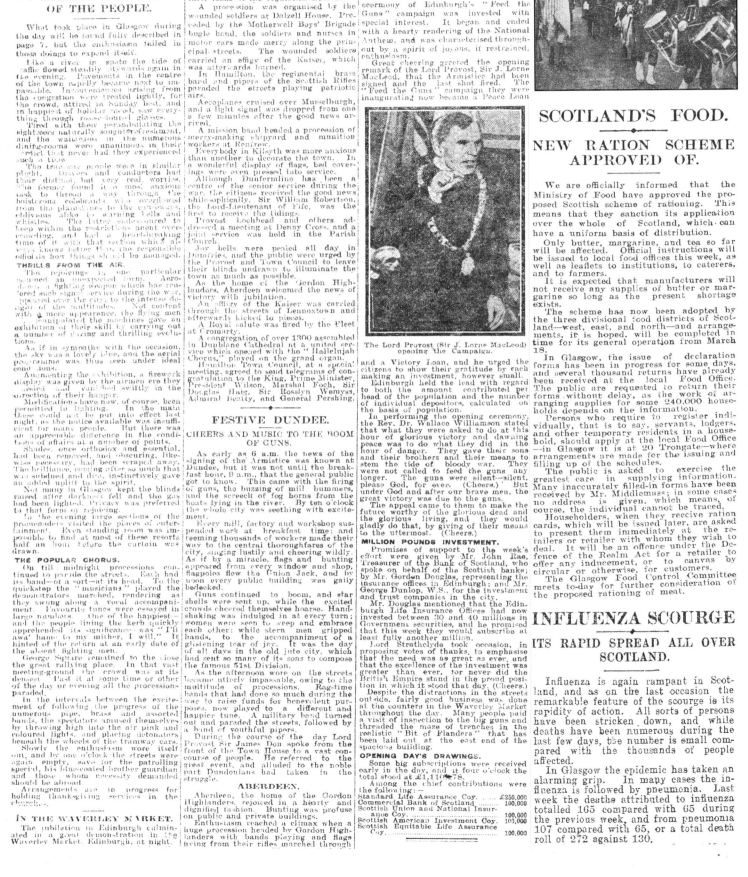

The Lord Provost (Sir J. Lorne MacLeod) opening the Campaign.

and a Victory Loan, and he urged the citizens to show their gratitude by each making an investment, however small.

Edinburgh held the lead with regard to both the amount contributed per head of the population and the number of individual depositors, calculated on the basis of population.

In performing the opening ceremony, the Rev. Dr. Wallace Williamson stated that what they were asked to do at this hour of glorious victory and dawning peace was to do what they did in the hour of danger. They gave their sons and their brothers and their means to stem the tide of bloody war. They were not called to feed the guns any longer. The guns were silent—silent, please God, for ever. (Cheers.) But under God and after our brave men, the great victory was due to the guns.

The appeal came to them to make the future worthy of the glorious dead and the glorious living, and they would gladly do that, by giving of their means to the uttermost. (Cheers.)

MILLION POUNDS INVESTMENT.

Promises of support to the week's effort were given by Mr. John Rae, Treasurer of the Bank of Scotland, who spoke on behalf of the Scottish banks; by Mr. Gordon Douglas, representing the insurance offices in Edinburgh; and Mr. George Dunlop, W.S., for the investment and trust companies in the city.

Mr. Douglas mentioned that the Edinburgh Life Insurance Offices had now invested between 30 and 40 millions in Government securities, and he promised that this week they would subscribe at least fully another million.

Lord Strathclyde took occasion, in proposing votes of thanks, to emphasise that the need was as great as ever, and that the excellence of the investment was greater than ever, for never did the British Empire stand in the proud position in which it stood that day. (Cheers.)

Despite the distractions in the streets outside, fairly good business was done at the counters in the Waverley Market throughout the day. Many people paid a visit of inspection to the big guns and threaded the maze of trenches in the realistic "Bit of Flanders" that has been laid out at the east end of the spacious building.

OPENING DAY'S DRAWINGS.

Some big subscriptions were received early in the day, and at four o'clock the total stood at £1,110,?78.

Among the chief contributions were the following:—

Standard Life Assurance Coy.	£250,000
Commercial Bank of Scotland	100,000
Scottish Union and National Insurance Coy.	100,000
Scottish American Investment Coy.	100,000
Scottish Equitable Life Assurance Coy.	100,000

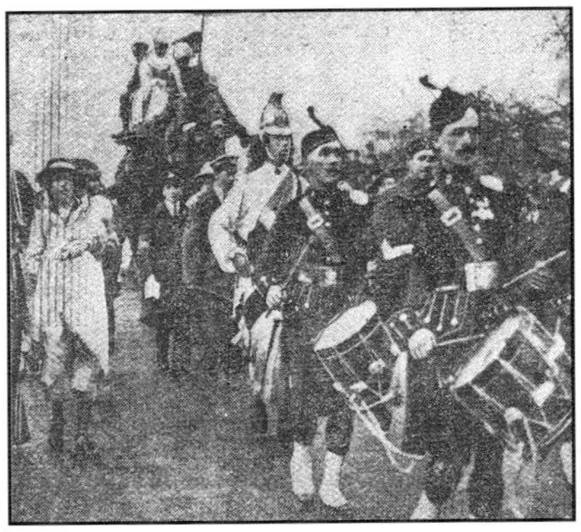

SCOTLAND'S FOOD.

NEW RATION SCHEME APPROVED OF.

We are officially informed that the Ministry of Food have approved the proposed Scottish scheme of rationing. This means that they sanction its application over the whole of Scotland, which can have a uniform basis of distribution.

Only butter, margarine, and tea so far will be affected. Official instructions will be issued to local food offices this week, as well as leaflets to institutions, to caterers, and to farmers.

It is expected that manufacturers will not receive any supplies of butter or margarine so long as the present shortage exists.

The scheme has now been adopted by the three divisional food districts of Scotland—west, east, and north—and arrangements, it is hoped, will be completed in time for its general operation from March 18.

In Glasgow, the issue of declaration forms has been in progress for some days, and several thousand returns have already been received at the local Food Office. The public are requested to return their forms without delay, as the work of arranging supplies for some 240,000 households depends on the information.

Persons who require to register individually, that is to say, servants, lodgers, and other temporary residents in a household, should apply at the local Food Office—in Glasgow it is at 20 Trongate—where arrangements are made for the issuing and filling up of the schedules.

The public is asked to exercise the greatest care in supplying information. Many inaccurately filled-in forms have been received by Mr. Middlemass; in some cases no address is given, which means, of course, the individual cannot be traced.

Householders, when they receive ration cards, which will be issued later, are asked to present them immediately at the retailers or retailer with whom they wish to deal. It will be an offence under the Defence of the Realm Act for a retailer to offer any inducement, or to canvas by circular or otherwise, for customers.

The Glasgow Food Control Committee meets to-day for further consideration of the proposed rationing of meat.

INFLUENZA SCOURGE

ITS RAPID SPREAD ALL OVER SCOTLAND.

Influenza is again rampant in Scotland, and as on the last occasion the remarkable feature of the scourge is its rapidity of action. All sorts of persons have been stricken down, and while deaths have been numerous during the last few days, the number is small compared with the thousands of people affected.

In Glasgow the epidemic has taken an alarming grip. In many cases the influenza is followed by pneumonia. Last week the deaths attributed to influenza totalled 165 compared with 65 during the previous week, and from pneumonia 107 compared with 65, or a total death roll of 272 against 130.

1918

JOY AS ARMISTICE ENDS THE WAR

THE opening ceremony of Edinburgh's "Feed the Guns" campaign in November held special interest, coming as it did so soon after the news that an Armistice had been signed and that the Great War was finally at an end. It began and ended with a hearty rendering of the National Anthem, and was characterised throughout by a spirit of joyous, if restrained, enthusiasm.

Many thousands of Clydebank people decided to join in the celebrations in Glasgow.

To the sound of music from the Motherwell Boys' Brigade bugle band, soldiers and nurses in motor cars paraded along the main streets of the town. The wounded soldiers carried an effigy of the Kaiser, which was afterwards burned.

In Hamilton, the regimental brass band and pipers of the Scottish Rifles paraded through the streets playing patriotic airs.

Aeroplanes cruised over Musselburgh, and a light signal was dropped from one a few minutes after news of the

Armistice arrived. In Dundee, the public heard the good news at 9am; and this was followed by the firing of guns, the buzzing of "mill bummers" (factory hooters) and fog horns from boats.

In Aberdeen, the home of the Gordon Highlanders, the people celebrated in the streets and public and private buildings were a mass of union flags and bunting. The celebrations reached a climax when a huge procession headed by the Gordon Highlanders with bands playing and flags flying from their rifles marched through the main streets.

COMINGS...

Muriel Spark
Writer

"Getting there!"

CARROLL'S SILK CUT CIGARETTES

4½ FOR 10   4½ FOR 10

P.J. CARROLL & CO. LTD.
DUNDALK & GLASGOW

'FLU EPIDEMIC GRIPS SCOTLAND

A particularly virulent 'flu virus was rampant throughout the country in October. It was reported that this particular strain of the disease seemed to spread much faster than previous outbreaks and in many cases, was often aggravated by an accompanying attack of pneumonia. Fortunately, in spite of the great numbers affected by the illness, there were relatively few fatalities.

Glasgow, however, was particularly badly affected and the death toll had risen from 130 to over 270 in just over a week. Schools also suffered heavily and in several cases, absence rates were so high amongst both staff and pupils that the education authorities were forced to close affected schools for several weeks.

If You Have Headaches Suspect Your EYES.

The ocular headache is well known to the medical man and optician, though often little suspected by the ordinary person. Proceeding from eyestrain it is a sure sign that all is not well with those invaluable workers—the eyes.

75% of the glasses now worn are for the relief of Headaches.

Again, eyestrain may declare itself by means of waterings of the eyes, inflammation, spots, or blurring. If you have the least suspicion of your eyes, get them examined. My private sight-testing rooms, equipped with the most modern apparatus, are at your service, and all examinations are free of charge.

J. Lizars

Ophthalmic Optician,
101 to 107 Buchanan Street, Glasgow,
Also at Edinburgh, Paisley, Greenock, Motherwell, Aberdeen, Belfast, and Liverpool.

FOOD RATIONING SYSTEM ESTABLISHED

In February, the Ministry of Food approved a new scheme for the rationing of butter, margarine and tea which, it was hoped, would result in a uniform distribution of the foodstuffs across the whole country. Scotland was to be divided into three divisional districts – east, west and north – and almost a quarter of a million households would be issued with ration cards.

These cards were to be presented to particular shops when obtaining any of the rationed items and it was an offence under the Defence of the Realm Act for shopkeepers to offer any inducements or to tout for business.

GOINGS...

Andrew Carnegie
Philanthropist

THIS SPORTING LIFE

FOOTBALL	RUGBY UNION	GOLF	HORSE RACING	SHINTY
Scottish Champions Rangers	*Scotland vs England* No game played	*British Open Winner* No competition held	*Scottish Grand National Winner* No race run	*Camanachd Cup Winners* No competition held
Scottish Cup Winners No competition held				

DO YOU WANT CASH?
£5 to £5000 at the Cheapest Possible Price.
No Security Required; Note of Hand Alone. Easy Repayments. No Fees. Distance no Object.
A. ADAMS (Est. 1889),
16 ST. ENOCH SQUARE, GLASGOW.
Also at
5 Hanover Street, Edinburgh.

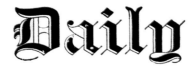

Daily Record and Mail.
The All-Scotland Newspaper. Sale Twice That of Any Other Morning Paper
ESTAB. 1847—No. 22,480 GLASGOW, SATURDAY, FEBRUARY 1, 1919 ONE PENNY

READ
Horatio Bottomley
in the
SUNDAY MAIL AND RECORD
TO-MORROW.

MILITARY READY TO DEAL WITH CLYDE RIOTERS.

SERIOUS STRIKE RIOT IN GLASGOW.

BATON CHARGES BY POLICE.

SHERIFF AND CHIEF CONSTABLE AMONGST INJURED.

STRIKE LEADERS ARRESTED.

Considerable bodies of military have been drafted into Glasgow for any emergencies which may arise after the disgraceful rioting scenes yesterday. This provision bears out the intention of the authorities rigorously to preserve order.

Following on the announcement of the Cabinet's intention not to intervene in the arbitrary 40-hours' week demand, the strikers massed in George Square in the morning.

Rioting developed immediately after noon, and the Riot Act was read—for the first time in half a century—by Sheriff-Principal Mackenzie.

Numerous baton charges against the strikers, who used all sorts of missiles, were made by the police, who, whether in George Square, or subsequently on Glasgow Green, managed to keep the disorders within controllable bounds. It was not necessary to call upon bodies of soldiers held in reserve.

The riot casualties numbered at least 30, and included the Sheriff-Principal, the Chief-Constable, and the Deputy Chief-Constable.

Two of the strike leaders, William Gallagher and D. Kirkwood, were arrested in George Square.

A considerable portion of the Central district of Glasgow was left without electric light; two dozen tramway cars were put out of action by the strikers, and cases of shop looting occurred in various districts.

One of the most promising features of the strike situation is the initiation of a movement among loyal Trades Unionists to organise anti-strike demonstrations.

TURMOIL STARTS

STRIKERS ATTACK THE POLICE.

The procession of Clyde strikers to George Square, Glasgow, yesterday forenoon, was the introduction to riotous disorders, of a grave nature. The demonstrators, well aware of the risks they were running, had no feasible purpose.

As a matter of fact, there was no reason whatever for a demonstration in force before the City Chambers. The answer returned by Mr. Bonar Law to the message from the Unofficial Strike Committee was common property in the early morning, for it had been published broadcast by means of the morning journals circulating in the city. Courtesy might, of course, have demanded that a visit should have been paid to Lord Provost Stewart for the formal intimation of that reply, but there was no justification whatever for an attendance in force, nor for the threatening attitude which those who composed the procession adopted towards the representatives of established order.

Hints of trouble were in the air from the breakfast hour, when it was seen that little groups of malcontents were assembling in various quarters of the city for the purpose of marching upon the Municipal Buildings.

Singing snatches of their favourite "Red Flag" as they swung along, the demonstration presented a menacing and truculent appearance. For the most part the ranks were composed of the 'prentice class, hefty young fellows, upon whom a sense of civic responsibility has not yet dawned.

Into George Square they poured, ignoring, in their desire for a vantage place, the kerbs which protect the little green places. Soon they formed a mass, which extended beyond the bounds of the Square, and overflowed in hundreds into all the side streets. View points were eagerly sought. Monuments, in the estimation of many, presented ideal platforms for this purpose, and it was one of the commonest sights of the forenoon to see young fellows perched aloft on these memorials, clinging to an arm or limb of the figure which supported their weight.

Anticipating the possibility of trouble the police were out in force. Men were lined up on foot in front of the City Chambers, and officers on horseback rode between points, seeing to the maintenance of order.

Even in the earliest stages, the constables had to endure a good deal of chaffing that was neither good-natured nor in good form. One young man, his face white with excitement, harangued a line of policemen from the pavement close to the Gladstone statue. "You had better join us," he added, "and you will get the 40 hours' week also."

Differing accounts are, of course, in circulation respecting the incident which led to the first collision between the mob and the police. There is reason to believe, however, that it was due to the interference of a band of young fellows, who tried to hold up the car traffic at the Square at Hanover Street corner.

One car particularly claimed attention from the strikers. Several soldiers in khaki were on the vehicle at the time, and they did their best to prevent either the car or the conductress from interference.

A baton charge by the police was decided upon.

With truncheons drawn, the constables hurried forward. Their advent appeared to irritate the men who had been indulging in horse-play, and on the instant the air became thick with flying missiles. The ammunition consisted of stones, rivets, and bottles, the latter having been taken from a passing lorry.

The contest for supremacy did not last long. Before the sturdy onslaught of the police the rioters melted like snow in summer. Directions, if the methods employed by the constables formed any basis for judgment, had been given to avoid striking demonstrators on the head, and the blows descended chiefly upon bodies, arms, and legs. Nursing their sores, those who had borne the brunt of the encounter crept from the scene as speedily as their hurts permitted.

A deputation, led by Mr. E. Shinwell, had, in the interval, been passed by the guard into the Municipal Buildings. Lord Provost Stewart, at the moment, was engaged in a private conference with several representative members of the Shipbuilding and the Engineering Federation, and the deputation were, accordingly, shown into the library, which adjoins his lordship's room.

Impatient at the delay in receiving them, the party left the apartment, and insisted upon an interview being granted immediately. On learning that such a proceeding was scarcely possible, the deputation left in anger, declaring that there had been a breach of confidence.

The re-appearance of the party in the open led to a fresh outburst of excitement, and the crowd surged forward eagerly to hear what had transpired.

Mr. William Gallacher, one of the leaders, then mounted a pedestal, and proceeded from that elevation to address the multitude, whose numbers at this stage are estimated at between 70,000 and 80,000, many, of course, having been attracted to the scene out of curiosity, and having no relation whatever to the dispute in progress.

Mr. Gallacher had not travelled far in his oration when the eloquence was cut short. The police promptly took him into custody. Hostility to the officers again manifested itself, and the display took the identical form of the earlier attack.

RIOT ACT READ.

At the height of the storm, Sheriff-Principal Mackenzie was seen to leave the Municipal Buildings, and in company with the Town Clerk (Sir John Lindsay), and Chief Constable Stevenson, proceed to the kerb.

The Riot Act was in the Sheriff's hand. As he was reading it the uproar was deafening, missiles began to descend all round the party, and the document was actually torn from the Sheriff's grasp. A broken bottle thrown from the heart of the throng in front cut the Sheriff on the hand.

The Chief Constable was struck by a missile on the cheek. After the hurt had been attended to, Mr. Stevenson resumed his interrupted duties of supervising the work of his staff.

Another arrest was made shortly afterwards. The man taken into custody in that instance was Mr. David Kirkwood.

For a period the loggia of the City Chambers presented the appearance of a field dressing station. Six doctors, with numerous assistants, were kept busily engaged dealing with patients for nearly two hours. As the dressings were completed those who had not been seriously injured retired and mingled with their friends.

Through the instrumentality of Mr. Neil M'Lean, **M.P. for Govan, the two** prisoners were allowed to address the demonstrators from the balcony fronting the Municipal Buildings.

ARRESTED LEADERS' APPEAL.

Speaking with a bandage round his head, Mr. Gallacher said:—

"Now, keep order. Understand it has been a very unfortunate occurrence. We appeal to you to get into order and get on the march away from the square for your own sake. We are all right. You don't have to trouble yourselves one little bit about us. You are only troubling us about you.

"We appeal to you to march away from the square. Logan, a discharged soldier, and some of the other discharged men will lead you to Glasgow Green or elsewhere, where the situation can be discussed. We appeal to you to go on the march, for God's sake. Are you going to do that for us? (Cries of "Yes" from the crowd.) Well, get into order and go."

Mr. Kirkwood then said:—"Fellow-workmen, we believe it is in your interest at the moment that you go away from the Square. We appeal to you to do that—the time is inopportune for you to do anything else.

"Don't do anything, fellow-workmen. Be advised at the moment. Leave George Square, and we will see what will happen later on."

The crowd cheered the remarks of the speaker.

Mr. Neil MacLean, M.P., also appealed in a word to go away to form up and march to the Green.

At this time the Lord Provost, the Town Clerk, and the Sheriff were standing on the pavement outside the Council Chambers.

SCENES ON WAY TO GREEN.

The advice was almost immediately followed by the greater portion of the strikers. A large body of men, however, proceeded up North Frederick Street, where stones and other handy missiles were freely thrown about.

Much damage was done in the neighbourhood. The crowd smashed windows as they went, and motor-cars which passed were made object target practice, the glass screens in a number of instances being smashed. The main body, which had continued on the way to the Green, had further encounters with the police.

The Southern Division constables to the number of 40 who were held in readiness, in answer to a telephone message, crossed the Albert Bridge to Saltmarket. There the rioters at once attacked the police with bottles and jelly jars, which are supposed to have been purloined from a lorry.

When the constables succeeded in driving the mob along Great Clyde Sttreet and across Glasgow Bridge several plate-glass windows in Bridge Street were smashed, as was also the window of a public-house in Adelphi Street.

TRAMCARS ATTACKED

In the Saltmarket the tramcar service was held up. Jumping on the cars the strikers detached and destroyed the trolly poles and smashed the windows. Many passengers narrowly escaped personal injury. Some twelve cars were thus thrown out of service for the time being.

In Jail Square, a large section of the strikers, after holding a meeting in the Green, threw bottles at the police and struck them with sticks and stones. This led to a baton charge, in which several constables and strikers were injured.

The strikers also attacked a vehicle

(Continued on Next Column.)

TROOPS READY.

THOUSANDS POURED INTO GLASGOW.

Thousands of troops have been poured into Glasgow in fulfilment of the Government's undertaking to protect life and property against the excesses of the strikers.

There is evidently no intention of permitting a continuance of the disorders which the rabble indulged in yesterday.

The disturbances were all at an end for the day when the first detachment of the troops arrived. The soldiers reached Queen Street station shortly after ten o'clock, and from that hour until the early morning there was a constant stream of men fully equipped for any and all emergencies.

The troops first marched to the Central Station, where they were provided with food and refreshment, and were then marched to quarters in different parts of the city, some of the contingents being headed by pipe bands.

They were accompanied by heavy ammunition wagons, and the general appearance of the long columns of khaki-clad men, who belong to the Seaforths, the Gordons, and other Highland regiments, suggested that at last the Government is in earnest in the measures to crush the new revolutionary spirit which has found expression in the Clyde area.

ORDER AT ALL COSTS.

LORD PROVOST TAKES A FIRM ATTITUDE.

The Lord Provost of Glasgow (Mr. Stewart) asks the citizens to have patience, and assures them that he and his colleagues will not shirk their duty in the crisis through which the city is passing.

His Lordship delivered this message last night when addressing repatriated prisoners of war in St. Andrew's Hall.

"I am almost sorry you have returned at this time," said his Lordship. "One could have hoped that there would have been more gratitude shown by those people who have created disturbances in the city for the sacrifices you have made for them. (Loud applause.)

"I am struggling to find an excuse for such conduct. My colleagues and I realise that these men have been labouring under prolonged physical strain for such a time that possibly it may have affected their nervous system. I hope that with some patience their mental balance may be restored.

"Conduct such as we have had to-day makes one despair that they have any mental balance, or are ever likely to have it.

"I don't like to refer to the subject, but I do take this opportunity of saying—and there is no threat in what I say—that, so far as I and my colleagues are concerned, we realise to the fullest extent our responsibilities in the matter, and the citizens of Glasgow must just have patience with us. **We will not shirk our duty. We assure them that the resources of civilisation are not yet exhausted."** (Loud applause.)

Continued from previous column.

conveying cripple school children, and broke several of the windows.

At Glasgow Cross traffic was momentarily held up a derelict car, This car, a green one going eastwards, was forced to halt by a crowd of rioters. The windows were smashed with missiles, and the conductor was roughly handled and thrown on the street. A car following immediately had one window broken, while the trolley was cut and severely twisted.

In Glasgow Green the strikers were addressed by Mr. Neil M'Lean, Labour M.P. for Govan, and others M'Lean said they were not out order but to conduct their a peaceably, but they were not g allow themselves to be dragooned and bludgeoned. In all likelihood they would hold another demonstration on Monday, when they would show that the city belonged to the citizens and not to those who gave instructions to batter them.

BACK AT GEORGE SQUARE.

In the evening again there was a renewal of the scenes. Crowds of curious people gathered in the neighbourhood of the City Chambers, expecting they scarcely knew what to happen. The police were out in force once more, and they kept moving the people on.

A menacing attitude developed among a section about nine o'clock, and the constables, forming up, cleared the way in the same manner as they did earlier in the day. It was deemed prudent to keep the public at a good distance from the City Chambers, and this was done promptly.

Additional Strike matter on Page 9.

ACTRESS DRUG DRAMA.

BILLIE CARLETON CASE IN POLICE COURT.

DE VEULLE TURNS ILL.

(From Our Special Correspondent.)

London, Friday.

A further stage was reached to-day in what has become known as the actress drug drama. Raoul Reginald de Veulle, a dress designer, appeared at Bow Street before Mr. Garrett to answer to a charge of manslaughter in connection with the death of Miss Billie Carleton, the Coroner's jury having found that cocaine was unlawfully supplied to her by the accused in a culpable, neglig[illegible] manner.

The accused, since his remand on [illegible], has been confined to bed. To-d[illegible] stood in the dock with his c[illegible] collar turned up and looking [illegible]

During the proceedings De [illegible] took ill, and he was allowed to [illegible] court for a few minutes. Later [illegible] counsel, Mr. Huntly Jenkin, d[illegible] the Magistrate's attention to the accused's weak state of health, and the case was adjourned for a fortnight. De Veulle is to be detained in custody, an appeal for bail not being granted.

PEOPLE IN THE DRAMA.

The chief people in the drama are:—

Miss Billie Carleton (22), one of the most popular actresses of the day. She was addicted to opium-smoking and to cocaine-taking. She died of cocaine poisoning on the afternoon following the Victory Ball at the Albert Hall, London, on November 27.

Raoul Reginald De Veulle ([illegible]), married, an ex-actor, latterly a theatrical dress designer with a firm of dressmakers in New Bond Street. It was at his flat in Dover Street that Miss Carleton gave the opium-smoking party, which has been called a "disgusting orgy. He denies that he ever supplied cocaine to Miss Carleton, but she often asked him for some, and lent him money to buy cocaine for himself.

Lionel Belcher, a young film actor He stated at the inquest that he bought cocaine in £10 packets at a chemist's for De Veulle. He once took Miss Carleton to an opium smoking den in Limehouse.

Miss Olive Richardson, a film actress, living with Belcher. She was present at some of the "cocaine parties."

Dr. F. Stuart, of Knightsbridge, Miss Carleton's doctor and friend, who managed her financial affairs.

Miss Longfellow, film actress, who warned De Veulle not to supply cocaine to Billie Carleton, with whom she was friendly.

THE ALLEGATIONS.

COUNSEL STATES CASE FOR THE PROSECUTION.

Sir Richard Muir, counsel for the prosecution, said the question to be considered was what was the actual cause of Miss Carleton's death. She was alive and asleep in her room at half-past 11 o'clock on the morning of that day when her maid, May Booker, noticed two things about her state of health. The first was that she was snoring, which the maid had never known her to do before, and the second was that she was very pale.

The maid left her undisturbed, and Miss Carleton continued her sleep, and continued to snore up till half-past three in the afternoon, when the snoring ceased, and the maid, becoming alarmed, tried to wake her, but failed to do so. Thereupon she telephoned to Dr. Stewart, who was a friend of Billie Carleton, and also her medical attendant for some years.

That was at four o'clock in the afternoon, and he arrived and found that the unfortunate young woman was dead. On December 2 a post-mortem examination was made by Dr. Jewsbury, pathologist at Charing Cross Hospital, and he could discover no cause for her death by natural means, and he also thought that the probable cause of death was narcotic poison, and the poison indicated was cocaine.

The contents of the nostrils, together with the necessary organs of the body were submitted to Professor Richards, of Queen's College, for analysis. The contents of the **nose showed signs of cocaine.**

The fluid taken from the body showed there was an alkaloid present, probably cocaine, and the other organs of the body were free from any indication of poisoning.

MISS CARLETON AND DRUGS.

"It appears from the medical evidence that cocaine alkaloid rapidly

(Continued in the Next Page.)

1919

'RED' CLYDE STRIKERS HIT STREETS

WITH the end of the war, the labour market in industrial Clydeside was under sever threat, with a flood of demobilised conscripts returning home coupled to a decline in orders.

The STUC and the Clyde Workers Committee proposed to solve the crisis by reducing the working week to 40 hours. This demand was backed by an unofficial strike which began in January.

Although the strike call was largely ignored elsewhere, and on Clydeside itself enjoyed only a limited support, the development of "flying pickets" threatened to bring Glasgow to a standstill.

One power station was closed down, voltage was reduced throughout the city, and there was talk of halting the tram service. To counter the possibility of public disorder, thousands of troops were drafted into Glasgow.

After the Cabinet announced their intention not to intervene in the dispute, the strikers marched into George Square on January 31. As the threat of trouble escalated, the Riot Act was read out to the crowds, for the first time in half a century.

When the crowds refused to disperse, the police launched a series of baton charges against the strikers in an attempt to clear the square. This action prompted a violent response from the workers and the air soon became thick with missiles – stones, rivets and bottles.

Over 40 people were injured, and the riot resulted in two of the strike leaders being arrested.

According to the Scottish Secretary, the riots in George Square revealed its true colours as a "Bolshevist rising".

Troops were rushed in to suppress the riot and by the following morning, six tanks and 100 army lorries were on the streets of Glasgow.

The strike subsequently collapsed after recriminations among the organising bodies. Hastily, the STUC backed away from militant action and Bloody Friday, as it was called, was seen as having discredited the revolutionary tactics of the CWC.

The two arrested strike leaders were convicted of incitement to riot and were given short prison sentences.

SPRING SUITS
of
Modern Cut
at
BAKERS

EXAMPLE—

The above illustration is one of the many new and popular fashions we are specialising for present wear.

The jacket is double-breasted – two buttons—long pointed lapels—outside breast pocket—slightly waisted.

Cut and fashioned by our own Expert Craftsmen, it is already most popular, but is only one of our many London and American fittings. We invite you to inspect—to compare our materials and prices.

LOUNGE SUITS
(MADE-TO-MEASURE)
£5 5/- to £9 9/-
BLUE SERGE SUITS,
£6 6/- to £10 10/-
And Intermediate Prices.

Every piece of material in our house has the price marked in plain figures, and you are welcome to call and examine freely.

When viewing ask to see our Spring Overcoats and Raincoats— to measure or ready for service— at prices to meet all demands.

NOTE—Open on Saturdays until 8 p.m.; Week Days, 7 p.m.; Tuesday (Half-Day), Closed at 1 o'clock.

ARTHUR BAKER & CO Ltd
MEN'S TAILORS.
17 UNION STREET
(Near Argyle Street Corner)

LOCAL AUTHORITIES IN RATES REVOLT

The financial burdens placed on local councils across Scotland by the Government's radical policies on housing, education and police pay led to an open revolt. Many authorities refused to impose the increased charges on their ratepayers, particularly the education rate, until their demands for a government grant were met. Parish councils such as those across Inverness-shire claimed that the ordinary people simply could not afford rates which had increased sixfold in three years.

Weak, Wasted Children

Grateful Mothers tell of Little Sufferers' Remarkable Cures by Dr. Cassell's Tablets

Dr. Cassell's Tablets

AN APPEAL TO EMPLOYERS.

IF YOU WANT THE SERVICES of an ex-officer, or ex-soldier of similar educational qualification, get into touch at once with the nearest Directorate of the APPOINTMENTS DEPARTMENT of the Ministry of Labour, with which ex-officers and soldiers of higher education are advised to register themselves for employment.

MAKE YOUR NEEDS KNOWN by telephone, telegram, or letter, to the nearest Directorate, where men who have fought for you are registered.

The Directorate for
LINLITHGOW, HADDINGTON, ROXBURGH, KIRKCUD-BRIGHT, WIGTOWN, LANARK (with all Glasgow area), SELKIRK, EDINBURGH, BERWICK, DUMFRIES, DUMBARTON, AYR, RENFREW, PEEBLES,

is situated at

BALMORAL HOTEL, PRINCES ST., EDINBURGH.

COMINGS...

Ludovic Kennedy
Broadcaster & Journalist

Chic Murray
Comedian

Hamish Henderson
Folklorist & Poet

PASSENGER FLIGHTS INAUGURATED

Scotland's first passenger air service was inaugurated early in May by a flight from Turnhouse in Edinburgh to Manchester. A similar service from Glasgow began a few days later. With fares of £19 compared to £2 13s 3d for a first-class train ticket, and the maximum number of passengers per flight being limited to five, the service was never likely to enjoy a widespread appeal.

THIS SPORTING LIFE

FOOTBALL	RUGBY UNION	GOLF	HORSE RACING	SHINTY
Scottish Champions Celtic	*Scotland vs England* No game played	*British Open Winner* No competition held	*Scottish Grand National Winner* The Turk at Bogside	*Camanachd Cup Winners* No competition held
Scottish Cup Winners No competition held				

ALL ____ the News
ALL ____ the Pictures
ALL ____ the Time

Daily Record and Mail.

The All-Scotland Newspaper. Sale Three Times That of Any Other Morning Paper.

THE PAPER WHICH GETS THINGS DONE.

ESTAB. 1847 No. 23,049. GLASGOW, FRIDAY, NOVEMBER 26, 1920. ONE PENNY

MYSTERIOUS OUTRAGE IN PHOENIX PARK, DUBLIN.

STILL BUILDING TANKS.

PARTS FOR 50 BEING MADE IN GLASGOW.

AMAZING SQUANDERMANIA.

QUESTIONS FOR M.P.'S TO RAISE.

Amazing Squandermania.—The amazing revelation, made by our Investigator in London, that the War Office is still building large numbers of tanks and armoured cars in this country, shows to what extremes the Squandermaniacs are still going in their waste of public money.

Building Tanks.—The nation's resources are being spent on the building of tanks—a Glasgow firm, Messrs. Beardmore and Co., is concerned in the contract—after hundreds of these mammoth war engines have been scrapped, and when the state of the country's finances preclude expenditure for necessary constructive work.

Question for Parliament.—Here is a glaring case of Squandermania which calls for the matter being raised in Parliament without delay, for either confirmation or denial, and a complete and satisfactory explanation of the whole circumstances given to the public.

WASTING PUBLIC MONEY ON WAR MATERIAL

TANKS AND ARMOURED CARS FOR "SIDE-SHOWS."

(By Our Investigator.)

London, Thursday.

Searching for leakages in Government spending departments that are draining the Nation's financial resources. I was astonished to learn that the War Office is still spending considerably on the manufacture of war materials.

Armoured cars and tanks are still being made in this country.

I doubted the statement, but I was positively assured of its correctness.

WHY NEW TANKS?

The manufacture of tanks at this late hour of the day, after so many hundreds of them have been broken up and sold as scrap, under the Disposals Board's scheme, seems an extraordinary method of wasting public money.

They are said to be for use in one or other of our foreign military "sideshows"; and this may partly explain, when other things are taken into account, the excessive drainage of money these vague enterprises are costing.

I was told that at the moment, the celebrated Glasgow steelmakers, Messrs. Beardmore & Co., are manufacturing the parts for fifty new tanks.

A GLASGOW CONTRACT.

Every economist will express his whole-hearted disapproval of such wasteful expenditure, especially when not a penny can be afforded even for constructive schemes.

One must be careful, of course, to exclude the Glasgow firm from any association with such criticism.

The Company is believed to be the best in the world at producing this particular kind of material, and any such contracts go to them as a matter of course.

That they have the work on hand is, rather than anything else, a high tribute to the excellence of their productions.

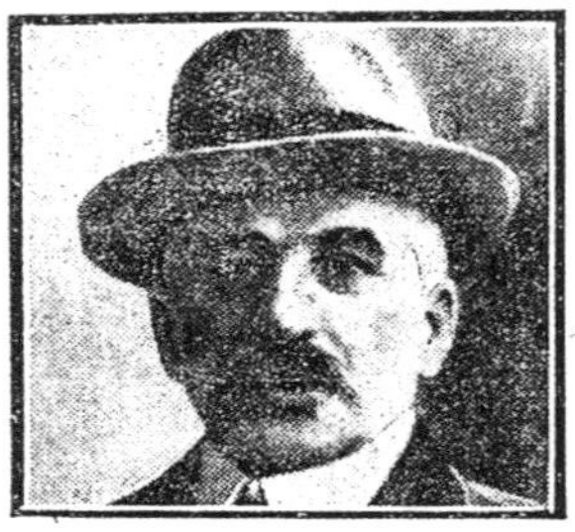

M. LEYGUES,
The French Premier, who is to discuss the Greek problem with Mr. Lloyd George to-day

PREMIERS MEET TO-DAY.

PROBLEMS OF NEAR EAST.

M. Leygues, the French Prime Minister, who was accompanied by M. Berthelot and others, arrived in London last night to confer with the British Prime Minister on the situation in the Near East, and the questions arising out of the peace settlement generally.

They were met at Victoria by Mr. Lloyd George, the Earl of Derby, the French Ambassador in London, and others.

The French party drove off to Hyde Park Hotel, and arrangements were made for them to visit Downing Street this afternoon.

Signor Giolitti, the Italian Premier, will not take part in the conversations, but will be represented by his Foreign Minister, Count Sforza.

M. VENIZELOS IN FRANCE.

Nice, Thursday.

M. Venizelos arrived here to-day, accompanied by a numerous suite.

In an interview, M. Venizelos said: "When I can speak, I shall be glad to make a declaration. One should not be too hard on the Greek people."—Reuter.

"TINO" WANTS REFERENDUM.

Lucerne, Thursday.

Dr. Streit, ex-Greek Foreign Minister, returned here to-day from a brief visit to Berne.

The object of his visit was to tell the British Minister there that ex-King Constantine fully approved the declaration recently made by the Greek Premier on the subject of cordial co-operation with the Entente.

Dr. Streit laid great stress on "Tino's" great desire for a referendum of the Greek people.—P.A.

ANOTHER DEPARTMENT?

FIGURES FOR COSTS, PROFITS AND PRICES.

The establishment of a permanent Costings Department to be set up under the Board of Trade is recommended in the report issued yesterday on costings in Government departments made by the Standing Committee on the investigation of prices.

The Committee state that they see no reason why general reports should not be issued based on records of prices given voluntarily and confidentially to Government departments provided that the names of the individual firms do not appear.

In view of the permanent value of the records collected during the war the Committee recommended that they should be assembled and housed under the charge of the Board of Trade.

The proposed Costings Department should be empowered to conduct surveys of the trade of the country and to publish regularly statistical information on the subject of costs, profits and prices.

MORE IRISH MURDERS.

MYSTERY OF A VOLLEY NEAR PHOENIX PARK.

THE SINN FEIN PLOTS.

WOMEN IN MANCHESTER WRECKING SCHEME.

Phœnix Park Mystery.—Five fresh outrages are reported from Ireland. Mystery surrounds the murder of a soldier and a constable who were shot dead shortly before the Curfew, near Phœnix Park, Dublin. A volley of about 20 revolver shots rang out, but no one appears to have seen who fired.

Sinn Fein Plots.—The statement in Parliament, by Sir Hamar Greenwood, that £3500 has been spent recently in Scotland by the Irish murder gang, supports the "Daily Record" Investigator's reports of the mystery traffic in arms and ammunition that has been going on in the West of Scotland.

Women in the Plot.—It transpires that the pass which enabled the Sinn Fein spy to gain admission to the Manchester electrical power station was obtained by one or two women.

DUBLIN MYSTERY.

SOLDIER AND CONSTABLE SHOT DEAD.

(From a Special Correspondent.)

Dublin, Thursday.

A constable and a soldier were shot dead in the immediate neighbourhood of Phœnix Park, Dublin, shortly before curfew last night

The affair is wrapped in mystery, and although many have been interrogated no light has yet been thrown to indicate who was responsible for the shooting.

20 SHOTS HEARD.

An official account states that about twenty shots were heard in the vicinity of Infirmary Road, near the avenue leading to King George Fifth Hospital.

A man was found dead, and he was subsequently identified as Constable Thomas Dillon, R.I.C., 28 years old, and a native of County Roscommon.

Later it was found that Lance-Corporal Turner, 15th Hussars, aged 19, had been shot dead in Infirmary Road, while in charge of a party of eight soldiers.

The firing appears to have come from all directions.

There were considerable numbers of people on the scene at the time.

It is reported that a number of men were stopped and searched, but afterwards released.

LABOUR LEADERS RELEASED.

Mr. Thomas Johnston, secretary of the Irish Labour Party and Trades Union Congress, and Mr. Thomas Farren, ex-president of the Irish Transport and General Workers' Union, who were arrested at the time of the raid on Liberty Hall last night, have been released.

Further information about the raid indicates that it was of a very thorough character.

A fireplace in a back room on the second floor appeared to have been recently renovated. It was examined and behind it were found a few bombs.

OTHER THREE DEATHS.

Prisoner's Fatal Dash for Freedom.

According to official reports issued from Dublin Castle to-day, Michael Moran, of Tuam, while being escorted on Wednesday night to camp at Galway, attempted to escape. He was fired upon, and died later.

The dead body of Denis O'Donnell, a tailor, of Mitchelstown, pierced by several bullets, was found on Wednesday night.

Martin Lyons, an ex-soldier, was attacked by armed men at Tinnymuch Moate, Co. Westmeath, this morning, and shot dead.

A WONDERFUL ESCAPE.

County Inspector Madden, of Cork, had a wonderful escape from death at 3 p.m. to-day.

He was fired at by a man with a revolver, and the bullet passed through both his cheeks, inflicting two slight wounds.

CROKE PARK VICTIMS.

At Glasnevin Cemetery, Dublin, yesterday, the remains of six of the victims of the shooting at Croke Park were buried. The funerals were private.

(Sunday Massacre Funeral Scenes—Page 2.)

SINN FEIN PLOTS.

£3500 SPENT ON ARMS IN SCOTLAND.

Sir Hamar Greenwood's announcement in Parliament that £3500 had been spent recently in Scotland, but particularly in Glasgow, in purchasing arms for assassins in Ireland bears out the statements in the "Daily Record" from time to time of the mystery traffic in firearms and ammunitions in the West of Scotland

Acting on information, the Lanarkshire police have paid surprise visits to houses of Sinn Feiners in the industrial villages and succeeded in seizing an odd gun or revolver here and there.

Since the Firearms Act came into operation recently the police have made effective use of their new powers, and they intend to prosecute a more vigorous search.

BOTHWELL RAID.

It is also known that several members of Saturday afternoon Sinn Fein brake clubs have been found to carry revolvers in their pockets, all of which goes to prove that the Sinn Feiners in Scotland have some secret organisation whereby they are supplied with arms.

The recent Bothwell raid, where a supply of R.I.C. uniforms came into the possession of the police, affords further proof of a traffic with Ireland.

GREENOCK MYSTERY.

'Derry Boat Passengers Closely Scrutinised.

There was unusual excitement at the Custom House Quay, Greenock, last night between nine and ten o'clock, when the steamer Rose left for 'Derry.

No one in authority could or would venture an explanation of the crowd of 200 people, mostly Irishmen, who gathered round to see the vessel off.

Greenock police guarded the gangway, and several plain clothes men moved among the crowd.

A close scrutiny of every passenger was made, and it was believed that an attempt to carry over munitions was being made in a round about way for the rebel forces.

A young woman of about 23 made her way through the crush laden with a heavy bag, and when she saw the police making an examination she withdrew.

As she was watched by the "Daily Record" investigator she transferred the bag to a man, who went westward, on the quayside, and about ten minutes afterwards another man appeared from the spot which they had chosen with something in a travelling rug, and went up the gangway without interference.

Neither the young woman nor the man who first took the bag attempted to get on board.

WOMEN IN THE PLOT.

How Pass to Manchester Power Station Was Got.

Mr. S. L. Pearce, the chief electrical engineer to Manchester Corporation, stated yesterday that the pass to visit the electrical power station in Stuart Street, used by Sinn Feiners in October, was obtained through an innocent employee at the request of one or two women.

Whether these women were or were not

(Continued on Page 2, Column 2.)

BIG FRENCH FAMILIES

OVER £80,000 DISTRIBUTED IN BOUNTIES.

Paris, Thursday.

Over £80,000 were distributed by the French Academy to-day to parents with large families in prizes of £1000 each.

Among the beneficiaries was one family of 20, some of 19, many of 14, some of 15, and others of 12 children.—Reuter.

RUSSIAN WAR RUMOUR.

SOVIET AND POLAND STILL NEGOTIATING.

Reuter learns in authoritative circles that no confirmation has been received in London of the alarmist report to the effect that the Peace negotiations between the Soviet and Poland at Riga have been broken off.

The negotiations at Riga were suspended last week owing to the failure of the Poles to evacuate troops from Volhynian territory, in accordance with the Armistice terms.

But the Soviet authorities accepted the Polish explanations, and resumed negotiations on November 21.

FRANCE TO TRADE WITH SOVIET

Paris, Thursday.

M. Leygues, the French Premier, told the Foreign Affairs Committee yesterday that the French Government had decided to permit French merchants and manufacturers to open commercial relations with Soviet Russia.—Reuter.

LEAGUE AMENDMENTS.

TURNED DOWN BY MAJORITY AT GENEVA.

Geneva, Thursday.

In the ballot held by the first commission of the League of Nations' Assembly relative to amendments to the covenant proposed by the Scandinavian Governments, 20 states voted against the amendments, and 8 for, while 3 abstained.

M. Lange (Norway) said the amendments were in no way contrary to the Treaty of Versailles.

M. Viviani (France), on the other hand, considered that the Commission should, as a matter of principle, reject any amendments, as the first meeting of the assembly must not convey the impression that it was revising clauses of the Treaty.—Reuter.

MORE U.S. STEEL ORDERS.

New York, Thursday.

The Carnegie Steel Company, competing with foreigners, has obtained from the Netherlands Government an order for 15,000 tons of rails at the price of 52 dollars per ton.

The American Bridge Company has secured an order for 5800 tons of steel for a bridge, connecting Santa Catharina Island, Brazil, with the mainland.—C.N.

190 MILES AN HOUR.

New York, Thursday.

Lieutenant Mosley (American Army) won the Palitzer Trophy at Mineola, Long Island, to-day, with a flying speed of approximately 190 miles an hour.—Reuter.

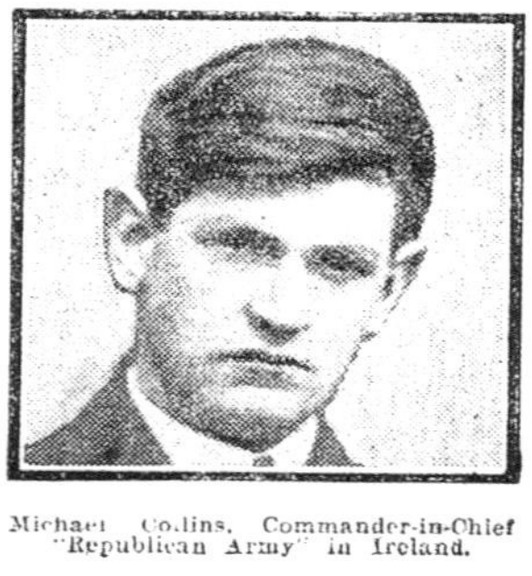

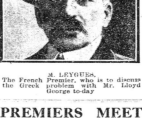

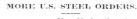

Michael Collins, Commander-in-Chief "Republican Army" in Ireland.

PROBE ON TANKS CASH 'WASTE'

INVESTIGATIONS were launched to discover the extent to which Government "squandermaniacs" were wasting public money.

Revelations made by a *Daily Record* investigator indicated that the War Office was still building large numbers of tanks and armoured cars in Scotland – a full two years after the end of the Great War.

The nation's resources were being spent on the building of tanks and Glasgow firm Beardmore and Co were contracted to produce them. This came after hundreds of tanks had been broken up and sold as scrap.

A question was raised in Parliament, demanding that the spending be confirmed or denied and that a complete and satisfactory explanation be given to the public.

The *Daily Record* investigator was searching for leaks in Government spending departments when he discovered the War Office spending on the manufacture of military materials. The building of tanks after so many had been scrapped under the Disposal Board's scheme seemed an extraordinary waste of public money.

Two influential associations representing practically the whole business world advised the Government that industry could not stand another "Squandermania Budget".

Businessmen pointed out that instead of searching for a substitute for Excess Profits Duty, the Chancellor should be concentrating on economy, as the taxable limit of the country had already been overstepped.

They declared that if squandering by the various departments was brought to an end, the Excess Profits Duty and the Corporation Tax could be dropped and wartime spending would be replaced by normal expenditure.

And they added that a very important element in reducing prices and the cost of living was that the Government should make smaller demands from the taxpayer.

It had been abundantly proved that not only could no further contribution be expected from industry, but the balance had already gone too far in this respect.

COMINGS...

Molly Weir
Actress & Writer

GOINGS...

John Bartholomew
Map-maker

OPEN GOLF VICTORY

Scotsman George Duncan won the British Open Championship at Deal in July. In a thrilling finish, Duncan made up 13 shots over the second 36 holes to finish two shots ahead of England's Sandy Herd. His score of 141 for the last 36 holes was not bettered for another 15 years. As well as taking the coveted title, Duncan also collected £100 prize money.

WHAT IT COST

POUND OF BUTTER
2s

POUND OF BACON
2s

PINT OF BEER
3d

CIGARETTES
10d (8 Players No. 3)

WOMEN'S SHOES
£1 18s

MEN'S SUIT
£5 10s

TON OF COAL
£1 9s 6d

POSTAGE
1½d

CAR
Morris Cowley £175

H.M.S. HOOD DEPARTS

Britain's largest warship, H.M.S. *Hood*, left her birthplace on the Clyde to begin her sea-trials. The massive warship was commissioned after the Battle of Jutland in 1916 and was hailed as a triumph of naval architecture, the greatest warship in the world. She was also the most expensive, having cost over £6 million to build. Sadly, the *Hood* met her end in May 1941 following a fierce exchange with the new generation of super-battleship, the Nazis' *Bismarck*.

THIS SPORTING LIFE

FOOTBALL	RUGBY UNION	GOLF	HORSE RACING	SHINTY
Scottish Champions Rangers	*Scotland vs England* England 13–4 Scotland at Twickenham	*British Open Winner* George Duncan at Deal, England (303)	*Scottish Grand National Winner* Music Hall at Bogside	*Camanachd Cup Winners* Kyles Athletic at Glasgow
Scottish Cup Winners Kilmarnock				

FOR LATEST STRIKE NEWS
— See —
'Noon Record.'

Daily Record and Mail.

The All-Scotland Newspaper. Sale Three Times That of Any Other Morning Paper.

ESTAB. 1847—No. 25,185. GLASGOW, THURSDAY, MAY 5, 1921. ONE PENNY.

SHELL is the ONLY Motor Spirit sold to dealers in bulk with the stipulation that it shall be stored and retailed separately, not mixed with Petrol of any other brand or grade.

SHELL

DISORDERS FOLLOW GLASGOW SINN FEIN OUTRAGE.

CITY AMBUSH MURDER.

SINN FEIN GUNMEN ATTACK POLICE VAN.

INSPECTOR SHOT DEAD.

18 ARRESTS INCLUDING 2 WOMEN AND A PRIEST.

At Prison Gate.—Desperate recklessness was shown by a Sinn Fein gang who ambushed a police van in a busy Glasgow thoroughfare at midday yesterday, killing an inspector and wounding a sergeant of police beneath the walls of Duke Street prison.

Attempted Rescue.—The object of the dastardly attack was to rescue from the police a Sinn Fein prisoner much wanted by the Irish authorities. The attempt was, however, frustrated by the courageous stand of the police escort, who returned their assailants' fire.

Arrests.—A pitched battle was waged in the street, and it was only by a miracle that the crowd which thronged the thoroughfare escaped without hurt, the only casualties being the unfortunate police officers. Eighteen persons, including two women, and a priest, were arrested in connection with the outrage later in the day. After these arrests, disorders took place in the evening leading to the apprehension of other 12 people.

Inspector Robert Johnstone, shot dead by Sinn Fein gunmen in Glasgow, yesterday.

GRIM FIGHT UNDER SHADOW OF GALLOWS

VAN SURROUNDED BY 3 BANDS OF GUNMEN.

Glasgow was yesterday the scene of a Sinn Fein ambuscade which equals in daring and recklessness many of the outrages in Ireland.

A police van was attacked by bands of armed men at mid-day in High Street, one of the city's busiest thoroughfares.

One police officer, Inspector Robert Johnstone, was shot dead, and Detective-Sergeant George Stirton was severely wounded.

Eighteen persons, including two women and a priest, suspected as being implicated in the crime, have been arrested.

Everything points to the ambush having been carefully planned.

PITCHED BATTLE.

The van was conveying to Duke Street Prison from the Central Police Court a prisoner named Frank Somers, who is urgently wanted by the Irish police on a number of serious charges.

Somers' rescue was undoubtedly the object of the dastardly attack

That object was not attained.

When about 200 yards from the prison gate the van was fired upon without warning of any kind.

The vehicle stopped in the shadow of the portion of the gloomy building where executions are carried out, and there Inspector Johnstone was murdered.

The police returned the fire of their assailants, and a pitched battle was waged in the street.

Bullet marks in the walls and windows of the neighbouring buildings bear mute testimony to the fury of the fight.

Remarkable to relate, however, the casualty list was confined to the unfortunate police officers.

Although the street was crowded with pedestrians and vehicular traffic, not a single civilian was hit in the wild exchange of shots.

POLICE PRECAUTIONS.

Prisoner Charged With Jail-breaking.

All the circumstances of the outrage point to its perpetrators being fully alive to the movements of the prisoner whose rescue they meant to effect.

Somers was arrested in Glasgow on April 29, and on Saturday last he appeared before the Central Police Court, when he was remanded until yesterday to permit of further investigation of his career.

Accordingly he appeared before the Court again yesterday charged with having.

(1) On November 25, in Sligo, stolen a revolver;
(2) On June 26, 1920, broken out of Sligo Jail, and
(3) On February 15 last broken out of Londonderry Jail.

Lieutenant Gray explained that particulars of the prisoner's case had not yet been received from Ireland, and asked for a remand until Saturday, pending more particular inquiry.

Suspecting that they had a prisoner of some considerable importance in the Sinn Fein movement,—suspicions which have been fully confirmed by yesterday's tragedy—the police observed especial precautions in conveying their man from the Central Police Office to Duke Street Prison.

The largest of the fleet of patrol wagons was used.

Posted beside the driver were Inspector Johnstone, Detective-Sergeant Stirton, and Detective-Constable M'Donald, all fully armed.

Somers, who is a stoutly built man of 32, was placed in a small compartment in the fore part of the van, where he had no more than standing room.

In adjoining compartments were two constables and another prisoner.

Shortly before half-past twelve the van left St. Andrew's Square and proceeded up High Street towards the Drygate entrance to Duke Street prison.

ATTACKERS IN 3 BANDS.

Prison Van the Centre of a Ring of Fire.

The police van had almost reached the prison corner, when suddenly the monotonous hum of the traffic was broken by two sharp cracks.

The prevailing impression was that a motor-car or cycle had sustained a puncture, and no one seemed to worry.

Then there broke out a perfect fusillade of shots, and the startled pedestrians saw three bands of men armed with pistols firing at the van from either side of High Street.

One party was stationed at the corner of Rottenrow, another at the angle of the prison wall, and a third fired from High Street, behind the van.

The "Black Maria" was thus practically surrounded by a ring of desperate gunmen.

The van stopped. Its wind-screen was smashed, and Inspector Johnstone, who was sitting in front, dropped dead into the street, shot through the heart.

Shot after shot was fired. Men gasped and women screamed. People ran excitedly in all directions.

Detective-Sergt Stirton and Detective Constable M'Donald jumped down into the street, and opened fire.

ASTRIDE DEAD BODY.

Sergeant's Brave Defiance of Desperadoes.

The sergeant stood astride Inspector Johnstone's body, and carried on firing until a bullet shattered his right wrist.

Realising that the prisoner inside the van was the object of the daring attack, Constable Ross, who was at the wheel, and who miraculously escaped the bullets of the gunmen, set the vehicle in motion and swung into Drygate.

One of the desperadoes, more daring than his fellows, ran into the roadway behind the van just before it started off.

Pointing his pistol at the doorway he fired a shot through the lock. The door swung open.

The Sinn Feiner remained in the street.

With his pistol hand held close in to his waist he launched round after round inside the van, which was now in motion. Then he bolted.

By this time the officers' fire seemed to have shaken the morale of the attackers, for they broke from their cover and fled in all directions.

One desperado ran along Rottenrow.

Despite his wounded wrist, Detective-Sergeant Stirton started off in pursuit, but loss of blood began to tell, and he had to give up the chase.

WOUNDED SERGEANT.

Strength Gives Way After Splendid Work.

He returned to where Inspector Johnstone lay and assisted in placing the unfortunate inspector's body in a motor delivery van which had come upon the scene.

Unselfishly refusing an offer of succour for himself, Sergeant Stirton turned into Drygate and, pointing his pistol, dispersed the crowd who had surged round the prison gate as the van was being manœuvred inside.

Once within the gate, the plucky sergeant's strength gave way, and he collapsed.

After his wound had been dressed by the prison doctor he was conveyed to the Royal Infirmary, whither the body of Inspector Johnstone had been removed.

During the daring attempt to rescue him, Somers made no demonstration of any kind inside the van.

But when he was removed in the prison yard it was noticed that his face was pale with excitement.

(Continued on Page 2.)

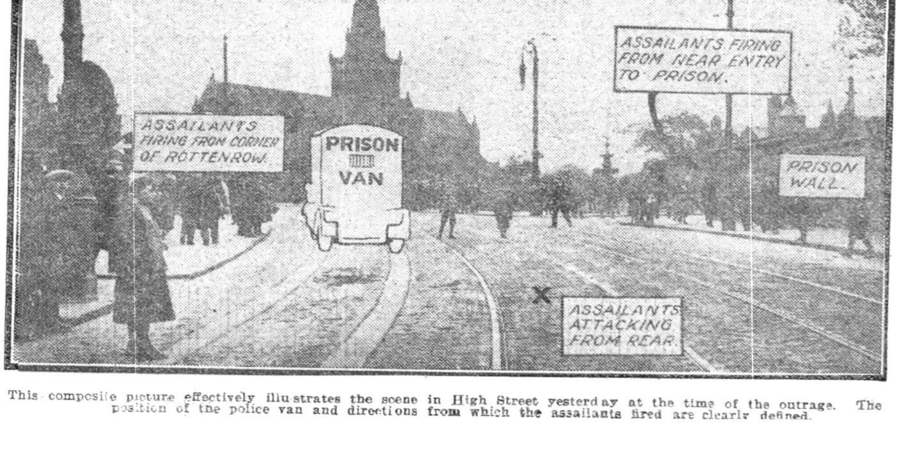

This composite picture effectively illustrates the scene in High Street yesterday at the time of the outrage. The position of the police van and directions from which the assailants fired are clearly defined.

POLISH REVOLT IN SILESIA.

ALLIED TROOPS IN ACTION.

REBEL COUPS.

Berlin, Wednesday.

All the large towns in the industrial region of Upper Silesia are surrounded by Polish insurgents.

According to semi-official advices received here, a suburb of Gleiwitz is actually in possession of the rebels.

Kiefferstaltze was also occupied this morning by bands of well-armed Poles.

In Rybnik, the Poles have occupied the railway station, post office, and the headquarters of the provincial Government, whilst the Polish flag is flying over the Town Hall

The occupation of Rybnik was preceded by sharp fighting with Italian troops, who are said to have suffered not inconsiderable loss.

The whole of the right bank of the River Oder, in the Ratibor area, is in the hands of the rebels.

Some French motor cars, which were advancing on the insurgents, were received with a lively rifle fusillade, and replied with machine guns.

This morning fresh bands of rebels assembled outside Kattowitz.

At present they are advancing on Bismarckhuette, where energetic counter measures are being taken.—Reuter.

21 ITALIAN CASUALTIES.

Berlin, Wednesday.

Fighting between Allied troops and the insurgent Polish bands is still in progress at Gleiwitz.

At Pless, two officers and 19 men of the Italian forces have been killed, and their commander seriously wounded.

At Antonienhutte, ten policemen were put to death.—C.N.

ALLIES' ULTIMATUM.

EXPIRES WEDNESDAY NIGHT AT TEN.

The Supreme Council sat till ten minutes past 12 this morning, when the ultimatum to Germany was signed.

This ultimatum makes reference to the question of disarmament, and that of the punishment of war criminals.

It will be handed to the German Ambassador in London by the Prime Minister this morning, and is timed to expire at 10 o'clock on the night of the 11th.

FOCH RETURNS TO PARIS.

Paris, Wednesday.

Marshal Foch, General Weygand, Admiral Grasset, and General Nollet arrived in Paris at five o'clock this evening from London.—Reuter.

GERMAN SENSATION.

UNANIMOUS RESIGNATION OF THE GOVERNMENT.

Berlin, Wednesday.

In view of the situation which has arisen following the American reply, the German Government to-day unanimously decided to resign.—Reuter.

MINES AND SUBSIDY.

SLIDINGSCALE PLAN.

M.P'S. AND PEACE

Considerable interest has been aroused by the suggestion, made by Mr. Frank Hodges, secretary of the Miners' Federation, in a letter to "The Times," yesterday, regarding the financial assistance offered by the Government to the miners.

Mr. Hodges, who stated that the miners would accept a reduction in wages of 2s per day, said this would mean a Government contribution of £36,000,000.

His suggestion, however, is that this State assistance should be related specifically to the cost of living, and be operated on a sliding scale basis, in which case, should the cost of living fall by the end of the year to a certain figure, the Government subsidy would disappear altogether.

Interviewed on the matter yesterday, Mr. Hodges said he had nothing to add to what was stated in his letter.

FEDERATION'S POLICY.

This proposal on the purely wages aspect of the dispute. the "Daily Record" learns, undoubtedly represents the official policy of the Federation, and is not a personal expression of opinion by Mr. Hodges.

No arrangement has been made by the Miners' Federation for calling the National Executive together in London.

The taking of a ballot on the Government's offer is regarded as a question of policy, on which only the Executive or a delegate conference could decide.

OWNERS' NEW FIGURES.

It is understood that the mineowners have decided to post new wage scales in the mining areas, showing the effect of the Government's offer of £10,000,000 upon the wages which would be payable if the men went back to work.

These figures, it is gathered, will show a very substantial advance upon those first exhibited, which precipitated the dispute.

MEDIATION PLEA.

M.P.'S URGE GOVERNMENT TO RENEW PARLEYS.

Mr. Hodges' proposal was referred to when the new emergency regulations—which give the Government further powers for restrictions on train services, lighting, summer time, etc.—came before the House of Commons last night.

Mr. Clynes said the country was looking to the Government to act as mediators in bringing the coal dispute to a close.

It was clear that the dispute could not be settled by the application of force.

One cause of the continuance of the deadlock was the feeling among the miners and their leaders that the Chancellor of the Exchequer had been acting as an advocate and exponent of the interests of the mineowners.

The Home Secretary defended the necessity of these continued regulations.

He indicated that the danger from the Triple Alliance was not yet over, particularly in the event of the Government having to import coal supplies from abroad.

MR. HODGES' PROPOSAL.

Colonel John Ward urged the Government to resume negotiations with the miners.

Mr. Hodges had that day made a suggestion of practically a new principle on which the dispute could be settled.

Mr. Renwick and other members supported the necessity for the regulations, and the resolution embodying the new regulations was carried by 215 votes to 54.

"THE END IN SIGHT."

MR. THOMAS SAYS STRIKE WILL BE OVER WITHIN A WEEK.

Acting upon medical advice, Mr. J. H. Thomas, M.P., is taking a few weeks' rest, and sailed yesterday from Southampton for America.

Before he sailed, Mr. Thomas predicted that the coal crisis would be over within a week.

He declined to state his reasons, but remarked that, if he did not think the end of the present deadlock was in sight, he would not have contemplated leaving the country at this juncture

(Other Strike Matter on Page 2, Col. 1.)

1921

IRA MURDER GLASGOW POLICEMAN

IRA terrorists ambushed a police van in Glasgow on May 5, killing an inspector and wounding a sergeant near Duke Street Prison.

The object of the attack was to rescue from police custody an IRA prisoner, Frank Somers, who was urgently wanted by the Irish police on a number of serious charges. About 200 yards from the prison gate, the van was fired on without warning. The police returned fire and a pitched battle was waged in the busy thoroughfare. The rescue attempt failed but not before the inspector had been fatally wounded .

Somers had been arrested in Glasgow on April 29, and the next day, at the Central Police Court, he was remanded until May 4, to permit further investigation. When he appeared before the court again, he was charged with:

BREAKING OUT of Sligo Jail on June 26, 1920.

STEALING a revolver on November 25, 1920, in Sligo.

ESCAPING from Londonderry Jail on February 15, 1921.

The court was told that the details of Somer's case had not yet been received from Ireland and a remand until May 7 was granted.

Police suspected that they had an IRA prisoner of some importance and they took special precautions while transferring Somers from Central Police Court to Duke Street Prison.

Eighteen people, including two women and a priest, were suspected of being implicated in the ambush and were arrested.

Disturbances in the evening in the east end of the city led to the arrests of 12 other people.

DOUBLE COLLISION DISASTER

In October, the Firth of Clyde was the scene of a disastrous double collision. The passenger steamer *Rowan,* bound for Dublin from Glasgow, was struck by an American freighter, the *West Camak,* in dense fog off Corsewall Point in Wigtownshire.

As the passengers and crew were abandoning the *Rowan,* she was then rammed a second time by another ship, the *Clan Malcolm,* (seen left after the incident) heading for Liverpool. Most of the 20 fatalities resulted from this second collision.

MALTONA
THE PERFECT
TONIC WINE.
4/6 per bottle; 2/4 per half-bottle.

GARDENING.
NATIONAL SAFETY!
GROW MORE VEGETABLES.
PURDIE'S CHOICE GARDEN SEEDS.
ONION SETS, SHALLOTS.
Royal Horticultural Society War Pamphlet,
"VEGETABLES AND HOW TO GROW THEM,"
Post Free, 5d.
D. G. PURDIE, 6 WATERLOO STREET, GLASGOW.

RITO (Horticultural No. 1) suits everything that grows. Wonderfully increases all crops. Allotment Holders and Gardeners should buy from W. Elliot, 243 Buchanan Street, Glasgow.

COMINGS...

George Wylie
Sculptor

Deborah Kerr
Actress

George Mackay Brown
Poet & Writer

GOINGS...

John Boyd Dunlop
Pioneer of the Pneumatic Tyre

THE END OF THE WORLD WAS NIGH

The Church of Scotland began an unofficial inquiry into a growing movement within its ranks which was predicting the imminent end of the world. At a packed meeting in Edinburgh in December, Pastor Fred Clark (right) declared, "The revival is to go on. It is coming to this city and dear old Glasgow is going to get her baptism of fire." And as the year drew to a close, in several of the fishing villages of the north east where the movement was strong, residents abandoned their usual chores and pursuits as they awaited "the crack o' doom". There is no record of their views on what was to happen once they realised the world had not ended.

THIS SPORTING LIFE

FOOTBALL	RUGBY UNION	GOLF	HORSE RACING	SHINTY
Scottish Champions Rangers	*Scotland vs England* Scotland 0–18 England at Inverleith	*British Open Winner* Jock Hutchison at St Andrews (296)	*Scottish Grand National Winner* Race abandoned	*Camanachd Cup Winners* Kingussie at Inverness
Scottish Cup Winners Partick Thistle				

Motor Insurance
Scottish Automobile and General Insurance Co. Ltd.
136-138 Hope Street, Glasgow.

Daily Record and Mail.
The All-Scotland Newspaper. Sale Three Times That of Any Other Morning Paper.
ESTAB. 1847—No. 23,516. GLASGOW, SATURDAY, MAY 27, 1922. ONE PENNY.

FOR LATEST DERBY NEWS
— See —
'Noon Record.'

SAXON AND SCOT IN FINAL OF GOLF CHAMPIONSHIP.

TO-DAY'S GOLF DUEL.

HOLDERNESS & CAVEN.

SCOTT'S FEAT.

HOW WETHERED AND HUNTER FELL.

(By Our Golf Expert.)

Prestwick, Friday Night.

The final contest for the supreme honour in amateur golf will be fought out, as it has been so often in the past, by representatives of English and Scottish golf; but there are new elements in the last stage of to-morrow.

Mr. Ernest Holderness, who will uphold the honour of England, is an Anglo-Indian, and is the first of that great sporting community to go so far in golf.

Mr. Caven, who will endeavour to bring the championship cup for the first time to Renfrewshire, belongs not to the leisured few, who usually play so prominent a part in these national conflicts, but to that great and ever-increasing class which takes recreation on the links after the day's business has been attended to.

CONTRAST IN STYLES.

The final promises to be an exposition in styles, for the Scotsman, who is short and stocky, plays with a compact, well controlled swing, while Mr. Holderness is full and free with his shots.

The final is over 36 holes, and the morning round starts at 10 o'clock, and the afternoon round at 2.30.

Since the inauguration of the event 36 years ago, there have been 12 English-Scottish finals; and the English have won on eight occasions.

The events of the penultimate day's golf were the overthrow of Hunter and Wethered.

The two appeared to be converging remorselessly from the extreme corners of the draw, but golf is a game of strange surprises.

SCOTT'S FEAT.

Robert Scott, of Glasgow, slew the English Goliath, and Holderness destroyed Hunter.

There is no gainsaying that the popular imagination pictured a final between the champion, who has now fallen, and the distinguished golfer who tied for the open championship.

Wethered lost so much in the first nine holes against the steady, straight, "the far and sure" Scott, that although the latter had a relapse on the first four holes in the return journey, and should have lost the lot, Wethered did not seize all his chances, and found the leeway too heavy; while Hunter was not able to cope with the flash of Holderness' brilliance after the turn.

THE FINALISTS.

Mr. Holderness was born at Lahore, India, in 1890, but it was on English links that he learned and perfected his game. He was in the Oxford University teams of 1910, 1911, and 1912, and it is notable that in the three championships since the war Oxford has been represented in the final, in 1920 by Cyril Tolley, last year by Allan Graham, and this year by Ernest Holderness.

Holderness has for some years been recognised as one of the most polished and elegant golfers in England.

His style leaves nothing to be desired, the only mark on his golfing reputation has been that he was not the best man in a tight match.

Mr. Caven was born at Dornoch 30 years ago, and is now in the counting-house of John Lang & Co., Johnstone.

His brother is the professional to the Cochrane Castle Golf Club, an eighteen hole course, a short distance from Milliken Park and Johnstone.

He has distinguished himself for a number of years in West of Scotland contests.

He has won the Tennant Cup (held at present by Robert Scott) and the Newlands Trophy.

His greatest achievement was a victory in the Eden tourney at St. Andrews last year, when he defeated the great English golfer, R. Montmorency, in the semi-final.

SURPRISE OF THE TOURNEY.

Mr. Robert Scott, of the Glasgow Club, it may be safely said, achieved the greatest surprise of the championship by his brilliant overthrow of Mr. Wethered yesterday forenoon.

A product originally of the public parks courses in Glasgow, having learned the game at Alexandra Park, Mr. Scott, in his twenty years' identification with the game, has done much to earn distinction; but none of his honours, not even his four Glasgow Championships, will compare, as a triumph, with this feat of ousting the brilliant Oxonian.

(Continued on Page 2, Col. 1.)

E. W. E. Holderness, of Walton Heath, who meets John Caven, of Cochrane Castle, in the final of the Amateur Golf Championship

PERILS AT HOME AND ABROAD.

PREMIER AND PEACE APOSTLES.

Britain is not out of danger.
The world is not out of danger.
Humanity is not out of danger.
There are perils abroad.
There are perils nearer our coast.
There are perils inside this Island.

Mr. Lloyd George gave these reasons for the people standing together in a spirit of combination and co-operation at a luncheon given by his supporters in appreciation of his work at the Genoa Conference.

Of the work at Genoa he said:—

"It has been begun, and, having been begun, it is going through to the end.

"We have undertaken a task of the greatest magnitude and the greatest complexity beset with difficulty at every turn, but a task which is vital to the well-being of humanity, not merely in the British Empire and throughout the Continent of Europe, but throughout the whole world."

WHAT AMUSED HIM.

Proceeding, he said that nothing had amused him more than the eagerness with which some of the greatest friends of peace had been trying to demonstrate that they had failed.

Over-eagerness to demonstrate the failure of an enterprise always indicated a real anxiety that it should fail.

So, when he saw some apostles of peace demonstrating their joy and satisfaction at every prediction of failure, showing gloom and wrath at every prediction of possible success, he came to the conclusion that the wish was father there to the thought.

TOO MUCH TO EXPECT.

It was too much to expect that in six weeks they would overcome the difficulties of Europe and abate all the suspicions.

They were deeper, more complex than that, but if they persevered they would accomplish in the end.

We mobilised 9,500,000 men.

Had we no right to say something as to what peace should be established in the world?

Our casualties in that war were 3,266,000.

Britain, who put her might into the fighting, would henceforth put forth all her great might to establish the peace of the world and good-will amongst men. (Cheers.)

QUEEN 55 YESTERDAY.

QUIET BIRTHDAY AMONG HER FAMILY.

The Queen was 55 yesterday, having been born at Kensington Palace on May 26, 1867.

The Queen was the recipient of innumerable congratulations from all parts of the Empire.

The Prince of Wales cabled from the Renown and Prince George from his ship offering their congratulations, while the various other members of the Royal family tendered theirs in person.

Princess Mary paid an early visit to her mother, and was subsequently joined by Viscount Lascelles.

The birthday was celebrated quietly at Buckingham Palace, where the members of the immediate Royal family met at luncheon.

A SALUTE FOR THE QUEEN.

A Royal salute was fired from the big gun battery at Stirling Castle, yesterday, in honour of Queen Mary's birthday.

Royal Artillerymen from Piershill, Edinburgh, were brought to Stirling to fire the salute.

DERBY DAY PUZZLE.

SCARE STORY ABOUT PONDOLAND.

BETTING STIR.

Next Wednesday is Derby Day. As the date of the greatest horse-racing event in the world approaches, interest in it becomes more and more pronounced.

The old classic Epsom event—it was instituted in 1790 by the 12th Lord Derby—brings out a host of punters who, perhaps, never risk a shilling on a horse in any other race of the whole season.

The number of sweepstakes organised for next Wednesday's event is said to constitute a record.

Preparations for the great cosmopolitan crowd which will assemble at Epsom Downs, on Wednesday, are being pushed ahead.

All that remains is successfully to "spot the winner."

People everywhere discuss and dogmatise on the chances or improbabilities of this or that horse, the mount of such and such a jockey, the tips from one stable or another, the hopes of the owners concerned.

PONDOLAND RUMOUR.

Thus, a report which got about yesterday that Pondoland, the Derby favourite, is unwell, created quite a stir all over the country.

These scare reports are usual on the eve of the race.

Late last night, Mr. Joel, the owner of Pondoland, issued the following statement:—

"I think Pondoland's prospects good. Whatever beats him will win.—Sol Joel."

An immediate effect of the rumour, however, has been to depose Pondoland from the position of favourite, and to re-establish St. Louis in the premier position of the wagering.

Pondoland, which was quoted in the betting yesterday morning at 3½ to 1, dropped back last night to 6 to 1.

The latest and most reliable news about all the horses and everything connected with the Derby will be found in the Noon Edition of the "Daily Record."

POINCARE'S THREAT.

NEED TO DEMONSTRATE TO GERMANY.

Paris, Friday.

M. Poincare, referring in the Chamber to-night to the German reparations payment due on May 31, said he was convinced that it would not suffice to appeal to the goodwill of Germany, and that it would be necessary to demonstrate to her, if she did not show goodwill, that France had the means to compel her.—Reuter.

POINCARE'S LONDON VISIT.

Paris, Friday.

It is stated that M. Poincare will visit London on 17th and 18th June in response to invitations received some weeks ago from the City of London and the British League of Help. He will be accompanied on his visit by General Petain.—C.N.

FILMING FLIGHT.

WORLD FLYERS OVER ALPS TO-DAY.

The following message was received last night from Major Blake:—

Paris, Friday.

After a variety of adventures in the fog, the second aeroplane (which is to accompany the world flyers to Athens) arrived at Le Bourget at 7 o'clock to-night.

A start will be made to-morrow soon after dawn for Rome, by way of Lyons and Turin. This will involve a stiff climb over the Alps.

Major Blake was unable to start from Paris on the second stage of the journey at six this morning, as he had intended, owing to the delay in the arrival of the second machine.

"We are naturally anxious," added Major Blake, "not to go on without her, as we want to get a full cinematograph record of this early stage of the journey taken by one of the passengers, Mr. Malins, who did such fine work for the British War Office on the Somme.

"Our own 'bus is now in absolutely perfect order."

Major Blake had the honour to-day, of being introduced to M. Millerand, President of the Republic, who cordially wished him good luck.—"Daily News," Copyright, per C.N.

BAKERS' STRIKE OFF.

John Caven, of Cochrane Castle, who meets E. W. E. Holderness in the final of the Amateur Golf Championship to-day.

DELICATE IRISH SITUATION.

TO-DAY'S BIG PARLEY IN LONDON.

Developments in regard to the discussions of the Irish situation which opened in London, yesterday, are of such a delicate nature as may necessitate an eleventh-hour change in the Premier's week-end plans.

It is now considered unlikely that he will be able to spend the week-end at Chequers as previously arranged.

It is probable that his presence will be necessary at the conferences which are expected to take place in London over the week-end.

Informal talks between Mr. Churchill, Mr. Griffith, Mr. O'Higgins and Mr. Kennedy were carried on until late yesterday afternoon.

Mr. Griffith laid before Mr. Churchill the Irish Provisional Government's view of the Collins-De Valera pact, and after discussion lasting three hours, it was learned that the Colonial Secretary intimated that he wished to consult the Prime Minister and his Cabinet colleagues before the discussions proceeded further.

A meeting of hte Cabinet Committee on Ireland was called, and met at 10 Downing Street in the afternoon.

BIG CONFERENCE TO-DAY.

The Prime Minister presided, and there were present Mr. Chamberlain, Mr. Churchill, Sir L. Worthington Evans, Sir Hamar Greenwood, with Lord FitzAlan standing by in case his advice was required.

To-day an important conference of British and Irish co-signatories to the peace agreement will be held at 10 Downing Street, at which the Premier will preside.

Then, it is expected, progress will be made as the result of the presence of Mr. Collins, who, it is understood will arrive in London this morning.

SIR H. WILSON IN BELFAST.

Sir Henry Wilson, M.P., arrived in Belfast yesterday, and was present at a meeting of the Northern Ireland Cabinet, presided over by Sir James Craig.

THROWN OVER BRIDGE.

MAN ATTACKED BY MOB IN BELFAST.

(From Our Own Correspondent.)

Belfast, Friday.

After another stormy night, Belfast to-day has been comparatively quiet.

Several desperate incidents occurred during last night.

When returning home over Albert Bridge, a man, supposed to be a gunman, was attacked and beaten by a mob and then thrown over the bridge into the River Lagan and drowned.

Information of a sinister character having reached the Ulster Government, steps were to-day taken to protect the Belfast harbour, shipping, and shipyards.

Military and police guards have been strengthened all over the docks area, and no one will be allowed inside the harbour premises without an official permit.

DESTROYER ARRIVES.

MASSING OF REBEL FORCES NEAR LONDONDERRY.

A British destroyer arrived in the River Foyle yesterday and anchored in mid-stream opposite the British military barracks in Londonderry.

The reason for the vessel's arrival is unknown, but opinion in Londonderry is that it is the sequel to the concentration of large I.R.A. Forces in the Free State close to the Londonderry-Donegal border, and only a few miles from Londonderry city.

SETTLEMENT TERMS.

WAGES & HOURS

5 O'CLOCK WEEK-DAY START.

The dispute in the Scottish baking trade was amicably settled after a five hours' conference between the operatives and employers held in Glasgow last night under the auspices of the Ministry of Labour.

The threatened strike of Scottish bakers, therefore, is now definitely off.

Mr. M'Kerrell, of the Ministry of Labour, presided, and Mr. Morrison M'Laughlan, also of the Ministry, was present at the conference, which was composed of representatives of the Scottish Association of Master Bakers, embracing truce employers in Glasgow, the Co-operative Societies in the baking trade, and the Scottish Operative Bakers' Union.

The settlement does not apply to the non-truce employers in Glasgow, whose men have been on strike for three weeks.

Under an arrangement arrived at last week, the operative bakers throughout Scotland were due to come out on strike to-night, but the operatives' officials are rescinding the strike notices in view of last night's settlement.

SETTLEMENT POINTS.

The following are the principal points in the settlement:—

WAGES.—Wages will be regulated in terms of the 1921-22 National Agreement, according to the cost of living index figures.

Overtime during the six week-days will be paid for at the rate of time-and-a-half.

HOURS.—Wages will be fixed on the basis of a 45 and a 47-hours week.

A committee will be appointed, consisting of three representatives from each of the parties to the agreement, to determine the application, and the daily allocation of the hours.

In the event of the committee failing to agree, they must make application to the Ministry of Labour to appoint an arbiter to determine the differences between them.

This reference must be finally disposed of within fourteen days of the date of the agreement, namely, June 10.

STARTING HOUR.—Early men will not start earlier than 4 o'clock, on the first five days of the week, and 3 o'clock on Saturday.

The general body of the men will start not earlier than 5 o'clock on the first five days of the week, and 4 o'clock on Saturdays. Allowance for early men will be 5s per week.

Maximum overtime allowed on Saturdays will be 1½ hours. Ovensmen to be exempted from this rule.

Holiday and Sunday work, exclusive of "sponging," will be paid for at double time rates.

All operative bakers and confectioners employed shall be members of the Scottish Union of Bakers and Confectioners.

ABOUT DIFFERENCES.

Local joint committees with a minimum membership of three operatives and three employers, and a maximum of seven are to be appointed to deal with local conditions in accordance with the Agreement.

Failing a settlement, difference which may arise will be submitted to the Reference Committee, whose decision shall be final.

In addition to the provisions already mentioned, the Agreement regulates the conditions of employment of pastry bakers, confectioners, and other trades, and apprentices.

The present practice in each district in regard to holidays will remain in force, and the new Agreement will remain in operation from June 12, 1922, till April 30, 1923.

THE DRESS-SPOILERS.

INK-SQUIRTER CAUGHT RED-HANDED.

Paris, Friday.

One of the dress spoilers who have been the terror of Parisiennes recently, was caught red-handed on the Metro last night.

After two complaints that girls had had their dresses ruined by ink, inspectors travelled to St. Surplice Station and caught a young man squirting ink on a girl's dress with a fountain pen filler.

Taken to the police station, he gave the name of Lebon, and said he was an artillery soldier on leave.

Several bottles of ink were found on him.—C.N.

1922

11TH HOUR DEAL HALTS STRIKE

THE dispute in the Scottish baking trade was settled amicably during a five-hour conference between the workers' union officials and employers held in Glasgow on May 26.

Bakers had been due to go on strike the next day under an arrangement decided the previous week.

But in view of the "11th hour" settlement, union leaders rescinded the strike notices.

The principal points of the deal were:

WAGES: These were to be regulated in terms of the 1921-22 National Agreement, according to the cost-of-living figures.

HOURS: Wages were to be set on the basis of a 45-hour and a 47-hour week.

STARTING TIMES: Early men were not to start before 5am on the first five days of the week and 3am on Saturday.

The general body of men was not to start earlier than 5am on the first five days of the week and 4am on Saturdays.

The allowance for early men was to be 5s a week while the maximum overtime allowed on Saturdays was to be 1 hour 30 minutes.

Ovensmen were to be exempt from this rule.

Holiday and Sunday work, exclusive of "sponging", was to be paid for at double time rates.

All operative bakers and confectioners employed were to become members of the Scottish Union of Bakers and Confectioners and local joint committees were to be appointed to deal with local conditions in accordance with the agreement.

ROUND-THE-WORLD FLIGHT ATTEMPT

Glasgow pilot, Captain Norman MacMillan, was part of the team which left Croydon Aerodrome in May

on what they hoped would be a record-breaking round-the-world flight. Captain MacMillan, together with his colleagues Major Blake (seen left) and Lt Col. Broome, hoped to cover the 30,000 miles in their De Havilland DH9 in a little over 90 days. The first leg of the journey to Paris was accomplished easily, causing Major Blake to comment: "This journey over France was quite uneventful, which is precisely what we want the whole journey to be." Unfortunately, he did not get his wish. After being reported missing for over a week, their aircraft was eventually forced to ditch in the Bay of Bengal and the crew rescued. At this point the adventure was abandoned.

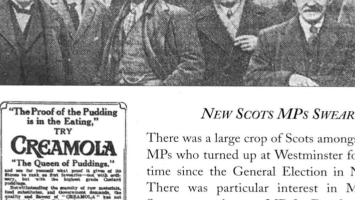

"The Proof of the Pudding is in the Eating," TRY

CREAMOLA

"The Queen of Puddings."

and see for yourself what proof it gives of its fitness to rank as first favourite—not with ordinary, but with the highest grade Custard puddings.

Notwithstanding the scarcity of raw materials, food substitutes, and Government demands, the quality and flavour of "CREAMOLA" has not depreciated in the slightest degree from its pre-war standard, which gained for it the reputation of being the "Queen of Puddings."

As for Economy, it contains the sustaining properties of fresh eggs, and a 7d packet carries about three times the quantity of any other high-class custard.

Sold by all Grocers and Stores, in 1¼d. 7d, and 1s 2d packets; and in large air-tight tins, 1s 6d.

D. K. PORTER & CO., GLASGOW,
Contractors to H.M. Government.

Send post card for Creamola Recipe Book, post free.

NEW SCOTS MPS SWEAR

There was a large crop of Scots amongst the new MPs who turned up at Westminster for the first time since the General Election in November. There was particular interest in Mr Edwin Scrymgeour, the new MP for Dundee, who had famously proclaimed to the local electorate that "the King would throw down his crown" when he was elected to Parliament. There was much speculation as to whether he would refuse to take the Oath of Allegiance. However, both he and the new Communist MP for Motherwell, Mr Newbold, did so without incident although it was noted that they, together with many of the Labour MPs, did so in the Scottish fashion. This involved raising their right hand and affirming their allegiance to the Crown, rather than the "English" method which involves invoking the name of God and kissing the Bible.

COMINGS...

Fulton Mackay
Actor

Cliff Hanley
Journalist & Writer

GOINGS...

Alexander Graham Bell
Inventor of the Telephone

THIS SPORTING LIFE

FOOTBALL	RUGBY UNION	GOLF	HORSE RACING	SHINTY
Scottish Champions Celtic	*Scotland vs England* England 11–5 Scotland at Twickenham	*British Open Winner* Walter Hagen at Sandwich, England (300)	*Scottish Grand National Winner* Sergeant Murphy at Bogside	*Camanachd Cup Winners* Kyles Athletic at Oban
Scottish Cup Winners Morton				

Daily Record

and Mail.

The All-Scotland Newspaper. Sale Three Times That of Any Other Morning Paper.

ESTAB. 1847—No. 23,932.   GLASGOW, WEDNESDAY, SEPTEMBER 26, 1923.   ONE PENNY.

GAS MANTLES

Ino XX., - - - 3/9 doz.
Searchlight XXXX., 5/- „
Estab. **PETER FISHER** 1816
57 HIGH STREET——GLASGOW

AVON
"DUROLITH"
CORD TYRES
for cars, motor cycles, cycles
"Throughout our 20 years of trading we have found no better tyres than AVON and no equal of that most excellent production the DUROLITH."
Messrs. J. W. Fryatt & Sons, York.

HEARTRENDING STORIES OF SCOTS PIT DISASTER.

43 MINERS ENTOMBED

ALL-NIGHT EFFORTS TO RESCUE THEM.

SCOTS PIT DISASTER.

SUDDEN RUSH OF WATER FOLLOWED BY BLACK DAMP.

All Scotland was shocked yesterday by the news of a pit disaster at Redding, Stirlingshire, which in magnitude may prove to be the most serious the country has experienced for the past 46 years.

While to date three bodies only have been recovered, it is feared that the lives of other 43 miners may be lost.

Slender as appears the hope of the entombed men being brought to the surface alive, all that is humanly possible is being done.

Since an early hour yesterday morning three rescue brigades have been performing heroic labours in order to reach timeously their comrades imprisoned in the pit bottom.

Several hours must yet elapse before it can be ascertained whether or not these exertions will be crowned with the success which they deserve.

Dusk was falling yesterday when the last member of the rescue party was drawn to the surface.

BLACK DAMP AND WATER.

Sadly the helmeted figures shook their heads in answer to the anxious inquiries which greeted them on emerging from the improvised cage.

Two terrors lurked below.

One was black damp, and the other, equally grave from the rescuer's viewpoint in this particular instance, was a flood of water

Walking about the bottom, the rescue brigade found themselves up to the thighs in inky black water.

Until both these evils had been overcome it was impossible, they asserted, to do anything further for the relief of their fellows.

PUMP AT WORK.

To this end, steps were speedily in progress, and by early evening a pump, capable of dealing with 2000 gallons of water per minute, was in action, and a fan, intended to ventilate the underground workings, was being placed in position.

Expert opinion considers that it may be about the breakfast hour this morning before the consuming anxiety of the dependents of the entombed men will be answered.

How grievous is the blow to the district may be gauged from the fact that the men imprisoned in the pit are believed to have upwards of 200 dependents.

CAUSE UNKNOWN.

PIT ONE OF THE DRIEST IN THE COUNTRY.

Sir Adam Nimmo, chairman of Messrs. James Nimmo & Company, the owners of the Redding Colliery, who visited the scene in the afternoon, was much distressed.

To a "Daily Record" representative Sir Adam made the following statement:—

The company cannot give an official statement at this juncture. No one can say exactly how the disaster occurred.

It was evidently due to an inrush of water from somewhere.

The flooding was the last thing we would have expected to occur.

As a matter of fact, we considered that the pit was probably the driest in the country. We never had any apprehensions about flooding.

It is a coalfield by itself, and in the daily experience the amount of water pumped from it was exceptionally small.

It had always been understood that a great, impregnable barrier existed to the south of the coalfield which cut it off absolutely from the other fields.

The old workings were higher than the new pit.

AN ABSURD STORY.

In Glasgow, to-day, I heard some ridiculous reports about water from the Forth and Clyde Canal having penetrated into the pit. That is an absurd idea.

We shall continue the rescue operations until we have cleared every ounce of water from the pit and recovered all the bodies, if, unhappily, the men cannot be rescued alive.

(Moving Stories of Disaster on Page 2.)

Sir Adam Nimmo, who informed a "Daily Record" representative that the pit where the disaster occurred was regarded as one of the driest in the country.

AMBASSADORS IN DILEMMA.

HITCH OVER JANINA REPORT.

Paris, Tuesday.

The Conference of Ambassadors cannot agree on the report which it has received from the Commission it appointed to investigate the murder of the Italian mission at Janina.

The Ambassadors intended to meet this morning, but a previous interview having proved unsatisfactory, the meeting was put off until 4.30 this afternoon.

They met then until seven o'clock, but without result, and another meeting will be held to-morrow morning.

ITALIAN REFUSAL.

The Italian Ambassador refuses to accept the report, which, there is good reason to believe, finds

1. That the crime was not a political one.
2. That Greece has in no way been romiss in trying to find the murderers.

On the second point there is not absolute insistence, and the Italian Ambassador maintains that the evidence shows that Greece has not done her best to clear up the authorship of the crime, and considers Italy will proceed to exact the sanctions provided for from Greece.

The conference appears to be in complete disagreement, and a serious situation may arise.

The Governments of the respective countries concerned are being asked for further instructions, and from Italian quarters it is suggested that unless a settlement is reached a less conciliatory attitude may be expected from Rome. —C.N.

END OF RESISTANCE.

GERMAN SURRENDER TO BE UNCONDITIONAL.

BACK TO WORK IN THE RUHR

REICHSTAG EXPECTED TO CONFIRM DECISION.

Reichstag To-Morrow.—It but remains for the Reichstag to-morrow to homologate the decision of the German Federal Premiers and the political parties in the occupied regions yesterday to abandon passive resistance in the Ruhr.

The Surrender.—The surrender is to be unconditional, though an official announcement lays it down that "the unity of the Reich" is to be safeguarded. The principle established is that the return to work should be ordered as a whole and not by isolated decrees.

NEWS IN FRANCE.

DENOUEMENT TAKEN FOR GRANTED.

Paris, Tuesday.

The news of the German Government's decision to terminate passive resistance is received here with calm satisfaction, but there is no tendency to premature jubilation — for various reasons.

Firstly—Such a denouement has been all along taken for granted in France.

Secondly—It is not yet clear that the Reich's capitulation is absolutely unconditional.

Thirdly—It is observed that Herr Stresemann's condemnation of resistance is based, not on principle but on mere expediency.

Fourthly—It is held that the bare official withdrawal of the decrees ordering resistance is simply an outward visible sign.

LESS VISIBLE.

Before General Degoutte is instructed to render the occupation less visible, the French Government must be satisfied that the capitulation of the Reich is unconditional, and have proofs that resistance has ceased.

Should, as may happen, Herr Stresemann follow up the cessation of resistance by forwarding concrete proposals to Paris, it goes without saying that these will be immediately communicated to Great Britain.—Reuter.

FIGHT'S FUTILITY.

WHAT SWAYED THE STATE PREMIERS.

(From A Special Correspondent.)

Berlin, Tuesday.

Now that the State Premiers, as well as the representatives of employers and workers in the Ruhr, are agreed that in unconditional surrender to France on the question of the abandonment of passive resistance in the Ruhr lies the sole hope of saving Germany from irremediable chaos, it only remains for Herr Stresemann to announce publicly that the Government regulations supporting the population of the Ruhr in their resistance are to be withdrawn.

He is expected to do this in his statement before the Reichstag on Thursday, or else before the Foreign Committee of the Reichstag to-morrow.

THE VITAL FACTOR.

The factor which more than anything else convinced the State Premiers to-day of the utter futility of continuing the fight in the Ruhr was the Chancellor's revelation that no less than 8000 milliard marks would be needed to finance the struggle during next week.

It was the need for finding such large sums, Herr Stresemann declared, that had caused the collapse of the mark and had chiefly influenced the Government in its decision to abandon the struggle.

The State Premiers, including, apparently, Dr. Von Knilling, the Bavarian Premier, were convinced by the facts and figures brought forward by the Chancellor of the hopelessness of Germany's position, and realised that unconditional surrender would have to be made, and that the question of the release of political prisoners and the return of those expelled from the Ruhr would have to be left to the generosity of the French at the eventual negotiations.

What is going to happen in Germany now is a question no one can answer.

OUTBREAK RUMOURS.

The air is full of rumours of impending outbreaks, either by Nationalists or by Communists, but these need not be taken very seriously.

There is not doubt that the ultra-Nationalists are furious at the collapse of passive resistance in the Ruhr and the Government's surrender to France.

They would joyfully welcome a coup, which would overthrow the Stresemann Government, but they are not at present strong enough.

In any case, whatever may happen, the Government is prepared for all the eventualities, and professes to have the utmost confidence in the Reichswehr in event of a "Putsch," whether from the Right or the Left.

HOLIDAY CURTAILED.

Mr. Ramsay Macdonald, speaking at an Independent Labour Party dinner in London last night, said that in view of the existing situation he had curtailed the duration of his visit to the Near East.

All the French victory meant was that a powerful and well-armed country had taken a country broken and disarmed, and had strangled it.

NEW EARTHQUAKE.

123 DEAD AND 100 INJURED IN PERSIA.

Teheran, Tuesday.

Considerable damage was caused by earthquake shocks on Thursday at Bujnurd, in the province of Khorassan. Several villages are reported to have been completely destroyed.

The casualties, so far as is known at present, are 123 dead and about 100 injured.—Reuter.

THE ANGUISH OF IT.

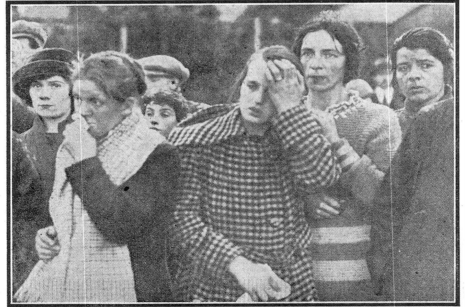

A picture to move every heart to deepest sympathy.

PIT DISASTER STUNS SCOTLAND

THE whole of the country was shocked by the news of a pit disaster at Redding in Stirlingshire. It was the most serious Scotland had experienced in almost 50 years.

The rescuers managed to bring up 21 of the miners but by the night of September 25, there were still 42 men entombed below ground.

Rescuers faced two major difficulties before they could even start their rescue operation.

The first was the black damp and the other was a flood. As rescuers walked at the bottom of the pit, they found themselves up to their thighs in inky black water and until these two hazards had been dealt with, it was impossible for them to do anything further to rescue their trapped workmates.

Steps to combat both these hazards were quickly taken and by early evening, a pump was in action, along with a fan to ventilate the underground workings.

The rescue brigades, with tireless determination, worked desperately round the clock to reach the helpless miners, but without success.

A spark of hope flared briefly for the relatives of those still trapped when, two days after the rescue of the 21 men, two rescuers emerged from the temporary shaft erected by the "Gutter Hole" where the first batch of men had been rescued with news that there was air in the mineshaft: "We found some mice scampered about the pit bottom" the rescuers reported.

But both the families and the rescuers alike knew from bitter experience that it would only be by a miracle that any of the 42 trapped men could still be alive. Sadly, that miracle did not happen.

COMINGS...

Bill McLaren
Rugby Commentator

Roddy MacMillan
Actor & Playwright

Gordon Jackson
Actor

GOINGS...

Andrew Bonar Law
Unionist Statesman

FASTEST FLIGHT TO GLASGOW

A new record was established in July for the fastest flight between London and Glasgow. F. T. Courtney covered the distance in 2 hours and 29 minutes during the King's Cup air race. Of the 17 entrants for the competition, 14 started and 11 finished the three-leg trip to Renfrew Aerodrome from Hendon via Birmingham and Newcastle. Courtney's was the first aircraft to arrive at Renfrew, having averaged speeds of 150mph, and the remaining pilots touched down over the space of the next 30 minutes. Courtney's performance gained him two prizes: a cup for the first aircraft to arrive at Renfrew and a £40 cheque for the fastest overall time from London to Glasgow.

DUNOON CENOTAPH UNVEILED

In scenes that were being echoed throughout the country, a war memorial to commemorate the 400 men from Argyll who made "the supreme sacrifice" was unveiled in Dunoon by General Sir Ian Hamilton. The memorial, which stands some 28 feet high, was designed in the Scottish Renaissance style. The unveiling ceremony was preceded by a church service and pipers played *The Flowers of the Forest* as the large crowd made their way after the service to the memorial. The Provost of Dunoon accepted the memorial into the keeping of the town council and the day ended with a large number of wreaths being laid.

ON RADIO

A Talk to Women

Boy's Life Brigade Bulletin

The Children's Corner

An Hour of Melody by The Wireless Trio

Classical Night of The Wireless Orchestra

THIS SPORTING LIFE

FOOTBALL	RUGBY UNION	GOLF	HORSE RACING	SHINTY
Scottish Champions Rangers	*Scotland vs England* Scotland 6–8 England at Inverleith	*British Open Winner* Arthur Havers at Troon (295)	*Scottish Grand National Winner* *Harrismith* at Bogside	*Camanachd Cup Winners* Furnace at Inverness
Scottish Cup Winners Celtic				

WOMAN WHO FIGHTS MEXICANS. Page 11.

Daily Record and Mail.

The All-Scotland Newspaper. Sale Three Times That of Any Other Morning Paper.

ESTAB. 1847—No. 24,180. GLASGOW, SATURDAY, JULY 12, 1924. ONE PENNY.

WASH FROCKS FOR THE HOLIDAYS
in a large variety of designs and styles in Ratine, Sponge Cloth and Striped Zephyrs.
In all leading colour effects and offered in two lots at
HOLIDAY PRICE......10/- & 15/-
The BONANZA Ltd.
173 to 185 ARGYLE ST.

HANDING OVER TSARIST £10,000,000 TO SOVIET.

TSARIST MILLIONS.

GIVING SOVIET BANK OF ENGLAND DEPOSITS.

CONFERENCE PROPOSAL.

GOVERNMENT "WATCHING" BRITISH CREDITORS' INTERESTS.

If an agreement under consideration by the Anglo-Soviet Conference in London is finally approved, the Soviet will get the £10,000,000 or £12,000,000 deposited in the Bank of England and other banks by the Tsarist Government.

It is understood that if an agreement, which is at present being considered by the Anglo-Soviet conference in London, is finally approved, it will have the effect of benefiting the Soviet Government to the extent of probably £10,000,000 or £12,000,000.

If the Treaty of Commerce is concluded, it will supersede the old trade agreement drawn up in 1921, and will enable the Soviet Government to claim money, now in the Bank of England and other banks, which belonged to the Russian Imperial Government.

The drawing up of the Treaty, so far as the British Government is concerned, has been left by the Prime Minister in the hands of Mr. Ponsonby, Under-Secretary for Foreign Affairs.

Well-informed circles in London state that there is nothing unexpected in the Treaty, since one of the principal objects of the conference was to put the Soviet Government in the position formerly occupied by the Tsarist Government.

The Treaty of Commerce has not yet been finally approved, and no further plenary session of the conference has been fixed.

It was pointed out last night that the agreement was not a separate matter, but was part of the general Treaty, which it would be the endeavour of the conference to draw up.

In the event of complete agreement being reached by the conference on all points, including Soviet indebtedness to this country, sums in the possession of the former Russian Government would be released in favour of the Soviet Government, but not as part of any partial agreement.

In this connection it was mentioned that it has been stated in the House of Commons that the Government were fully aware of the situation and were watching the interests of the people who had lost money in Russia.

HERRIOT REPLIES TO POINCARE.

BIG SENATE VOTE OF CONFIDENCE.

Paris, Friday.

M. Herriot replied this afternoon, in the Senate, to the speech made by M. Poincare yesterday.

If the Allies were not to agree on the Dawes plan, were they, he asked, to return to the policy of enclosing the Ruhr and mass expulsions.

The French Government must hurry up and substitute an inter-Allied Agreement for the Agreement which now exists between France and Belgium.

He pointed out that Germany, in January next, would retake her economic liberty so far as France was concerned, and it was therefore in the interests of France that some agreement should be arrived at.

GERMAN LOAN.

It was not sufficient to issue bonds in connection with the Dawes plan.

It was necessary to place these bonds—and the British and American Governments were constantly occupied with this task—so that there would be no loss of confidence between the interests of the future bearers of bonds and the Government.

The Experts' Report depended clearly on the co-operation of the Allies and Government.

M. Poincare interrupted, and said M. Herriot implied that each Government was left with its political freedom.

M. Herriot maintained that if one accepted the Dawes plan, one must also accept its directing principles, and one of those principles was that the problem of Reparations must henceforth pass into the economic domain.

There was another interruption regarding Mr. MacDonald's speech yesterday.

M. Herriot said he had not read the text of the speech.

He explained that it was the Reparations Commission which would present to the London Conference suggestions for the putting into operation of the Dawes Plan, and that the Commission would say when the plan was really put into operation.

The Premier added that Italy and Belgium had already accepted the bases of the Franco-British Note.

M. Herriot received a vote of confidence by 246 votes to 18.—C.N.

BRITISH MEETING.

A meeting was held in the Premier's room at the House of Commons yesterday to consider questions connected with the forthcoming Inter-Allied Conference. There were present:—

Mr. Ramsay MacDonald.
Mr. Philip Snowden.
Mr. J. H. Thomas.
Mr. Sidney Webb.
Hon. Peter Larkin (High Commissioner for Canada).
Sir Joseph Cook (High Commissioner for Australia).
Sir James Allen (High Commissioner for New Zealand).
Mr. James M'Neill (High Commissioner for Irish Free State).
Lord Olivier (Secretary of State for India).

SCOTCH EXPRESS.

Eric Liddell, the Scottish champion, yesterday won the 400 metres Olympic race in the world's record time of 47 3-5 secs.

METAGAMA AGAIN ASHORE.

CRIPPLED LINER'S FATE.

St. John's (N.F.), Friday.

The crippled Canadian-Pacific liner, Metagama, which has been undergoing repairs here since June 20, after her collision with the Italian steamer, Clara Camus, off Cape Race, went ashore this afternoon off the entrance to the harbour.

The Metagama was leaving for Quebec for permanent repairs. The vessel is now surrounded by tugs trying to get her off.

The ship took on a bad list. It became difficult to control her, and the wheel chains broke when she was swinging around for exit.

It will be remembered that after the collision on June 19, the Metagama contrived to reach port, but the captain, owing to her sinking condition, had to beach her on a mudbank.—Reuter.

LLOYD GEORGE'S ALTERNATIVE TO STATE MINES. Page 5.

REBELS' COUP.

BRAZIL CITY HELD, DESPITE HEAVY GUN FIRE.

Buenos Aires, Friday.

A message to "La Nacion" states that the Government of Sao Paulo has been deposed, and that a revolutionary junta headed by General Rondon has formed a temporary Government.

The rebels are reported to be continuing their operations successfully, and it is feared the movement may extend.

Efforts by the Federal Authorities to take Sao Paulo have failed in spite of violent bombardments which have inflicted many casualties on the inhabitants.

Disquieting reports from other quarters indicate that the Federal troops are joining the rebels, and even the navy is believed to be tainted with the revolutionary spirit.—C.N.

VERA CRUZ MURDER.

New York, Friday.

A message from Mexico City states that a British subject named Herbert Vereker has been killed at Potrera Bellano (in the northern district of the State of Vera Cruz) by bandits because of his refusal to give over his money to them.—C.N.

SCOTS RUNNER'S FEAT.

E. H. LIDDELL'S TRIUMPH AT OLYMPIC GAMES.

WINS 400 METRES RACE.

CREATES NEW WORLD'S RECORD AFTER THRILLING FINISH.

Eric H. Liddell, an Edinburgh University student, and Scottish champion sprinter, won a notable victory for Britain at the Olympic Games in Paris, yesterday. Not only did he win the 400 metres race, but he created a new world's record by covering the distance in 47 3-5 secs.

A GREAT RACE.

LIDDELL BREAKS TAPE THREE YARDS AHEAD.

Paris, Friday.

The Union Jack flew in proud majesty over the Colombes Stadium to-day, for the only final down for decision, the 400 metres flat, resulted in a great victory for Britain.

The brilliant running of E. H. Liddell, the Edinburgh University sprinter, was responsible, and in covering the distance in 47 3-5 seconds he created the third world's record in two days for this event.

Guy Butler, the old Light Blue was third, being separated from the winner by Fitch, the American, who, in the semi-final returned 47 4-5 seconds, beating Imbach's 48 seconds dead of yesterday.

SKIRL OF THE PIPES.

The race was the one bright spot in the afternoon's sport, for with the Decathlon events occupying most of the programme, the crowd had sunk into more or less apathy.

There had been nothing to applaud. The 100 metres times were all mediocre compared with the recent performances of the cream of the world's sprinters in the event proper.

It looked like being a dull afternoon. Suddenly the pipers of the Cameron Highlanders, who had assembled in the middle of the stadium began playing, and the crowd broke into cheers at the lively strains of a Scotch air.

SEMI-FINAL THRILL.

It was the prelude to better things. It was time for the 400 metres semi-finals, and the Decathlon was relegated to the centre of the stadium.

The first was a thrilling race. Butler, one of the British representatives, reproduced his brilliant form of yesterday, and confident of qualifying, slowed up nearing the tape, to finish a comfortable second.

Even then he was only beaten by inches by Fitch, who returned a world's record time.

The crowd were stirred, and when the time was announced there was a remarkable demonstration of enthusiasm.

STIRRING RACE.

However, there was better to come, for the final was even more thrilling.

There was a gasp of astonishment when Eric Liddell, one of the most popular athletes at Colombes, was seen to be a clear three yards ahead of the field at the half distance.

Nearing the tape Fitch and Butler strained every nerve and muscle to overtake him, but could make absolutely no impression on the inspired Scot.

With 20 yards to go Fitch seemed to gain a fraction, but Liddell appeared to sense the American, and with head thrown back and chin thrust out in his usual style, he flashed past the tape to gain what was probably the greatest victory of the meeting.

So far, certainly, there has not been a more popular win.

FRENZY OF ENTHUSIASM.

The crowd went into a frenzy of enthusiasm, which was renewed when the loud speaker announced that once again the world's record had gone by the board.

The day really closed on this glorious note.

Far away in a remote corner of the Stadium a few decathlon competitors were hurling themselves at the high jump, but they were almost unobserved for the crowd had gone with the thrill of Liddell's victory fresh in their minds.

'VARSITY STUDENT.

HOLDER OF THREE SCOTTISH CHAMPIONSHIPS.

Eric H. Liddell, who was born in Tientsin, China, on January 16, 1902, comes of a sterling sporting ancestry.

His father was a missionary in the Far East, but before that he was a gymnast and fencer of marked ability. His father had strong family associations with Greenock and Loch Lomondside, while his mother was born in the Scots Border country.

Young Liddell received his early education at Eltham College and succeeded his brother, R. V. Liddell, as captain of the school.

In his youthful schooldays he gave promise as an athlete, but it was when he went to Edinburgh University that he showed his real mettle.

TRIPLE SCOTS CHAMPION.

He has held the 100 yards and 220 yards Scottish amateur championships since 1921, and last month at Hampden at the S.A.A.A. championship meeting he completed the triple event by adding to his list of triumphs the 440 yards race.

Two years ago Liddell gave the English athletes a taste of his ability by romping home in the 100 yards and 220 at the British championship gathering, and this year he won the 440 yards.

If there have been ups and downs in his running career, it is due to the fact that he is a student first and an athlete afterwards.

NOT TO WRECK IT.

MR. ASQUITH AND THE HOUSING BILL.

Speaking at Norwich last night in connection with the Liberal campaign, Mr. Asquith said neither of the opposite parties was for the moment in good trim for aggressive work.

The Labour Government had produced a good, wholesome Free Trade Budget, but what else was there to their credit?

Their path week by week was strewn with unfulfilled pledges and broken promises. While they had enjoyed the almost unexampled tolerance and no lack of good will or helpful co-operation, they had shown a singular incapacity for constructive statesmanship.

Referring to housing, Mr. Asquith declared that no attempt had been, or would be, made by the Liberal Party to wreck the Government Bill.

They wished it well so far as it was an effort to deal on a comprehensive and continuous scale with a grave and urgent national problem. Mr. Asquith, however, strongly criticised the finance of the scheme.

RAILMEN'S BILL.

LEADERS TO FRAME MEASURE FOR NATIONALISATION.

The National Union of Railwaymen, sitting in conference at York, yesterday, adopted a re-drafted resolution:—

(1) Welcoming the grouping of the railways, and

(2) Calling upon the Executive to frame a Bill to be submitted to Parliament having for its object the nationalisation and democratic control of the railways.

Mr. Figgins, of Glasgow, opposed the resolution as not going far enough.

The working class, he contended, had very little to learn in regard to the control of industry.

It was not the few men who sat on Boards of Directors and drew big salaries who really administered the Railway industry.

It was the workers, and particularly the supervisory grades who were organised in that Union who were responsible for the actual administration.

LIDDELL GRABS OLYMPIC GOLD

EDINBURGH University student and Scottish champion sprinter, Eric Liddell, won a famous victory for Britain at the Olympic Games in Paris in July.

Not only did he win the 400 metres race, but in doing so he created a new world record, covering the distance in 47.35 seconds.

There was a gasp of astonishment when Eric Liddell, one of the most popular athletes at the Games, was seen to be a clear three yards ahead of the field at half the distance.

Then, with 20 yards to go, the great American runner Fitch seemed to gain on him a fraction.

But Liddell appeared to sense Fitch's presence and with his head thrown back and chin thrust out in his characteristic style, he shot through the tape to secure victory.

The crowd went into a frenzy, which increased when it was announced that Liddell's final charge had broken the world record.

During the Games, Liddell was at the centre of a controversy.

The Scots sprinter was a deeply religious young man and refused to run one of his events because it was due to take place on a Sunday.

Eric Liddell showed promise as an athlete in his schooldays, but it was when he went to Edinburgh University that his true talent was fully realised.

He had held the 100 yards and 200 yards Scottish amateur championship titles since 1921 and in June 1924, he completed a "hat trick" by adding the 400 yards title to his list of triumphs.

Later in the century, Liddell's record-breaking win at the Paris Games provided the climax for the Oscar-winning film *Chariots of Fire*.

COMINGS...

Eduardo Paolozzi
Sculptor

Rikki Fulton
Actor & Comedian

GLASGOW BOMB PLOT FOILED

An ambitious plan by Irish Republican terrorists to dynamite important public buildings and utilities in Glasgow was uncovered by police in May. *The Sunday Mail* reported that the likely targets were believed to be the Post Office in George Square, the City Chambers, various docks and the Dawsholm gas works in Maryhill. The perpetrators of the planned outrage were said to be Republican extremists living in Glasgow who were unhappy with the recent Anglo-Irish Treaty and the resulting partition of Ireland. Following a tip-off from an informer, the police were able to prevent the bombers from carrying out their plan although the terrorists escaped.

LABOUR'S FIRST PM

James Ramsay MacDonald became Britain's first Labour Prime Minister in January following the fall of the Tory minority government on a vote of confidence. Lossiemouth-born MacDonald, the MP for Aberavon, had become Labour leader in November 1922. On becoming PM, he warned that as a minority government leader, he was in office but not in real power and that Labour MPs, particularly the "Red Clydesiders", would have to limit their expectations of a Socialist revolution. In the event, a general election in November ousted him from office.

GOINGS...

Peter Mackie
Distiller & Founder of White Horse whisky blend

THIS SPORTING LIFE

FOOTBALL	RUGBY UNION	GOLF	HORSE RACING	SHINTY
Scottish Champions Rangers	*Scotland vs England* England 19–0 Scotland at Twickenham	*British Open Winner* Walter Hagen at Hoylake, England (301)	*Scottish Grand National Winner* Royal Chancellor at Bogside	*Camanachd Cup Winners* Kyles Athletic at Kingussie
Scottish Cup Winners Airdrie				

WOMEN IN THE PULPIT. Page 2.

Daily Record and Mail.

ESTAB. 1847—No. 24,555. GLASGOW, THURSDAY, SEPTEMBER 24, 1925. ONE PENNY.

LOAF TOO DEAR? Page 9.

MINERS' TRUMP CARD IN AGREEMENT DISPUTE.

TO-DAY'S EXECUTION.

FAMILY'S LAST INTERVIEW WITH KEEN.

BAILIE MRS. BELL'S ORDEAL

FIRST WOMAN TO ATTEND GRIM CEREMONY IN OFFICIAL CAPACITY.

THIS morning in Duke Street Prison, Glasgow, John Keen is to be executed for the murder of an Indian pedlar. Official intimation was received yesterday morning that the reprieve petition had failed, and in the afternoon the condemned man's wife, little boy, and father and mother had an interview with him in his cell.

For the first time in the history of this country a woman will attend the execution in an official capacity. As one of the junior magistrates, Bailie Mrs. Bell is deputed to be present at the grim ceremony, and in an interview yesterday with the *Daily Record* she said she had no intention of shirking the duty, disagreeable as it was.

KEEN'S VISITORS.

LAST INTERVIEW WITH WIFE AND PARENTS.

Lord Provost Montgomery had the unpleasant duty yesterday of conveying to John Keen, sentenced to death for the murder of an Indian pedlar in the Port Dundas district of Glasgow, the news that the reprieve petition had failed.

The sentence is accordingly being carried out in Duke Street Prison at 8 o'clock this morning, Pierpont being the executioner.

There was a tragic moment in the prison when his Lordship and Sir John Lindsay, the Town Clerk, conveyed the intelligence to the condemned man, who had been brought out to a reception room by the Governor of the jail.

THE OFFICIAL MESSAGE.

Keen bore the ordeal stolidly. When asked by the Lord Provost if he understood the significance of the letter from the Secretary for Scotland, the prisoner bowed his head slightly.

The official message was in the following terms:—

My Lord Provost,

With reference to the case of John Keen, now lying under sentence of death in His Majesty's Prison, Duke Street, Glasgow, I have to inform you that after careful consideration I regret that I am unable to discover sufficient grounds to justify me in advising His Majesty to interfere with the due course of the law.

You will be so good as to acknowledge receipt of this intimation by telegram.

I am, etc.,

JOHN GILMOUR.

After having heard the letter read Keen was taken back to his cell.

FAMILY'S DISTRESS.

A *Daily Record* representative, who called at the residence of the Keen family in the Port Dundas district yesterday, found them in a state of deep distress. Up to the last they had been buoyed up with hope that the petition for reprieve would be successful.

Seated in a nicely furnished room, which bore evidence everyhere of good housewifery and scrupulous cleanliness, the father, mother and sons expressed their disappointment at the failure of their efforts to obtain a reprieve.

LAST INTERVIEW.

"We had our last interview with John in the prison this afternoon," said his father. "It was terrible for everyone of us, but he kept up like a hero.

"There were the four of us, the same as yesterday—his mother, his wife, his wee son, and myself. I needn't tell you that we were all in an awful state.

"We all know that he is innocent, and that made it all the harder for us to see him as he was, and to think of what he had to face in the morning.

"At a time like this it heartens us to know that 113,000 people signed the petition.

"Our family wish to express thanks to all who have shown their sympathy. We would like to mention specially the Lord Provost, Mr. W. T. Doherty, one of the Cowcaddens Councillors, and the Governor of Duke Street Prison, who has been very kind to us."

MUST DO MY DUTY.

BAILIE MRS. BELL AND HER CIVIC OBLIGATIONS.

A feature of this execution is that for the first time in Great Britain a woman will be present as one of the representatives of the civic authorities.

Mrs. Bell, in her capacity of Magistrate of the City of Glasgow, has been deputed to attend the tragic ceremony.

This is a duty which devolves, according to custom, upon the two junior bailies of the city, who in this case are Mrs. Bell and Dr. James Dunlop, one of the Dennistoun representatives.

A GRAVE RESPONSIBILITY.

In course of conversation at the City Chambers yesterday afternoon with a *Daily Record* representative, Mrs. Bell said it was a grave responsibility that confronted her, but she was determined to see it through.

"When I accepted this important office," she remarked, "I took over with it all the tasks, pleasant or unpleasant, which it might have in store for me. This is, naturally, one of the most disagreeable duties which anyone in my position could be called upon to face. Still, it has to be done, and I have no intention of shirking it.

"Women, as has often been proved, can often survive ordeals much better than men. They are placed face to face nowadays with situations which would not have been thought of before.

WOMEN ON THE JURY.

"Take the trial itself, for instance. There were nine women on the jury, and for four days and nights they were cooped up and compelled to listen to all sorts of details in the evidence. That was a big ordeal, wasn't it?

"Yet they did not flinch. They heard the evidence and they brought in their verdict. It was their duty.

"Well, they did their duty, and I mean to do mine, hard though I feel it will be. I was elected a Magistrate, and I must fulfil the obligations the position carries with it.

DUTY ALONE.

"It is not a matter in which our sex should claim privileges. At all events, that is how I see the matter—from the standpoint of duty alone.

"No, I do not believe in the abolition of capital punishment," she replied, in answer to a question

POWER OF THE PRESS.

Geneva, Wednesday.

The Sixth Commission of the League of Nations has decided to ask the Council to call a meeting of experts of the Press, with a view to seeking means for enlisting the help of the Press in the cause of peace.—C.N.

LOST WITH ALL HANDS.

Lloyd's agent at Concepcion (Chile) telegraphed yesterday—"Chilean steamer Mercedes, totally lost. All on board lost."

FIRST WOMAN TO ATTEND EXECUTION.

Bailie Mrs. Bell, one of the Junior Magistrates of Glasgow, who is to attend the execution in Duke Street Prison to-day of John Keen. She will be the first woman in this country to be present at an execution in an official capacity.

STILL LOVED BY WIFE.

MAX REINHARDT'S DIVORCE SUIT.

Duisburg, Wednesday.

The divorce suit which Max Reinhardt, the famous theatrical producer, is bringing against his wife, Else Heims, came again before the Court to-day after repeated postponements. The hearing will be private at the request of both parties.

Max Reinhardt has produced many witnesses in the effort to prove his wife's guilt, and in turn the wife has deposited with the Court photographs of all the ladies with whom she alleged her husband had been on intimate terms. The witnesses, in fact, number 60.

For some years Else Heims has refused to grant the divorce requested of her, and she will not hear of an amicable separation.

AS OBSCURE ACTOR.

At the last hearing of the proceeding she maintained that she still loved her husband, whom she met when he was an obscure actor, and whom she maintained she has helped in every way domestically and in his artistic career.

Frau Reinhardt is living in Berlin with her two boys, aged 12 and 16. She has expressed herself as reluctant to bring trouble on people not actually connected with the divorce proceedings.—Central News.

DEPORTED CHRISTIANS.

Geneva, Wednesday.

The Council of the League of Nations will sit to-morrow to consider the British request for representatives of the League to be sent to Irak to investigate the deportation of Christians by the Turks on the Mosul frontier.—C.N.

Capt. Reginald Kingscote Hewer, M.C., 7th (Queen's Own) Hussars, whose marriage to Miss Elizabeth I. L. Findlay, younger daughter of Mr. and Mrs. Leslie Findlay, of 10 Eton Terrace, Edinburgh, and Muirton, Craigellachie, takes place at the Church of St. Margaret, Aberlour, on October 6.

NO PIT CRISIS NOW.

WHAT SUBSIDY PAPER STATED.

MINERS' TRUMP.

(From Our Political Correspondent.)

London, Wednesday Night.

There is not likely to be any crisis over the hitch in the coal truce.

To-day, the miners' leaders met the Prime Minister, who promised to give his reply to-morrow.

In view of a new factor which has come to light, it looks as if the men's contention is completely upheld, and that the Prime Minister will find that no reductions should be made under the terms of settlement.

MINERS' TRUMP CARD.

The miners have produced for Mr. Baldwin's consideration a very strong argument. It is nothing less than a copy of the Paper, containing the supplementary estimate for £10,000,000, which was circulated from the Treasury, under date of August 3, and on which the House of Commons voted on Thursday, August 6.

This Paper stated that the ten million pounds was "provision for a temporary subvention to enable the coal mining industry to continue the payment of wages at rates not less than those obtaining in July, 1925. The subvention will be calculated in accordance with the arrangements set out in White Paper C.M.D. 2488."

The motion that this sum be granted was carried by the House by 351 votes to 16.

Therefore, Parliament voted to continue the July wage rates without reduction.

If this provision had appeared also in the White Paper, the misunderstanding could hardly have arisen.

BRITISH SHIPS SEIZED.

SUSPECTED OF CARRYING CONTRABAND.

New London (Conn.), Wednesday.

A British four-masted schooner suspected of carrying liquor concealed beneath a cargo of 2,000,000 feet of timber was brought into port to-day by coastguards, who placed a coastguard crew on board and then permitted her to proceed to her destination of New York City, where she will be unloaded.

The schooner hails from St. John, and has long been on the officials' list of suspicious vessels.—Reuter.

Three Prince Rupert (B.C.) boys (amateurs) have established two-way wireless communication with Sydney, N.S.W., a distance of about 8000 miles.

CAILLAUX IN U.S.

DISGUST AT A QUESTION.

DEBT PAYMENTS.

OFFER OF £15,000,000 A YEAR.

New York, Wednesday.

M. Caillaux, accompanied by the other members of the French mission which is negotiating for a settlement of the French war debt, landed here to-day from the liner Paris.

The Minister was visibly perturbed by the pressmen's first question, "We know that you were not convicted of treason, but will you tell us just of what you were convicted?"

M. Caillaux threw up his hands in obvious disgust.

Asked whether he expected to get the same terms for France as Great Britain had got, M. Caillaux replied with emphasis, "Better."

BASIS OF OFFER.

It is believed that M. Caillaux will make an offer on the basis that £25,000,000 a year is the limit of France's capacity to her American and British creditors.

M. Caillaux is credited with the hope that the British offer will eventually be scaled down to £10,000,000 annually, which would leave £15,000,000 for the American payments.

On the other hand, the lowest suggested in America as an adequate payment is well over £20,000,000. The French debt to the United States with accrued interest is now in the neighbourhood of £900,000,000.

AMERICAN VIEW.

The view most generally held on the American side is that all pre-Armistice and post-Armistice loans to France should be consolidated together with the debt incurred by the purchase of United States Army stocks, and funded for paying off in 62 years—the same as the British debt—at a flat rate of interest of 3½ per cent.

This reduced rate of interest would be made retroactive, so that the present accumulation of interest which has accrued at 5 per cent. would be very considerably reduced.

The resultant figure, however, would still be largely in excess of what is claimed by the French to be their capacity to pay.—C.N.

T.U.C. COLD DOUCHE.

NO INTERVENTION IN SEA STRIKE.

That they could not at the present juncture usefully intervene in the seamen's strike was the decision reached by the General Council of the Trades Union Congress yesterday.

A communication had been sent to the Council from some of the shipyard trade unions requesting the Council to intervene in the dispute at Southampton and other seaports.

One of the questions raised was the suggested withdrawal of shipyard labour from ships employing "blackleg" crews.

The communication came from only six of the 17 unions who were invited to take part in the conference at which the decision to approach the General Council was reached.

The larger unions, including the Boilermakers, the Shipwrights, the Amalgamated Engineering Union, and the Transport Workers, were not parties to the request made to the General Council.

REBUFF TO STRIKERS.

Sydney, Wednesday.

The Waterside Workers' Union has unanimously turned down the overseas seamen strikers. It is believed that this decision will have a far-reaching effect on the strike, so far as Australia is concerned.

The Watersiders have intimated that they will work all overseas vessels, with the exception of the Port Hobart and the Lycaon.—C.N.

1925

WOMAN BAILIE TELLS OF ORDEAL

FOR the first time in Britain, a woman was present at an execution as one of the representatives of the civic authorities.

And she told the *Daily Record* of her feelings.

Mrs Bell, in her capacity as Magistrate of the City of Glasgow, was deputed to attend the hanging of John Keen, sentenced to death for the murder of an Indian pedlar in the Port Dundas district.

This was a duty which devolved, according to custom, upon the two junior bailies of the city.

Lord Provost Montgomery had the unpleasant task of giving Keen the news that his reprieve petition had failed.

The sentence was to be carried out in Duke Street Prison on the morning of September 24.

During a meeting with a *Daily Record* representative, Mrs Bell said it was a grave responsibility that confronted her, but she was determined to see it through.

She said: "When I accepted this important office, I took over with it all the tasks – pleasant and unpleasant – which it might have in store for me. This is naturally one of the most disagreeable duties which anyone in my position could be called upon to face. Still, it has to be done and I have no intention of shirking it."

When Mrs Bell was interviewed after the execution, she told the *Daily Record* representative that she felt no ill effects from the ordeal through which she had passed.

She said: "I think it is only right, that I should describe how it affected me and prove that a woman can carry out her duties equally as well as a man could do it.

"What impressed me most was the solemn, decorous manner in which the execution was conducted, its expedition, and the great self-control of the young man Keen, who had wonderful command over himself.

"There was nothing to harass the onlookers unless one allowed the imagination to run away with one's feelings.

"We were all deeply impressed with the unflinching way in which the young man faced his death."

SCOTS EARTHQUAKE.
SEVERE SHOCK ON ISLAND OF MULL.
TIDAL WAVE IN PACIFIC.
IMPORTANT CABLE CENTRE LAID WASTE.

AN earthquake shock, which was particularly severe on the Island of Mull, was experienced in Argyllshire yesterday. Houses were shaken violently, and muffled underground rumblings created alarm among the people. No damage, however, was caused to property. In the Southern Pacific, one of the principal islands of the Caroline group in the Yap, one the principal islands of the Caroline group in the Yap, one the principal important cable centre, is reported to have been laid waste by a tidal wave which has left not a house standing.

HOUSES SHAKEN.
ARGYLLSHIRE ALARMED BY RUMBLING.

COMINGS...

Walter Carr
Actor

EARTH MOVES ON MULL

The island of Mull was the focus of a series of violent earth tremors just before Christmas. The "earthquake" lasted up to ten seconds and was felt throughout Argyll as far north as Oban. People reported hearing a muffled underground rumbling sound which increased in intensity before windows began rattling and objects fell from surfaces.

Unfortunately, the scale of the tremors was not recorded as the Paisley Observatory seismograph was broken.

UNDERWEAR
for FATHER and SON
The policy of this House is to provide Underwear that can be guaranteed unshrinkable and yet sold at a MODERATE PRICE.

KEEP YOUR EYE ON
Paisleys
JAMAICA STREET
Broomielaw Corner, Glasgow, C1

THE GREAT FIRE OF GLASGOW

A blaze of unparalleled proportions devastated a large area of the Kelvingrove district of Glasgow. At its peak, some 30,000 square yards were on fire and a number of important buildings were destroyed, including the Kelvin Hall (in which it was thought the fire began) and the Kelvin United Free Presbyterian Church.

Strong winds fanned the flames and caused them to spread from the Hall to adjacent tenements, particularly in Blantyre Street which was almost completely destroyed in the conflagration.

Fortunately, in spite of the scale of the blaze, only two minor injuries were reported.

THIS SPORTING LIFE

FOOTBALL	RUGBY UNION	GOLF	HORSE RACING	SHINTY
Scottish Champions Rangers	*Scotland vs England* Scotland 14–11 England at Murrayfield	*British Open Winner* Jim Barnes at Prestwick (300)	*Scottish Grand National Winner* Gerald L at Bogside	*Camanachd Cup Winners* Inveraray at Inverness
Scottish Cup Winners Celtic				

TO-DAY'S WIRELESS PROGRAMMES Page 5

Daily Record and Mail.

ESTAB. 1847—No. 24,744. GLASGOW, TUESDAY, MAY 4, 1926. ONE PENNY.

PREMIER WITH A "DOUBLE" Page 7

LAST MINUTE PEACE BIDS FAIL.

The Hon. Mrs. Hoare, daughter of Viscount and Viscountess Deerhurst, who will be presented at Their Majesties' Court this season.

TRAINS & TRAMS.

STATE APPEAL TO MOTORISTS.

POSITION TO-DAY.

Reports received from areas in Glasgow and the West of Scotland early this morning indicated that the strike of all classes of transport workers has been more or less complete. The exact situation, however, will not be known until about noon.

The trains from Glasgow to the South left as usual under the control of drivers whose home stations are in England, and, despite the fact that they were warned that the companies could not guarantee that the trains would reach their destinations, large numbers of passengers travelled. The Belfast and Dublin boats left as usual.

'BUS SERVICES.

With regard to the 'bus services the position last night was very obscure. A large proportion of the drivers are non-union men and they may be at work as usual to-day. It is said that the local authorities operating the emergency measures may take over the 'buses.

The Scottish Motor Transport Company will run 'buses on all routes from Kilmarnock to-day.

All work was stopped at the docks at an early hour this morning, only certain "safety" men being permitted to remain on duty.

GLASGOW TRAMS.

Following instructions from their society, the Transport and General Workers' Union, Glasgow tramwaymen are expected to join in a sympathetic strike to-day.

By the programme, drivers and conductors on late cars were expected to finish duty at midnight, and the all-night men were due to finish at 4 a.m.

The Subway, which is also under the management of the Tramways Department, is similarly involved in the dispute.

To-day people who rely on these conveniences are likely to experience great difficulty in getting to their destination, as, at the best, only a skeleton service would be provided.

OFFICIAL'S EXPLANATION.

Tramway employees, to the number of nearly 400, including a dozen conductresses, met in the Berkeley Hall, Glasgow, last night, to hear an explanation of the situation from Mr. Arthur Gee, group secretary of the Transport and General Workers' Union.

Mr. Gee stated that the meeting was not called for the purpose of taking a decision on the question of a strike or no strike, but to pass on instructions. Instructions had been given to strike, and they were carrying out these.

Subsequently, meetings for a like purpose were held at the tramway depots throughout the city.

A meeting of the Road Transport Section of the Transport and General Workers' Union was held in Glasgow last night, when all the stables and garages represented in this organisation endorsed ...ion of the British Trade Union ... to commence work this

BIG STRIKE BEGUN.

LAST MINUTE PEACE MOVES END IN FAILURE.

PREMIER'S REVIEW OF CRISIS.

"THE General Strike is on." This dramatic message was flashed over the wires from London shortly after 11 o'clock last night. Earlier in the evening an optimistic feeling prevailed that a settlement might be reached when it was reported that the Prime Minister was again in contact with the miners' leaders and the T.U.C. Negotiating Committee.

A faint flicker of hope was also raised by a short exchange between Mr. Churchill and Mr. Thomas in the concluding stages of the Chancellor's speech in the House of Commons. The significant passages were these:—

Mr. Churchill said that the Government were bound to face the position unflinchingly, rigorously, rigidly, and resolutely to the end.

"Then this is the end?" inquired Mr. Thomas. "The door is always open," replied the Chancellor. "The T.U.C. have only to cancel the general strike challenge."

"Does that specific statement apply equally to the lock-out notices?" asked Mr. Thomas.

These exchanges afforded a slight hope that negotiations would be resumed. As a matter of fact no further negotiations took place, and the House of Commons dissolved in the knowledge that all efforts at a settlement had completely failed.

Members of the Miners' Executive who had been waiting in the Committee corridor during the evening left the House of Commons soon after the House rose at 11.7. Mr. Thomas and several other members of the T.U.C. remained, as did one or two members of the Cabinet.

There was a great crowd outside the Houses of Parliament, a section of which sang the "Red Flag," and raised cheers for the miners. Another section sang "God Save the King." The police kept the crowd in check. There was no disorder.

DRASTIC ORDERS.

AUTHORITIES' WIDE POWERS.

Wide discretion given to authorities under the Emergency Powers Act is revealed by the regulations published last night. In addition to powers taken to maintain services essential to the life of the community, such as the supply and distribution of food, coal etc., and organisation and direction of transport, there are stringent penal provisions.

Persons will be held guilty of offence against the regulations by any attempt to cause mutiny, sedition, or disaffection among His Majesty's Forces, or forces under civic authorities, or to interfere with organisation and distribution of supplies, the usual exception being made for participation in a strike or peaceful persuasion.

HEAVY PENALTIES.

Measures are included to provide against the possession, for the purposes of circulation, of documents aiming at a contravention of the regulations, and the Secretary of State, or persons authorised by him, may prohibit or disperse any public meeting or procession likely to occasion grave disorder.

There is a regulation against unlawful drilling, and the billeting sections of the Army and Air Force Act may be enforced.

Failure to comply with, or an offence against, the regulations, entails liability on summary conviction to imprisonment for three months, or a fine not exceeding £100, or to both imprisonment and fine.

The police may arrest without warrant any person acting in such a manner as to endanger the public safety, and are given extensive powers of search in this connection.

IN CLYDE YARDS.

CONFUSING POSITION OF THE UNIONS.

What is going to happen in the shipbuilding and engineering establishments on Clydeside is not yet known.

Some of the unions have issued instructions to their men to stop; others have not.

In any case, the works may very soon be affected by the shortage of power supplies.

PROFITEERING WARNING

Sir Arthur Rose, the emergency commissioner for Glasgow, issues a warning regarding food profiteering.

Prices, he said yesterday, appeared to be inclined to rise generally, and it was difficult to see any real justification for that at the moment. He had powers to fix maximum prices, and if material increases took place it might be necessary to put these powers into operation, although they did not want to do so.

"If prices run away, however," he concluded, "drastic action will have to be taken."

PETROL SUPPLIES.

RATIONING OR PERMITS NOT NECESSARY

It is considered unlikely that a system of rationing or permits for motor spirit will be necessary, says an official announcement.

The principal motor spirit distributing companies state that the retail price of motor spirit will remain unaltered.

No action will be taken by the police during the present emergency in respect of the use of a mechanically propelled vehicle for which an Excise licence is not in force, or one which is used for purposes not covered by any such licence, provided that the vehicle is registered and carries its proper number plates.

The police will not, however, permit a vehicle to be used in any manner inconsistent with the safety of the public.

APPEAL TO MOTORISTS.

The Ministry of Transport appeals to the owners of motor vehicles of all kinds for assistance in maintaining national and local services essential to the wellbeing of the community.

Owners of commercial and mechanical transports not fully used should notify the haulage committees of their areas.

It should be clearly understood that the Government is prepared to assist in the transport of foodstuffs and other essential services.

STRANDED.

RAIL PASSENGERS' ADVENTURE.

A large number of Scottish travellers to the South found themselves in an awkward predicament in the early hours of the morning as a result of the cessation of railway traffic.

Late trains left Glasgow and Edinburgh with fairly large complements who had decided to take the risk attached to travel under such conditions.

When Carstairs was reached, however, the trains proceeded no further. They were coupled to another train which arrived from Aberdeen and run back to the Central Station, Glasgow.

It appears that they were unable to go as far as Carlisle on account of the large number of trains already held up there.

NIGHT IN CARRIAGES.

When a *Daily Record* representative visited the Central Station about 2 a.m., he found that most of the passengers had remained in the carriages.

Some of them had resigned themselves to the situation and had settled down as comfortably as possible for the night.

Others were too worried as to how and when they were to get to their destinations to follow this philosophical example.

One family with whom the *Daily Record* representative chatted were gravely concerned about the prospects of their reaching London in time to catch a boat which was to convey them to Natal.

"It we have to take a taxi all the way, we must get to London," was how the matron of the little party expressed herself.

COAL FOR BRITAIN.

DUTCH DOCKERS URGED NOT TO HANDLE IT.

Rotterdam, Monday.

The Transport Workers' Federation to-day distributed a manifesto to the Rotterdam dockers exhorting the men not to assist in coal loading to Great Britain from Tuesday next, nor to work vessels entering the New Waterway for bunkering which, under normal conditions, would have bunkered in Great Britain. The manifesto also urges the men not to enrol for British ships.—Reuter.

Lady Cunliffe, wife of Lord Cunliffe of Headley, who will be presented at Their Majesties' Court.

PREMIER'S POSITION.

HOW HE FOUGHT FOR PEACE.

WAGES CRUX.

There was a tense atmosphere in the House of Commons when the business began yesterday.

The Prime Minister was greeted with loud cheers when he entered the House. A Conservative member shouted "Here he is," and the whole of the Ministerialists rose and cheered and waved their order papers.

Mr. J. H. Thomas entered the House shortly after the Prime Minister, and on his entrance the whole of the Labour Party rose and cheered him.

On the motion for the adjournment the Prime Minister said—

"I would like to express my view at the outset that these difficulties have been considerably increased for many years past by the organisation of the industry itself and the extraordinary machinery they have for wages adjustment."

TWO ESSENTIALS.

There were no doubt historical reasons for this—the nature of the industry and the isolation of many of the mining villages had something to do with it. But the industry would have caused far less anxiety to itself and to the nation had it succeeded in conducting its affairs through such organisations as were employed in the cotton and iron and steel industries and the railways.

Moreover, the conditions of the industry had been interfered with many times by successive Governments. ("Hear, hear.") He was quite convinced there would be and could be no settlement in that industry until two things were attained—

First, a very different spirit, and

Secondly, a very different organisation for the discussion and arrangement of wages. ("Hear, hear.")

The whole machinery required, in his view, a radical overhauling.

"One Government prescription after another has been tried and administered, and yet the health of the patient has been but little improved.

INTO DECIMALS.

"Something is done at the last moment because up to that last moment both sides have been too prone to manœuvre for a favourable position with the public, and the public themselves are incapable of forming a sound judgment because the mysteries of minimum percentages and datum lines, bonus terms, and percentages and allowances and subtractions going into two decimals.

"One of the great difficulties is that you can never get the agreed amount the miner is earning, for neither the miner nor owner will ever agree on a figure, and then a Cabinet Minister, not necessarily a mathematician or a chartered accountant by profession is called in, and expected to understand these matters and expected with a divine impartiality to make these two sides agree —and this is the peculiar feature time after time—at the last minute of the eleventh hour that is left.

Continued on Page 2, Column 1.

1926

CLASS STRIKE SPLITS SCOTLAND

The first General Strike in British history began at midnight on May 5 following the total breakdown of talks between miners' unions and pit owners.

Both sides had been locked in lengthy and acrimonious negotiations following the announcement in March of plans to cut miners' wages by up to 13% and increase their working day to eight hours. Strikes and lockouts followed as each side adopted entrenched positions.

The TUC's General Council called for all essential services to walk out in support of the miners and the strike was on.

The strike call was seen by the Government as the work of extremists within the TUC and a direct attack on democracy and constitutional government.

A state of emergency was declared and as a precaution against expected violence, troops were deployed in cities throughout Britain. In Scotland, there were isolated reports of actual attacks: a policeman was stabbed in Edinburgh, another was set upon by a mob in Irvine and beer lorries were looted in Bathgate. In Glasgow, large crowds of strikers attempted to immobilise public vehicles and there were sporadic cases of looting.

An important feature of the strike was the way in which the middle classes turned out to take over the running of public and essential services. The Secretary of the Post Office for Scotland later thanked those who gave assistance in person or by the loan of their vehicles. However, the sight of white-collar professionals operating trams and buses led to many confrontations and all over Scotland, volunteer drivers were roughly handled by strike supporters. Often, only the presence of the military prevented serious trouble.

The TUC called off the strike after nine days when it was clear that support for it was crumbling. The embattled miners continued the fight alone for another five months.

COMINGS...

Stanley Baxter
Entertainer

Johnnie Beattie
Entertainer

ON RADIO

The Week's Good Cause

Choral Evensong

Epilogue

HEARTS STAR DIES

Robert Mercer, the Hearts and Scotland half-back, collapsed and died shortly after the start of a match between the Edinburgh team and Selkirk in April. The large crowd which had turned up at Ettrick Park in Selkirk for the game were stunned when Mercer simply dropped to the ground a few minutes after kick-off. He was carried off the field unconscious and given first aid on the touch-line before being moved to a local hospital where he later died. Mercer had been a prominent figure in football in the Borders where his loss was particularly mourned.

MAN WEDS AS WOMAN SHOCK

A bizarre story came to light in March regarding a cross-dressing Clydebank painter who married an unsuspecting Linlithgow man.

The painter, whose landlady in Dalkeith described him as "young, slim and rather artistic look-ing" passed him-self off as an actor whose special talents lay in impersonating women, a ruse that allowed him to attend local entertainments in stylish dresses and high heels. The success of his "impersonation" was such that he married the Linlithgow man in unspecified circumstances. A doctor was subsequently called to verify the obvious state of the "bride's" gender which in turn led to a rapid annulment.

THIS SPORTING LIFE

FOOTBALL	RUGBY UNION	GOLF	HORSE RACING	SHINTY
Scottish Champions Celtic	*Scotland vs England* England 9–17 Scotland at Twickenham	*British Open Winner* Bobby Jones at Royal Lytham, England (291)	*Scottish Grand National Winner* Estuna at Bogside	*Camanachd Cup Winners* Inveraray at Oban
Scottish Cup Winners St Mirren				

COMFORT IN SPECTACLES
Shell frames give nose comfort.
Toric lenses give eye comfort.
This combination gives the ideal reading spectacle.
JOHN TROTTER LIMITED
40 Gordon Street, Glasgow and 100 George St., Edinburgh

Daily Record and Mail.
ESTAB. 1847—No. 24,989. GLASGOW, FRIDAY, FEBRUARY 25, 1927. ONE PENNY.

The Finest Whisky Simply Means "OLD KEG"

"INDIGNITY" OF THE PARISH RELIEF LOAN IN SCOTLAND

DOUR SCOTS FIGHT.

POOR LAW BILL CARRIED A STAGE FURTHER.

GRANT INSTEAD OF LOAN

UNDERTAKING BY THE LORD ADVOCATE.

AFTER a dour fight, the Scottish Poor Law Emergency Bill was carried through the Committee stage of the Commons last night by a majority of 93.

The Clause empowering Parish Councils to give relief in the form of a loan which can be recovered later met with the strongest opposition, and the Lord-Advocate undertook to reconsider the Clause on the Report stage.

HUMILIATING PRINCIPLE FOR SCOTLAND.

LORD ADVOCATE TAUNTS ANGRY SCOTS.

From Our Parliamentary Representative.
Westminster, Thursday.

The Scottish Poor Law Emergency Bill got through the Committee stage to-night by 200 against 107 votes, and the Report stage will be taken on Monday.

Scots Conservatives were suspicious. Mr. Kidd (Linlithgowshire) moved an amendment to provide that before the relief proposed in the Bill is given, the Parish Council should take a ballot of ratepayers on the question of whether or not the proposed relief should be allowed.

The Lord Advocate pointed out that this would be impracticable, and eventually this amendment was withdrawn.

Then Sir Alexander Sprot moved an amendment, the effect of which was to make the Bill apply only to the present emergency. He argued that the provisions regarding the issue of relief to dependants of those engaged in an industrial dispute should end on March 31 next, instead of in 1930, as provided for by the Bill.

UP IN ARMS.

He had an unexpected supporter in Sir Robert Horne, who took exactly the same line. But again the Lord Advocate could not agree, and this amendment also was withdrawn.

The big fight came over Clause 3 of the Bill. This clause gives power to Parish Councils in Scotland to give relief in the form of a loan, which can be recovered later, and the Scottish Labour Members were up in arms against it.

Mr. Johnston (Dundee) protested that the clause would import into the Scottish Poor Law something that has never been there—a loan, instead of a grant.

"Why should this bad provision of English law be forced upon Scotland?" demanded Mr. Stewart (St. Rollox).

LORD ADVOCATE'S TAUNT.

The Rev. James Barr (Motherwell) joined in the protest. So did the veteran, Mr. James Brown (Ayrshire), whose point was that the clause "introduces a humiliating and crippling principle into Scottish Poor Law—it will place an indignity on Scottish people who cherish their independence."

The Lord Advocate taunted the Scottish Labour members with trying to get some benefits of the English system of Poor Law administration incorporated in the Scottish law without any of the limitations.

This kind of relief to dependents by way of loan had existed for centuries in England, and the experience was that substantially it had been very little used, except in connection with circumstances arising out of a trade dispute.

Experience had proved, he asserted, that over 50 per cent. of the loan had been recovered, and in some cases 100 per cent. That meant that a substantial portion of the relief given by way of loan to dependents of unemployed men never came on the rates at all.

That was one of the material reasons why the Government had given the 40 per cent. grant. It would not be fair that the Parish Councils should bear the whole cost of the £650,000 granted in relief during the recent strike.

This clause was an essential part of the Bill, and the powers it granted to Parish Councils were purely optional.

MR. ROSSLYN MITCHELL.

Mr. E. Rosslyn Mitchell said he did not think that any man, whose family was in want and whose family was relieved because they were in want through no fault of his own, should at the end of a dispute or period of unemployment have to set out to maintain his family burdened with the debt that had been incurred during that period.

He objected to the clause because it introduced a new principle in Scottish parochial life and because it placed members and officials of Parish Councils in a position of being subjected to outside pressure to compel payment of loans made to families of unemployed men.

Mr. Neil M'Lean also strongly resisted the clause.

AN UNDERTAKING.

The Lord-Advocate gave an undertaking to reconsider on the Report stage of the Bill the closing sentence of the clause which empowers a Parish Council to recover as an alimentary debt relief given as a loan.

Finally, the Secretary of State for Scotland assured the angry Scotsmen that, in introducing this clause, the Government had no other desire than to produce similar conditions in the administration of Poor Law relief in England and in Scotland.

But the Scots went to division all the same, and, as stated, the Bill emerged from the Committee stage by a majority of 93.

Scottish Deputation's Interview—Page 2.

BOMBING 'PLANE EXPLODES.

Helsingfors, Thursday.

A terrible accident occurred here yesterday during bomb-throwing practice from a Finnish Army aeroplane. The aeroplane was at an altitude of 350 feet when a number of bombs exploded.

The machine was blown to pieces, and the two occupants killed on the spot. The cause of the explosion is unknown. —Reuter.

MR. MACDONALD FOR U.S.

Our Lobby Correspondent understands that Mr. Ramsay MacDonald hopes to pay a visit to the United States at Easter.

EX-KAISER'S WIFE ILL.

Amsterdam, Friday.

The wife of the ex-Kaiser is suffering from a slight attack of influenza, but her complete recovery is expected within the next few days.—Reuter.

Mr. R. H. Death, a London taxi-cab driver, who has just taken out a patent for a device for harnessing the tides.

BLEEDING MAN AS EVIDENCE.

DRAMATIC ACT BY BELGRADE M.P.'S.

Belgrade, Thursday.

A sensational incident occurred during the sitting of the Jugo-Slavian Parliament to-day when a half-naked and badly wounded man was brought before the deputies as a concrete proof of police cruelty.

M. Maximovitch, the Minister of the Interior, was speaking in repudiation of the charges of cruelty made against his subordinates in the gendarmerie when the dramatic interruption occurred.

A door was flung open and several Opposition deputies appeared carrying the bleeding figure of a man, who was thereupon exhibited as a victim of police treatment the previous night. There were horrible wounds on the man's body.

The incident created such a sensation that the President of the Chamber, M. Marko Trifkovic, was forced to suspend the session amidst tumult. It is expected that M. Maximovitch will resign. —B.U.P.

CHILIAN "REDS" ARRESTED.

Santiago De Chile, Thursday.

All Anarchist and Communist leaders have been arrested, and their newspapers suspended.—Reuter.

8 NURSES IN FLAMES.

ETHER EXPLOSION HORROR.

SWIFT DEATH.

Giessen, Nassau, Thursday.

In an evangelistic home and training school for nurses a terrible mishap caused the death of one of the sisters and frightful burns to seven others.

Eight of the nursing sisters were in the kitchen of the establishment engaged in refilling bottles of ether when suddenly there was a terrific explosion and all of them became enveloped in flames.

One of them, who was actually holding a bottle, was so quickly enveloped that she was a charred corpse before anything effectual could be done to prevent her incineration.

Two others, with their clothing a mass of flames, ran out into the street, where some passers-by rolled them over and over in the snow and thus extinguished the flames.

Five of the sisters were seriously burnt before help arrived on the hands and face and will be disfigured for life.—Reuter.

TANKER TRAGEDY.

CHARRED BODIES FOUND ON BRITISH SHIP.

New York, Thursday.

Two bodies burned beyond recognition have been found on the British oil tanker Black Sea, which caught fire following an explosion on board.

The company states that four other members of the crew are missing. Their names are withheld.

Fire boats and tugs got the fire under control, and the ship was beached at Redhook. Three of the crew, including the assistant engineer, are in a serious condition.

The ship, which was about to leave for London with a full cargo, is badly burnt.—C.N.

[The Black Sea, 2961 tons, belongs to the British Black Sea Shipping and Oil Company, London.]

WANTED—A CHANGE OF TUNE.

The Man With The Note: "Look here, the other tenants are complaining of the goings-on in this flat. Better mend your ways or you may get notice to quit."

SCOTS GUN DRAMA.

WIFE AND GIRL WOUNDED.

HUSBAND'S ACT

COMMITS SUICIDE AT DOOR.

A tragic affair occurred in the village of Sandbank, near Dunoon, yesterday morning, when William M'Nae (53), after shooting at his wife and daughter with a double-barrelled sporting gun, turned the weapon on himself with fatal results.

Mrs. M'Nae was wounded in the head, and her daughter Agnes (15) received a discharge of pellets in her side, but neither is in a serious condition.

Mrs. M'Nae occupies Rockbank, a room and kitchen cottage east of the village, while her husband resided in Ellenwood, at the other end of Ardnadam. They had been living apart for about three months.

BROKE KITCHEN WINDOW.

About 5.30 a.m. M'Nae arrived at his wife's house, and, after breaking the kitchen window with the butt of the gun, fired into the bed, where his wife and daughter Agnes were sleeping.

Mrs. M'Nae was hit on the right side of the head. Her daughter, who was lying to the inside of the bed, threw herself over her mother to protect her, and got the second shot, five pellets entering her side.

Evidently under the impression that he had killed his wife, M'Nae then shot himself, putting the muzzle of the gun into his mouth.

An account of the tragic happenings was given by Mrs. M'Nae to a *Daily Record* reporter, who called at Rockbank. Her head was swathed in bandages.

"I had a feeling," she said, "that something terrible was going to happen. I was wakened with the sound of the window being smashed, and I thought to myself, 'He has come for me at last.'

"Almost simultaneous with the sound of the window being broken I heard a shot and felt blood trickling down my face. I shouted to Agnes, 'He has shot me!' and she threw herself over me to protect me.

"There was a succession of shots, and Agnes was hit on the side while trying to save me. I distinctly heard my husband say—'I have got you now, and I am going to do for myself too.'

AWAKENED BY SCREAMS.

"Our screams awakened my son, John, who was sleeping in a cubicle in the kitchen, and when he rushed outside he found his father lying dead at the door.

"I fully believe he intended to kill me. After breaking the glass of the window, he must have taken careful aim at my bed, and it is little short of marvellous how I escaped so lightly."

Mrs. M'Nae volunteered the information that a letter had been found at her husband's house.

In it he indicated what he intended to do, and gave instructions that he and his wife were to be buried together, and, if possible, side by side.

The letter also stated that certain articles were to be given to his daughter Bessie.

The daughter Agnes, who is employed as a maid in a local house, had only gone to sleep with the mother for the night, because the latter was afraid something might happen.

The M'Naes have been resident in Sandbank for about three years, prior to which they resided in Glasgow.

COURT PROCEEDINGS.

The dead man, it is stated, was to have appeared at a J.P. Court to-day, on a charge of assaulting his wife.

Mrs. M'Nae contemplated taking an action for legal separation, and the first stage of the case was to have been heard in Dunoon Sheriff Court yesterday.

M'Nae was a native of Dalbeattie, Kirkcudbrightshire, and at one time owned several fruit shops in Glasgow.

COMMONS FIGHT OVER POOR LAW

THE Scottish Poor Law Emergency Bill got through its Committee Stage in the Commons after a hard fight. The majority was 93.

Strongest opposition came over the clause empowering parish councils to give relief in the form of a loan which could be recovered later and the Lord Advocate undertook to reconsider the clause for the Report Stage of the Bill.

Sir Alexander Sprot moved an amendment to make the Bill apply only to the present emergency.

He argued that the provisions regarding the issue of relief to dependants of those engaged in an industrial dispute should end on March 31, 1927 and not in 1930.

The Lord Advocate taunted the Scottish Labour members, accusing them of trying to get some benefits of the English system of Poor Law administration incorporated in the Scottish law without any of its limitations.

This kind of relief to dependants by way of loan had existed for centuries in England, he said, and in practice it had been very little used, except in connection with circumstances arising out of a trade dispute.

Experience proved, he asserted, that in most cases, more than 50 per cent of the loan had been recovered, and in some cases 100 per cent.

This meant that a large portion of the relief given never came from the rates at all.

Mr Reynard, clerk to Glasgow Parish Council, asked that the term "involved in a trades dispute" should be more clearly defined.

He suggested that, as in the Unemployment Insurance Act, before dependants of strikers could insist on relief being provided by the parish council, there should be a waiting period of not less than six weeks from the commencement of the dispute.

He dealt also with the question of loans and asked that a period should be permitted during which each of the parish councils could repay the remaining portion of the 40 per cent deduction which had been granted by the Government from the money expended on strikers' dependants during 1928.

EDINBURGH'S ROYAL VISIT

In July, King George V and Queen Mary received the enthusiastic greetings of large Edinburgh crowds as they drove in an open carriage to Holyrood from Waverley Station. The king and queen later visited Glasgow to open the new Kelvin Hall.

HURRICANE HITS SCOTLAND

In January, winds reaching over 100 mph lashed Scotland for more than three days, bringing chaos to many parts of the country and claiming the lives of 22 people. Trees and trams alike were blown over and many buildings suffered structural damage. There were several instances recorded of whole tenements collapsing, the worst case being in Kinning Park in Glasgow. At its height, on the night of January 28, Paisley Observatory recorded a wind speed of 102mph, the strongest gust ever recorded since records began in 1883.

COMINGS...

Kenneth McKellar
Singer

POLICE PROTECTION

In a bid to reduce the casualty rate amongst police on traffic duty, constables in Edinburgh were issued with gleaming white helmets and gauntlets.

THIS SPORTING LIFE

FOOTBALL	RUGBY UNION	GOLF	HORSE RACING	SHINTY
Scottish Champions Rangers	*Scotland vs England* Scotland 21–13 England at Murrayfield	*British Open Winner* Bobby Jones at St Andrews (285)	*Scottish Grand National Winner* Estuna at Bogside	*Camanachd Cup Winners* Kyles Athletic at Inverness
Scottish Cup Winners Celtic				

ARNOTT'S UNTRIMMED STRAWS ARE NOW OFFERED AT 1/11½
SECURE YOURS EARLY
ARNOTT & CO. LTD., JAMAICA ST., GLASGOW, C1

Daily Record and Mail.

ESTAB. 1847—No. 25,427. GLASGOW, SATURDAY, JULY 21, 1928. ONE PENNY.

TO-DAY'S BONANZA OFFER
Check Flannel Suitings in all the new colourings. 40 in. wide. Worth 3/11. Now, per yard, 2/6½
BONANZA LTD. 173-185 ARGYLE STREET, C.2

SCOTS PRIEST'S FATAL FALL FROM TRAIN AT LARBERT.

SLATER'S TRIUMPH.

MURDER CONVICTION QUASHED.

MISDIRECTION BY JUDGE.

PROMINENT MEN'S VIEWS ON THE DECISION.

"IN these circumstances we think that the instructions given in the charge amounted to misdirection in law, and that the judgment of the Court before whom the appellant was convicted should be set aside."

This was the conclusion arrived at by the Court of Scottish Criminal Appeal in the High Court of Justiciary, in Edinburgh, yesterday, in connection with the appeal by Oscar Slater against his conviction and sentence for the murder of Miss Gilchrist, of Glasgow, twenty years ago. Full text of the judgment is on Page 12.

There was a large attendance to hear the decision, the passages leading to the Court being crowded.

The Lord Justice General, Lord Clyde, presided, and the other Judges present were the Lord Justice Clerk, Lord Alness, Lords Blackburn, Sands, and Hunter.

Oscar Slater was present in Court, and followed the proceedings with eager interest.

He seemed to be greatly relieved in mind when the final sentences of the judgment of the Court were realised.

A number of Glasgow people were also

Oscar Slater's Own Sensational Story will appear in TO-MORROW'S *'Sunday Mail'*
The only Scottish Newspaper to have his own story.

in Court, including the Rev. E. P. Phillipps, the Jewish Rabbi.

Sir A. Conan Doyle was not present; but Mr. Wm. Roughhead, W.S., the writer on criminology, who was a new witness at the hearing of the appeal, sat within the bar.

The counsel for Slater, Mr. Craigie Aitchison, Mr. Watson, and Mr. Clyde were in attendance; and Mr. Montgomery, Advocate-Depute, sat in the Crown side of the Court.

The agents in the case were Sir John Prosser, Crown Agent; and for Slater, Messrs. Norman Macpherson and Dunlop.

The opinion of the Court was read by Lord Clyde, and took half an hour in delivery.

QUESTIONS BY M.P.'S.

WILL COMPENSATION BE PAID TO SLATER?

(From Our Political Correspondent.)

The judgment in the Slater appeal has now to be considered by the Secretary for Scotland and the Home Secretary, with a view to deciding what action should be taken by the Government.

Sir John Gilmour informed me yesterday that, pending this consideration, it was not possible to express any definite opinion.

I gather, however, that there is every probability that some recompense will be granted to Slater. It is likely that this will take the form of an annuity, together with a free pardon.

An announcement of the Government's intentions will probably be made in the House of Commons on Monday, when two questions on the subject will be put to the Secretary for Scotland.

Mr. Campbell Stephen, M.P. for Camlachie, will ask the Secretary of State for Scotland if he can state whether he has given consideration to the verdict of the Court of Appeal in the Slater case, setting aside the verdict of a former Court, and whether he can state what steps he proposes to take in the way of compensation, and otherwise, to this man for his 20 years of imprisonment.

Mr. G. Buchanan, M.P. for Gorbals, will also ask if the Secretary of State is aware of the decision, and if it is his intention to have any compensation granted, or to take any other steps to repair the damage done.

HELEN LAMBIE'S RELIEF.

Relief at the finishing of the case was expressed by Mrs. Gillon (formerly Helen Lambie, Miss Gilchrist's maid), when she learned of the result of Slater's appeal at her home in Peoria, Illinois. U.S.A., yesterday.

PROMINENT PEOPLE'S VIEWS.

Mr. Craigie Aitchison, K.C., Slater's senior counsel was warmly congratulated by many of his colleagues in Parliament Hall.

In conversation with the *Daily Record*, he said:

"The appeal has been successful, and the conviction has been quashed.

"It was a moral victory," he added, "over a bad conviction."

Asked as to the question of compensation, Mr. Craigie Aitchison said:

"Of course, they must compensate the man."

Slater's faithful friend from the time of sentence almost, the Rev. Mr. Phillips, when interviewed by the *Daily Record*, said:

"I am delighted at the judgment, and hope sincerely that the next pronouncement will be one of compensation to Slater for the great wrong that has been done him.

"I trust, further, that the public will realise the significance of the judgment, and that Slater will now be accepted by everybody as a guiltless man, as all along I believed him to be, and as the Court now formally declared him in actuality.

"Slater, I may say, has been very depressed during these last few days, and I hope that the verdict will bring him the bright spirits he deserves after the prolonged ordeal through which he has passed."

Sir Arthur Conan Doyle, who has been one of the foremost of Slater's champions, interviewed in London yesterday, said:

"I am, naturally, very glad, but I do not see how there was any possibility of any other decision being arrived at.

"I think the Crown conducted the case with great dignity and moderation, and the whole proceedings were quite satisfactory.

"I hope some good will come out of this case by resulting in the various responsible officials, who for years have refused to do anything in the matter, being pulled up very sharply.

"It was the same with Parliamentarians. The only one who has ever given me any encouragement in this case is Mr. Ramsay MacDonald.

Mr. Ramsay MacDonald said:

"The decision is exactly what everyone who has read the latest statements made by Sir Conan Doyle and others expected.

"Thinking over what has happened, and what might have happened, it fills one with horror.

"It is now clearly the duty of the Government to consider compensation, and it must be in proportion to the wrong done."

Legal Expert on Slater Appeal Decision.—Page 2.

Miss Jean Scott, whose father, the prominent American criminal lawyer, states, that her engagement to Mr. N. C. D. Colman, M.P. for Brixton, has been broken off on account of differences in temperament.

FELL OUT OF EXPRESS.

CATHOLIC PRIEST KILLED.

NEAR LARBERT.

Father Michael Boyle (54), a Roman Catholic clergyman, who resides at the Monastery, Perth, lost his life in tragic circumstances yesterday afternoon near Larbert Railway Station.

He fell from an express train as it was slowing down at Larbert, and was so severely injured that he died shortly afterwards. Death was due to a fracture of the base of the skull.

Father Boyle, who was accompanied by two other Catholic clergymen, was travelling from Perth to Glasgow on his way to Waterford.

It is stated that Father Boyle, who had awakened from a sleep, opened the door of the compartment apparently under the impression that the train had stopped.

GREAT NEWS FOR THE CHILDREN
Meet the BUDDS
See Page 19

CONDITION VERY GRAVE.

DAME ELLEN TERRY RAPIDLY LOSING STRENGTH.

Late last night, Dame Ellen Terry was stated to be rapidly losing strength.

"Her breathing," stated the bulletin, "is very difficult, and her condition very grave."

INDIAN RAIL STRIKE.

Madras, Friday.

A general strike was called at midnight on the South Indian Railway by the Labour Union in order to secure the redress of certain alleged grievances, including the wages of the menial staff.—Reuter.

Oscar Slater, whose appeal against his conviction for the murder of Miss Gilchrist has been unanimously sustained by the Court of Criminal Appeal in Edinburgh.

DIVORCE VEIL LIFTED.

SENSATIONAL EVIDENCE IN BONN CASE.

VERDICT FOR SIR MAX.

JUDGE ON TESTIMONY OF "PAID WATCHERS."

THE first phase of the sensational Bonn divorce case, after a hearing of unprecedented length, came to an end yesterday, when, in the London Divorce Court, Sir Max Bonn, the banking magnate, was found not to have committed adultery, on any of the occasions alleged by Lady Bonn.

Sir Max's cross-petition for divorce against Lady Bonn will not be heard till next term.

WOMAN WHO WAS DEPORTED.

CROSS-PETITION TO STAND OVER.

The veil of privacy which had, necessarily, hung over the long proceedings was lifted yesterday by the President's summing up.

Lord Merrivale's speech, which occupied three hours, was heard by a packed Court, in which sat many fashionably dressed women.

It was an exhaustive examination of the evidence, and, at one point, his Lordship drew out from a bundle of photographs, which had been produced, the picture of a young woman, to whom reference had been made.

"A young woman, not unattractive," he commented.

QUESTION OF RELIABILITY.

He commented on the fact that the allegations against Sir Max were supported only by the testimony of "paid watchers" and the door-keeper of a house of ill-fame.

"After all," said Lord Merrivale, "if a man was paid to find out adultery, the jury must consider for themselves what effect it might have on his mind."

He added that the evidence given by keepers and door-keepers of houses of ill-fame had become a by-word.

Referring to the evidence of two women, Cecile Benoist, who was deported in 1925, and Marie Carossa, Lord Merrivale said:—

"The Court has been relieved of their presence for some days. I sincerely hope that they may never appear again."

The Judge also adverted to a statement that for three years before the war a young woman had been Sir Max's mistress, and that there had been another young woman, to whom he was profoundly attached.

The jury only took 20 minutes to come to their decision.

FORENSIC DUELS.

The case has been notable, not only for the length of time which it has occupied, but for the forensic duels indulged in by counsel, these being described by the Judge as "tremendous conflicts" and "passionate appeals."

Among the array of counsel were seven noted K.C.'s.

In his cross-petition, to be heard next term, Sir Max cited Sir Ronald Waterhouse and Mr. Arthur Marcus Hanbury as co-respondents, all the parties denying the allegations made against them.

"TREMENDOUS CONFLICT" EXPLAINED.

JUDGE ON ISSUES AT STAKE.

In his summing up, the President intimated that the questions he proposed to leave to the jury, on the present part of the case, were:—

(1) Whether Sir Max Bonn committed adultery with a woman, or women, unknown, at Maddox Street?
(2) Whether Sir Max committed adultery with a woman, or women, unknown, at Conduit Street?
(3) Whether he committed adultery at Rue Lavoisiere, Paris?
(4) Whether he committed adultery with Cecile Benoist?

PASSIONATE APPEALS.

The jury, the President continued, had listened to passionate appeals, invective, and arguments.

Counsel, on both sides, had not spared themselves.

Sir Max Bonn was a member of a great city firm.

In all these specific matters, which were within his knowledge, more particularly than in the knowledge of anyone else, he must have committed perjury, if Cecile Benoist were to be believed.

That explained the tremendous conflict there had been in this case.

Starting from September, 1920, when the parties married, they lived a life of passionate affection, until 1926, or the latter part of 1925.

In 1927, two holidays were taken by Lady Bonn abroad.

By October 10 it was apparent that all possibility of amity had gone. On the 15th there was a flaming quarrel.

On September 29 watchers were engaged, and on November 3 Lady Bonn filed a petition alleging that Sir Max had committed adultery during his Paris visit.

Lady Bonn had gone to her solicitors on September 29, and what was being discussed by Sir Max Bonn was a proposal, as was said, for unconditional separation, and, alternatively, a proposal that Sir Max Bonn should submit to divorce.

The jury must consider how the matter would have stood if Sir Max Bonn had consented to a petition for divorce and was not going to defend the case.

The evidence of watchers and the doorkeeper of a disused house of ill fame were all very well if there were no contest and if the accused party were silent, but it became a much more serious matter if there were a contest and the accused party were the sort of fighting man Sir Max Bonn had proved himself to be in this case.

The case came before the jury in that extraordinary condition

The evidence as to Maddox Street and Conduit Street was the evidence of September and October last year, and was the evidence of three paid watchers.

THE PARIS EVIDENCE.

The evidence as to Paris was the evidence of the paid watchers, corroborated by the doorkeeper

The jury would see why Cecile Benoist and Marie Carossa were very material factors in the case.

There was no woman at Maddox Street or Conduit Street, but the evidence only of paid watchers; no woman from Paris, where there were said to be a number of women in the house; no observer outside either of the places, except paid watchers; no independent

Continued on Page 2.

SLATER WINS MURDER APPEAL

THERE was a large attendance in January to hear the decision of the Court of Scottish Criminal Appeal in the High Court of Justiciary on the Oscar Slater case.

Slater had appealed against his conviction and sentence for the murder of Miss Gilchrist of Glasgow, twenty years previously, a case which had attracted massive public interest at the time and subsequently as the arguments over Slater's guilt or innocence gathered momentum.

The opinion of the court took half an hour to read and was delivered by Lord Clyde, President of the Court of Session and also Lord Justice General.

During the trial, it was reported that Slater's association with prostitutes were disclosed and Lord Clyde said:

"It cannot be affirmed that any member of the jury was misled by their feeling that a man who supports himself on the profits of prostitution is regarded by all men as a blackguard or that this weighed in the question of the appellant's guilt. But neither can it be affirmed that none of them was.

"What is certain is that the judge's direction entirely failed to give the jury the essential warning against allowing themselves to be influenced by any feelings of the kind referred to.

"It is manifestly possible that, but for the prejudicial effect of denying to the appellant the full benefit of the presumption of innocence, and allowing the question of his means of support to go to the jury as a point not relevant to his guilt of Miss Gilchrist's murder, the proportion of 9 to 5 for 'guilty' and 'not proven' respectively, might have been reversed.

"In these circumstances, we think that the instructions given in the charge amounted to misdirection in law, and that the judgement of the court before whom the appellant was convicted should be set aside."

With this, Oscar Slater was a free man.

COMINGS...

Jimmy Logan
Actor

Ian Bannen
Actor

TO-DAY—
athletes the
world over train
on this delightful
food!

Grape=Nuts

10¼ per pocket

BOXING CROWD'S DISAPPOINTMENT

A massive crowd of 40,000 people turned out to watch Scots boxer Tommy Milligan take on Welshman Frank Moody in Glasgow in an eagerly-anticipated fight. However, the contest had barely started before a vicious Moody right hook brought it to an abrupt end just two minutes into the first round. The Scotsman fell like a log and was counted out in spite of the crowd's cries of "Get up, man! Get up!" In fact, it took Milligan a full 30 seconds to regain consciousness.

RED MINERS OUSTED

Vigorous attempts were made in July to oust Communists from the executive of the Scottish Mineworkers' Union.

The "Reds", who were particularly strong in Lanarkshire and Fife, were branded as disruptive extremists at the national mineworkers' conferences in Llandudno which overwhelmingly voted to support the Scottish Executive's efforts to confront and exclude Communists from their ranks, in keeping with official Labour Party policy.

WAR ON 'RED' MINERS
SCOTS LEADERS' APPEAL
TO CONFERENCE.
BAN ON COMMUNISM.

GOINGS...

Charles Rennie Mackintosh
Architect & Designer

Douglas Haig
First World War Military Commander

THIS SPORTING LIFE

FOOTBALL	RUGBY UNION	GOLF	HORSE RACING	SHINTY
Scottish Champions Rangers	*Scotland vs England* England 6–0 Scotland at Twickenham	*British Open Winner* Walter Hagen at Sandwich, England (292)	*Scottish Grand National Winner* Aedeen at Bogside	*Camanachd Cup Winners* Kyles Athletic at Glasgow
Scottish Cup Winners Rangers				

COMFORT IN SPECTACLES
Shell frames give nose comfort.
Toric lenses give eye comfort.
This combination gives the ideal reading spectacle.
JOHN TROTTER
LIMITED
40 Gordon Street, Glasgow
and 100 George St., Edinburgh

Daily Record and Mail.

SCOTLAND'S NATIONAL NEWSPAPER

ESTAB. 1847—No. 25,593. GLASGOW, FRIDAY, FEBRUARY 1, 1929. ONE PENNY.

SLASHING ATTACK ON HIGHLAND ELECTRICITY SCHEMES

DEATH SENTENCES ON REBELS.

SPANISH REVOLT NOT YET QUELLED.

BIG INSURRECTIONARY MOVEMENT.

ACCORDING to reports from the Spanish frontier, the abortive revolt at Ciudad Real was only part of a much larger insurrectionary movement, which is likely to break out over the week-end. An attempt is already being made to foment general strikes in the industrial centres.

GENERAL STRIKE CALLED.

SECRET MEETING OF LEADERS.

NEWS of the unrest of Spain, owing to the extreme rigidity of the censorship, still comes mainly from Hendaye on the frontier.

A frontier correspondent of *Le Quotidien* of Paris (quoted by Reuter) reports the rebellion has not been nipped in the bud, as announced officially in Madrid.

Other garrisons besides that of Ciudad Real are in the movement, though they have not yet passed to open revolt.

The movement, continues the correspondent, is thus all the more dangerous for the Directorate, and for General Primo de Rivera, the Dictator, against whom it is specially directed.

Phil Scott wins the big fight. Report on Page 9. Pictures on Page 12.

The revolt will, inevitably, soon begin again, perhaps even this week, adds the correspondent.

The Hendaye correspondent of the *Quotidien* says that the Spanish Government's attitude shows great concern.

Banks have received orders to effect no exchange operations with abroad, and this has been a hard blow to trade.

The Paris *Intransigeant* publishes a message from Hendaye stating that Senor Sanchez Guerra, the Conservative ex-Premier, instead of having been arrested, as at first reported, surrendered voluntarily.

Finding that the artillery officers at Valencia, on whom he had counted to foster the revolt, were disinclined to join him, at the last moment, Senor Sanchez Guerra is reported to have exclaimed, in desperation—

"Arrest me, and me only. I am solely responsible for this unsuccessful plot."

The message adds that attempts to declare general strikes have been made at Bilbao, Granada, and Cordova.

It is reported from Hendaye, says the B.U.P.'s Paris correspondent, that, at a court-martial at Cuidad Real, Col. Paz, Lieut.-Col. Brits, and Commandant Cejador, the ringleaders of the revolt there, were sentenced to death.

The executions, however, may not be carried out.

The Spanish Government is considering its policy, and it is considered likely that a civil trial will also be held.

PLANNED IN PARIS.

The police have discovered that the revolt, which was revealed by the premature uprising of the regiment in Ciudad Real, was planned by prominent Spanish exiles in Paris.

It is alleged that a meeting of Spanish rebels, including Senor Guerra, Doctor Maranon, and General Ochoa, took place in Paris on January 13.

Numerous arrests are reported to have been carried out in the Spanish provinces.

It is thought these are measures of precaution, to prevent any attempt on the life of the King, who left Seville last night for Madrid, his train passing through Ciudad Real.

It is also reported that a regiment of infantry has been ordered to Valencia.

GOLF CHAMPION "DESERTED."

WALTER HAGEN SUING FOR DIVORCE.

Los Angeles, Thursday.

Mr. Walter Hagen, the American golfer and holder of the British open golf championship, is suing for divorce, alleging that despite his best efforts to provide for the happiness and welfare of his wife, she deserted him three years after the marriage.—B.U.P.

RADIUM SUPPLY HOPES.

BRITISH GROUP NEGOTIATING FOR IMPORTS.

Negotiations are in progress between a British group and the Czecho-Slovakian Government for the importation into this country of radium at a lower price and in greater quantities than at present.

If this scheme materialises it is hoped to assist to a great degree medical practice and research by a regular supply of radium.

"Unless influences over which we have no control should intervene," said Mr. A. H. Tysser, managing director of the British Continental Press, who is one of the negotiators, yesterday, "the scheme will go through in its present form."

ENGLAND WINS TOSS.

START OF FOURTH TEST MATCH.

Adelaide Oval, Friday.

Although Adelaide's share of this year's Tests was shorn of much of its glory owing to the rubber having been won on the three previous matches, the stimulus afforded by the fact that Australia was fighting to win their first match and that England, on the other hand, was trying to complete a clean sweep and so avenge Warwick Armstrong's achievement here in 1921, lent to to-day's match an interest keen enough to bring thousands to the ground at an early hour.

If superstition entered into England's calculations, then they had more to contend with than appeared on the surface, as this is their thirteenth Test Match at Adelaide. Of the previous twelve, they have won only three. The last Test played here was that memorable match which kept English cricket "fans" up all night only to meet a disappointing dawn, for Australia won by 11 runs.

CHAPMAN CALLS "TAILS."

A. P. F. Chapman, the England skipper, won the toss and decided to bat first. Chapman called "tails" for the first time in the Tests. "So you switched it on me, Percy?" said J. S. Ryder, the Australian captain, as he returned to the pavilion, smiling. "Yes," replied Chapman, "I beat Vic Richardson with tails the other day, and thought to try it again." Both captains laughed, although Chapman's seemed to be the heartier.

There was no rain at all yesterday and after that of the previous day or two, the wicket was as perfect as a wicket could be. It was as hard as concrete and as fast as any batsman could wish. England's highest in a Test at Adelaide is 501—1911-12—and to-day everything looked favourable for a repetition of this feat.

A SLOW START.

A'Beckett bowled the first over to Hobbs. Hendry bowled from the other end. Both batsmen made a slow start, their desire being to get the pace of the wicket, and against the good quality attack they had to exercise care.

Ryder was anxious that they should lay themselves in quickly, however, and when 16 runs had been made, he called on Grimmett. The South Australian, who was, of course, on his own wicket, bowled to a normal field, but without a silly point.

This was a position which Richardson filled with such distinction in previous matches. Grimmett found he had to have one, however, and Woodfull was brought in there later.

Oxenham, with the conditions all against his bowling came on at 29, at A'Beckett's end, but Hobbs and Sutcliffe were very steady and kept one another company, Hobbs being 12 and Sutcliffe 14 when the total stood at 30.

ENGLAND—First Innings.

Hobbs, not out	16
Sutcliffe, not out	20
Extras	4
Total (no wicket)	40

"EXPLOITING" THE HIGHLANDS.

HOSTILITY TO ELECTRICITY SCHEMES.

WHY THE POWERS SOUGHT ARE OPPOSED.

COUNTY, city, and town councils, the Forestry Commissioners, education authorities, harbour trustees, railway and other public companies and landlords and fishery boards are among the petitioners against the two proposed Highland electricity schemes.

The case against the schemes is forcibly stated by Mr. Evan W. Barron, editor of the *Inverness Courier*.

NOT NATIONAL PROJECTS.

VITAL QUESTIONS AT ISSUE.

By EVAN M. BARRON,
Editor of the "Inverness Courier."

THERE is only one standpoint from which the two proposed Hydro-Electric schemes in the Highlands can be regarded by Highlanders, and that is—Are they for the good of the Highlands or are they not?

Many people seem to imagine that the Highland Hydro-Electric schemes are in some undisclosed way national schemes in the sense that the Government or the Electricity Board is really, though not nominally, behind them, or is somehow or other responsible for them.

That is nothing but a delusion. There is not a vestige of reason for any such belief.

The schemes, it cannot be too often or too emphatically pointed out, are being promoted simply and solely for private purposes and for private profit.

Two groups of financiers are trying to exploit the Highlands for their own benefit.

If the schemes go through in anything like their present form the result will be not only that the greatest and the most important of the water resources of the Highlands will be controlled by two companies trading for profit, but that a wide belt of magnificent Highland country, stretching practically from sea to sea, will be at the mercy of two great financial trusts.

TO GAIN FAVOUR.

Supporters of the schemes are trying to gain favour for them, and attempting to divert attention from the real questions at issue, by raising anew the bogey of landlordism and representing the opponents of the schemes as nothing but selfish Highland landlords.

The truth is that the promoters are asking Parliament to confer powers on them far beyond anything which any Highland landlord possesses.

As things are, Highland landlords are ordinary individuals, subject to the same laws and the same restrictions on their actions as the rest of us.

But our would-be new landlords, the two financial groups promoting the schemes, will be in many respects above the existing law and not subject to the present restrictions, if their schemes go through.

POWERS OF EVICTION.

They will, for instance, have power to evict any landholder be he crofter, smallholder, farmer or landlord, if they covet his land for the purpose of their schemes.

They will have power to close rights-of-way that have existed from time immemorial.

They will have power to divert rivers, lochs and burns from their natural courses, to the great loss of all manner of people, dwellers in towns and villages as well as dwellers in the country.

They will have power to remove their neighbours' landmarks as and when they like—houses, churches, schools, churchyards, anything, in fact, that interferes with their plans.

They will have power to ruin the natural beauty of one of the most glorious parts of the Highlands, and deprive those who love its glories of many of the rights of access and many of the other privileges in regard to it which they at present enjoy.

VAST TERRITORY.

Nothing but national necessity of the gravest kind, or the prospect of national gain on a great and desirable scale, could justify such a tremendous interference with public and private rights and with the natural resources of a vast national territory.

But of either of these essentials there is not the slightest trace in either of the schemes.

One scheme, the West Highland, is being promoted ostensibly in the interests of certain industries which it is proposed to establish on the western seaboard of Inverness-shire, in order that by the aid of a plentiful supply of cheap electricity the profits of the owners of these industries may be increased.

For that purpose a large area of the Highlands is to be devastated and its water stolen.

A still larger area is to have its supplies of water diminished to an enormous extent, its prosperity placed in grave jeopardy, and its interests imperilled in countless ways by the diversion from east to west of the waters of lochs and rivers which at present flow through it on their way to the eastern seaboard.

GRAMPIAN SCHEME.

The other scheme, the Grampian Scheme, is being promoted entirely in the interests of the promoters.

Its purpose is simply and solely to give the Grampian Company a large supply of electricity *for sale outside the Highlands.*

It is not conceived in the remotest degree in the interests of the Highlands, there is no guarantee that any of the supply will be available for use in the Highlands, and, like the West Highland, it will have the most injurious effect on a very large tract of country.

While I said that the West Highland scheme was "ostensibly" promoted in the interests of the district, my belief is that it will no more benefit the area concerned than will the Grampian project.

TEARING VEIL AWAY.

There is, of course, nothing inherently wrong in one promoting schemes which will benefit oneself.

When, however, as in the present case, the specious plea is advanced that these hydro-electric schemes are conceived in the interests of the Highlands it is necessary to tear the veil aside and expose them for what they really are—schemes conceived in the interests of the promoters alone.

Moreover, it is estimated that on the completion of the schemes there will be a "saving" of a million tons of coal annually in the production of electricity.

(Continued On Page 2.)

BY TELEPHONE LINE.

Sandwina appeals against the referee's decision, which disqualified him in the fight against Scott in London last night. — Picture by "Daily Record" telephone line. Other pictures on Page 12.

1929

PROTESTS AT ELECTRIC SCHEMES

THERE was great opposition to the two electricity schemes planned for the Highlands.

Among the many petitioners against the schemes were county, city and town councils, the Forestry Commissioners, education authorities, harbour trustees, railway and other public companies and landlords and fishery boards.

They said that supporters of the schemes were trying to gain favour for them, and attempting to divert attention from the real questions at issue, by raising a new bogey of landlordism and representing the opponents of the schemes as nothing but selfish landlords.

The truth was that the promoters were asking Parliament to confer powers on them far beyond anything which any Highland landlord possessed.

As things were, objectors argued, Highland landlords were ordinary individuals subject to the same laws and the same restrictions on their actions as normal citizens.

But if the schemes went through, the would-be new landlords, the two financial groups promoting these schemes, would be in many respects above the existing law and not subject to the present restrictions.

They would have the power to evict any landholder, be he crofter, smallholder, farmer or landlord, if they desired his land for the purpose of their schemes.

They would have the power to close rights of way and divert rivers, lochs and burns from their natural courses, to the great loss of all manner of people. They would also be able to remove landmarks.

CLYDE TANKER INFERNO

A spent match resulted in a massive blaze which destroyed the Glasgow-based oil tanker *Vimeira* and claimed the lives of fifteen of her crew and the stevedores working on her while she was berthed in Rotterdam. The match ignited petrol floating on the water near to the tanker and the fire then spread to the ship itself. Some 60 people were on board when she caught fire amidships and many tried to escape the flames by leaping into the burning water.

GOINGS...

Robert Lorimer
Architect

John Dewar
Whisky Distiller

David Buick
US Car Manufacturer

NEW!

Another Triumph—
for "His Master's Voice"

His Master's Voice

SCOTTISH FISHING FLEET CRIPPLED

The Scottish fishing fleet was facing economic ruin following a major gale which struck the boats off the Norfolk coast in November. Some 600 vessels, fishing out of Lowestoft and Yarmouth, lost over 30,000 nets and other gear when they were caught in the storm. Without nets, many of the trawlers were forced to return home to an uncertain future.

GALE RUINS SCOTS FISHERMEN.
£150,000 LOSS OF NETS BY STORM.
RELIEF FUND QUESTION RAISED IN PARLIAMENT.

COMINGS...

Magnus Magnusson
TV Presenter

Winnie Ewing
Nationalist Politician

'It's quite right what they say ... CRAVEN 'A' DON'T AFFECT THE THROAT AND THEY NEVER VARY'

CRAVEN 'A'

THIS SPORTING LIFE

FOOTBALL	RUGBY UNION	GOLF	HORSE RACING	SHINTY
Scottish Champions Rangers	*Scotland vs England* Scotland 12–6 England at Murrayfield	*British Open Winner* Walter Hagen at Muirfield (295)	*Scottish Grand National Winner* Donzelon at Bogside	*Camanachd Cup Winners* Newtonmore at Spean Bridge
Scottish Cup Winners Kilmarnock				

FOR EVENING WEAR

WHITE GOLD, RIMMED, & RIMLESS SPECTACLE WEAR

W. W. SCOTT & Co., Ltd.
Ophthalmic Opticians
180 SAUCHIEHALL ST., C.2

Daily Record and Mail.

SCOTLAND'S NATIONAL NEWSPAPER

ESTAB. 1847—No. 25,878.　　GLASGOW, WEDNESDAY, JANUARY 1, 1930.　　ONE PENNY.

69 DEAD IN CINEMA DISASTER.

AWFUL SCENES AT PAISLEY.

CHILDREN'S FIGHT FOR LIFE.

AGONISING FATE.

THE biggest and most terrible cinema disaster ever experienced in Great Britain occurred in Paisley yesterday afternoon.

Sixty-nine children perished in a panic which followed a film fire in the Glen Cinema at Paisley Cross—also known as the Good Templars' Hall—about half-past two.

By the grimmest of irony, the incident which caused the panic was comparatively trivial. A spool of film caught fire in the re-winding room where a young man was at work. He seized the case containing the burning film and threw it into a passage leading to the hall.

Great clouds of smoke from the film case entered the hall, the children were stricken with panic and rushed in a screaming, struggling mass to two exists at the screen end of the hall.

These led to two passages which led in turn to a stairway. Some of the children fell on this stair and were at once overwhelmed by the masses of scared youngsters in the rear. In a moment the stairway was piled breast-high with little bodies.

DIED FROM SUFFOCATION.

None of the children received burning injuries. Many died from suffocation in the stairway, others were suffocated by the fumes from the burning film.

One of the fire officers who was present states that there was also coal gas in the hall, but the part, if any, this played in causing the death-roll has not been definitely ascertained.

The smoking case lay in the passage for only a few moments before the manager, who had been told of the accident, dashed up and threw it out of the cinema on to a piece of vacant ground. But the damage had already been done.

JOY TURNED TO TRAGEDY.

HOLOCAUST IN FEW MINUTES.

THE show was a special children's matinee which started at 2.15, and about 600 children were present.

The first picture was a cowboy one, and as is usual at these matinees the children were being violently partisan—the villain was greeted with boos and jeers, and when the hero appeared the cheers were loud enough to raise the roof.

Scarcely had the fun started when a cloud of smoke from the film burning in the vestibule belched into the area.

In an instant hilarious joy was turned to panic. Like a wave the children surged towards the screen and two exits leading to Terrace Walk, a lane at the back of the cinema overlooking the Cart.

STRUGGLING MASS.

The two passages culminated in a single one and then there were nine or ten steps leading down to the door on the Walk.

The mass was too great to get out by the doorway. A few of the first children fell and in a matter of seconds the stairway and the passage leading to it were several feet deep in struggling bodies. The struggles of some did not last long. The weight behind was so great that they died almost immediately.

The throng which is always at Paisley Cross and Dunn Square learned of the disaster when a handful of screaming children dashed out of the smoking vestibule.

Several policemen and civilians valiantly tried to enter but were driven back by the smoke. Others ran round to the exit in the Walk overlooking the Cart.

HEROIC FIREMEN.

Two minutes after the alarm was raised Paisley Fire Brigade pulled up at the door of the Cart.

"For God's sake, get your smoke helmets. The hall's full of children," shouted some civilians to the firemen.

"My men," said Deputy-Firemaster Wilson, to the *Daily Record* afterwards, "did not wait for smoke helmets or anything else when they heard that the children were inside."

Into the smoke-laden corridor the firemen hurried, and at the back of the area one party under Mr. Wilson took the passage to the left and another party took the right.

In the hall the air was thick with the fumes from the burning film, though they were not so dense as in the passage.

SCENES OF TERROR.

Children lay on the floor of the hall, children were standing dazed in the clearer area, children were scrambling on seats, on the stage, near the screen in an effort to get away from the terror they had sensed at the rear of the hall. From the passages at the far end there came the screams and moans of the children jammed there.

"Half-a-dozen youngsters grabbed me as soon as I reached them," said a fireman. "I could not get them to understand what to do, so I simply turned and went back up the hall to the main entrance with them clinging to me.

BLACKENED FACES.

"You could not put your foot on the floor for still bodies, some of them with blackened faces. I doubt if some of the children who escaped will ever recover from the horror of that experience.

"I saw one little lad in a corner with bodies piled up above his waist. He wasn't looking at the bodies. He was looking upwards and gesticulating as if pushing something back with his hands. I suppose he still imagined he was fighting for life in that mad crush."

MANY VOLUNTEERS.

The firemen had many volunteer helpers in their work. Some men got ladders and ascended to windows in the side of the wall, which were broken open. Through them the rescuers got into the hall and aided in the work of evacuating the children, a number of whom were passed to men standing on the ladders and thence lowered to the ground.

OTHER DISASTER NEWS

Fire Chief's Statement . Page 2
List of Victims . . . . Page 2
Hospital Scenes . . . Page 3
Interview with Survivors Page 3
Provost's Message . . Page 4

FATHER'S ORDEAL.

FIREMAN WHO THOUGHT HIS CHILDREN WERE THERE.

On the way to the fire a fireman sidenly recalled that his wife had sken of sending the two children to the matinee. The pang of that memory sirred him to an even fiercer energy in the rescue work.

He scanned the face of child after child as he worked, hoping—or fearing—to find his own among them. They were not among the survivors, as he had hope, nor among the dead, as he had fear.

When he returned to the station he found that his children had not gone to the show.

VICTIMS' GARMENTS.

Other parents had sadder experiences. One mother hurried to the spot and found his child lying apparently senseless among some injured outside the cinema. He took it up and rushed home. When the body was examined he was found to be dead.

The hospital mortuary was packed with bodies and at no time during the evening was it without the little groups of parents going a silent round in search of their missing child.

All evening men and women came and went. Many of them left with reddened eyes, carrying bundles of stained garments.

The infirmary staff laboured nobly with the appalling number of cases, and my Paisley doctors lent their services. More than one of the doctors

THE FATAL GATE.—It was here that the children piled up in their attempt to get through the narrow doorway.—"*Daily Record*" photograph.

was going about his work with white overalls over evening clothes which had been donned for some Hogmanay festivity.

EMERGENCY AMBULANCES.

While the children were being taken out of the hall the ground outside was like an hospital. Two ambulances made numberless trips between the hall and the Royal Alexandra Infirmary, and tramcars, private motor cars, and commercial vehicles were all pressed into service to take the dead and injured to hospital.

News of the disaster flashed like lightning round the district and from many homes distracted mothers rushed to the Cross to learn the fate of their children.

MOTHERS AID DOCTOR.

A typical story of the ghastly experience of hundreds of Paisley mothers was told by Mrs. Brown, 5 Hunter Street.

Three of her children were at the matinee, and the first news she got was that all had perished. She ran round to a temporary dressing station

HOGMANAY HUSH.

THE New Year came in mournfully in Paisley. When the clock on the tower of the Clark Town Hall chimed the hour of twelve, there was a large crowd at the Cross, where the cinema stands; but all attempts to sing "Auld Lang Syne" feebly died away. People contented themselves with greeting each other in hushed tones. It was an occasion for tears, not rejoicing, in a town which has experienced the saddest Hogmanay in its history.

in a workshop where many little bodies were laid out on the floor, and a doctor was passing from one to the other looking for signs of life.

The place was crowded with hysterical women trying to find their little ones.

"The doctor," said Mrs. Brown, "appealed to us to help him, and showed how artificial respiration should be applied. Several of us at once started to work on the children despite the fact that we were almost frantic with our own grief."

BABY VICTIM.

The youngest victim was a girl of 18 months, Minnie M'Crann, of 11 Storie Street, whose sister, Nellie M'Crann, also lost her life. Minnie, a *Daily Record* reporter was told, did not want to go to the pictures but was persuaded to go along with her sister.

MANAGER'S STORY.

EFFORT TO STEM EXIT RUSH.

OPEN DOORS.

Mr. Darwood, the manager of the cinema, said in an interview of the

"I was informed by the assistant-operator of what had taken place. I rushed to the vestibule, lifted the box containing the burning film, and threw it out of a side-door into a piece of vacant ground facing Dunn Square.

"Inside the hall, by this time, pandemonium had broken out among the children, who naturally rushed to the exits farthest from where the smoke was coming.

"I endeavoured to get the children to come back and go through the other doors that had been thrown open, but they refused.

"They were soon lying on top of one another, and many of them were rescued from the exits leading to Terrace Walk and Dyers' Wynd."

RELIEF FUND.

FILM DIRECTOR'S OFFER FOR RELATIVES.

The *Daily Record* was informed last night that Mr. James V. Bryson, managing director of the Universal Pictures Corporation, has offered £1000 to start a fund for the relief of the relatives of the victims.

FOOTBALLERS AS RESCUERS.

A. Gebbie, an inside forward of the St. Mirren Football Club, along with Dave M'Millan, a well-known local player, worked heroically in rescuing children from the building.

A small boy, David Allison, son of the trainer of the St. Mirren Club, who had attended the performance with his little sister, saved many of the children. He showed them a way of exit known only to a few, the boy being familiar with the building, having been a frequent visitor there.

FATHER'S PITIFUL TASK.

Mr. Cairns, of 38 Gordon Street, Paisley, had the pitiful experience of running with his boy, Johnnie, in his arms from the cinema to the Infirmary, only to discover at the Infirmary that the child was dead.

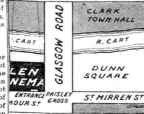

sketch map showing the location of the cinema.

Wireless Programmes—Page 9.

FIRE PANIC CLAIMS 69 LIVES

SIXTY-NINE children perished in a panic which took place after a New Year fire at the Glen Cinema at Paisley Cross.

The grim irony of the tragedy was that the incident which caused the panic was trivial. A spool of film caught fire in the rewinding room, where a young man was at work. He seized the case containing the burning film and threw it into a passage leading to the hall.

The smoking case lay in the passage for only a few minutes before the manager, who had been alerted to the incident, threw the case out of the cinema on to a piece of vacant ground but by then the panic had begun.

Clouds of smoke from the film case had entered the hall and the children began to panic. They rushed to two exists at the screen, screaming and pushing.

The two passages led to a stairway. In their rush to escape, some of the children fell on the stair and were soon crushed by other children pushing on from behind them.

The manager tried to get the children to exit through another set of doors that had been opened, but the terrified youngsters refused.

Firemen and local men soon arrived at the scene and began the rescue operation to save the panicking children still trapped inside the building. Tragically, 69 of the children did not survive. None of the children received burn injuries but many died from suffocation in the crush, while others suffocated on the fumes from the burning film.

Because of the tragedy, the New Year came in mournfully in Paisley.

When the clock on the tower of the Clark Town Hall chimed the hour of midnight, there was a large crowd at the Cross where the cinema stood, but all attempts to sing "Auld Lang Syne" feebly died away.

People contented themselves with greeting each other in hushed tones on what was the saddest Hogmanay in the town's history.

COMINGS...

Ronnie Corbett
Comedian

Sean Connery
Actor

GOINGS...

Arthur Conan Doyle
Creator of Sherlock Holmes

Neil Munro
Author of The Vital Spark

BEN LOMOND UNDER THE HAMMER

The Duke of Montrose felt it necessary to sell off land because of the burden of post-war taxation and in April, Ben Lomond went up for grabs. The popular 3192-foot peak and the public approaches were included in the Rowardennan and Inversnaid blocks of land for sale. A campaign was started to raise a fund to keep the mountain for the nation and eventually the ben became part of the Queen Elizabeth Forest Park.

CLYDE YARDS SET TO SHUT

Two shipyards on the Clyde were facing closure in November – Napier & Miller at Old Kilpatrick and the south yard of Ardrossan Dockyard Ltd. They had been acquired by National Shipbuilding Securities Ltd under the scheme for eliminating redundant yards. An official statement said: "The Clyde's capacity was increased to a greater extent than any other district to meet war needs. It is desirable that the industry now operates at maximum efficiency."

WHAT IT COST

POUND OF BUTTER
1s 2¼d

POUND OF BACON
1s 6d

PINT OF BEER
5d

CIGARETTES
6d (10 Gold Flake Mild)

WOMEN'S SHOES
£1 11s 6d

MEN'S SUIT
£6 11s

TON OF COAL
£1 3s 2½d

POSTAGE
1½d

CAR
Ford De Luxe Saloon £135

THIS SPORTING LIFE

FOOTBALL
Scottish Champions
Rangers

Scottish Cup Winners
Rangers

RUGBY UNION
Scotland vs England
England 0–0 Scotland
at Twickenham

GOLF
British Open Winner
Bobby Jones
at Hoylake, England
(291)

HORSE RACING
Scottish Grand National Winner
Drintyre at Bogside

SHINTY
Camanachd Cup Winners
Inveraray
at Oban

COMFORT IN SPECTACLES

Shell frames give nose comfort.
Toric lenses give eye comfort.
This combination gives the ideal
reading spectacle.

JOHN TROTTER,
LIMITED

40 Gordon Street, Glasgow,
and 100 George St., Edinburgh.

Daily ✠ Record
and Mail.

SCOTLAND'S NATIONAL

NEWSPAPER

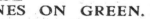

ESTAB. 1847—No. 26,425.   GLASGOW, FRIDAY, OCTOBER 2, 1931.   ONE PENNY.

50,000 IN GLASGOW WORKLESS RIOTING.

WILD RIOTING IN GLASGOW.

POLICE INJURED IN STREET FIGHTING.

SHOPS LOOTED.

MR. JOHN M'GOVERN, M.P. for the Shettleston Division of Glasgow, was among those arrested when mounted and foot police charged a demonstration of 50,000 unemployed on Glasgow Green, last night.

After warning the organisers that their procession would not be allowed to leave Glasgow Green, where it had congregated from all parts of the city, the police charged the crowd.

Several policemen were among those injured. Shop windows were smashed and looted.

Twelve persons were arrested, one of them being a woman.

AMAZING SCENES ON GREEN.

PANDEMONIUM IN DARKNESS.

FOR half an hour there was pandemonium in the darkness of the roadways and paths in the Green—shouts and jeers, screams of terrified women and children, and shrill blasts of police whistles summoning officers to fresh charges.

Many people were injured, including several policemen, and among those who had to be taken to the infirmary were two sergeants and a constable.

As the mob was driven from the Green it began to attack shop windows, hundreds of which were smashed and looted.

Long after midnight mounted and foot police were still patrolling the chief streets of the city dispersing hostile crowds.

MASS DEMONSTRATION.

In the afternoon, about 10,000 unemployed took part in a demonstration outside the City Chambers in George Square while a meeting of the Town Council was going on. The Town Council heard a deputation of unemployed, which asked that the Government be petitioned to rescind the dole cut decision. The Council, however, declined to do anything in the matter.

While the deputation was inside, Mr. John M'Govern, M.P., and a number of other speakers addressed a huge mass meeting in North Hanover Street, and it was announced that another monster demonstration would be held at night.

THE GATHERING.

Contingents of unemployed were to assemble in their respective areas and march to Glasgow Green, near the High Court, for a great demonstration through the streets at 8 o'clock.

Amid great excitement the contingents assembled and marched into the main avenue of the Green.

Strangely enough there was not a single policeman to be seen, though the crowd was so dense that it stretched across Saltmarket to the wall of the High Court.

Just before 8 o'clock three police inspectors made their way through the crowd and told one of the organisers that the demonstration was not to be allowed to leave the Green.

COLUMN OF POLICE.

On the stroke of eight the police appeared marching eight abreast along Greendyke Street from the Central Police Office. At the junction of Greendyke Street and Saltmarket the police halted, a move which seemed rather to puzzle the crowd. They very soon realised, however, what was afoot.

Before the crowd realised what was happening, 15 mounted men, who had come down Saltmarket in sections of four, spread across the wide thoroughfare in one rank, and headed for the mass of humanity jammed in the semi-circular space around the gates of the Green.

CROWD SCATTERED.

Behind the mounted men came the foot police, who tackled what the mounted people had left. The crowd scattered in every direction, and as they

scattered the crash of shattered windows could be heard along Saltmarket.

As the mounted police rushed into the Green women and children sought refuge in shops in the vicinity.

Those at the head of the procession offered resistance and attempted to drag the officers off their saddles. The officers immediately drew their batons and two of the organisers of the demonstration were felled to the ground.

M.P. FROG-MARCHED.

Mr. John M'Govern was approached by half a dozen policemen on foot and was requested to "move on." He refused, and as one of the officers caught him by the arm he offered resistance, whereupon the constables were ordered to use force.

A remarkable scene followed. Shettleston's M.P., struggling violently for his freedom as the officers frog-marched him out of the Green to the Central Police Station.

Mr. M'Govern shouted appealing remarks to the demonstrators in the vicinity, but by this time they were rushing up side streets and along the Saltmarket away from the onrushing constables.

The Central police chambers were reached within a few minutes, and after being searched and charged Mr. M'Govern was conveyed to the cells. He will appear before Stipendiary Smith at the Divisional Court to-morrow morning.

Great excitement prevailed as the crowds rushed up Saltmarket and, amid

(Continued on Page 2, Column 4.)

Lady May Cambridge photographed when leaving her dressmakers in Grosvenor Street, London, where she had been calling to make arrangements regarding her wedding gown.

VALUE OF £ ABROAD.

	Yesterday.	Wed.	Tues.
New York	16/4½	16/1½	15 9½
Montreal	18/4½	18/9½	17 8½
Paris	16 10½	16	15/8½
Brussels	16/2	16/	15/8½
Berlin	16/4½	16/4½	16/4½
Geneva	18/4	15/10½	15 5½
Rome	16/9	16/6½	17/1
Amsterdam	16/3	16/0½	15 11
Oslo	19/6	19/10	19/10
Copenhagen	19/6	19/6	19/6
Stockholm	18 8	19/	18 9

SILKS TRIAL SURPRISE.

POSTPONEMENT TILL NEXT YEAR.

TO-DAY'S MOVE.

The *Daily Record* understands that application will be made in the High Court to-day for a postponement of the Scottish silks trial, the opening of which had been fixed for October 12.

This move has been mutually agreed upon by the parties.

It is probable that the case will not now come up until January.

LUXURY HOME FOR SALE.

LADY MOUNTBATTEN AND HIGH TAXES.

Because "increased taxation has made it impossible for her to keep the house open," Lady Louis Mountbatten has given instructions for the sale of her magnificent Park Lane mansion, Brook House, London, which she inherited from her millionaire grandfather, Sir Ernest Cassel.

In his will Sir Ernest expressed the wish that Brook House and its contents should never be sold.

Lady Louis feels, however, that he could by no possibility have foreseen the present high level of taxation, and the modern cost of maintaining such a place.

FORTUNE SPENT ON IT.

Hundreds of thousands of pounds were spent on Brook House, after Sir Ernest bought it from the executors of Lord Tweedmouth, in making the grand hall and staircase.

Hundreds of tons of beautiful marble were used, and the specially-built dining-room seats 100 guests.

Lady Louis is to join her husband, Lord Louis Mountbatten, the recently-appointed Fleet Signal Officer with the Queen Elizabeth at Malta, where he will be stationed for two years. Upon her return to London Lady Louis may live in a flat.

FORCED DOWN BY ILLNESS.

BAD LUCK DOGS KINGSFORD SMITH.

PLUCKY BID.

Athens, Thursday.

AIR-COMMODORE KINGS-FORD SMITH was compelled by indisposition to land at Milas, 90 miles south of Smyrna, yesterday, while attempting to beat Mr. J. A. Mollison's record flight from Australia to England, which he accomplished in 8 days, 13 hours and 35 minutes. He made a safe landing and his machine was undamaked.

In spite of not feeling well, the airman was determined to cintinue his flight and pluckily telegraphed to his friends here that they might expect him at Tatoi Aerodrome this afternoon. At eight o'clock to-night he had not arrived and the aerodrome officials were wondering whether he might be able to continue his flight to-day.

DOGGED BY SICKNESS.

Air-Commodore Kingsford Smith has been dogged by sickness during the greater part of his flight. An attack of sun-stroke on the second day out brought on

FLIGHTS COMPARED.

THE FOLLOWING IS THE COMPARATIVE RECORD OF MOLLISON'S AND KINGSFORD SMITH'S FLIGHTS:—

Mollison.	Kingsford Smith.
Day.	Day.
1st—Batavia.	1st—Cheribon, Java.
2nd—Singapore.	2nd—Victoria Point, Burma.
3rd—Rangoon.	
4th—Calcutta.	3rd—Rangoon
5th—Karachi.	4th—Jhansi.
6th—Basra.	5th—Bushire.
8th—Rome.	6th—Leaves Bushire for Aleppo.
9th—Croydon.	7th—Forced landing at Milas.

fainting fits, but he persevered in spite of bad luck.

It now looks as if he has little chance of beating the record as he would have to arrive in Tngland before 6.30 to-morrow. —Reuter.

MESSAGE TO LONDON.

A wireless message received at Le Bourget, confirming the landing at Milas, stated that the airman hoped to continue on to Athels last night.

In a cable received by the Vacuum Oil Company in London last night from Milas, and timed 4.55 p.m., Air Commodore Kingsford Smith said:—"Awaiting permission to leave. Will advise."

SIR THOMAS LIPTON EASIER.

IMPROVEMENT IN CONDITION LAST NIGHT.

The *Daily Record* learns that there was an encouraging improvement, last night, in the condition of Sir Thomas Lipton, who has been seriously ill at his London home for several days.

He is suffering from a chill, which he caught 10 days ago, and four doctors are attending him.

His robust constitution has helped him to maintain his strength so far, and his friends are greatly cheered by the improvement noted last night.

LOSS TO DUNDEE COUNCIL.

Three prominent members of Dundee Town Council, Messrs. John Reid, John Phin, and R. J. Larg yesterday intimated that they were not to seek re-election at the November municipal elections.

Councillor Reid is at present convener of the Housing Committee, Councillor Phin convener of the Works Committee, and Councillor Larg convener of the Police Committee.

The scene during the rioting in Glasgow last night in the vicinity of the entrance to Glasgow Green at Jail Square.—"Daily Record" photograph.

Wireless Programmes—Page 21.

POLICE BATON CHARGE RIOTERS

A DEMONSTRATION against the high levels of unemployment in the country took place on Glasgow Green in October. Over 50,000 people from all parts of the city and further afield congregated in the park to listen to speakers and vent their frustrations.

When the crowd tried to move on from the Green, police officers warned the organisers that their procession would not be allowed to leave the park.

Shortly after this, the police charged the crowd with truncheons drawn in an attempt to disperse them.

For half an hour there was pandemonium in the darkness of the roadways and paths in and around the vicinity of the Green.

There were shouts and jeers, screams of terrified women and children, and the shrill blasts of police whistles as more officers were summoned to provide reinforcements for fresh charges.

Many people were injured and among the policemen hurt and taken to the infirmary were two sergeants and a constable.

As the mob was driven from the Green it began to attack shops. Windows were smashed and then looting began.

The disturbances lasted long after midnight, when mounted and foot police officers were still patrolling the main streets of the city and dispersing hostile crowds.

ROUGH GOING FOR MOSLEY

Sir Oswald Mosley, leader of the New Party, was given a rough reception in September when he addressed more than 20,000 people at Glasgow Green. He had verbal duels with hecklers, was hit by stones and other missiles and he was mobbed by a jeering crowd on his way to his car. Fiercely attacking the last Labour Government, the New Party leader had to struggle to be heard. At one point, a column of people marched on to the Green singing *The Internationale*. Sir Oswald refused to be intimidated and smiled and waved to the hostile crowd as his car drove away after the rally.

QUAKING WITH FEAR

Scotland and the rest of Britain was hit in June by the most severe earthquake ever experienced here. Two tremors were felt in the middle of the night in many parts of Scotland, particularly in the north east. Houses were shaken, chimney stacks shattered and many people were terrified. In Portknockie, householders ran into the streets in panic. Aberdeen people told of hearing a frightening roaring that accompanied the second of the tremors along with a wave of intense heat. The earthquake was believed to have had its epicentre in the North Sea.

COMINGS...

Hugh Fraser
Businessman

Lonnie Donegan
Skiffle Star of the '60s

GOINGS...

Thomas Lipton
Businessman & Yachtsman

THIS SPORTING LIFE

FOOTBALL	RUGBY UNION	GOLF	HORSE RACING	SHINTY
Scottish Champions Rangers	*Scotland vs England* Scotland 28–19 England at Murrayfield	*British Open Winner* Tommy Armour at Carnoustie (296)	*Scottish Grand National Winner* Annandale at Bogside	*Camanachd Cup Winners* Newtonmore at Inverness
Scottish Cup Winners Celtic				

COMFORT IN SPECTACLES
Shell frames give nose comfort.
Toric lenses give eye comfort.
This combination gives the ideal reading spectacle.
JOHN TROTTER
LIMITED
40 Gordon Street, Glasgow,
and 100 George St., Edinburgh

Daily Record and Mail.
ESTAB. 1847—No. 26,784. GLASGOW, FRIDAY, NOVEMBER 25, 1932. ONE PENNY.
SCOTLAND'S NATIONAL NEWSPAPER

BLUE BONNETS OFF TO SIR A. SINCLAIR

Sir A. Sinclair.

Sir R. Horne.

Mr. John Buchan.

Sir Godfrey Collins.

GREAT DEBATE ON HOME RULE.

What The Government Offers.

BRAVO! SIR A. SINCLAIR.

A Scots Parliament Within The British Union.

IN the momentous debate on Home Rule in the House of Commons, last night, Sir Archibald Sinclair (who was the first Secretary for Scotland in the National Government) seemed to be the only speaker who grasped the possibilities of a practical solution to the present Scottish demand that we should be allowed to look after our own domestic affairs.

Without going into detail, he indicated the possibility of a Scottish Parliament which, while sustaining all the merits of the Union of 1707, would allow of the Scottish M.P.'s sitting in Edinburgh as a separate body, controlling such vital concerns as Scotland's agriculture, education, fisheries, land laws, social services and national amenities.

Sir Robert Horne pronounced definitely against a separate Parliament, while outlining a series of suggestions for the centralisation of Scottish Departments in Edinburgh and other reforms.

Sir Godfrey Collins, the Secretary for Scotland, who also declared against Home Rule, promised administrative centralisation, financial considerations permitting.

The absence of the Prime Minister was regrettable, as, to judge from his recent utterances, he holds practically the same point of view as Sir Archibald Sinclair.

KEEN INTEREST IN DEBATE.

M.P.'S PRESENT IN FULL FORCE.

From Our Parliamentary Correspondent.

LAST night's momentous debate on the Scottish Home Rule issue in the Commons revealed that the Government's reforms in Scottish administration, as disclosed by the Secretary of State, go no further than the forecast. Indeed, in some respects they fall short of them.

A bigger proportion of Scottish Private Bill legislation is to be heard in Scotland, but national financial considerations in the meantime preclude the establishment of a new set of Scottish Offices in Edinburgh, or even the appointment of an additional Under-Secretary.

SCENE IN THE HOUSE.

The debate, let me say, was one of the most earnest and important, in an experience extending over a quarter of a century, I have ever heard at Westminster concerning Scotland's purely domestic affairs.

The Scottish M.P.'s were forward almost in their full strength. All the Scottish Ministers were in their places on the Treasury Bench.

Mr. Baldwin was also there, looking grave and preoccupied; but I did not see the Prime Minister.

The general atmosphere of the House seemed to be that with the recent manifestation of Scottish public opinion on this matter the issue had now to be faced seriously by the House of Commons.

Up in the Peers' Gallery I saw Lord Elibank and Lord Hutchison, and the whole air of the assemblage was one of expectancy, not to say tension.

CASE AGAINST HOME RULE.

The opening speech of Sir Robert Horne was a subtle performance. The Member for Hillhead surveyed the problem from many angles, and finally reached the conclusion that Scotland and England are now so interlocked and interwoven in their interests that they could not be dragged asunder without grievous injury to both countries.

There was not a murmur of dissent to anything he said, and his concrete suggestions, which came at the end, were of the same character as those dealt with later by Sir Godfrey Collins, the Secretary of State for Scotland.

SIR A. SINCLAIR SCORES.

It was a striking contribution which Sir Archibald Sinclair, the former Secretary for Scotland, made to the debate.

He said that if he were to choose between Separation or Dominion status on the one hand, and the Union as it existed at present with the hope of administrative reform, on the other, he would unhesitatingly choose the Union.

But Sir Archibald said there was a third and a better course—a measure of Home Rule which would preserve the representation of Scotland in this Parliament, with ample safeguards against the rupture of any of the business and commercial ties between the two countries, and which would leave Scotland free to manage her own domestic affairs.

There was an amusing little interlude in the debate when Sir Robert Horne was speaking.

Sir Robert referred to the amount of Departmental work that the Secretary of Scotland had to do, and observed that the salary attaching to the post was only £2000 a year.

EX-MINISTER BLUSHES.

"£2500," interjected Mr. Churchill.

Sir Robert paused, and then appealed to Sir Archibald Sinclair, sitting immediately below him, as to what was the correct figure.

Sir Archibald blushed at his inability to answer the query straight away, and the House laughed uproariously when, the next minute, they observed the ex-Scottish Secretary looking up an official text book to discover what his recent salary had been.

(FULL DEBATE ON PAGE 2.)

END OF YEARS OLD STRIFE.

LOSSIE DISPUTES SETTLED.

LEASE OF SQUARE

The long drawn-out strife between Captain Brander, Dunbar, Pitgaveny, and the Town Council of Lossiemouth, regarding the ownership of the town's square, has, the *Daily Record* learned last night, been amicably settled.

In terms of the arrangement reached, the Council will be given control of the square on a 99 years' lease for an annual payment of 20s.

The further controversy between the parties regarding the acquisition by the Council of a vacant piece of ground near the Marine Hotel has also been settled, the terms having been adjusted whereby the Council has now secured the ground for recreation purposes.

THREAT TO PLOUGH.

The settlement reached regarding the square puts an end to a dispute which has been going on for years, and which culminated in April this year when, by instructions of the laird, it may be recalled, part of the ground was ploughed up owing to the Council's refusal to grant a licence to a travelling circus.

Following upon this, the laird threatened to plough up the entire square by holding a public ploughing match, and later intimated his intention of using it as a place of interment for the body of a lunatic.

DUKE OF GLOUCESTER.

VISIT TO ANNAN BEFORE TRIP AFTER BIG GAME.

H.R.H. the Duke of Gloucester arrived at Annan yesterday morning on a visit to Captain E. W. Brook, of Kinmount, where he will remain for the next few days.

The Duke is to leave England shortly after Christmas for a big game shooting trip in the Sudan, and he will be accompanied by Captain Brook, who was with the Duke on both his previous African expeditions.

TRAGEDY OF STORM IN BUCHAN.

MAN FOUND DEAD IN DITCH.

IN the first severe storm of the winter, in the Buchan district of Aberdeenshire, a tragedy came to light yesterday morning at Kininmonth, Crimond, when the body of Alexander Marshall (45), casual labourer, was found in a ditch, in which was three inches of running water.

It is not yet known whether he died from drowning or from exposure.

Marshall, who is stated to be a native of Maud, travelled about the country in search of casual labouring work, and was in receipt of a disability pension of 28s per week.

On Wednesday afternoon he hired a car at New Pitsligo, and, after being driven to Maud, continued on his way to a lodging-house at Kininmonth.

Scottish Economy Proposals —Page 17.

There he dismissed the car, but did not enter the lodging-house, and his body was discovered in the daylight, yesterday morning, lying in a ditch.

The weather during the night was intensely cold, with showers of sleet and snow.

SKI-ERS HOPEFUL.

Hopes of winter sports are running high on Deeside. Snow has fallen in most parts of Aberdeenshire, and a keen frost is being experienced.

At Braemar, yesterday, snow was lying to a depth of about six inches at different parts. There was a fairly heavy fall on Wednesday, and yesterday the frost was sharp.

So far there has been no ski-ing, but the curlers are making preparations in the event of the frost holding.

There were five degrees of frost in Dundee early yesterday morning, and curling took place on several local ponds.

Slight showers of snow fell in the earlier part of the day on the Forfarshire hills.

DRIFTER SUNK IN NORTH SEA.

CREW RESCUED BY BUCKIE BOAT.

The crew of the drifter Cedron, BF. 991, were rescued yesterday when their boat sank off Scurdyness Light, near Montrose.

The drifter Rochomie, of Buckie (Skipper W. G. Clark), while returning home from the Yarmouth fishing, saw distress signals, and with difficulty got alongside the Cedron, which had sprung a leak.

The Rochomie took the Cedron in tow, but after an hour the latter boat showed signs of sinking, and her crew was transferred to the Rochomie, which stood by till the Cedron sank with all the crews' clothing and gear.

The Rochomie reached Fraserburgh Harbour in the afternoon, and will remain there till the storm abates. The Cedron's crew left for their homes.

HEART TO HEART TALK TO NATION.

King To Broadcast On Christmas Day

NEW DEPARTURE.

IT is announced that the King will broadcast from Sandringham on the afternoon of Christmas Day. This is the first occasion on which the King has broadcast direct to the nation.

Previously, his voice has only been heard on the wireless on occasions when he has been speaking at an official function.

The *Daily Record* learns that the broadcast will take the form of a Christmas message from the King to his people.

FINAL DETAILS

Arrangements for the broadcast are not yet entirely complete, and officials of the B.B.C. and members of the Royal household are still discussing final details.

The King will speak from Sandringham House, his Norfolk home, where he and the Queen invariably spend Christmas.

The broadcast will probably be made from the King's study, through a special microphone which is to be installed by B.B.C. engineers.

HEARD ALL OVER EMPIRE.

This first "heart to heart" talk to his people ever made by a British monarch marks another stage in the history of broadcasting.

The occasions when the King's voice has been heard on the wireless in the last few years have included such official ceremonies as the India Round Table Conference, the London Naval Conference, and the opening of the Shieldhall Dock at Glasgow.

The King possesses one of the best "wireless voices" in the world. It has excellent carrying power, as has been demonstrated several times when people all over the Empire have been able to pick up transmissions and understand clearly every word.

£2100 FOR INFIRMARY.

CARNOUSTIE WOMAN'S BEQUEST TO DUNDEE.

Dundee Royal Infirmary directors yesterday announced a gift of £2100 from the estate of the late Miss Catherine Gray, Carnoustie, to endow two beds in memory of her mother and father.

In addition to the Royal Infirmary legacy Miss Gray left £200 for the poor of St. Stephen's Church, Carnoustie; £200 to Dundee Mission for the Outdoor Blind; £100 to Salvation Army Eventide Home, Dundee; and £100 to Carnoustie, Barry and Panmure Nursing Association.

ALARMING INVERNESS FIRE.

TRANSPORT OFFICES DESTROYED.

AN alarming fire took place in Inverness last night. Premises occupied as the head offices of the Highland Motor Transport Co., and situated in Bank Lane, were destroyed, and only the prompt work by Firemaster Treasurer prevented the spread of flames to business premises and dwelling houses in the vicinity.

The building, a two-storey one—was a mass of fierce flames when the Brigade arrived. The fire was in grave danger of spreading to commodious offices of Stewart, Rule, & Co., a firm of local solicitors, of which Sir Alexander M'Ewen, one of the leaders of moderate Scots Home Rulers, is chief partner.

Within a few yards of the blazing building was also an electric sub-station, owned by the Inverness Corporation's Electricity Department. Thanks to the speed with which the alarm was given, firemen soon had the fire under control, but some time elapsed before it was extinguished.

The damage is extensive. Large crowds thronged Bank Lane and watched the firemen's strenuous fight with the flames.

The offices, which were tenanted by Transport Co., were the property of Sir Alexander M'Ewen. It was discovered later that the fire originated in a store adjacent to the Transport offices.

Wireless Programmes—Page 24

SCOTS HOME RULE – <u>IN</u> THE UNION

A MOMENTOUS debate on Home Rule for Scotland took place in the House of Commons in November.

The *Daily Record* reported that Sir Archibald Sinclair, the First Secretary for Scotland, seemed to be the only speaker who grasped the possibilities of a practical solution to the Scottish demand that Scotland should be allowed to look after her domestic affairs.

He indicated that a form of Scottish Parliament could be set up that could sustain all merits of the Union of 1707.

The new institution would allow a system whereby Scottish MPs would sit in Edinburgh as a separate body, controlling such vital concerns as Scotland's agriculture, education, fisheries, land laws, social services and national amenities.

A bigger proportion of Scottish Private Bill legislation is to be heard in Scotland, but national and financial considerations precluded the establishment of a new set of Scottish Offices in Edinburgh, and even the appointment of an Under Secretary.

The debate was seen as one of the most earnest and important on the Home Rule issue to take place in almost a quarter of a century.

The general atmosphere of the House seemed to reflect the awareness that the issue had to be faced seriously by all MPs.

CENSORS GAG COMPTON MACKENZIE

Scots author Compton MacKenzie became a victim of political censorship when, in October, his book *Greek Memories* was banned on the day it was due to be published. It was the third of four books chronicling events in Athens during the First World War and dealing with moves and counter-moves in international espionage. War Office officials refused to comment on why the book had been withdrawn.

In the first of the books, Compton MacKenzie claimed that in 1915 the Allies had thrown away Greek support through "gross bungling". Later, at the Old Bailey, the author admitted an offence against the Official Secrets Act and was fined £100.

ON RADIO

Keeping Fit in Winter

Music Hall

The End of Savoy Hill

A Talk for Scottish Farmers

New Ways for Hard Times – Starting with Chickens

Reginald New & His Organ

MOLLISON FLIES INTO THE RECORD BOOKS

Flying Scotsman Jim Mollison smashed the record for a flight from Britain to Cape Town when his Puss Moth plane landed in South Africa on March 29. It had taken him 4 days, 17 hours and 19 minutes, almost 16 hours less than the previous record. He had the huge crowds awaiting his arrival at the newly-opened municipal aerodrome worried … for he landed on a nearby beach and stumbled out of the plane looking dazed. Mollison said that because of fatigue, he had been seeing his plane's instruments in double for two days. He did not want to risk landing in the glare of lights and opted for the beach.

COMINGS…

Jimmie MacGregor
Folksinger & Broadcaster

Jeremy Isaacs
TV Executive

GOINGS…

Kenneth Graham
Author of
Wind in the Willows

THIS SPORTING LIFE

FOOTBALL	RUGBY UNION	GOLF	HORSE RACING	SHINTY
Scottish Champions Motherwell	*Scotland vs England* England 16–3 Scotland at Twickenham	*Home Internationals* Scotland 8 - 7 England Scotland 11½ - 4½ Ireland Scotland 9 - 6 Wales	*Scottish Grand National Winner* Clydesdale at Bogside	*Camanachd Cup Winners* Newtonmore at Glasgow
Scottish Cup Winners Rangers				

Daily Record

and Mail.

SCOTLAND'S NATIONAL NEWSPAPER

ESTAB. 1847—No. 27,105.   WEDNESDAY. DECEMBER 6, 1933.   ONE PENNY.

Which means a George Younger

George Younger & Son, Ltd.,
BREWERS, ALLOA.

LOCH NESS MONSTER PHOTOGRAPHED

WHAT IS IT?

Sworn Statement By Foyers Photographer.

A PUZZLING PICTURE.

Let Our Readers Judge.

WHAT will be the most discussed photograph of our time appears on the back page of the "Daily Record" to-day. The photographer is Hugh Gray, employed at the British Aluminium Works, and living at The Bungalow, Foyers.

Yesterday, before a magistrate of Inverness, and other witnesses, he swore to the fact that his remarkable snapshot was taken of the monster which he saw in all its great length moving on the surface of Loch Ness.

The "Daily Record" leaves the picture itself and the evidence which has been collected to the judgment of its readers.

WHAT THE EXPERTS SAY.

Negative Not Tampered With.

YESTERDAY the *Glasgow Herald* published the following report about the Loch Ness monster:—

The Loch Ness monster has been photographed by Mr. Hugh Gray, fitter, Aluminium Works, Foyers.

The negative reveals a creature about 30 feet long with a head like a seal and an elongated body like an eel, with two lateral fins.

Mr. Gray was walking on the afternoon of Sunday, November 26, when he saw the monster in the loch a distance of about 100 yards away. He had his camera with him and took five snapshots, only one of which has been successful.

The monster was seen no fewer than four times last week, once by Alexander Shaw, roadman, Whitefield, who saw it on a previous occasion during the summer. It was also seen from the opposite side of the loch on Wednesday and Thursday.

The distance mentioned in the above report does not coincide with Mr. Gray's considered statement. He can only say that he was standing some distance off and at a certain height. It looks as if the photographer had taken the picture at a distance of some 50 feet and that the elevation from which he took it meant he had to point his camera downwards.

Investigation.

A similar report appeared in the Aberdeen *Press and Journal*, which added that Hugh Gray was being made offers from many sources for the negative. Actually, offers involving large sums of money were received by Mr. Gray, but as the *Daily Record* had already secured the picture on Monday afternoon these offers were ineffective, Mr. Gray preferring that the reproduction should be made in our columns.

(CONTINUED ON PAGE 2.)

Nothing was published about the case yesterday, as it was felt that the fullest possible investigation was necessary. Immediately the negative arrived in the *Daily Record* Office from Foyers, a group of photographic experts were invited to inspect the film. These gentlemen were:—

Mr. M. C. Howard, of Kodaks.
Mr. C. L. Clarke, of "The Kodak Magazine."
Mr. S. Ballantyne, of Lizars.
Mr. Cameron, of Blackadder's.

Experts' Views.

They one and all agreed that the negative bore no trace of having been tampered with in any way, although, naturally, they expressed no opinion on the nature of the object photographed, having no means of verification. The attempted verification had to be conducted, yesterday, in Foyers, where the *Daily Record* representative, along with Bailie Hugh MacKenzie, J.P., of Inverness, and Mr. Peter Munro, an official of the British Aluminium Coy., interviewed Mr. Gray.

For the purpose of taking a sworn statement Mr. MacKenzie, J.P., was specially asked by the *Daily Record* to accompany our representative, and they travelled from Inverness to Foyers by motor car to see Mr. Gray.

It was felt that the statement made by Mr. Gray should amount to a sworn statement.

Our readers will be as puzzled as ourselves as to the nature of the object which is contained in this photograph. A print was submitted to Professor Graham Kerr, M.A., F.R.S., Professor of Zoology at Glasgow University, and he and his staff were naturally non-committal.

Does Not Recognise It.

Professor Graham Kerr said:—

"I see nothing in the photograph with a head like a seal, nor do I see a body like an eel, nor do I see two lateral fins, such as have been described by the photographer.

"What I do see is a curved

The winter sport season now being on, both in Scotland and on the Continent, makes sports fashions important. Here is a really smart all-wool winter sports outfit in brown and orange.

MAN WHO TOOK THE PICTURE.

Mr. Gray Tells His Story.

"GLAD TO HELP."

(From Our Own Reporter.)

Inverness, Tuesday.

A *DAILY RECORD* representative who visited Foyers to-day was told how the photograph of the Loch Ness monster was taken.

Mr. Hugh Gray, one of the employees of the British Aluminium Company at Foyers, had had a glimpse of the monster on a previous occasions, but often after that he was very dubious that the object was a real monster, so many stories had been published.

However, it was his custom on Sundays to go along the Loch Ness side, especially where the River Foyers enters the loch, and scan the loch, if the water was very calm.

"Four Sundays ago," Mr. Gray said, "after the church service, about one o'clock, I went to a part of the lochside where I could get a good view of the loch, taking with me my camera, as was my usual custom.

"The loch was as still as a mill pond, and the sun was shining brightly. I had no idea that I would see the monster, or the great black object that has so often been reported as making its appearance in the loch.

Up It Comes.

"I had hardly sat down on the bank overlooking the loch when, lo and behold! an object of considerable dimensions rose out of the water not so very far from where I was sitting. I immediately got my camera into position and snapped the object, which was two or three feet above the surface of the water. I did not see any head, but there was considerable motion from what I thought was the tail.

"The object only appeared for a few minutes. I cannot give any definite opinion as to its size or appearance except that it was of great size, and had apparently come up to the surface then sank out of sight.

"I afterwards went home thinking that, from the brief view I had of the object, so far as the photograph was concerned, nothing would show on the surface of the water. The spool lay in my mother's house at Foyers until Friday of last week, when my brother took it to a chemist's business in Inverness, where the negative was developed, and I understand that a very good picture of the monster, or whatever the object is, was seen.

"No one was with me," said Mr. Gray, "when the photograph was taken.

A Delight To Him.

"I might have had it developed long before I did, but I was afraid of the chaff which the workmen and others would shower upon me if I said I had a photograph of the monster, as there are many who do not give credence to the story that there is anything unusual in the loch."

Asked by Bailie Mackenzie, J.P., if he swore to all he had said, Mr. Gray said that he did.

"In fact," he said, "if the photograph shows something that will be helpful in elucidating the identity of the strange thing in the loch, it will be a delight to me. I am glad that the *Daily Record* has shown such a great interest in the strange creature that has got into the loch, and I am glad to give them the negative to be published."

ABERDEEN CYCLIST KILLED.

In Collision With Motor Car.

ANOTHER street fatality occurred in Aberdeen last night.

The victim was David Main Youngson (37), who resided at 141 Ruthrieston Circle, Aberdeen, the same area as that in which a little girl who was killed by a motor lorry the previous night resided.

Youngson, who was an attendant at Woodend Hospital, was cycling down Anderson Drive, and when nearing its junction with Great Western Road he was struck by a motor car.

He was conveyed to Aberdeen Royal Infirmary where it was found that life was extinct. He is survived by his widow and a family of three.

MR THOMAS REPLIES TO MR DE VALERA

If A Republic Is Declared.

IRISHMEN'S STATUS.

"THE contingency has not arisen, and, I hope, will never arise."

Mr. J. H. Thomas, the Dominions Secretary, made this statement in the House of Commons yesterday in replying to a question on the status of Irish Free State subjects after the declaration of a republic.

Subsequently Mr. Thomas read despatches on the subject between the British Government and the Free State Government, and stated that the British Government could not believe that the Free State Government contemplated final repudiation of their Treaty obligations.

"HAS NOT ARISEN."

The Dominions Secretary was asked by Major-General Sir Alfred Knox if he would take immediate steps to bring to the notice of the natives of the Irish Free State, both in this country and the Free State, the disadvantages which they will suffer, both in status and in the way of

PROHIBITION KILLED.

New York, Tuesday.

After some delay, Utah, the last of the States to act, has ratified the repeal of Prohibition, which is now dead.
—Reuter.

entering this country, from the declaration of the Irish Free State as a republic.

Mr. Thomas: "No, sir. I do not feel that any steps such as those indicated are necessary. The contingency has not arisen, and, I hope, will never arise. Further, the advantages enjoyed by British subjects, as compared with aliens, in this country are sufficiently well known and appreciated to need no emphasis from me." (Cheers).

DISADVANTAGE OF ALIENS.

Sir Alfred Knox—Is it not a fact that, in the event of the declaration of a republic by the Irish Free State, no longer immigrants from Ireland would be allowed to come here and compete in the British labour market, or take advantage of our schemes of social insurance? Is it also not a fact that all natives of the Irish Free State domiciled in this country would be liable to be returned to Southern Ireland if they do not accept British nationality?

Mr. Thomas—There can be no doubt whatever as to the disadvantages of aliens in this country compared with British citizenship.

"DOOR NEVER CLOSED."

Sir William Davison—Will he assure the House that the status of British citizens, which was guaranteed by the Treaty to the loyalists in Southern Ireland, will be guaranteed by this House whatever happens?

Mr. Thomas—I have already said that I still refuse to believe that such a contingency will ultimately arise. When it does the Government will deal with it.

Mr. Hannon—May I ask whether the House is to understand that the door is still open for negotiations if the Irish Free State desire it?

Mr. Thomas—The door has never been closed.

Full Text of Despatches—Page 11.

WIRELESS—Page 20

DID CAMERA 'CAPTURE' NESSIE?

ONE of the most discussed Nessie photographs of our time appeared in the *Daily Record* in December. The photographer was Hugh Gray and he appeared before an Inverness magistrate and other witnesses to swear to the authenticity of his remarkable snapshot of what he took to be the monster on the surface of Loch Ness.

As soon as the photograph arrived at the *Daily Record* office, a group of photographic experts were invited to inspect the film. They all agreed that the negative bore no trace of having been tampered with in any way, although, they expressed no opinion on the nature of the object photographed.

Mr Gray made a statement to the news-paper detailing the events surrounding the photograph.

He said: "Four Sundays ago, after church service about one o'clock, I went to a part of the lochside where I could get a good view of the loch, taking with me my camera, as was my custom. The loch was still as a mill pond, and the sun was shining brightly.

I had no idea that I would see the monster or the great black object that has so often made an appearance in the loch. I had hardly sat down on the bank overlooking the loch when an object of considerable dimensions rose out of the water not so very far from where I was sitting.

I immediately got my camera into position and snapped the object, which was two or three feet above the surface of the water. I did not see any head, but there was a considerable motion from what I thought was a tail."

The *Record* left it to its readers to make up their own minds as to whether this really was the elusive monster.

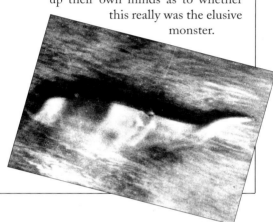

FRESH SET-UP FOR MILK

Milk producers in Scotland got their act together in September with the launching of a milk marketing scheme that would have control of the output area from the Border to the Grampians. A poll of registered producers resulted in 4746 in favour, with only 1417 "turning sour". The HQ was to be in Glasgow, with up to five regional offices.

There was also a warning for milk producers – register soon, or you could be prohibited from selling milk.

ON RADIO

In Town Tonight

Scrapbook

COMINGS...

Hugh MacIlvanney
Sports Journalist

David McCallum
Actor

Andy Stewart
Entertainer

EVEREST CONQUERED – BY AIR

Two Scots pilots managed to "conquer" Mount Everest by flying over its 29,000ft summit in April. When they took off in two Westland aircraft, the Marquis of Clydesdale, Lieutenant-Colonel Blacker, and Flight-Lieutenant McIntyre had intended only to carry out a trial flight before going for a serious attempt. But with the wind in the upper atmosphere dropping considerably, they managed to achieve the aim of the expedition. They hoped their survey photos would help climbers.

THIS SPORTING LIFE

FOOTBALL	RUGBY UNION	GOLF	HORSE RACING	SHINTY
Scottish Champions Rangers	*Scotland vs England* Scotland 3–0 England at Murrayfield	*British Open Winner* Densmore Shute at St Andrews (292)	*Scottish Grand National* *Winner* *Libourg* at Bogside	*Camanachd Cup Winners* Oban at Keppoch, Lochaber
Scottish Cup Winners Celtic				

Daily ✤ Record
and Mail.

Issued to commemorate the launch of the Cunard - White Star liner "Queen Mary," at Clydebank

This second supplement is incorporated in the Daily Record, Scotland's National Newspaper, for 27th September, 1934.

"QUEEN MARY"

SOUVENIR SUPPLEMENT

Issued to commemorate the launch of the Cunard - White Star "Queen Mary," at Clydebank

This second supplement is incorporated in the Daily Record, Scotland's National Newspaper, for 27th September, 1934.

CHEERS FOR PRIDE OF THE CLYDE

THE crash of a bottle against a towering prow, two sentences in the clear voice of Her Majesty the Queen and 40,000 tons of graceful steel slid into the rain-lashed Clyde.

Ship No.534 had been given a name and launched as the new Cunard White Star liner, *Queen Mary*.

Speculation followed swiftly about her successor liner for it had been the intention for years that there would be a sister ship.

And Sir Percy Bates, chairman of Cunard White Star, reaffirmed that intention within a few minutes of the launch.

The means to attain success in this particular industry, he said, included the provision of a second ship of similar status to the new Clydeside Queen, although he did not give further details.

The thousands who gathered on the south bank of the Clyde will always remember the extreme thrills of the launch of the Cunarder *Queen Mary*.

A vast throng assembled in the specially built stands and on the rising ground overlooking one of the greatest Clydeside scenes of all time.

They saw the unforgettable spectacle of the *Queen Mary* driving towards them stern first as she gathered speed after her first quivering into new life.

But the most breathtaking time of all was the minute during which the mammoth hull ploughed her way into the river, leaving a wake of crashing steel chains, shattered woodwork, and clouds of red dust.

THE RECORD'S COLOUR REVOLUTION

The *Daily Record* of May 21 was hailed as the world's most remarkable newspaper. For the first time in daily newspapers, it introduced the use of real colour printing at speed and on normal newsprint, something that had previously been thought impossible. The colour attempts of other daily newspapers were poor and outdated and limited to what was simply an elaboration of what had been produced by the old *Record* presses as far back as 1909. The *Daily Record* was described as the pioneer of modern journalism and it maintains that pioneering spirit today.

COMINGS...

Alasdair Grey
Novelist

ON RADIO

Vaudeville
The Foundations of Music

TRAGEDY PLUNGE FROM TRAIN

The governor of Glasgow's Barlinnie Prison, Mr Robert Wilkinshaw, was killed when he fell from an express train in January. The Glasgow-Ayr train was hitting 50mph near Beith when Mr Wilkinshaw stood up near a carriage door that suddenly opened. Three other passengers tried to grab his coat, but he fell onto the line. Someone pulled the communication cord and the train halted at Glengarnock. Police and railway officials searched back and found the governor's body.

THIS SPORTING LIFE

FOOTBALL	RUGBY UNION	GOLF	HORSE RACING	SHINTY
Scottish Champions Rangers	*Scotland vs England* England 6–3 Scotland at Twickenham	*Home Internationals* Scotland 10-5 England Scotland 10½ - 4½ Ireland Scotland 9½ - 5½ Wales	*Scottish Grand National Winner* Southern Hero at Bogside	*Camanachd Cup Winners* Caberfeidh at Inveraray
Scottish Cup Winners Rangers				

Mr. Baldwin's Smoke

Presbyterian Mixture
A. GALE & CO.,
1 Dundas Street,
GLASGOW, C.1

Daily Record
and Mail.

ESTAB. 1847—No. 27,452.　　THURSDAY, JANUARY 17, 1935.　　ONE PENNY.

SCOTLAND'S NATIONAL NEWSPAPER

LORD SNOWDEN BACKS "L.G."

Dramatic Intervention In "New Deal" Campaign

VISCOUNT SNOWDEN.　　　　MR. LLOYD GEORGE.

"SPEEDY TRIUMPH" BLESSING

Lady Snowden On Mr. Lloyd George's Platform To-Day

THE sensational announcement is made, on the eve of Mr. Lloyd George's first explanation of his "New Deal" campaign at Bangor, to-day, that Viscount Snowden has given his blessing to the former Liberal Premier's crusade.

"I hope that under your inspiring leadership," Lord Snowden yesterday wrote to Mr. Lloyd George, "it will be carried to a speedy triumph."

It is understood that Lord Snowden's health will not permit him to carry on an extended campaign of speech-making, but it is likely that he will occasionally speak from the same platform as Mr. Lloyd George.

It may be noted also that among those who will be present at the inauguration of Mr. Lloyd George's campaign at Bangor, to-day, will be Lady Snowden, who is representing her husband.

LORD SNOWDEN'S LETTER

In his letter to Mr. Lloyd George, Lord Snowden says:

"The crusade you are beginning for a great and united national effort to revive industry and to rescue the mass of our population from the hardship and suffering of unnecessary poverty, deserves, and I believe will receive, the support of earnest and sympathetic men and women of all parties, and of that large and increasing number of electors who have no party affiliations.

"There is a widespread feeling in the country that the national situation demands bold and enterprising measures. Complacency and timidity in the face of grave evils, if continued, will bring disastrous consequences.

TIME FOR ACTION

"This is a time for action. There is a vast field for national effort which, while avoiding wild and revolutionary policies, will rebuild our industrial and social life.

"The country is waiting for an inspiring lead on a programme of courageous national reconstruction.

"It is obvious to every thinking person that our national resources are being wasted, and that, if they were

FIRST LABOUR CHANCELLOR

VISCOUNT SNOWDEN retired from active politics in August, 1931.

In 1893 he joined the I.L.P., from which he resigned in 1927.

He entered Parliament in 1906 as Labour Member for Blackburn. Losing his seat in the 1918 election, he won Colne Valley for Labour in 1922, and retained it with an increased majority in 1924 and 1929.

He became the first Labour Chancellor of the Exchequer in 1924, and again held that office when the financial crisis of 1931 occurred.

He joined the National Government, but subsequently took exception to the tariff proposals. He was elevated to the Peerage in November, 1931.

organised and our great productive power fully utilised, unemployment and kindred evils could be abolished and a far higher standard of life for the workers could be attained.

CO-OPERATIVE EFFORT

"It is a sad reflection on our civilisation that, with all the possibilities of universal comfort, we should have millions of persons out of work, and that the insecurity of employment should always be like a nightmare before every wage-worker, and that a large part of our population in town and country should be herded in pos-

Continued On Page 2, Column 2

"WAR" ON OVERCROWDING

DRASTIC SCOTTISH HOUSING BILL

Far-Reaching Powers For Local Authorities

PLANS for the most determined drive ever undertaken to end the evils of overcrowding in Scotland are contained in the Government's new Housing Bill, details of which were published last night.

Overcrowding is to become an offence. Under the proposed Scots national housing standard, not more than two persons may be accommodated in a single apartment, and not more than three in a house of two rooms. In computing this standard, children under 10 years will be counted as half persons.

It is estimated that 100,000 new houses will be required to rehouse those who will be living in officially "overcrowded" buildings when the new legislation takes effect. An additional 60,000 houses will be needed for slum-clearance purposes.

FAR-REACHING POWERS

Very far-reaching powers, as well as duties, are conferred on local authorities. They are given compulsory powers regading the reconditioning of working-class houses and for the acquisition of the necessary land. They are under the obligation of carrying out surveys of overcrowding in their districts.

A new subsidy of £10 per house is to be given for a period of 40 years.

FULL REPORT ON P. 3. PROPERTY OWNERS' PROTEST, P. 2

Steamer In Distress Off Jura

THE Port Askaig (Islay) lifeboat put out to sea last night in search of a vessel reported to be burning distress flares and sending up rockets west of the island of Jura.

The lights were seen by one of the lighthouses on the west coast of Jura, and word was sent to the lifeboat station.

The vessel in distress has not been definitely identified, but she is not believed to be a passenger-carrying ship.

There is no telephone communication with Islay, and it was not known early this morning what the result of the lifeboat's search had been.

The Northern Lighthouse Commissioners' vessel Hesperus, which was due in Oban last night, did not dock when expected.

She was on a passage from the Clyde, and it is thought she may have seen the distress signals and gone to the scene of the mishap.

WIRELESS—Page 18

HANGED IN CELL

Detained Woman Sensation

A SENSATION was caused in North Manchester last night when it was learnt that a woman detained at Goulden Street Police Station had been found hanged in her cell.

The woman was immediately rushed by ambulance to hospital, but she was dead upon arrival and was removed to a police mortuary.

The discovery was made by a police matron. The dead woman, who was aged 57 had been hanged with a scarf.

It is understood that she had been detained by the police in connection with an alleged shoplifting offence and had not yet appeared before the Magistrates.

NOTTS CRICKET

"No Confidence" Vote On Committee

By a majority of at least two to one, a crowded meeting of members of the Notts County Cricket Club, in Nottingham yesterday, carried a resolution of "no confidence" in the present committee, on the threefold count of their action in respect of the apology to Australia regarding "direct attack" bowling, the alleged subterfuge which prevented Voce from continuing to bowl in the match against the Australians at Trent Bridge, and the deposition of Mr. A. W. Carr from the captaincy.

A statement signed by Voce was produced to the effect that he was fit to play against the Australians. However, the evidence of a doctor and two of the team was that Voce had complained of pains, and was declared unfit.

One of the opponents of the committee's actions declared that if the committee did not resign, they would consider appropriate action at the annual meeting next month.

The committee's statement in defence revealed that the Australians, Lancashire and Middlesex had all made charges against Notts of unfair bowling.

HUSBAND AND WIFE DEAD

Found Shot In Home In Dumfriesshire

MR. T. GIBSON, a retired tea planter, and his young wife were found shot dead in their house, Bellview, Keir, Dumfriesshire, last night.

Some relatives of Mrs. Gibson called at the house, and were unable to gain admission. Doors were locked, and blinds drawn.

The police were informed, and they forced an entry.

Search was made in the house, and Mr. Gibson was found dead on the stairs. He had been shot through the head.

His wife was found dead in bed. She also had been shot through the head.

MALARIA SUFFERER

Mr. Gibson is stated to have been ill with malaria for some weeks. He was 49 years of age, and his wife was 26.

The couple took over Bellview about three years ago, and carried on poultry farming.

Both were natives of Dalbeattie, Kirkcudbrightshire.

BID TO BEAT THE HOUSING EVIL

OVERCROWDING was to be "outlawed" in Scotland, under the terms of a drastic new Housing Bill by the Government which contained far-reaching proposals for ridding the country of the overcrowding evil.

More than 100,000 houses, it was estimated, were needed to be built to re-house those who were living in overcrowded dwellings in Scotland.

In addition, more than 60,000 houses were needed for slum clearance.

To meet the needs in connection with overcrowding, the Scottish Bill made the following provisions:

A new subsidy of £10 per house was to be given during a period of 40 years, of which sum, £6 15s per house per annum was to be provided by the Treasury and £3 5s by the local authorities. Additional Exchequer aid was to be given in certain circumstances.

A national standard of overcrowding was also defined. Infants of less than a year would not counted while children between one and ten years of age were to be counted as "half persons". The standard said that there would be deemed to be overcrowding where there were:

Two persons in a single apartment.

Three in a house of two rooms.

Five in a house of three rooms.

7$1/2$ in a house of four rooms.

Ten in a house of five rooms.

And an increase of two persons for each additional room over five.

This standard, laid down by statute for the first time, was to apply to a house with a rent or rateable value of not more than £90 per annum.

GENERAL ELECTION RE-POLL DEMANDED

Following the election of the Conservative Walter Elliot in the November General Election, the Scottish Socialist Party petitioned the Court of Session for a re-poll of the Glasgow Kelvingrove ward. At the first count, Mr Elliot defeated the Socialist candidate, Hector McNeil, by only two votes. On a recount, an uncounted ballot box was discovered which increased the Tory majority to 149. The SSP later claimed they lost the election because they had less cars than their opponents to ferry their supporters to the polls. The petition was ultimately abandoned on grounds of cost.

COMINGS...

Archie Macpherson
Sports Commentator

John McGrath
Founder of 7:84 Theatre Co.

GOINGS...

Samuel Peploe
Scottish Colourist

John Menzies
Bookseller & Wholesaler

ON RADIO

*The American Half Hour
(with Alistair Cook)*

Promenade Concert

*Harry Gordon (The Man frae
Inversnecky) & His Band*

Herring Fishing Bulletin

ABDINE

Is the Health Drink Symbol that distinguishes the CHIEF from the Mediocre. "ABDINE" is the original and only genuine Fruit Drink, and has over 40 years' reputation as the Best & Safest Health Drink for all ages. Sold everywhere. Packets, 1½d Each.

JUBILEE ROW

Greenock Town Council, with a socialist majority, voted not to take part in the Royal Jubilee celebrations. But after suggestions that this did not reflect the feeling of the community, the *Daily Record* was asked to conduct a survey to find out. Meanwhile, the Moderates formed a committee to try to bring Greenock into line with other Scottish towns. They called for subscriptions to fund celebrations.

THIS SPORTING LIFE

FOOTBALL	RUGBY UNION	GOLF	HORSE RACING	SHINTY
Scottish Champions Rangers	*Scotland vs England* Scotland 10–7 England at Murrayfield	*British Open Winner* Alf Perry at Muirfield (283)	*Scottish Grand National Winner* Kellsboro' Jack at Bogside	*Camanachd Cup Winners* Kyles Athletic at Inverness
Scottish Cup Winners Rangers				

COMFORT IN SPECTACLES

Shell frames give nose comfort.
Toric lenses give eye comfort.
This combination gives the ideal
reading spectacle

JOHN TROTTER
LIMITED
40 Gordon Street, Glasgow
and 100 George St., Edinburgh

Daily Record
and Mail.

ESTAB. 1847—No. 28,046.   FRIDAY, DECEMBER 11, 1936.   ONE PENNY

SCOTLAND'S NATIONAL NEWSPAPER

A SCOTS QUEEN

King George VI And Queen Elizabeth To Be Proclaimed

CORONATION NEXT MAY

FUTURE PLANS OF EDWARD VIII.

AS the unparalleled drama of the abdication of King Edward VIII. unfolded itself yesterday, a wave of relief swept over the country, spreading right throughout the Empire, the succession of the Duke and Duchess of York to the Throne being hailed as not only the best but the only solution to the crisis.

To Scotland the crowning of the Duchess of York as Queen Elizabeth will be particularly gratifying and the Empire will welcome, with warmest loyalty a Scottish Queen.

KING GEORGE VI.

The new King will be Proclaimed to-morrow afternoon.

It is understood he will assume the title of King George VI.

The Coronation will probably take place on the date arranged for King Edward—May 12.

The House of Commons will meet at 2.45 to-morrow afternoon for members to take the Oath of Allegiance to the new King. The swearing-in will be continued at Monday's sitting.

King Edward will renounce with the Throne all his titles. After abdicating, he will be plain Mr. Windsor.

ACCESSION PLANS

The *Daily Record* learns that, while the Duke of York, who will be 41 on Monday, has not yet made a final decision as to what title he will take, it is likely that he will choose to be known as George VI., rather than Albert I.

Princess Elizabeth

When her father comes to the Throne, Princess Elizabeth will be Heiress Presumptive, as the Duke of York has been Heir Presumptive during his brother's reign.

Princess Elizabeth will not be Heiress Apparent, as this title would follow to any future son who might be born to the new King and his Queen.

For this reason, it is considered unlikely that Princess Elizabeth will be given the Duchy of Cornwall. Most probably she will continue to be known as Princess Elizabeth.

It was authoritatively stated last night that the Accession Council at St.

The New King

MOVING SPECTACLE STIRS HEARTS

Premier's Ordeal In Memorable Commons Scene

BY OUR PARLIAMENTARY REPRESENTATIVE
WESTMINSTER, THURSDAY.

NEVER IN THE LONG HISTORY OF PARLIAMENT, EXTENDING OVER 700 YEARS, HAS THERE BEEN THE SCENE AND THE DRAMA COMPARABLE WITH TO-DAY, WHEN KING EDWARD VIII. RENOUNCED THE THRONE OF THE GREATEST EMPIRE IN THE WORLD.

So moving was the spectacle that not only women were moved to tears, but members of Parliament, seasoned in public affairs, wiped their eyes as the irrevocable decision was made known.

Cheers For Premier

At 3.35, Mr. Baldwin came in by the doors behind the Speaker's chair. He carried two sheets of typescript bearing the red Royal Seal at the head.

He hesitated for a moment before emerging into the full view of the House, as if somewhat nervous. Two or three colleagues patted him on the back and, as if encouraged, he stepped forward. When the House saw him they cheered long and mightily.

The demonstration of loyalty and affection was unanimous exceeding anything seen like it previously.

Mr. Baldwin looked a trifle haggard. His hands moved rather nervously. Sitting down between Mr. Ramsay MacDonald, Lord President of the Council, and Mr. Neville Chamberlain, Chancellor of the Exchequer, he talked with them at some length.

Wife's Encouragement

While waiting for questions to finish, Mr. Baldwin looked up and saw his wife in the Gallery above. Both exchanged a slight smile—it seemed as though it was a smile of encouragement.

Question time ended at 3.42. When the Speaker, looking very grave, stood up and said, " Mr. Baldwin," a great hush fell upon the proceedings. The very silence itself stirred the emotions.

Mr. Baldwin nervously rose to his feet, and with the typescript in his hand walked to the far end of the Chamber and stood at the Bar. The three clerks

(Continued on Page 2, Column 4)

King Edward To Broadcast To-night

KING EDWARD will broadcast to-night at 10 o'clock.

An announcement made by the B.B.C. last night stated:—

" King Edward desires, immediately he has ceased to be King, to broadcast. His broadcast to-morrow evening will be in the character of a private person owing allegiance to the new King.

" Arrangements have been made to enable what he says to be transmitted all over the world."

The King will make his broadcast from outside London, it is understood. He may broadcast from Sunningdale, or, alternatively, it is possible that, should he leave the country earlier in the evening, he may speak to his peoples from abroad.

After the King has spoken all B.B.C. transmitters will close down.

James's Palace will be held by the new King as the first act of his reign to-morrow morning.

The Proclamation of the new King will take place to-morrow afternoon.

Queen Mother

It is probable that, with the accession of the new King and the presence of a Queen Consort again, Queen Mary will be known as Mary the Queen Mother.

"MR. WINDSOR"

King Edward, the *Daily Record* understands, will leave the country as soon as he has completed his abdication by signing the Act of Abdication,

Continued On Back Page

ON OTHER PAGES

	Page
Royal Statement	2
Revelations By Premier	3
The New King	6
The New Queen	8
Edward VIII.	11
Historic Scots Visits	12
Empire's Scots Queen	13
How Scotland Heard	36

Great Ovation For Duke

THE DUKE OF YORK was given a loyal ovation when he returned by car to his London residence, 145 Piccadilly, last night.

Many hundreds of people had assembled in the locality, and when the Duke arrived he was cheered lustily. So enthusiastic was his reception that the police, in spite of their numbers, were unable to clear a passage for the Royal car for nearly five minutes.

The Duke, who was sitting in the back of the car, raised his hat repeatedly and smiled his acknowledgements to the tremendous crowd.

After the Duke had entered the house a man in the crowd started to sing the National Anthem, which was immediately taken up by the hundreds of people thronging the vicinity.

Men and women climbed the railings around the house, and every vantage point was used to catch a glimpse of the Duke. Traffic was unable to proceed for several minutes.

The New Queen

RADIO—Page 27

WARM WELCOME FOR SCOTS QUEEN

A WAVE of relief swept the country and spread through the Empire as Prince Albert, Duke of York succeeded to the throne as George VI after the unparalleled trauma of the abdication of his brother, King Edward VIII, after a reign of only 10 months.

And for Scotland, the crowning of the Duchess of York as Queen Elizabeth was to be particularly gratifying, as the Empire welcomed, with warmest loyalty, a Scottish Queen.

Before her marriage to the King in 1923, Her Royal Highness was of course Lady Elizabeth Bowes-Lyon, the daughter of the 14th Earl of Strathmore and Kinghorne. Queen Elizabeth is able to trace her line of descent back to Robert the Bruce and her love of Scotland is well-known, stemming from the happy times of her childhood spent at the family home of Glamis Castle.

The crisis in the monarchy came about after Edward VIII refused to give up his intention to marry an American divorcee, Mrs Wallis Simpson. The abdication drama unfolded over several months and the succession of the King's brother and his popular wife was hailed as not only the best, but the only, solution to the crisis in the British monarchy.

The final curtain of that great constitutional crisis came when the King announced his intention to abdicate in a radio broadcast to his subjects at home and overseas on December 11.

The following day, the King left Britain aboard a British warship to join Mrs Simpson in France, leaving the nation stunned. The royal couple married and subsequently became the Duke and Duchess of Windsor.

ANOTHER COLOUR FIRST

On Monday, June 22, the *Daily Record* became the first newspaper in the world to print a colour photograph of a news event in the course of the paper's normal production – a picture of Mrs Simpson, the woman the King gave up his throne to marry. The *Record* had been pioneering the use of full colour for layout and advertising for two years, but this was a milestone and the achievement of being able to print the photo in conjunction with the coverage of an important "on the day" story was acclaimed by newspapers throughout the world.

SCOT HELD ON GUN CHARGE

George Andrew MacMahon, a Scots journalist living in London, was arrested in July after a loaded revolver was thrown on to the road as the King was returning to Buckingham Palace after presenting Colours to troops in Hyde Park. MacMahon was charged with "being in possession of a revolver with intent to endanger life" and was subsequently jailed for 12 months with hard labour for "intending to harm the King".

COMINGS...

William McIlvanney
Novelist

GOINGS...

R.B. Cunninghame Graham
Writer,
First President of the
Scottish Labour Party &
First President of the
Scottish National Party

THIS SPORTING LIFE

FOOTBALL	RUGBY UNION	GOLF	HORSE RACING	SHINTY
Scottish Champions Celtic *Scottish Cup Winners* Rangers	*Scotland vs England* England 9–8 Scotland at Twickenham	*Home Internationals* Scotland 8 – 7 England Scotland 8 – 7 Ireland Scotland 9½ – 5½ Wales	*Scottish Grand National* *Winner* *Southern Hero* at Bogside	*Camanachd Cup Winners* Newtonmore at Spean Bridge

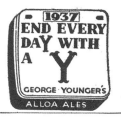
1937 END EVERY DAY WITH A Y — GEORGE YOUNGER'S ALLOA ALES

Daily ✠ Record
and Mail.

SCOTLAND'S NATIONAL NEWSPAPER

ESTAB. 1847—No. 28,079.   WEDNESDAY, JANUARY 20, 1937.   ONE PENNY

GLASGOW BOXER'S WORLD TITLE
Benny Lynch's £2600 Share Of Record Purse

Lynch (right) ducks to avoid a lead to the jaw during his fight with Small Montana in London last night.
—Picture by wire.

NOW UNDISPUTED CHAMPION

Montana's Craft Saves Him From Knock-Out

By ELKY CLARK, Ex-European Flyweight Champion

London, Tuesday Night

BENNY LYNCH OF GLASGOW IS NOW THE UNDISPUTED FLYWEIGHT CHAMPION OF THE WORLD.

At the Wembley Pool, here, to-night he defeated Small Montana of America on points over fifteen rounds.

Lynch won, I thought, with a bit in hand. Benny has always been noted as a fighter depending mostly on a big punch to bring him victory, but on his display to-night he surprised his most ardent admirers by the way he boxed and brought into play a clever craftsmanship.

Lynch throughout was the aggressor, and although he failed to land a knock-out punch, he obviously worried Montana with wicked lefts and rights to the body.

Against a less crafty fighter, Lynch would surely have gained his objective, as he did against Jackie Brown and Pat Palmer.

The purse for the contest amounted to £6000, of which Lynch claimed £2600. Several hundreds of pounds were guaranteed Montana for travelling and training expenses in addition to what the Filipino actually received.

There were 13,600 people at the fight, and they paid £14,000.

MONTANA did not prove the lightning spark he was cracked up to be, but nevertheless he proved to be seven stone nine pounds ten ounces of tough material.

The Filipino, although not so fast on his feet, possessed a nice swerve from the hip that was delightful to watch. It was with this movement that he prevented the Scot from landing a knock-out. Montana was coolness personified throughout the Scot's rugged onslaught. It was by keeping a cool head that he managed to stay the distance.

Montana proved a splendid boxer, but

(Continued on Back Page)

TRAGEDY OF DEATH OF COL. BAILLIE-WRIGHT

Was Preparing For Ex-Officer Son's Release From Jail

LIEUTENANT-COLONEL C. H. BAILLIE-WRIGHT, father of Norman Baillie Stewart, known as the "Officer in the Tower," died at his home in Woodstock Road, Redland, Bristol, yesterday.

The tragedy of his death is that he and his wife had just begun making preparations for the homecoming of their son.

Baillie Stewart is serving a sentence of five years' penal servitude for imparting information to a foreign Power, and is expected to be released early next month from Maidstone Prison, it being assumed he will be granted the usual good conduct remission.

It is understood that an application has been made to the Home Office for the release of Baillie Stewart earlier than would otherwise have been, the case owing to his father's death.

Recent Serious Illness

Inquiries early this month at the home of Col. and Mrs. Baillie-Wright met with the response that they had both left Bristol for the time being, and apparently Col. Baillie-Wright returned to Bristol only a few days before his death.

Col. and Mrs. Baillie-Wright were living at Southsea when their son was tried by court-martial in April, 1933, found guilty, sentenced and cashiered.

On two occasions since Col. Baillie-Wright had had serious attacks of illness, and only the hope of seeing his son free again and established on another business had enabled him to recover. He had received offers from several people to take his son into business.

Throughout ex-Lieutenant Baillie Stewart's imprisonment his father and mother, who have lived very quietly and in seclusion in Bristol, have maintained their belief in his innocence.

"My son still maintains his innocence, and so do I," his mother once wrote.

Mrs. Baillie-Wright has been seeing

Lt.-Col. Baillie-Wright.

Baillie Stewart in prison fairly regularly—the last time early this month.

His father stated recently, "I know my son has a talent for writing, and I understand that while at Maidstone he has been writing lyrics and some music which showed considerable promise."

It was as a result of the publicity of the trial of the "Officer in the Tower" that Lieut.-Colonel Baillie-Wright adopted the name of Lieut.-Colonel C. H. B. Wright.

Royalty And Youth Festival

It is officially announced from Buckingham Palace that the King and Queen will visit the Festival of Youth at Wembley Stadium, on Saturday, July 3.

Well, Gorbals Have It...

By MISS BILLIE HOUSTON

WELL, Gorbals have it. When I saw little Benny, our own Benny, pursue the Filipino, Montana, round the ring, sticking out that gorilla left of his as though measuring the distance between Montana's nose and the floor, I thought what a pity this Filipino is portable.

Benny seemed to be hitting the top of Goat Fell. Every punch was a paralyser had it landed. But the Filipino had all the pimpernels skinned from the row of gooseberries. He was a ghost who would not be handcuffed to anything that was coming from Gorbals.

Lynch A Fighter

I was desperate. My own feeling was that Montana is the greatest boxer I have ever seen in the ring, but Lynch was a fighter. The beauty and mathematical precision of Montana amazed me. But Lynch had guts. I think he won on the last two rounds, because Benny suddenly went all out.

But, partisanship aside, Montana is the most marvellous thing I've ever seen.

Come On, Glasgow

Now I can breathe freely, as I did at the ringside when Benny Lynch's arm was held up as the winner. I felt like the fellow at the back of the hall who kept yelling, "Come on, Glasgow."

Every bone in my body, everything I had got in me, echoed that shout. Right or wrong, I wanted Gorbals to win . . . and it did win.

Lynch, with his dour, wee face, that awful punch coming up that seemed to threaten—did it connect—to knock Montana toward Hollywood, was my one hope. How I wanted Lynch to win. And he won. So here's to us.

STIRLING TO PLANT "ROYAL" TREES

The Commissioners of Crown Lands have informed Stirling Town Council that they are prepared to pay for the planting of a tree in the King's Park, Stirling, in commemoration of King George V.

RADIO—Page 8

U.S. Offer To Lynch

NORMAN HURST, Boxing Correspondent of Allied Newspapers, writes that yesterday afternoon he received a message from the manager of Madison Square Garden, New York.

"Tell Lynch that if he defeats Montana in a clear-cut manner he will be matched for a fight at Madison Square against Sixto Escobar for the bantamweight championship of the world."

This would give Lynch an opportunity of gaining the unique distinction for a British boxer of holding two world titles at the same time.

"I'M MIGHTY PROUD"

Benny Lynch's Message To The "Daily Record"

By "WAVERLEY"

In the early hours of this morning I had a telephone conversation with Benny Lynch, who was then in the Euston Hotel, London, where he is staying. He returns home to-morrow, arriving in the Central Station, Glasgow, at 9.35 p.m.

"How are you, Benny?" I queried

"I'm feeling very fit. Let me give this message to the 'Daily Record.' I'm not the least bit damaged, and I'm mighty proud that once again I have won for Scotland. Just now I feel proud I am a Scot, and that I have kept the title for my country."

"It was a hard fight, I believe."

"I found him very elusive, but I think I have proved that I can both box and fight, and that I am not just a strong puncher as some people seem to think. It was a battle of tactics.

"There was a time, nearing the half-way stage, when Montana foxed that he was tiring. I pretended I was weary, too. In the seventh round he let go, but I was ready for him, and proved myself as strong as he was. I think he realised that."

"Was he a hard puncher?"

"He was guilty of hitting with the inside of the glove and I suspected that those in his corner warned him about

it. But he was a great little sport, and one who fought fairly and squarely, asking for no mercy and proffering none.

"And now I'm off to bed, but tell your readers once again that I'm so happy at keeping the championship in Scotland."

Tommy Morgan, the famous Scots comedian, who is a close friend of Benny, was with me during the conversation. He also had a word with the champion.

"We're all waiting to give you a great welcome," said Tommy.

BENNY PROVES HE'S GREATEST

BENNY LYNCH became the undisputed Flyweight Champion of the World in January, defeating America's Small Montana on points over 15 rounds at the Wembley Pool.

The Glasgow boxer was the aggressor throughout, and although he failed to land a knockout punch, he got the better of Montana with his combination lefts and rights.

It had been generally expected that Lynch would win by a knockout, and even though he failed to achieve this, Lynch still showed himself to be a worthy champion by out-pointing a boxer who came with the reputation of being one of the toughest in the world.

The American did not prove to be the lightning spark he was cracked up to be, but he did prove to be tough. Montana was coolness personified throughout Benny Lynch's rugged onslaught. Although not fast on his feet, he possessed a swerve of the hip, which prevented the Scot from landing the knockout blow and it was due to this that he managed to stay the distance.

Montana was a great boxer and a fighter but Lynch seemed to rise to the occasion and often he beat him to the punch.

The contest was also one of the cleanest that could have been witnessed. Both men punched crisply and the referee, Mr C.B. Thomas, of Wales, had little trouble in controlling the fight.

It was obvious after the 10th round that Montana needed to put Lynch on the floor to get the verdict but Benny never slackened his pace and kept building up the points with a powerful display of combination punching.

In the final few rounds, the American stepped up the pace in a last dying effort to steal the fight but Lynch was always there to meet him more than halfway.

SCOTS WELCOME FOR KING AND QUEEN

Thousands turned out in Edinburgh in July for the visit of King George VI and Queen Elizabeth. Trains and buses brought people from all over Scotland to witness the occasion and Prince's Street was jam-packed from seven in the morning.

STOP! THESE VERMIN WITH **RODINE** THE RAPID RAT REMOVER

COMINGS...
Donald Dewar
Scotland's first First Minister
Ronnie Browne
Folksinger
Roy Williamson
Folksinger

GOINGS...
J. M. Barrie
Creator of Peter Pan
Ramsay MacDonald
First Labour Prime Minister

ON RADIO
Monday At Seven

34 KILLED IN RAILWAY CRASH

One of the worst disasters in the history of British Railways happened in December near Castlecary, Dumbartonshire. During a snowstorm, the 4pm train from Edinburgh to Glasgow crashed into a standing train that had travelled from Fife and Dundee, also heading for Glasgow. Thirty-four people were killed and 96 were injured. Three coaches were shattered and wreckage was piled 40 feet high as rescue workers and Castlecary villagers searched for survivors.

THIS SPORTING LIFE

FOOTBALL	RUGBY UNION	GOLF	HORSE RACING	SHINTY
Scottish Champions Rangers *Scottish Cup Winners* Celtic	*Scotland vs England* Scotland 3–6 England at Murrayfield	*British Open Winner* Henry Cotton at Carnoustie (290)	*Scottish Grand National* *Winner* *Right'un* at Bogside	*Camanachd Cup Winners* Oban Celtic at Keppoch

EMPIRE EXHIBITION SPECIAL

Daily *and Mail.* Record

SCOTLAND'S NATIONAL NEWSPAPER

ESTAB. 1847—No. 28,475   THURSDAY, APRIL 28, 1938   ONE PENNY

THE CLACHAN

Empire Exhibition, Glasgow 1938

THE ROYAL SEAL OF APPROVAL

KING GEORGE and Queen Elizabeth opened the Empire Exhibition at Bellahouston Park, Glasgow in May, during their first visit to the city after their accession to the throne.

Their Majesties were joined by over 150,000 people who visited the Exhibition on its opening day. The aim of the event was to illustrate the progress and achievements of the British Empire both at home and abroad and to stimulate Scotland's stagnant economy, still struggling to overcome the problems that had befallen it earlier in the decade.

Under the guidance of Architect-in-Chief, Thomas Tait, designers had turned the 175-acre park into a magnificent blend of strikingly modern pavilions, avenues, cascades and fountains.

Pride and pleasure in the completed achievement were the keynotes of the proceedings throughout the opening day, notes struck by His Majesty at the opening ceremony at nearby Ibrox Stadium.

In a speech which did not fail to pay due tribute to the share borne by all parts of the Empire in promoting the exhibition, Lord Elgin, President of the Exhibition, was also lavish in the praise

he showered upon Scotland: "Scotland is proud to have the privilege of staging this symbol of unity of the British people … There have been gathered together exhibits illustrating the resources of the whole British Empire, resources which are limitless, produced by a people whose capacity for work is also limitless, whose capacity for play at the proper time is boundless and whose desire is for peace."

In the five months it was open, some 12 million visitors saw the Exhibition, and in spite of a poor summer and the shadows of war looming, it was viewed generally as a memorable achievement.

CHEERS AS QUEEN OF THE CLYDE IS LAUNCHED

The Clyde shipyard of John Brown was packed as the Queen launched the world's biggest liner in August, and gave her name to the ship. A bell rang at 3.37pm and hammering broke out from under the keel of the *Queen Elizabeth*. "Oh, she's away," said the Queen when the massive vessel began to move. And cheers rang out as the liner continued down the slipway and hit the water. Earlier, on the launching platform, there were speeches and the Queen was given a souvenir. Taking a great interest in the proceedings was the young Princess Elizabeth. It wasn't all sweetness and light, however, for the possibility of war with Germany was on the horizon and during the launching ceremony, the Queen took the opportunity to send out a message from the King on the growing European crisis.

COMINGS…

Allan Massie
Novelist & Journalist

Moira Anderson
Singer

David Steel
Last Leader of the Liberal Party

ON RADIO

Band Waggon

DEATH IN THE CITY FOG

It was Black Tuesday in Glasgow on January 3 when the city was hit by the worst fog for several years. Two men drowned when they fell into the Clyde in the mirk and traffic was thrown into chaos. Trams, buses, cars and lorries crashed into each other and ships collided on the river. Hundreds of people were stranded at Central Station, unable to get transport home. Ironically, the suburbs enjoyed sunshine during the day.

THIS SPORTING LIFE

FOOTBALL	RUGBY UNION	GOLF	HORSE RACING	SHINTY
Scottish Champions Celtic	*Scotland vs England* England 16–21 Scotland at Twickenham	*Home Internationals* Scotland 6½ - 8½ England Scotland 9½ - 5½ Ireland Scotland 8½ - 6½ Wales	*Scottish Grand National* *Winner* *Young Mischief* at Bogside	*Camanachd Cup Winners* Oban at Oban
Scottish Cup Winners East Fife				

CRISES MAPS —Page 65

Sunday ✠ Mail

Scotland's National Sunday Newspaper

No. 1615   28 Pages   E   SUNDAY, SEPTEMBER 3, 1939   TWOPENCE

"Red Tape" The Whisky

MIDNIGHT CABINET MEETING

AT 11.10 last night it was announced that the Cabinet had been summoned again. Within five minutes Ministers were trudging through blackened streets of Westminster to Number 10 in what appeared to be a violent electric storm.

Every second the sky was lit up with violent flashes of blue light. Emergency fire and A.R.P. patrols were called to their stations The meeting ended at 12.10. No statement to be issued until to-day.

No hint was given as to the purpose of the discussions, though it was believed that it was some further communication from France after last night's House of Commons debate which necessitated the calling together of the Cabinet.

WE DON'T MAKE WAR AGAINST CIVILIANS

"THE GOVERNMENTS OF THE UNITED KINGDOM AND FRANCE SOLEMNLY AND PUBLICLY AFFIRM THEIR INTENTION, SHOULD A WAR BE FORCED UPON THEM, TO CONDUCT HOSTILITIES WITH A FIRM DESIRE TO SPARE THE CIVILIAN POPULATION AND TO PRESERVE IN EVERY WAY POSSIBLE THOSE MONUMENTS OF HUMAN ACHIEVEMENT WHICH ARE TREASURED IN ALL CIVILISED COUNTRIES.

"IN THIS SPIRIT THEY HAVE WELCOMED WITH DEEP SATISFACTION PRESIDENT ROOSEVELT'S APPEAL ON THE SUBJECT OF BOMBING FROM THE AIR. FULLY SYMPATHISING WITH THE HUMANITARIAN SENTIMENTS BY WHICH THAT APPEAL WAS INSPIRED, THEY HAVE REPLIED TO IT IN SIMILAR TERMS.

Lebrun's Stirring Message

Paris, Saturday.

PRESIDENT LEBRUN sent a stirring message to the French Senate and Chamber which was read at this afternoon's sitting.

"With great calm, with cool resolution, and in perfect order, France has taken the measures that her security and fidelity to her obligations demand," stated M. Lebrun.

"As spokesman of the nation," continued M. Lebrun, "I address to our forces on land and sea and in the air an affectionate greeting and the expression of the unanimous confidence of the country.

"The union of citizens more sacred than ever has again been spontaneously realised. Firmness of spirit, discipline and hope animate them to their very depths.

"They understand that even beyond the fate of the Motherland the liberty of the world and the future of civilisation are at stake

These are the opening paragraphs of an official joint Anglo-French declaration which was published last night, and which continues as follows:—

"They (the Governments of the United Kingdom and France) had indeed some time ago sent explicit instructions to the commanders of their armed forces prohibiting the bombardment, whether from the air or from the sea, or by artillery on land, of any except strictly military objectives in the narrowest sense of the word.

"Bombardment by artillery on land will exclude objectives which have no strictly defined military importance, in particular large urban areas situated outside the battle zone.

"They will, furthermore, make every effort to avoid the destruction of localities or buildings which are of value to civilisation.

ANGLO-FRENCH DECLARATION

"As regards the use of naval forces, including submarines, the two Governments will abide strictly by the rules laid down in the Submarine Protocol of 1936, which have been accepted by nearly all civilised nations.

"Further, they will only employ their aircraft against merchant shipping at sea in conformity with the recognised rules applicable to the exercise of maritime belligerent rights by warships

"Finally, the two allied Governments re-affirm their intention to abide by the terms of the Geneva Protocol of 1925 prohibiting the use in war of asphyxiating or poisonous or other gasses and of bacteriological methods of warfare.

"An inquiry will be addressed to the German Government as to whether they are prepared to give an assurance to the same effect.

"It will, of course, be understood that in the event of the enemy not observing any of the restrictions which the Governments of the United Kingdom and France have thus imposed on the operations of their armed forces, these Governments reserve the right to take all such action as they may consider appropriate."

NO REPLY FROM HITLER

"HERR HITLER has not yet replied to the warning message delivered by Britain and France on Friday. The British and French Governments are in communication as to the limit within which it would be necessary for them to know if Germany is prepared to effect a withdrawal of her troops from Poland."

This statement was made by the Prime Minister and Lord Halifax in the House of Commons and the House of Lords last night.

The Prime Minister said it was possible that delay in Germany's reply had been due to a proposal put forward by the Italian Government that hostilities should cease and that there should be immediately a conference between Great Britain, France, Poland, Germany and Italy.

His Majesty's Government, said the Premier, will be bound to take action unless the German forces are withdrawn from Polish territories.

Full Report on Pages 4 and 5.

Germans Claim Corridor Victory

POLAND is now nearly cut off from the sea, if German claims last night, that their forces from the Reich proper have almost effected a junction with German troops from East Prussia, are accurate.

The following communique was issued by the High Command of the German Army at 7.30 p.m., yesterday, according to the official German News Agency:—

"German troops have gained further rapid successes on all fronts.

"Troops operating south of the industrial region in Upper Silesia are approaching Biala and have taken Pless. Further north a Polish bunker line has been penetrated. North of the industrial region our troops are nearing the River Warther.

"Motorised columns are advancing on Radolsk, north of Tschenstochau. Wielun has been captured. Units operating opposite Kem are pushing briskly towards Sieradz.

Pomeranian detachments have crossed the Brahe and reached the neighbourhood of the Weichsel, south of Graudenz. A junction with the troops operating in the direction of Graudenz from East Prussia has thus nearly been made."

The Germans last night announced that they had bombed a number of Polish aerodromes, while reports from

Polish sources yesterday claimed that the German army had been unable to develop its offensive.

Reports received in Paris by wireless from Warsaw stated that the German troops had not been in a position to follow up their surprise offensive and that they had suffered heavy losses and had had to make bloody sacrifices.

Germans Repulsed

M. Lukasieicz, Polish Ambassador in Paris, announces: "Reports that fighting has ceased are entirely wrong. German army tried to break through the Polish defences this morning, but were unsuccessful. They were repulsed everywhere.

"Two German attempts to raid Warsaw from the air were made between 5.45 a.m. and 6.35 a.m. They were driven off. The German bombers were

unable to reach Warsaw and dropped their bombs in the suburbs. They were driven off by anti-aircraft batteries and Polish fighting aeroplanes.

A military report in Warsaw stated that the Poles had repulsed the Germans at one point near Mlawa, south of the East Prussian frontier and at another point near Teschen in the south-west.

A Polish attack on Danzig where the Heimwehr entrenched themselves three days ago was said to be progressing.

Authoritative quarters in Warsaw denied that Polish aircraft had bombed points on the German side of the frontier. On the other hand Warsaw reported that 60 people had been killed in Lvov in German air raids since hostilities started.

A raid on Gdynia yesterday is admitted to have caused serious damage.

LATER NEWS

Any later crisis items to hand will be found in the stop press column on the back page

BRITAIN PLUNGED INTO WAR AGAIN

BRITAIN once again found itself at war in September following Germany's invasion of Poland and its subsequent refusal to withdraw its troops.

The invasion signalled the end of the Government's policy of trying to appease Hitler. It was now clear that the Nazi's efforts at expanding the Third Reich would not be limited to the German-speaking parts of Europe.

On September 3, Prime Minister Neville Chamberlain formally announced to an anxious nation that Britain was at war.

Broadcasting to the Empire later that day, the King said:

"For the second time in the lives of most of us, we are at war. We have tried to find a peaceful way out of the differences between ourselves and those who are now our enemies, but it has been in vain.

"We have been forced into conflict, for we are called, with our allies, to meet the challenge of a principle. It is the principle which permits a state to disregard its treaties and its solemn pledges, which sanctions the use of force or the threat of force against the sovereignty of other states.

"Such a principle, stripped of all disguise, is surely the primitive doctrine that 'might is right'.

"The task ahead will be hard. There may be dark days ahead, and war can no longer be confined to the battlefield, but we can only do right as we see that right. Reverently, therefore, we commit our cause to God."

SPECIAL LATE NEWS

BRITAIN DECLARES WAR (OFFICIAL)

Announced officially by Prime Minister at 11.15 a.m. to-day. Britain is now at war with Germany.

THE PREMIER'S STATEMENT

The Prime Minister on radio to-day stated:—

"I am speaking to you from the Cabinet room at 10 Downing Street. This morning the British Ambassador in Berlin handed the German Government a final note stating that unless we heard from them by 11 o'clock that they were prepared at once to withdraw their troops from Poland a state of war would exist between us.

"I have to tell you now that no such undertaking has been received, and that consequently this country is at war with Germany. You can imagine what a bitter blow it is to me that all my long struggle to win peace has failed.

"Yet I cannot believe that there is anything more or anything different that I could have done, and that would have been more successful.

"Up to the very last it would have been quite possible to have arranged a peaceful and honourable settlement between Germany and Poland, but Hitler wouldn't have it.

"He had evidently made up his mind to attack Poland whatever happened, and although he now says he put forward reasonable proposals which were rejected by the Poles, that is not a true statement. The proposals were never shown to the Polish Government, and although they were announced in the German broadcast on Thursday night, Hitler did not wait to hear the comment, but had ordered his troops to cross the frontier.

His actions showed convincingly that this man will never be trusted. He can only be stopped by force, and we in Britain and France are going to help Poland, so bravely resisting the attack upon her people. We have done more than any other country to establish peace, and any people or country should know that we have resolved to go to war. I think you will play your part with calmness to the finish.

GETTING READY FOR THE BOMBINGS

In May, 103,000 people "saw" Glasgow being bombed, a building burst into flames, rescue services at work, heard the wail of air-raid sirens and anti-aircraft guns bark defiance at enemy planes. But it wasn't for real for the crowd that packed into Hampden Park. It was an elaborate and spectacular demonstration of what people could expect to happen if Britain was to find itself at war and air raids took place. Sadly, the experience was soon to become all too real.

COMINGS...

Jackie Stewart
Grand Prix Champion

ON RADIO	
For Housewives: Health & Evacuation	*From My Postbag* Memory Lane

CREST OF A HEATWAVE

Thousands of Scots headed to resorts to paddle, sunbathe and enjoy ice-cream cones in the heatwave in June. Temperatures hit a record 88°F in the shade and over 100°F in the sun.

THIS SPORTING LIFE

FOOTBALL	RUGBY UNION	GOLF	HORSE RACING	SHINTY
Scottish Champions Rangers	*Scotland vs England* Scotland 6–9 England at Murrayfield	*British Open Winner* Dick Burton at St Andrews (290)	*Scottish Grand National Winner* *Southern Hero* at Bogside	*Camanachd Cup Winners* Caberfeidh at Inverness
Scottish Cup Winners Clyde				

Shopping's A Pleasure
at Glasgow's Modern Jewellers

David DOW

68 ARGYLE STREET
and 325 Sauchiehall Street.

Daily ✠ Record
and Mail.

ESTAB. 1847—No. 29,005   TUESDAY, JANUARY 9, 1940   F   ONE PENNY

SCOTLAND'S NATIONAL
NEWSPAPER

More Drastic Sacrifices For War Effort

No Early Call On M.P.s

(By Our Political Correspondent)

THE Prime Minister may make a passing reference to Mr. Hore-Belisha's resignation in his Mansion House speech this afternoon, but he will reserve his statement on the affair until the House of Commons meets next Tuesday.

PARLIAMENT WILL NOT BE CALLED TOGETHER ANY EARLIER BECAUSE OF ATTEMPTS TO MANUFACTURE A CRISIS AND THERE IS NO QUESTION OF A SECRET SESSION ON THE SUBJECT.

There were indications of an attempt to stampede the Opposition into premature expression of views, but the Socialist Parliamentary Party appears to be content to await the statement of the facts in the House before declaring any attitude or taking any action.

Same line is likely to be adopted by the National Council of Labour, which meets to-morrow.   F. T.

Any restrictions to come will not be imposed because of actual shortages, but in order to restrict consumption, particularly of non-essentials, and so economise shipping space and keep down the risks of inflation through rising prices.

At the same time, efforts will be directed towards increasing our exports.

The whole object will be to concentrate upon our war effort in the economic sphere and to ensure that, as far as possible, all our resources in foreign currency and shipping are devoted to actual war requirements.

The Government believe that the people are prepared to respond to greater efforts in this direction.

We are a long way from the position of Germany and its ration to the citizen of one new suit a year.

THE LONG VIEW

But, if it became necessary because of the demand upon raw materials for war purposes, the Government would not hesitate to introduce some standardisation in clothing.

This, of course, is merely an extreme instance of the long view which is being taken in official quarters.

One of the basic factors in the situation is the enormous demand upon shipping. Setting off the losses due to enemy action against new building and the capture of German vessels, we are, so far, about square.

STILL BE SHORTAGE

The position is, however, that even if there were no sinkings, there would still be a shipping shortage, partly because of the inevitable delays of the convoy system and the operation of the contraband control.

Meantime, every effort is being made to extend and speed up our shipbuilding programme.   F. T.

RATIONING MAY INCLUDE SUITS

By Our Political Correspondent

INTENSIFICATION OF THE NATION'S WAR EFFORT WILL BE CALLED FOR IN THE COMING MONTHS. THE PRIME MINISTER, IN HIS LONDON MANSION HOUSE SPEECH, THIS AFTERNOON, WILL TELL THE COUNTRY THAT FURTHER RESTRICTIONS AND SACRIFICES MUST BE FACED.

The necessity will be further explained by other members of the War Cabinet at big meetings between now and the end of February.

The country will be told that it must prepare for the war entering upon a much more serious and strenuous phase; for food rationing, which commenced yesterday, was only the forerunner of more drastic restrictions to come.

ITALY WILL FIGHT FOR HUNGARY

A DEFENSIVE military alliance between Italy and Hungary is said to have been agreed upon by Count Ciano and Count Csaky.

Italy will undertake to go to the assistance of Hungary in the event of aggression against her by either Russia or Germany, it is said in a "highly authoritative source" in Budapest, quoted by the New York wireless.

DALADIER BREAKS ANKLE BONE

Paris, Monday.

M. DALADIER, the French Premier, fractured an ankle bone in an accident yesterday, it is officially announced.

Professor Henri Mondor, who made an X-ray examination, set the bone.

M. Daladier has already resumed his duties at the War Office.—B.U.P.

WAS "DEAD" BUT—

BELOW are Flight-Lieut. William M. Penman, R.A.F., eldest son of Mr. and Mrs. Penman, of Edinburgh, and Miss Peggy MacCorkindale, former winner of the Scottish junior tennis championship, after their wedding at Christ Church, Harrow, yesterday. Flight-Lieut. Penman, who was a Scottish Rugby Internationalist, was reported killed in the air raid over Wilhelmshaven in the first week of the war, but managed to 'phone his fiancee before the rumour reached her.

YESTERDAY HE WED

3 TRAINS IN FRENCH FOG CRASH

Paris, Monday.

SEVEN soldiers travelling home on leave were killed and 19 injured in a train accident near Orly, about six miles outside Paris, on Saturday.

Publication of the news was delayed so that the families of those concerned could be officially informed first.

Three trains were involved, and there was thick fog at the time. As the first train carrying soldiers stopped outside Orly the second, also carrying troops, ran into it. It was, however, travelling slowly.

The occupants of both trains got out, but as they were crossing the down line another train passed, killing seven and injuring 19.—Reuter.

MAN-POWER NOT USED

By OUR POLITICAL CORRESPONDENT

THE CONTINUANCE OF A SUBSTANTIAL AMOUNT OF UNEMPLOYMENT AT A TIME WHEN SO MUCH NATIONAL EFFORT IS NEEDED FOR WAR PURPOSES IS GIVING THE GOVERNMENT SOME CONCERN.

The returns published to-day show that there are still 1,361,525 on the unemployment register and while many of these are moving from one job to another and there is a "hard core" of unemployable, the total is still regarded as too high.

In the early months of this year the Government will devote special attention to the problem of absorbing a much greater number of the unemployed into the national effort.

UNFAVOURABLE EFFECT

A matter which the Government also have to consider is that the spectacle of this large body of unemployed is having an unfavourable effect upon French opinion.

The French Government no longer have any feeling that this country is not pulling its weight in the war, but the ordinary Frenchman cannot understand our unemployment.

French man power has been practically fully mobilised, with the result that there are great shortages of male labour in industry and large numbers of women have to be employed.

The suggestion has been made by French Ministers—quite informally and unofficially — that they could absorb our unemployed in French industry. There is, for example, a great shortage of labour in the French coal mines.

For obvious reasons, a transfer of British unemployed to France does not offer any solution. Apart from any other consideration there is the disparity in wages, and conditions of employment.

MORE DIVISIONS

One way of relieving the strain upon France, in the interests of the common effort in which both countries are united, would be to increase as rapidly as possible the number of our Army divisions in France.

This would enable some of the older Frenchmen to be released from the colours and resume their civilian work.

The matter is one which arouses differences of opinion, but the British Government are conscious of the heavy burden which the French nation is bearing.

On the home front the Government is pursuing its efforts in consultation with trade union leaders to speed up the absorption of the unemployed.

In addition to these efforts, the Government's war programme will eventually involve the employment of a very large number of women.

Workless Figures—Page 2

From Jock's C.O. And Jock

HERE are two voices from France saying "Thank you" to Jock's Box, the voice of the C.O. and one from the ranks.

"May I say that it would have been impossible for you to have chosen a more useful or more acceptable list of presents to send out, and I cannot exaggerate the enthusiasm with which they were received. Please accept our most sincere thanks for your generosity."—Lieut.-Col. W. Tod, commanding 2nd Bn. The Royal Scots Fusiliers.

"I am not very good at writing my thanks because I don't know what to say, but I would like you to print my few words in your paper so that readers may know that all the things they sent, or money given, was well spent, and that all the men of the 2nd Bn. Cameronians received a good parcel."—Rifleman James Walsh, 2nd Bn. Cameronians (S.R.).

TIGHTENING BELTS – AND BRACES

IT was reported in January that intensification of the nation's war effort would be called for in the following months.

The Prime Minister was to address the country and alert it to the further sacrifices that would have to be made.

Food rationing, which was already in operation, was only the forerunner of more drastic restrictions to come – and that could include restricted supplies of men's suits.

The country was to be told that it must prepare for the war entering upon a much more serious and strenuous phase.

Restrictions that were to come were not to be imposed due to shortages, but in order to restrict consumption, particularly of non-essentials.

The aim of this was to economise shipping space and keep down the risks of inflation through rising prices.

Although the restrictions would be in place, efforts were to be directed towards increasing the exports.

The main objective of this scheme was to concentrate upon the war effort in the economic sphere and to ensure that, as far as possible, all resources in foreign currency and shipping were devoted to war requirements.

The Government believed that the people were prepared to respond to greater efforts in that direction.

If it became necessary – because of the demand upon raw materials for war purposes – the Government said that it would not hesitate to take the step of introducing some standardisation.

AIR RAIDS TAKE THEIR TOLL

Three areas of Scotland bore the brunt of the Nazis' air attacks with high explosive and incendiary bombs on July 13. In the south-west, an elderly man was killed and six houses were damaged in the same street. Several other casualties were reported in the target areas. Royal Air Force fighter planes shot down 10 enemy bombers and anti-aircraft guns brought down another. In the Battle of Britain, Germany's Luftwaffe lost 34 of their aircraft.

KING HONOURS HEROINE

Elizabeth Lyle was the first ARP warden in Scotland to receive a Royal commendation for bravery during an air raid. She had rescued a baby from a bombed tenement in Leith.

GOINGS...

John Buchan
Author of
The Thirty-Nine Steps

COMINGS...

Gus Macdonald
Media Executive & Politician
Dennis Law
Footballer
John Byrne
Artist & Playwright

WHAT IT COST

POUND OF BUTTER
1s 3d

POUND OF BACON
1s 6d

PINT OF BEER
9d

CIGARETTES
1s 5d (20 Players No. 3)

WOMENS' SHOES
16s 3d

MEN'S SUIT
10s 6d

TON OF COAL
£1 14s

POSTAGE
2½d

CAR
Hillman Minor £175

THIS SPORTING LIFE

FOOTBALL	RUGBY UNION	GOLF	HORSE RACING	SHINTY
Scottish Champions No competition held	*Scotland vs England* No game played	*British Open Winner* No competition held	*Scottish Grand National Winner* No race run	*Camanachd Cup Winners* No competition held
Scottish Cup Winners No competition held				

Nazi Leader Flies To Scotland

BASSETT'S ORIGINAL LIQUORICE ALLSORTS
The sweets of Victory
IN CARTONS 4ᵈ 8ᵈ & 1/-   *Also loose. Of all good Confectioners*

Daily Record
and Mail.

ESTAB. 1847—No. 29,430   TUESDAY, MAY 13, 1941   E   ONE PENNY

RUDOLF HESS IN GLASGOW HOSPITAL

Herr Hess, Hitler's right-hand man, has run away from Germany and is in Glasgow suffering from a broken ankle. He brought photographs to establish his identity.

An official statement issued from 10 Downing Street at 11.20 last night said:—

"Rudolf Hess, Deputy Fuhrer of Germany and Party Leader of the Nationalist Socialist Party, has landed in Scotland under the following circumstances:

"On the night of Saturday, the 10th, a Messerschmitt 110 was reported by our patrols to have crossed the coast of Scotland and be flying in the direction of Glasgow. Since a Messerschmitt 110 would not have the fuel to return to Germany this report was at first disbelieved.

"Later on a ME.110 crashed near Glasgow with its guns unloaded. Shortly afterwards a German officer who had baled out was found with his parachute in the neighbourhood suffering from a broken ankle.

"He was taken to a hospital in Glasgow, where he at first gave his name as Horn, but later on he declared he was Rudolf Hess.

"He brought with him various photographs of himself at different ages, apparently in order to establish his identity. These photographs were deemed to be photographs of Hess by several people who knew him personally.

"Accordingly an officer of the Foreign Office who was closely acquainted with Hess before the war, has been sent up by aeroplane to see him in hospital."

A later official statement said Hess has been identified beyond all doubt.

THIS WAS HIS 'PLANE

Two pictures of the wreckage of the Messerschmitt 110 in which Rudolf Hess flew to Scotland.

"Insanity" —Rubbish

THE flight of Hess must have tremendous repercussions in Germany, where he was not only powerful but immensely popular, writes a Press Association political correspondent.

Although there is no official comment, the Berlin attempt to anticipate the news by speaking of Hess's "mental disorder" won't hold water, and there is every reason for drawing the conclusion that the flight was a deliberate one.

And Hess, significantly, chose a 'plane which would not have enough petrol to take him back.

It requires possession of all one's faculties to fly a fast fighting 'plane, and "hallucinations" are not associated with piloting such a machine to a given point. The possession of photographs for identity purposes indicate that Hess knew where he was going.

Rudolf Hess

"I Found German Lying In Field"

DAVID M'LEAN, A PLOUGHMAN, WAS THE MAN WHO FOUND RUDOLF HESS. HERE IS M'LEAN'S OWN STORY AS TOLD TO THE "DAILY RECORD," FIRST NEWSPAPER ON THE SCENE:—

"I was in the house and everyone else was in bed late at night when I heard the 'plane roaring overhead. As I ran out to the back of the farm, I heard a crash, and saw the 'plane burst into flames in a field about 200 yards away.

"I was amazed and a bit frightened when I saw a parachute dropping slowly earthwards through the gathering darkness. Peering upwards, I could see a man swinging from the harness.

Good Morning! Another Day Nearer Victory!

1941

HITLER'S DEPUTY HAS LANDED

THE Reich's second most powerful man, Rudolf Hess, was reported to be in a hospital in Glasgow in May after a drama that saw him land in Scotland by parachute.

An official statement from 10 Downing Street said that Hess, the Deputy Fuhrer of Germany's Nationalist Socialist Party, had landed under the following circumstances.

"On the night of Saturday the 10th, a Messerschmitt 110 was reported by our patrols to have crossed the coast of Scotland and be flying in the direction of Glasgow.

Since a Messerchmitt 110 would not have the fuel to return to Germany this report was at first disbelieved.

Later on a ME110 crashed near Glasgow with its guns unloaded. Shortly afterwards a German officer who had baled out was found with his parachute in the neighbourhood.

The man was suffering from a broken ankle. He was taken to a hospital in Glasgow, where he at first gave the name as Horn, but later on he declared he was Rudolf Hess."

He brought with him various photographs of himself at different ages, apparently in order to establish his identity.

And these photographs were deemed to be photographs of Hess by several people who knew him personally.

According to Hess, his object had been to convince the British of the wisdom of a negotiated peace.

But he admitted that he had left Germany solely on his own initiative and his action has generally been regarded ever since as that of an unbalanced man .

After the war, Hess was tried for major war crimes and sentenced to life imprisonment. He entered Spandau Prison, in Berlin, early in 1946 and thereafter was out of the public eye. He remained in jail for the next forty years, with much of his time spent in effective solitary confinement as the only prisoner in the massive prison. In 1987, he committed suicide in Spandau.

NO LET-UP IN THE WAR HORROR

German bombers intensified their raids on the central belt of Scotland early in May. Houses were reduced to rubble and ARP wardens, ambulance crews and firefighters were at full stretch as they tried to rescue and treat the injured and contain the damage. A bomb also fell on a first-aid post and emergency services gave it priority as the air strike continued. One town in the west of Scotland suffered a huge attack of incendiary bombs as well as ones delivering devastating high explosives.

When reporting such strikes, it was the policy of the *Record* and other papers not to identify which towns had been hit, in order not to aid enemy intelligence.

ON RADIO

The Brains Trust

Worker's Playtime

London Calling Europe

Sincerely Yours, Vera Lynn

The Kitchen Front

"Ici La France"

Lift Up Your Hearts

THREE KILLED IN TRAMCAR CRASH

A Glasgow tramcar overturned going down a steep hill in February and three of the passengers were killed. More than 20 others were injured in the accident which happened between Thornliebank and Barrhead. The tram left a bend in the track alongside Darnley Fire Station after crossing Nitshill Road and ran 15 yards before hitting a power standard and overturning into a field. The standard virtually cut the upper deck away from the lower deck and the chassis.

THIS SPORTING LIFE

FOOTBALL	RUGBY UNION	GOLF	HORSE RACING	SHINTY
Scottish Champions No competition held	*Scotland vs England* No game played	*British Open Winner* No competition held	*Scottish Grand National Winner* No race run	*Camanachd Cup Winners* No competition held
Scottish Cup Winners No competition held				

Presbyterian Mixture

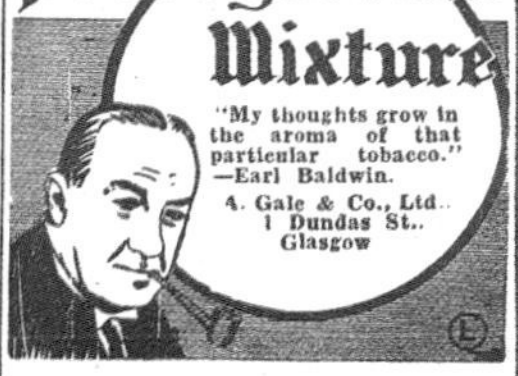

"My thoughts grow in the aroma of that particular tobacco."
—Earl Baldwin.

A. Gale & Co., Ltd., 1 Dundas St., Glasgow

Daily Record and Mail.

EST, 1847—No. 29,827 BLACK-OUT—Back Page THURSDAY, AUGUST 27, 1942 RADIO—Page 6 ONE PENNY B

To-day

Lord Kemsley
Gravity of the Battle for Fuel .... *P. 2*

Lawrence Fairhall
'Planes or Navies? .... *P. 5*

James Hogg
Hitler Stole Our Football Gifts ...... *P. 2*

SCOT SOLE SURVIVOR OF ROYAL CRASH

MORE THAN 24 HOURS AFTER THE SUNDERLAND FLYING-BOAT CARRYING THE DUKE OF KENT HAD CRASHED ON A LONELY HILLSIDE IN THE NORTH OF SCOTLAND CAME THE DRAMATIC NEWS LAST NIGHT THAT THERE WAS ONE SURVIVOR OF THE TRAGEDY — A SCOTSMAN.

He is Flt.-Sergt. Andrew Simpson Wilson Jack, aged about 24, of Grangemouth, rear-gunner in the plane.

He was thrown clear when the plane hit the hillside and was not seriously hurt, although he was burned on the face, arms, and legs.

Stunned and semi-conscious he wandered away from the scene of the crash before searchers arrived.

Saved By A Miracle

For three miles he staggered through the heather until crofters found him and took him to a village. Here his wounds were tended and in the afternoon he was taken to hospital.

It was then that it became known that there had been a survivor. Previously it had been officially stated that all the crew and passengers, said to number 15, perished, though late last night it was revealed that one occupant of the plane was still unaccounted for.

It is believed that Jack jumped clear in the nick of time and survived the accident by a miracle. "I don't know where I am, but I am glad to be in bed," he said when interviewed in hospital.

Although dazed and suffering from shock, he walked nearly three miles to bring the news of the disaster to the occupants of a lonely moorland cottage.

He was on the point of collapse when he reached the cottage.

The local doctor who went to the scene of the crash with search parties which set out from neighbouring villages and hamlets was passing the cottage in his car when he was stopped and taken to the injured airman.

"I found him seriously ill," he told the *Daily Record*. He was badly shocked and I removed him to hospital. It is difficult to understand how he was able to cover the distance over rough moorland from the wrecked 'plane to the cottage."

Hon. Michael Strutt

Hon. John Lowther

HEARD CRASH

First news of the crash came from a farmer's son.

With his father, Mr. David Morrison, he was out searching for straying sheep on the hillside two miles from the hamlet.

"My son Hugh and I suddenly heard the noise of a 'plane overhead," said Mr. Morrison to a *Daily Record* reporter.

Continued on Back Page, Col. 4

Prayer Services For All

ARRANGEMENTS are being made by the three Services and many factories to allow men and women to listen to a special 15 minutes service on the National Day of Prayer, September 3, which the B.B.C. is broadcasting on both Home and Forces from 11 a.m.

The B.B.C contemplates that this service will be one of the most widely listened to during that day. It will replace the usual 10.15 a.m. service with special prayers.

Everything is being done for all ranks to attend or listen to a service.

Other special services which will be broadcast during the day include a two-minute period of intercession in the Home and Forces programmes at 7 a.m.

The Cardinal Archbishop of Birmingham will give a ten-minute address in the Home Service at noon, and a Joint Service of Prayer and Dedication will be broadcast from a studio in the Home service at 9.20 p.m. The Rev. C. W. G. Taylor, Moderator of the General Assembly of the Church of Scotland, will give the first address at this service. The second will be given by the Archbishop of Canterbury.

Egypt Battle May Be Renewed Any Moment

GENERAL WILSON'S appointment as Commander of the Ninth Army is criticised in Ankara as an indication that Britain intends to build up its army in Iraq and Persia to hold the Germans should they cross the Caucasus.

Turkish opinion does not believe that the Germans will attempt that. There are only three routes—the Black and Caspian Sea coasts, and the Georgian Military Highway. The Caspian route is only 25 miles wide.

Air activity and artillery duels mounting day by day to a climax add fresh evidence to the view of observers in the Western Desert that the great battle for Egypt may berenewed at any moment. Both the official communique from British H.Q. in Cairo and yesterday's Italian reports tell of increased air activity by both sides. Allied operations appear to be on a much greater scale than Rommel's.

CRASH VICTIMS

The Duke's body, which was at first laid with his dead comrades, will be taken to London.

It is understood that the Chief Inspector of Accidents has left for the scene of the disaster.

Among the victims were Lt. John Lowther, R.N.V.R., the Duke's private secretary—who was grandson and heir to Viscount Ullswater, former Speaker of the House of Commons—the Hon. Michael Strutt, son of Lord Belper and brother of the Duchess of Norfolk, and Leading-Aircraftman Hale, the Duke's valet.

Mr. Lowther, who had been the Duke's secretary for seven years, travelled to Scotland by train on Tuesday with the Duke's party.

Mr. Strutt, who was 28, was taking the place of Squadron-Leader D. J. Ferguson, who was prevented by illness from accompanying the Duke.

The Lord Chamberlain announces that the Court will go into mourning for four weeks until September 23.

CALAIS AIR RAID

Squadrons of R.A.F. fighters returning from the Calais district crossed the coast near Folkestone between nine and ten o'clock yesterday morning.

On his return from Moscow, Mr. Churchill visited the 8th Army's forward areas in Egypt and held discussions in Cairo covering the whole field of operations from India to Malta. Mr. Churchill in siren suit and topee converses with General Alexander.

BOCK'S STALINGRAD DRIVE HELD IN SOUTH

PLAN TO STRIKE FROM REAR

STALINGRAD, gravely imperilled by the immense weight of men and metal unleashed against it from north and south, is now facing the prospect of a siege whose bitterness may parallel Moscow's ordeal last year.

Although to the south-west, above Kotelnikovo, Bock's panzer forces have during the last 24 hours been held and in some places thrown back by Red Army counter-attacks to their starting point, the thrust from the north-west, supported by a constant sream of tanks and motorised troops across the Don bend, has assumed a still darker turn.

According to German reports, large fires are blazing in many parts of Stalingrad, subjected to large-scale Luftwaffe assaults throughout the day, but the city's A.-A. defences are taking a heavy toll of the raiders.

Meanwhile, other units of the Nazi air fleet of 2000 'planes are maintaining a colossal air umbrella over the reinforcements crossing the Don to the bridgehead on the north-eastern loop of the "elbow."

From here Stockholm reports say the panzers are continuing their thrust towards Dubovka, about 40 miles up-stream from Stalingrad, apparently apprehensive of the cost of a frontal assault and planning to by-pass the city and strike at it from the rear.

Bitter Soviet resistance is slowing up the German advance from Kachalinsk, but the Germans are slowly deepening their wedge on the east bank of the Don.

In the south-west, about 50 miles from Stalingrad, the Russians are reported to have isolated and destroyed advanced units of the German panzer wedge.

But the Germans are continuing their violent attacks, and, despite heroic resistance, further progress must be expected in this sector.

TIMO WAITING

Generally, it is apparent that the Soviet position at Stalingrad is slowly deteriorating.

Only a large-scale frontal counter-offensive by Marshal Timoshenko's reserves can halt the German assault. Though no signs of this are so far visible, it may yet come.

It is quite possible, as was the case at Moscow, that the Russians are waiting until the Germans and their vassals have been bled white against the fortifications covering the approaches to the city before they launch their counter-blows

There is little precise news of the position in the North Caucasus and Kuban regions, though it is clear that the Germans are still advancing.

PORTS UNDER FIRE

Unconfirmed reports say that the Black Sea port of Anapa is already under German artillery fire and that Novorossisk naval base is seriously menaced by a German column striking from Krymskaya.

German pressure at Prokhladaya has been held during the past 24 hours, but Red Army troops there are outnumbered by the Germans, who are using strong panzer units.

Battles have been going on around two populated points, one of which is an important town.

Latest despatches say that the enemy is attempting to throw pontoon bridges across the Terek River, which indicates that the main direction of their advance is still towards the Grozny oilfields, 80 miles from the river bend.

Stalingrad Prepares for Siege —Page 4

Stalin Starts Offensive

A LATE Moscow flash message announces that Soviet troops on the Central and Kalinin fronts have passed to the offensive.

They have driven the Germans back between 30 and 50 miles.—Reuter.

NEW "CONVOY CARRIERS"

"Daily Record" Air Correspondent

American naval men are full of praise for the new "convoy carriers" which are being launched in the U.S. at an amazing rate.

These air carriers, many of which are in commission, are converted merchantmen, with a smoke-stack at one side. They are powerfully-gunned and can give a good account of themselves amongst attacking aircraft or sea raiders.

Each accommodates about 30 fighters. This is impressive when compared with the British aircraft-carrier Eagle, recently sunk, which carried 20 aircraft. In time a convoy-carrier will accompany every merchant convoy in dangerous waters.

17 Rioters Killed

Lucknow, Wednesday.

Seventeen rioters were killed in an exchange of fire between an armed gang and a patrol in United Provinces, it was officially announced to-night.—Reuter.

Big Jap Attack Repulsed

Washington, Wednesday.

A BIG Jap attack on Guadalcanal in the Solomons has been repulsed, and the situation is regarded as encouraging, says a U.S. Navy Department communique to-night.

The Japs are suffering very heavy losses. Six small ships were hit and 12 'planes brought down.

"It is still too early to estimate the outcome of the battle at sea being fought off the Solomon Islands, says the communique, "but reports to date disclose that the U.S. forces at Guadalcanal are holding their positions in face of strong enemy thrusts and in each action have inflicted heavy damage on the attacking Japanese forces.

"The performance of our fighter aircraft based on Guadacanal has been outstanding.

CRUISER ABLAZE

"As previously reported a strong enemy air attack on Guadacanal during the afternoon of August 23 was intercepted by these fighters.

"Twenty-one enemy 'planes were shot down. Our loss was three 'planes."

First Axis reference to the Solomons battle came from Berlin when the German News Agency confirmed a Washington announcement that a Jap cruiser was burning fiercely.

It was also claimed that an American heavy cruiser had been sunk.

ADVERTISER'S ANNOUNCEMENT

YOU'LL FEEL BETTER WHEN YOU'VE HAD A GUINNESS

GUINNESS IS GOOD FOR YOU

G.E.1107 H

1942

SCOT SURVIVES ROYAL CRASH

THE ROYAL FAMILY was in mourning in August following the death of The Duke of Kent who was killed along with thirteen aircrew when the Sunderland flying boat in which he was travelling crashed on a lonely hillside in the north of Scotland.

And more than 24 hours after the Duke's death was announced came the dramatic news that a survivor had been found.

Flight Sergeant Andrew Simpson Wilson from Grangemouth had been the Sunderland's rear gunner and he had been thrown clear of the aircraft on impact. Although he was not seriously hurt in the crash, suffering only minor burns, he was in a dazed state when he was eventually found by crofters. He had wandered away from the crash site and had roamed the hills in a confused state for the best part of a day.

The crash had been heard over a wide area and crofters David Morrison and his son Hugh were the first on the scene. The aircraft had hit the hillside with terrific force and wreckage was spread over a wide area.

The Morrisons found some of the victims in the smouldering wreckage while others had been thrown some distance away from it. No survivors had been expected.

The Duke, the youngest brother of King George VI, had been on board the aircraft heading for Iceland where he was due to inspect air training facilities. A keen pilot since the 1930s, the Duke had joined the RAF in 1940 and regularly made unpublicised trips across the Atlantic and elsewhere to visit training schools in his role as welfare officer. His body was brought down from the hills and taken to Dunrobin Castle. Draped in the RAF flag, his coffin was then taken by train to London for a private burial.

SERVICEMEN JUMP TO THE RESCUE

Soldiers, sailors and airmen going home on leave leapt from a crashed train in January to help rescue victims of the collision. They helped bring out more than 30 people from the Edinburgh to Glasgow express after it ran into a light engine at Eastfield, Springburn – but 11 people died in the smash. The first three coaches of the train were wrecked and a broken rail burst through the bottom of the tender. The train had been slowing down as it approached the Cowlairs tunnel, otherwise the fatalities could have been higher. Polish soldiers from another train also helped rescuers.

ON RADIO

Desert Island Discs

The Radio Doctor

COMINGS...

Billy Connolly
Actor & Comedian

John Greig
Footballer

John Bellany
Artist

FUEL WASTE ILLEGAL

From June it became an offence to waste fuel through its excessive or inappropriate use, including advertisements, in shop window lighting and for show cases. Government-appointed inspectors were given the right to inspect premises to test the use of fuel.

● Men under 33 who are being

DE-RESERVED

The **RAF** needs you for flying duties

Get yourself one of the finest of all fighting jobs — fly as a pilot or observer in the R.A.F.

Even if you didn't express a preference for flying duties with the R.A.F. when you registered with your age group for National Service, you can do so now, provided you have not yet been posted to any other Service. *Make your decision now. Volunteer for flying duties at the R.A.F. Section of your nearest Combined Recruiting Centre (address below), or post the coupon below for full details.* (Unsealed envelope — 1d. stamp.)

To Air Ministry Information Bureau, Kingsway, London, W.C.2.
Please send " Flying Duties" leaflet.

AGE.................

NAME.................

ADDRESS.................

GW 51/2/1.

JOIN THE R.A.F. AT GLASGOW
St. Mungo Grand Hall, Moffat Street

THIS SPORTING LIFE

FOOTBALL	RUGBY UNION	GOLF	HORSE RACING	SHINTY
Scottish Champions No competition held	*Scotland vs England* No game played	*British Open Winner* No competition held	*Scottish Grand National Winner* No race run	*Camanachd Cup Winners* No competition held
Scottish Cup Winners No competition held				

Brightens the Black-out!
WILLIAM YOUNGERS BEER

Daily Record
and Mail.

EST. 1847—No. 30,190   RADIO—Page 7   TUESDAY, OCTOBER 26, 1943   BLACK-OUT—Back Page   ONE PENNY   F

"BLACK & WHITE"
ITS THE SCOTCH

★

"Suddenly Mrs. Galloway saw him."

Mrs. Galloway Greets Her Boy

At first, Mrs. Galloway couldn't see him. Perhaps her excitement was blinding her, but eagerly as she scanned every face she admitted with heavy heart that her boy wasn't there. She had come from her home in Perth—at 6 Tulloch Street —to greet him.

She clutched the hand of Mrs. Moncrieff, who also had come from Perth to see a son. Together they watched, sharing each other's disappointment and then—

Suddenly Mrs. Galloway saw George and flung herself forward through the protecting cordon round the station into his arms. "I thought I'd get into trouble afterwards for breaking through," she said, ' 'but I don't think they could blame me.

"I DID NOT BELIEVE IT"

" My son was expected in the original mercy ship which did not sail, and I did not believe until this moment that he was really coming this time."

Young George Galloway himself was radiant. He has lost his right hand, but does not mind since it has brought him home before the end of the war.

There were several hours more of waiting for Mrs. Moncrieff and in the end it was her daughter who spotted young Alec as he was carrying his kitbag up the platform.

At first Mrs. Moncrieff could not speak and then she said: "He was only 18 when he went away and a man has come home."

London: Brief Alert

AN alert of brief duration sounded in London early last night. There were several short bursts of gunfire in one district.

Enemy aircraft flew over the London outskirts but made off after several bursts of gunfire. No bombs were dropped.

High explosives fell in one district in South-East England. Slight damage was caused, but no casualties were reported.

GRAND NEWS

" I spoke to the son of Mr. Lindsay, the minister, and Mr. Ross, the fishmonger. It will be grand news for them when we get back to-night," said Mrs. Galloway.

123 JAP PLANES DESTROYED

General MacArthur's communique this morning stated that Allied planes destroyed 123 Japanese planes at Rabaul over the week-end.—B.U.P.

Last Ashore Was Baby In Great Homecoming

It was a great home-coming. That was the verdict of the 3694 prisoners and internees who disembarked at Leith, yesterday.

Last night, when the tumult of welcome was over, the youngest and the oldest of the internees were the last to come ashore— eleven-weeks old Baby Sandall and 76-year-old Frederick Oates,: of Bradford.

" Everyone has been so kind to us since we left the enemy," said a woman returning to friends.

Disembarkation began before dawn and was completed under flood-lighting.

Special Pictures and Stories—Pages 4, 5 and 6

RED ARMY TRAP CLOSING SWIFTLY

DNEPROPETROVSK TAKEN BY STORM

Moscow, Monday.

DNEPROPETROVSK, SOVIET " CITY OF STEEL AND IRON," AND THE LAST GERMAN POSITION IN THE NORTH-EASTERN CORNER OF THE VAST DNIEPER " ELBOW," WAS TAKEN BY STORM BY THE RED ARMY TO-DAY.

Marshal Stalin, calling for a salute from the Moscow garrison of twenty salvos from 224 guns, disclosed this dramatic extension of the base of the Kremenchug bridgehead in an Order of the Day broadcast to-night.

His Order also announced the fall of Dneprodzherhinsk-Kamenskoye, 20 miles west of Dnepropetrovsk, on the south bank of the river.

The fall of these towns means that the base of the big bridgehead smashed across the Dnieper for 80 miles towards Krivoi Rog, in the heart of the river bend, is now nearly 90 miles in length.

AT DISASTER POINT

It means also the collapse of the German position on the river " elbow " where the loss of Melitopol and Dnepropetrovsk within the last 48 hours intensifies to disaster point the danger created for the Germans by the fall of Zaporozhe some days before.

The road is open now for a drive along the southward road to the great manganese city of Nikopol, opposite Zaporozhe, whence the last German " escape " railway from the bend swings to the south-west.

To the west the line is already threatened by the armoured spearheads' fresh penetration of three to five miles towards Krivoi Rog, whose last defences are now being hammered.

May Be Trapped

The German left flank in the Dnieper bend is evidently falling back as fast as it can, presumably pivoting on Krivoi Rog, writes a military correspondent.

It is probable that a considerable portion of the garrison was trapped by the various Soviet converging movements, as the only path of escape was across country and was threatened from north and south.

In any case, the congestion on all these roads running west and south-west must be embarrassing for the Germans and provide a marvellous target for the Russian bombers.

Continued on Back Page—Col. 4

ADVERTISER'S ANNOUNCEMENT

EYES AT WAR

WAR-TIME conditions are hard on your eyes. Long working hours in office and factory or out in the wind, impose a strain upon them. They grow red with fatigue. They feel heavy. Dust gets into them and provokes inflammation. *Look after your eyes—they are precious.* Soothe and relieve them by the daily use of 'Valopto', the scientifically prepared antiseptic eye lotion. It takes but a minute to bathe your eyes with 'Valopto'. Its gentle refreshing antiseptic action keeps your eyes fighting fit. It is safe and beneficial for everybody's eyes. The regular use of ' Valopto' relieves and prevents conjunctivitis, blepharitis, inflamed eyelids, styes and watery eyes.

How do I use ' Valopto' ?

First cleanse eyelids with cotton wool soaked in the lotion (use fresh piece for each eye). Then fill eyebath one third full of 'Valopto.' Apply to eye with head tilted back, keeping eyelids open. Try a 'Valopto' eye bath *to-day*—see how much better your eyes feel right away. *Your doctor should be consulted if you have the slightest reason to suspect serious eye trouble.* At all chemists 2/- a bottle (inc. tax).

VALOPTO
REGD BRAND
Eye Lotion

FOR TIRED EYES

DAE HEALTH LABORATORIES LTD., 25/27 Berners Street, London, W.1

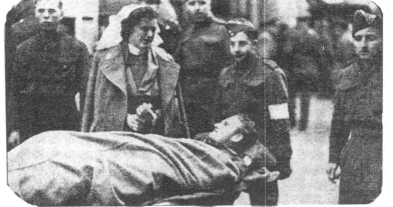

A stretcher case is brought ashore, gently, tenderly, and all who see him wish him in their hearts a sure and speedy recovery.

1943

WOUNDED JOCKS REPATRIATED

A MERCY ship docked at Leith in October bringing home almost 3700 wounded prisoners of war and civilian internees from the clutches of the Nazis.

The repatriation ship had sailed from Gothenburg in neutral Sweden and the troops had been taken there by rail in cattle trucks from prison camps across Poland and Germany.

Many of the men came from the 51st Highland Division who had been captured after the fall of St Valery in France in 1940.

Also on board were a number of Australian and New Zealand troops.

As the ship docked at the Edinburgh port, shipyard workers downed tools and cheered and sirens and hooters were sounded throughout the docks.

The reception sheds were hung with flags and bunting and military and pipe bands played a medley as the men disembarked.

The men started coming ashore at daybreak and they were still disembarking under floodlight into the evening while their relatives waited anxiously to catch a glimpse of their loved ones on the boat or on the quayside. The oldest – a 76-year-old civilian from Bradford – and the youngest – an 11-week-old baby – were the last to leave the ship.

The women of the WVS and other voluntary groups were on hand to make the new arrivals feel welcome and comfortable. While most of the soldiers were categorised as "walking wounded", there were many whose injuries had been so serious that they came ashore on stretchers.

From Leith, trains took the men to hospitals across Scotland and south of the border.

BATTLING THE SCOURGE OF TB

Mass radiography outfits were to be established in Scotland to combat the growing menace of tuberculosis in the country. Although in the period between the two world wars the tuberculosis figures had been cut in half, there had been a reversal of that position in the years from 1939 to 1943. In this period, the figure had risen by 40 per cent. Aberdeen's increase was a massive 64 per cent and Glasgow's increase was 35 per cent.

In March 1943, it was reported that there were 800 more TB beds than in the pre-war years. In addition, there were a further 650 cases waiting to be dealt with. In response to this, the Department of Health was arranging for another 800 beds to be provided. Three mass radiography outfits were also to be made available to enable the disease to be more easily diagnosed in its early stages.

The Department of Health referred to the serious shortage of nurses. There was an urgent need for at least 250 new nurses for the tuberculosis hospitals.

The Department of Health also attacked the economic motive discouraging the early notification of TB. To date in 1943, there had been no scheme of financial assistance to dependants. To correct this, a scheme was to be introduced to enable local authorities to pay allowances to a breadwinner who had to enter a TB hospital

KING'S FLYING VISIT

King George paid a visit to Scotland in February and spent the day inspecting troops and watching them train. The visit was meant to have been a surprise, yet children appeared in the streets with Union Jacks – one of those "well-kept" official secrets that often leak out. Some of the troops were caught on the hop, however. The King was often cheered by soldiers in battle dress … side by side with others wearing gym shorts.

ON RADIO	
Sunday Half Hour	Radio Newsreel
Hi, Gang!	Saturday Night Theatre
Music While You Work	Dance While You Dust

THIS SPORTING LIFE

FOOTBALL	RUGBY UNION	GOLF	HORSE RACING	SHINTY
Scottish Champions	Scotland vs England	British Open Winner	Scottish Grand National Winner	Camanachd Cup Winners
No competition held	No game played	No competition held	No race run	No competition held
Scottish Cup Winners				
No competition held				

FAMOUS FOR NEARLY 200 YEARS.

George Younger's

Alloa BEER

Daily and Mail. Record

EST. 1847—No. 30,382   RADIO—Page 7   WEDNESDAY, JUNE 7, 1944   BLACK-OUT—Back Page   ONE PENNY   F

GOURLAY'S for TYPEWRITERS
AT REASONABLE PRICES
44 ST. VINCENT PLACE
GLASGOW C.1
PHONE: CENTRAL 7944-5
BUY SELL or EXCHANGE

S.H.A.E.F. Communique No. 2.

23.30 Hours, June 6.

Shortly before midnight on 5th June, 1944, Allied night bombers opened the assault. Their attacks in very great strength continued until dawn.

MINEFIELDS SWEPT

The naval forces, which had previously assembled under the over-all command of Admiral Sir Bertram Ramsay, made their departure in fresh weather and were joined during the night by bombarding forces which had previously left northern waters. Channels had to be swept through the large enemy minefields

This operation was completed shortly before dawn, and, while mine-sweeping flotillas continued to sweep towards the

LATEST COMMUNIQUE

enemy coast, the entire naval force followed down swept channels behind them towards their objectives.

Shortly before the assault three enemy torpedo boats with armed trawlers in company attempted to interfere with the operation and were promptly driven off. One enemy trawler was sunk and another severely damaged.

The assault forces moved towards the beaches under cover of heavy bombardment from destroyers and other support craft while heavier ships engaged enemy batteries which had already been subjected to bombardment from the air.

Some of these were silenced. Allied forces continued to engage other batteries. Landings were effected under cover of the air and naval bombardments and airborne landings involv-

ing troop-carrying aircraft and gliders carrying large forces of troops were also made successfully at a number of points.

Reports of operations so far show that our forces succeeded in their initial landings Fighting continues

Allied heavy, medium and light and fighter bombers continued the air bombardment in very great strength throughout the day with attacks on gun emplacements, defensive works and communications

CONTINUOUS COVER

Continuous fighter cover was maintained over the beaches and for some distance inland and over naval operations

Allied reconnaissance aircraft maintained continuous watch by day and night over shipping and ground forces.

Our aircraft met with little enemy fighter opposition or anti-aircraft gunfire.

Naval casualties were regarded as being very light.

LANDINGS ON 100-MILE FRONT ARE REPORTED

Germans Say Paratroops Of Both Sides Are Battling West Of Le Havre

First day of the Allied assault on the Western "Wall" has gone well. A communique from Allied Supreme Headquarters at midnight announced: "Reports of operations so far show that our forces succeeded in their initial landings." These landings, according to German accounts, are taking place at a series of points extending over a 100 miles line from Cherbourg to Le Havre.

According to a German news agency report shortly after the midnight communique the Allies now hold bridgeheads on both sides of the Orne estuary, roughly midway between Cherbourg and Le Havre and further west in the area north-west of Bayeux.

A small Allied group consisting of light tanks and armoured scout cars now stands a few kilometres in the dunes north-east of Bayeux and is trying to establish contact with the main bridgehead, according to the Germans.

FIGHTING 10 MILES INLAND

Allied paratroops have been dropped on the road between Carentan and Valognes-Cherbourg-Paris road, said Paris Radio last night. "Very heavy fighting is going on here," the radio said.

Mr. Churchill reported to the House of Commons last night that landings along the whole front have been effective and that fighting is taking place in the town of Caen, ten miles inland.

At Allied H.Q. the invasion army was stated to be "over the first four or five hurdles" in its tremendous opening task in the liberation of Europe.

The Allied troops went in at dawn yesterday under the greatest air umbrella in history and got on to the beaches without the coastal defences proving nearly as effective as was expected.

The Luftwaffe made only 50 sorties in reply to the Allies' devastating air blow, in which over 10,000 bombs were hurled by the R.A.F. at the German defences between midnight and 8 a.m., and 7000 sorties flown by all armadas supporting our ground troops during the day.

Airborne troops engaged in the biggest parachute descent in military history suffered little loss and are now established.

Losses among the huge naval armada which accompanied the invaders have been "very very light."

Air and ground battles between Allied and German paratroops took place yesterday afternoon west of Le Havre, according to Berlin.

"PARIS SIEGE"

Several British and Canadian battalions of paratroops and airborne troops in gliders were being landed when German gliders landed German paratroops. Heavy fighting took place partly while the men were still in the air, said the radio.

The German Overseas News Agency said last night: "Un-
Continued on Back Page, Col. 1.

INVASION PICTURES
Pages 3, 4, 5, and 8

In looking at this map of the invasion areas, the southern English coast is behind you

Greatest Air Armada Out Again Last Night

THE greatest air armada of the war was crossing the East Coast for two hours yesterday evening.

The thunder of the first wave of heavy bombers flying south-east brought people running into the streets from their tea tables and stampeded cattle.

The armada continued without a moment's respite as fighters and heavy bombers flew out in a dozen streams simultaneously in every part of the sky.

"It dwarfs anything we have ever known here," said an observer on the coast. "It is like all the heavy night attacks of the last few weeks put into one."

First German Prisoners

FIRST German prisoners and first casualties to reach a British port were landed late yesterday afternoon, states a correspondent representing the combined American press.

They belonged to the 352nd infantry division, holding the sector between Isigny and Bayeux and to the 21st panzer division from the Caen sector, it was stated.

"5th" Beyond Ostia

Allied H.Q., Italy.

Allied troops advancing south of Rome advanced beyond the Tiber at all points and cleared Ostia harbour.

See Story—Page 6

Weather Worry

WEATHER is still biggest worry of invasion, reports Reuter's correspondent. A strong north-west wind shows no sign of moderating.

It will not halt flow of reinforcements, but an improvement would make the operation very much easier.

Threat To French

THE Commander of the German forces in France last night broadcast this order to the people of France:

German troops have been given the order to shoot at any person who is seen to be co-operating with the Allied invasion forces or who gives shelter to Allied soldiers, sailors or airmen.

Frenchmen who co-operate with Allied troops will be treated as bandits.

—And Appeal

Radio France (Algiers) addressed this appeal to the French police and gendarmerie last night.

Policemen, gendarmes, and members of the Garde Mobile join the Patriot forces with all your equipment.

Police officers and prison wardens, political prisoners are in your charge. When opportunity presents itself, open the doors and let them go!

U.S. BOMB GALATZ

Scores of U.S. heavy bombers heavily escorted by fighters, took off from the American Heavy Bomber Base in the Soviet Union yesterday, and roared over the Soviet-German front to shower many tons of high explosive and incendiary bombs on aerodrome installations at Galatz.

Saw 100 Gliders 15 Miles In

TANKS MOVING ON CAEN

From LAWRENCE FAIRHALL, "Daily Record" Air correspondent with the Allied Expeditionary Air Forces in England.

Tuesday Night.

THE Air Vice-Marshal this afternoon visited airfields under his command and spoke to Typhoon pilots who have been flying over the invasion beaches since dawn this morning.

He heard first-hand stories of how the Luftwaffe has failed to put up any resistance to the great fleets of Allied aircraft which have kept up a day-long offensive against targets in the invasion zone.

Two high-flying ME's were the only enemy aircraft which have so far been reported over the landing areas. One of these, after finding itself flying in the middle of some Spitfires, shot up into the clouds and was lost.

We Hold Beaches

Flying Officer F. M. Botting, a Canadian, reported seeing a number of gliders lying in a big field.

"The field was about 10 to 15 miles inland, and I saw somewhere between 50 and 100 gliders lying all over the ground," he added.

R.A.F. pilots who had been flying at low level over the fronts all day told me this evening that they saw our tanks moving on Caen, ten miles up the River Orne.

"In the area inland we saw several fires which may have been petrol dumps going up," they said.

When we left after our last sorties we could see no enemy infantry at this point near the coast."

There was no longer any opposition on the beaches, which were in our hands.

Lack of Opposition

The lack of air opposition was fantastic, they added.

"We saw our ships closing in on the beaches as we went over the French coast. When we turned at the end of our patrols and were over them again a few minutes later we could see them already unloading supplies which were moving off from the beaches inland almost as we watched.

"The whole business from the
Continued On Back Page—Col. 4

"WE ARE HERE NOW," SHOUTED PARATROOPS AT LE HAVRE

From CYRIL MARSHALL, "Daily Record" Special Correspondent.

Stockholm, Tuesday.

"WE are here now!" shouted Allied paratroops as their feet touched ground at Le Havre, and the same shout came from more of them as they reached the earth at Caen, according to a Berlin report.

The paratroopers immedi-

ately started shooting, putting up a barrage behind which they tried to get possession of a number of concrete forts.

In this, the Berlin report says, they were not successful, but they managed to entrench themselves and the greater part of them resisted death or capture until other Allied troops, coming by sea, landed and joined them.

Berlin opinion is that Eisen-

hower's aim is to drive straight for Paris if he succeeds in establishing strong beach-heads The places chosen for landing, in the neighbourhood of Caen, in the region between the mouths of the rivers Orne and Vire, give rise to this opinion.

Big paratroop formations which landed west of Le Havre and near Boulogne are supposed to have had for their task, the luring of large

numbers of German troops from the landing beaches but the Germans claim that the ruse was not successful.

"Dummies"

It is reported that German divisions have been locked in fierce combat since the morning with both paratroops and disembarked troops.

One Berlin report says that parachute troops were made to

appear more numerous by the sending down of life-sized dummies.

Large German air forces have been dispatched to the scenes of the landings and are hotly engaged with Allied naval and air forces.

Later Berlin reports declare that there were 12 landing places and that the Allies penetrated three miles inland at three or four points.

1944

TROOPS BATTER GERMAN 'WALL'

THE first day of the Allied forces D-Day assault on the Germans' European "Western Wall" in June went well.

A communiqué from the Allied Supreme Headquarters announced:

"Reports of operations so far show that our forces succeeded in their initial landings."

These landings, according to German accounts, took place at a series of points extending over a 100-mile line from Cherbourg to Le Harve.

The German news agency reported that the Allies held bridgeheads on both sides of the Orne estuary.

These were roughly midway between Cherbourg and Le Harve and further west in the area north-west of Bayeux. The Prime Minister, Winston Churchill, reported to the House of Commons that the landings along the whole front in France had been effective and that fighting had taken place in the town of Caen, 10 miles inland.

At Allied HQ, the invasion army was stated to be "over the first four or five hurdles" in its tremendous opening task in the liberation of Europe.

The Allied troops went in at dawn on June 6 under the greatest air "umbrella" in history.

And they got on to the beaches without the massive German coastal defences proving nearly as effective as had been expected. The Luftwaffe made only 50 sorties in reply to the Allies' devastating air blow.

More than 10,000 bombs were hurled by the RAF at the German defences between midnight and 8 am.

And 7000 sorties were flown by air armadas supporting the ground forces during the day.

Airborne troops engaged in the biggest parachute descent in military history and suffered little loss.

The losses at sea had been less than feared and the resistance of enemy batteries had been greatly weakened by bombings from war planes and ships.

By nightfall, the Prime Minister revealed, the Allied forces had penetrated several miles inland on a broad front.

SCOTS SURGEON HERO

Surgeon-Lieutenant Maurice Hood from Glasgow made the supreme sacrifice in March while saving the life of a US seaman. Lieut. Hood had transferred to the American freighter to attend to the sailor who was suffering from acute appendicitis. He elected to stay with him to tend him rather than return to his own ship and shortly afterwards, the freighter was sunk by torpedoes. Lieut. Hood was not amongst the survivors. Lieut. Hood had previously won the Distinguished Service Cross for a similar selfless act in helping to tend a large number of men wounded in action.

SCOTS FRONT THE NORMANDY BREAKOUT

Scots troops were at the forefront of the Allies' push out of Normandy. Late in June, Scottish infantry and armoured units were in action seizing vital bridges over the River Odon. The fighting around Granville and Mondranville was particularly hard against strong enemy defensive positions but, inspired by the pipers leading them into the battles, the Scots had managed to establish and secure an important corridor through the Odon defences.

ON RADIO

Variety Bandbox

D-Day War Report

Up In The Morning Early

Tunes of the Town

Garrison Theatre

COMINGS...

Margot Macdonald
Nationalist Politician

Jimmy Johnstone
Celtic Footballer

THIS SPORTING LIFE

FOOTBALL	RUGBY UNION	GOLF	HORSE RACING	SHINTY
Scottish Champions No competition held	*Scotland vs England* No game played	*British Open Winner* No competition held	*Scottish Grand National Winner* No race run	*Camanachd Cup Winners* No competition held
Scottish Cup Winners No competition held				

GEORGE YOUNGER'S ALLOA BEER

Daily ✠ Record
and Mail.

EST. 1847—No. 30,669   1d   WEDNESDAY, MAY 9, 1945   A KEMSLEY NEWSPAPER

Carnival Spirit For "Last All Clear"

On the balcony at the Palace, the Royal Family greets the cheering crowds.

VICTORY, BUT JAPS REMAIN

IN their speeches yesterday both His Majesty the King and Mr. Churchill drew attention to the tasks that lie ahead.

The King said: "In the Far East we have yet to deal with the Japanese, a determined, cruel foe. To this we shall turn with the utmost resolve and with all our resources."

Mr. Churchill declared: "Japan remains unsubdued. The injury she has inflicted on Great Britain, the U.S. and other countries call for justice and retribution. We must now devote all our strength and resources to the completion of our task."

Much hard work awaits us, both in the restoration of our own country after the ravages of war, and in helping to restore peace and sanity to a shattered world.

This comes upon us at a time when we have all given of our best. For five long years and more, heart and brain, nerve and muscle, have been directed upon the overthrow of Nazi tyranny. Now we turn, fortified by success, to deal with our last remaining foe.

King's Speech Page 2
Mr. Churchill Page 4

EDINBURGH WILL SEE THE KING

THE KING AND QUEEN, accompanied by Princess Elizabeth and Princess Margaret Rose, will visit Edinburgh on Wednesday, May 16, and will attend a service of thanksgiving in St. Giles' Cathedral.

The visit is for one day only. London had its opportunity to cheer the King yesterday when crowds stood outside the Palace.

When Mr. Churchill had finished the King appeared smiling and radiantly happy.

VE-NIGHT OF JOY IN GLASGOW

Mr. Churchill

*L*IKE a European city on the eve of liberation, Glasgow went daft with joy last night. Victory celebrations were still in full swing in the early hours of this morning as thousands of happy citizens, hundreds left with no means of transport, made their way home.

Royal Family Hailed As They Bow From Palace Balcony

THE KING AND QUEEN, PRINCESS ELIZABETH and PRINCESS MARGARET stood in the sunshine on the balcony of Buckingham Palace yesterday. Beneath them were thousands upon thousands of their cheering people.

That picture was a symbol and emblem of the Empire's VE-Day rejoicings, which had culminated in the Prime Minister's broadcast of the end of the war in Europe.

Mr. Churchill had said, "We may allow ourselves a brief period of rejoicing"—the people were seeing to that already, "but let us not forget for a moment the toil and efforts that lie ahead," he warned.

Buckingham Palace and Whitehall were the magnets which drew multitudes of people.

They saw the Prime Minister go to lunch with Their Majesties at the Palace before making his historic pronouncement.

—And Again

They saw him again when, with the members of the War Cabinet and Chiefs of Staff, he was received by the King some hours later to receive his congratulations on victory.

All day Londoners, reinforced by many from the provinces, and by Service men and women of all nationalities had given a full rein to their rejoicing.

The King and Queen came on to the balcony again just before half-past midnight. A few minutes later the floodlights were switched off and gradually the crowds disappeared.

Police estimated that there were more than a quarter of a million people within a quarter mile of the Palace last night.

Garlanded with twinkling, coloured fairy lights, George Square was packed with crowds such as it has never seen before.

Nearly 100,000 people jostled, sang, danced, whistled, shouted, leapt on to passing buses, cars, taxicabs, tramcars, and formed "human chains" to guide them through the milling throng.

VE-NIGHT DELIGHT

Tramcars and buses were jammed. There were only inches to move around in. Men, women and children went delirious with pent-up VE-Night delight.

Almost one-tenth of Glasgow had come to George Square.

Young men and girls climbed on to statues to watch the historic scene. Gaily-clad in coloured paper hats, waving streamers, Union Jacks and Allied flags, the great Glasgow public "went to town" in real Victory spirit.

The police were not "kill-joys." They warned a few people who were climbing dangerously high upon the Square's statues, but watched with benevolent eye two sailors on an air raid shelter throwing cigarettes with magnificent prodigality to the crowd beneath them.

And everywhere among the throng were the flag and favour sellers. Whatever else ran short in the city, their stocks seemed endless.

DANCE AND SONG

Where they could find room people danced eightsome reels and couples jitterbugged to the music that echoed through the square. Servicemen led rival groups in community singing.

A Dutch marine drew a large crowd in Exchange Square.

Perched on the equestrian statue in front of the Royal Exchange, he began with an imitation of Hitler, addressing a mob.

Then, in serious vein, he thanked the British people for all they had done for the Dutch, with a special tribute to Scots folk who had received them so kindly into their midst. He got a rousing cheer.

I watched the scene from a

Continued on Back Page, Col. 2

DANCING ON THE STREETS
Kemsley House The Mecca

*K*EMSLEY HOUSE, in Hope Street, Glasgow, was the Mecca of Glasgow's VE-Day celebrations, last night.

"The Daily Record" and "Evening News" provided the music from loud speakers wired along the gaily decorated and illuminated facade of the building, and the joyous crowd did the rest.

For hours they danced—not your master of ceremonied ballroom stuff, but real hard reeling and jigging on the tram lines. If the music was suitable, the crowd danced to it in rings or long wriggling lines; if it was not suitable, they just danced to their own yelling.

Pipe Music

But to see the crowd of sailors, soldiers, airmen, W.A.A.F.s, A.T.S., Wrens and "civvies" of all types go really crackers you had to be there when the loud speakers gave out the pipe music, especially the reels.

Usually the dancers made way for the trams, buses and private vehicles good naturedly.

But not when there was an eightsome in the air. Glasgow, especially Hope Street, belonged to them so long as that music was on.

As the night went on the dancing became more and more hilarious.

Couples, especially sailors, even jumped on the drivers' platforms of cars and danced

No 'Daily Record' To-morrow

IN accordance with the expressed desire of the Government that workers generally should enjoy a VE-Day's holiday the "Daily Record" will not be published to-morrow, but will be out as usual on Friday.

The "Evening News" has its holiday to-day but reappears to-morrow.

The "Sunday Mail" will be published as usual.

A midnight flash: outside Kemsley House, and the cheering, dancing crowds are still there. Other pictures of scenes outside Kemsley House are on Pages 4 and 5.

GOING DAFT AT VICTORY PARTY

LIKE a European city that has just been liberated, Glasgow went daft with joy as victory celebrations were in full swing to celebrate VE-Day.

Almost one tenth of the city went to George Square.

Some 100,000 people were jostling good-naturedly, singing, dancing, leaping on to passing buses, cars, taxis, tramcars and forming human chains to guide them through the milling throng.

The square, decked with garlands with twinkling coloured fairy lights, had never seen the like before.

Young men and girls climbed onto statues to watch the historic scene and waved flags as Glasgow celebrated.

Where they could find room, people danced eightsome reels and couples jitterbugged to the music that echoed through the square. Servicemen led groups in community singing.

A Dutch Marine drew a large crowd in Exchange Square, perched on the equestrian statue. He began with an imitation of Hitler addressing a Nazi rally. He then became serious and thanked the British people for all they had done for the Dutch. He paid a special tribute to Scots folk who had received them so kindly into their midst and got a rousing cheer from the crowd.

Squibs and rockets flashed through the midnight sky and bonfires left a victory glow in the morning sky. Thousands of people walked through Kelvingrove to see the floodlit Glasgow University, glowing like a symbol of light and learning.

Celebrations took place all over Scotland and throughout Britain.

Each one followed the same format, of music, dancing and festivals of colour as people dressed up and waved flags.

Church services were held to remember the dead and give thanks that the war was finally over.

Outside Kemsley House in Hope Street, Glasgow, crowds gathered to wait for Prime Minister Winston Churchill's speech and the formal announcement of VE-Day.

ATTLEE SWEEPS LABOUR INTO POWER

A sensational General Election result in July saw wartime hero Winston Churchill toppled from office and Labour's Clement Attlee take over as Prime Minister. It was a landslide victory for the Labour Party and it astonished the world as British voters opted for the radical left wing policies of Attlee and his colleagues.

COMINGS...

Aly Bain
Folk Musician

Maggie Bell
Rock Singer

Ken Buchanan
Boxer

GOINGS...

Cosmo Lang
Anglican Archbishop of Canterbury

ON RADIO

Family Favourites

World Theatre

Today in Parliament

In August, the atomic bombing of Hiroshima and Nagasaki in Japan finally brought the war to a close but in doing so ushered in a new era, the dangers and horrors of which had been so terrifyingly demonstrated with over 100,000 deaths from just two bombs.

DOWNPOUR ALMOST KOs FIGHT

Scotland's first big peace-time sporting event was almost washed out in September. Over 40,000 people braved a torrential downpour that lasted for over an hour during the Empire Bantamweight title fight between Jackie Paterson and Jim Brady at Hampden. The conditions in the ring were so atrocious that both boxers had difficulty keeping their feet. Paterson eventually won on points.

THIS SPORTING LIFE

FOOTBALL	RUGBY UNION	GOLF	HORSE RACING	SHINTY
Scottish Champions No competition held	*Scotland vs England* No game played	*British Open Winner* No competition held	*Scottish Grand National Winner* No race run	*Camanachd Cup Winners* No competition held
Scottish Cup Winners No competition held				

Bailey's
Quality Wine Merchants

GLASGOW. EDINBURGH,
PAISLEY, GREENOCK,
AYR, IRVINE. TROON.

Daily Record
and Mail.

EST. 1895—No. 15,739   1d.   MONDAY, MARCH 18, 1946   A KEMSLEY NEWSPAPER

Above them a'
LANG'S
Old Liqueur
SCOTCH WHISKY
Bottle 25/9, Half-Bottle 13/6
Maximum Prices, as fixed
by the Scotch Whisky Assoc.

Aground In Gale Off Kintyre Coast—14-Hour Ordeal

This dramatic picture of the American Liberty ship, Byron Darnton, wrecked and broken in two off the Island of Sanda, south of the Mull of Kintyre, yesterday, was taken by "Daily Record" photographer, James Morison, from a Scottish Airways plane at six o'clock last night. Flying conditions were next to impossible when the plane took off from Renfrew and battled its way south through snow and rain showers in a south-westerly gale. Fortunately there was a clear weather patch round the wreck, and the pilot was able to come down to about 200 feet to allow Morison to take this picture.

I Saw No Sign Of Life

By Eddie Campbell

"Record" Reporter

WHEN I flew over the wreck yesterday afternoon the heavy seas had completed their work of breaking up the Byron Darnton.

The vessel lay on her side on the rocky shore, her back broken just forward of midships, and the two halves separated by some fifteen or twenty feet.

The bow and stern sections had fallen over opposite sides of the rocks as the tide receded, lending to the picture of the stricken vessel, a curiously animate appearance.

In the distorted perspective of an aerial view, the ship seemed, from one angle, to be lying on the rocky base of the lighthouse.

Apart from a solitary wheeling gull, there was no sign of life on the island or on the wreck.

As we flew over the upper reaches of the North Channel, a destroyer, the H 84, and a submarine could be seen travelling north-east, away from the scene of the wreck.

The weather, which had apparently calmed slightly since the Byron Darnton ran ashore, was still wild enough to send huge breakers over the wreck.

Wavell's Son-In-Law Killed

Major the Hon. Simon Astley, son-in-law of Lord Wavell, Viceroy of India, and Lady Wavell, died on Saturday at Quetta, capital of British Baluchistan, in North-West India, as a result of a motor-car accident.

SHIP BREAKS BACK; 54 RESCUED

LESS THAN TWO HOURS AFTER THE PASSENGERS AND CREW OF THE AMERICAN LIBERTY SHIP, BYRON DARNTON, WHICH RAN AGROUND ON SANDA ISLAND, OFF THE MULL OF KINTYRE, WERE RESCUED BY THE CAMPBELTOWN LIFEBOAT YESTERDAY, THE SHIP BROKE IN TWO.

The survivors—39 of a crew and 15 passengers—were landed at Campbeltown.

Destroyers, tank landing craft, tugs, and lifeboats from Portpatrick, Girvan and Portrush had raced through heavy seas to assist in the rescue—only to find that the Campbeltown lifeboat, which had set out for Sanda just before midnight on Saturday, had succeeded in taking the survivors on board.

RAN INTO STORM

The Byron Darnton (7000 tons) was inward bound from Copenhagen when, late on Saturday night, she ran into a storm of rain and sleet.

Visibility had fallen to a few yards and a gale was rising when the vessel ran aground on Sanda, a small island which lies some two miles to the south of the Mull of Kintyre.

First indications of a ship in
Continued on Back Page, Col. 3

Slammed Door On Gunmen

LATE last night a Glasgow man opened the door of his house at 447 Sauchiehall Street in answer to the bell, and was confronted by three men.

"Give him the works," shouted one of the trio, as a gun was thrust at the body of the occupant, Mr. J. Harvey.

Mr. Harvey, who is well-known in greyhound circles, immediately slammed the door in their faces, at which the trio ran down the stairs.

Early this morning detectives of the Central and Marine Divisions were searching for the men.

Princess At Greenock

Princess Elizabeth left Euston last night on the 9.20 express for Glasgow.

She will embark at Greenock to-day for Belfast, where she is to launch the new aircraft carrier H.M.S. Eagle to-morrow.

New Air Service: Prestwick To N.Y.

From CLIFFORD HULME, "Daily Record" Special Correspondent
New York, Sunday.

PIONEERING a Prestwick-New York air service, a Liberator owned by the Scottish Aviation Company, carrying the Duke of Hamilton, Mr. Walter Elliot, Captain David M'Intyre and an all-Scottish crew of five, arrived here this morning three hours ahead of schedule after an uneventful journey in excellent weather.

Flying time was 16 hours with one halt in Iceland.

Mr. Elliot, whose first Atlantic flight it was, told me the company plans a charter service by the northern route, using for a start two passenger planes and one freighter. He said the Icelanders showed keen interest.

On the return flight, beginning April 26, Mr. Elliot will take back his wife who is at present in Canada. Meanwhile he will visit Canada

FOSTER CLARK'S SOUPS

are first class soups

OXTAIL   KIDNEY
GREEN PEA   TOMATO

54 SAVED BY LIFEBOAT HEROES

THE American liberty ship, *Byron Darnton*, was inward bound from Copenhagen when, late on March 16, she ran into a violent storm of rain and sleet.

Visibility had fallen to a few yards and a gale was rising when the vessel ran aground on the island of Sanda, which lies some two miles south of the Mull of Kintyre.

First indications of the ship's distress signals were seen by a coastguard at Southend, near Campbeltown.

The rescue services immediately swung into operation and within an hour, the Campbeltown lifeboat was on its way out to the scene.

Some 54 passengers and crew of the *Byron Darnton* endured a 14-hour ordeal before they were finally taken aboard the lifeboat.

For hours, the lifeboat men fought against the mountainous seas and increasingly hazardous conditions, but in the end they succeeded in their bid to take the crew and passengers on board.

Crammed into the lifeboat, the survivors – 39 crew and 15 passengers – presented a bedraggled appearance when they stepped ashore at Campbeltown.

They had all lost their belongings.

Passengers and crew of the *Byron Darnton* were warm in their praise of the courage of the lifeboat crew.

Less than two hours after the rescue, the ship broke in two and sank.

COMINGS...

Bill Forsyth
Film Director

Robin Cook
Labour Politician

GOINGS...

John Logie Baird
Inventor of the TV

AIR AMBULANCE TRAGEDY

A Royal Navy air ambulance plane flying out of Abbotsinch Airport near Glasgow and carrying a crew of three plus a doctor and a patient crashed into a mountain in September. Everyone in the aircraft was killed. The wreckage of the plane, which had been heading for Stretton, Warrington, was found on Mickledore Crag on the west side of the highest peak in England, 3210ft Scafell Pike in Cumberland. It was reckoned that if the aircraft had been flying just 100 feet higher, it would have cleared the crag.

ALL-SCOT BATTLE FOR PRESTWICK

Sixty peers and MPs and members of the Scottish Council on Industry met in the City Chambers in Edinburgh in January and unanimously decided to petition the Government to make Prestwick a trans-oceanic airport of an equal standing with Heathrow in London. They demanded that Scotland should control and administer the air services within Scotland and the direct services between Scotland, the UK and other countries or else the country's economic future would be undermined.

ON RADIO

Letter from America	*Dick Barton, Special Agent*
Woman's Hour	*Down Your Way*

THIS SPORTING LIFE

FOOTBALL	RUGBY UNION	GOLF	HORSE RACING	SHINTY
Scottish Champions No competition held *Scottish Cup Winners* No competition held	*Scotland vs England* No game played	*British Open Winner* Sam Snead at St Andrews (290)	*Scottish Grand National Winner* No race run	*Camanachd Cup Winners* No competition held

Daily ✠ Record
and Mail.

EST. 1895.   No. 16,264   FRIDAY, NOVEMBER 21, 1947   A KEMSLEY NEWSPAPER   1d.

To Romsey In The Moonlight

By "Daily Record" Reporter

Romsey, Hants, Thursday.

IT was just half past six to-night when Princess Elizabeth and her husband, the Duke of Edinburgh, drove slowly through the iron gateway at Palmerston Lodge entrance to Broadlands, Romsey, to start their honeymoon.

The Princess dressed in blue and radiantly happy, smiled delightedly to the crowd, while her husband, in naval uniform, laughed and waved his hand. "Isn't she lovely . . . isn't she beautiful," was the remark made by almost every woman in that homely crowd of country folk. For hours hundreds of the townsfolk and their neighbours from the country-side waited as darkness fell on this damp November day.

The town is still suffering from its wartime blackout and street lamps are few. But the Council borrowed spotlights from Southampton to floodlight the gateway with is flags of all nations and red and yellow banner declaring "Welcome to Romsey."

Wish Respected

In the little villages all along the main road from Winchester to Romsey people had come out of their houses to wave and shout good luck to the Royal honeymooners.

A few moments before they arrived a misty moon peeped out from behind the heavy rain-clouds and as the gates shut behind them the bells of the 800 year-old Romsey Abbey pealed out to add to the people's welcome.

Because of the Royal wish for privacy, the Mayor and Corporation of Romsey waived their desire to give a brief civic welcome at the borough boundary.

Instead, they chose two of the youngest members of the Town Hall staff to deliver a letter of welcome.

While nearly half of Romsey's 7000 population were gathered at the iron gates trying to get a glimpse of the newly-married couple, these two changed into their party-frocks to deliver the letter.

The two girls were Miss Beryl Stone, aged 16, of Ganger Cottage, Woodley, Romsey, and 19-year-old Miss Mildred Harding, of Elmscote, Cuppernham, near Romsey.

Both are daughters of gardeners working in the district.

They were suddenly summoned from their office desks to get ready to take the letter which was enclosed in an envelope sealed with the borough arms.

In the letter, the Mayor and Corporation said: "We offer to Your Royal Highnesses our most sincere greetings and loyal affection on behalf of the townspeople of this ancient borough and we express our earnest hope that you will both enjoy great happiness during your residence in this town which is graced and enriched by your Royal presences."

Better View

At Waterloo Station, London, when the Royal couple set out, a small Corgi dog followed them into their honeymoon train.

Princess Elizabeth at the last moment decided to take her pet with her.

Her blue going-away attire the contrast in the colour of the Duke of Edinburgh's naval uniform, coupled with the general colourful effect of the carpeted platform, the shining brand new Pullman coaches — "Rosemary" and "Rosamund" — and the two huge baskets of mixed chrysanthemums on either side of the coach door, brought gasps of admiration from those privileged to be on the platform.

Many thousands of people who packed the station to cheer the royal couple got a better view than many spectators who for many hours lined the Mall, Whitehall and other points of the wedding route.

Factory girls, housewives and their children and the working men saw what was perhaps the most romantic and impressive scene of all.

The streets of London were fast becoming dark when into the station and underneath the big archway of Waterloo came an escort of mounted policemen and six Life Guards in full dress.

THEY were married yesterday in Westminster Abbey.

The King and Queen stood at the gates of Buckingham Palace yesterday afternoon waving good-bye to their daughter, as with her husband she drove off on her honeymoon.

It was a family touch, setting the seal on a day memorable for pageantry, for colour, and for splendour.

A few minutes earlier, watched by the milling thousands outside the Palace railings, the bridal pair had been showered with rose petals thrown by the Royal family.

Philip Is A Prince Again

FULL style and title of the former Lieut. Philip Mountbatten is His Royal Highness Prince Philip, Duke of Edinburgh, it was officially stated at Buckingham Palace, last night.

He will sign himself "Philip," not "Edinburgh," and he ranks as a British Prince. Close friends are to address him as "Prince Philip."

Princess Elizabeth will henceforth be known officially as Her Royal Highness the Princess Elizabeth, Duchess of Edinburgh.

While the crowd outside the Palace waited for the departure of the bride and bridegroom for Waterloo Station, four stalwart pipers in full Highland dress were given a little cheer to themselves as they threaded their way through the crowd. They were workers from the Royal Estates at Balmoral.

HER BOUQUET

Gracie Fields and Bob Hope watched the procession from a window in Whitehall, near Trafalgar Square. After all the guests had left the Abbey, Gracie sang many of her favourite songs from the window.

Princess Elizabeth's bridal bouquet of white orchids, car- nations and other white flowers was laid on the Unknown Warrior's Tomb in the Abbey last night.

As a wedding gesture, strike pickets with their placards and posters were withdrawn for one day only from Claridge's Hotel, where Royal guests are staying.

Scaffold workers in Trafalgar Square were prevented by police from selling their seats at £10 each.

The marriage register containing the Royal couple's signatures will be on view to the public in Westminster Abbey to-day, to-morrow and on Monday from 10.30 a.m. until 6 p.m.

'I WILL OBEY' SAYS QUEEN-TO-BE

HER Royal Highness, Princess Elizabeth, heiress presumptive to the throne, was married in November and vowed to obey her sailor bridegroom.

In bridal white before the High Altar of ancient Westminster Abbey, in a low voice, she said "I will" and promised "to love, cherish and obey" her husband.

The ceremony was simple and intimate and after the wedding, Buckingham Palace officially announced that Lieutenant. Philip Mountbatten had been given the title of His Royal Highness Prince Philip, Duke of Edinburgh.

And Princess Elizabeth was to be known officially as Her Royal Highness the Princess Elizabeth, Duchess of Edinburgh.

The occasion was marked by a huge crowd of well-wishers which had gathered outside trying to catch a glimpse of the young couple.

It was a great day all over Britain and not only for Princess Elizabeth and the Duke of Edinburgh. It was the people's day too. In Scotland, bonfires, displays of flags, concerts, parties and dances, marked the royal wedding.

King George and Queen Elizabeth stood at the gates of Buckingham Palace waving goodbye to their daughter and new son-in-law as they drove off to start their honeymoon tour of the world aboard the royal yacht, *Britannia*.

It was a family touch setting the seal on a day memorable for pageantry, for colour and for splendour. A few minutes earlier, watched by the crowd, the bridal pair had been showered with rose petals thrown by the Royal Family.

NEW FESTIVAL FOR THE CAPITAL

Flying in the face of postwar austerity and gloom, Edinburgh inaugurated an International Festival of Music and Drama in August. In what was hoped to be an annual event, the city played host to over 800 performers from over 20 countries. At the same time, the first Edinbugh Military Tattoo was held, with dancing and band displays in Princes Street Gardens from locally based troops. In true Scottish fashion, the Festival began with a dedication service in St Giles attended by many civic and foreign consular dignitaries.

HARDY HAS TROUBLE WITH SCOTS WINDBAG

International superstars Laurel and Hardy were in Edinburgh in July with their wives visiting the Empire Scotland Exhibition. At Stan's prompting and to his wife's mock horror, Ollie tried his hand at a set of miniature bagpipes but couldn't even blow up the bag. "I'm scared I'll kill the beast," he joked. In the exhibition itself, Scotland's latest golf clubs held the men's attention while their wives were more interested in "things for the kitchen". Mrs Hardy later described an all-electric cooker as "a housewife's dream".

COMINGS...

Barbara Dickson
Singer & Actress

Gerry Rafferty
Pop Singer

Liz Lochhead
Poet & Playwright

ON RADIO

Round Britain Quiz   *Twenty Questions*

The Critics

GOINGS...

Will Fyffe
Singer, Comedian & Actor

THIS SPORTING LIFE

FOOTBALL	RUGBY UNION	GOLF	HORSE RACING	SHINTY
Scottish Champions Rangers	*Scotland vs England* England 24–5 Scotland at Twickenham	*Home Internationals* Scotland 7-8 England Scotland 10-5 Ireland Scotland 11-4 Wales	*Scottish Grand National Winner* *Rowland Roy* at Bogside	*Camanachd Cup Winners* Newtonmore at Oban
Scottish Cup Winners Aberdeen				

RARE GOOD SCOTCH
JOHNNIE WALKER
BORN 1820 — STILL GOING STRONG

Daily Record
and Mail

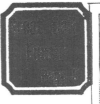

Absolutely
A1
FINEST COOKING SALT
COOKING SALT

ESTABLISHED 1895. No. 16,389   FRIDAY, APRIL 16, 1948   A KEMSLEY NEWSPAPER   1d.

EXPLOSIVES FOUND IN GLASGOW RAIDS

Alba House, Dundas Street, Glasgow, headquarters of "Young Scotland."

SWOOPS by detectives and Special Branch investigators throughout the West End of Glasgow yesterday, in which a mass of explosives and detonators was discovered, culminated last night in a raid on the Alba House, Dundas Street, headquarters of "Young Scotland" Movement.

From various houses three young men were arrested and detained at Marine Police Office.

Det.-Inspector William Kerr, chief of the Special Branch in Glasgow, last night told the "Daily Record":

"These men will appear in court in the morning, charged with contravention of the Explosives Substances Act.

Police inquiries, started some time ago, were geared up within the last few days when a check-up was conducted.

Detectives moved out into the various parts of the West End and made surprise raids on houses in residential areas.

LOADED CARS

Police cars were loaded up with a wide selection of dangerous explosive missiles, which were taken to Marine Divisional Headquarters for examination.

Shortly before eight o'clock last night a police squad car drew up outside 48 Dundas Street, a few yards from Queen Street railway station, and detectives rushed into the close.

They ran upstairs to the third floor, smashed open the door of Alba House and combed the premises. During their search, in the rafters of the roof, they found a considerable quantity of high explosives.

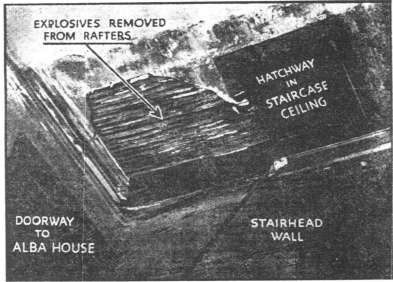

EXPLOSIVES REMOVED FROM RAFTERS

HATCHWAY IN STAIRCASE CEILING

DOORWAY TO ALBA HOUSE

STAIRHEAD WALL

The stairway roof outside Alba House, above which a quantity of explosives were found.

C.I.D. Swoop On "Young Scotland"

So thorough was the search that the ceiling over the stairway caved in and littered the landing below with broken plaster.

Two police vans were called and a large number of boxes were carried downstairs and loaded gently into the waiting vehicles. Sheaves of papers were also taken from the premises.

The raid was over in about half an hour.

Before the detectives left they called at an adjacent office and borrowed a hammer from the caretaker, elderly Mrs. Mary Howat, in order to jam the smashed door back into place.

When a "Daily Record" reporter called, Mrs. Howat was sweeping away the debris from fallen ceiling outside her door.

CLATTER OF FEET

"The first thing I knew about the raid," she said, "was when I heard the clattering of running feet up the stone stairs. This was followed by the sound of heavy objects being dragged across the floor next door."

Of the occupiers of the premises, she said: "They seemed to be a nice bunch of boys. They gathered here practically every night and held sing-songs."

Up till a late hour last night the documents which had been found were being studied by the police.

FOOTNOTE.—"Young Scotland" has extreme Scottish national views. It is not connected with the Scottish National Party or the Scottish National Convention.

Det.-Inspector William Kerr, chief of the Special Branch in Glasgow, who is in charge of the investigations.

B.E.A.C. Form SOS Fleet

BRITISH European Airways Corporation is forming an air ambulance service for the Orkneys.

Two De Havilland Rapides three pilots and three radio operators will carry out the mercy flights under the command of 43-year-old Captain David Barclay.

Westray, the Orkney island which sent out two S.O.S. calls this week and had them refused by B.E.A.C., will be surveyed at the week-end by Captain Barclay.

FAIR ISLE TOO

Accompanied by a Civil Aviation ministry official he will also fly to Fair Isle and Foula.

The new service was planned with the Ministry of Civil Aviation and the Health Department.

No Jobs For Them

Glasgow's unemployed total 20,100—15,953 men and 4,157 women.

Dublin SOS For Scot

EFFORTS were made in Dublin last night to notify Mr. Alexander Bruce Cheyne Dawson, labourer, 66 Bank Street, Alexandria, shortly after his arrival in the city by air, to return home immediately as his father had died earlier in the evening.

Alexandria police passed an urgent phone S.O.S. to Dublin, but up till a late hour Mr. Dawson had not been traced.

BREADBOARD STRETCHER

A BAKER'S breadboard was used as a stretcher for a 15-year-old message boy, William Nicolson, Smellie Street, Greenock, when he lost control of his bicycle in Bow Road, Greenock, yesterday, and was thrown to the ground, injuring his hips.

The occupants of a baker's van found the boy lying on the road and took him to hospital.

TO-DAY'S WEATHER — WARM

S.E., Mid and S.W. Scotland.—Moderate southerly winds. Fine generally after local morning fog. Warm.

Rest of Scotland.—Fresh S.W. winds. Cloudy with some rain. Warm.

Tension Rises In Italy

Rome, Thursday.

SCATTERED outbreaks of violence throughout Italy were reported to-day as electioneering tension rose before Sunday's vital poll, which will determine Italy's place in the future European pattern.

Seravalle, town of Mantua in Northern Italy, was gripped by a general strike called in protest against the arrest of the Communist mayor after a machine-gun, three German rifles and a quantity of ammunition were found in his house.

No visas for foreigners to enter Rome are being granted until after the election, the Italian Embassy in Paris announced to-day.

Fans First

The Hope Street entrance of the Central Station opposite Waterloo Street will be used for Hampden cup final queues only to-morrow. No traffic will be allowed.

Train Mail Bags Rifled

From Our Own Reporter

EXPERIENCED mailbag thieves, working with inside knowledge, are believed to be behind an epidemic of mailbag thefts from trains coming into Liverpool from Crewe and the South and West of England.

First disclosure of the robberies came last night with the news that a mailbag and empty envelopes had been found by platelayers working on the track at Hartford Junction, north of Crewe, and at Roseley Hill, Liverpool.

Other letters, believed to have been taken at the same time, were found late last night in a compartment of the afternoon train from Plymouth to Liverpool.

Twice last week on successive days, the mail "brakes" had their seals broached and packages stolen from them.

Each time only bags containing registered mail were involved.

Reinforcements of uniformed and plain clothes railway police were keeping a special check on all trains coming into Liverpool (Lime Street Station), said a railway police official last night.

DUPLICATE KEY

"We suspect that the theft from the Plymouth train was carried out by someone with a duplicate corridor key who made his way from an ordinary compartment to the mail brake," he said.

Last week's attempts were different. The seals on the brake were found to be broached when the train reached Liverpool.

Truman's Hope

PRESIDENT TRUMAN expects to be re-elected.

Questioned on a controversy over whether he should have built a balcony on to the classical portico of the White House, Mr. Truman said he thought he would be using the balcony during the next four years—if he were not too busy.

Dive To Safety
Air Crash Miracle

A MILLION to one chance saved the life of the 38-year-old American, sole survivor in the air crash at Shannon Airport, Eire, just before dawn yesterday, which cost the lives of 30 people.

The survivor, Mark Worst, European maintenance base manager of the Lockheed Aircraft Corporation, makers of the machine which crashed, was flying to Shannon, where his wife was waiting for him.

The plane, a Constellation, the Empress of the Skies, struck a wall 600 yards from the main runway, hit the ground again 100 yards further on, and then a hole appeared in the cabin floor in front of Mr. Worst. In a split second he had freed himself from his safety straps and slipped through the hole.

EXPLOSION FOLLOWED

He tumbled through the belly luggage compartment to the ground and flung himself clear of the plane as it exploded and burst into flames.

His wife, a qualified nurse, rushed out from the airport to help in the rescue work and did not know he was safe for half an hour.

Mr. Worst, with hands, arms and face severely burned, said in a Limerick hospital last night, "The aircraft was functioning perfectly. We circled the field to land and made a pass at the main runway.

ANOTHER RUN

"We overshot it and circled to make another landing run.

"Suddenly I felt a bump and then another bump. A hole opened up before me in the cabin floor. I unstrapped myself and dropped through the hole to safety.

"When I was clear I looked to see if any of the other passengers were with me, but I was alone."

£2 On Rents

Kilsyth Town Council have decided to raise the rents of two-apartment houses in the burgh by £2 per annum, with an additional 10s per extra apartment for larger houses.

BRUSH... UP... YOUR... SMILE...

WITH THE CORRECT-SHAPE TOOTHBRUSH

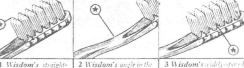

1 Wisdom's straight-line head reaches all the awkward corners.

2 Wisdom's angle in the handle is the secret of its comfortable control.

3 Wisdom's widely-spaced tufts "comb" between teeth clean there deep, too.

Wisdom
REGD.

ADDIS LTD. OF HERTFORD, MAKERS OF THE FIRST TOOTHBRUSH IN 1780

1948

EXPLOSIVES SEIZED IN SWOOP

DETECTIVES and Special Branch investigators carrying out surprise raids after months of police enquiries, uncovered a large quantity of explosives and detonators in April.

The explosives were found during a raid on the Alba House headquarters of the Young Scotland movement in Dundas Street, Glasgow. The group was known to hold extreme Scottish nationalist views.

Officers discovered the explosives hidden in the rafters of the premises.

Their search was so thorough that the ceiling over the stairway caved in and littered the landing below with broken plaster.

The quantity of explosives uncovered was large enough to require two extra police vans to take the dangerous materials to the Marine Division headquarters for examination.

During the raids, the police visited several houses in the west end of Glasgow.

They arrested several young men who were later detained and questioned about any connections they may have had with the Young Scotland movement and the explosives found at the headquarters.

In addition to the explosives, large quantities of documents were also found during the raid on Alba House and these were also taken away for analysis by the police.

COMINGS...

Jim Watt
Boxer

Lulu
Singer & Entertainer

Dick Gaughan
Folksinger

CASH BOOST FOR SCOTS

Hopes were high that 150 new firms would begin production in Scotland during the year and latest figures revealed that almost £14million had been invested in the country by companies in the previous year. This represented the biggest cash injection for over two decades according to the Scottish Council for Development and Industry. The Council also said that 100,000 jobs had been created since the end of the war in 1945 and added: "This year should see the largest advance in the establishment of new industry. Never again will Scotland be the poor relation of the United Kingdom."

ON RADIO

Any Questions?	*Take It From Here*
Mrs Dale's Diary	*Top of the Form*

AIRLINER DOWNED NEAR LARGS

In April, a B.O.A.C. Viking airliner travelling between Glasgow and London came down in thick mist in the hills above Largs as it made its final approach to Renfrew airport. The passengers and crew managed to scramble to safety before the plane burst into flames. The alarm was raised by the pilot and one of the passengers who walked for two hours in poor weather to reach Largs. They later guided the rescue parties back to the location of the wreckage and the other passengers.

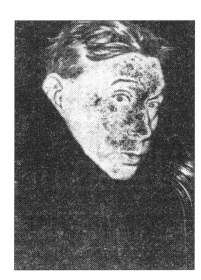

THIS SPORTING LIFE

FOOTBALL	RUGBY UNION	GOLF	HORSE RACING	SHINTY
Scottish Champions Hibernian	*Scotland vs England* Scotland 6–3 England at Murrayfield	*British Open Winner* Henry Cotton at Muirfield (284)	*Scottish Grand National Winner* *Magnetic Fin* at Bogside	*Camanachd Cup Winners* Newtonmore at Inverness
Scottish Cup Winners Rangers				

ROBERTSON'S JAMS
On a million tables every day

Daily ✠ Record
and Mail.

ESTABLISHED 1895. No. 16,898.   FRIDAY, DECEMBER 2, 1949.   A KEMSLEY NEWSPAPER.   1d.

Housing warning Page 5.

Your smalls and dainties have longer life when you use
Clypsol
WASHES EVERYTHING
A Sunshine Bleach Product

They saw it happen...

No govt. help for railways

From HAROLD TURNER

Westminster, Thursday

BRITAIN'S railways, faced with a working loss of £20,000,000 this year, and probably worse to come in 1950, must stand on their own feet.

There is to be no Government subsidy to help them.

In the Commons to-night, Mr. Alfred Barnes, Minister of Transport, made this plain to M.P.s who had gathered to debate the report of the Transport Commission.

Mr. Barnes was moving the acceptance of the report and the Opposition had tabled a motion regretting the losses and the marked deterioration in the position with the mounting costs and increased fares and rates "so detrimental to the public."

Mounting expenses

Mr. Barnes said that he must not anticipate the Government's decision.

But he thought is rested on him to remind the House that it would be unwise within two years to go back on the main responsibility which Parliament placed on the British Transport Commission and certainly before the integration of the services had had time to be decided.

"The deterioration in 1949," he said, "is, of course, due in the main to the mounting costs of railway expenses. Certainly it is not due to inefficient management."

Staff costs had increased by 160 per cent. and these represented 62 per cent. of the operating costs.

Scottish voice not heard

In the last minutes of the debate Col. Hutchison (Unionist, Glasgow Central), addressing Mr. Speaker, said: "Would I be in order in protesting at the farcical amount of time allowed for these discussions which has allowed for no Scottish voice being heard in the debate, and the docks not being mentioned?"

Mr. Speaker did not reply.

Mr. Callaghan, Parliamentary Secretary to the Ministry of Transport, finished his winding-up speech two minutes before his time, and Col. Gomme-Duncan (Unionist, Perth) seized his opportunity.

"The voice of Scotland has not been heard," he said, and he hoped that another opportunity of discussing this report would be provided, when Scotland's particular problems could be ventilated.

The Opposition motion was defeated by 303 votes to 149.

Hughie Quinn
"I saw a gun."

Mrs. Helen McGhie
Thought they were fooling.

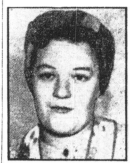

Stewart Robertson
He took car's number

... at this bank

GUNMEN GRAB £17,600 AT BANK

West Scotland hunt for 4 men

POLICE in Glasgow and Lanarkshire last night threw a cordon round a wide area in the hunt for the four bandits in a car with faked number plates, two of whom, in the biggest Scottish robbery for 30 years, snatched a £17,600 payroll outside the Commercial Bank of Scotland in Motherwell yesterday afternoon.

Early to-day Motherwell Police were still conferring with detectives at Glasgow C.I.D. headquarters.

Jumped into waiting car

In a breathless sixty-second attack, two men jumped at small, middle-aged Hugh Richardson, cashier of Colvilles Dalzell works, and ex-police sergeant, 48-year-old Stewart Young, Colvilles security officer, as they took a double-handed leather bag, containing the money in £5, £1 and 10s notes, into their car outside.

The bandits ran with the bag a few yards down Airbles Road, where the bank is situated, and into a waiting car, in which two other men are believed to have been sitting. It raced down the road in the direction of Hamilton.

The car is believed to be an Austin 8 or 10 fitted with registration number BG 835, the number of a car which was destroyed several years ago.

The bandits had watched Richardson and Young put two other bags, containing silver, into the car before they made their attack.

One of them sprang at Richardson from a shop doorway, jabbed him on the knuckles with a gun, and wrenched the bag from him.

Coming behind Richardson and Young as they left the bank was 15-year-old messenger Hughie Quinn, of Missen Lane, Motherwell.

He said: "One of the men just seemed to spring out from nowhere I saw a gun in his hand and he brought it down quickly on Richardson's hand

Continued on Back Page. col. 1

Mr. Hugh Richardson
... wrenched the bag from him.

N. Atlantic defence—

12 nations agree

Paris, Thursday.

AFTER a five-hour meeting here to-day the Defence Ministers of the 12 North Atlantic powers announced "unanimous agreement."

A communique to-night said the Ministers gave full approval to strategic concept for integrated defence of North Atlantic area, provision of programme for production and supply of armaments and equipment.

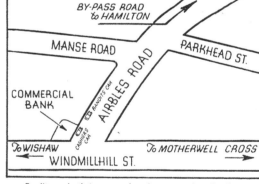

Bandits made their escape along by-pass road to Hamilton.

£100,000 damage in blaze

POLICE held back crowds in the centre of Aberdeen last night while every available fire unit fought a spectacular blaze which gutted a large printing works.

The damage is estimated in the region of £100,000. Valuable linotype and lithographic machinery, as well as half the firm's stock of Christmas cards and calendars waiting to be despatched to all parts of the country, were destroyed.

Shortly after six o'clock flames were seen coming from the works of Middleton's (Aberdeen) Limited, in Rose Street, and within half an hour the whole building was ablaze, and flames leaping a hundred feet into the sky were seen over the whole city.

200 workers thrown idle

By concentrating on preventing the flames spreading, the firemen saved nearby tenements, shops and business premises.

After three hours the outbreak was under control and the tenants, who were warned out of adjoining properties were permitted to return.

Over 200 employees will be thrown idle. The factory and stores were gutted and the only part of the firm's premises to remain intact was the offices.

Christmas food up in smoke

HUNDREDS of tons of food, mainly Christmas provisions, went up in flames shortly before midnight last night when fire broke out at a three-storey warehouse of wholesale grocers at Plaistow.

The store adjoins the police station and policemen off duty were called from their beds to help push a score of lorries out to safety.

Scene of yesterday's hold-up in Motherwell.

Map: BY-PASS ROAD to HAMILTON / MANSE ROAD / PARKHEAD ST. / AIRBLES ROAD / COMMERCIAL BANK / BANDITS' CAR / CASHIER'S CAR / To WISHAW / WINDMILLHILL ST. / To MOTHERWELL CROSS

Photo labels: THE COMMERCIAL BANK / THE COMMERCIAL BANK OF SCOTL. / HOLD-UP TOOK PLACE HERE

THE REDHEAD FROM GLASGOW

A RED-HEADED girl from Glasgow confronted Canadian Finance Minister Douglas Abbott in Ottawa yesterday and told him she would not pay a higher rent sanctioned by Parliament.

She was Mrs. Jean Parent, of Montreal, formerly Miss Jean Dunbar of Parliamentary Road, Townhead, Glasgow, who came to Canada four years ago as a war bride.

With a delegation of 300 Montreal tenants she protested against a 20 per cent. rent increase, and said: "I am not going to pay it and I am not going to move." The delegation cheered her.

Dollars from Butlins

MR. W. E. BUTLIN will open his dollar-earning holiday camp in the Bahamas on January 28 for American "middle-income group" at 12 dollars (about £3 sterling) a day in summer and 15 dollars (about £5 sterling) in winter.

FOR EASY STARTING THIS WINTER

Castrol
WAKEFIELD
MOTOR OIL

"GIVE ME CASTROL EVERY TIME"

RAIN. — Moderate north-westerly winds; scattered showers at first; becoming fair, but chance of rain again in evening.

1949

POLICE HUNT ARMED ROBBERS

POLICE were looking for four armed bandits who snatched a £17,600 payroll outside the Commercial Bank of Scotland in Motherwell on December 1.

Officers in Lanarkshire and Glasgow threw a cordon round a wide area in the hunt for the bandits who made off with the money in a car with faked number plates.

The attack, which lasted just 60 seconds, occurred as two men jumped at Hugh Richardson, cashier of Colville's Dalzell works and Stewart Young, the company's security officer.

They were carrying the bag containing the money in £5, £1 and 10s notes to their car outside the bank.

The bandits snatched the bag and then ran a few yards to their own car which was parked near the bank in Airbles Road.

Two other men were waiting and when the raiders got in, it raced down the street in the direction of Hamilton.

The car was believed to be an Austin 8 or 10 and had been fitted with a false registration number BG835, taken from a car which had been destroyed a few years previously.

Before the robbery, the bandits had watched as Mr Richardson and Mr Young emerged from the bank and put two other bags containing silver into the car.

An eye witness said one of the men seemed to spring from nowhere. He jabbed Richardson and hit him on the knuckles with his gun before snatching the bag from his hands.

Then he ran to the waiting car for the getaway.

CLOTHES GO OFF THE RATION

Harold Wilson, the President of the Board of Trade, announced that all clothes rationing would end on March 15. He said: "It would have been easy to abolish it at any time in the past three years. We could have done so by retarding the export drive and putting the home market first, but we were never prepared to contemplate such a course." No one expected a great spending spree with the end of the rationing, except for items like sheets, etc., for the purchase tax on all non-utility goods still remained prohibitive.

COMINGS...	GOINGS...
Andrew Neil Newspaper Executive	*Jessie M. King* Designer & Illustrator

GIRL IN STORE BLAZE DEATH LEAP

Hundreds of shoppers watched in horror as a young woman died after jumping from a blazing building in Argyle Street, Glasgow, in May. Twelve other girls died in the fire when they were trapped inside Grafton's fashion store. Firemen rescued 19 other girl employees, some of whom had escaped from the building by walking across a six-inch ledge to the roof of the cinema next door. It took two hours to bring the blaze under control.

ON RADIO

Book At Bedtime	*Billy Cotton's Band Show*
Morning Story	*Ray's A Laugh*

THIS SPORTING LIFE

FOOTBALL	RUGBY UNION	GOLF	HORSE RACING	SHINTY
Scottish Champions Rangers	*Scotland vs England* England 19–3 Scotland at Twickenham	*Home Internationals* Scotland 5-10 England Scotland 4½-10½ Ireland Scotland 8½-6½ Wales	*Scottish Grand National* *Winner* *Wot No Sun* at Bogside	*Camanachd Cup Winners* Oban Celtic at Glasgow
Scottish Cup Winners Rangers				

Rely on the Quality
ballito
Stockings

Daily ✠ Record
and Mail.

ESTABLISHED 1895. No. 17,230 TUESDAY, DECEMBER 26, 1950 A KEMSLEY NEWSPAPER. 1d.

GRANITE HOUSE
FAMOUS
DRAPERY DEPT.
OFFERS
UTILITY CURTAIN
MATERIAL
in Rust, Gold and Sand
Colours. 36ins.
wide. Yard.... **7/6**
TRONGATE STOCKWELL STREET CORNER.

Police check-up on Scots-bound cars

YARD DIRECTS SEARCH FOR STONE OF DESTINY

The Stone of Destiny below the Coronation Chair.

"Daily Record" Reporter

POLICE road blocks were established yesterday on main roads from England to Scotland following the removal earlier in the day of the Stone of Destiny from Westminster Abbey.

The stone, on which the ancient Scottish Kings were crowned, weighs about three hundredweights. Police, searching for a Ford Anglia car seen near the Abbey yesterday, received reports last night that a similar car had been seen heading north near Birmingham.

In the car are stated to be two men and a woman, who have Scottish accents. They called at a service station in Hockley Heath yesterday morning and drove off towards Birmingham.

A Scotland Yard description of the woman was that she was about 25 years of age, had long dark hair, long, pointing nose, dark eyes, fresh complexion, thin lips, and wore a green checked coat with long collar.

One of the men was between 26 and 29 years of age, had a snub nose and fresh complexion. He was of medium build and had fair hair which had not been combed.

It is certain that the plot to remove the Stone of Destiny was planned in Scotland and was carried out by a raiding party.

But leaders of the chief home rule movements, the Scottish National Party and Scottish Convention, last night promptly disowned any part in the scheme.

Prominent independent home rulers would not reveal whether they knew of the plot. Said one of them in Glasgow— "Obviously at this stage we are not going to give a hint of who might be involved.

"But it will probably appear at some Scottish national monument — the Wallace Monument at Stirling for instance."

None of the thousands who attended the Christmas Day services in the Abbey conducted

The fake stone plot that failed—see Page 7.

by the Dean of Westminster, Scottish-born Dr. A. C. Don, knew that the stone had been stolen.

Afterwards Dr. Don said: "The Stone was stolen in the early hours of this morning but we hope Scotland Yard will lay their hands on it"

McNEIL HORRIFIED

Secretary of State for Scotland Hector McNeil was horrified when he heard.

"I think it is mean and atrocious," he stated last night.

Referring to the possibility of Scottish Nationalists having organised the "removal," he said, "I cannot see how it furthers any argument."

Immediately it was discovered the Stone was missing Scotland Yard sent out a terse message to all police forces in Midland and Northern England: "Coronation Stone stolen from Westminster Abbey. Suspect work of Scottish Nationalists. Stop and search all cars heading north."

Special road blocks were set up on the main roads in Lancashire. All cars driving through the county towards Scotland were stopped while police searched them.

Chief Inspector Owen
Continued on Back Page, Col. 1.

THE DUKE OF MONTROSE said last night that if the Stone was on its way back to Scotland, he did not regret it. "Our old Scottish charters are now being returned to Edinburgh and everyone agrees that that is right and as it should be."

"I fail to see why the Scone Stone should be treated differently. It is part of our early Celtic history.

"England has plenty of good solid history to her credit and to be proud of, and she has no reason to weep if the Scone Stone should come again to Scotland and be restored to the old capital, which it should never have left."

"King" John MacCormick, chairman of the Scottish Covenant, whose petition for a greater measure of Home Rule was signed by nearly two million Scots last year, said that "whatever the outcome of the present adventure," he hoped the Stone would ultimately be kept in Scotland except on Coronation occasions.

"The Stone of Destiny properly belongs to the people of Scotland," he said. "Under the terms of the Treaty

The Duke of Montrose.

Duke says "it should be here"

of Northampton, in 1328, the Stone, which is the ancient symbol of Scottish nationality, was to be returned to Scotland, but the clause was never observed."

Mr. Nigel Tranter, one of the leaders of Scottish Covenant, said: "We in that movement stick to constitutional methods, but as an individual I would be the last to deplore initiative and enterprise shown by any person in Scotland—even if it is misplaced as this is—if it will waken people up to the feeling in Scotland.

"It takes a lot to get any news of Scotlands' national existence into the English press and this sort of thing is the only type of Home Rule story that gets a break in the English newspapers."

Reds send out 'probe' patrols

From RICHARD HUGHES
Tokio, Monday.

INCREASED Chinese activity was reported to-night by battlefront officers on the left, or Yellow Sea flank, of the United Nations forces.

There was, however, no development of the anticipated all-out Communist offensive during the second night of the full moon. Action by Chinese spearheads which have crossed the Parallel is described as "probing."

Fifth Airforce fighter-bombers hurled a Christmas Day offensive against all sectors in North Korea, but significantly concentrated their heaviest attack on the Chorwon-Pyongyang-Kumhwa area, where the strongest massings of Chinese troops have been reported.

16 MILES SOUTH

Reports have been received of "enemy movement" as far as 16 miles south of the 38th Parallel, and 14 miles south of Kaesong, but these groups may be North Korean guerrillas.

With traditional efficiency the U.S. Navy has rung down the curtain on one of the most tragic and wasteful offensives in U.S. military history.

Evacuation of the Hungnam area on the north-eastern coast has been satisfactorily and officially completed.

The successful withdrawal of 105,000 troops and 100,000 refugees under the covering fire of a crushing naval bombardment and unchallenged air cover was described in grim talks as "re-deployment."

DR. A. C. DON
The Dean of Westminster.

A native of Broughty Ferry, Dr. Don was educated at Rugby School and Magdalen College, Oxford, and from 1908-1909 was in business in Dundee. He entered the Church and became a curate in 1912. From 1936-46 he was Chaplain to the Speaker of the House of Commons. He is a member of the R and A. St. Andrews.

Fog halts buses, ships and planes

GLASGOW was "blacked-out" by fog yesterday, which reduced visibility over most of the city to only a few yards.

Roads in many places were icy, and there were a number of crashes. Transport services were disorganised and buses were running as much as two hours behind schedule.

By early evening all shipping on the Clyde was brought to a standstill.

Renfrew airport had to close down and all services were diverted to fog-free Prestwick.

Full story—Page 7.

Bells brought lost Clyde ferry to safety

By "Daily Record" Reporter

FIFTEEN passengers and the crew of two aboard Glasgow's small Linthouse-Whiteinch ferry will never forget Christmas Day, 1950. For an hour and a quarter they were lost on the Clyde in thick impenetrable fog on a journey which normally would have taken only a few minutes.

At last, with handbells clanging and whistles blowing to let them know they were near safety, they came to the river bank a mile from the landing place. In the fog the ferry had to move very slowly, constantly at the mercy of the swift current of the ebbing tide.

Almost as soon as it left Linthouse, the ferry was in trouble. Passengers heard the clatter of riveters at work and discovered they were going down stream past Stephens' yard instead of across the river

The ferrymen headed out into the river, but the swift current carried the boat down stream again and it landed close to Connell's shipyard on the north side. Out of Connell's they steamed, narrowly escaping the stern of a ship under construction.

"ALMOST HIT BANK"

"Once or twice in the search for the landing place we almost hit the bank," said 21-year-old John McKillen, 1090 Dumbarton Road, Glasgow, who had boarded the ferry on his way home from the abandoned football match at Hampden. "We were gathered round the wheel house, but could see absolutely nothing for a long time.

"When we came to the bank again, one of the passengers jumped ashore, saying he was going to get help. After that we went upstream, and soon we heard the bells and whistles from the north bank signalling to us to come in. We found we were in Mechan's works, where the men passed out a plank on which we walked ashore."

SHIP GROUNDS AGAIN

THE 7242-ton British steamer Domingo de Larrinaga, refloated from Redcar sands yesterday, went aground two hours later at the entrance to the Tees.

MALT VINEGAR
must be
BREWERY BOTTLED

● TO STAY BRIGHT AND USABLE TO THE LAST DROP

● TO BE FREE FROM SEDIMENT

● TO STAND UP TO ANY TEST

Always insist on the name

GRIMBLE'S GOLD MEDAL SCOTTISH DISTILLED MALT VINEGAR LEITH

GRIMBLE'S
OF LEITH

THE ONLY MALT VINEGAR BREWED IN SCOTLAND

SHOWERS—Light northerly winds; scattered showers and bright intervals; keen frost early and late.

1950

HUNT FOR THE STONE AFTER RAID

THE Stone of Destiny was stolen from its resting place beneath the Coronation Throne in Westminster Abbey early on Christmas Day.

Immediately after the stone was discovered missing, Scotland Yard issued instructions to all police forces in Midland and Northern England, "to stop and search all cars heading north as the Coronation Stone was stolen from Westminster Abbey and Scottish Nationalists were the prime suspects."

The police were searching for a Ford Anglia car and two men and a woman who had been seen near the Abbey in the early hours. The car was spotted heading north near Birmingham and as a result, special road blocks were set up by police on the main roads to Lancashire.

All cars driving through the county towards Scotland were stopped while police searched them.

Despite the presence of police patrols on all the main roads in England, and reports of sightings of the Ford in various parts of the country, Scotland Yard stated that there was no trace of the Stone and the search continued.

The Duke of Montrose commented that if the Stone was on its way back to Scotland, he did not regret it.

"Our old Scottish characters are now being returned to Edinburgh. I fail to see why the Scone Stone should be treated any differently. It is an important part of our early Celtic history."

The Stone – on which traditionally, kings of Scotland were crowned at Scone in Perthshire – had been taken from Scotland in the late thirteenth century by King Edward I of England, "The Hammer of the Scots".

After its "retrieval" in 1950, it was eventually handed back to the authorities in London. No charges were ever brought

---

COMINGS...

Robbie Coltrane
Actor

Ian Charleson
Actor

GOINGS...

Harry Lauder
Entertainer

SCOTS TROOPS FOR KOREA

The Argyll and Sutherland Highlanders were amongst the first British troops to arrive in Korea at the end of August. The Argylls formed part of the United Nations force sent in to help counter the invasion of South Korea by its Communist neighbour to the north.

In the following months, some 4,000 British troops including the Black Watch and the K.O.S.B. took part in bloody battles against North Korean and Chinese forces.

WHAT IT COST

POUND OF BUTTER
1s 6d

POUND OF BACON
2s 7d

PINT OF BEER
1s 3$\frac{1}{4}$d

CIGARETTES
1s 7$\frac{1}{2}$d (box of 50 Pearl)

WOMEN'S SHOES
£3 9s 11d

MEN'S SUIT
£5 13s 11d

TON OF COAL
£7 13s 2d

POSTAGE
2$\frac{1}{2}$d

CAR
Austin 7 £335

AYRSHIRE PIT RESCUE

A subsidence at Knockshinnoch Castle colliery in New Cumnock trapped 128 men underground in November. Rescue parties from pits throughout Ayrshire, Lanarkshire and Dumfriesshire worked tirelessly to reach the men, which they did by drilling through to them from neighbouring old workings. Unfortunately, 13 of the miners were separated from the main body of trapped men and could not be reached.

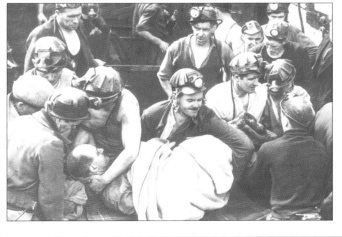

THIS SPORTING LIFE

FOOTBALL	RUGBY UNION	GOLF	HORSE RACING	SHINTY
Scottish Champions Rangers	*Scotland vs England* Scotland 13–11 England at Murrayfield	*British Open Winner* Bobby Locke at Troon (279)	*Scottish Grand National Winner* Sanvina at Bogside	*Camanachd Cup Winners* Newtonmore at Oban
Scottish Cup Winners Rangers				

ballito
Mirrasilk
SHEER AS NYLONS
NOW AVAILABLE - 12'11 A PAIR

Daily ✠ Record
and Mail.

ESTABLISHED 1895.   No. 17,529.   TUESDAY, DECEMBER 11, 1951   A KEMSLEY NEWSPAPER.   1½d.

Threat
to Truce
—Page 5

Double Breasted 95/-
MEN'S SUITS
One of the Granite's
Greatest-ever Bargains
Two Piece in Fine
Worsteds. Blues
Browns. Greys.
GRANITE HOUSE
TRONGATE STOCKWELL STREET CORNER

CID men patrol at two courses

WHILE statements and information about the alleged doping of racehorses continued to reach Scotland Yard, detectives and extra police mingled with racegoers at Birmingham and Newcastle yesterday.

At Birmingham Mr. R. Renton, the Ripon trainer whose horse Q.E.D. won the Ashby Handicap 'Chase by ten lengths at 4 to 1, said he had been told by the C.I.D. before racing started that they had reason to believe that Q.E.D would be interfered with before the race.

"The horse was never out of anybody's sight after that," said Mr. Renton. *(Full story, Page 7.)*

Racehorse owner goes to Yard

Another "doping" development yesterday was a three hours visit to Scotland Yard by Mr. Alex Barnett. Newcastle-on-Tyne racehorse owner, and Mr. Ernest Street, who formerly trained a string of 22 horses at Malton. Yorks.

Mr. Barnett's horse Rock Star was disqualified as the result of a report of the Jockey Club's analyst after finishing third in the Clarence House Stakes at Ascot Heath on September 27 last, and Mr. Street had his training licence withdrawn.

Since then Mr. Barnett has been campaigning to have his promising horse reinstated and to get back his trainer's licence. He offered a £50 reward for information leading to the arrest of whoever "nobbled" his horse.

"Placed our cards on the table"

After his visit to Scotland Yard, Mr Barnett, 56-year-old general merchant, said:

"We had an interview with one of the 'chiefs.' I can't tell you his name because that would impede his work in investigating this doping business

"We placed all our cards on the table and gave him our views. He seemed to be very interested in what we had to say, and we came away feeling very pleased with the interview.

"Now it's up to all the other owners who know anything to come forward and tell the authorities what they can. I've done my duty."

Mr. Barnett, whose lifelong interest in the Turf began when he used to bet in sixpences more than 30 years ago, describes himself as "a small, modest owner, struggling to make racing pay."

He has had several horses from time to time, but at present has only four, including Rock Star—"one of the best horses in the country."

The Deputy Chief Constable of Cambridgeshire, Supt. H. Unwin, told the Press Association last night:

"Lord Rosebery has been in communication with the Chief Constable, and stated that he intends to place before the Yard, the facts relating to the doping of his horse.

"Lord Rosebery hopes that anybody who has any information will now send it to the Commissioner at Scotland Yard and not to him."

(C.I.D. guard horse—Page 7)

Three K.O.S.B. heroes win awards in Korea

SCOT IS FIRST CALL-UP D.S.O.

Wounded, he fought on, saved his men

2nd Lieut. Purves, D.S.O.

TWO young Scots National Service officers and a private have won awards for their part in the "gunpowder plot" battle in Korea, when the Reds launched 6000 men in an all-out attack on a vital ridge on the eve of Guy Fawkes' Day.

Twenty - year - old Second Lieut. William Purves, ex-bank clerk, of Ednam, near Kelso, has been awarded the D.S.O., and Second Lieut. Ralph Alister Brooks, of Kelso, the Military Cross.

BOTH WITH K.O.S.B.

Both officers are serving with the King's Own Scottish Borderers.

Second Lieutenant Purves is the first National Service man to receive the Distinguished Service Order. An Army spokesman said the D.S.O. normally goes to officers of field rank, major and above, and few subalterns have received it.

In the same battle Private John Rodger Pender, of Pilton, Edinburgh, won the Military Medal.

The citation accompanying the award to Second-Lieutenant Purves said that although he was "in great pain from a serious wound in the right shoulder" he fought an eight-hour battle on a partly overrun position under intense artillery fire. He later extricated his men "with great skill and coolness."

"Not until he had received a direct order did he give any consideration to his painful wound."

BROUGHT BACK 12 WOUNDED

After another hour of fighting, the ridges of Hill 317, 400 yards from Second-Lieutenant Purves' position, "were in enemy hands and overlooked his position which was now completely exposed," the citation said. "He fought on for almost five hours more."

Forced to attempt to extricate the two platoons under his command, Purves "brought down a precipitous feature 12 wounded men and all the platoons' arms and equipment.

"The outstanding leadership, bravery and resource of this young officer, together with his sense of responsibility, were an inspiration to all. The stubborn defence of this feature contributed materially in preventing the battalion from being overrun."

The main weight of "Charlie Chinaman's gunpowder plot," as the troops called it, fell on three companies of the 1st Battalion King's Own Scottish Borderers holding a vital ridge-line position on the Korean front.

The Chinese, blowing bugles and shouting, deluged the companies, but the Kosbies
Continued on Back Page

Minutes of terror for 18 families

"Daily Record" Reporter

MR. JAMES McGUIRE was playing billiards in a Glasgow social club last night. His wife was at the theatre. In their absence flames raged through the empty ground-floor house at 55 Wigton Street, Port Dundas, and 10 minutes of smoky terror began for 18 tenement families.

A woman ran shouting from the close as suffocating clouds swirled up the four-floored well of the block. Women and children screamed as the gas lights on the landings went out and left them stumbling in the dark.

John Corbett, 50-year-old labourer, had just left his 76-year-old mother's home at No. 55 and gone to his own house nearby at 21 Rodney Street, when the alarm was raised.

He dashed back with 20-year-old neighbour John Cully, and met his mother on the first landing. While he carried her to safety, Cully and another man battered at the door of the blazing McGuire home. There was no one inside.

John Cully

Cully raced upstairs. As he reached the first landing an elderly woman coming down with Mrs. Margaret Bell collapsed in a dead faint. Cully and a neighbour carried her down to the street.

John Corbett

Then Cully climbed back upstairs, and found four screaming children in a top-floor house. He guided them into Mr. Archie Craig's home next door.

"There were about seven kids in there," he said afterwards. "But I don't know what happened then. I couldn't see and I couldn't breathe.

Continued on back Page, foot of Column One

Germany to pay us £51M. less

A TREASURY announcement last night on the conclusion of the tripartite talks in London on German debts arising from post-war assistance given by Britain, France and the U.S. to Germany, states that all three countries have made considerable concessions, amounting in the case of Britain to £51M.

When the Tri-partite Commission on German debts and the German delegation on external debts began their meeting the claims were:—U.K. £201M.; France, 15.7 million dollars; U.S., about 3200 million dollars.

The British Government were prepared to accept £150M. to waive all interest on this amount and accept repayment over 20 years.

King revokes Order

THE KING signed a warrant yesterday revoking the appointment of five Counsellors of State made on September 27.

The Order of September 27 —made four days after the operation on the King—authorised the appointment of the Counsellors to deal temporarily with "current business in the U.K. and the Colonies."

The five were the Queen, Princess Elizabeth, Princess Margaret, the Duke of Gloucester, and the Princess Royal.

£6000 jewel haul probed

"Daily Record" Reporter

POLICE were making inquiries yesterday into the theft of jewellery worth £6000 from the London hotel suite occupied by Frank Sinatra and Ava Gardner.

The jewellery—a diamond and emerald platinum necklace, belonging to Ava, and a platinum ring, set with sapphires, and gold cuff-links embossed with Wedgwood china, belonging to Frank—was stolen from jewel boxes in their bedroom between Saturday and Sunday night.

Egypt may decide on break to-day

From JOHN FISHER

THE Egyptian Cabinet meets to-day to decide whether to break off diplomatic relations with Britain

Foreign Office experts on procedure were trying yesterday to decide the possible effects of this step, if taken.

In its extreme form, the breaking off of diplomatic relations means the withdrawal of all diplomatic staff, except perhaps an attache who would be left in charge of the Embassy records.

Egypt's move might, however, mean merely the withdrawal of the ambassador, Amr Pasha, from London and his replacement by a Charge d'Affaires.

There would then exist the same kind of relationship that Britain now has with Communist China, where we have no ambassador, or that she had until recently with Spain.

CONSULS MIGHT REMAIN

At present there are British consuls or consular representatives at more than a dozen Egyptian centres. These might remain.

Our consuls would be able to protect the rights of British subjects and merchants and to take up injustices with the local police. They could not, however, approach the Egyptian Government on behalf of British interests in Egypt.

What follows a Christmas Dinner?

HENNESSY, of course, the Brandy that made Cognac famous

As a liqueur, as a beverage, as a safe and quick stimulant, Hennessy Brandy is unequalled.

Is there a Hennessy in the House?

Storm halts keepers' relief

ROUGH seas prevented the lighthouse tender Pole Star from leaving Stromness yesterday to carry out the Christmas relief of the lightkeeper and his assistant at Suleskerry Rock, 40 miles west of the Orkneys.

The more northerly areas of Scotland took the brunt of yesterday's storm, which showed signs of abating in the evening. Overnight snow had fallen in some areas to a depth of four inches, and the temperature dropped to 29 degrees. Showers of hail and sleet accompanied the snow.

Ski-ers were out at Dalwhinnie, Inverness-shire. Lorry drivers and motorists had to cope with drifts between two and three feet deep over the Dava Moor on the Grantown-on-Spey to Forres road.

Ice and snow hindered transport on the Glasgow to Oban road yesterday.

—and to-day an improvement in the weather will begin in the south-west, spreading to the north by evening.

BRAVERY AWARD FOR KOREA SCOT

A YOUNG Scottish National Service officer won an award for his part in the "gunpowder plot" battle in the Korean War.

Second Lieutenant William Purves from Ednam, near Kelso, who had worked as a bank clerk before his call-up, was awarded the Distinguished Services Order, becoming the first National Service man to receive the gallantry award.

Korean Communist forces launched 6000 men in an all-out attack on a vital ridge on the eve of Guy Fawkes' Day and the actions of 20-year-old Second Lieutenant Purves were, according to his official citation, "an inspiration to all".

The main weight of "Charlie Chinaman's Gunpowder Plot" as the troops called it, fell on three companies of the 1st Battalion King's Own Scottish Borderers who were holding the ridge line position.

The citation accompanying the award to the young officer said that although he had been in great pain from a serious wound in the right shoulder, he fought an eight-hour battle on a partly overrun position under intense enemy artillery fire.

He later brought his men to safety with great skill and coolness and it was not until he had received a direct order from his commanding officer that he sought medical attention for his wounds

His citation continued: "The outstanding leadership, bravery and resource of this young officer, together with his sense of responsibility, were an inspiration to all. The stubborn defence of this feature contributed materially to preventing the battalion from being overrun."

CLAN MARCH FIASCO

An estimated half a million people crowded into Edinburgh's Princes Street to see a parade of hundreds of pipers as part of the International Clan Gathering in August. The crowd overwhelmed the police on duty and the march ended in chaos as the crowds pressed forward and forced it to a stop.

COMINGS...

Gordon Brown
Labour Chancellor

ON RADIO

Listen with Mother
Life with the Lyons
The Archers
Crazy People

ON TV

Watch with Mother
Bat Masterson
What's My Line

ESCAPE ATTEMPT BUNKERED

Mrs J.F. Milligan of Riddrie in Glasgow got more than she bargained for when she went to fetch coal from her bunker. Cowering in the corner was an escaped convict from nearby Barlinnie Prison!

"I nearly fainted," she said. "He just looked up at me and shook his head as if to say 'don't tell anyone'. Well, I dropped the lid and ran round the front of the house shouting, 'There's a man in my bunker! There's a man in my bunker!'" The convict's freedom was short-lived: he was caught trying to board a bus nearby.

THIS SPORTING LIFE

FOOTBALL	RUGBY UNION	GOLF	HORSE RACING	SHINTY
Scottish Champions Hibernian	*Scotland vs England* England 5–3 Scotland at Twickenham	*Home Internationals* Scotland 8-7 England Scotland 6½-8½ Ireland Scotland 8-7 Wales	*Scottish Grand National Winner* Court Painter at Bogside	*Camanachd Cup Winners* Newtonmore at Inverness
Scottish Cup Winners Celtic				

ROSS'S LIQUEURS
Sloe Gin
Cherry Whisky

Daily ✤ Record
and Mail.

ESTABLISHED 1895. No. 17,610.   SATURDAY, MARCH 15, 1952.   A KEMSLEY NEWSPAPER. 1½d.

CALCUTTA CUP Page 6

Ask for **Red Tape** THE WHISKY *you may be fortunate*

Maximum Retail Prices as fixed by the Scotch Whisky Association. Small sizes available

The tartan on television

TV "HELLO" TO SCOTLAND

Reception was near perfect, says expert

THROUGHOUT Central and South Scotland TV's opening programmes last night from the Kirk o' Shotts transmitter were reported generally as " very clear reception and sound good."

Summing-up, an engineer attached to a large firm of manufacturers, which was getting first-hand reports by phone from its representatives throughout the country, said in Glasgow: reception was as near perfect as we could possibly have expected. Most areas within a 30-mile radius of the transmitting station were getting first-class images.

" We're not greatly concerned at the moment about places farther afield. Their reception might not be a hundred per cent. at present, but when more power is added to the Kirk o' Shotts transmitter sometime in July they will see a marked improvement."

In some outlying districts viewers reported fading an interference.

Freak reception

There was freak reception at Aberdeen, which is outwith the transmission area, but it was fading badly.

Belfast viewers who have been unable to tune into Holme Moss, received the Kirk o' Shotts transmission with only slight fading.

Over on the east coast of Scotland reception was almost perfect. A Kirkcaldy report stated there was no fading and very little interference. Dundee viewers also said it was nearly perfect.

Crowds gathered at shop windows in many towns where firms had sets operating. There was slight interference at some of these shows, probably due to passing traffic.

In Oban last night reception was surprisingly good notwithstanding the surrounding mountains.

Reports from other parts—
Kelso — Interference and slight fading.
Berwick—Fading at times.
Ayr — Good reception but some interference.
Greenock—Perfect reception.
Rothesay—Fair reception subject to slight fading.

● Members of the Royal Scottish Country Dance Society in the Duke of Edinburgh Reel on last night's television programme from Edinburgh. Watching from the platform are Mr. James Stuart, Secretary of State for Scotland; Lord Provost James Miller of Edinburgh, Lord Tedder and the Very Rev. Charles L. Warr. Below, in the studio, Miss Mary Malcolm and Alistair MacIntyre, the announcers, maintain the tartan motif for Scotland's big night.

...and it's rather awe-inspiring
Shop window displays attract crowds

"DAILY RECORD" REPORTER

SCOTLAND faced the television cameras —shyly and timidly—for the first time last night and home Scots seemed to find the experience awe-inspiring.

There was something uncanny about it all. Mr. James Stuart, Secretary of State for Scotland, nervously fingered his tie; Lord Tedder smoothed his jacket, and the subdued breathing of over 200 people could be heard in the deathly silence.

Suddenly a voice said—" Thirty seconds to go " and the breathing seemed to stop.

The man who had spoken—a technician with earphones over his head, raised his hand and then pointed to the far corner of the room. A woman's voice said—"This is the B.B.C. television programme" — and Scotland's television service was on the air.

Another page had been added to Scotland's history and the new medium had reached the land of J. Logie Baird—one of television's pioneers.

The scene was set in the B.B.C. headquarters in Scotland. The colourful evening dresses of the women showed up against the sombre black of the men.

At a table in the back of the studio were Lord Tedder, vice-chairman of the Board of Governors of the B.B.C.; Mr Stuart, Lord Provost James Miller of Edinburgh, and the Very Rev. Charles L. Warr, Dean of Thistle.

Fixed on those four men from different parts of the room were the large triple-lensed TV cameras, red lights flicking on and off as each one in turn took note of the scene.

BURST OF APPLAUSE

Everyone was excited. It could be seen in the nervous fingers of Mr. Stuart, the tapping of the Lord Provost, and restless hands and feet of the audience.

Exactly at 7.45 p.m. when Mr. Stuart officially declared the Kirk o' Shotts station open, the atmosphere, which had been so strained it could almost be felt, suddenly broke, and the nervousness dissolved in a burst of applause.

Mr Stuart sat down, obviously relieved that the nerve-shattering eye of the camera had now moved to the chief Scottish announcer, Mr. Alistair McIntyre.

For the whole gathering it was a memorable event, from the notabilities who overflowed into the foyer, to the Pressmen in the galleries, and the technicians behind the cameras.

Mr. Stuart condensed all our thoughts with his words: " One can imagine the scene and the visible restlessness of the

Continued on Back Page

Touch of brilliance

IT was a brilliant touch to make Scotland's first presentation the graceful dances which followed the speech making. Those gently swaying kilts, and charming figures, made a handsome picture at the close of " Rouken Glen."

Scots viewers will see so many red-nosed comedians and hard-boiled tap-dancers in future that they will be glad to think that their country's contribution was first offered in so happy an example of national grace and skill. Many will hope to see more of these dancers.

Alastair Sim's talk would have been a triumph at any time, but last night it came as a happy Scots contribution to a usually-serious feature.

Car crashed Through Vestibule

WHILE a motorist stood window-gazing in Stirling last night at Scotland's first TV show, his car ran off down a hill and crashed into the vestibule of the Regal Cinema in Maxwell Place.

It smashed through the swing doors after running up three steps leading to the cinema and finished up with its nose resting against the pay-box, where Mr. Edward Kelly, of 25 Cowan Street, Stirling, was buying a ticket.

FRIGHT OF LIFE

Mr. Kelly and the 19-year-old cashier, Barbara McLaren, of Tullibody, were showered with broken glass and wood as the car ripped through the entrance.

Miss McLaren escaped injury, but Mr. Kelly was taken to Stirling Royal Infirmary suffering from shock.

Miss McLaren, who sits with her back to the door, told the " Daily Record "—" I didn't see a thing.

" When I looked round, I got the fright of my life to find the car with its headlamps inches from me."

Inside, the audience were watching " Home to Danger "

for **SPEED— ACTION— SAFETY—** TAKE 'ASPRO'

There are plenty of colds about—particularly feverish ones. To arrest them at the onset you need a medicine which acts with MAXIMUM speed—and dispels the first shivery, uneasy symptoms as soon as they appear. That means you need 'ASPRO'. You can take 'ASPRO' at any time, anywhere—and directly you take it 'ASPRO' combats the cold in three different ways—it acts as an anti-pyretic, quickly reducing feverishness— it soothes away the aches and pains—it promotes the action of the skin, too, helping you to get rid of the cold through the pores.

DON'T TOLERATE SORE THROAT— Gargle with— 'ASPRO'

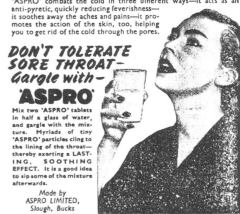

Mix two 'ASPRO' tablets in half a glass of water, and gargle with the mixture. Myriads of tiny 'ASPRO' particles cling to the lining of the throat— thereby exerting a LASTING, SOOTHING EFFECT. It is a good idea to sip some of the mixture afterwards.

Made by ASPRO LIMITED, Slough, Bucks.

BREAD DEARER FROM TO-MORROW

THE price of bread in Scotland will be increased by 11½d a 1lb 12oz loaf from to-morrow.

The Wholesale and Retail Bakers of Scotland decided this at a meeting in Glasgow yesterday when the Budget proposals on the bread subsidy were discussed.

A sliced and wrapped pan loaf is to cost 9d, unwrapped a penny cheaper. Plain batch loaves, sliced and wrapped, will be priced at 8½d and unwrapped at 7½d.

The 14 oz. pan or fancy loaf is to cost 4½d.

The bakers have also recommended price increases for morning rolls in the Glasgow area. Cost is to be raised from to-morrow by threepence to one shilling by dozen. Plain tea-bread, which used to sell at four for threepence, goes up to four for fivepence.

CLOUDY—Moderate or fresh south-easterly winds; mainly cloudy and dry with bright periods.

1952

SCOTS SWITCH ON TO THE TELLY

SCOTLAND faced the television camera, shyly and timidly, for the first time on the night of Friday, March 14.

The first TV programme to be broadcast was a scene filled with evening dresses and the sombre black evening dress suits of men as they celebrated the opening of the Kirk o' Shotts station in Lanarkshire.

Members of the Royal Scottish Country Dance Society performed the Duke of Edinburgh Reel.

Because comparatively few people owned television sets, crowds gathered outside shops in many towns where firms had the new technological "miracle" operating in their front windows.

There was slight interference reported but this was thought to be due to the passing traffic, interfering with the transmission – vehicles did not come fitted with signal suppressors in those days.

Throughout Central and South Scotland TV's opening programmes from the Kirk o' Shotts transmitter were reported generally as giving "a very clear reception and good sound".

An engineer who was involved with the gathering of reports from representatives throughout the country, said in Glasgow that the reception had been as near perfect as could be expected.

Most areas within a 30-mile radius of the transmitting station were getting first-class images.

However, in some outlying districts, viewers reported the picture fading and also interference to both the sound and vision.

Their reception was not 100 per cent but it was expected that when more power was added to the Kirk o' Shotts transmitter, then the viewers would see a marked improvement and "normal service would be resumed as soon as possible".

TRAGEDY STRIKES THE FASTEST MAN ON WATER

John Cobb, the fastest man on land, died in September as he was attempting to break the world speed record on water using a jet-propelled boat on the dark waters of Loch Ness. After his first run, Cobb was recorded travelling at speeds of 206.89 mph, 28mph faster than the world record, previously held by the American, Stanley Sayers.

As he prepared for the reverse run along the measured mile of the loch, Cobb's 400hp jet boat exploded to the obvious horror of the hundreds of people who had turned out to watch his record attempt.

MALAYSIAN TERRORISTS AMBUSH SCOTS TROOPS

In February, an officer and six men of the 1st Battalion Gordon Highlanders were killed in an ambush on a rubber estate, 53 miles south of Ipoh in southerrn Malaysia.

The Gordons had been in Malaysia since early 1951 as part of the effort to defeat the Communist guerrillas fighting for independence from British rule. They had gone to the estate following reports that terrorists were intimidating estate workers when they were attacked by around twenty bandits from prepared positions on high ground.

COMINGS...

Irvine Welsh
Author of Trainspotting

David Hayman
Actor & Director

James Naughtie
Radio Broadcaster

ON RADIO

The Goon Show

Science Review

Sportsreel

Hints for Housewives

Variety Playhouse

ON TV

Dragnet

The Appleyards

The Flowerpot Men

THIS SPORTING LIFE

FOOTBALL	RUGBY UNION	GOLF	HORSE RACING	SHINTY
Scottish Champions Hibernian	*Scotland vs England* Scotland 3–19 England at Murrayfield	*Home Internationals* Scotland 9-6 England Scotland 9½-5½ Ireland Scotland 10-5 Wales	*Scottish Grand National Winner* *Flagrant Mac* at Bogside	*Camanachd Cup Winners* Inverness at Glasgow
cottish Cup Winners Motherwell				

Daily and Mail. Record

ESTABLISHED 1895.   No. 17,990.   WEDNESDAY, JUNE 3, 1953   A KEMSLEY NEWSPAPER.   1½d.

ELIZABETH R

1953

DAWN OF A NEW ELIZABETHAN ERA

QUEEN ELIZABETH was taken to her coronation at Westminster Abbey by a golden, horse-drawn coach.

And millions heard – and saw on television – her take the Coronation Oath, binding her to the service of her people in Britain and the Commonwealth.

During the ceremony, the Duke of Edinburgh was by her side and he was the first to place his hands between those of the Queen in an act of homage.

Millions of people around the world were able to watch the ceremony.

They were almost able to feel they were present at the ceremony as they could finally hear the words that had sworn in kings and queens for centuries. The gold coach was a memorable sight as it travelled through the streets of London.

Despite the rain and the cold, the people did not seem to mind as they waited to catch a glimpse of their Queen.

In the abbey, the Duke of Edinburgh, wearing his duke's robes over the uniform of an Admiral of the Fleet, paced to the third chair.

The Queen and her ladies-in-waiting entered.

With the Archbishop, Her Majesty faced east, south, west and north.

The Archbishop said: "I here present unto you Queen Elizabeth, your undoubted Queen.

"Wherefore of all you who are come here this day to do homage and service, are you willing to do the same?" There were shouts of approval.

The Queen curtsied graciously in acknowledgement.

Her responses to the questions by the Archbishop followed: "I solemnly promise so to do" … "I will" … "All this I promise to do" … "The things which I have here promised, I will perform and keep, so help me God."

The Queen was then anointed by the Archbishop, who then took St Edward's Crown, took one pace forward, raised it high and held it there before placing it slowly and gently on the head of Her Majesty.

This was met with shouts of "God save the Queen".

LOCHABER LASHED

In late May, pedestrians all across the Lochaber district of Inverness-shire had to wade through surging waters to get to work and local bus services were suspended, following the worst thunderstorm that Scotland had experienced for half a century. Houses and business premises were flooded and landslides blocked roads and swept away sections of railway track. Telephone lines were put out of action and electricity supplies disrupted. Mountain torrents swept down steep hill roads in the upper reaches of Fort William tearing huge holes in the road surface and leaving masses of debris in their wake.

ON RADIO		
The Eye Witness You May Like to Hear	Saturday Night Theatre	Twenty Questions A Life of Bliss

IRISH FERRY DISASTER

In January, the Stranraer-to-Larne steamer *Princess Victoria* ran into the full force of a 110mph hurricane which had been battering Scotland for more than a day. The boat was blown 20 miles off course before she capsized. Only 45 survivors were picked up by rescue ships out of the 177 men, women and children passengers.

THIS SPORTING LIFE

FOOTBALL	RUGBY UNION	GOLF	HORSE RACING	SHINTY
Scottish Champions Rangers *Scottish Cup Winners* Rangers	*Scotland vs England* England 26–8 Scotland at Twickenham	*British Open Winner* Ben Hogan at Carnoustie (282)	*Scottish Grand National Winner* Queen's Taste at Bogside	*Camanachd Cup Winners* Lovat at Fort William

GOLDEN SHRED

puts the taste on the toast

SCOTLAND'S NATIONAL NEWSPAPER

Daily Record

ESTABLISHED 1895.   No. 18,333.   FRIDAY, JULY 9, 1954.   A KEMSLEY NEWSPAPER.   1½d.

SLOANS
Restaurant AND LOUNGE BAR
make it YOUR INN WHEN OUT
ARGYLL ARCADE
GLASGOW

- Scotland's £20M. hope comes true
- For hundreds in Motherwell—JOBS

COLVILLES STEEL PROJECT MEANS A BOOM

Industrial Reporter

PLANS for a new £20M. iron and steel plant at Motherwell were announced yesterday by Colvilles, the Scottish steelmakers.

It is the most important industrial development in Scotland for years.

Colvilles have received permission from the Iron and Steel Board and the Iron and Steel Holding and Realisation Agency to go ahead with expansion plans which have been on ice for several years.

The new plant is to be built on a site of more than a square mile at Ravenscraig, east of Colvilles' Dalzell Works and near their subsidiary, the Lanarkshire Steel Company.

Work is to begin immediately and should be completed by the autumn of 1957. There will then be jobs for between 700 and 800 more steelworkers.

And this is only a first instalment. The layout has been designed to provide for further expansion in the future.

The plant could ultimately be doubled in size and production stepped up to 800,000 ingot tons a year.

THE START

To begin with there will be two batteries of 35 coke ovens, a giant blast furnace capable of producing 1000 tons of pig iron a day, and a melting shop with three furnaces of 220 tons capacity which will produce 400,000 tons of steel a year.

Some of Colvilles' older furnaces will be demolished when the initial scheme matures and there will be a net increase in their output from 1,800,000 ingot tons to 2,045,000 tons a year.

With the new coke ovens will go a boiler plant and power station generating electricity from surplus gases, and a by-products plant to strip the coke oven gases of valuable chemicals before they are used as fuel.

Vast quantities of coking coal and imported ore — between 500,000 and 600,000 more tons of each—will be needed to keep the new blast furnace supplied.

The ore handling facilities at Rothesay Dock, Clydebank, could not cope with this demand and an entire new installation is to be provided at General Terminus Quay, Glasgow, which will make it possible to unload there simultaneously two of the largest type of ore-carrying vessels.

THE TRAINS

A shuttle service of special trains will operate between the terminus, the existing Clyde Iron Works and the new works at Motherwell, where the latest mechanised handling methods will enable Colvilles' men to empty a whole train load in 45 minutes.

Sir Andrew McCance, deputy chairman and joint managing director of Colvilles, said yesterday that one of the reasons for the long delay with this project was that there had been some controversy about the choice of a site for the new integrated plant.

The alternative was a waterfront location in Renfrewshire, first advocated many years ago, but it is now clear that the

Continued on Back Page

God bless you... real big

In a way, this was evangelist Billy Graham's happiest moment of the year. He got back to New York yesterday after five months' "crusading" in Europe. And there was Ruth, his wife, and the children.

Between Billy and Ruth is the other Ruth, aged 3, while Anne (6) got up on the shoulders of Virginia (8) to welcome Daddy home. The baby son was at home.

To-day, the whole family will be together at their mountain home in Tennessee. . . . Billy's to pray in peace and quiet about whether he's to come back to Scotland in 1955.

And also to play with the kids. When he's home, he allows an hour every day to romp about with them. But for most of the year, he's away preaching —and so it has been for the 11 years of their married life.

Even at home there are interruptions—sightseers. "It's not good for the children," says Ruth, so they're planning to move house up the mountain.

M.P.s get the rise

M.P.s last night got their pay-rise. But the Tories have not got their "pairs."

The Prime Minister in Parliament announced: "We give £2-a-day on Mondays, Tuesdays, Wednesdays and Thursdays . . . but not Fridays."

He named it a "sessional allowance," decreed it applicable only when Parliament is sitting, and left M.P.s to calculate it as a gross gain of between £250 and £280 a year.

His statement ended the pay wrangle. Its terms had been accepted by Socialists at a private meeting yesterday morning.

A fortnight earlier they had raised the roof, decided in private they would take nothing other than a straight pay rise.

In their private party meeting yesterday many Socialists are believed to have voted, still, against accepting the Government's compromise. Many, too, abstained.

ONE ISSUE

But to-day Sir Winston remains faced with the "pairs war." for Labour M.P.s last night refused an armistice.

"We do not support the Prime Minister's announcement on pay. . . . We merely acquiesce," was their attitude as they insisted on continuing their guerilla warfare against the Government.

On pay there remains only one issue on which to argue. The day the new allowance starts. It is not likely to cause much trouble. It will probably be May 24, the day Parliament voted on the pay issue. If so, M.P.s already have a "bonus" of nearly £50 to claim as "back-pay."

There will be no escaping the Tax collector. These expenses will be set against a member's total expenses claim — leaving more of his actual salary than hitherto liable to Tax deduction.

Many M.P.s calculate they will be little more than £150 a year in pocket from the new allowance.

The Government itself expects the Exchequer to be little more

Continued on Back Page

Individually MADE TO MEASURE *that's the point!*

At HEPWORTHS the words *"individually Made-to-Measure"* mean exactly what they imply. All bespoke garments are individually cut by hand to the customer's own measurements and then tailored by skilled craftsmen. Such suits—perfect in every detail—cost only . . .

£8.15   £10.15   £12.15

Hepworth's

Where the *GOOD CLOTHES* come from

H200

Branches at ABERDEEN · AIRDRIE · ALLOA · ARBROATH · AYR · BATHGATE · BUCKIE · CUPAR · COATBRIDGE · DINGWALL · DUNDEE · DUNFERMLINE · DUMFRIES · EDINBURGH (SOUTH BRIDGE AND TOLLCROSS) · ELGIN · FALKIRK · FORRES · FORT WILLIAM GREENOCK · HAMILTON · HAWICK · KEITH · INVERNESS · KILMARNOCK · KIRKCALDY KIRKWALL · LEITH · LERWICK · LEVEN · PERTH · THURSO · MOTHERWELL · PAISLEY PETERHEAD · ST. ANDREWS · STIRLING · STORNOWAY

£20M GO-AHEAD FOR STEEL PLANT

IT was announced in July that a £20million iron and steel plant was to be built at Motherwell by the Scottish steel makers, Colville's.

This was one of Scotland's biggest industrial projects.

After being on hold for years, the extension plans were finally given the go-ahead by the Iron and Steel Board and the Iron and Steel Holding and Realisation Agency.

The new plant was to be built on a site of more than a square mile at Ravenscraig, east of the Colville's Dalzell works.

Construction was intended to be completed by the autumn of 1957 and it was thought that there would be jobs for between 700 and 800 more steelworkers.

This was to be only the first instalment, for the plant layout had been designed for expansion.

It had the capacity to be doubled in size and its production stepped up to 800,000 ingot tons a year.

The plant was to be a great boost to Scottish shipbuilding and other industries.

To begin with, there were to be two batteries of 35 coke ovens and a giant blast furnace capable of producing 1000 tons of pig iron a day. There was also to be a melting shop with three furnaces of 220 tons capacity which it was estimated would produce 400,000 tons of steel a year.

And there was to be a net increase in the output of the furnaces from 1,800,000 ingot tons to 2,045,000 tons a year.

Sir Andrew McCance, deputy chairman and joint managing director of Colville's, said that one of the reasons for the long delay with this project was that there had been some controversy about the choice of a site for the new integrated plant.

HOME TOO SOON

The Scottish football squad left for their first World Cup campaign in June. Smiles soon turned to tears as the Scots were completely outclassed by their group opponents. World Champions Uruguay thrashed them 7-0 and the Scots eventually finished the tournament without gaining a point.

ON RADIO	ON TV
Hancock's Half Hour	Rin Tin Tin
Hello Playmates	The Grove Family

COMINGS...

Annie Lennox	Iain Banks	Marcella Evarist
Pop Singer	Author	Dramatist

PRESTWICK AIR CRASH

Thirty-two people were killed on Christmas morning in an air crash at Prestwick airport. Their plane, a B.O.A.C. four-engine Strato-cruiser, crashed on the main runway and burst into flames. There were only 4 survivors. The blaze was seen for many miles around as seven units of Prestwick Fire Brigade raced to the airport. Rescue teams and local doctors were called from their homes to assist in the rescue.

THIS SPORTING LIFE

FOOTBALL	RUGBY UNION	GOLF	HORSE RACING	SHINTY
Scottish Champions Celtic	Scotland vs England Scotland 3–13 England at Murrayfield	Home Internationals Scotland 6-9 England Scotland 6-9 Ireland Scotland 9-6 Wales	Scottish Grand National Winner Queen's Taste at Bogside	Camanachd Cup Winners Oban Celtic at Inverness
Scottish Cup Winners Celtic				

SUNDAY MAIL

Scotland's National Sunday Newspaper.

No. 2426. MARCH 20, 1955. A KEMSLEY NEWSPAPER 2½d.

Scotland can give a lead to the whole world but . . .

DO NOT LOOK FOR MIRACLES, SAYS BILLY

ANOTHER COAL SHOCK

By J. D. MARGACH

BIG increases in coal prices are coming. They'll be the biggest since the war, with drastic increases in the prices of coal for major industries and nationalised industries like the railways.

And the cost of the stiff increases in industry's overheads will have to be passed on to the ordinary coal consumers.

Facing a total deficit of £17M., the National Coal Board have agreed big price rises are necessary to put their finances on a healthier level.

Wage rises

The Board also have an eye on the proposed new wage increases which will cost them £13M. extra a year.

But all the increased prices will be concentrated almost wholly on coal for industrial users, to relieve domestic and household coal of any additional burden.

Tanker got stop order

The crew of the Finnish tanker Aruba, carrying 13,000 tons of jet fuel for Communist China, have agreed to sail her into the Indian Ocean and wait in international waters between Ceylon and Malaya for further orders.

The decision was announced in Helsinki to-day by the Finnish Seamen's Union, which has authorised the crew to refuse to sail in "dangerous waters."

Singapore Port authorities will refuse bunkering facilities to the Aruba if she calls there. The Western powers have claimed that she is breaking a ban on strategic exports to China imposed by the United Nations, of which Finland is not a member.

In Peking, the official People's Daily accused the United States to-day of sending five warships to Singapore to interfere with the tanker's voyage to Whampoa, the port of Canton.

Report in Hong Kong say that the "Aruba" is operating under a contract which is valid only if the tanker reaches Communist China.

Nehru's war fears

The dangers of war were increasing, Mr. Nehru, the Indian Premier, told a rally at Chandigarh, yesterday. In the event of war, he said, India would stay away from it.

AFTER 16 YEARS MRS. NOIMA SEES DAUGHTER

FROM Communist China, 76-year-old Mrs. Sura Noima arrived at London Airport yesterday to meet her daughter and son-in-law for the first time in 16 years.

Her son-in-law, Mr. Arnold Thompson, of Peel Grove, Longsight, Manchester, said that he was married while serving with the Lancashire Fusiliers in China in 1938.

His mother-in-law was a White Russian and for the past four years he had been trying to get her to join him.

"But we had some difficulties with the authorities in China and finally, through the international Committee for European Migration, we were Ur . . 'aiom faiom faiom faiaoa advised that my mother-in-law would be joining us."

Mrs. Noima was flown from Hong Kong by the I.C.F.M. together with a number of European refugees.

Her three grandchildren—Arnold (14), Raymond (eight) and Ellie (six) were at the airport to greet her.

"The problem isn't the hydrogen bomb or the Communists . . ." Billy Graham talking to the Press yesterday.

Baby in pram disappeared

LEAVING their four-month-old baby girl asleep in her pram outside yesterday, a young couple went into the new house they had .bought in Garfield Street, Dennistoun, Glasgow. Minutes later the mother looked from a window and was horrified to see that the baby and pram had disappeared.

After a frantic search of the area the baby was found—still sleeping in her pram—being wheeled through a busy shopping area by a six-year-old toddler.

The baby, Fiona Anderson, is the daughter of Sergeant George Anderson, a 25-year-old national serviceman in the R.E.M.E., and his wife, Georgina.

When Mrs. Anderson saw that the pram had disappeared, she almost collapsed.

Sergeant Anderson and his father, Mr. George Anderson, raced downstairs, but the street was deserted. Running in opposite directions, they scoured the area while a "999" call was sent to police headquarters.

Began to cry

It was Sergeant Anderson who spotted the pram—being wheeled along Bellfield Street by a small girl.

"I asked the toddler why she had taken the baby," said Sergeant Anderson afterwards, "and she just started crying and ran off through a close.

And the mystery girl? She disappeared leaving only one clue behind—a green, imitation crocodile handbag.

He broke siege of Leningrad

MARSHAL Leonid Govorov, who broke the siege of Leningrad in the last war, died yesterday after a long illness, Moscow Radio announced.

Marshal Govorov was Deputy Defence Minister.

The early stages of the war saw Marshal Govorov in command of artillery on one of the sectors of the Soviet-German front. When the Germans closed in on Leningrad he was chosen to command that front and the skill with which he conducted operations there led to the smashing of the blockade of Leningrad.

36,360 new cars

Cars registered for the first time in January numbered 36,360. New motor cycles totalled 11,264.

BOY (15) SWORE AT HEAD

WHEN the father of a 15-year-old Caithness boy was summoned because of the boy's irregular attendance at school, the boy went to his headmaster's house to get an explanation, the procurator-fiscal, Mr. C. J. H. Campbell, told Wick Juvenile Court yesterday.

The headmaster refused to discuss the matter and said that he would see the boy at school. And when the boy was ordered out of the house, he started shouting and swearing at the headmaster.

Mr. Campbell said the boy thought that he was being blamed for non-attendance on August 31 whereas he was actually at school on that date.

Later in the day, the boy went to see the headmaster in the school staffroom and again demanded an explanation about the date.

A policeman who was on premises was attracted by the noise of the boy shouting. The boy then calmed down and went away.

The warning . . .

The boy was charged with having: (1) Within the schoolhouse occupied by the headmaster conducted himself in a disorderly manner and committed a breach of the peace. (2) Within the headmaster's staff room threatened the headmaster and conducted himself in a disorderly manner.

Sheriff Peter Thomson, in admonishing him, warned the boy that if he appeared in court again he would have to be disciplined.

"We cannot tolerate behaviour like this towards a headmaster," he said.

JAMAICAN INVASION

OFFICIALS of Salvation Army and Y.M.C.A. hostels and borough councils in London's coloured communities are planning emergency measures this week-end to meet an invasion by Jamaicans.

One thousand are due to land at Plymouth.

WITH his Bible...

WITH his Bible in one hand and his hat in the other, Billy Graham acknowledged his enthusiastic welcome to Scotland yesterday with the message: "The eyes of the world are on you. You can be the start of a religious revival that will sweep the world."

But he counselled: "DON'T EXPECT MIRACLES. DON'T EXPECT TOO MUCH FROM US."

Billy Graham—"Call me plain mister. I haven't earned my degree of doctor"—obviously wasn't expecting the tremendous welcome that awaited when he arrived in Glasgow for the start of his six-week All-Scotland Crusade.

Certainly, he didn't expect the reception he got en route—at Dumfries, time 7 a.m.

In fact he was almost caught napping by the hymn singing crowds who had gathered to see him pass.

"I was still in bed when I heard them singing outside," he told reporters. "I decided if they had got up that early to greet me, I could get up to speak to them. I did, flinging my overcoat on top of my pyjamas. But it became rather difficult when they wanted me to pose for pictures . . . I had to explain my position."

WELCOME HYMN

In Glasgow, over 3000 people crowded St. Enoch Station to welcome the tall, sun-tanned, wavy-haired preacher with the film-star looks. As he stepped from the train they started to sing a hymn. A man with a Salvation Army hat played a cornet, while another accompanied the singing with a concertina.

A diminutive, grimy-faced porter elbowed his way through the official reception party on the platform to grab Mr. Graham's hand and pump it up and down with great gusto. And a woman with a little girl broke from the crowd and put her arm round his waist. She accompanied the smiling evangelist as he

ALL-NIGHT PRAYERS

As Billy Graham was travelling to Scotland, an all-night prayer meeting for the success of his campaign was held in Aberdeen Gilcomston South Church.

When it began at 10 p.m. on Friday, there was a congregation of about 400. At the conclusion at 6 a.m. yesterday about 50 people were in the church.

There were sessions of hymn singing, scripture reading, and prayers.

pushed his way through the cheering, singing throng.

Before leaving to meet almost 100 reporters in a hotel, he told the crowd from a balcony window overlooking the station: "We have been praying all the way across the Atlantic that God may start a spiritual revival here in Glasgow."

And to reporters he said: "This mission to Glasgow is all-important. The eyes of the Christian world are on us. I believe we will have the start of a religious revival that will sweep the whole world.

Continued on Back Page

It is the
Quality
of your
Sleep
which counts

That
is why countless thousands drink delicious

Ovaltine
The World's Best Nightcap

1/6, 2/6 and 4/6 per tin.

No other beverage can give you better sleep

Look out for rain

It will be fine, despite fog patches over most of the country early to-day. Rain or sleet possible later.

In the west and south-west it will be mainly cloudy with a chance of rain.

1955

'NO MIRACLE CURE' SAYS BILLY

AMERICAN evangelist Billy Graham was enthusiastically welcomed to Scotland in March and gave the country this message:

"The eyes of the world are on you. You can be the start of a religious revival that will sweep the world."

But he warned people not to expect miracles or to expect too much from him.

Billy Graham had not been expecting the welcome that awaited him when he arrived in Glasgow at the beginning of his six-week crusade.

More than 3000 people crammed into St Enoch Station to welcome the preacher with the film star looks.

As he stepped from the train, he was greeted by a hymn-singing audience.

Mr Graham said: "This mission to Glasgow is all-important. The eyes of the Christian world are on us.

"I believe we will have the start of a religious revival that will sweep the world.

"Most of us realise that we are living in one of the most tense and critical periods in the world history. Our only hope for survival is to turn to religion and Glasgow can play its part."

Mr Graham said that in his opinion there was still a point of contact between East and West and this was in the realm of the spirit. Americans, Russians, Chinese and Japanese had the same longing and yearnings and the same spiritual capacity as the Scottish people.

He added: "The problem of mankind is not with the hydrogen bomb or the Communists.

"It is the basic problem of human nature. Men and women are the problem and until they can change, we are never going to solve the world's problems."

Mr Graham believed that his campaign in Scotland would prove to be greater than his London campaign in 1954.

In answer to a question indicating that, given the crime rate in America, he would be better preaching at home, Mr Graham said:

"My campaign in Scotland will have a greater impact on America than any campaign I ever held there.

"They hold you, the old country, in awe. They are willing to follow your lead."

"TEN BOB WIDOWS" PROTEST

The "Ten Bob Widows Protest Association" travelled from Edinburgh to open a branch in Glasgow. They were widows who received a pension of only 10 shillings (50p) a week because they were under 50 when their husbands died. The pension increased when they reached 60, but women widowed at 60 or over got a pension of £2.00 per week. The president of the Glasgow association, the redoubtable Mrs Gallacher of Garriochmill Road, highlighted the injustice to the gathering of hundreds of middle-aged women: "I brought up two boys on that measly pension, only to have it stopped when they reached 15!"

ON RADIO

Workers' Playtime	The Jimmy Logan Show
Music To Remember	Family Favourites

COMINGS...

Alex Salmond
SNP Leader

PLANS FOR ATOMIC TRAINS STOPPED IN THEIR TRACKS

In January, the *Daily Record* reported on the British Transport Commission's ambitious plans to electrify Scotland's railway system using energy generated at the nuclear plant at Dounreay. However, a secondary plan to create an integrated road and rail transport system in Scotland's largest urban centre was vetoed by Glasgow Corporation on the grounds that it would lead to an increase in fares for passengers.

THIS SPORTING LIFE

FOOTBALL	RUGBY UNION	GOLF	HORSE RACING	SHINTY
Scottish Champions Aberdeen	*Scotland vs England* England 9–6 Scotland at Twickenham	*British Open Winner* Peter Thomson at St Andrews (281)	*Scottish Grand National Winner* Bar Point at Bogside	*Camanachd Cup Winners* Newtonmore at Glasgow
Scottish Cup Winners Clyde				

Daily Record

TUES AUG 28 1956

SCOTLAND'S NATIONAL NEWSPAPER

2ᴰ

No. 18,978

WHY THIS MADNESS?

Shipyard bosses and men in head-on clash

By Andrew Hargrave
'Record' Industrial Correspondent

THE Clyde is faced with a complete shut-down of its busy shipyards.

Bosses and 5500 key men are lined up for a head-on clash over guaranteed pay.

● The **BOSSES** declare the Clyde will be forced out of the cut-throat world market if they gave in.

● The **MEN** declare modern methods are threatening their pay packets and they demand security.

There are only three days left to stop the madness of a prolonged dispute.

WHAT IS THE SITUATION?

Yesterday Clyde shipbuilding employers gave a flat "No" to the "black squad" demand for guaranteed pay.

5500 INVOLVED

They have rejected the strike ultimatum by 3000 key craftsmen—platers, caulkers and burners, who yesterday were joined by 2500 welders, making a total of 5500.

Which means as from 5.30 p.m. on Friday the biggest industrial war on the Clyde since the General Strike of 1926.

WHAT IS AT STAKE?

The livelihood of 5500 workers and their families?

The business prospects of 28 yard owners and their shareholders?

THIS AND A GREAT DEAL MORE. The prosperity of the Clyde is the prosperity of Britain.

CLYDE'S SHARE

At the moment more than 600,000 tons of new shipping worth £50M. is being built on the Clyde—one ship in every three in the whole of the country.

Orders for nearly 1,500,000 tons worth about £115 million are on hand.

But those ships will **NOT** be started if the 5500 strike.

For platers, caulkers, burners and welders are INDISPENSABLE for the smooth working of the rest of the 27,000 shipbuilding men of the Clyde.

Their work is indispensable to thousands more in outside firms who serve the Clyde yards.

So you see a complete shut-down is inevitable unless a compromise is reached.

Said the Clyde Shipbuilders' Association after its crisis talks yesterday:

"The meeting was conscious of the serious consequences which would result from the strike . . . both as regards the suspension of thousands of other workpeople who are in no way parties to the dispute, and also of its effect on the output and the reputation of the shipbuilding industry on the Clyde."

No illusions

Nor are the officials of the union — the Boilermakers' Society—under any illusion.

Last night their local officials —Mr. Robert Neilson and John Chalmers, of Glasgow, and Mr. Tom Canning, of Greenock— were studying the employers' statement and drafting a reply.

But Mr. Chalmers assured me once again:

"We are ready and willing to meet the employers any time to see if we can reach a settlement."

The men want security. "They want to know what to expect in their wage packets at the end of the week," an official told me.

They are afraid of new methods and techniques making inroads in

Continued on Back Page

BAND MAN RAY SWEPT HER OFF HER FEET

BAND leader Ray Ellington carried off his bride yesterday . . . and didn't the bride like it!

Ray, aged 40, and TV actress Ann Wuest, aged 21, were off to a honeymoon in Majorca after their wedding at Caxton Hall Register Office, London.

But it wasn't a swept-off-her-feet romance altogether . . . Ray and Ann became engaged last September, broke it off a couple of months later . . . then re-discovered they really loved each other.

For superb tailormades Watt Brothers always!

INDEED, the new Autumn collection of classic coats and suits now on show in these famous Fashion Salons are already attracting many ladies to make an early selection from what is the most comprehensive display of Quality tailormades to be seen anywhere, with the widest variety of styles . . . sizes . . . and prices too!

The New Autumn Coats and Suits at Watt Brothers are Simply Irresistible!

STYLED by London's finest Designers in ladies' Couture clothes, the cut is superb . . . the finish, perfection . . . the tailoring is by craftsmen . . and the quality of the materials maintain that wonderful reputation for high-class garments which Watt Brothers have SO long enjoyed . . . and which SO many ladies appreciate.

Definitely! For Superb Tailormades! It's Watt Brothers . . . ALWAYS!

Prices from 8½ Gns. to 30 Gns.

Watt brothers

OF SAUCHIEHALL STREET, GLASGOW

Flood can make this ghost village

THE tiny village of Broom of Moy, Morayshire, is in an even more desperate position now than when the floods swept in for the second time two weeks ago.

Only a two-foot thick bank keeps the River Findhorn at bay, and meanwhile damage to cottages mounts every day.

WALLS are cracking and water drips from the ceilings.

CARPETS have been ruined by the muddy morass.

FURNITURE is being affected by mould.

AND THEY WILL BE UNINHABITABLE IF THE FINDHORN STRIKES AGAIN. BROOM OF MOY MAY BE A GHOST VILLAGE.

Stuart shocked

Devastation in the area shocked Scottish Secretary James Stuart yesterday.

Mr. Stuart toured the district with Provost Robert Braid of Forres and talked with farmers whose crops have been laid waste by the muddy waters.

Provost Braid said after the tour: "**Mr. Stuart said he was shocked by the destruction he had seen.**

"Plans for the strengthening of the banks and added protective measures will be discussed by the Scottish Secretary and the magistrates today."

Constant vigil

Villagers are being given financial help from a local fund started by Brigadier H. Houldsworth, Lord Lieutenant of Morayshire.

But if the rains come again the villagers are ready to quit. A day and night vigil is being kept on the river.

Mrs. Ferguson of Westermoy Farm, whose husband William helped to rescue the villagers in the past, said: "The fishermen are nervous.

"The river rises so quickly they cannot help watching it. They are afraid of the rain."

● In Forres police check the river every few hours. Sandbags are kept ready in case of a break-through.

Unions pass Suez motion

Midlothian County Trades Council, meeting at Penicuik, passed an emergency resolution viewing with concern Britain's Suez policy.

1956

SHIPYARDS STRIKE SHUTDOWN

THE Clyde was faced in August with a complete shutdown of its busy shipyards as owners and workers lined up for a head-on clash over guaranteed pay.

The shipyard owners claimed that they would be forced out of the cut-throat world market if they agreed to the union's demand. The men declared that modern working methods were threatening their pay packets. They demanded security.

The employers' side flatly rejected the demand for guaranteed pay, in the face of the strike ultimatum issued by the 3,000 caulkers, platers and burners. The tradesmen were later joined in their demands by the 2,500 welders. On August 31, the biggest industrial conflict on the Clyde since the General Strike of 1926 began.

At the time of the strike, more than 600,000 tons of new shipping worth £50m was being built on the Clyde. A third of all British shipbuilding was taking place in west central Scotland. Further orders for nearly 1.5m tons, worth about £115m, were on hand. These new ships could not be started however if the 5,500 tradesmen stayed on strike. The rest of the 27,000 workforce could not work without them.

However, the threat of automation stiffened the resolve of the men of the Clyde. Welders, caulkers and burners wanted £14 7s 6d (£14.38), with the platers demanding £13 5s 6d (£13.28) for a 44-hour week.

Summary sackings by the yard owners did not at first weaken their resolve. However, the knock-on effect was having serious implications throughout Clydeside as families struggled to get by. The Lord Provost of Glasgow and community leaders pleaded with both sides to reach a compromise. The strike was finally settled on September 20. However, 5,000 jobs had been lost and the men had to return to work without guaranteed pay, although they were offered improved terms and a measure of job security.

'THEFT OF THE CENTURY' TRIO JAILED

Three men were imprisoned in January for what was rather excitedly known as 'the theft of the century'. After a nine-day trial, John Lappen, John Blundell and Charles McGuinness were found guilty at Glasgow's High Court of holding up a bank van and stealing £44,000 the previous July.

Three other men had 'not proven' verdicts returned on them and they were freed.

Only a small quantity of the stolen cash was ever recovered.

PUSHKAS TRIED TO FLEE TO SCOTLAND

It was revealed in October that Ferenc Pushkas, Hungary's footballing genius, had planned to slip away from the Hungarian team during its visit to Scotland in December 1954 and seek asylum here. It was claimed he was sick of the restrictions in Communist Hungary and had expressed an interest in playing for Celtic. Unfortunately, the plan came to nothing and was kept secret until after Pushkas' death in the Hungarian Uprising.

ON TV

Highway Patrol

Hancock's Half Hour

Lassie

Gunsmoke

Opportunity Knocks

ON RADIO

17 Sauchie Street

Have A Go!

THIS SPORTING LIFE

FOOTBALL	RUGBY UNION	GOLF	HORSE RACING	SHINTY
Scottish Champions Rangers	Scotland vs England Scotland 6–11 England at Murrayfield	Home Internationals Scotland 9½ - 5½ England Scotland 8 - 7 Ireland Scotland 10½ - 4½ Wales	Scottish Grand National Winner Queen's Taste at Bogside	Camanachd Cup Winners Kyles Athletic at Oban
Scottish Cup Winners Hearts				

Daily Record

TUES
MAR 12
1957

2ᵈ   No. 19,145   SCOTLAND'S NATIONAL NEWSPAPER

25,000

Sensational start for Scotland's drive to beat TB

Watch for it here too...

- Aberdeen
- Ayr
- Kilmarnock
- Lanarkshire
- West Lothian
- Edinburgh
- Midlothian
- Perth
- Port Glasgow
- Dundee

MORE than 25,000 people rushed to be X-rayed yesterday as Scotland's newest drive to beat TB got off to a sensational start in Glasgow.

All world records were smashed. Volunteer workers offered to stay at their posts until midnight to clear long queues who were still outside the X-ray centres at their scheduled closing times.

At one such centre the machine became overheated AND HAD TO BE WRAPPED IN TOWELS SOAKED IN COLD WATER.

At another the machine broke down for three hours while hundreds of people waited outside.

The staff worked until midnight to make sure everyone was X-rayed.

Home by taxi

Police were called when an impatient-queue threatened to get out of hand in one area.

Again the staff worked overtime. Then they were sent home—most of them stay in Motherwell, about 20 miles away—by taxi.

A couple who are both deaf and blind waited in a queue of hundreds to go before the machine.

In another a woman of 94 was given priority.

Also given priority was an 80-year-old woman whose husband and son died of TB.

Confident

Late last night officials were talking of the amazing first day of the five-week campaign in Glasgow—Europe's worst TB spot.

And they were confident that the drive will get the same response when it moves to Perth, Dundee, Edinburgh and other towns and districts.

Bailie John Mains, Glasgow's health convener, spoke for his city. He said: "It's the greatest day we've ever had here."

An average of only 9000 a day is needed to reach the target of 250,000.

Zero hour ...

In the morning the atmosphere was strained. Zero hour was approaching.

Around the city 28 mobile x-ray units were in position. More than 20,000 volunteer workers were standing by.

Thousands of pounds had been spent on publicity ... thousands of man-hours had been worked in preparing the campaign.

WOULD THE GLASGOW PUBLIC RESPOND?

The praise

Soon they got their answer. From every centre came reports: "We're being flooded out with people."

After the doors opened the workers' big problem was how

A 'FLOOD'

to cope with the number of "patients."

BY 8.30 P.M. it was clear that the previous world record for one day's x-ray . . . 17,000 at Los Angeles four years ago . . . was going to be beaten.

AT 9.30 P.M. the official figure was 20,6000 . . . but that failed to take account of EIGHT centres for which there were no returns at that time.

AT 10 p.m. it was clear that the final figure for the day would be AT LEAST 25,000.

'Keep it up'

From officials there was praise for . . .

- The voluntary workers at the centres. "They have

Big George Young was there

Rangers and Scotland captain George Young (above) has an X-ray check-up yesterday. And awaiting their turn (left) are teammates George Niven and Sammy Baird.

...And so were other men of Rangers

done tremendous work," said Bailie Mains.

- FOR THE DOCTORS of the Public Health Department who planned the campaign and the publicity which has gone with it.

But most of all . . .

- FOR THE PUBLIC. "KEEP IT UP," said Dr. William Horne, the city's M.O.H. "AND WE WILL SMASH T.B. IN GLASGOW FOR ALL TIME...."

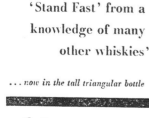

Sir Compton Mackenzie, famous author of 'Whisky Galore' says:

'I back my opinion of 'Stand Fast' from a knowledge of many other whiskies'

... *now in the tall triangular bottle*

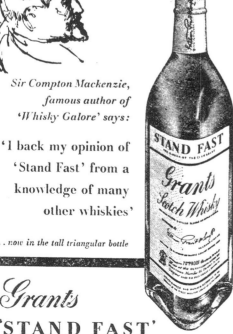

STAND FAST
Grants
Scotch Whisky

Grants
'STAND FAST'
SCOTCH WHISKY

Mick's swan song nearly

A STRAY mongrel yesterday cocked a snoot at a police cordon, fought against a strong ebb-tide, won a race for life against 100 angry swans . . . and vanished.

Hundreds watched from the bridge at the Shore, Leith.

Traffic was stopped as they watched the mongrel swim desperately up-river with a trail of hissing angry swans behind him.

Into trouble

Before that two policemen had cornered Mick the cheeky mongrel—who has a large streak of collie in him.

Mick looked desperately round

as the cops closed in. There was a warehouse on one side—a high wall flanking the dock waters of Leith on the other.

He chose the wall. Up and over he went . . . plunging 20ft. into the water.

He could not get out on the other side, so he luged up-river against the strong out-going tide.

The swans that wait for scraps to be thrown from passers-by on the bridge scattered alarmed.

Nearer and nearer they came, necks outthrust.

They were almost within beak distance of Mick when a friendly hand reached down from an iron ladder and scooped Mick to safety.

The arm belongs to 30-year-old

joiner Henry Main, of 25 Comely Bank Road, Edinburgh. He said later:

"I once saw a dog drowned by swans. I couldn't let that happen to the mongrel.

"When I got it ashore I thought it was exhausted. But it just shook itself and ran off."

And Mick the cheeky mongrel was still keeping clear of dog-catchers late last night.

SCOTS AIRPORTS ARE BOOMING

Last year Scotland's 13 civil aerodromes handled 925,619 passengers. And the Ministry of Transport and Civil Aviation confidently forecast that the million mark will be topped this year.

Renfrew set up a new passenger record with 373,958. Prestwick also had its busiest year ever with 243,307 and Edinburgh's total of 94,433 was 35 per cent up on the previous year.

SIR HARTLEY JOINS BIG PETROL FIRM

SIR HARTLEY SHAWCROSS, Labour M.P. for St. Helens, Lancs., who has given up his law practice, is to become a legal consultant for one of the country's biggest industrial concerns.

A spokesman for Shell Petroleum, said yesterday: "Sir Hartley will act as a legal consultant for companies in the Royal Dutch-Shell group.

'Rock' and soup for the First Lord

The First Lord of the Admiralty, the Earl of Selkirk, yesterday played a Bill Haley record on a juke box in Chatham naval barracks cafeteria.

He also tasted the soup in a galley during a 12-hour visit

1957

CROWDS FLOCK TO X-RAY UNITS

MORE than 25,000 people rushed to be X-rayed as Scotland's drive to beat TB got off to a sensational start in Glasgow.

Thousands of pounds were spent on publicity and manpower to promote the campaign. The big question was would the public respond?

That question was soon answered as reports from every centre said they had been flooded with people.

All world records were smashed as volunteer workers offered to stay at their posts until midnight to clear long queues who were still outside the X-ray centres after their scheduled closing times.

When the doors were opened, the workers' big problem was how to cope with the number of patients.

By 8.30pm in Glasgow, it was clear that the previous world record for one day's X-ray – 17,000 at Los Angeles in 1953 – was going to be soundly beaten.

At 10pm, it was clear that the final figure for the day would be at least 25,000.

Officials were talking of the amazing first day of the five-week campaign in Glasgow – the city which has Europe's worst record of the killer disease.

Bailie John Mains, Glasgow's Health Convener, said: "It's the greatest day we've had here."

An average of only 9000 a day is needed to reach the health organisers' target of 250,000.

Around the city, 28 mobile X-ray units were in position, manned by more than 20,000 volunteers.

Dr William Horne, the city's Medical Officer of Health, said, "If the public keep this up, then we will smash TB in Glasgow for all time."

CLYDE CRUSH

The problem of crushing at football games in Scottish stadiums, where tens of thousands turned up every Saturday, was a cause of concern for many years. The dangers were most graphically highlighted in the Ibrox Disaster of 1971, but incidents on a smaller scale were a common feature in earlier decades. A game at Shawfield Stadium, the home of Clyde FC, attracted such numbers that a wall collapsed, killing a 12-year-old boy and injuring many others. The tragedy prompted the Clyde Supporters' Association to demand a separate enclosure for boys and the elderly – a development far in advance of its time.

CINEMA GUTTED BY HUGE BLAZE

Forty families had to be evacuated when a huge blaze ripped through the Partick Picture House in Glasgow in February. Firemen on turntable ladders struggled to contain the fire as it roared 50 feet into the night sky. However, a series of explosions almost tore the roof off the cinema, one of Glasgow's oldest, and by the morning the Picture House was reduced to a smouldering shell.

COMINGS...

Michael Caton-Jones
Film Director

Ricky Ross
Pop Singer

ON TV

Emergency Ward 10

Pinky and Perky

The Sky at Night

ON RADIO

Gardeners' Question Time

Saturday Night on the Light

My Word!

Is There A Doctor In The House?

At Home & Abroad

THIS SPORTING LIFE

FOOTBALL	RUGBY UNION	GOLF	HORSE RACING	SHINTY
Scottish Champions Rangers	*Scotland vs England* England 16–3 Scotland at Twickenham	*British Open Winner* Bobby Locke at St Andrews (279)	*Scottish Grand National Winner* Bremontier at Bogside	*Camanachd Cup Winners* Newtonmore at Spean Bridge
Scottish Cup Winners Falkirk				

Daily Record

FRI MAY 30 1958

2½ᴅ SCOTLAND'S NATIONAL NEWSPAPER
No. 19.525

SENTENCED TO DEATH

PETER ANTHONY MANUEL, WHOSE PICTURE IS ON RIGHT, WAS SENTENCED TO DEATH AT GLASGOW HIGH COURT

He was found:—

Not guilty

of the murder of Anne Kneilands.

GUILTY

of the capital murders of Marion Watt, Margaret Brown, and Vivienne Watt.

GUILTY

of the murder of Isabelle Cooke.

GUILTY

of the capital murders of the Smart family.

GUILTY

of stealing the Smarts' car.

GUILTY

of breaking into a house at Bothwell, and firing a gun into a mattress.

GUILTY

of breaking into a house at High Burnside, and stealing jewellery and other items.

Not proven

on a charge of breaking into a house at North Mount Vernon.

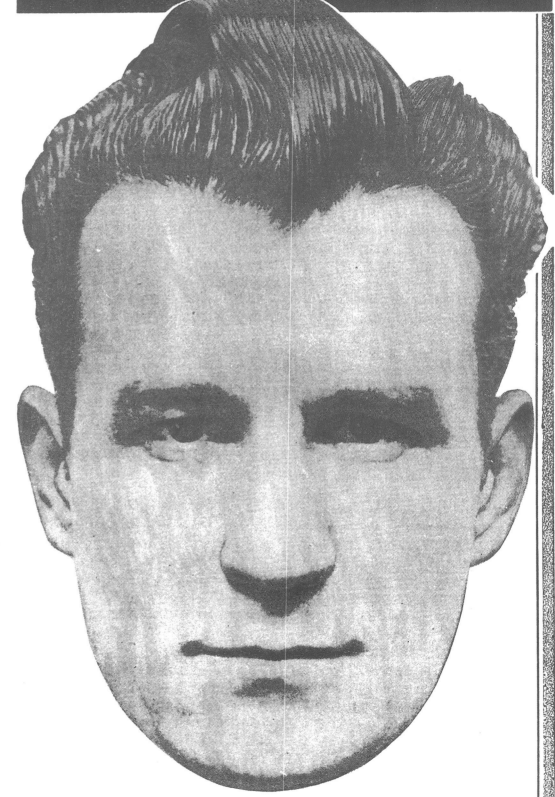

● PETER MANUEL . . . found guilty of seven murders

MASS MURDERER MANUEL TO HANG

SEVEN times murderer Peter Manuel was sentenced to the gallows by the High Court in Glasgow in May after what was dubbed "The Trial of the Century".

New York-born Manuel moved to Scotland as a child with his Scottish parents in the 1930s.

His murdering spree began in 1956 but he was not arrested until 1958.

Manuel's first victim was thought to be 17-year-old Anne Kneilands who was murdered in January 1956.

He was eventually charged with killing her by striking her on the skull with a piece of iron. However, at his trial, he was found not guilty.

Eight months later, Manuel, armed with a gun, broke into the Burnside home of baker Mr William Watt. Manuel killed Mrs Watt, her daughter Vivienne and the girl's aunt Mrs Brown.

Mr Watt had been on a fishing trip but became a prime suspect for the murders. Manuel came forward to offer evidence which led to Mr Watt's release, but Manuel was not charged with the crime at that point.

In December 1957, Isabelle Cooke, 17, disappeared in Glasgow.

Manuel was finally caught after the murders of an Uddingston family. He shot three members of the Smart family in their home and was later caught spending traceable, new bank notes.

Manuel stood trial for the murders of the Smarts, the Watts, Isabelle Cooke and Anne Kneilands in May 1958.

Throughout his trial, there were twists and turns.

It culminated in Manuel dismissing his defence counsel and representing himself.

He told his story for 88 sensation-packed minutes, not once faltering in his 17,000-word testimony.

On May 29, Manuel was sentenced to death after being found guilty of the murders of Marion and Vivienne Watt and Margaret Brown, Isabelle Cooke and the Smart family.

He was found not guilty of the murder of Anne Kneilands.

Manuel was hanged on July 11, 1958, at Glasgow's Barlinnie Prison.

'GENTLE JOHN' OUT AGAIN

In December, police were once again scouring Aberdeen for 'Gentle John' Ramensky, Scotland's most notorious safe-blower and jailbreaker. He had escaped for the third time this year from Peterhead's maximum security prison.

Ramensky spent more than 40 of his 67 years behind bars and his safe-cracking talents led to his release from prison during the war to join a special commando unit that stole documents behind enemy lines. After the war, he couldn't resist returning to his old ways.

ON RADIO

Beyond Our Ken

Roundabout

ON TV

77 Sunset Strip

M Squad

The Larkins

Casey Jones

Whirly Birds

Zorro

Grandstand

COMINGS...

Elaine C. Smith
Singer & Actress

POP SENSATION CAUSES DUNDEE TEEN RIOT

Singing star Tommy Steele fainted as hundreds of screaming teenagers mobbed him near the end of his show in May at Dundee's Caird Hall.

Steele and members of his band were forced to run as many of the 3000-strong audience mobbed the stage. Within minutes the passage to the dressing room was blocked with bodies and during the uproar that followed, Steele had his hair torn out and his clothing ripped by his fans. It was during this fracas that the pop star fainted.

He was later smuggled out of the hall through an underground passage.

THIS SPORTING LIFE

FOOTBALL	RUGBY UNION	GOLF	HORSE RACING	SHINTY
Scottish Champions Hearts	*Scotland vs England* Scotland 3–3 England at Murrayfield	*Home Internationals* Scotland 7 - 8 England Scotland 8½ - 6½ Ireland Scotland 10½ - 4½ Wales	*Scottish Grand National Winner* Game Field at Bogside	*Camanachd Cup Winners* Newtonmore at Inverness
Scottish Cup Winners Clyde				

Daily Record

SAT SEPT 19 1959

2½ᴰ

SCOTLAND'S NATIONAL NEWSPAPER

No. 19,933

DISASTER PIT FLOODED

ALL HOPE GONE....

Wives collapse at tragic news

ALL HOPE WAS GIVEN UP EARLY TODAY FOR 46 MEN TRAPPED 1000FT. BELOW GROUND BEHIND A WALL OF FLAMES.

Rescue teams were brought up and the blazing section of Auchengeich Colliery, at Chryston, Lanarkshire, was flooded.

For hours before the official announcement it seemed that no one could possibly have survived . . .

But hope lingered on—because of the Miracle of the Bell.

The bell — which connects with the section where the men were trapped—was pulled five times by one of the rescue team.

Seconds later an answer was received.

An answer

One of the rescue team, Stan Devren, 24, of 22 Maxweltown Road, Blackhill, Glasgow, said: "After that the bell rang continuously.

"It couldn't be a fault because the fire hadn't reached that part of the tunnel to cause a fall and set the bell off . . ."

But half an hour before midnight . . . 16 hours after the men had taken a bogey ride to death . . . came the official announcement:

"There is practically no hope of there being any survivors.

"A collection of firedamp has made it necessary to withdraw men engaged in fighting the fire. Arrangements are now in hand to flood part of the road and put out the fire."

The statement came from Mr. Ronald W. Parker, chairman of the Scottish Division of the National Coal Board.

Trip to death

When the pit section has been cleared of gas . . . when the red heat of the blaze has died . . . and when the water has been drained away . . .

The rescuers will go back down to the horror section—the section where 48 miners laughed as an underground train took them on a journey to death.

Scotland's worst pit disaster as 47 laughing and joking miners left the early morning sunshine

behind them to ride on the bogey-train to the coal face.

It became a mile-long train ride to death.

They were travelling to the coal face for their first shift after a three-day strike.

But deep down along the haulage system an electric fan is believed to have short-circuited and burst into flames.

Deadly carbon - monoxide fumes gushed along the airways into the path of the oncoming miners.

Thin wisps of smoke quietened the joking miners. Then they were in the middle of the gas.

They rang the haulage bell, signalling to winchman Tommy Campbell to haul them back. The line of bogies retreated before the fumes.

But they were not fast enough for one man.

Tommy Green, 50, of 75 Manor Drive, Marnoch, Glenboig, jumped off the little wagons and made his own way back.

Still ringing

He was found unconscious by other miners. And last night he was the only one of the 47 on that railway of death known to be alive.

Rescue teams from all over the county raced in to help. Miners waited grim-faced at the pithead.

Then, as the news spread around the surrounding groups of mining villages and towns, the womenfolk, many with

● TOM GREEN . . . the only survivor. For the full dramatic story of his rescue turn to Page 6.

● Mrs. FLEMING (right) is helped by another woman from the scene of the disaster
● BELOW— A mother waits and hopes . . . but the strain is too much for her little son

DEATH-ROLL HITS VILLAGE HARDEST

THE worst hit area of the pit disaster at Auchengeich Colliery, Chryston, Lanarkshire, is Bridgend—only a few hundred yards from the pithead.

For almost all the families in the small, brick miners' rows have lost relatives.

Forty-seven men are believed dead in the disaster—the biggest death-roll since 1889, when 63 men died in an underground fire at Mauricewood, Penicuik, Midlothian.

Last night the N.C.B. issued the names of the men. They are:—

Matt Cannon, 58, of 5 Queenslie Street, Glasgow; Alex Sharpe, 54, of 114 Easterhouse Road, Glasgow; Henry Clayton, 62, of 98 Monkland View Crescent, Bargeddie; R. McCoid, 55, of 16 Kenmore Street, Shettleston.

William Lafferty, 2 Delburn Street, Parkhead, Glasgow; John McAuley, 42, of 30 Searhill Street, Kirkshaws, Coatbridge; Peter Kelly, 40, of 4 Slakiewood Avenue, Gartcosh; James McPhee, 51, of 56 Raith Drive, Bellshill; W Meechan, 22, of Douglas Street, Viewpark, Uddingston; A Crombie, 42, of 129 Clydesdale Avenue, Hamilton; W Skilling, 55 of 5 Chriss Avenue, Eddlewood, Hamilton; Joseph McDonald, 53, of 14 East Springfield Terrace, Bishopbriggs.

Peter McMillan, 55, of 7 Drumsack Avenue, Chryston; George

McEwan, 20, of 94 Holyknowe Road Lennoxtown; Michael Fleming, 47, of 33 Bridgend Chryston; Thomas Stokes, 32, of 60 Bridgend Chryston; Martin Fleming, 51, of Frankfield Road, Stepps; George McIntosh, 58 of 2 Oxgang Place Kirkintilloch; James Devine, 39 of 80 Greenlea Road, Chryston; Gerald Martin, 54, of 5 Beauly Place, Chryston; Thomas Bone, 27 of 2 Meadowhead Avenue, Gartferry; John Mulholland sen., 50, of 72 Dalshannon Road Condorrat;

William Brynes, 54, of 20 Knowe Road, Chryston; John Muir, 38, of 14 Dalshannon Road Condorrat; Edward Henery, 61, of 45 Pentland Road, Chryston; Pat Harvey, 39, of 2 Jasmine Place Condorrat; John Shevlin, 46, of 20 Coronation Place, Mount Ellen, Chryston; George Jackson, 21, of 34 Fleming Avenue, Muirhead; F. Broadley, 38, of 10 Lochend Avenue, Mount Ellen; D. McElhaney, 49, of 15 Holyknowe Road, Lennoxtown; Frank Fisher, 49, of 158 Loch Road, Kirkintilloch; Aaron Price, 50, of 71 Redbrae Road, Hillhead, Kirkintilloch.

A McKenna, 42, of 6 Lennox

JAMES DEVINE

DONALD WEIR

Continued on Back Page

Continued on Back Page

1959

46 KILLED IN MINING DISASTER

MINER Thomas Green was the sole survivor of the Auchengeich disaster which claimed 46 lives – the country's worst mining tragedy of the century.

It began as 47 laughing and joking miners left the sunshine behind them to ride on a bogey train to the coal face.

They were travelling to the coal face after returning to work after a three-day strike.

The miners were unaware that deep down along the haulage system, an electric fan was believed to have short-circuited and burst into flames. Carbon monoxide fumes gushed along the airways into the path of the oncoming miners.

The smoke worried the miners and they began to ring the bell, signalling for the winchman, Tommy Campbell, to haul them back.

The lines of the bogies retreated before the fumes and Thomas Green jumped off the back wagon and began to make his own way back.

He was later found unconscious by other miners - the only survivor.

The alarm was raised and relayed to the Scottish Mine Rescue headquarters at Coatbridge, Lanarkshire and it brought out 21 full-time heroes, ready to fight disaster.

These were ordinary men, all veteran miners and trained to fight the often deadly dangers that can strike at the coal face or in the mine workings without warning.

As the rescue operation swung into action, the call went out to part-time rescue men at pits around Scotland and from Ayrshire, Renfrew and Dumfriesshire, men came to do what they could to try to save the lives of their fellow miners.

However, in the now blazing shafts of Auchengeich, dense clouds of smoke beat the rescuers back. Six times they pushed forward but each time they were forced to retreat.

They kept trying while there was still hope of bringing out survivors but in the end, the dreadful official announcement of the final death tally was made.

THE £30,000 SIGNATURE

Dave Mackay, the Hearts and Scotland skipper, signed for English First Division giants, Tottenham Hotspur, in March for a record fee of £30,000.

Mackay had won all the domestic honours with the Edinburgh club since joining them from Newtongrange Star in 1953. He had also just been acclaimed as Scottish Footballer of the Year when the shock move was announced.

However, the lure of playing with a major English club coupled to the record transfer fee proved irresistible for the talented midfielder.

ON RADIO
Pick of the Week

ON TV
No Hiding Place
Laramie
The Ken Dodd Show
Noggin the Nog

FREAK WAVES SINK FISHERIES VESSEL

The fisheries cruiser, *Freya*, was caught in a fierce January gale not far from Wick and was heading for the safety of the Cromarty Firth when she was swamped by a succession of freak waves.

Two waves struck the 274-ton ship in quick succession, crippling her and throwing her over into a heavy list. The crew barely had time to launch a life raft before a third wave capsized the *Freya* which quickly sank.

For over four hours, the crew clung to their dinghy before one of their distress flares was spotted by the Wick coastguard who alerted the local lifeboat.

THIS SPORTING LIFE

FOOTBALL	RUGBY UNION	GOLF	HORSE RACING	SHINTY
Scottish Champions Rangers	*Scotland vs England* England 3–3 Scotland at Twickenham	*British Open Winner* Gary Player at Muirfield (284)	*Scottish Grand National Winner* Merryman II at Bogside	*Camanachd Cup Winners* Newtonmore at Glasgow
Scottish Cup Winners St Mirren				

Daily Record

TUES. MAR. 29 1960

SCOTLAND'S NATIONAL NEWSPAPER

2½ᴵᴰ

No. 20,096

Nineteen die as a whisky store explodes

INFERNO!

● High on a turntable ladder, a fireman fights the flames.

Death of Mr. C. B. Livingstone

WE regret to announce the death of Mr. C. B. Livingstone, Chairman of the Daily Record and Sunday Mail Ltd.

Mr. Livingstone had been seriously ill for some time. A week ago he underwent an operation in a Glasgow hospital and he died there early last night. He was 51.

Mr. Livingstone was a great newspaperman in the Scottish tradition. His personal success was remarkable.

He joined the Daily Record when he was 15. Before he had reached his 29th birthday he was editor.

Great 'scoop'

Among newspapermen his name will always be associated with the Record's 'great scoop' on the arrival in Scotland of Rudolph Hess.

His organising ability was outstanding and at one period he edited both the Sunday Mail and the Daily Record. In September, 1945, he became director and general manager.

In August, 1958, Mr. Livingstone was appointed Chairman of the company. He was a Justice of the Peace, and a past President of the Scottish Daily Newspaper Society.

Mr. Livingstone is survived by Mrs. Livingstone and their daughter and three sons.

TRIBUTES—SEE PAGE 5

ELECTRIC IRON KILLS A WOMAN

PRETTY Catherine Galloway, 23, offered to iron shirts for her young brothers last night . . . and was ELECTROCUTED.

Just after she started to iron in the living-room of her home at 110 Corsock Street, Dennistoun, Glasgow, her parents heard her scream.

And when Mr. Alex. Galloway, 51, and his wife, Jean, 41, rushed into the room, they found Catherine lying on the floor on top of the iron.

Plug out

Mr. Galloway said later: "The iron was warm but the plug had been pulled from the socket when Cathie fell. And the switch was turned off. We can't explain that.

"Cathie was moaning and I held her head in my arms. But she died before the ambulance arrived.

"We are stunned by the tragedy. She was a lovely girl and a great help in the house.

"Only a few minutes before this happened she offered to iron shirts for her brothers—Alex, 10, and Robert, 6—so that they would be tidy when they went to school in the morning."

● Flames envelop a fire engine buried in the rubble.

Crashing wall traps firemen

A FANTASTIC ERUPTION OF FLYING BRICKS AND LANCING FLAME LAST NIGHT TURNED A GLASGOW DOCKSIDE BLAZE INTO ONE OF SCOTLAND'S WORST-EVER FIRE DISASTERS.

For under the tons of broken masonry that was once the 60-foot wall of a warehouse NINETEEN FIREMEN WERE TRAPPED.

And early today it was officially stated

BLACKEST DAY

that there could be no hope for them.

Up until the time of the explosion—just after 7 p.m.—all that could be seen was smoke seeping from the building in Cheapside Street, Anderston.

Then came the blast. The

Continued on Back Page

For the **Easter Bride!**

In our Model Gown Salon we are showing

AN EXCLUSIVE COLLECTION of **SUPERB BRIDAL GOWNS** 20 Gns. to 48 Gns.

CHARMING BRIDESMAIDS' GOWNS 15 Gns. to 30 Gns.

In our Budget Dress Salon **LOVELY BRIDAL GOWNS** 9 Gns. to 14 Gns.

SMART BRIDESMAIDS' GOWNS 8 Gns. to 12½ Gns.

* These attractive Gowns are available in all exquisite materials Short and Full-length Styles

brothers

OF SAUCHIEHALL STREET, GLASGOW

1960

19 DIE IN WHISKY STORE BLAZE

NINETEEN firemen died after a 60-foot wall fell on them as they tackled a whisky warehouse blaze in Cheapside Street, at Anderston Quay, Glasgow.

It was one of Scotland's worst fire disasters.

Before the explosion that killed the men, all that could be seen was smoke seeping from the building … then came the blast.

The wall seemed to explode and no one had a chance, as the wall was turned into a mass of broken masonry.

Six firemen were snatched from their turntable ladder.

Others working from three fire tenders on both sides of the warehouse were blasted off their feet and tons of debris rained down on the men below. Flames shot more than 100 feet into the air as 21,000 barrels of whisky exploded and about £2million worth of tobacco went up in smoke.

One man, Fireman Charles Bickerstaff, was pulled from the wreckage but he had to have a leg amputated.

There was no sign of the other firemen and three fire engines were buried under the mounds of rubble.

The dead men's mates stood stunned by the situation, before returning their attention to beating the blaze that claimed the lives of their friends.

After five hours, with no sign of the fire being controlled, extra units were sent from Paisley, Dumbarton, Coatbridge and Shotts. Assistant Fire Chief Alec Swanson said:

"In the intense heat and smoke after the explosion, it would have been impossible for anyone to have lived, even if they had not been struck by the debris."

Hours after their colleagues had died in the blaze, firemen all over Britain paid tribute to them and their families.

And at a conference in London, delegates representing the country's 21,000 firemen accepted a pay rise and elected to give all of the first week's pay increase to the dependants of the men who died in Glasgow.

The total amount that would be raised for the families was expected to be about £21,000.

REAL MADRID – KINGS OF EUROPE

The first-ever European football final to be staged in Scotland was held at Hampden Stadium in May between Real Madrid and Eintracht Frankfurt.

The Spaniards were the bookies' favourites but they soon found themselves trailing to a brilliant goal by Kress. This was the spur the men from Madrid needed and they proceeded to treat the 127,000 fans to one of the greatest displays of soccer wizardry ever seen in Scotland.

At the final whistle, the score was 7-3 to Madrid and the Spanish champions were greeted by roar after roar from the appreciative crowd as they trotted round Hampden with their well-earned trophy.

THE YANKS ARE COMING!

In May it was announced that US nuclear submarines would soon be setting up base in the Holy Loch in Argyll. The PM, Harold MacMillan, assured the Commons that while the new base may bring anxieties, he hoped that people would feel that it did not add to the risks to which the nation was inevitably exposed in the nuclear age.

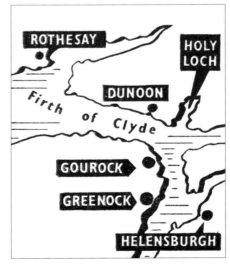

WHAT IT COST
POUND OF BUTTER
2s 8d
POUND OF BACON
4s
PINT OF BEER
1s 5d
CIGARETTES
3s 6d (20 Rocky Mount)
WOMEN'S SHOES
£2 19s 11d
MEN'S SUIT
£10 10s
TON OF COAL
£15
POSTAGE
3d
CAR
Triumph Herald £702

THIS SPORTING LIFE

FOOTBALL	RUGBY UNION	GOLF	HORSE RACING	SHINTY
Scottish Champions Hearts	*Scotland vs England* Scotland 12–21 England at Murrayfield	*British Open Winner* Kel Nagle at St Andrews (278)	*Scottish Grand National Winner* *Fincham* at Bogside	*Camanachd Cup Winners* Oban Celtic at Oban
Scottish Cup Winners Rangers				

Daily Record

THURS MAY 18 1961

3D SCOTLAND'S NATIONAL NEWSPAPER

No. 20,451

THE AMAZING IBROX BRAWL

Arrests as fans attack Italian flag

● TROUBLE . . . as the Italians' star right-winger, Hamrin, tries to reason with assistant trainer Chiapella over that Rangers' penalty.

● TROUBLE again as Chiapella attempts to push his way through (right) . . . and TROUBLE as players mill aimlessly around the pitch (above) with referee Steiner working in vain to sort them out.

● TROUBLE . . . as Mr. Steiner warns two of the Fiorentina cracks that HE is the boss.

● TROUBLE . . . as the Italians seek to keep on arguing and referee Steiner walks away.

FISTS, boots, bottles and beer-cans. Those were the ingredients last night in the seething bowl that was Ibrox Stadium, Glasgow.

The ugliest incident of all came when the final whistle gave Fiorentina a 2-0 first-leg win over Rangers, in the final of the European Cup for cup-winners.

Angry fans ripped down the Italian flag from its place of honour above the covered enclosure.

IT WAS ALMOST IN PIECES WHEN POLICE STORMED INTO THE ENCLOSURE, SAVED THE FLAG — AND BROUGHT THEIR NIGHT'S TOTAL OF ARRESTS TO FIFTEEN.

Meanwhile, the dark-shirted Fiorentina players stood in the middle of the Ibrox pitch—saluting the crowd.

Warnings

A few seconds before, six policemen had been needed to man-handle a struggling fan across the field. That was the tense finish to a torrid match.

Bottles and beer-cans had flown behind the Italian goal whenever Fiorentina players fouled a Ranger.

Warning after warning came from "no-nonsense" referee Steiner, of Austria.

Three Fiorentina players were booked and Orzan, their captain, was told to warn his players.

The most fantastic scenes of all came in the 18th minute, just after Fiorentina snatched their first goal.

Rangers were awarded a penalty when Ian McMillan was pulled down.

'Invasion'

Tempers rose to boiling point as the Italians almost downed referee Steiner with their gesticulating arms.

Fiorentina assistant trainer Chiapella sped across the turf. It took 90 seconds to restore order.

Then it happened.

As Rangers skipper Eric Caldow ran up to take the kick, 'keeper Albertosi began to jump about his goal.

When Caldow kicked the ball, the prancing, dancing 'keeper was about as close to him as to his own goal line.

'Take it again'

Fans howled for the kick to be re-taken, but play was waved on.

So it went on . . . roars, touls, catcalls, until just before the final whistle when Milan netted the Italians' second goal.

It was all over.

Police mounties guarded the players' exit after the game as

3 FIORENTINA MEN BOOKED

the Fiorentina team left in their bus.

Their tactics, such as they were, gave them a victory, but NOT the admiration of the Scots football fans.

● Third Lanark began their American visit last night with a 4-1 win over English tourists Birmingham City. Rex Kingsley's report—Page 21.

● WAVERLEY'S IBROX REPORT—PAGE 23.

● ANGER as fans rip down the green, red and white Italian flag.

Someone isn't using Amplex

Top rowing team of the season but . . . someone isn't happy about it! You've guessed—it's the man in the middle. The reason of course—he isn't an AMPLEX man and all this extra exertion makes it quite obvious. Other men use Amplex just as naturally as they have three meals a day. They don't talk about it—they just use it. One or two tiny tablets taken once or twice a day make all the difference. Why? Because Amplex tablets stop breath and body odours at source. Make sure your 'team' spirit leaves nothing to be desired . . .

take

AMPLEX

and be sure

30 TABLETS 1/10

AN ASHE LABORATORIES PRODUCT

1961

GERS FANS IN EUROPEAN FURY

ANGRY Rangers supporters ripped down the Italian flag from its place of honour at Ibrox Stadium, Glasgow.

The incident happened as Fiorentina won 2-0 against Rangers, in the second leg of the final of the European Cup Winners Cup.

The flag was almost in pieces when police stormed into the enclosure and saved the flag, bringing the night's total of arrests to 15.

Fists, boots, bottles and beer cans were the ingredients of the violence at the match. At one point, six policemen were needed to manhandle a struggling fan across the field.

It was a tense finish to a fiery match that saw bottles and beer cans being thrown behind the Italian goal whenever a Fiorentina player fouled one of the Rangers players.

The referee handed out warnings and Fiorentina captain Ozan was told to warn his players after three of them had been booked.

In the 18th minute, just after Fiorentina snatched their first goal, Rangers were awarded a penalty when Ian McMillan was pulled down.

Tempers began to rise as the Italians surrounded the referee and began to protest.

The Italian trainer went onto the pitch to restore order.

The final event which caused outbursts of bad temper happened as Rangers skipper Eric Caldow ran to take the penalty kick, and Italian keeper Albertosi began to jump about his goal.

When the kick was taken, Albertosi was as close to Caldow as to his own goal line. Fans howled for the kick to be taken again, but play was waved on.

The roars and catcalls continued until just before the final whistle when Milan scored the Italians' second goal.

Mounted police guarded the players' exit after the game. The Fiorentina team may have won the match but their team tactics did not win the admiration of the Scottish fans.

QUEEN OF THE GORBALS

The Queen and Prince Philip visited Glasgow's notorious Gorbals district in July. Both were relaxed and happy as they stopped and talked to the crowds of locals who had turned out to see the royal visitors. They also visited several homes, including a traditional 'single-end' tenement, where the Queen was clearly surprised by the conditions, asking the family, "Is this all you have?"

ON RADIO

Afternoon Theatre

In Touch

ON TV

Dr Kildare

The Avengers

Maigret

Perry Mason

Peter Gunn

The Rag Trade

Supercar

The Flintstones

Rawhide

Songs of Praise

HOLY LOCH PROTESTERS

Anti-nuclear protesters tried to make their presence felt as the advance guard of the US Navy's Polaris fleet, the depot ship *Proteus*, arrived on the Clyde in March. The small flotilla of demonstrators bobbed about the choppy water to no great effect and several had to be fished out by local police and navy personnel.

THIS SPORTING LIFE

FOOTBALL	RUGBY UNION	GOLF	HORSE RACING	SHINTY
Scottish Champions Rangers	*Scotland vs England* England 6–0 Scotland at Twickenham	*Home Internationals* Scotland 12½–2½ England Scotland 11½–3½ Ireland Scotland 8-7 Wales	*Scottish Grand National* *Winner* *Kinmont Wullie* at Bogside	*Camanachd Cup Winners* Kingussie at Fort William
Scottish Cup Winners Dunfermline				

Daily Record

WED. SEPT. 5 1962

3ᴰ SCOTLAND'S NATIONAL NEWSPAPER
No. 20,857

250,000 take a...
SENTIMENTAL JOURNEY

TRAMCAR SOUVENIR

● The CAVALCADE of "CAURS" heads South over the Clyde at the Jamaica Street bridge.

AN AMAZING FAREWELL TO THE 'CAURS'

A QUARTER of a million people turned out last night to wave goodbye to Glasgow's last tramcar.

They HUNG OUT of tenement windows and JOSTLED on the pavements, even CROWDED out to the tramlines for a moment of history which touched every one of them.

CHEERED

And how they waved and cheered as a horse-drawn tram led the procession of 20 "caurs" of all ages.

Mobile patrols and squads of mounted police were drafted in to handle the huge crowds packing the city centre.

CLOUDBURST

And how the city's youngsters — who have seen only the modern trams — and the old folk cheered . . .

Not even a cloudburst could dampen their fond farewell as an era ended.

● FULL STORY and more amazing pictures on Centre Pages.

Cross-fire! As Reds get tough on U-2

THE Russians got tough again yesterday over America's foreign-based, high-flying U-2 "spy" planes. But almost immediately there were counter-blasts.

A Soviet Note, handed to an American envoy in Moscow, protested that a U-2 had "violated" Russian territory—Sakhalin Island, north of Japan. And the Note repeated the warning of possible "retaliation" against countries where U-2 planes are based.

Almost immediately, WEST GERMANY accused Russia of violating West German air space. Police at Helmstedt said two Russian jets crossed the border and stayed on the wrong side for about five minutes.

Later, a Western Allied spokesman said in Berlin that Russian MIG fighters "flew near" three Western airliners in the Berlin air corridor. He said the fighters "accompanied for

Continued on Back Page

YOUR MATTRESS RE-MADE
AT MUCH LESS COST

IN ONLY 3 DAYS

Have your mattress re-made in the Stoddart Factory. Only finest materials used. A top quality job guaranteed at much less cost than a new mattress.

HAIR MATTRESSES RE-MADE OR CONVERTED INTO SPRING INTERIORS ● SPRING INTERIORS RE-MADE ● BASES OR OPEN TYPE SPRINGS RENOVATED ● QUILTS RE-COVERED

Write, or phone GLASGOW BEL 2897

Open all day Tuesdays

No matter how bad condition your present mattress is in, the Stoddart Re-making Service will return it to you as good as new.

Stoddart
FOR SERVICE & SATISFACTION

Our van has a regular collection and delivery service for Glasgow and a weekly service for certain Ayrshire, Renfrewshire and North Lanarkshire areas.

THOS. STODDART LTD., HUNTER ST., GLASGOW, C.4. ESTAB. 1910

1962

END OF THE LINE FOR THE 'CAURS'

THOUSANDS of Glaswegians lined the streets of the city to bid farewell to the famous Glasgow tramcar.

Twenty trams, of eight different types – one was drawn by horses – drove in procession along the three-mile route from the Dalmarnock depot to Coplawhill.

In scenes reminiscent of the end of war, almost a quarter of a million people cheered in the torrential rain as the "caurs" made their way along London Road, Trongate, Argyle Street, Hope Street, St Vincent Street, Union Street, Jamaica Bridge and Eglinton Street.

The Lord Provost of Glasgow, magistrates, councillors and the city's MPs were joined by guests from all over Britain.

Even royal visits to the city had never attracted such numbers and never had Glasgow seen so many cameras. Onlookers risked limb if not life as they placed coins in the tracks of the trams for a commemorative "flattening". Appropriately, the largest crowds were at the junction of Hope Street and Argyle Street, near to the "Hielanman's Umbrella", the part of Glasgow most closely associated with the trams.

In keeping with tradition, one of the trams broke down on London Road. In true tramway fashion, all those behind it were held up. They then "speeded" up to catch the rest of the trams.

For one of the tram drivers, Robert Cooper, aged 64, it was an emotional day. He had been driving trams for 33 years. As he travelled the "eight fare stages" to Pollokshields, people leaned into the cab to shake his hand and wish him all the best. He said later: "You can't drive a route for more than 30 years without knowing your regulars."

A part of Glasgow life for as long as anyone could remember, the "caurs" were to be sadly missed.

On Radio

The Men From the Ministry

Go Man Go

On TV

Dr Finlay's Casebook

Z Cars

The Saint

Mr Ed

Naked City

Animal Magic

Mr Magoo

That Was the Week That Was

Out of This World

Comings...

Ally McCoist	**Gavin Hastings**
Footballer	Rugby Player

CAPITAL SPECTACULAR

Edinburgh's most spectacular royal visit took place in October as huge cheering and flag-waving crowds lined the streets to watch King Olav of Norway drive in an open carriage with the Queen and Prince Philip from Waverley Station to the Palace of Holyroodhouse. In the evening, the King was guest of honour at the lavish candle-lit State banquet, the first at Holyrood since 1603.

Meanwhile, the threat of nuclear war between the Superpowers loomed ever closer. The USA warned the USSR not to deliver nuclear missiles to Cuba or else it would retaliate. As the Soviet ship carrying the rockets sailed on to its destination, the world held its breath and waited...

THIS SPORTING LIFE

FOOTBALL	RUGBY UNION	GOLF	HORSE RACING	SHINTY
Scottish Champions Dundee *Scottish Cup Winners* Rangers	*Scotland vs England* Scotland 3–3 England at Murrayfield	*British Open Winner* Arnold Palmer at Troon (276)	*Scottish Grand National Winner* Sham Fight at Bogside	*Camanachd Cup Winners* Kyles Athletic at Inverness

SUNDAY MAIL

5ᴰ SCOTLAND'S NATIONAL SUNDAY NEWSPAPER
No. 2866   SEPTEMBER 22, 1963

DRIVER IN BUS CRASH DRAMA

THE BRAVEST MAN IN GLASGOW

That's what they're calling Joe after he saves sixty

SUNDAY MAIL REPORTER

BUS driver Joseph Leahy was being hailed as the bravest man in Glasgow last night after his split-second thinking stopped another bus toppling to disaster.

Twenty-eight-year-old Mr. Leahy had just turned his bus into busy Stirling Road, Glasgow, from Castle Street.

Suddenly he saw a bus in front of him collide with a van.

Saved

The bus, packed with passengers, was rocking wildly.

Mr. Leahy slammed on his brake. His ten passengers scrambled off.

Then he roared up to the other bus to prop it up.

His gamble paid off. The other bus didn't capsize. The passengers were saved . . .

Last night Joseph, who lives at 60 Priesthill Road, Priesthill, said:

"One minute I was on a routine tea-time run. The next there was chaos.

"I wouldn't like to live through it again."

Full load

Driver of the other bus was 23-year-old Pakistani, Anwar Haq, of 50 Burnbank Terrace, Kelvinbridge.

The van collided with the side of his cab.

Badly shaken, but unhurt, he said afterwards: "I was just coming up to Castle Street when I saw the green van coming towards me. I swerved to try and get out the way.

"But we collided and the bus began to rock.

"If it hadn't been for Driver Leahy I would have been right over.

"I had a full load of about 60 passengers. I hate to think of what might have happened if we had toppled over."

The conductress of Mr. Leahy's No. 4 bus, dark-haired Willemina MacKay, of 18 Hatton Drive, Crookston, said: "*Joe deserves a medal for what he did. The other bus could have fallen and crushed him in his cab.*"

Mr. William Thomson, of 25 Torryburn Road, Barmulloch, was standing at a bus stop.

34 hurt

He said: "The man who saved the day was Mr. Leahy.

"I have never seen anything as brave as what that man did."

A third busman, 34-year-old Bernard Harkin, of 203 Millburn Street, Garngad, drove his bus into the rear of the toppling bus to steady it after Mr. Leahy.

Four ambulances took 34 people to the Royal Infirmary with cuts, bruises and shock. No one was seriously injured

Crowds gather around the scene after the crash. Inset—Driver Leahy.

IT'S ALL IN THE MAIL

SPARE PART SURGEONS

Amazing story of the men who save lives.
—PAGE 8

THE GREAT CAR JUNGLE

THE JUDGE gives you all the facts.
—PAGE 10

Z-CARS AND ME

INSPECTOR BARLOW tells of his big break.
—PAGE 13

RANGERS v. REAL

A full-page special.
—PAGE 24

WOMAN STOPS RIOT

A WOMAN yesterday stopped a riot by hundreds of angry football fans.

It happened outside Pittodrie Park, Aberdeen, after the Dons had crashed to their fourth successive defeat.

Hundreds of shouting supporters gathered in the street outside the ground, yelling for Aberdeen's manager.

Then up stepped 56-year-old grandmother Mrs. Jemima McFarlane.

Jeers

Facing the crowd, Mrs. McFarlane pleaded with them to go home.

As more than 30 police, led by Chief Superintendent Hugh McQueen, deputy chief constable of Aberdeen, rushed to clear the street, she stepped into the crowd.

Moving from group to group Mrs. McFarlane, secretary of the Aberdeen Supporters' Club, pleaded: "This sort of thing will not help. Go home and be quiet."

The riot, outside the players' entrance, happened after Aberdeen were beaten 2-0 by St. Mirren.

The dejected Aberdeen players left the field to the jeers of their fans.

Then, minutes later, more than 300 young supporters gathered outside the players' entrance chanting: "We want Pearson."

They were referring to Aberdeen manager Tommy Pearson, the former Newcastle and Aberdeen outside-left.

CHIEF SUPERINTENDENT McQUEEN SAID: "I HAVE NEVER SEEN SCENES LIKE THESE AT PITTODRIE BEFORE."

Discover for yourself the secret in the blending!

To enjoy Scotch Whisky at its best ask for "Black & White".

You'll discover at once that the special "Black & White" way of blending fine individual whiskies achieves a smoothness and satisfying character that makes this superb Scotch first favourite everywhere.

'BLACK & WHITE'
SCOTCH WHISKY

THE SECRET IS IN THE BLENDING

Retail Prices U.K.—Bottle 41/6, Half Bottle 21/9, Quarter Bottle 11/3, Miniatures 4/-

1963

PRAISE FOR COURAGE OF DRIVER

BUS driver Joseph Leahy was hailed the bravest man in Glasgow after his quick thinking stopped another bus from toppling over.

Mr Leahy was on a routine tea-time run, when chaos broke out. He had just turned his bus from Castle Street into Stirling Road in Glasgow when he saw a bus ahead of him collide with a van.

The bus in the collision was packed with passengers and it began to rock wildly from side to side.

Quick-thinking Mr Leahy stopped and instructed his passengers to get off before driving his bus up to the other bus to prop it up.

His gamble paid off. His swift action saved the bus from toppling over and saved the passengers.

A third bus driver arrived at the scene and drove his vehicle to the rear of the tottering bus to stabilise it.

Mr Leahy, of Priesthill, said: "One minute I was on a routine tea-time run. The next there was chaos. I wouldn't like to live through it all again."

The bus ahead of Mr Leahy's was driven by Mr Anwar Haq.

He was not injured but was badly shaken as the van collided with the side of his vehicle.

Talking later about his ordeal, he said: "I had a full load of about 60 passengers.

"I hate to think of what might have happened if we had toppled over."

A witness to the incident stated that he had never seen anything quite as brave as the swift action taken by Mr Leahy.

Four ambulances arrived at the scene but fortunately, the passengers in the bus hit by the van suffered only from minor cuts and grazes.

JUST CHAMPION

Jim Clark became the first Scot and the youngest British driver to become the Grand Prix world champion. His victory at Monza in September was his fifth win of the season and was sufficient to secure him the championship with three races left.

SCOTS LINK TO GREAT TRAIN ROBBERY

Scotland Yard detectives were investigating the possibility that a Glasgow post office worker tipped off the gang who snatched over £2 million from the Glasgow to Euston mail train in August in what was Britain's biggest-ever train heist. Although 15 men were later caught and given lengthy sentences, the indentity of "Mr Mac" as the informer was known was never discovered.

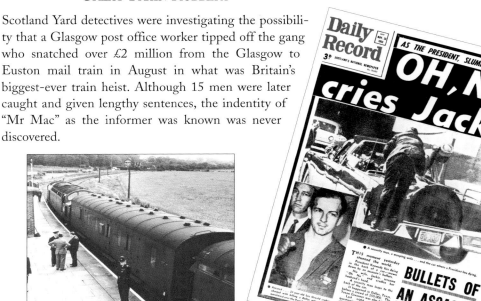

ON TV
The Fugitive
Dr Who
Candid Camera

ON RADIO		
Roundabout	Twelve O'Clock	Treble Chance
Take Your Partner	Spin	Semprini Serenade

In Scotland,
as everywhere else,
everyone could remember what they
were doing when they heard the news
from Dallas that President John F.
Kennedy had been assassinated.

THIS SPORTING LIFE

FOOTBALL	RUGBY UNION	GOLF	HORSE RACING	SHINTY
Scottish Champions Rangers	Scotland vs England England 10–8 Scotland at Twickenham	Home Internationals Scotland 10½ – 4½ England Scotland 5 – 10 Ireland Scotland 10½ – 4½ Wales	Scottish Grand National Winner Pappageno's Cottage at Bogside	Camanachd Cup Winners Oban Celtic at Glasgow
Scottish Cup Winners Rangers				

Daily Record

SAT. SEPT. 5 1964

3ᴰ SCOTLAND'S NATIONAL NEWSPAPER

No. 21,482

19 to 1 double

THAT was yesterday's great performance by KLONDYKE at Epsom.

FIVE MEETINGS TODAY

—including the big race at Lanark, the Silver Bell.

All the tips
—Pages 20 and 21

★

IT'S DERBY DAY

● The biggest club day in Scottish soccer, with derby games throughout the country.

The top news on today's programme.
—Pages 22 and 23

AN OLD FIRM WARNING

A STERN warning was handed out to Old Firm fans last night on the eve of the big game.

Celtic and Rangers fans were warned by Glasgow's Chief Constable Mr. James Robertson that "stringent measures" will be taken against . . .

1—Anyone waving banners or any kind of placard.

2—Anyone using obscene or provocative language inside or outside the ground.

He appealed to the thousands of fans who will flock to Parkhead . . . "Come early and co-operate with police in traffic and crowd movement."

Mr. Stan Lind, president of the Rangers Supporters' Association, said: "It looks like being the best league game of the season."

And Mr. Hugh Delaney, secretary of the Celtic Supporters' Association, said: "There has been no trouble the last five times the teams have met. I think it could be a cracker of a game."

Off on the Royal trip to history

THEN, A FEW HOURS LATER

CRASH UNDER THE BRIDGE

● *HALFWAY ACROSS . . . spectators cheer as the Royal car with the Queen and Prince Philip (inset) make the historic crossing of the bridge.*

THOUSANDS of cars poured bumper - to - bumper over the newly-opened Forth Road Bridge last night.

There were dozens of minor collisions on the approach roads.

One on the Fife side brought the first '999 call.

A woman passenger was taken to hospital with shock.

There was even a collision UNDER the bridge in mist.

The flagship of the Home Fleet, the cruiser Lion, was still at anchor after the bridge-opening ceremony by the Queen . . .

The frigate Lowestoft was getting under way.

Suddenly there was the crunch of tearing metal as the Lowestoft's bows bit into the Lion.

On board the Lion at the time was Vice-Admiral Twiss. Flag Officer Home Flotillas.

Damage was not serious but both ships are to go into Rosyth Dockyard for repairs.

★ **THE QUEEN'S** opening of the bridge: Full reports and sparkling pictures of Scotland's great day—

Pages 10 to 15

"An inquiry will be held," said a Navy spokesman.

The bridge opening brought a fantastic flood of cars—far more than expected. At one point 3000 an hour were crossing.

On the Edinburgh side queues were reported seven miles back on the approach roads.

On the Fife side there was a four-mile queue of 2000 cars.

After six hours "clearing" the bridge following the Royal opening, cars had started to roll at 5.50 p.m.

FIRST MAN to pay the 2s 6d toll was Mr. Jack Hamilton, resident engineer of the bridge project.

He handed over the cash then his dark green Jaguar

moved off . . . first across the bridge.

Next through the barrier were Mr. Charles Grimm and his wife from **Brechin,** Angus.

From the Fife side two motorists claimed a joint "first."

In one lane was Robert Morrison, 42, of 132 Balgillo Road, Broughty Ferry, **Dundee** with his wife Jemima and daughter Donna, four.

'Made it'

"I wanted to go across on the first day but I had no idea that I would be the first, or first equal," Mr. Morrison said.

Driving alongside him was 28-year-old Jimmy Archibald, a cigarette salesman, of 59 Wedderburn Crescent, **Dunfermline.**

"For a long time now I've had the idea of being first across the bridge," said Mr. Archibald. "Now I've finally made it."

At 10.30 p.m. with thick mist covering the bridge, the traffic eased off.

expected again today and tomorrow.

FINE NOTE: An extra £5 was added to the bridge receipts yesterday . . . fines from three motorists who broke down on the crossing.

● *TOLL QUEUE . . . columns of motorists wait to cross the bridge last night at South Queensferry.*

1964

BUMPY TIME AT FORTH BRIDGE

THE £20m Forth Road Bridge was opened by the Queen ... and almost immediately there was a crash! However, the collision didn't take place on the bridge itself, but underneath it. The cruiser, HMS *Lion*, still at anchor after the opening ceremony, was hit by HMS *Lowestoft* as the frigate manoeuvred itself into position.

The Queen officially opened the 3,300 foot span bridge in a ceremony at South Queensferry. One of the main figures involved in the construction of the bridge, the resident engineer, Mr J.A.K. Hamilton, was the first to pay the 2s 6d toll (13p)

when the bridge was opened to traffic.

In the first three and a half hours, some 20,000 cars crossed. The bridgemaster, Mr Robert Wilson, said that at the peak period, cars were crossing at between 5,000 and 6,000 an hour.

However, the thick mist denied drivers the chance to fully appreciate the experience of driving over the Forth. The very heavy traffic also reduced much of the journey to a slow crawl. At one point, the journey from one side to the other was taking as much as 45 minutes.

Vehicles had queued for many hours on both sides before the bridge was finally

opened to the public. With horns sounding and workmen cheering, the long processions finally started to move. The first member of the public to cross the bridge from the south was Mr Charles Grimm of Brechin, who had been visiting Edinburgh with his wife: "We were just going home and had absolutely no intention of being the first to cross." Mr Arthur Hutton of Falkirk was the first member of the general public to make the crossing from the north.

Described by the Queen as "this immense engineering project", initial plans for a road bridge across the Forth were first drawn up in the 1920s.

COMINGS...

Stephen Conroy
Artist

Pat Kane
Journalist & Pop Singer

Liz McColgan
Athlete

ON TV

Crossroads

Redcap

Just Jimmy

Steptoe & Son

The Singing Ringing Tree

Car 54 – Where are You?

Top of the Pops

BEATLEMANIA COMES TO SCOTLAND

The Beatles' trip to Scotland ended with 24 girls in hospital suffering from hysteria and more than 300 fainting cases. Eight thousand fans had mobbed the 'Fab Four' on their arrival at the Odeon cinema in Glasgow's Renfield Street and had tried to break through a 100-strong police cordon. Ambulance men rushed forward to rescue fainting girls, in danger of being trampled in the chaos. After the show, the group slipped out of a side exit into a waiting hired car. Disappointed fans refused to believe they had gone and thousands of young girls blocked Renfield Street and West Nile Street in the hope of catching a last glimpse of their idols.

LAST WINTER STORMS CAUSE CHAOS

Blizzards caused havoc across Scotland, just six days before the start of Spring. The north-east was blanketed in deep snow and hundreds of motorists, including a complete wedding party, had to be rescued from their vehicles after becoming trapped. In Inverness, hotels were forced to cope with over 100 unexpected guests after attempts to keep the main road open were abandoned.

ON RADIO

Roundabout

The Joe Loss Pop Show

Starlight Serenade

Movie Time

Saturday Night Theatre

Saturday Club

THIS SPORTING LIFE

FOOTBALL	RUGBY UNION	GOLF	HORSE RACING	SHINTY
Scottish Champions Rangers	*Scotland vs England* Scotland 15–6 England at Murrayfield	*British Open Winner* Tony Lema at St Andrews (279)	*Scottish Grand National Winner* Popham Down at Bogside	*Camanachd Cup Winners* Kilmallie at Fort William
Scottish Cup Winners Rangers				

Daily Record

MON. JUNE 7 1965

4D. SCOTLAND'S NATIONAL NEWSPAPER No. 21,716

As Skye boats sail on a Sunday

14 ARRESTED IN FERRY BLOCKADE

By GORDON ARGO and JIM LAWSON

THE road to the Isles was blocked by a line of human bodies yesterday—when the first Sunday ferry went over the sea to Skye.

After months of protest and petition against the ferry plan, the day had come when the islanders massed their ranks.

But the day ended with 14 of them on a breach of the peace charge . . . and the ferries sailing on.

'Sad day'

The blockade drama flared at Kyleakin as the first ferry crossed the short stretch from the mainland.

As the Rev. Angus Smith, a Free Church minister, watched the boat approaching, he said: "It's a sad, sad day for this God-fearing island of ours."

Then, looking at the islanders massed behind him, he added: "We are all witnessing for the Lord our God against the breach of the Fourth Commandment, which says the Lord's Day should be kept holy.

"*The Caledonian Steam Packet Company, who run the ferry, should respect our wishes and no tourists should come to Skye on a Sunday.*"

Police took up position as the islanders moved on to the quayside to make the ferry trippers aware that, on Skye, they are looked on as Sabbath-breakers.

Praying

As the boat sailed nearer, the waiting islanders began to pray and sing psalms and press against the police cordon.

Then, at eight minutes past one, the boat tied up alongside the quay and the first car rolled ashore . . .

Under an escort of 25 police it nosed up the quay through a crowd of visitors.

Islanders flung themselves on the ground and, as police sought to shift them, Mr. Smith, the minister, threw himself in front of the leading car.

There was a Gaelic shout of "Seas aig an thoiseach" ("Down in front of them").

People cheered and the singing reached a crescendo as Mr. Smith was picked up and carried away by four burly policemen.

202 cars

The 300-strong crowd surged forward with islanders shouting: "Remember the Sabbath Day and keep it holy."

Soon the police—50 strong, plus plain clothes men—had marched, carried and bustled other demonstrators into a nearby office.

In the first car, George Pueretz with his wife Sydney, from Dallas, Texas, said: "The last time I saw so many police

Continued on Back Page

● THE SCENE at Kyleakin after a cordon was broken and islanders, including Free Church minister Mr. Angus Smith, threw themselves in front of cars from the Sunday ferry.

Pat Crerand ordered off

SCOTLAND wing-half Pat Crerand was ordered off in last night's Fairs Cities semi-final between Manchester United and Ferencvaros.

It was a rough house with a difference in Hungry—even the REFEREE was involved.

Full report—See Page 18.

✱ For the racing fans there are NINE cards today. All the tips—Pages 15, 16, 17.

A FREE HOLIDAY

● . . . That's just one of the prizes in our great new contest—PAGE 6.

WINNING POP FANS

● Ticket winners in our Rolling Stones contest are named—PAGE 4.

● It was a losing battle against the ferry for the islanders. Above are some who sang psalms and prayed as the tourist cars rolled on to the isle.

FEEL LIKE A MILLION ON THE BEACH

GET IN SHAPE FOR SUMMER NOW!

Various Courses can be arranged to suit you
PAYMENT CAN BE MADE WEEKLY
RING CEN 8570 TODAY
TAKE INCHES OFF OR PUT INCHES ON

FOR MEN
★ BODY BUILDING
★ FITNESS CONDITIONING
★ REDUCING
★ MUSCLE TONING
★ STEAM ROOM
★ SUNRAY
★ VIBRO-MASSAGE

FOR WOMEN
★ SLENDERISING
★ BUST DEVELOPMENT
★ FIGURE CONTOURING
★ BODY BUILDING

7 DAYS A WEEK
10 a.m. - 10 p.m.

OLYMPIC HEALTH STUDIOS
40 Queen St., Glasgow C.1. Tel. CEN 8570

PROTEST BY SKYE BOAT THRONG

PROTESTERS made a bid to block the Road to the Isles as the first Sunday ferry went over the sea to Skye.

After months of protest and petition against the ferry plan, the day arrived when islanders closed their ranks.

The day, however, ended with 14 of the islanders being arrested for breach of the peace.

The drama began at Kyleakin as the first ferry crossed the short stretch from the mainland.

Police took up position as the islanders moved onto the quayside to make ferry trippers aware that on Skye, they were regarded as Sabbath breakers.

Under an escort of 25 police officers, the first car ashore from the ferry moved up along the quay through a crowd of visitors.

As Islanders flung themselves on the ground, local minister Mr Smith threw himself in front of the leading car and was greeted with a cheer from the 300-strong crowd.

The throng surged forward with the islanders shouting: "Remember the Sabbath day and keep it holy."

Then the crowd was eventually cleared and the cars were allowed through.

The day ended with the 14 arrests … and the ferries continuing to sail.

CELTIC LEGEND FINALLY REVEALS WHY HE LEFT PARKHEAD

Looking a bit heavier and somewhat hampered by his hat and coat, Celtic legend Charlie Tully was again on the pitch at Parkhead, demonstrating his famous "scissors kick". Now in his forties, Tully was back in the stadium he left as a player in 1959 to make the draw for the Celtic Pools. The Celtic-Hibernian game had been called off, so Tully thought he'd provide some entertainment of his own. Asked why he had left Celtic, where he was long regarded as a hero, Tully replied: "When you marry an Irish girl, you marry her mother! We had to go back to Belfast."

KO COMA DRAMA

Scots boxer John O'Brien made a sensational comeback to the ring in September when he knocked out Jesus Saucedo of Mexico in the fourth round at Earls Court. Saucedo was rushed to hospital after failing to respond to ringside medical attention and needed an emergency operation to remove a blood clot. He later made a full recovery.

ON TV		ON RADIO
Peyton Place	Captain Pugwash	Round the Horne
Beverly Hillbillies	The Man from UNCLE	The World At One
The Likely Lads	The Virginian	I'm Sorry I'll Read That Again
Not Only… But Also	Call My Bluff	

THIS SPORTING LIFE

FOOTBALL	RUGBY UNION	GOLF	HORSE RACING	SHINTY
Scottish Champions Kilmarnock	*Scotland vs England* England 3–3 Scotland at Twickenham	*Home Internationals* Scotland 3½ - 11½ England Scotland 5½ - 9½ Ireland Scotland 9 - 6 Wales	*Scottish Grand National Winner* Brasher at Bogside	*Camanachd Cup Winners* Kyles Athletic at Oban
Scottish Cup Winners Celtic				

Daily Record

WED. NOV. 2 1966

4D SCOTLAND'S NATIONAL NEWSPAPER

No. 22,155

SEVEN-STOREY BUILDING COLLAPSES

4 DEAD IN TOMB OF STEEL

IBROX OFFER TO EDDIE TURNBULL

—Full story Page 27

discovered!

Here's wealth worth looking for: a golden, subtle-tasting whisky in a distinctive, diamond-cut bottle. And it's amazingly easy to find: just go into any licensed premises and say the heart-warming words, "Lang's Scotch Whisky". Discover this great whisky for yourself today.

LANG'S OLD SCOTCH WHISKY

also available LANG'S GOLD LABEL DE-LUXE 75° PROOF

● Out and alive . . . steel man Jimmy Cattanach is carried to safety. Four of his mates died.

FOUR men died under hundreds of tons of steel and concrete when the seven-storey skeleton frame of a building crashed to the ground yesterday.

Late last night rescuers were searching by floodlight for a fifth man also feared dead in the wreckage.

The disaster happened on the construction site of Aberdeen University's new zoology department building.

As an ear-splitting roar shattered the lunchtime quiet, many people thought it was a jet plane going through the sound barrier.

When they ran to the spot, however, at St Machar Drive and Tillydron Road, they found a tomb of rubble where moments earlier the 90-foot high framework of the building had stood.

Last night as rescuers still

By JIM GILLESPIE and ROBERT STEWART

toiled at the scene, police named the four known dead. The men, all from Aberdeen, were:

Robert Will, middle-aged, of Ashgrove Gardens, North.

Albert Shand, father of one, of Wallfield Crescent.

John Hekelaar, of 27 Invercauld Gardens, Mastrick.

James Matthews, of 57 Victoria Road, Torry.

Albert Shand's young wife Maureen was told of his death

Named

when she arrived at the site to get news of him.

As police, firemen and rescue volunteers flocked to the scene there were stories of amazing heroism . . . and tragedy

HEROISM like that of Bobby Cowe, who calmly rolled cigarettes as he lay trapped in the rubble, then cut himself free with a blow-torch that the rescuers passed through to him

Tried to run

Bobby, 20, of 49 Fernhill Road, Aberdeen, was taken to hospital with two other men who were brought out alive.

TRAGEDY like that faced by site agent George Kelman

whose stepfather Robert Will was one of those killed

George told police: "My stepfather is somewhere in there" . . . and went on determinedly directing the rescue operations

The two men who went to hospital with Bobby Cowe were: steel fixer Jimmy Cattanach, of Stonehaven, Kincardineshire, the first to be rescued; and father of two John Burnett, 34, of 149 Cairngorm D r i v e, Aberdeen.

Last night two of the rescued told their own dramatic stories.

Hunt goes on

Continued on Back Page

1966

HEROISM AND TRAGEDY AS 4 DIE

FOUR men died under hundreds of tons of steel and concrete when a seven-storey skeleton frame of a building crashed to the ground.

The disaster happened on the construction site of Aberdeen University's new zoology department building.

As an ear-splitting roar shattered the lunch-time quiet, many people thought it was a jet plane going through the sound barrier. However, when they ran to the scene at St Machar Drive and Tilydrone Road, they found the tomb of rubble where until just a few moments earlier, the 90-foot high framework of a building had stood.

As police and firemen arrived at the scene, they were accompanied by rescue volunteers. Scores of rescuers attacked a 12-foot heap of steel girders with oxy-acetylene cutters, picks – and even their bare hands – to save their mates who were trapped underneath.

As the rescue operation took place, there were stories of both amazing heroism and of tragedy.

HEROISM like that of Bobby Cowe, who calmly rolled cigarettes as he lay trapped in rubble, then cut himself free with a blow-torch that the rescuers passed through to him.

TRAGEDY like that faced by site agent George Kelman, whose stepfather Robert Will was one of those killed.

George told police: "My step-father is somewhere in there", but went on directing the rescue operation until all the survivors were freed.

GOINGS...

Willie Gallacher
*"Red Clydesider" &
Longest-serving
Communist MP*

TAY BRIDGE OPENS

Dundee drivers were celebrating the opening of a new road link in August as the new £6 million bridge linking the city to the Kingdom of Fife was opened.

The new bridge, over 7,000 feet in length and three years in the making, was formally opened by Her Majesty The Queen Mother.

ON TV

Softly, Softly

The Baron

The Frost Report

Get Smart

Green Acres

The Monkees

Till Death Do Us Part

Daktari

It's A Knockout

WORLD CHAMP WALTER

Hamilton flyweight Walter McGowan became Scotland's latest world title holder when he defeated the Italian Salvatore Burruni at Wembley in June. In spite of nursing a badly cut eyebrow which all but blinded him for a large part of the fight, 23-year-old McGowan outclassed Burruni over the 15 rounds. It was an emotional victory for McGowan who had tears of joy streaming down his cheeks as he was presented with his championship belt.

THIS SPORTING LIFE

FOOTBALL	RUGBY UNION	GOLF	HORSE RACING	SHINTY
Scottish Champions Celtic	*Scotland vs England* Scotland 6–3 England at Murrayfield	*British Open Winner* Jack Nicklaus at Muirfield (282)	*Scottish Grand National Winner* *African Patrol* at Ayr	*Camanachd Cup Winners* Kyles Athletic at Inverness
Scottish Cup Winners Rangers				

Daily Record

FRI. MAY 26 1967

4D SCOTLAND'S NATIONAL NEWSPAPER No. 22,329

CHAMPIONS OF EUROPE

CELTIC

CUP SPECIAL

V-E NIGHT '67!

IT'S THE GREATEST MOMENT IN THE LIFE OF CELTIC'S MANAGER JOCK STEIN AS HE PROUDLY GRASPS THE EUROPEAN CUP IN LISBON LAST NIGHT. SHARING JOCK'S JOY IS RIGHT-HALF BOBBY MURDOCH.

CELTIC are champions of all Europe. The European Cup manager Jock Stein held last night will come to Britain for the first time.

Tonight it will be in Glasgow. The team are due to fly in from Lisbon about 6.30 p.m. following their wonderful European Cup victory over Inter Milan.

But the fans are advised NOT to go to Glasgow Airport.

As soon as the team touch down, they—and the Cup—will be driven to Parkhead where the big fan welcome is planned.

World match

Celtic will meet the champions of South America in a two-leg match for the title of World Champions.

Present world club champions are Penarol of Uruguay, who beat Real Madrid 4-0 in last season's decider.

In Lisbon about 10,000 Celtic fans — including some from America and Ireland — celebrated throughout the night.

At the end of the game there were fantastic scenes as hundreds jumped the moat to invade the pitch.

Some were hurt in the crush, but none seriously.

Liveliest

Chanting and cheering, the fans mobbed the players and hacked at the turf to carry off bits of grass as souvenirs.

Bar and cafe owners in the city braced themselves for one of the liveliest-ever nights. And what a night it was . .

DONALD BRUCE tells the Lisbon story on Page 19. Celtic's glory goals in pictures are on the Centre Pages and the full match report on Pages 38 and 39.

Wilson to see De Gaulle ● Middle East crisis BACK PAGE

1967

A GRAND OLD TEAM TO CHEER FOR

THE European Cup was brought to Britain for the first time when Celtic became the champions of Europe in May.

Their attractive, attacking play overwhelmed and outclassed the arch-villains of defensive, negative football, Italy's Inter Milan. And the Celts ran out 2-1 winners in Lisbon.

The game began badly for the Scots. Inter Milan player Mazzola scored the first goal of the match in seven minutes after a penalty had beenawarded against Celtic.

The Glasgow team's spirit wasn't broken but they spent long periods of frustration as their brilliant moves and fierce shooting failed to get them the goal they needed.

Their efforts were finally rewarded with a brilliant goal scored by Tommy Gemmell – a goal that sent Celtic fans everywhere jumping with joy.

Celtic were back in the game, and in with a chance.

With five minutes to go, a cleverly-worked move ended with a goal from Steve Chalmers to secure Celtic's victory, and Jock Stein's all-Scots side finished as worthy European champions.

The next day more than 60,000 screaming, cheering, chanting fans packed into Celtic Park to welcome home their European Cup heroes.

As they drove in from the airport to Parkhead, the team were greeted by an estimated 200,000 jubilant fans lining the streets.

Cars hooted their horns, barmen and drinkers stood at pub doors to cheer and women in bingo halls streamed onto the streets to voice their support for the winners.

At Celtic Park itself, thousands sang the praises of their team as the Bhoys paraded the huge trophy round the stadium on the back of an open lorry.

THE NEW QUEEN

In September, excited crowds cheered wildly as the latest Clyde-built 'royal' liner eased down the slipway at John Brown's. The 58,000-ton *Queen Elizabeth 2*, launched by Her Majesty, maintained the tradition of naming the great Cunard liners that began with the *Queen Mary*, named after her grandmother and the *Queen Elizabeth*, named after her mother.

ON RADIO

My Music!

The World This Weekend

The Jimmy Young Show

Just A Minute

NATS' SENSATIONAL VICTORY

COMINGS...

Tommy Smith
Jazz Musician

GOINGS...

Duncan Macrae
Actor

In a night of high drama and wild emotion, the SNP won a sensational by-election victory in November, seizing the traditionally safe Labour seat of Hamilton. The new MP, Winnie Ewing, secured the biggest recorded anti-Labour swing of the century to overturn a 16,500 majority and snatch victory by 1,800 votes from the Labour candidate, Alex Wilson. In what was always going to be a two-horse race, the Tory candidate came a very poor third. As the result was announced amidst a sea of saltires and lion rampant flags, the large crowd of SNP supporters and activists went wild, singing and chanting their new MP's name.

ON TV

Callan

The Forsyte Saga

Ironside

Man In A Suitcase

All Gas and Gaiters

Hogan's Heroes

The Golden Shot

The Prisoner

Mission Impossible

THIS SPORTING LIFE

FOOTBALL	RUGBY UNION	GOLF	HORSE RACING	SHINTY
Scottish Champions Celtic *Scottish Cup Winners* Celtic	*Scotland vs England* England 27–14 Scotland at Twickenham	*Home Internationals* Scotland 8 - 7 England Scotland 8½ - 6½ Ireland Scotland 8 - 7 Wales	*Scottish Grand National Winner* *The Fossa* at Ayr	*Camanachd Cup Winners* Newtonmore at Glasgow

Daily Record

TUES. JAN. 16 1968

4d SCOTLAND'S NATIONAL NEWSPAPER No. 22,525

20 KILLED BY HURRICANE

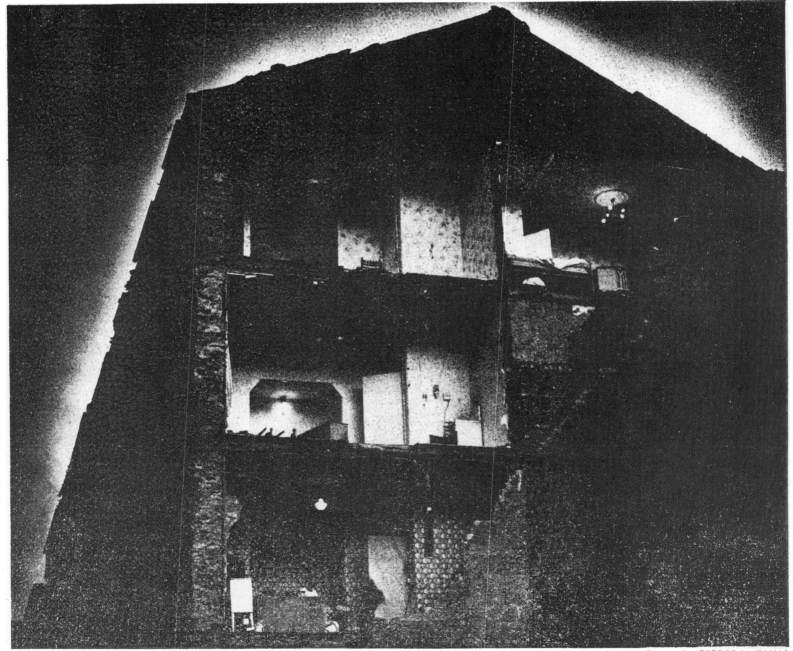

Picture by GEORGE McEWAN

THE PICTURE OF DESTRUCTION...

THIS dramatic picture is vivid witness of the force of the hurricane that wrenched homes apart and killed 20 people in Central Scotland yesterday.

It came in the night as families slept, a howling terror of destruction.

From this building in Maryhill, Glasgow, 12 families escaped . . . without time even to put out the lights. Their story is told on Page 16.

Elsewhere, in other buildings, other families were not so lucky. For this was the night when death was blowing in the wind.

NOW TURN TO BACK PAGE
Disaster Special: Pages II-17

1968

DEADLY STORM LASHES SCOTLAND

A KILLER hurricane brought havoc to Scotland in January. Twenty people were killed in the central belt and homes were wrecked.

The hurricane was the worst storm in memory and as the wind lashed through the country, it left behind it a trail of death, destruction and tragedy.

Several children were among the people who died.

Hundreds of other people were left homeless.

The worst tragedy hit the Partick area of Glasgow where two mothers and two girls were crushed to death when tons of rubble swept away three floors of a tenement.

It happened after a chimney toppled on to the roof at 555 Dumbarton Road.

On the morning after the hurricane struck, the city looked as if it had been hit by a bombing raid.

Streets were littered with fallen masonry, broken roof slates and crashed chimney heads, and some buildings had been torn open like grotesque doll's houses.

In Glasgow alone, 500 people were left homeless.

The number for the whole of Scotland was estimated at more than 1,000.

As the disaster struck, there were teams who worked tirelessly while facing constant danger.

The police and ambulancemen who answered distress calls; the firemen who dug for victims in a tenement collapse; the linesmen who repaired the damaged power links that had blacked out a lot of the city; the welfare workers who responded to help calls.

Then there were the hundreds of neighbours and friends who acted selflessly to help those in need.

FORMULA ONE'S FLYING SCOTSMAN KILLED

World champion grand prix driver, Jim Clark, died in April following a horrific crash at Germany's notorious Hockenheim circuit.

The 32-year-old Scot, the top driver in both 1963 and 1965, lost control of his Lotus in the wet and slippery conditions while taking a sweeping curve at 170 mph and shot over the rim of the track. Rescue teams were quickly on the scene and Clark was rushed to hospital but the Flying Scot was already dead.

JAMES WATT ST BLAZE

Glasgow once again lived up to its unenviable reputation as 'tinderbox city' following a factory fire in November that claimed the lives of 22 employees.

The workers in Stern Upholsterers in James Watt Street were unable to escape as flames shot through the two-storey building because of bars on the windows and padlocked doors. The bars, installed when the building had been formerly used as a whisky bond, had been retained by the new owners for security reasons. In spite of this the Corporation had granted the building a fire safety certificate which officially cleared the building as having adequate means of escape. Immediately after the fire, orders were issued for the inspection of all city buildings with barred windows in the hope of preventing a similar tragedy.

ON RADIO

Late Night Extra	The Tony Blackburn	Fresh Start
Night Ride	Show	Home This Afternoon

ON TV

Journey to the Unknown	Dad's Army	Nearest and Dearest
	Please, Sir!	Captain Scarlet
Never Mind the Quality, Feel the Width	The Champions	Rowan & Martin's Laugh-in

THIS SPORTING LIFE

FOOTBALL	RUGBY UNION	GOLF	HORSE RACING	SHINTY
Scottish Champions Celtic	*Scotland vs England* Scotland 6–8 England at Murrayfield	*British Open Winner* Gary Player at Carnoustie (289)	*Scottish Grand National Winner* Arcturus at Ayr	*Camanachd Cup Winners* Kyles Athletic at Oban
Scottish Cup Winners Dunfermline				

Daily Record

WED JULY 16 1969

5d **SCOTLAND'S NATIONAL NEWSPAPER** No 22,988
**

A policeman: A boy: 2 women: 9 men

13 SHOT IN CITY STREETS

RECORD EXCLUSIVE

Cameraman Bob Hotchkiss had to dodge bullets to take this exclusive picture of the gunman in the attic.

THIRTEEN people were wounded by a gunman during 105 minutes of terror in Glasgow yesterday.

They were a policeman, a seven-year-old boy, two women and nine men.

The gunman opened fire when police went to interview him in connection with the death of Mrs. Rachel Ross, 72, in Ayr.

From an attic window bullets rained down into Holyrood Crescent, Woodside, at the start of the running battle with police.

.. GUNMAN AT THE WINDOW

Even ambulances arriving to take away the injured had to run the gauntlet of shots from the third-floor window.

The detectives—who had been looking for James Griffiths, a 34-year-old man from Rochdale, Lancs—called for reinforcements.

The battle went on through the streets of the city in a 60 m.p.h. car chase . . . even into a pub, where the gunman stopped for a drink of brandy.

It ended in a cul-de-sac five miles from Holyrood Crescent.

By then, 13 people had been shot

The gunman himself was dead—shot as police cornered him in a block of flats.

POLICEMEN AT THE READY..

Policemen during the siege with .22 B.S.A. Martini International rifles . . . guns of the same calibre and similar to those used by American snipers in Vietnam.

The only picture of the sniper before he died

Full story—Back Page ● more pictures—Pages 13, 14 and 15

GUNMAN RUNS AMOK IN CITY

THIRTEEN people were shot by a gunman during 105 minutes of terror in Glasgow in July. The victims were a policeman, a seven-year-old boy, two women and nine men.

From 10.50am until 12.35pm, the desperate gunman blasted his way through the north of the city in a bid to flee from the law.

Detective Chief Inspector Sam McAllister of the Scottish Crime Squad, and a senior detective investigating the death of a 72-year-old Ayr woman, went "on information received" to a house in the city's West End. The man, armed with a rifle and shotgun, sat at an attic window keeping police pinned down with a volley of fire.

Entrenched in his stronghold, the gunman continued to fire.

Then he scrambled over roofs and ran through back courts to Lansdowne Terrace and on to Henderson Street.

There he shot 57-year-old James Kerr in the neck and stole Mr Kerr's car.

At 60mph he drove through a police cordon, steering with one hand and shooting with the other.

Then came another hijacking, this time a lorry, and three more men were shot before the gunman was cornered in a Springburn cul-de-sac.

He blasted open the door of an empty house at 26 Kay Street, Springburn, and made his last stand.

From a window, he fired more shots and at 12.35 his life ended. CID boss Tom Goodall said afterwards: "I cannot confirm how the man died.

"I cannot confirm whether it was as a result of a shot from a policeman's gun or whether he shot himself."

The gunman was a 34-year-old man who was being sought by police on both sides of the border.

SCOTLAND'S NEW GRAND PRIX CHAMP

Jackie Stewart clinched the Formula One championship with a victory at the Italian grand prix in September. In a close, thrilling race, the 30-year-old Scot just managed to take the chequered flag half a car length ahead of Jochen Rindt to secure his sixth victory of the season. He became the second Scot to lift the coveted title following the late Jim Clark.

COMINGS...

Stephen Hendry
Snooker Player

ON RADIO

Waggoner's Walk

Album Time

Ed Stewart

Scotch Corner

ON TV

Department S

Randall & Hopkirk (Deceased)

Doctor in the House

Up Pompeii

The Clangers

Star Trek

Far removed from the concerns of the Earth, Neil Armstrong was taking giant steps forward in the conquest of space as he and fellow NASA astronaut, Buzz Aldrin, became the first men on the moon on July 20th. The mission, Apollo 11, went without a hitch and after a few days' stay on the moon, the two men blasted off to rejoin their colleague Michael Collins who had been orbiting the planet while the others were on the surface. On their return to Earth, the astronauts were placed in quarantine to allow scientists to check whether they had picked up any infections while on the moon. Once they were given the all-clear, the heroes welcome awaiting them got into full swing.

THIS SPORTING LIFE

FOOTBALL	RUGBY UNION	GOLF	HORSE RACING	SHINTY
Scottish Champions Celtic *Scottish Cup Winners* Celtic	*Scotland vs England* England 8–3 Scotland at Twickenham	*Home Internationals* Scotland 10-5 England Scotland 10-5 Ireland Scotland 10-5 Wales	*Scottish Grand National* *Winner* *Playlord* at Ayr	*Camanachd Cup Winners* Kyles Athletic at Oban

SUNDAY MAIL

8d   3222   JULY 26, 1970

PANIC BUYING EMPTIES SHOPS

SUNDAY MAIL REPORTER

SCOTTISH housewives felt the first effects of the dock strike yesterday when panic buying left scores of shops without sugar, tinned fruit or bacon. As the "sold-out" signs went up, rationing started in two Scots cities and there was talk of it spreading.

Wholesalers and suppliers are likely to impose indirect rationing for in many cases stocks are low and some shops are being told: "Sorry. No more deliveries meantime."

Shops were packed yesterday as canny housewives stocked up—afraid of a prices explosion later in the week.

The manager of one big chain of shops in the **FALKIRK** area said: "People are panic buying. Some bought as much as 28lb of sugar.

"We're sold out and other shops are in the same position. And my suppliers have told me they cannot guarantee further deliveries.

"Danish bacon is the same. I have been told to expect no more meantime."

Prices are holding steady meantime, but Mr Thomas Brechin, head of one of Scotland's largest meat businesses, said: 'There MUST be an increase by the end of this week.'

Bulk ban

Mr David Campbell, manager of Woolworth's store in **STIRLING**, ran out of sugar and had to turn away local shop owners who had gone to him for supplies.

Mr Campbell said suppliers seemed to be holding back stocks and that he had received only a third of his weekly order.

In **ALLOA**, Clackmannanshire, one store manager said he would not allow people with money to buy in bulk "leaving none for folk who couldn't afford to do that."

In **EDINBURGH** a spokesman for the Edinburgh and Dumfriess-shire Dairy Co. said his firm was low on sugar, but that rationing was not being considered yet.

Sugar shoppers in **GREENOCK** were disappointed yesterday. Supplies that should have reached Massey's on Friday never arrived.

A spokesman said: "We don't know when our next load of sugar will arrive."

Where rationing has already started — in Glasgow and Dundee—some big stores are

(Continued on Page 2)

Double Scotch!

IAN AND ROSEMARY GRAB TWO MORE GOLDS

THIS was the moment that sent all Scotland wild with excitement yesterday — Ian Stewart winning the Commonwealth Games 5000 metres, with fellow-Scot Ian McCafferty second and Kenya's Kip Keino trailing third.

Making it a "double Scotch" gold medal finale, Ian's girl-friend, Rosemary Stirling, surged to victory in the womens' 800 metres.

Immediately Ian crossed the finishing line, Rosemary rushed forward (right) to congratulate him with a hug.

What an end to the biggest and friendliest Games in the history of the event.

The climax came as 2000 athletes flooded into the Meadowbank arena in a display of international friendship.

After the Queen's closing speech the athletes and officials danced and dined the night away at a farewell party at Murrayfield Ice Rink.

Games Special—See Pages 30, 32.

The Secret Of A Perfect Complexion

BY TOP SWEDISH MODEL
GUNILLA KNUTSON
—PAGE 22

Home Truths About Council Houses

SUNDAY MAIL
SPECIAL REPORT
—PAGES 4 AND 5

1970

FOOD PANIC OVER DOCK STRIKE

HOUSEWIVES in Scotland felt the effects of the dock strike in July when panic-buying left scores of shops without sugar, tinned fruit or bacon.

As "sold-out" signs went up, rationing started in two Scottish cities and it was predicted that the cutback by food outlets would spread.

Wholesalers and suppliers were thought likely to impose "indirect rationing", as many shops with low stocks were being told: "Sorry, no more deliveries meantime".

The manager of one chain of shops in the Falkirk area said: "Some people bought as much as 28lb of sugar. We've sold out and other shops are in the same position

"My suppliers have told me that they cannot guarantee further deliveries. Danish bacon is the same. I have been told to expect no more."

Rationing had already began in Glasgow and Dundee and housewives were restricted to 4lbs of sugar at a time. It was thought that shops would next put bacon and butter on their rationing list.

Shops were packed with housewives stocking up, afraid of a price explosion. Prices had remained steady but Thomas Brechin, head of one of Scotland's largest meat businesses, said: "There MUST be an increase in the next few days", a view endorsed by wholesalers generally who were predicting that price increases would be inevitable if the dock strike continued.

Meanwhile, in a bid to beat the strike, Scottish air charter companies were expecting to begin a big airlift of food and supplies. It had already started in england and was expected to spread to Scotland.

The switch to aircraft would end the worries of the Scottish islands. It was hoped that operators would quickly establish an air bridge to get vital supplies to places like Orkney and Shetland.

GOLDEN BOY OF THE GAMES

In July, Lachie Stewart's surprise victory in the 10,000 metres gave Scotland its first gold medal of the ninth Commonwealth Games in Edinburgh.

Running the best race of his life, Stewart out-ran the British record holder, Dick Taylor, and beat the race favourite, Australian Ron Clarke, into second place.

Stewart's win was just the start of what proved to be a great day for Scotland at the Games. Rosemary Payne took the gold medal in the woman's discus with a Commonwealth record throw and Bill Sutherland took the bronze in the 20-mile walk.

ELECTRICITY SCANDAL HITS NEW BRIDGE

There were chaotic scenes on Glasgow's new Kingston Bridge as November's black ice caused dozens of cars to spin out of control and crash. Angry motorists were paying the price of a year-long argument between the Corporation and the Electricity Board over the cost of power needed to run the heating system built into the bridge to keep it ice-free. The spate of accidents led to a resolution of the argument and the restoration of electricity to the bridge.

WHAT IT COST

POUND OF BUTTER
17½p

POUND OF BACON
34p

PINT OF BEER
12p

CIGARETTES
27p (20 Senior Service)

WOMEN'S SHOES
£4.99

MEN'S JEANS
£5.95

TON OF COAL
£16.00

POSTAGE
3p

CAR
Austin Allegro £973

THIS SPORTING LIFE

FOOTBALL	RUGBY UNION	GOLF	HORSE RACING	SHINTY
Scottish Champions Celtic	Scotland vs England Scotland 14–5 England at Murrayfield	British Open Winner Jack Nicklaus at St Andrews (283)	Scottish Grand National Winner The Spaniard at Ayr	Camanachd Cup Winners Newtonmore at Kingussie
Scottish Cup Winners Aberdeen				

SUNDAY MAIL

9d   3245   JANUARY 3, 1971

108 injured, and boys are among the dead

66 KILLED IN IBROX DISASTER

SIXTY-SIX spectators were killed and another 108 injured—three critically —in Britain's biggest-ever football tragedy at Ibrox Park, Glasgow, yesterday.

It came at the end of a trouble-free match between Rangers and Celtic watched by 80,000 spectators.

Just before the end of the match, Rangers fans on their way out heard the roar of the crowd when Rangers scored a last seconds equalising goal.

They tried to get back up the steps to the terracing but were engulfed by hundreds of jubilant fans swarming down after the final whistle.

Crash barriers on the stairway were broken by the crowds . . . and fans fell on top of one another.

Lord Provost Sir Donald Liddle, weeping at a press conference, said: "It is quite clear a great number died of suffocation."

The Chief Constable, Sir James Robertson, said it was clear that barricades had burst and people had piled on top of each other.

Fans help injured

Ambulances, fire engines and police cars were rushed to the stadium. Some had difficulty in reaching the scene because home-going crowds leaving the match were unaware of the tragedy.

As well as the official figures, many more were treated on the spot by first aid men and volunteers from among the spectators.

Police appealed to spectators who had escaped the disaster to help in carrying stretchers.

Many friends, still wearing their club colours, helped to carry dead and injured to the pavilion.

Club officials worked in their shirt sleeves, giving help to injured spectators.

The first bodies were extricated and brought

Continued on Page Two

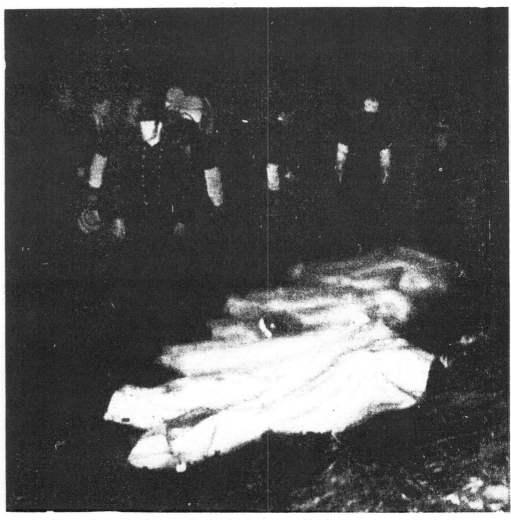

Shrouded bodies lie in rows on the Ibrox turf.

POLICE NAME THE DEAD—SEE BACK PAGE

PICTURES PAGES 3, 4, 5, 7, 9

TRAGEDY AT OLD FIRM MATCH

SIXTY SIX football fans died and another 108 were injured when tragedy struck at Ibrox Park in January.

The disaster came at the end of a trouble-free match between Rangers and Celtic, watched by some 80,000 spectators.

Just before the end of the match, Rangers fans on their way out of the ground heard the roar of the crowd when their team scored an equalising goal in the last few seconds of the game.

They tried to get back up the stairs to the terracing to join in the celebrations but they were engulfed by hundreds of jubilant supporters swarming down after the final whistle. In the resulting crush, crash barriers on the stairway gave way and fans began to fall on top of one another.

Ambulances, fire engines and police cars rushed to the stadium, some being delayed by the home-going crowds leaving the match, unaware of the tragedy.

When rescue services arrived, they found scenes of chaos with fans injured and what they described as "a mound of dead".

Police appealed to spectators who had escaped to help carry the stretchers. The volunteers and the rescue squads carried the dead and the injured onto the pitch.

Fifty three bodies were laid out on the field and the other 13 victims were taken to hospital where they were to be found dead.

A weeping crowd gathered at Ibrox to find out if their relatives or friends had been killed or injured.

Players from both of the Old Firm rival teams paid their respects at the funeral services for the victims.

After the tragedy, pleas were again made to change the safety legislation on football stadiums.

GAS EXPLOSION DESTROYS SHOPS

In October, a massive mid-afternoon gas explosion destroyed a busy shopping centre at Clarkston Toll on the outskirts of Glasgow. Twelve people were killed in the blast and dozens more were injured as over a dozen premises collapsed in the modern complex. A passing bus was also caught by the explosion and suffered severe damage.

ON TV

The Onedin Line

Upstairs, Downstairs

Bless This House

Sale of the Century

Follyfoot

Here Come The Doubledeckers

The Generation Game

GOINGS...

John Boyd Orr
Nobel Prize-winning Nutritionist

John Reith
First Director-General of the BBC

ON RADIO

The Long March of Everyman

JAGS JUBILANT

In one of the greatest upsets in Scottish football history, Partick Thistle thrashed Celtic 4-1 to lift the League Cup in October. The 63,000 crowd had turned up expecting Celtic to win with ease but were stunned to see the Jags score four goals in 37 minutes. Thistle's young goalkeeper, Alan Rough, was in superb form and his efforts ensured that Celtic's only reward for relentless pressure in the second half was a single Dalgleish goal.

THIS SPORTING LIFE

FOOTBALL	RUGBY UNION	GOLF	HORSE RACING	SHINTY
Scottish Champions Celtic	*Scotland vs England* England 15–16 Scotland at Twickenham Scotland 26–6 England at Murrayfield	*Home Internationals* Scotland 8 - 7 England Scotland 8½ - 6½ Ireland Scotland 12 - 3 Wales	*Scottish Grand National Winner* Young Ash Leaf at Ayr	*Camanachd Cup Winners* Newtonmore at Inverness
Scottish Cup Winners Celtic				

Daily Record

3p Thursday, May 25, 1972   No. 23,877

BARCELONA BATTLE

Rangers win Cup ..then fans riot

THE SHAME IN SPAIN

Players mobbed on the pitch

Rangers captain John Greig mobbed by wildly excited fans as they invade the pitch.

BARCELONA: MIDNIGHT
Alex Cameron reports

THOUSANDS of Rangers fans fought a pitched battle with baton-swinging Spanish police here last night.

It happened at the end of the most unruly major European soccer match ever.

The scenes after Rangers had beaten Moscow Dynamo 3-2 in the Cup Winners' Cup final were fantastic.

It was chaos. A total shambles. A blot on sport and those who watch it.

Charged

It took Rangers players nearly 10 minutes to fight their way through the mobbing, milling thousands, who rushed on to the pitch in the worst mass invasion ever at a big game in Europe.

And it was the **FIFTH** time that the fans had scurried madly on to the great Barcelona pitch from their seats on the steep tiers of concrete.

Finally the pistol-packing policemen, who had shown a total apathy, lost their heads at the end of the match.

They charged into the crowd with batons swinging madly. Fans were bludgeoned to the ground.

White-suited ambulance men rushed around to attend to fans with blood streaming from their faces.

Yelling

The police charged the unruly mob three times, foot-long batons swinging like windmills among the Scots.

But the most astonishing scene of all was when hordes of yelling fans leapt from the terracing and chased the police halfway across the pitch in disorder.

Other fans hurled

CONTINUED ON BACK PAGE

THE TENSE TRIUMPH ● VICTORY AND VIOLENCE

See Page 27

See Centre Pages

THE MAD BATTLE OF BARCELONA

THOUSANDS of Rangers fans fought a battle with Spanish riot police at the end of the European Cup Winners Cup Final in Barcelona in May.

Rangers fans had gone wild when the final whistle was blown and rushed onto the pitch to celebrate their team's famous 3-2 victory over Moscow Dynamo.

It took the players almost 10 minutes to fight through the throng of fans and the policemen who had shown total apathy throughout the match, lost control. They charged into the crowd with batons swinging madly.

There had been two pitch invasions previously in the game.

When Colin Stein scored Rangers' first goal with a magnificent shot from in 24 minutes, many of the 25,000 Scottish supporters ran on to the pitch cheering and singing. And the same happened when Willie Johnston hit the net after 40 minutes to score the Gers' second goal.

The Scots fans began celebrating wildly on the terracing because at this point, Rangers looked as if they had the game won and they looked home and dry when Johnston scored a third goal, just three minutes after half-time.

However, the Russians refused to accept defeat and after 55 minutes, Estrokov scored their first goal.

This was later followed by another goal two minutes from the end when Makorikov scored. Rangers were in trouble. but they held their nerve and the lead to the final whistle.

As Rangers brought the cup to Ibrox, they were greeted by thousands of fans celebrating in the rain.

Although the ugly scenes in Spain took the edge off the victory for the players, they were clearly overjoyed with the reception they received at home.

STIRLING STUDENTS ABUSE QUEEN

Drunken students at Stirling University heckled and jostled the Queen during a royal visit to the campus in October. What began as an orderly sit-in at the McRobert Theatre to protest at the money spent by the university on the visit, quickly degenerated into a drunken rabble whose abusive behaviour outraged many onlookers. At one point, the police had to form a protective barrier between the Queen and the bottle-waving students.

GOINGS...

John Grierson
Pioneer of Documentary film-making

Compton Mackenzie
Author of Whisky Galore

STEEL JOBS BLOW

Hopes of a giant steel complex being built at Hunterston in Ayrshire were dashed in October by British Steel boss Lord Melchett. He announced instead that only a smaller scale plant would be built, employing up to 500 people rather than the 10,000

which the unions had been hoping for if the major project had been given the thumbs-up. More ominously, Lord Melchett also stated that Scotland would be likely to lose over 7000 steel jobs during the next decade.

ON RADIO

I'm Sorry I Haven't A Clue

The Last Goon Show of All

Words

ON TV

Colditz	*Are You Being Served?*
Emerdale Farm	*Record Breakers*
Lord Peter Wimsey	*Mastermind*

THIS SPORTING LIFE

FOOTBALL	RUGBY UNION	GOLF	HORSE RACING	SHINTY
Scottish Champions Celtic	*Scotland vs England* Scotland 23–9 England at Murrayfield	*British Open Winner* Lee Trevino at Muirfield (278)	*Scottish Grand National Winner* *Quick Replay Leaf* at Ayr	*Camanachd Cup Winners* Newtonmore at Glasgow
Scottish Cup Winners Celtic				

Daily Record

SCOTLAND'S BIGGEST DAILY SALE

3p   Friday, October 26, 1973   24,315

World on the alert

A "YES" from the Americans and Russians last night ended a day of war fears.

A day when President Nixon put his country's world-wide nuclear forces on "alert" . . . and could not explain why.

A day when he yet again called off a major public address . . . and handed over to Secretary of State Henry Kissinger.

For long hours Kissinger—and the Western world—lived with the threat that Russia might send troops in to the Middle East in answer to a peace-force plea from Egypt.

Questions were asked in the Commons about Britain's possible role—and about President Nixon's "unbalanced" decision.

It was from the UN in New York that reassurance came. The Security Council voted to send a peace force to the Middle East—without Big Power participation.

The Russians and Americans both voted "yes" and the emergency was over.

Full stories of the crisis and the growing Nixon riddle—Back Page and Page 2.

A PAGE ONE EMERGENCY CALL

999 PLEASE COME BACK!

THE (NEVER-ENDING) BATTLE OF TINDERBOX CITY

Firemen fight a whirlwind of flames in a Glasgow dockland timber warehouse. The date: Sept. 26 . . . but what if it happened today—Oct. 26?

THINK AGAIN. Please come back to work! This is the Record's emergency call to Glasgow's 660 firemen.

At 8 a.m. today, you are on official strike according to your unofficial leaders.

Or unofficially on strike according to your union's official leaders.

Whichever way you look at it, you will be Britain's **FIRST** firemen to walk out on the job.

And as you do that, so you lose the most important ally in your fight for a better deal—public opinion.

So far, you have had the public on your side.

MOST PEOPLE agree that you are under-paid and under-staffed . . . that you work long and dangerous hours.

THE RECORD shares these views.

WE ALL want you to get the best deal possible under Phase 2 of the Incomes Policy.

Gallant

And if anyone qualifies for an exceptional "unsocial hours" payment under Phase 3 surely you do!

But at the same time the Record agrees with S T U C General Secretary James Jack that a strike "won't get you anywhere."

YOU ARE THE FIRE EXPERTS.

● **DON'T** get your fingers burned by telling the public, and your official negotiators, to go to blazes!

Settle today for the extra cash offer.

● **DON'T** destroy your gallant record by letting the troops take over the Battle of Tinderbox City.

On the Centre Pages today we picture troops practising yesterday to do your job.

The picture on the left is a reminder that it is just that: **YOUR JOB.**

So please . . . answer the Record's 999 call.

HOPES RISE FOR PEACE — CENTRE PAGES

1973

PLEA TO THE STRIKING FIREMEN

GLASGOW'S firemen became the first in Britain to stage a walkout during a dispute. In October, the city's firefighters reported for work outside their stations, then made history by refusing to take up their duties.

Glasgow, with the worst fire record of any British city, was left without protection. The authorities had to rely on the military for fire cover, and soon the "Green Goddesses" – Army fire engines – were a common sight on the streets.

Within hours of the strike starting, an arsonist struck in the Dennistoun area, starting three fires all within a few streets of one another. However, the well-equipped soldiers were well up to the task. But as the strike dragged on, the strain began to tell on these stand-in firemen.

Certain public places had to limit their opening hours. Libraries had to close at 6.00pm although the city's bingo halls were allowed to stay open.

The firemen had gone on on strike for better wages and conditions. After 15 years' service, a fireman was paid £33.53 per 40-hour week with eight hours compulsory overtime. The men went on strike for a £5-a-week pay rise because Glasgow Corporation offered the men only £2.48.

As the strike continued, many of the firemen's families began to suffer. Neighbours and friends organised food parcels while the firefighters themselves collected cash outside the city's football stadiums. Not everyone was so supportive however, including the Fire Brigades Union.

The strike ended after eight weeks with a degree of success for the firemen, some of whom received rises of up to £9.13.

POWER CRISIS GRIPS THE NATION

In December, Prime Minister Edward Heath made a dramatic TV appeal to the nation, asking people to rally round the Government's emergency measures to beat the fuel crisis. This had been caused by a train drivers' strike and a miner's overtime ban which together threatened to curtail or disrupt the movement of coal to power stations and other industries. The Government's response was to introduce a three-day working week in priority industries beginning in January 1974, together with selective power-cuts for domestic users.

In a series of austerity measures of a type not seen since the Second World War, the country was asked to adopt voluntary restraints on their use of heating and lighting in order to conserve energy.

ON TV

Within These Walls	Reilly – Ace of Spies
	New Faces
The Tomorrow People	Some Mothers Do
Kung Fu	'Ave 'Em

GOINGS...

Robert Watson-Watt
Pioneer of Radar

Neil Gunn
Writer

ON RADIO

Music Weekly

Kaleidoscope

Checkpoint

The Radio 1 Roadshow

The Story of Pop

SCOTLAND'S BOUNCING BABIES

The *Record* reported in May 1973 that Scottish babies were healthier than they had ever been before. Better housing conditions, better food and improved medical knowledge were cited as the main reasons. In fact, doctors were reporting a new problem: babies that were too fat. One doctor called for a public information campaign to debunk the myth that a fat baby was a healthy baby: "Fat babies tend to grow into fat people, and that can't be healthy". The increasingly early onset of puberty, and the implications for young teenagers, was also seen as a cause of some concern.

THIS SPORTING LIFE

FOOTBALL	RUGBY UNION	GOLF	HORSE RACING	SHINTY
Scottish Champions Celtic	*Scotland vs England* England 20–13 Scotland at Twickenham	*British Open Winner* Tom Weiskopf at Troon (276)	*Scottish Grand National Winner* Esban at Ayr	*Camanachd Cup Winners* Glasgow Mid Argyll at Fort William
Scottish Cup Winners Rangers				

Daily Record

SCOTLAND'S BIGGEST DAILY SALE

4p   Thursday, February 7, 1974   No. 24,400

As election fever grows, a moment of confrontation..

FACE TO FACE

NO two men in crisis-hit Britain have more to talk about than miners' leader Joe Gormley and Premier Edward Heath.

That is, they would have, if they **WANTED** to get together.

Yesterday they did meet ... but only socially.

And definitely not on the conversation agenda were a miners' strike or an election.

Of course, it was hardly the time or the place. The two men came face to face at a reception in the Soviet Embassy, in London.

And last-minute negotiations would have been, well, undiplomatic.

BALLOT

Last night, as election fever mounted, it looked as if the Prime Minister might have more to say shortly.

Opinion among top Tories hardened that Polling Day would be on February 28 or March 7.

And one Cabinet minister, Mr James Prior, Leader of the House, went as far as to say:

" The miners have now had their ballot. Perhaps we ought to have ours."

CRISIS COUNTDOWN
—Page 2

 New Seekers split   **SONG GIRLS GO THEIR OWN WAYS**   SEE BACK PAGE

NUM STRIKE SPARKS ELECTION

THE Prime Minister Edward Heath called a general election for February 28 in the wake of the decision by the National Union of Mineworkers to begin a national strike from February 9.

Support for the miners grew as the General Secretary of the TUC, Len Murray, declared that all affiliated unions should not cross picket lines: other unions had to back the miners if their strategy − halting the flow of coal and oil to industry − was to succeed.

A pithead ballot resulted in 81% of miners voting for industrial action. The Government's offer of a further meeting with the Employment Secretary, Willie Whitelaw, was rejected. Lawrence Daly, General Secretary of the NUM said that hard cash, not more talks, was the only way to avoid the strike.

James Jack, General Secretary of the Scottish Trades Union Congress said: "The question of whether or not there should be a strike is very much in the hands of the miners."

However, Jack hinted at the nervousness among many in the Labour movement at the prospect of fighting a general election while the country had been brought to a standstill by striking trade unionists.

"I think they should defer any action until the result of the election is known. It might damage Labour's cause." He believed that every wage- and salary earner in the country would look forward to February 28 and the chance to get rid of "an idiotic and unfair government."

Campbell Adamson of the CBI looked to the longer term. In his view, whatever government was returned, the problem of major strikes and their effects of British industry had to ne addressed. "We have to invent another way of settling wage disputes," he said.

BIGGEST NORTH SEA STRIKE YET

In April, the Scottish-based oil company Burmah announced that it had made the biggest discovery yet of North Sea oil.

The new Ninian oilfield was lying 180 miles north east of Shetland. The company predicted that oil production could reach as much as 900,000 barrels a day. This would amount to a staggering 45 million tons a year − half of Britain's consumption of oil for the whole of 1974.

The find, along with predictions of more massive oilfields nearby, was expected to make Britain a net exporter of oil by the early 1980s, news that was seized upon by Scottish Nationalists to support their slogan, "It's Scotland's Oil".

COW CABARET PRODUCES RESULTS

Uphall, West Lothian was the centre of attraction for dairy farmers throughout Scotland in August, as news spread of an innovative method for increasing milk production. The secret? Croon to your cattle! Bill Cowie, a dairyman at Oatridge College Farm, noticed that if he sang while milking the cows, the yield from the herd increased. College authorities were sceptical at first, and decided to conduct a study. The results were startling. The 109 cows milked in silence produced around 115 gallons a day. When subjected to the 'cow cabaret', this figure increased to 200 gallons a day!

ON TV		
The Pallisers	It Ain't Half Hot Mum	Porridge
The Waltons		TISWAS
Harry O	The Six Million Dollar Man	Rising Damp

THIS SPORTING LIFE

FOOTBALL	RUGBY UNION	GOLF	HORSE RACING	SHINTY
Scottish Champions Celtic	*Scotland vs England* Scotland 16–14 England at Murrayfield	*Home Internationals* Scotland 4½ - 10½ England Scotland 9 - 6 Ireland Scotland 9 - 6 Wales	*Scottish Grand National Winner* Red Rum at Ayr	*Camanachd Cup Winners* Kyles Athletic at Oban
Scottish Cup Winners Celtic				

Daily Record

5p   SCOTLAND'S BIGGEST DAILY SALE

Friday, July 25, 1975   No. 24,853

The happiest honeymoon in the world
CENTRE PAGES

YOU'VE HAD YOUR FISH AND CHIPS
PAGE NINE

What the Record said last month

Down .. and out !

JOHNNY NO-JOB!

- In Britain there are 1,087,869 on the dole
- In Scotland 129,836
- With ONE job for every FIVE school leavers

BRITAIN'S army of jobless crashed through the million mark yesterday.

And from the 1,087,869 figure of gloom one shattering fact emerged.

In Scotland, there is just **ONE** job for every **FIVE** school-leavers.

The plight of the youngsters—nearly 16,000 are out of work, with only 3000 vacancies open to them—yesterday prompted Strathclyde chief Mr Geoff Shaw to refer to this week's controversial TV documentary "Johnny Go Home."

He said: " Problems

*By DOUGLAS MALONE
Record Industrial Editor*

highlighted in this programme result from long-term unemployment, forcing young people to leave their homes in search of work."

For Scottish TUC leader James Jack, the figures were " nothing short of a tragedy.

Emergency

" The tragedy is that a substantial number of young people are not only without work . . . but without any signs that suitable work will become available," he said.

Last night the STUC and the Scottish Council of the Labour Party called for a state of emergency to deal with Scotland's

129,836-strong dole-queue.

Neither body wants to wait for the formation of the Scottish Development Agency.

Instead they want a special employment agency to be set up—with Government cash backing —to start training schemes and special projects for jobless youngsters.

On the Scottish unemployment total in general, they are demanding urgent talks with Scottish Secretary Willie Ross, Employment Secretary Michael Foot and Premier Harold Wilson to press for an " emergency package " including :

DOUBLING the present Regional Employment

Continued on Back Page

1975

CALL FOR ACTION ON DOLE MISERY

THE number of jobless people in Britain went over the million mark in July, with a total of 1,087,869 on the dole.

From this figure emerged the staggering fact that in Scotland, there was only ONE job for every FIVE school leavers.

For Scottish TUC leader James Jack, these figures were "nothing short of a tragedy".

He said: "The tragedy is that a substantial number of young people are not only without work, but without any signs that suitable work will become available."

The STUC and the Scottish Council of the Labour Party called for a state of emergency to be declared to deal with Scotland's dole queue which had reached 129,836.

They wanted a special employment agency to be set up with Government backing to start training schemes and special projects to help the jobless youngsters.

Both organisations stressed that should the jobless total in Scotland reach the then predicted level of 200,000, the cost to the country in unemployment benefits would be £6 million a week.

They claimed that the money would be better spent keeping people in employment. And they promised a "revolt" if anything were done to cut back on public service expenditure.

Meanwhile in the House of Commons, Employment Secretary Michael Foot revealed that a £10 million package of emergency measures had been worked out with the Government-backed Manpower Services Commission and was to be put into effect immediately.

It was stated that this would make it possible for a further 6000 young people to obtain skilled training during the year.

SOLDIERS CLEAR UP

With no end in sight to a lengthy strike by dustcart drivers in Glasgow, the Government decided in March to use troops to clear the backlog of rubbish in the city which had begun to pose a serious health threat. The soldiers began clearing the huge piles of refuse which had been piling up in dumps, back courts and streets for the previous nine weeks. Rats were a major concern, with the soldiers killing several hundred a week as they removed the rotting waste. In fact, it was the fear of a plague of the rodents infesting the city which had been the deciding factor to send in the troops.

OPEN ALL HOURS?

Plans to liberalise Scotland's drinking laws were given a great boost in September. An experiment to test a "continental" style of al fresco drinking and extended opening hours in Edinburgh during the Festival was hailed a great success. More than 100 pubs, hotels and restaurants had taken part in the experiment and the police reported that there had been no extra problems as a result. Charles Gray, Vice Convener of Strathclyde Region, was impressed and commented that "relaxation of the drink laws can only be a good thing. It's drinking against the clock that causes bother."

GOINGS...

James Robertson Justice	Lex Maclean
Actor	Comedian

ON TV

Angels

The Sweeney

The Good Life

Jim'll Fix It

Celebrity Squares

Space: 1999

THIS SPORTING LIFE

FOOTBALL	RUGBY UNION	GOLF	HORSE RACING	SHINTY
Scottish Champions Rangers	*Scotland vs England* England 7–6 Scotland at Twickenham	*British Open Winner* Tom Watson at Carnoustie (279)	*Scottish Grand National Winner* Barona at Ayr	*Camanachd Cup Winners* Newtonmore at Fort William
Scottish Cup Winners Celtic				

Daily Record

SCOTLAND'S BIGGEST DAILY SALE

6p   Monday, November 15, 1976   No. 25,259

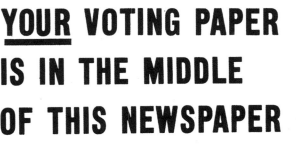

YOUR VOTING PAPER IS IN THE MIDDLE OF THIS NEWSPAPER ▶

WHAT DOES THE NATION THINK?

Scotland's National Newspaper invites our Two Million Readers to join the Greatest Political Debate for 269 years

PLEASE TURN TO PAGE 3 ▶

1976

A RECORD REFERENDUM

ALMOST half the people of Scotland want the country to become independent. That was the stunning result of the *Daily Record* Referendum of November 1976.

Over two days, November 15 and 16, the *Daily Record* issued a questionnaire with each copy of the paper – a staggering 2,132,513 in total. Although by no means the most rigorously scientific poll, the answers on the 45,475 ballots which were returned sent shock waves through the Scottish political establishment.

Just over two years earlier, in October 1974, the SNP had gained over 30% of the vote in the general election, and had returned 11 MPs. The *Record* Referendum showed the nationalist bandwagon was still on a roll, indicating a massive 22% swing from Labour to the SNP.

The Labour Government was deeply unpopular and the day after the publication of the poll, St Andrews Day, it was due to publish its Devolution Bill, in a clear attempt to deflect support for independence. Jim Callaghan, who had succeeded Harold Wilson as Prime Minister earlier in the year, was struggling to deal with increasing unemployment and a weak pound. On 28 September, the Chancellor, Denis Healey, at Heathrow Airport en route to an international conference, had to turn back to deal with the sterling crisis.

Everything pointed to sweeping nationalist gains at the next election. The majority of those under 40 wanted independence, while the SNP was attracting the support of two-thirds of teenagers. However, the *Record* gauged the mood of the voters quite accurately when it stated that the SNP was vulnerable to a rapid loss of support, as the Scottish electorate was in a pretty volatile state. In the general election of May 1979, support for the nationalists fell sharply. Only three of their 11 MPs held on to their seats. Devolution and independence were off the political agenda for the next 20 years.

ROLLERMANIA SELLS OK!

Scotland's main contribution to the music scene in the 1970s was the teen pop sensation, the Bay City Rollers. They were seldom out of the headlines, often for the most trivial reasons. In October, Stuart 'Woody' Wood and the newest member of the band, Ian Mitchell, found themselves in the same private hospital in London. There was nothing seriously wrong with either of the stars – Woody was having a splintered bone in his nose dealt with, and Mitchell was having a node removed from his throat – but their appearance in the *Record* was guaranteed to boost sales, especially among teenage girls.

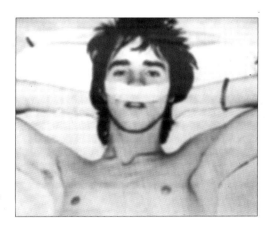

On TV

Poldark	*Open All Hours*
I, Claudius	*The Krypton Factor*
Starsky and Hutch	*Man from Atlantis*

On Radio

Quote...Unquote

A Good Read

You the Jury

Folkweave

Jack de Manio Precisely

The World Tonight

Sounds of Scotland

GOLDEN BOY WILKIE

Scots swimmer David Wilkie finally achieved his dream at the Montreal Olympics in June. He picked up the gold medal in the 200 metres breaststroke and shattered the world record by more than three seconds. Wilkie was the first Briton for almost seventy years to win a swimming gold in this competition.

THIS SPORTING LIFE

FOOTBALL	RUGBY UNION	GOLF	HORSE RACING	SHINTY
Scottish Champions Rangers	*Scotland vs England* Scotland 22–12 England at Murrayfield	*Home Internationals* Scotland 10-5 England Scotland 10-5 Ireland Scotland 9-6 Wales	*Scottish Grand National Winner* *Barona* at Ayr	*Camanachd Cup Winners* Kyles Athletic at Inverness
Scottish Cup Winners Rangers				

Jubilee Record

25 YEARS

..and here's a welcome from the people of Scotland

1977

JUBILEE JOY FOR GLASGOW

AROUND a quarter of a million people lined the streets of Glasgow to welcome the Queen and other members of the royal family, as they visited the city as part of the celebrations to mark the monarch's silver jubilee.

About an hour before the Queen arrived, workmen removed nationalist slogans which had been daubed on the Cenotaph in George Square. But there was no mistaking the warmth of the welcome as the Queen stepped from the royal train at Central station. Thousands more packed into George Square, where the Queen was due at a City Chambers reception. The enthusiasm of the crowd led to an unscheduled appearance and royal wave from the balcony.

The city saw the Household Cavalry in all its finery for the first time, while the sound of the 21-gun salute from the Custom House Quay, another first, startled many.

The rest of the day was taken up with a service at Glasgow Cathedral and a trip to Hampden Park to watch a Glasgow Select play an English Select. Fears that jeering might drown out the playing of God Save the Queen proved unfounded. The one moment of controversy came in fact at the Cathedral, where the Moderator of the General Assembly of the Church of Scotland, the Rt Rev Thomas Torrance, gave what was later described as an anti-nationalist political speech.

Then it was on to the Royal Variety Show at the King's Theatre in Glasgow, where Ronnie Corbett and Frankie Howerd topped a bill that included Sydney Devine and Lena Zavaroni.

There had been fears that the people of Glasgow would not respond to the royal visit. A spokesman for the royal household said the Queen had been delighted with the welcome.

SCOTS INVADE AFTER ENGLISH DEFEATED

Thousands of Scots fans invaded the pitch to celebrate their team's 2-1 victory over the Auld Enemy at Wembley in June. Not only was the hallowed turf invaded, some £15,000 worth of it was carried back north as souvenirs. The goalposts also bore the brunt of the fan's celebrations and were soon lost in the melée that followed the final whistle. Although the fan's behaviour was treated as being reprehensible, their general good nature ensured that there were no ugly scenes in or out of the stadium and the 300-odd arrests were largely for minor, drink-related offences.

ON TV

Roots

Jesus of Nazareth

Secret Army

The Sullivans

Charlie's Angels

The Professionals

Citizen Smith

Ripping Yarns

Blankety Blank

Robin's Nest

How the West Was Won

Raffles

GOINGS...

Matt McGinn
Folksinger

NESSIE SNAPPED AGAIN

Once again, Scotland's resident loch-monster made headline news in June with the latest reported sighting also being captured on camera. Or at least that's what the photographer claimed. Tony Shiels was in no doubt that he had captured Nessie on film shot from the grounds of Urquhart Castle. What raised most eyebrows amongst the sceptics, however, were Mr Shiels' claims that he was a professional wizard and that he had summoned the monster by telepathy.

THIS SPORTING LIFE

FOOTBALL	RUGBY UNION	GOLF	HORSE RACING	SHINTY
Scottish Champions Celtic	*Scotland vs England* England 26–6 Scotland at Twickenham	*British Open Winner* Tom Watson at Turnberry (268)	*Scottish Grand National Winner* Sebastian V at Ayr	*Camanachd Cup Winners* Newtonmore at Glasgow
Scottish Cup Winners Celtic				

THURSDAY June 8 1978

Daily Record

8p   SCOTLAND'S BIGGEST DAILY SALE   No. 25,742

FANS STONE TEAM BUS

2 am: The anger erupts into violence

Faces of fury . . . jeering fans howl abuse at the Scotland team as they leave the pitch   **Picture ERIC CRAIG**

THE worst night in Scottish football history ended last night with Scots fans stoning the team bus.

They had waited outside to jeer and boo.

But, as the players who let them down so badly appeared, their anger boiled over.

The fans raced towards the coach. Some spat at the windows. Some hurled stones they had picked up. Some hurled themselves.

And Cordoba Stadium and the streets outside were littered with discarded tartan.

The fans' disbelief grew as Scotland trailed to a miserable 1-1 draw with underdogs Iran.

As the game dragged on, their songs became weaker and weaker until they finally faded away.

On the final whistle, they screamed abuse and threw their scarves at team manager Ally MacLeod and the players as they walked within a few feet on their way to the dressing room.

Abuse

The players walked with heads down. MacLeod hurried past.

John Robertson could only shake his head and Joe Jordan held out his hands as if to say " there's nothing we could do."

Security officers stood by anxiously in case any of the Scots supporters tried to jump over the low fence towards the team.

The crowds waited

From
KEN GALLACHER in CORDOBA

outside the stadium until the players emerged.

Each man was booed as he appeared.

Sirens

But the worst abuse was reserved for MacLeod.

One fan screamed: "We've walked a million miles for f---all."

The coach eventually made its way through, protected by police cars with sirens wailing.

The world's Press watched in amazement at the booing and jeering continued while the bus sped away.

There was not one single fan at the game who wasn't bitterly disappointed by Scotland's performance.

Alan Hately, 40, a computer salesman of 46 Jordan Lane, Edinburgh, said: "It has

Continued on Back Page

CRY FOR US ARGENTINA

THE songs of Scotland died in our throats last night.

Barring a miracle, our team is out of the World Cup in a way no fan imagined possible.

Shamed. Humiliated. And shown up to be fourth rate in front of the whole world.

In two million Scottish homes last night families sat stunned, silent and saddened as they watched an unbelievably bad Scotland

PAGE ONE OPINION

team stumble to a 1-1 draw with Iran.

Ally MacLeod will take a lot of stick, and he deserves his share of it. But he can't be blamed for the gutless display of many of the players.

WE CHEERED the team that didn't qualify in the last

World Cup because they fought and played and gave everything they had and made us feel proud.

WE CHEERED the present squad when they lost to England at Hampden because they played their hearts out and made us feel proud.

Today there is only emptiness and anger.

Cry for us, Argentina. For last night was the bitter end.

THE FACE OF FAILURE BACK PAGE   **CHAMPAGNE AND TEARS** PAGE FIVE

ANGRY RETREAT BY ALLY'S ARMY

ONE of the worst campaigns in Scottish World Cup football history ended with Scots fans stoning the team bus in Argentina in June.

The supporters had waited outside the stadium simply to jeer and boo but as the players emerged, the Tartan Army's anger boiled over and infuriated fans ran towards the bus, spitting and throwing stones.

Shamed and humiliated, the supporters had witnessed their team being shown up as fourth-raters in front of the world.

They had also to cope with the scandal of winger Willie Johnston being sent home in disgrace after he had failed a routine drugs test.

The Scottish team, under their manager Ally McLeod, were shamed after losing 3-1 to Peru and only managing to draw 1-1 with Iran.

Both opponent countries were teams that Scotland believed they should have been able to beat.

The footballing fiasco continued when the Scots were put out of the World Cup, even although they had won 3-2 against much fancied Holland, going out on goal difference, thanks to the disastrous earlier results.

The Scottish team did, however, manage to gain some pride in their magnificent performance against Holland.

They also regained the support of the same fans who had jeered the team four days previously. Ally's Army chanted, waved flags and sang their heads off as the jeers turned to cheers.

Ironically, Scotland's Archie Gemmell was later given the Goal of the Tournament award for a brilliant solo strike against the Dutch.

NEW OWNERS FOR TROUBLED LINWOOD

Scotland was rocked with the news that the French car giant Peugeot-Citroën was taking over Chrysler's European operations, including the troubled Linwood plant. Gavin Laird of the engineering union expressed his astonishment, while government spokesmen could not conceal their shock at the news. Public money had been pumped into Chrysler since January 1976, as the Labour Government tried desperately to save the ailing car giant's British operations. While most of the plant's 9,000 workers welcomed the news, believing it would secure their employment, MP Tam Dalyell warned of troubled times ahead. Peugeot-Citroën had a reputation for dealing with strikes ruthlessly.

GLASGOW HOTEL GUTTED

The prestigious Grosvenor Hotel in Glasgow's fashionable west end was destroyed in January in a spectacular blaze which ripped through the listed Victorian building. The fire began in the kitchens and quickly spread, and smoke and flames soon engulfed the entire length of the hotel. Fortunately, all staff and guests escaped unharmed. The blaze happened in the middle of a firemen's strike and it was left to military firefighters to try to control it.

ON RADIO	ON TV	
The Hitchhiker's Guide to the Galaxy	*Pennies from Heaven*	*Butterflies*
	Dallas	*3-2-1*
	Hazell	*Blake's 7*

THIS SPORTING LIFE

FOOTBALL	RUGBY UNION	GOLF	HORSE RACING	SHINTY
Scottish Champions Rangers	*Scotland vs England* Scotland 0–15 England at Murrayfield	*British Open Winner* Jack Nicklaus at St Andrews (281)	*Scottish Grand National Winner* King Con at Ayr	*Camanachd Cup Winners* Newtonmore at Fort William
Scottish Cup Winners Rangers				

SATURDAY March 3 1979

Daily Record

8p   SCOTLAND'S BIGGEST DAILY SALE   No. 25,955

	YES	NO
WESTERN ISLES	6218 28%	4833 22%
ORKNEY	2104 15%	5439 39%
SHETLAND	2020 14%	5466 37%

YES: 33% NO: 31%

A NATION DIVIDED

	YES	NO
HIGHLAND	44,973 33%	43,274 32%
GRAMPIAN	94,944 28%	101,485 30%
TAYSIDE	91,482 31%	93,325 32%
FIFE	86,252 35%	74,436 31%
LOTHIAN	187,221 33%	186,421 33%
BORDERS	20,746 27%	30,780 40%

1,230,937 voted for an Assembly

1,153,502 voted against

THE YES MAJORITY WAS...

77,435

36% DIDN'T VOTE

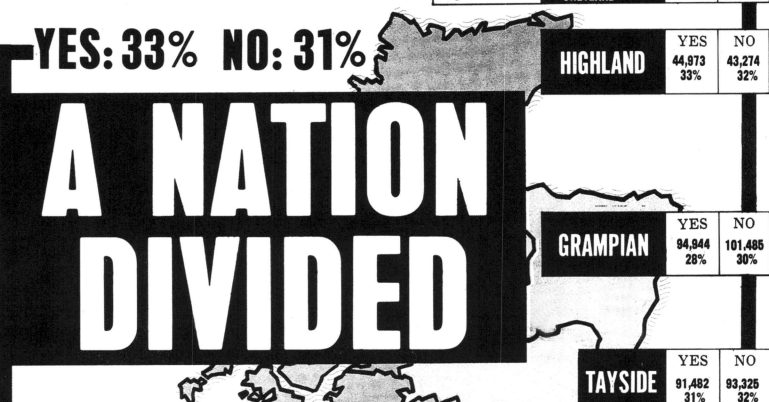

	YES	NO
CENTRAL	71,296 36%	59,105 30%
STRATHCLYDE	596,519 34%	508,599 29%
DUMFRIES and GALLOWAY	27,162 26%	40,239 39%

FULL STORY AND ANALYSIS—Pages 2 and 3

1979

DEVOLUTION DOWN BUT NOT OUT

THE March referendum on the Scottish Assembly produced the worst possible result – no clear-cut decision.

With around a third of the electorate voting Yes for a devolved assembly for Scotland, another third voting against it and the remaining third not voting at all, the required 40% threshold in favour of devolution was not reached, causing headaches for the Callaghan Government.

The decision on whether Scotland was to have its own Assembly was returned to Westminster where the Government faced an agonising choice which would put their survival even until the autumn in doubt.

If they tried to push the Scotland Act through Parliament they would face defeat at the hands of Labour anti-devolution MPs.

If they abandoned the Act because the 40% level had not been reached, they would lose the support of the 11 Scottish Nationalist MPs.

Either defection could have resulted in the Labour government losing its working majority in Parliament and so lead to a general election.

The 'yes' side actually won the poll with 1,230,937 votes to 1,153,502 – a majority of 77,435. There was a 64% turn out, with 51.5% voting for and 48% against. However, the Yes campaign failed by a large margin, some 267,917 to reach the 40% threshold of the total electorate.

Strathclyde, Highland, Lothian, Fife, Central Regions and the Western Isles all had 'Yes' majorities while the 'No' vote predominated in Tayside, Borders, Dumfries and Galloway, Orkney, Shetland and Grampian.

It was clear that the Tory pro-devolution vote had vanished. The Scottish Conservatives came out in support of the official party NO line. The result was a triumph for party leader, Margaret Thatcher. However, some 70% of young Scots voters had voted Yes which was being seen by the bitterly disappointed pro-devolutionists as a vital pointer to the future.

BOAT PEOPLE SEEK REFUGE

Scotland played its part in helping those who became known as the Vietnamese boat people. Wars, first with Cambodia and then with China in early 1979, led to thousands fleeing the country. Many crowded onto boats ill-equipped for the purpose, flooding into Hong Kong and other parts of the Far East. Britain agreed to accept a limited number of the boat people. Around 40 arrived in Edinburgh, before being resettled in other parts of Scotland.

ON RADIO

Breakaway

The Food Programme

ON TV

Danger UXB

Lou Grant

Telford's Change

Shoestring

Minder

Mork & Mindy

The Dukes of Hazzard

Sapphire and Steel

To The Manor Born

Not the Nine O'clock News

Worzel Gummidge

HISTORIC ELECTION VICTORY

History was made in May when Margaret Thatcher entered 10 Downing Street as Britain's first woman Prime Minister.

But a chill wind blew in from the north for the new PM, a wind that had cut down her staunchest supporter in Scotland, her former Shadow Scots Secretary, Teddy Taylor. The signal was clear – Labour were the dominant party in Scotland.

Some Tory strategists believed that Scotland's swing to Labour was due to Mr Callaghan's firm pledge that if he was returned to power devolution would be back on the agenda. But for now, according to the out-going Scots Secretary Bruce Millan, the subject was dead.

And it remained to be seen how Mrs Thatcher would deal with the massed ranks of opposition to her north of the border.

THIS SPORTING LIFE

FOOTBALL	RUGBY UNION	GOLF	HORSE RACING	SHINTY
Scottish Champions Celtic	*Scotland vs England* England 7–7 Scotland at Twickenham	*Home Internationals* Tournament cancelled Scotland 17-13 England	*Scottish Grand National Winner* *Fighting Fit* at Ayr	*Camanachd Cup Winners* Newtonmore at Oban
Scottish Cup Winners Rangers				

SATURDAY July 26 1980

Daily Record

10p SCOTLAND'S BIGGEST DAILY SALE No. 26,476

TOUCH AND GOLD!

Super Wells wins glory for every Scot

Scots reject music peace plan

By FRANK SULLIVAN

THE BBC are to drop their controversial plan to scrap the Scottish Symphony Orchestra . . .

But only if striking musicians agree to the axing of the Scottish Radio Orchestra.

Last night an angry and emotional meeting in Glasgow of more than 70 musicians from the two orchestras threw out the peace plan.

Rodney Mount, a member of the strike committee, said the Scots might well reject the result of the forthcoming ballot and continue strike action.

He said: "There is a distinct bias against Scotland, not only from the BBC but also from the Musicians' Union, which is London-based.

"In England there is more work for freelance players so it is much easier for players there to make up their earnings.

Action

"Our colleagues in England regard it as a reasonable offer, but there is no way BBC musicians in Scotland can make up their earnings."

Mr Mount said they would not give up until both Scottish orchestras had been saved. The strike committee will meet today to discuss further action.

Under the deal, the SSO, the Northern Ireland Orchestra and the London Studio Players would be saved.

The SRO, the Midland Radio Orchestra and the Northern Radio Orchestra would be scrapped in March, but the members would be given a pay-off and then guaranteed 66 per cent of their earnings by working for the BBC on a freelance basis for five years.

THIS is the moment that at one time looked like never happening—Scotland's Allan Wells proudly wearing the coveted 100 metres Olympic Gold Medal.

The medal he won by a hairsbreath from Cuban Silvio Leonard, left, with Petar Petrov of Bulgaria trailing third.

But Allan's golden glory came only after an agony of waiting . . .

TEN nerve-wracking

From ALEX CAMERON in the Lenin Stadium

minutes before the judges decided he had taken first place with a nod and a push of the chest to cross the line just ahead of Leonard.

A HOLD-UP of two and a quarter hours before the Edinburgh sprinter was able to pass the drugs test.

Then the tension ended and 28-year-old Allan climbed the podium in the Moscow stadium to receive the Gold.

The race produced one of the most dramatic finishes of the Games.

Not even the sophisticated

electronic timing equipment could split the Scot and the Cuban—each had a time of 10.25 seconds.

When Allan saw the action replay on the stadium's huge TV screens, he was certain he had won, throwing his arms in the air and doing a lap of honour.

But for millions watching TV—and Allan's wife Margot —there were nagging doubts.

As the two sprinters crossed the line, 27-year-old Margot cupped her head in her hands, crying: "He's lost. He's lost."

Tears were streaming down her cheeks, and when the final

TURN TO PAGE TWO

OUR MESSAGE TO ALLAN LAST NIGHT

TO ALLAN WELLS
OLYMPIC VILLAGE, MOSCOW
CONGRATULATIONS FROM
EVERYONE IN SCOTLAND.
YOU'VE DONE US PROUD.
MAKE IT A DOUBLE ON MONDAY.
DAILY RECORD, GLASGOW.

GOLDEN ALLAN RUNS UP THE FLAG

SCOTLAND'S Allan Wells won the 100 metre gold medal at the Olympics in July. He won by a hairsbreadth from Cuban Silvio Leonard and Peter Petrov of Bulgaria.

And he said he was flattered to be flying again the Scottish track gold medal standard last flown by the great Eric Liddell 56 years previously.

Allan's golden glory came after an agony of waiting.

First, there was a 10-minute wait until the judges decided he had taken first place with a nod and a push of the chest across the line just ahead of Leonard.

Even the electronic timing equipment could not split the Scot and the Cuban, and each was given a time of 10.25 seconds.

Then came a hold-up of two and a quarter hours before the Scots sprinter was able to pass the drugs test.

Commenting on his win, Allan said that his only regret as he stood on the winners podium was that the National Anthem and not *Flower of Scotland* was ringing round the ground.

He said: "There can be no better moment in a man's life, and the truth is I felt very Scottish.

I would have liked this to have been more obvious on such a memorable occasion for me.

Now I have the title of the fastest man on earth, it stills seems a bit incredible."

He was the first Scot to win the Olympic 100 metres gold and the first Briton to do it since Harold Abrahams in 1924.

WATT RETAINS HIS TITLE

Jim Watt retained his world lightweight title in ten minutes of furious action against Ulsterman, Charlie Nash. Knocked down in the first round, the Scottish champion recovered to put Nash down three times in the next three rounds and badly cut the Irishman's eye. The referee stopped the fight in the fourth.

GOINGS...

John Laurie
Actor

NORTH SEA RIG HORROR

The North Sea witnessed its worst accident in March when the accommodation platform, *Alexander Keilland*, collapsed during a Force 10 gale. One of the rig's five supporting legs was thought to have buckled after being hit by a huge wave. The biggest ever peacetime rescue operation swung into action and although 60 were saved, 137 workers died in the freezing waters.

WHAT IT COST

POUND OF BUTTER
42$\frac{1}{2}$p

POUND OF BACON
£1.12$\frac{1}{2}$

PINT OF BEER
41p

CIGARETTES
74p (20 B&H King Size)

WOMEN'S SHOES
£21.99

MEN'S JEANS
£15.99

TON OF COAL
£35

POSTAGE
12p

CAR
Renault 5 £4,100

THIS SPORTING LIFE

FOOTBALL	RUGBY UNION	GOLF	HORSE RACING	SHINTY
Scottish Champions Aberdeen	*Scotland vs England* Scotland 18–30 England at Murrayfield	*British Open Winner* Tom Watson at Muirfield (271)	*Scottish Grand National Winner* *Salkeld* at Ayr	*Camanachd Cup Winners* Kyles Athletic at Kingussie
Scottish Cup Winners Celtic				

Daily Record

12p   SCOTLAND'S BIGGEST DAILY SALE   No. 26,649

THE BEEB PAID £4m FOR IT . .

GONE WITH THE WIND

NOW YOU CAN READ ALL ABOUT IT ON THE CENTRE PAGES

LATE NIGHT NEWS

After 201 days captive in Iran..

JEAN IS FREED

JEAN WADDELL

SHE'S READY TO FLY HOME

SCOTS missionary Jean Waddell has been freed from her Iranian prison cell.

After 201 days in captivity, her ordeal ended last night when she was moved to a "halfway house" with the two other British missionaries waiting to be allowed to fly home.

Meal

The dramatic events in Teheran were announced in a terse message that the three Anglicans had been released from jail and were "ready for return home."

The position of a fourth Briton, businessman Andrew Pyke, was unclear and he was

By LACHIE KENNEDY and DEREK MASTERTON

believed to be still in detention.

Miss Waddell, 58, of Arbroath, and her fellow missionaries Dr John Coleman and his wife Audrey, spent their first hours of freedom at an Iranian Government reception centre.

With them was Mr Terry Waite, the Archbishop of Canterbury's special envoy who has battled for their release.

They celebrated the occasion together with a small religious service, followed by a meal and a long chat.

Before they fly out of Teheran—within the next few days—an Ayatollah will go on Iranian TV to say they are being released because the spying charges against them were false.

A Foreign Office spokesman in London said: "We are keeping in touch with the Archbishop of Canterbury to try to sort out the details."

Last night, Miss Waddell's family celebrated this first step of her return home.

At her home in Arbroath, Jean's sister, Mrs Doris Tymiec, said: "We are overjoyed. It really is wonderful news. I hope Jean will be home very soon.

"The last few weeks have been pretty terrible. Every day it seemed that Jean was to be released. Then our hopes were dashed. Now it looks like her ordeal is over at last."

Treated

Miss Jean's niece, Mrs Marya Gorny, of Bishop's Stortford, Hertfordshire, said: "We have just opened a bottle of champagne.

"We are overwhelmed. After all the disappointments, our hopes of seeing my aunt have never been higher."

TURN TO PAGE FIVE

THE AGONY OF A HOSTAGE—Page Five

Step into Spring WITH £1000 IN OUR EXCITING NEW CONTEST

TURN TO PAGE 6

IT'S ALL IN THE PAPER YOU CAN'T PUT DOWN

£150 for doing nothing

Dockers' deal to save cash

CONTAINER port dockers on Clydeside are to be paid £150 every third week —for sitting at home doing nothing.

The seemingly amazing deal, which comes into effect today at Greenock on the lower Clyde, is the result of the drop in traffic at the terminal.

And the peculiar nature of the container trade.

Under the agreement about a third of the 104 dockers will stay at home each week and only turn out if they are needed.

Levels

The "free week" system will be worked on a rota basis, unlike other guaranteed pay systems.

The Clyde Port Authority believe that the whole package will SAVE money, as it includes a reduction in manning levels.

And the dockers' average earnings—now running at £12,000 a year—are expected to drop in 1981.

At Greenock, many of the container ships arrive at the weekend or on Mondays.

So while a full complement of dockers is needed on these days, not so many men are wanted mid-week.

Similar

The terminal used to be busy on weekdays until trade dropped by a third when its biggest customer, Seatrain Lines, sold their North Atlantic interests to a

TURN TO BACK PAGE

1981

MISSIONARY FREED BY IRANIANS

IN IRAN, Scottish missionary Jean Waddell was released after spending six months in prison on suspicion of spying for the West. With several other Anglican missionaries, Miss Waddell had been held on charges which the Iranian authorities later admitted were false.

Jean Waddell was secretary to the Anglican bishop of Iran and found herself caught up in the Islamic fervour which swept the country following the fall of the Shah in 1979.

The arrival back in Tehran from Paris of the exiled Ayatollah Khomeini in February 1979 sparked a wave of fanaticism, in which anything regarded as Western was attacked and destroyed. Europeans were attacked on the streets, as religious fundamentalists set about establishing an Islamic republic. The Americans and the British were particular targets, given their perceived support for the detested Shah.

In November 1979, a mob stormed the US embassy in Tehran and took 53 Americans hostage. Many of them remained captive until January 1981.

Violence had also spilled over into the streets of London, where militant Islamic students staged protests. Many of them were subsequently deported.

As relations between Britain and Iran sank to new depths, Jean Waddell's situation became more dangerous. A couple of months before her arrest, she had been shot at and wounded.

The Archbishop of Canterbury's special envoy, Terry Waite, who played a major role in the release of the missionaries, insisted that the Britons should not be compared with the recently released US hostages. There were reports that the missionaries wanted to return to Iran at the earliest opportunity and comparisons with the American situation would not be helpful.

Miss Waddell's only sister, Doris, could not contain her joy at the news: "This is great. We have waited so long to hear this".

GOINGS...

Jack Coia
Architect

A. J. Cronin
Writer

ON RADIO

Priestland's Progress

Stop The Week

ON TV

Brideshead Revisited

Bergerac

Hill St Blues

Only Fools and Horses

Bullseye

Postman Pat

Brookside

IN REMEMBANCE OF 4,500 JOBS, BORN 16ᵗʰ MAY 1963 DIED 22ⁿᵈ MAY 1981 R.I.P.

END OF THE ROAD FOR ROOTES

Scotland's manufacturing base took another severe blow in June with the closure of the Linwood car plant and the loss of almost 5,000 jobs. When Lord Rootes first announced his grand plan in the early 1960s to create Scotland's first motor industry since the 1920s, it was hailed as central Scotland's economic saviour. The new Linwood plant was intended to act as a magnet for support industries which in turn would attract other car manufacturers to Scotland. Sadly, the dream was never realised. Difficult industrial relations and unspectacular production levels did not help in attracting the inward investment necessary to keep the plant going in the harsh economic climate.

SCOTTISH FILM HIT

The must-see film of the year was *Gregory's Girl*, starring Dee Hepburn and John Gordon Sinclair. *Gregory's Girl* had its world premiere in Glasgow in May and the story of how a girl's determination to play football is rewarded when she becomes the star of the team, proved an unlikely success. It cost only £200,000 to make and was filmed mainly at two schools in Cumbernauld. Despite its humble origins, the film attracted international acclaim for director Bill Forsyth.

THIS SPORTING LIFE

FOOTBALL	RUGBY UNION	GOLF	HORSE RACING	SHINTY
Scottish Champions Celtic	*Scotland vs England* England 23–17 Scotland at Twickenham	*Home Internationals* Scotland 11½ - 3½ England Scotland 9 - 6 Ireland Scotland 9½ - 5½ Wales	*Scottish Grand National* *Winner* Astral Charmer at Ayr	*Camanachd Cup Winners* Newtonmore at Glasgow
Scottish Cup Winners Rangers				

WEDNESDAY June 2 1982

Daily Record

15p   SCOTLAND'S BIGGEST DAILY SALE   No. 29,040

COLOUR SOUVENIR SPECIAL

MILES OF SMILES!

—and sunshine at every step

■ IT WAS Scotland's hottest day of the year — and for 270,000 Catholics, the most joyous day ever.

Laughing, singing, waving, they greeted the Pope as he toured Bellahouston Park, Glasgow, yesterday.

For all its religious dignity, it was a day of carnival—one which the Pope enjoyed as much as his people.

GOD BLESS THEM ALL
—PAGES 8 AND 9

PILGRIM'S PROGRESS
—PAGE 17

WELCOME TO THE CARNIVAL
—CENTRE PAGES

UNITED IN JOY   —BACK PAGE

1982

BASKING IN THE POPE'S VISIT

THERE were miles of smiles and sunshine at every step and never before had so many gathered for just one man as they did for Pope John Paul II in April.

With temperatures soaring to almost 80 degrees, the sun bathed Bellahouston Park and more than a quarter of a million Scottish Catholics basked in it.

From Barra to Bishopbriggs, by bus, by charter plane and, for some, on foot, they poured into the vast parkland for the open-air Mass which was to be the centrepiece of the Pope's visit to Scotland.

His Holiness had begun his visit to the United Kingdom several days earlier and had held historic talks with the Archbishop of Canterbury, the first time that leaders of the two great faiths had met on British soil since the Reformation.

When he arrived in Scotland, the Pope delighted nationalists of all faiths when, having stepped from his aircraft, he knelt to give his now-customary kiss to the ground, taken to signify that he was now in a new country.

Two days before the Bellahouston gathering, the Pope celebrated Mass at Hampden Park for Scottish school-children, where he was greeted with football-style chanting of his name and a show of teenage enthusiasm usually reserved for popstars. At times, the chanting threatened to drown out his address to the young congregation.

In Bellahouston, the hillside was dominated by the elegant lines of the papal altar and earlier opposition from more fundamentalist Protestants about the temporary removal of trees to make way for the altar was soon forgotten.

Following the service, the Pope waved to his devoted followers from the window of his helicopter as he left for the next stop on his tour.

JENKINS BREAKS THE MOULD

Roy Jenkins swept to a decisive by-election victory in Glasgow Hillhead in March, smashing the mould of Scottish and British politics. The former Labour Chancellor's victory came exactly a year to the day since he helped found the Social Democratic Party.

VICTORY IN THE FALKLANDS

After waging a ten-week campaign culminating in a short but fierce series of battles in June, British administration was restored to the Falkland Islands, one of the last and most remote outposts under its control. Argentinian forces had invaded and occupied the South Atlantic islands in April, claiming sovereignty over the Malvinas, as they called them.

The Scots Guards played a vital role in capturing the heavily defended Tumbledown Mountain, sustaining some 50 casualties in the process. The Guards' victory signalled the prelude to the Argentinian surrender on June 14.

On TV		
Harry's Game	*Dynasty*	*Treasure Hunt*
Boys from the Blackstuff	*Cagney and Lacey*	*Countdown*
	The Young Ones	*OTT*

GOINGS...

Alex Harvey
Rock Singer

THIS SPORTING LIFE

FOOTBALL	RUGBY UNION	GOLF	HORSE RACING	SHINTY
Scottish Champions Celtic	*Scotland vs England* Scotland 9–9 England at Murrayfield	*British Open Winner* Tom Watson at Royal Troon (284)	*Scottish Grand National Winner* Cockle Strand at Ayr	*Camanachd Cup Winners* Newtonmore at Inverness
Scottish Cup Winners Aberdeen				

SATURDAY October 29 1983

Daily Record

17p   SCOTLAND'S BIGGEST DAILY SALE   No. 29,478

HUTCHINSON

Agony mum's plea to shoot son

AN anguished mother said last night that if her son had killed three people, the police should shoot him.

Mrs Louise Reardon, 78, is the mother of Arthur Hutchinson, wanted in connection with the Sheffield wedding killings.

At her home at Hartlepool, Co. Durham, she said:

"I can't believe he could have done these things. He is the best son a mother could have.

"But if he has killed three innocent people I have no sympathy for him. He has become a monster."

Expert

Police believe Hutchinson, 42, who has a reputation as a ladies' man, may have sought help from a girlfriend. She could be shielding him.

Last night police were pointing to striking similarities between Hutchinson and triple killer Barry Prudom, who shot himself at Malton, Yorkshire, last year.

Like Prudom, he is an expert at surviving in the wild and evading massive police dragnets.

In another parallel, Hutchinson is a petty crook who could have snapped, and a fitness fanatic who ate only health food.

ON THE DAY JOHN GREIG QUIT IBROX

MY SADNESS

JOHN GREIG was at a secret hideaway with his wife and son last night after leaving Rangers Football Club "a saddened man."

And he was quoted as saying: "I'm finished with the game."

The manager, who gave 25 years of his life to the club, was not in the famous Blue Room to hear his resignation announced yesterday.

A few miles away in Lenzie, the Greig family home was deserted.

By FRANK SULLIVAN

And the strain the last few weeks at Ibrox placed on his family life was revealed in a short statement read on his behalf.

Future

It said: "This is obviously a very sad and emotional day for me as Rangers Football Club has been my whole life."

It went on: "As you will understand it has recently been a very trying time for both my family and myself . . ."

Greig told a friend: "I don't see myself staying in the game. I will be thinking about my future over the next week or two.

"But after spending so long with one club — and at the top in football — it would be very difficult to go anywhere else."

He added: "The worst thing of all for me is the thought of not going into Ibrox in the morning any longer."

Greig insisted on personally informing his team of his decision . . . before leaving Ibrox for the last time.

THE MAN WHO LIVED FOR RANGERS
PAGES 8 AND 9

JOHN GREIG'S PRIVATE HELL
PAGES 34 and 35

FERGIE'S THE FAVOURITE
—BACK PAGE

SORRY END TO GREIG ERA AT IBROX

THE reign of John Greig as manager of Rangers came to an end with the announcement of his resignation by the club chairman, Rae Simpson. A clearly emotional Simpson paid tribute to the man who had dedicated all his working life to the club, as a player for 18 years and as manager from 1978 to 1983.

John Greig was the most successful Rangers captain in the history of the club. Between 1960, when the 18-year-old Hearts supporter signed from Whitburn Juniors, and 1978, when he took over from Jock Wallace in the dugout, Greig amassed a phenomenal array of trophies and awards:

five championship medals, six Scottish Cup medals, four League Cup medals and, the greatest achievement of all, a European Cup Winner's Cup medal in 1972. He was the Scottish football writers' Player of the Year in 1966 and 1976 and was awarded the MBE for his services to football.

In 1978, Jock Wallace left Rangers for Leicester City and Greig moved straight from the dressing room to the manager's office. With hindsight, it was not a wise move.

Yet his first season as manager was successful, with both the Scottish and the League Cups going to Ibrox. However, this

proved to be a false dawn. In his remaining four years in charge, Rangers won only two more trophies, again the Scottish Cup and the League Cup. The big prize – the championship – was beyond him.

Rangers' dismal start to season 1983–84 was more than Rangers fans could take. The defeat by Aberdeen in September saw hundreds of supporters demonstrating against the manager and the 2-1 defeat by Motherwell in October proved to be the last straw.

A Ranger's fan to the end, Greig declared he was going solely in the best interests of the club.

ABERDEEN EURO TRIUMPH

Aberdeen joined the elite band of Scotttish teams to win a European trophy in May when they defeated Spanish giants Real Madrid in the final of the European Cup Winner's Cup.

The game in the Gothenburg stadium was tied at one goal apiece following strikes from Black and Juanito when the Dons substitute John Hewitt headed home the vital winner with just eight minutes remaining.

ON TV

St Elsewhere

Taggart

Auf Wiedersehen, Pet

Blackadder

Shine On Harvey Moon

Cheers

ON RADIO

When the Wind Blows

Ralph McTell & Friends

Roundtable

The Friday Rock Show

PM

McGregor's Gathering

MAGGIE HOLDS ON TO POWER

In June, Margaret Thatcher became the first prime minister for more than thirty years to gain re-election after a full term in office. Her widely predicted landslide victory gave the Tories almost twice as many seats overall as Labour who were almost wiped out electorally in southern England. In Scotland, however, it was a very different picture, where, by a margin of three to one, voters rejected Mrs Thatcher and her policies and returned opposition parties. In the UK, the Tories won 397 seats, Labour 209, the Alliance 23, the SNP 2 and others 19. The Tory majority was 144. In Scotland, the Tories won 21 seats, Labour 41, the Alliance 8 and the SNP 2.

THIS SPORTING LIFE

FOOTBALL	RUGBY UNION	GOLF	HORSE RACING	SHINTY
Scottish Champions Dundee United	*Scotland vs England* England 12–22 Scotland at Twickenham	*Home Internationals* Scotland 8½ - 6½ England Scotland 5½ - 9½ Ireland Scotland 8 - 7 Wales	*Scottish Grand National Winner* Canton at Ayr	*Camanachd Cup Winners* Kyles Athletic at Fort William
Scottish Cup Winners Aberdeen				

THURSDAY October 11 1984

Daily Record

18p   FORWARD WITH SCOTLAND   No. 29,772

20 years for the ice cream killer

THIS MAN MURDERED 6 PEOPLE

TRAGIC AGONY OF DIANA DORS' HUSBAND

I CAN'T LIVE WITHOUT HER

—BACK PAGE

THE man who killed six people in Scotland's most horrific mass murder was jailed for life yesterday.

And Thomas Campbell will spend at least **TWENTY YEARS** in prison.

Campbell, 31, was one of six men jailed at the end of the 27-day trial at the High Court in Glasgow.

He and Joseph Steele were found guilty of the horror blaze which killed

Andrew Doyle and five members of his family in April...

The blaze which was the last horrific act in a violent seven-month ice-cream van war in Glasgow housing schemes.

Campbell, known as TC, was the mastermind behind the war. He hoped to reap a fortune from his fleet of vans.

But not from selling ice cream. For

Campbell planned to flood Glasgow's schemes with heroin sold over the van counters.

Steele, 23, said to have been paid £300 by TC for the "torching" of the Doyle home when the front door — the only entrance to the top floor

TURN TO BACK PAGE

DRUGS DREAM THAT ENDED IN DEATH

PAGES 4 AND 5

ICE CREAM WAR KILLER JAILED

ICE Cream War killer Thomas "TC" Campbell, the man who was alleged to have ordered the deaths of six people, was jailed for life by the High Court in Glasgow in October.

And the judge recommended that Campbell spend at least twenty years in prison.

Campbell was one of six men jailed at the end of the 27-day trial.

He and Joseph Steele were found guilty of the horror blaze which killed Andrew Doyle and five members of his family in April 1984.

The blaze was the last horrific act in a violent seven-month Ice Cream War in Glasgow's housing schemes.

Campbell was the mastermind behind the war over vans selling round the streets. He planned to make a fortune from selling heroin over the van counters in Glasgow's sprawling schemes.

Andrew Doyle died because he was one of the traders who stood up to TC's evil empire.

TC decided to make an example of him, and was said to have paid £300 to Steele for the torching of the Doyle home.

The sentences came at the end of an inquiry by detectives into the power struggle.

Throughout their investigation detectives found that witnesses were scared to talk at first, but they were so horrified by the crime that, eventually, they did.

However, both men were protesting their innocence and in the 1990s, embarked on a high-profile campaign, which included a hunger strike by Campbell, to have their case reviewed, arguing that new evidence had come to light. Despite an appeal, Campbell was still in prison in 1999.

POLMONT EXPRESS CRASH

Thirteen people died and more than seventy were injured when a busy Edinburgh to Glasgow commuter train crashed near Polmont in Stirlingshire.

The accident came when the packed train hit a cow at around 80 mph after it wandered onto the line. Several carriages were derailed and hurtled up an embankment.

A fleet of ambulances ferried the injured to hospitals in both Falkirk and Stirling.

ON TV

The Far Pavilions

Lace

The Thorn Birds

The Bill

Miss Marple

Brass

Spitting Image

Thomas the Tank Engine

The A-Team

Robin of Sherwood

Scarecrow & Mrs King

ON RADIO

It's Your World

On the Air

WHAM BAM SLAM!

In March, Scotland's rugby heroes secured the Grand Slam with an emphatic 21-12 victory over the French at Murrayfield. The game had begun badly for the Scots and they allowed the French to dominate the first half. They soon found themselves trailing 9-3 and the French seemed set to control the game.

But from early in the second half, the Scots fought their way back into the game under the inspired leadership of skipper Jim Aitken. Urged on by the huge Murrayfield crowd, the Scots scored 18 points to secure victory and the championship. Aitken said afterwards, "I wasn't happy at half time but when we levelled the scores at nine-all, things began to click."

THIS SPORTING LIFE

FOOTBALL	RUGBY UNION	GOLF	HORSE RACING	SHINTY
Scottish Champions Aberdeen	*Scotland vs England* Scotland 18–6 England at Murrayfield	*British Open Winner* Seve Ballesteros at St Andrews (276)	*Scottish Grand National Winner* *Androma* at Ayr	*Camanachd Cup Winners* Kingussie at Oban
Scottish Cup Winners Aberdeen				

SATURDAY September 14 1985

Daily Record

20p   FORWARD WITH SCOTLAND   No. 30,058

The Lisbon Lions join football's greats to mourn Jock Stein

THE PRIDE AND THE GRIEF ... Lisbon greats Tommy Gemmell, Jim Craig and Billy McNeill join other mourning stars.

TEARS FOR THE BIG MAN

Denis Law bites back the tears.

■ Football mourned a legend yesterday ... Jock Stein, The Big Man. There were stars of the past, like Celtic's immortal Lisbon Lions, and the present, like Scotland's World Cup squad. Stars of showbiz, like Rod Stewart, and stars of TV sport, like Lawrie McMenemy, Denis Law and Pat Crerand.

■ The unknown stars were there, too ... the fans who cheer Scotland from the terracing. In their thousands they turned out to line the funeral route. It was a day for unashamed grief. And hundreds, like Denis Law, simply could not contain their tears.

HE WAS JUST MAGIC ... Pages 8 and 9.

FOOTBALL MOURNS LEGEND JOCK

THE football world went into mourning for the legendary Jock Stein – The Big Man – in September.

Jock, the Scotland team manager, died after collapsing at the end of a World Cup qualifying match against Wales in Cardiff which saw his team go through to the final stages of the tournament in Spain.

As the fans said farewell to Jock, the rich and the famous, the poor and the unknown stood three deep at the pavements as his funeral cortege passed by. More than 10,000 fans, unashamed of their tears, paid their last respects on the funeral route.

A competent player in the 1950s, injury forced Stein to retire prematurely but his love of the game was such that there was no question that he leave it. He served a successful managerial apprenticeship at Dunfermline and Hibernian before his appointment to Celtic in 1965.

Over the next 13 years, Jock Stein established himself as the most successful Scottish football manager ever. His tactical and motivational genius created teams which won an unprecedented nine League championships in succession in the mid 1960s and '70s as well as achieving numerous League and Scottish Cup triumphs. His most successful season was, of course, 1966–67 when Celtic swept all before them in every competition, and secured the greatest victory of all, the European Cup. After he left Celtic, he was briefly the Leeds manager before being given charge of the national side.

Jock's body was taken from his home in Glasgow to the city's Linn Crematorium where over 500 of soccer's top names, past and present, gathered to pay tribute … Sir Matt Busby, Denis Law and Pat Crerand, Jock's Lisbon Lions and numerous present-day stars.

The feelings of the day were perhaps summed up best by a football fan from Castlemilk who said: "See that Big Man, he was magic."

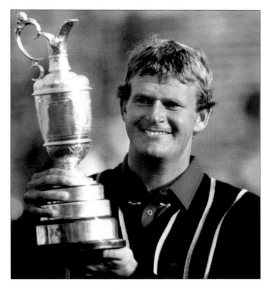

Lyle's Open Honour

In July, Sandy Lyle became the first Scot for 54 years to win the British Open Championship. A last round of 70 at Sandwich was sufficient to secure the £65,000 first prize with a total score of 282, one shot ahead of the USA's Payne Stewart. Receiving the title, Lyle told the delighted crowds, "It's a great honour. I'd like to thank the greenkeeper for putting the pins in the right position."

On TV		
Jewel In The Crown	Miami Vice	Blind Date
Eastenders	Girls On Top	Friday Night Live
Howard's Way	Supergran	Edge of Darkness

Brighton Bomber Captured

Despite Scotland's own sectarian strife, the Troubles in Ireland had largely passed the country by. However in June, the people of Glasgow were shocked to discover the existence of one of the Provisional IRA's most feared cells in their midst. Police raids in the Govanhill and Shawlands areas of the city led to several people being detained – one of them, Patrick McGhee, wanted in connection with the Brighton Bomb of October 1984, which almost killed the entire British Cabinet. Police also discovered plans for a time-bomb campaign in 12 English holiday resorts, aimed at causing widespread public panic.

Goings...

Chic Murray
Comedian

THIS SPORTING LIFE

FOOTBALL	RUGBY UNION	GOLF	HORSE RACING	SHINTY
Scottish Champions Aberdeen	*Scotland vs England* England 10–7 Scotland at Twickenham	*Home Internationals* Scotland 9½ - 5½ England Scotland 10½ - 4½ Ireland Scotland 10 - 5 Wales	*Scottish Grand National Winner* *Androma* at Ayr	*Camanachd Cup Winners* Newtonmore at Kingussie
Scottish Cup Winners Celtic				

Daily Record

20p   FORWARD WITH SCOTLAND   No. 30,228

Relieved Kathryn, left, and Wilma, right, are met at Heathrow by their friend Roopa.

PETER HUDSON

Shame of the beasts

■ PORTLY Peter Hudson and dapper David Swift discovered a common interest in jail...a lust for young boys. And when they were released after serving time for child sex offences, they teamed up for a six-month orgy of assaults on boys in parks.

■ But the odd couple were eventually trapped by their tiny victims' descriptions of "The Fat Man" and "The Thin Man." The police knew who they were looking for. And yesterday the beastly perverts were back in jail... for 14 years each.

BEASTS OF THE PARKS .. Page 23

DAVID SWIFT

HEARTS ARE TRUMPS

THE TEAM ONE MATCH FROM GLORY

IN COLOUR CENTRE PAGES

JULIE'S LOVE IS ON THE ROCKS

Page Three

ALL CLEAR

Champagne welcome for students

By BRIAN CULLINAN

SCOTS students arrived home from the shadow of nuclear horror late last night.

And a popping champagne cork signalled a message of joy to their anxious parents . . . "We're all well."

The Scots, and other British students, had already been screened several times for radioactivity on their journey from Kiev.

Many had been studying in the city and were just 30 miles from the scene of the world's worst nuclear accident.

RUSSIA IGNORES NUCLEAR HORROR—Page 2

Safety men carrying radiation detection equipment boarded their plane at Heathrow and clothing, shoes and luggage were confiscated.

The students had been asked to strip on the flight home and seal their clothes in plastic bags. They were given British Airways tracksuits to wear.

Hugged

Then, early today after two hours of checks, the party emerged through customs and declared their good health to waiting families and friends.

Kathryn Walker, 21, of Irvine, Ayrshire, and Wilma Clark, of Dundee, were both studying in Kiev when the blast happened.

Kathryn hugged her mother Christine and said: "I have to admit I was frightened, and I did begin to cry at one point.

"We got too little information from the Russians and too much from the West. We didn't know who to believe.

"We took the advice not to drink the water, but we ate the food."

And a relieved Wilma said: "We weren't aware of any danger in Kiev. But it seemed the rest of the world was going hysterical."

A spokesman for the National Radiological Protection Board later declared the students were "in no danger whatsoever."

WIN a trip to the World Cup —Page 9

SCOTS STUDENTS FLEE CHERNOBYL

Scots and other British students arrived home one week after the world's worst civil nuclear disaster. Many had been studying in Kiev, just thirty miles away from the accident site at Chernobyl in the Soviet Union.

Reactor No. 4 at the Chernobyl power station in the Ukraine was seriously damaged by an explosion on 26 April 1986. Two people were killed and some 15,000 people were evacuated from the surrounding area, as three other reactors were shut down. American satellite pictures indicated that the top of the reactor had blown off in the explosion and that a large cloud of radioactive particles had been released into the atmosphere. Initial fears that the molten hot white core was melting through the reactor's concrete floor on its way to contaminating the Dnieper River, were denied by Soviet scientists, who also said there was no immediate threat to Western Europe. They indicated that the situation was under control and planned to encase the reactor in concrete to avoid the spread of radioactive fallout.

Prevailing winds blew the contaminated cloud released by the explosion over Western Europe and in Scotland and the north of England, there were fears that the heavy rainfall at the time would lead to the radioactive particles entering the food chain through livestock eating contaminated grass. It would be several years before this could be verified.

The students had been screened several times on their journey from Kiev but, as an additional precaution for the return flight, their own clothing was confiscated and sealed in plastic bags. After two hours further checking at customs, they emerged and were warmly greeted by their anxious parents and friends, after safety officers had declared them free from radioactivity.

HOUSING CONDITIONS DISGRACE

Glasgow District Council commissioned a probe into housing conditions in the city – and the results were horrifying. The inquiry, led by Professor Robert Grieve, identified 40,000 homes in Glasgow as being in need of urgent repairs. Leaking roofs, lack of repairs and dampness were making life a misery for tens of thousands of families. Conditions in parts of Easterhouse, Castlemilk, Drumchapel and Pollok were appalling. Professor Grieve, brought up in a Glasgow tenement in the 1920s, described some of the houses as a "disgrace to humanity". The council believed it would take a decade to solve the problems.

TROUBLE AT THE CHALKFACE

Scottish teachers had been working to rule for almost 18 months in their campaign for improved salaries and conditions when representatives of the Church of Scotland and the Catholic Church offered to act as mediators in February. Parents nights, sports events and school trips had been affected. Higher and O-Grade examinations were among the next targets. The local authorities had agreed to a pay rise of 15% – 7% above inflation – but the Conservative Government refused to fund the award. There were high hopes that the recently appointed Scottish Secretary, Malcolm Rifkind, would adopt a more conciliatory approach.

ON TV

Casualty

The Singing Detective

Neighbours

The Equalizer

Boon

Bread

The Golden Girls

Naked Video

ON RADIO

Good Morning Scotland

In Concert

Some of These Days

Taking Issue with Colin Bell

THIS SPORTING LIFE

FOOTBALL	RUGBY UNION	GOLF	HORSE RACING	SHINTY
Scottish Champions Celtic	Scotland vs England Scotland 33–6 England at Murrayfield	British Open Winner Greg Norman at Turnberry (280)	Scottish Grand National Winner Hardy Lad at Ayr	Camanachd Cup Winners Newtonmore at Glasgow
Scottish Cup Winners Aberdeen				

WEDNESDAY January 7 1987

Daily Record

20p   FORWARD WITH SCOTLAND   No. 30,438

THE SIEGE OF BARLINNIE

OFFICERS HELD HOSTAGE —34 ARE INJURED

TROPHIES OF TERROR

They'll kill me Pages 2 and 3

POWDER-KEG PRISONS Centre Pages

FIVE masked prisoners display the trophies of battle. They wear officers' hats. One holds an officer's baton. And one flaunts a riot shield.

This was the scene yesterday on the roof of B-Block in Glasgow's Barlinnie Jail ...

moments after a brief and bloody battle between rioters holding prison officers hostage, and colleagues attempting to rescue them.

The would-be rescuers, wearing full riot gear, stormed the cell-block where their mates were

trapped. But they had to retreat, 34 of them injured, under a hail of missiles, dropping their equipment as they fled.

Later some of the trapped officers were freed. But late last night three were still being held hostage.

Picture: ALISTAIR DEVINE

ROYAL RIDDLE

EDWARD TO QUIT MARINES? Back Page

1987

RIOT AT POWDER KEG PRISON

A PROTEST over alleged brutality at Glasgow's Barlinnie Prison turned into a siege in January, as rioting prisoners held officers at knifepoint.

It was sparked off after two prisoners started a fight in the dining room. Another prisoner, Sammy Ralston, became involved and was marched off to the punishment block, known as The Wendy House.

After the evening recreation period at 8pm, trouble broke out on the top floor of B Hall. Prisoners attacked a prison officer who later needed nine stitches.

The alarm bells were sounded and officers raced into B Hall to try to suppress the riot. Some had grabbed riot shields and helmets but their charge was a disaster. They were outnumbered and a barrage of flying beds, lockers and heavy slabs crashed down on them.

Even the stairs had been sprayed with liquid detergent so that the officers slipped and fell.

In the heat of the battle, 41 officers found themselves cut off and trapped on the second floor. They had no option but to lock themselves into the empty cells.

Their nightmare got worse …

During the next 17 hours, rioting prisoners ran amok throughout B Hall.

They tried to hammer their way through the doors into the cells and set fire to mattresses placed against the doors. The terrified trapped officers used makeshift ropes from sheets to pull radios up the outside wall, so that they could keep in contact with the governor's office.

Finally, the officers decided to break out.

As they made a dash for freedom the prisoners showered them with missiles. A total of 34 officers were injured. Five officers remained trapped in the cells until the prisoners eventually burst in and grabbed them.

Then followed hours of negotiations in which authorities promised unbiased legal advise, independent medical examinations and access to family and friends visiting the prison after the siege.

PLOT TO MURDER MAGGIE IN SCOTLAND

An IRA plot to murder the Prime Minister on a visit to Edinburgh in April was foiled by Special Branch detectives. The police were tipped off by the disgruntled girlfriend of an IRA activist and several people in both London and Belfast were arrested under the Prevention of Terrorism Act. Mrs Thatcher's visit to the capital went ahead as scheduled, although the police in both Edinburgh and London officially denied the incident.

WELCOME HOME

Scots engineer Robert Maxwell arrived back home in Scotland in April to a family welcome of tears and cheers, having spent more than six years in a Libyan jail. Maxwell had been found guilty in 1980 of industrial espionage, although he always denied the charges and branded the trial "a sham". He was sentenced to 12 years' imprisonment and fined £85,000.

Maxwell paid tribute to Leith MP Ron Brown who had made a personal appeal to the Libyan leader, Colonel Gadaffi, which led directly to his release.

GOINGS…

Alistair Maclean	Fulton Mackay	Hugh Fraser
Writer	Actor	Businessman

ON TV

Fortunes of War	LA Law	Star Cops
Tutti Frutti	French & Saunders	Matlock
Inspector Morse	Strike It Lucky	The New Statesman

THIS SPORTING LIFE

FOOTBALL	RUGBY UNION	GOLF	HORSE RACING	SHINTY
Scottish Champions Rangers	Scotland vs England England 21–12 Scotland at Twickenham	British Open Winner Nick Faldo at Muirfield (279)	Scottish Grand National Winner Little Polveir at Ayr	Camanachd Cup Winners Kingussie at Fort William
Scottish Cup Winners St Mirren				

Daily Record

22p   FORWARD WITH SCOTLAND   No 31 052

THIS WAS No.13

Maurice and Dora ... Engulfed in seconds in the holocaust

Where the bungalow once stood, there is only a crater where salvage workers sift through the rubble

■ THIS was the trim bungalow home of Maurice and Dora Henry ... No 13 Sherwood Crescent, Lockerbie. Today it no longer exists. Where retired builder Maurice, 62, sat with his 55-year-old wife, there is only a gaping crater strewn with rubble.

■ IN a few terrible seconds, No 13 was swallowed up in the holocaust that hit the quiet town as Pan Am Flight 103 plunged from the skies. In a few terrible seconds, Maurice and Dora were engulfed in flames and debris — like the 15 other townsfolk who died.

LOCKERBIE AIR DISASTER..PAGES 2 and 3

LOCKERBIE HIT BY AIR DISASTER

HORROR came to the quiet town of Lockerbie in December when a giant airliner crashed onto it after a mid-air explosion.

Pan Am Flight 103 had been en route to America from Germany when a bomb in its cargo hold exploded. All 259 people on board the Boeing 747 were killed, as were 11 townspeople on the ground.

Many of the passengers on the plane were returning to America to be reunited with loved ones for the Christmas holidays.

The flight left Heathrow after a short stopover from Frankfurt and contact was lost 54 minutes later. Witnesses reported a gigantic ball of flames as the aircraft exploded and broke in two.

Part of a wing ploughed into a street in the town, immediately engulfing it in a giant fireball.

Firefighters raced to the scene and struggled to put out the flames in a huge crater beside the A74, with wreckage strewn over a wide area and several houses blazing furiously.

The aircraft's forward section landed three miles east of Lockerbie and other pieces of the wreckage were found throughout the streets of the town and in the neighbouring countryside.

No one claimed responsibility for planting the bomb although suspicion quickly turned to Middle Eastern terrorists. After three years, the offer of a £2.5 million reward and one of the largest international investigations ever mounted, two Libyan intelligence agents were named as prime suspects in the case – Abdel Baset Ali Mohamed al-Megrahi and Al-Amin Rhalifa E'himah.

For seven years, all attempts to bring the men to trial remained deadlocked until Libya, the UK and the USA all agreed that they could be tried in neutral Holland under Scots Law before a Scottish judge.

NORTH SEA RIG DISASTER

A massive blast ripped through Occidental Petroleum's Piper Alpha oil rig in July, in spite of it having passed a regulation safety check the previous week. A gas leak led to two explosions which engulfed the stricken rig in a huge fireball, forcing men to leap for their lives into a sea covered in blazing oil, some 200 feet below them.

NATO warships on exercise were amongst the many craft who rushed to the scene, some 120 miles off Wick. Although 167 men died in the inferno, incredibly 63 survivors were pulled from the sea by rescuers in high-speed dinghies who had to dodge in and out of the flames to reach the men.

GLASGOW'S GREENER STILL

In April, Glasgow, the "Dear Green Place", got even greener with a spectacular fireworks opening to its Garden Festival. The 120-acre wasteland site alongside the Clyde had been transformed into a glorious park filled with soaring modernistic towers, futuristic pavilions and, of course, fabulous flowers of every colour, variety and arrangement. The five-month-long festival was the largest public event held in Scotland since the Empire Exhibition of 1938.

ON TV		
London's Burning	You Rang, M'Lord	Fifteen To One
Hale & Pace		Mouse and Mole
Red Dwarf	The Tracy Ullman Show	The River

THIS SPORTING LIFE

FOOTBALL	RUGBY UNION	GOLF	HORSE RACING	SHINTY
Scottish Champions Celtic	*Scotland vs England* Scotland 6–9 England at Murrayfield	*British Open Winner* Seve Ballesteros at Royal Lytham, England (273)	*Scottish Grand National Winner* Mighty Mark at Ayr	*Camanachd Cup Winners* Kingussie at Inverness
Scottish Cup Winners Celtic				

FRIDAY   March   31   1989

Daily Record

Incorporating DAILY MIRROR   Record sale 778,836

22p   FORWARD WITH SCOTLAND   No. 31,135

Pam is hurt in bike smash

COMMONS scandal girl Pamella Bordes has been hurt in a motor cycle accident.

The alleged £1000-a-night call-girl slipped on rocks and fell on a remote mountain track on Bali, her tropical island hideout.

Bordes was rushed to hospital – where she gave a false name – and was treated for a broken hand and facial cuts.

Model

Later Peter Amardi, who rents the cottage next to Bordes' friend Shaban Crampton, said: "She will never model again."

But last night a spokesman at the hospital – in the island's capital Denpasar – said the facial cuts were not severe.

However, he confirmed a fracture of the left hand.

He said the former Miss India refused to stay in hospital.

Bordes fled her friend Shaban's cottage when discovered by reporters.

She is now believed to be hiding three miles away in a tiny village.

I'VE GOT MY POLL TAX

EXCLUSIVE

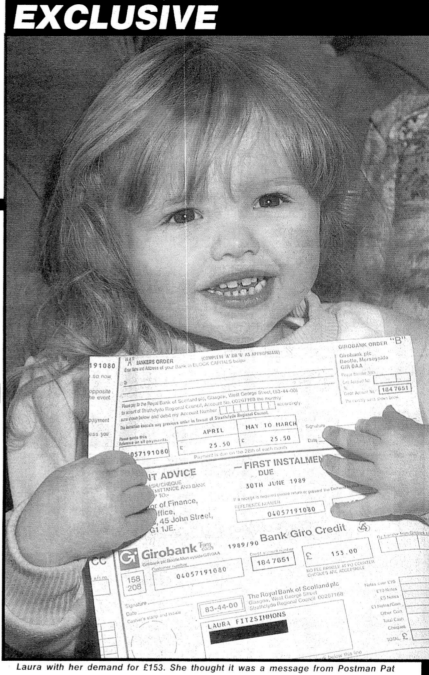

Laura with her demand for £153. She thought it was a message from Postman Pat

HI folks! My name's Laura and I'm two.

Like the rest of you, I've just received my poll tax form.

I know tomorrow's April Fools Day – but I don't think this is a joke!

Now little Laura Fitzsimmons is counting the pennies in her piggy bank . . .

Although it's unlikely that the tiny tot will have enough saved to pay her **POLL TAX BILL.**

By JIM DAVIS

When a demand for the first of two instalments of £153 popped through her letter box this week, Laura thought it was "a message from Postman Pat."

But her mum, Dorothy, and dad, John, knew it was a letter from a very grown-up organisation – Strathclyde Regional Council. And last night, Dorothy, 40, of Mosspark, Glasgow, slammed the region for the poll tax shocker.

Mrs Fitzsimmons said: "It gave us a laugh. But it just shows how crazy this system is.

"We are totally against the tax. But as responsible people we did not want to break the law.

"So we registered as directed. And this is what we got – a demand for Laura to pay up as well!"

Mr Fitzsimmons, unemployed, said: "I complained to the region but they just said it was our fault, not theirs."

A spokesman for Strathclyde Region said: "Laura's name had been entered on the form by her mum. But the child's date of birth looked like 1966, instead of 1986.

"If the demand is sent back to us, we will be more than happy to set the matter straight.

"Laura thought Postman Pat had delivered her poll tax demand. Well, 'Uncle Jack' Wood, the community charge officer, will gladly take it back."

● IF Laura had wanted to pay her poll tax monthly, it would have cost her £25.50.

IT'S NO JOKE...Pages 18 and 19

1989

POLL TAX IS NO LAUGHING MATTER

THE Poll Tax started on April Fool's Day but thousands of Scots did not see the joke – especially when mix-ups were leading to two-year-old girls being sent cash demands.

Tory politicians insisted that the new system, which replaced the rates, marked the start of a bright new tomorrow. But opponents said it unfairly switched the burden of domestic taxation from property owners to the poor.

There would be WINNERS, mostly the high rate payers, who would see their bills slashed.

Brian and Sheila Gilmore were presented as Poll Tax winners as they both worked and their rates in 1988 were £1242 for their seven-room house, whereas their Poll Tax bill was £784. Brian said: "I can quite clearly afford to pay the Poll Tax.

"But since my bill is going down so substantially it leads me to wonder who is being made to pay the extra."

There would also be LOSERS – Scotland's breadline families who were already struggling to make ends meet.

In Glasgow, where the Poll Tax was worked out to be £306 per person, shipyard worker Tom Dunlop was a certain loser as his rates bill for his council flat in Yoker had been £445.

However, counted with his wife Mary, and if his three grown-up children were in employment, he would have to find more than £1500.

The lightest charge was in Orkney where adults had to pay just £148 compared to the hardest-hit adults in Edinburgh who had to pay £393 each.

One of the biggest protest petitions ever raised in Scotland, with 300,000 signatures, was handed in to 10 Downing Street.

And the STUC-backed Committee Against the Poll Tax geared up for a fresh flood of support as people were seeing for the first time in black in white what they were expected to pay.

Committee organisers expected the anger from that to increase opposition. Anti-tax organisers said that the first payment demands would give the people their first opportunity to protest against the tax.

LORD CHANCELLOR GUILTY AS CHARGED

In May Lord Mackay of Clashfern, the Lord Chancellor, was found guilty – of attending the Catholic funerals of two top judges. Lord Mackay, Britain's senior lawman and an elder in the fundamentalist Protestant Free Presbyterian church, was appealing to the church authorities against a ban on taking communion. However, a spokesman for the church commented that if Lord Mackay "goes to a place such as a Mass which contaminates his soul then he must expect to be disciplined." After the failure of his appeal, the Lord Chancellor announced that he would be considering his position in relation to the church.

Daily Record

THE WALL COM TUMBLING DOWN!

And the Wall came tumbling down… In November, the Berlin Wall, which had split the city for almost 30 years, was knocked down as the Communist regime in East Germany collapsed. As the ultimate symbol of the Cold War was removed piece by piece, not only the Germans but the rest of the world had something to celebrate.

On TV	
Thirtysomething	*Birds of a Feather*
Home and Away	*Pingu*
Absolutely Fabulous	*Max Headroom*

Goings…
John Wheatley
Judge
Ewan MacColl
Folksinger

THIS SPORTING LIFE

FOOTBALL	RUGBY UNION	GOLF	HORSE RACING	SHINTY
Scottish Champions	*Scotland vs England*	*British Open Winner*	*Scottish Grand National*	*Camanachd Cup Winners*
Rangers	England 12–12 Scotland	Mark Calcavecchia	*Winner*	Kingussie
	at Twickenham	at Royal Troon (275)	*Roll–a–Joint* at Ayr	at Oban
Scottish Cup Winners				
Celtic				

THURSDAY November 29 1990

Daily Record

Incorporating DAILY MIRROR   Record sale 768,594

FORWARD WITH SCOTLAND

No10 – A DAY OF CHANGES
A TEAR

GOODBYE!

AND HELLO TO THE NEW BOYS

THIS was the moment when the Iron Lady could hold back the tears no longer . . .

She'd said goodbye to the staff at Number 10 Downing Street, goodbye to the waiting pressmen – but above all, goodbye to eleven years of POWER! And as Mrs Thatcher took one last look at No 10, her composure finally broke. Then the car sped off, carrying her and husband Denis to Buckingham Palace with her resignation. The Thatcher years had ended in tears.

EXCLUSIVE PICTURE by KEN LENNOX

THE TOP SCOT	TRANSPORT	CHANCELLOR

IAN LANG	MALCOLM RIFKIND	NORMAN LAMONT

SCOTS IN MAJOR CABINET SHUFFLE

Pages 2 and 3

1990

"REJOICE" – THATCHER TOPPLED

THE Thatcher era came to an end when the Prime Minister was finally persuaded by her Cabinet colleagues that she faced humiliation if she stayed in the race for the leadership of the Conservative Party.

Challenged by her long-time adversary, Michael Heseltine, following an extraordinary Commons speech by the former Deputy Prime Minister, Sir Geoffrey Howe, Mrs Thatcher failed to win enough votes to see off her former Defence Secretary. Emerging from the British Embassy in Paris after the first round of voting had been announced – Thatcher 204 votes, Heseltine 152 – she declared: "I fight on. I fight to win". However, once back in London, she was made aware of a distinct haemorrhaging of support among Tory MPs, fearful of the result of the next general election if Mrs Thatcher was to remain as Conservative leader.

The Prime Minister saw her Cabinet colleagues individually. She had appointed all of them, and was now being told that she could not rely on the support of a significant number of them.

As was her habit, Mrs Thatcher slept on her decision to step down. The following morning she told her husband Denis and telephoned her son and daughter, both in America.

The right wing of the Conservative Party began organising almost immediately to "stop Heseltine". However, a key factor in Heseltine's success thus far was his potential appeal in Scotland and the north of England.

The unpopular poll tax had been deployed in Scotland first. Along with the Government's economic policies and incidents like the infamous "Sermon on the Mound" in 1988 when she told the General Assembly of the Church of Scotland that the Good Samaritan could only help people because he had money, it did little to increase her popularity north of the border.

CITY OF CULTURE

The Queen and Prince Philip were serenaded into Glasgow by choirs as they arrived at Central Station to inaugurate the city's year as "cultural capital of Europe". The official handover of the title was made by the mayor of Paris, Jacques Chirac, before 1,500 invited guests at the King's Theatre. The popular year-long festival brought art and culture in every form to every part of the city.

FLOWER OF SCOTLAND INSPIRES GRAND SLAM HEROES

Scotland's unofficial national anthem, *Flower of Scotland*, echoed around Murrayfield in March as over 50,000 fans urged on their team at the start of the Grand Slam decider with England. In a rousing match, Scotland eventually ran out the winners 13-7. Coach Ian McGeechan acknowledged the inspiration the team got from the crowd: "I have never known such an atmosphere at Murrayfield. We had to find another gear and we did … England just didn't have any answers."

WHAT IT COST

POUND OF BUTTER
71p

POUND OF BACON
£2.58

PINT OF BEER
97p

CIGARETTES
£1.91 (20 Senior Service)

WOMEN'S SHOES
£29.99

MEN'S SUIT
£120

TON OF COAL
£42.36

POSTAGE
22p

CAR
Ford Escort £8,123

THIS SPORTING LIFE

FOOTBALL	RUGBY UNION	GOLF	HORSE RACING	SHINTY
Scottish Champions Rangers	*Scotland vs England* Scotland 13–7 England at Murrayfield	*British Open Winner* Nick Faldo at St Andrews (270)	*Scottish Grand National Winner* Four Trix at Ayr	*Camanachd Cup Winners* Skye at Fort William
Scottish Cup Winners Aberdeen				

Daily Record

Incorporating DAILY MIRROR

Record sale 772,042

27p FORWARD WITH SCOTLAND No. 33,737

8 SUPER PAGES FOR WOMEN

With Lynne Ewart's great star guide

Starts on page 17

OUTRAGE!

Israel makes shock peace offer

ISRAEL shocked its Arab neighbours last night by offering to take part in peace talks.

Foreign Minister David Levy suggested Israel might work with the eight Arab members of the anti-Iraq coalition.

He also said there could be talks with Palestinians, but NOT the PLO who they regard as a terrorist organisation.

Backed

The concessions came yesterday during talks in London with Foreign Secretary Douglas Hurd.

"It is the first time that, as a result of Arab conflict, Israel finds itself in the same camp as eight Arab countries," an Israeli diplomat said.

British sources said Mr Levy backed the Arab moves to stabilise the Gulf.

And he was quoted as saying that "there was a possibility for the eight to become eight plus one, to include Israel," once the threat of violence ended.

LOST IN CARNAGE – Page Two

A protester with banner – and teddy – yesterday **Picture: ANDY HOSIE**

❝ **My daughter asked if she'd been sent away because she was bad. It would break any mother's heart** ❞

READ JULIA CLARKE on Page 5

Families weep as 'ritual sex' case kids held 21 days

FURIOUS families demonstrated their anger outside a court yesterday after social workers got "place of safety" orders to hold nine children for 21 days.

Today, shocked parents from the Orkney island of South Ronaldsay will appeal against the children's panel decisions – which follow allegations of ritual sex orgies.

Hearings in Kirkwall were told yesterday of:

● "Acts of lewd and libidinous behaviour".

By DEREK MASTERTON

● Sex between adults and children during the hours of darkness with "ritualised music, dance and dress".

● Sex between adults, watched by children.

A crowd of more than 100 friends and supporters gathered outside the children's panel offices in Kirkwall to show their solidarity with the parents.

Police had to close the town's East Road to traffic because of the crowd.

News of the panel's decision was greeted with disbelief by the crowds waiting outside.

The children were taken from their homes at 7 am last Wednesday. Now fear is clouding island life.

South Ronaldsay mother of two Christina Sargent, 36, said: "I cried for two days after the raids.

"I have never been so terrified."

Power

"I am afraid that my presence here could put me at risk of losing my children."

She added: "I believe the families whose children have been taken from them have been victimised by the social

Turn to Page Four

RECORD NEWS SPECIAL
PAGES 4 & 5

PARENTS IN DEMO OVER SEX CASE

FURIOUS families demonstrated their anger outside a court after social workers obtained "place of safety" orders to hold nine children for 21 days.

The shocked parents from the Orkney island of South Ronaldsay appealed against the children's panel decisions, which came after allegations of ritual sex orgies.

Hearings in Kirkwall were told of:
ACTS of lewd and libidinous behaviour.
SEX between adults and children during the hours of darkness with "ritualised music, dance and dress".

INTERCOURSE between adults, watched by children.

The Orkney scandal began after three children in care claimed to have taken part in bizarre sex rituals in a quarry with their parents and other adults. They claimed the local Church of Scotland minister was the "master" of the sex ring.

The nine children, aged between eight and 15, were seized from their homes on South Ronaldsay by police and social workers.

Most were placed in foster homes on the mainland, but one boy was sent to a List D school and locked up with teenage crooks.

The youngsters were held for five weeks before a sheriff ordered the authorities to take them home.

The scandal prompted a public inquiry, which lasted almost a year. And, in his conclusions, Judge Lord Clyde slammed the authorities for the way the case was handled.

The families at the centre of the Orkney child abuse scandal were set to receive big payouts.

Their lawyers thrashed out deals with Orkney Islands Council, who faced 20 claims for damages, totalling approximately £1million.

SCOTS TROOPS LEAD THE CHARGE INTO KUWAIT

In January, Operation Desert Storm opened with a massive air bombardment as the Allied forces massing in neighbouring Saudi Arabia began their push to oust Saddam Hussein's invading Iraqi forces from Kuwait. After a month of intensive air attacks which crippled much of the Iraqi forces, infantry and armour poured into Kuwait for a short, sharp land war to finish the job.

Men from The Royal Scots Dragoon Guards, the Royal Highland Fusiliers and the King's Own Scottish Borderers were to the front in this attack, with several soldiers from each regiment receiving gallantry awards for their actions.

YANKS GO HOME

After thirty years, the US Navy bade farewell to the Holy Loch in February. With the Cold War over, the controversial submarine base was deemed to be surplus to requirements. While the news was greeted with unrestrained joy by anti-nuclear campaigners, local shopkeepers and hoteliers were shocked by the likely loss of the £30 million a year that the Americans put into the Dunoon and Cowal economy.

ON TV			GOINGS...
Northern Exposure	Soldier, Soldier Prime Suspect	Men Behaving Badly	Jack House Journalist

THIS SPORTING LIFE

FOOTBALL	RUGBY UNION	GOLF	HORSE RACING	SHINTY
Scottish Champions Rangers	*Scotland vs England* England 21–12 Scotland at Twickenham Scotland 6–9 England at Murrayfield (World Cup)	*British Open Winner* Ian Baker Finch at Royal Birkdale, England (272)	*Scottish Grand National Winner* *Killone Abbey* at Ayr	*Camanachd Cup Winners* Kingussie at Inverness
Scottish Cup Winners Motherwell				

Thursday January 9 1992

Daily Record

Incorporating DAILY MIRROR   No. 34,000

YOUR PAPER - MADE IN SCOTLAND   27p

WANTED

FOR MURDERING THE HEART OF SCOTLAND..

THE CRAIG KILLER

BLACK Bob Scholey, the man who murdered Ravenscraig, didn't have the courage to show his face yesterday.

The cold-hearted boss of British Steel had promised that the record-breaking plant would remain open until 1994.

It was the pledge of a man who has never given a damn about Scotland . . .

A pledge which turned out to be a double-cross.

He delivered the final death blow to the heart of industrial Scotland along with 1220 workers and another 15,000 whose jobs are dependent on steel.

But the Government, who hired him to do their dirty work, will not escape his axe.

For Scholey did the dirty on them as well – by announcing his

Turn to Page Two

DEATH KNELL FOR RAVENSCRAIG

BRITISH STEEL announced the closure of the Ravenscraig steel complex at Motherwell, with the loss of 1,500 jobs. The works would shut by September 1992, with the "domino effect" threatening another 15,000 jobs in what was already a jobs blackspot.

In 1990, the hot-strip mill was closed with the loss of 700 jobs. The following year, another 1,100 were made unemployed when one of the two blast furnaces was shut down.

The political fallout of the announcement left the Scottish Conservatives reeling, only months before the general election had to take place.

Since Prime Minister John Major had promised to help Lanarkshire, opposition parties were quick to condemn the move as a betrayal. Shadow Scottish Secretary Donald Dewar demanded the resignation of Secretary of State for Scotland, Ian Lang, and blamed British Steel's "misjudgment and malice".

SNP spokesman Ian Lawson called for the nationalisation of the Scottish steel industry. He referred to the demise of Ravenscraig as "the final betrayal of an anti-Scottish company". He challenged the Shadow Scottish Secretary to commit a future Labour administration to public ownership of the company.

With nine seats, the Scottish Conservatives were the third party in Scotland. Privately, party activists feared a wipe-out at the imminent general election. Some predicted the survival of only two Tory MPs – Allan Stewart in Glasgow Eastwood and Malcolm Rifkind in Edinburgh Pentlands. If the Conservatives won the election, the Scottish Office would comprise of Scots-born English MPs, a prospect viewed with alarm by Scots Tory activists.

Only months earlier, Mr Lang had predicted a Tory revival in Scotland. Asked to comment on the political effects of the closure, he replied tersely:"It's not helpful."

CLYDE SHIPYARD REPRIEVED

Yarrows, the Clyde shipbuilder, secured an order in January to build three Type 23 frigates for the Royal Navy, and in doing so was given a reprieve from closure. A specially commissioned report had forecast that up to 10,000 jobs in total from the surrounding community would be lost were the yard to close, and management workers and regional councillors began a vigorous campaign to secure the orders.

ON TV		
Heartbeat	The Jack Dee Show	Teenage Health Freak
Between the Lines	Murphy Brown	Nurses
A Touch of Frost	Love Hurts	Riders

HERE COMES THE JUDGE

Scotland's first woman judge was appointed in October. The appointment of Sheriff Hazel Aronson QC as Lady Cosgrove, a temporary judge at the Court of Session in Edinburgh, and at High Court hearings elsewhere, brought the centuries-old male domination of the bench to an end.

The Glasgow-born lawyer who had a meteoric rise through her profession spoke modestly about her historic elevation: "I am very honoured to be the first woman to sit on the Court of Session and High Court Bench. I hope that this will be a source of encouragement to all women in the legal profession."

THIS SPORTING LIFE

FOOTBALL	RUGBY UNION	GOLF	HORSE RACING	SHINTY
Scottish Champions	Scotland vs England	British Open Winner	Scottish Grand National	Camanachd Cup Winners
Rangers	Scotland 7–25 England	Nick Faldo	Winner	Fort William
	at Murrayfield	at Muirfield (272)	Captain Dibble at Ayr	at Glasgow
Scottish Cup Winners				
Rangers				

WEDNESDAY January 6 1993

Daily Record

Incorporating DAILY MIRROR

No. 34,310

YOUR PAPER - MADE IN SCOTLAND · 27p

SHETLAND OIL HORROR

SCRAP THE 'COFFINS'

Stranded on the rocks and battered by monstrous seas, the crippled tanker spews its filthy cargo on to the Shetland coastline

Why did we wait for a disaster?

DISASTER hits the Shetland Isles in the nightmare we've all dreaded since North Sea oil began to flow.

Because an old-style "coffin ship" was allowed to sail near our coast – and is now spewing its filthy cargo on to **OUR**

RECORD VIEW

coastline.

It's the same type of tanker the Americans banned after the Alaskan oil disaster.

And which **SHOULD** have been banned here.

Why the hell do we in Britain

always wait for the disaster to happen before taking any action?

The 18-year-old US-owned, Japanese-built Braer, sailing under a Liberian flag of convenience with a polyglot crew of Poles and Filipinos, wasn't up to the job.

Modern tankers are fitted with "double-skin" hulls designed to stop

Turn to Page Two

FULL STORY – PAGES 2, 3, 4, 5, 8 AND 9

SHETLAND OIL TANKER NIGHTMARE

SHETLAND woke up to its worst ecological nightmare as a seven-mile-long oil slick started creeping round the islands.

The slick came from the massive *Braer* tanker which had run aground in rough weather with a full cargo of oil and was in danger of breaking its back.

The spill grew larger by the hour. Oil was seen 12 miles north of the disaster scene and it was estimated that three quarters of the tanker's 84,500-ton cargo leaked out.

A massive clean-up operation costing millions of pounds swung into action as soon as the *Braer*'s distress call was heard.

Tons of specialist equipment arrived on the islands along with six special anti-pollution Dakota planes.

The aircraft flew in sorties 20 feet above the waves to spray special dispersal liquids on the black water.

Some of the worst pollution was on land, where 70 mph winds whipped oil-rich sea spray onto farmland, leaving roads and green fields slimy and black.

The Greek captain of the stricken tanker was dubbed "Captain Quitter" by the press for allegedly having abandoned his ship too soon.

But the angry skipper said that he and

his crew had been made scapegoats.

The battle to save wildlife caught up in the tragedy got under way immediately.

Teams of volunteers and vets came from all over the world, helping to combat the effects of the catastrophe on birds, seals, otters and other sea life.

The wildlife in Shetland was doomed for years, according to the man in charge of dealing with the environmental effects of the oil spill, Dr Jerome Montague, as thousands of dead sea birds began to be washed up on the shores around Quendale Bay. "We are in the hands of God," said one wildlife expert.

ROSYTH JOBS BLOW

Workers were left shattered at Rosyth naval dockyard in June when they discovered that they had lost a major battle for jobs. The contract to refit Trident submarines was to be moved to Devonport, in spite of Rosyth's 25 years' experience in this field.

The Government announced that the Forth base would lose 450 jobs as a result of the transfer of the work, although workers feared the ultimate closure of the yard. To soften the blow, it was announced that £100 million would be spent equipping the yard to refit 18 warships over the course of the next 12 years, although this was much less work than the yard had been used to.

RECORD HOSPICE APPEAL

Suzanne Sutherland was just three-years-old when she appeared on the front cover of the *Daily Record.* Suzanne was terminally ill, suffering from a progressive disorder of the nervous system which had confined her to a wheelchair.

At the time, Scotland lacked a hospice where children like Suzanne and their families could spend time together in an environment which met both the needs of the child and the family.

A vigorous campaign was launched by the newspaper, appealing to the Scottish people to fund the building of a children's hospice. An incredible £4 million poured in and in 1996, Rachel House in Kinross was opened by Princess Anne.

ON TV	
Goodnight, Sweetheart	Cracker
Peak Practice	Chef!
Sharpe	Power Rangers

THIS SPORTING LIFE

FOOTBALL	RUGBY UNION	GOLF	HORSE RACING	SHINTY
Scottish Champions Rangers *Scottish Cup Winners* Rangers	*Scotland vs England* England 26–12 Scotland at Twickenham	*British Open Winner* Greg Norman at Sandwich, England (267)	*Scottish Grand National Winner* Run For Free at Ayr	*Camanachd Cup Winners* Kingussie at Fort William

FRIDAY May 13, 1994

Daily Record

Incorporating DAILY MIRROR

No.34,730

YOUR PAPER – MADE IN SCOTLAND   27p

SPECIAL ISSUE
The tragedy that stunned Britain

WE CAN'T BELIEVE HE'S GONE

TODAY all Britain is still stunned by the sudden death of John Smith, a great Scot and the man who was certain to be Prime Minister.

On the front of this Special Issue we depict him as John would want to be remembered – a dedicated family man, with his wife Elizabeth and daughters Jane, Catherine, and Sarah (front).

He was a great friend of the Record. He'll be sadly missed.

FULL STORY PAGES 2,3,4,5,6,7,8,9,31 and CENTRE PAGES

JOHN SMITH'S DEATH STUNS MPs

BRITAIN was stunned by the sudden death of John Smith, a great Scot and the man almost certain to be Britain's next Prime Minister.

Shocked MPs were given the news at Westminster and political friend and foe alike paid tribute to him.

The Queen sent her condolences to the Opposition leader's wife Elizabeth and their three daughters.

And Premier John Major and former Prime Minister Margaret Thatcher joined Mr Smith's Labour colleagues in praising the man whose rapier wit had so often savaged the Conservatives at the dispatch box.

The evening before his death, the Labour leader had been in excellent health. The first sign of a problem was when he complained of chest pains. The pains got steadily worse until he collapsed.

His wife managed to resuscitate him, but just before the paramedics arrived, Mr Smith stopped breathing and no pulse could be found.

The paramedics and the ambulance crew continued the efforts to restart his heart using adrenaline and atropine.

However, shortly afterwards all hope of saving Mr Smith had gone.

He was declared dead 70 minutes after his collapse.

As the news spread through Westminster, business in both Houses of Parliament was cancelled.

The Commons was silent and sombre when speaker Betty Boothroyd, in a shaking voice, announced Mr Smith's death.

A shocked John Major said: "I will miss him not only as a formidable opponent but also as a man whom I liked and respected."

Labour's deputy leader, Margaret Beckett, who was to take over for an interim period, made an emotional speech honouring her friend and colleague.

She told how, at a gala dinner the Wednesday before his death, Mr Smith had talked of "the opportunity to serve our country. That is all we ask."

She said that they were almost the last words she had heard him speak and she added:

"Let them be his epitaph."

NEW BROOM SWEEPS CLEAN AT CELTIC PARK

An era came to an end at Celtic FC, when the Kelly and White families sold their controlling interest in the club to businessman Fergus McCann. It had been a far from friendly transformation. The previous board were held responsible by the club's supporters for Celtic's desperate condition, on and off the field of play. The catalyst for change came in the shape of Celtic's bankers, who were no longer prepared to finance the club's debts. McCann cleared the debt and set about transforming the club.

FERGUSLIE FLOODED

December storms brought chaos to the central belt with Paisley being particularly badly affected. More than 150 people had to be evacuated from their homes in Ferguslie Park as flood water up to five feet deep swamped the area.

The Government refused to help the stricken flood victims, many of whom had lost everything and had not been able to afford insurance. However, the *Daily Record* donated 10p from the sale of every copy on a given day to raise £75,000 for the victims.

ON TV

Cardiac Arrest

Middlemarch

Melrose Place

Cadfael

Hamish Macbeth

Dangerfield

NYPD Blue

The Day Today

Fantasy Football League

The Vicar of Dibley

Frasier

Knowing Me, Knowing You… With Alan Partridge

Heartbreak High

THIS SPORTING LIFE

FOOTBALL	RUGBY UNION	GOLF	HORSE RACING	SHINTY
Scottish Champions Rangers	*Scotland vs England* Scotland 14–15 England at Murrayfield	*British Open Winner* Nick Price at Turnberry (268)	*Scottish Grand National Winner* *Earth Summit* at Ayr	*Camanachd Cup Winners* Fort William at Inverness
Scottish Cup Winners Dundee United				

TUESDAY, MARCH 28, 1995

Daily Record

Issue No. 34,993

27p

1895   SCOTLAND'S CHAMPION   1995

WIN A FORTUNE

With our great new **SCRATCHCARD** Inside today

Daily Record **PLUS** £100,000 SHO

£50,000 SPENDING SPREE

PAGE 13

| STICK YOUR TOKEN 1 HERE | STICK YOUR TOKEN 2 HERE | STICK YOUR TOKEN 3 HERE | STICK YOUR TOKEN 4 HERE |
| STICK YOUR TOKEN 8 HERE | STICK YOUR TOKEN 9 HERE | STICK YOUR TOKEN 10 HERE | STICK YOUR TOKEN 11 HERE |

THEY CAME IN THEIR THOUSANDS TO SAY FAREWELL TO A FOOTBALL LEGEND...

TEARS for DAVIE

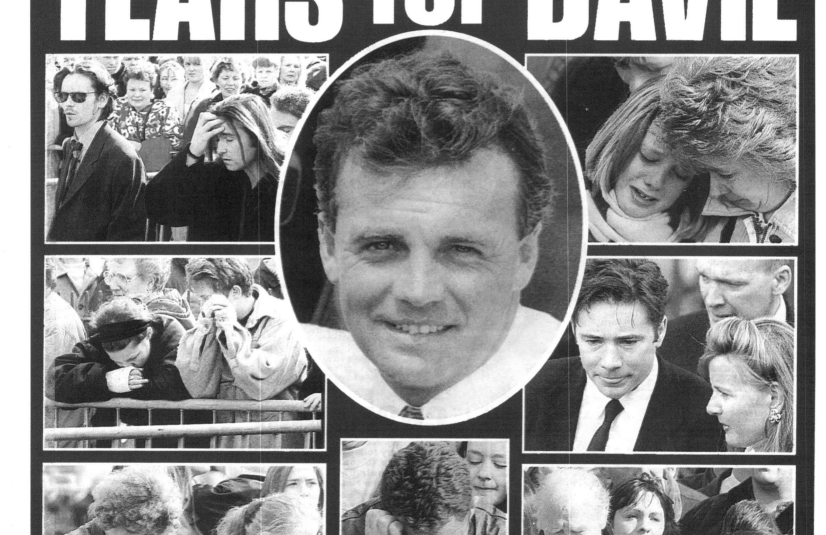

TRIBUTE TO A MAN OF THE PEOPLE – PAGES 2,3, 20,25, 42,43 and 44

THOUSANDS WEEP FOR STAR DAVIE

THE town of Hamilton in Lanarkshire was brought to a standstill as thousands of mourners turned out to pay their last respects to Davie Cooper, who died of a brain haemorrhage at the age of 39.

Friends and former colleagues from the world of football joined the family of the ex-Rangers and Scotland player at Hillhouse parish church for the funeral service. Rangers FC was represented by, among others, Richard Gough, Andy Goram, Donald Findlay QC and John Greig.

The former Rangers manager Graeme Souness was also in the congregation. One of the most poignant moments came with the arrival of the former Celtic player Charlie Nicholas, bearing a wreath. Nicholas was with Cooper when he collapsed.

Tributes were paid by Ally McCoist, a friend as well as a former team-mate, and the Rangers manager Walter Smith. The Reverend Jim MacKenzie spoke of the shock of Cooper's early death: "His life came to such an abrupt end. But even in our sadness we should celebrate that life."

Although some of the stars of Scottish football could not attend the service – the national squad had a European qualifying match in Moscow – all of Scotland's 40 league clubs were represented.

Wreaths from around the world were laid outside the church, including one from a famous Celtic supporter, Rod Stewart, with the message: "One of Scotland's greatest."

Cooper began his career with Clydebank before moving to Ibrox in 1977. After 12 years with Rangers, he moved to Motherwell, before returning to his first club as player-coach in 1993.

His parents Jock and Jean, his brother John, his girlfriend Liz Thomson and his estranged wife Christine, led the mourners in the church.

Many more gathered outside and lined the route of the funeral cortege to Bent Road cemetery, where the private burial ceremony took place.

ON TV

Band of Gold

ER

Pride and Prejudice

The Politician's Wife

The Fast Show

Father Ted

Friends

The Mrs Merton Show

The Thin Blue Line

Top Gear

The X-Files

GOINGS...

Fitzroy Maclean
Author, Soldier &
Diplomat

SKIER SURVIVES AGAINST THE ODDS

Cross-country skier Andy Wilson survived for three days in blizzard conditions in Glen Shee with only a Mars bar to keep him going. The harsh February weather had caught the experienced outdoorsman by surprise. In blinding storms and with temperatures plummetting to -38˚F, Andy at first tried to fight his way out of the glen. On his first night a rescue helicopter passed within 200 feet of him but failed to see him because of the poor conditions. When he was eventually picked up on the third day, his rescuers admitted they were surprised to find him alive as no-one had ever lasted that long on the freezing hills before.

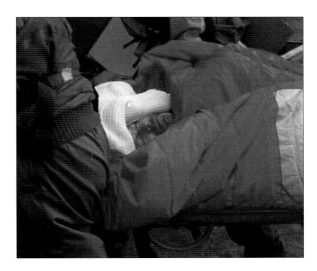

STIRLING'S BRAVEHEART PARTY

The *Braveheart* bandwagon rolled into Stirling – the heart of William Wallace country – as the Mel Gibson movie took much of Scotland by storm. Based on the life of the Scottish hero (with a sizeable amount of poetic licence), the film was described by actor James Cosmo as the "most important film Scotland has ever made – both politically and emotionally". Mel Gibson arrived in full Highland regalia as Stirling town centre was turned over to partying, albeit in the pouring rain. Scottish Secretary Michael Forsyth arrived to a less enthusiastic welcome.

THIS SPORTING LIFE

FOOTBALL	RUGBY UNION	GOLF	HORSE RACING	SHINTY
Scottish Champions Rangers	*Scotland vs England* England 24–12 Scotland at Twickenham	*British Open Winner* John Daly at St Andrews (282)	*Scottish Grand National* *Winner* *Willsford* at Ayr	*Camanachd Cup Winners* Kingussie at Oban
Scottish Cup Winners Celtic				

Daily Record

Saturday. March 16, 1996   28p

SCOTLAND IN MOURNING

Major is moved to tears

Teachers' silent tribute to Gwenne and her class

Brave little Amie fights for life

DUNBLANE survivor Amie Adam was fighting for her life in hospital last night.

And doctors feared the five-year-old could become evil Tom Hamilton's 18th victim.

Amie, shot in the thigh by the madman, was rushed to intensive care just 24 hours after docs said she was on the mend. She was put on a ventila-

CRITICAL... Amie

tor at Yorkhill Sick Kids hospital, in Glasgow, as medics fought to save her.

Doctors think a tiny piece of marrow from her thigh bone broke off and floated into her blood stream. Yorkhill medical director Alistair Miller said: "She seemed to be doing so well and talking, eating and drinking.

"She is now very seriously ill."

Amie's parents, of Albert Street, Dunblane, were said to be at her bedside.

IN LOVING MEMORY

TEACHERS from Dunblane Primary carry flowers to the school gates to honour the 17 victims of the massacre.

They were remembering a lost friend – teacher Gwenne Mayor – and the young pupils who died with her.

There were words of comfort yesterday for headmaster Ron Taylor, right, and his staff.

John Major and Tony Blair came to Dunblane to honour their courage. The VIPs also met the parents of the tiny victims, and paid tribute to the medics who cared for the survivors.

DESPAIR OF DUNBLANE – PAGES 2, 3, 4, 5, 6, 7, 8, 9, 10 and 11

1996

HORROR AT DUNBLANE

ALL of Scotland was stunned and horrified by the murder of 17 infant school children and their teacher at Dunblane Primary in Perthshire by a crazed gunman.

The killer was local man Thomas Hamilton, a former Scout master who had been forced to resign from the movement because of inappropriate behaviour towards boys in his charge. He had also run youth clubs in the area which had been investigated by both the police and social services. Because of this, Hamilton felt persecuted by the authorities and it was suggested that the school attack was his revenge.

The crazed killer began his indiscriminate shooting as soon as he entered the school grounds. Two teachers were injured as he fired pistols at random before making his way to the school gym where the 29 five- and six-year-olds were playing. Their teacher, Gwenne Mayor, was one of those killed during the rampage while another 12 children were also injured.

At the end of the senseless slaughter, the killer turned the gun on himself.

Frantic parents rushed to the school, gave their names to police and then waited anxiously to find out if their children were alive or dead.

The immensity of what had happened was felt throughout the small town. Almost everyone knew someone who was involved.

In the days that followed the tragedy, the streets surrounding the school became carpeted with floral tributes that poured into Dunblane from across Britain and the world. Hundreds of teddy bears were mixed with the flowers and notes of condolence.

Respecting the declared wishes of the town, the world's media withdrew from Dunblane shortly before the funerals, to allow the grieving families and towns-people to mourn their dead out of the glare of publicity.

BACK WHERE IT BELONGS

Seven hundred years after Edward I carried it off to England, the Stone of Destiny, the ancient symbol of Scottish nationhood, was installed in Edinburgh Castle in December. The Stone, on which Scottish kings were traditionally crowned, was driven amidst much pomp and circumstance from the Palace of Holyroodhouse up the Royal Mile to the Castle. There, before an invited audience of the nation's Establishment elite, comprising nobles, politicians, business chiefs and celebrities, it was formally handed over to its new keepers. It was all a far cry from the last time the Stone was in Scotland in 1950, when its daring theft from Westminster Abbey caused a national crisis.

THE BIG THAW

Normally it's the big freeze that causes the problems, but in January it was the big thaw that caused havoc all over the country. Burst pipes, flooding and water and power failures led to families having to be evacuated in Edinburgh, Glasgow, Dundee, Stranraer and throughout Perthshire. Emergency services and council staff were stretched to breaking point trying to cope with the public's pleas for help.

ON TV

Our Friends in the North	*Dalziel and Pascoe*	*Third Rock from the Sun*
Moll Flanders	*The Knock*	*Rugrats*
This Life	*Murder One*	*Star Trek: Voyager*
American Gothic	*Ballykissangel*	*Police/Camera/Action*

THIS SPORTING LIFE

FOOTBALL	RUGBY UNION	GOLF	HORSE RACING	SHINTY
Scottish Champions Rangers	*Scotland vs England* Scotland 9–18 England at Murrayfield	*British Open Winner* Tom Lehman at Royal Lytham, England (271)	*Scottish Grand National Winner* Moorcroft Boy at Ayr	*Camanachd Cup Winners* Kingussie at Inverness
Scottish Cup Winners Rangers				

TONY'S TRIUMPH ENDS 18 YEARS OF MISERY

Daily Record

28p VICTORY EDITION

LABOUR LANDSLIDE SENSATION

WIPE-OUT

Scotland boots out all ten Tories

IN SAFE HANDS ... New Prime Minister Tony Blair hugs wife Cherie last night.

THE Tories were wiped out in Scotland last night as Tony Blair swept to power in a landslide.

He romped home with an incredible majority to end 18 years of Tory hurt.

Blair, at 43, will be the youngest Prime Minister this century.

And he'll have the biggest Labour majority **EVER**.

In Scotland, all 10 Tory MPs were turfed out.

Scots Secretary Michael Forsyth was first to lose his seat.

By 3am, the rout was complete when the Tories' last hope – Foreign Secretary Malcolm Rifkind – was beaten.

In England, the biggest casualty

TURN TO PAGE 2

OUT

FORSYTH

OUT

LANG

OUT

RIFKIND

BLAIR: I WON'T LET YOU DOWN (2&3) WE'RE A TORY-FREE ZONE (4&5)

SCOTLAND'S TORIES TOPPLED

THE Conservatives were wiped out in Scotland as Tony Blair swept to power in a landslide victory. He put an end to 18 years of Tory rule by gaining the biggest Labour majority ever.

All 10 Scottish Tory MPs lost their seats as the "doomsday scenario" predicted to befall the party finally happened.

Scottish Secretary Michael Forsyth was the first to lose his seat and by 3am the Tory defeat was inevitable as Foreign Secretary Malcolm Rifkind was beaten.

And when Phil Gallie's Ayrshire seat was lost, the rout was complete and Scotland became a Tory-free zone for the first time.

But in spite of the major swing against the Conservatives, the SNP failed to capitalise and its share of the vote remained constant.

In England, too, senior Conservatives found themselves being rejected by the electorate. One of the the biggest casualties of the night was Michael Portillo, the Defence Secretary, who had been tipped to replace John Major as party leader. Other prominent Tory MPs to lose their seats included Cabinet member William Waldegrave and former Health Minister David Mellor, ex-Chancellor Norman Lamont and Sir Marcus Fox, chairman of the powerful backbench 1922 Committee.

Tony Blair was near to tears as Labour swept to power in a landslide. He told the British people: "I will not let you down."

After winning his Sedgefield seat with a 25,000-vote majority, Mr Blair said: "It is an honour to serve you, and I feel a deep sense of honour and humility."

"You have put your trust in me and I intend to repay that trust."

In the new Cabinet, Scottish politicians featured prominently, including Gordon Brown as Chancellor, Robin Cook as Foreign Secretary, and George Robertson as Defence Secretary.

A NEW PARLIAMENT ON ITS WAY

Pro-devolution campaigners celebrated a historic landslide victory in September's referendum. Over 74% of voters backed the creation of a Scottish parliament while 63% supported its right to vary tax rates. Scottish Secretary Donald Dewar, one of the chief architects of home rule, declared: "This is one of the greatest days in our history. We are a nation that believes in ourselves." It was hoped that the new parliament, the first in Scotland for almost 300 years, would open in 1999.

ON TV

King of the Hill

TFI Friday

Spin City

Teletubbies

Xena: Warrior Princess

Eurotrash

Shooting Stars

WORLD'S WORST FOOD-POISONING OUTBREAK

The world's worst outbreak of *E. Coli* poisoning claimed the lives of 21 people in Lanarkshire during January. The outbreak centred on John Barr's butcher shop in Wishaw which had sold contaminated meats for several functions over the preceding Christmas period. The shop was closed once the outbreak was traced.

Mr Barr was prosecuted over the supply of the infected meat and a lengthy public inquiry was set up under the chairmanship of the world-renowed bacteriologist, Professor Hugh Pennington of Aberdeen University. Professor Pennington's subsequent report recommended sweeping changes to the way in which food for public consumption was to be prepared, stored and sold.

THIS SPORTING LIFE

FOOTBALL	RUGBY UNION	GOLF	HORSE RACING	SHINTY
Scottish Champions Rangers	*Scotland vs England* England 41–13 Scotland at Twickenham	*British Open Winner* Justin Leonard at Royal Troon (272)	*Scottish Grand National Winner* Belmont King at Ayr	*Camanachd Cup Winners* Kingussie at Fort William
Scottish Cup Winners Kilmarnock				

Daily Record

Wednesday, June 24, 1998

SCOTLAND'S CHAMPION

30p

Heartbreak as Scotland crash to 3-0 World Cup defeat

OUT

By ROGER HANNAH

THE nation's heart was broken last night as Scotland's World Cup dream was destroyed in St Etienne.

A day of destiny which had promised so much ended in disappointment when we were beaten 3-0 by Morocco.

Two goals by striker Bassir and another from Hadda shattered the prospect of a second round clash with three-times world champions Italy in Marseille on Saturday.

To rub salt in the wounds, Craig Burley – a goal hero against Norway – was sent off in the second half.

But in the end, the result in St Etienne was rendered academic by Norway's 2-1 victory over world champions Brazil in Marseille. Brazil and Norway will now progress to the

TURN TO PAGE TWO

1998

WE'LL SUPPORT YOU EVER MORE

THE Scottish national football team's involvement in the World Cup in France came to an end with a humiliating 3-0 defeat at the hands of Morocco, one of the unfancied sides of the tournament.

It was a bitter pill to swallow for the thousands of Tartan Army foot-soldiers, who had watched their team perform well in the opening game of the tournament against reigning world champions Brazil. The Scots lost that game 2-1, but had put on a reasonable show against the team who would again get to the World Cup final.

The second game against Norway ended 1-1, a game the Scots deserved to win. However, in what has become something of a World Cup tradition, it was the so-called 'little team' in Scotland's group who sent Craig Brown's team home to think again. Morocco had joined Peru, Iran and Costa Rica in Scottish football's hall of infamy.

The Scotland manager bemoaned the lack of a Zidane or a Ronaldo in his team, freely admitting that the hard work of the Scots could not make up for the deficit in talent: "When we reach this level, we cannot quite hack it." Brown also hinted at the problems being created in the Scottish game by the increasing reliance on foreigners in the Scottish leagues: "We just don't have the quality players coming through in our domestic game."

A crowd of 2,500 greeted the team on their return to Glasgow Airport, but Brown was in philosophical mood: "You cannot kid the fans. They know we tried. They would never have forgiven us if we hadn't given 100%."

Brown remained confident that Scotland would qualify for the Euro 2000 tournament in the Low Countries, but the lack of world-class talent in the Scottish team did not bode well for the future.

BRITANNIA *RETIRES TO LEITH*

The Royal Yacht *Britannia* is set to spend the rest of her days in Leith as a floating museum following her decommissioning. The Edinburgh port beat off fierce competition from other cities around the country to provide a permanent berth for the former royal flagship.

Princess Anne had wanted the ageing ship scuttled as previous royal yachts had been once they were taken out of service but Defence Minister George Robertson believed Edinburgh to be a fitting home for *Britannia* where she would have a considerable contribution to make to the economy of the rejuvenated Leith as a tourist attraction, restaurant and conference centre.

SAPPHIRE *GRIEF CONTINUES*

A year on from the loss of the Peterhead fishing boat *Sapphire*, the families of the four missing crew remembered their lost loved ones in private ceremonies. The failure of the Government to back a salvage operation to raise the sunken trawler caused great resentment in the fishing community and added to the tragedy for the families. The ship was eventually raised and the four bodies recovered.

ON TV

Changing Rooms

Jonathan Creek

The Jerry Springer Show

You've Been Framed!

Who Wants to Be A Millionaire?

THIS SPORTING LIFE

FOOTBALL	RUGBY UNION	GOLF	HORSE RACING	SHINTY
Scottish Champions Celtic	*Scotland vs England* Scotland 20–34 England at Murrayfield	*British Open Winner* Mark O'Meara at Royal Birkdale, England (280)	*Scottish Grand National Winner* *Baronet* at Ayr	*Camanachd Cup Winners* Kingussie at Oban
Scottish Cup Winners Hearts				

Daily Record

Friday, May 7, 1999   32p

SCOTLAND'S CHAMPION

THE NEW SCOTLAND - DAY ONE

- **Coalition on the cards**
- **Turnout is below 55%**
- **Shock swing to SNP**
- **Rebel Canavan is back**

FIRST MINISTER: But Dewar will have to seek coalition

DONALD HAS TO DO A DEAL

By CHRIS DEERIN

LABOUR fought off an SNP surge last night to win the historic battle for Holyrood.

Donald Dewar, on course to lead 58 Labour MSPs, is now expected to do a deal with the Lib Dems to run Scotland's first Parliament in almost 300 years.

But Labour were rocked by a shock victory for expelled MP Dennis Canavan, who thrashed the official party candidate by more than 12,000 votes in his Falkirk West constituency.

There was also a large swing to the SNP in traditionally safe Labour seats.

Fatigue

Early results dashed Mr Dewar's dream of an overall majority and left him well short of the total he needed to govern without help.

A poll by the BBC put the Nats on 44 seats, which would establish them as a powerful opposition and guarantee Alex Salmond's position as leader.

The Tories appeared to have returned to the political map, knocking the Lib Dems into fourth place with 14 seats to 13.

Labour blamed heavy rain throughout polling day for an abysmal turnout, estimated at less than 55 per cent.

But experts said voter fatigue and a lacklustre campaign were major factors.

Labour held the first five seats to declare – all in safe territory for them – despite some major swings to the Nats which will prompt a post-mortem for Dewar's team. The honour of

TURN TO PAGE TWO

HOW YOU VOTED FOR FIRST PARLIAMENT IN 300 YEARS: Pages 2,3,4,5,6,7,8,9,10 &11

1999

NEW ERA DAWNS FOR SCOTLAND

ON May 6, the people of Scotland voted for the first Parliament to sit in Edinburgh in almost 300 years. In September 1997 they had overwhelmingly endorsed a tax-raising legislature in Scotland's capital. 129 MSPs would be elected by a system of proportional representation, combining the traditional first-past-the-post method with a regional list system.

However, Scotland's new dawn wasn't one of spring sunshine. Thick mist and rain covered much of the country on polling day, contributing to the disappointing turnout of only 58%.

Ever since the referendum, the main question had been who would form the largest bloc in the new Parliament –

Donald Dewar's Labour or Alex Salmond's SNP? A year earlier, opinion polls put the nationalists well in front, with independence, their greatest prize, seemingly within reach. A degree of panic engulfed much of the Labour campaign as the prospect of sweeping SNP victories loomed large. As polling day approached, Prime Minister Tony Blair appointed Chancellor Gordon Brown to take the fight to the nationalists.

The Liberal Democrats and the Conservatives fought their own election for third place. David McLetchie's Tories were confident of overtaking Jim Wallace's party.

In the event, the Labour Party emerged as the largest bloc, winning 56 seats, all but three of them under the first-past-the-post system.

The election was a disappointment for the SNP. Of their 35 MSPs, 28 were elected by the regional top-up method. The greatest disappointment, however, was their lack of success in Glasgow Govan, where the winning Labour Party had experienced all kinds of difficulties in the preceding years.

The Conservatives became the third party in the Parliament, with 18 seats, one ahead of the Lib Dems. Three independents were elected.

After several days of secret negotiations, the Lib Dems and the Labour Party agreed to form Scotland's first devolved coalition government.

CULTURE CITY NOW CITY OF ARCHITECTURE

Glasgow added to its growing list of accolades with the opening of its year as City of Architecture and Design. It had beaten Liverpool and Edinburgh for the title with promises of high-profile events, community involvement and urban improvement, and promised that unlike the 1990 City of Culture event, this award would have a sustainable legacy for the city. One of the most important parts of that legacy will be The Lighthouse, the UK's only museum of architecture and design, which is housed in the former *Glasgow Herald* building designed by Charles Rennie Mackintosh. Another key development, on a notorious gap site near Glasgow Green in the heart of old Glasgow, involves the building of up to 80 "homes for the future".

ON TV

Psychos

Wonderful You

The Ambassador

Buffy the Vampire Slayer

Night Fever

Ground Force

Animal Hospital

SMILE, YOU'RE ON TOO CANDID CAMERA!

Donald Findlay, the colourful QC, resigned in May as Vice-Chairman of Rangers FC after being caught on video singing sectarian songs at a players' party to celebrate the team's Scottish Cup victory earlier that day. In spite of previously claiming that "bigots have no place at Ibrox", the video plainly showed Findlay singing a medley of anti-Catholic songs with great gusto and to the obvious approval of many of those at the party. Given the public efforts that both Old Firm teams had been making to counter the sectarian rivalry between sections of their respective support, Mr Findlay's position was clearly untenable.

THIS SPORTING LIFE

FOOTBALL	RUGBY UNION	GOLF	HORSE RACING	SHINTY
Scottish Champions Rangers	*Scotland vs England* England 24–21 Scotland at Twickenham	*British Open Winner* Paul Lawrie at Carnoustie (290)	*Scottish Grand National Winner* Young Kenny at Ayr	*Camanachd Cup Winners* Kingussie at Kingussie
Scottish Cup Winners Rangers				

Watch this space…